MARKETING MANAGEMENT
Operating, strategic, and administrative

MARKETING MANAGEMENT
Operating, strategic, and administrative

JOHN A. HOWARD   Professor of Marketing
Graduate School of Business, Columbia University

 Third Edition • 1973

RICHARD D. IRWIN, INC.   Homewood, Illinois   60430
IRWIN-DORSEY INTERNATIONAL   London, England   WC2H 9NJ
IRWIN-DORSEY LIMITED   Georgetown, Ontario   L7G 4B3

The previous editions of this book were published under the title: *Marketing Management: Analysis and Planning*

Third Edition

First Printing, May 1973

ISBN 0-256-00227-4

Library of Congress Catalog Card No. 72–95396

Printed in the United States of America

Preface

I WISH TO SHARE with you the sense of excitement I have experienced in revising this book. Since the first edition was published in 1957, marketing management has become a more intensely challenging field of study. Let me explain, and in the explanation I shall use "we" to refer to all those in the field of marketing—teachers, researchers, and practitioners alike.

First, through research in buyer behavior, we have learned the power of theory. We have learned that theory permits us to compress a great amount of knowledge into a few relatively simple ideas, as shown in Chapter 3. I believe this book is a step toward achieving Wroe Alderson's idea of functionalism.[1] Thus, the method of the book is to bring as much theory, as much structure as possible to bear on marketing problems. In this way, I hope to have made some progress in pulling us out of the morass of detail which has in the past weighted down our marketing management texts. Still more structure is needed, for example, to aid us in adequately integrating consumer and industrial marketing. Equipped with structure, the student can learn faster on the job.

We have learned not only to design theoretical complex systems,[2] but also to test them empirically. Effective marketing information systems require this intellectual underpinning, for example. This is almost a

---

[1] K. Tim Hostuick and David L. Durtz, "Alderson's Functionalism and the Development of Marketing Theory," *Journal of Business Research*, forthcoming.

[2] J. A. Howard, "Are Systems Systematic" in D. M. Slate and Robert Feber, *Systems: Research and Applications for Marketing*, University of Illinois Bulletin, Vol. 65, No. 144, 1968.

quantum jump in sophistication because of the interrelated and subtle theoretical, factual, and statistical issues encountered, as we will see, especially in Chapter 8.

Also, we have learned how to apply these ideas to some practical problems. In Chapters 6, 7, and 8, we see how theory can help clarify thinking and guide marketing research in what facts to collect. Beyond this, theory guides the analysis and interpretation of those facts. As a result, we have also realized that quantification alone is aimless—but when guided by theory, it can be powerful indeed.

Second, we are beginning to see how these same theoretical ideas carry over into problems of consumerism and other issues of public policy. As discussed in Chapters 1, 15, and 16, the upsurge of consumerism has opened up a vast, uncharted, yet vitally important set of practical problems. Research efforts by marketing people have been in the vanguard of attempts to solve problems of consumerism, and have caused social scientists in other disciplines to look at marketing with a new respect. Nowhere was this illustrated better than at the Hearings on Modern Advertising Practices, held by the Federal Trade Commission in late 1971.[3]

Third, nonprofit organizations of immense variety—musical groups, ballet companies, and health agencies, for example—are asking whether the field of marketing can help them with their problems. Chapters 1 and 17 point out how this interest is leading to the development of a new and fascinating subfield, social marketing.

Finally, adding to the excitement in the field is the opportunity to make the emerging structure in the field more useful to the manager. Is the current technology being used? My observation is that it is only in scattered and unsystematic ways. Perhaps the best evidence on this is with advertising, which appeared in the Hearings on Modern Advertising Practices. As one of the industry representatives wrote, the hearings "produced surprise that so little was really known about the effects of advertising. This surprise was common to all parties, commissioners, and industry representatives alike." [4]

Our capacity to apply widely these ideas will be enhanced if we better understand company organization. Textbooks in marketing management, including my own, have been derelict in not dealing systematically with organization. Organization places severe constraints on using new technology; the political forces operating inside an organization may at some time suggest to the manager that he should, in a sense, be able to rig the system. To do this, he must fully understand it. Further, organization

[3] J. A. Howard and J. Hulbert, *Advertising and the Public Interest,* Chicago: Crain Communications, Inc., 1973.

[4] Herbert E. Krugman, "Why Three Exposures May Be Enough," *Journal of Advertising Research,* December 1972, pp. 11–14.

poses particular problems for innovating—new products or new marketing technology—as we shall see in Chapter 13. Less dramatically, organization conditions almost everything that goes on within it.

Also, the quality of the output of our teaching—the MBAs—is being questioned. For example, a number of company managers raise some serious doubts.[5] The reasons for this in actionable terms are not clear. The massive wave of acquisitions in the past decade may have drawn company attention away from marketing training. In my opinion, our failure to deal systematically with organization also accounts for a part of the criticism. Our teaching has lacked organizational realism.

A structure of organization permits us to introduce and give insightful perspective upon the relation between marketing strategy and corporate strategy. These concepts of marketing and corporate strategy in turn give us entrée to the highest levels of marketing issues in the company and the relation between marketing and such other issues as diversification, for example.

Hence, a purpose of this book is to redress this imbalance of too little emphasis on organization. It attempts to do this in Chapter 5, in part, by bringing concepts of buying choice to bear on managerial choice.

These are some of the reasons for the sense of excitement which I hope you share.

ACKNOWLEDGMENTS

Insofar as this edition meets the demands now laid upon an introductory text at the graduate level and an advanced text for the undergraduate level, it is because a number of people have been willing to contribute their advice and counsel generously in the preparation of it. John D. Henry, Manager of Market Research, Procter and Gamble Company, was most helpful with Chapters 6, 7, and 8. To pull together this set of ideas into a coherent whole proved difficult. His incisive mind and splendid experience added immensely to whatever merit the chapters on the brand manager possess. Working with him was an exciting adventure.

Dr. Albert Rohloff also reviewed Chapters 6, 7, and 8 and contributed insightfully on the nature of the brand manager's activities.

Robert Klath, Vice President, Corporate Planning, General Foods Corporation, clarified issues of corporate control and the brand manager, especially those in Chapter 7.

Richard D. Harriman, Associate Brand Manager, General Foods Corporation, critically commented upon two drafts of the entire manuscript. In doing this, he added substantially to fact, framework, and clarity.

Professor Abraham Shuchman, my colleague, gave generously of his

---

[5]David L. Hurwood, *New Generation of Marketers: A Management View,* Conference Board Report No. 582 (New York: The Conference Board, 1973).

ideas about the relation between corporate strategy and marketing strategy, as did Professor John O'Shaughnessy. Another colleague, Professor Neil Beckwith, contributed in a number of ways, but especially to Chapter 7. Professor Donald R. Lehmann also was kind enough to comment upon several chapters. Professor David W. Cravens, University of Tennessee, critically read every draft and contributed his splendid insights and grasp of the literature. Professor Harold W. Fox, De Paul University, carefully evaluated two drafts. Professor Mark I. Alpert, University of Texas at Austin, critically examined one draft.

Professor John U. Farley bears no direct responsibility for this book, but he has been an ideal colleague in providing stimulation and intellectual support.

The Alcoa Foundation's grant to develop industrial marketing was timely in supporting research on marketing organization. It is reflected most strongly in Chapter 5, but appears in numerous contexts.

Mrs. Bernice Schuddekopf, with skill, tact, and imagination, saw the manuscript through a number of drafts.

Finally, I am indebted to Deans Courtney C. Brown, George S. James, and Samuel B. Richmond for encouraging an unusually pragmatic intellectual environment in the School of Business. It emphasizes the development of principles, but looks upon principles as means to the end of better administration, not as an end in themselves.

Scarsdale, New York   JOHN A. HOWARD
April 1973

Contents

ix

Conventional accounting methods contrasted. Example 2: Cost estimates and a marketing decision. Example 3: The statistical analysis of product cost —an ideal case. Summary.

part I

Marketing

MARKETING is the process of:

1. Identifying customer needs.
2. Conceptualizing these needs in terms of an organization's capacity to produce.
3. Communicating that conceptualization to the appropriate locus of power in the organization.
4. Conceptualizing the consequent output in terms of the customer needs earlier identified.
5. Communicating that conceptualization to the customer.

Marketing management is the planning and controlling of the marketing process to achieve some end.

Marketing by *organizations* is the topic of this book. Individuals are concerned with the marketing of their products and services. Only organizations, however, typically have the resources to be explicit in the management of their marketing activities.

1

What is marketing management?

INTRODUCTION

ALL HUMAN ORGANIZATIONS—churches, universities, government agencies, corporations, and so forth—have marketing problems. Each organization must produce a service or product needed by an adequate number of people to justify its resource expenditure, or it cannot survive for long. It must let these potential "customers" know that it has this service or product available, and tell them how it will meet their needs. This activity is marketing.

The techniques set forth in this book are applicable to all types of human organizations. One of the best students of consumer behavior the author has ever had the pleasure of working with was a Marine chaplain enrolled in Union Theological Seminary who wanted a better understanding of how to improve relations between American servicemen and native Vietnamese. The same sophisticated ideas about consumers set forth in the following chapters are being applied in studying population control for the government of Kenya in Africa.

Though the techniques are the same, the more fundamental ideas—the underlying assumptions—that guide the implementation of the techniques are quite different. Even when we confine ourselves to physical products, we find substantial differences among countries. The Soviet Union, for example, believes in a highly centralized system. The United States relies on one that is less centralized and takes as its patron saint Adam Smith instead of Nikolai Lenin. As the architect of private enterprise, Smith asserted the following principle:

2

Consumption is the sole end and purpose of all production; and the interest of the producer ought to be attended to, only so far as it may be necessary for promoting that of the consumer. The maxim is so perfectly self-evident that it would be absurd to attempt to prove it.[1]

In order to protect the consumer while applying the concept of private enterprise that Smith endowed us with, the government often finds it necessary to formulate rules of the game for the guidance of the producer. In a complex society like ours, agencies such as the Federal Trade Commission are developed to carry out this rule-administering function. Thus we have those who are regulators and those who are regulated.

The purpose of this book is to serve both, and the purpose of this chapter is to give an overview of these ideas. There must be mutual understanding between the two, regulators and regulated, for effective adjustments to occur. Otherwise there may be chaos, and both will be less effective in performing their respective tasks. We believe that the regulators should understand the marketing system and, moreover, know the means by which regulation enters into the decision processes of the regulated, that is, the professional marketer. The marketer should understand the techniques of marketing, the marketing system in which he is operating, and the nature of the regulatory process if regulation is a central feature of the environment of that marketing system, as it is, increasingly, in the United States.

To an earlier generation, a book serving both sides might seem heretical. The younger generation feels differently. As an associate brand manager with three years' experience for one of the largest advertisers in the country put it:

In the past, business made its decisions through its stockholder constituency. But to make business decisions is no longer a right. It is a privilege that must be earned. We will be permitted to make these decisions in the future only if we can prove our right to do it well.

We have used the term "marketing system" without defining it. Our system is highly complex, as it is in any modern society with advanced technology in mass communication and great amounts of new-product innovation. Therefore we will examine it in some detail; the reader who is already familiar with it can skip the following section.

THE MARKETING SYSTEM

Introduction

The term "system" is used because it aptly describes the phenomenon we are dealing with: a set of elements that interact with one another. The

---

[1] Adam Smith, *Wealth of Nations* (New York: Random House, Inc., 1937), p. 624.

key elements of a *marketing* system are two: the *companies* which produce and market goods and services and the *households* which purchase these goods and services for its members. There are many kinds of each element.

In the part of the American marketing system that deals with consumer products, these elements are manufacturers, wholesalers, retailers, and ultimate consumers. In the part dealing with industrial products (those bought to be used in further manufacturing), the terms are a little different—manufacturers, mill supply houses, and users—but the functions served are roughly the same. The manufacturer provides the product which is the *input* to the marketing system, and this product directly or indirectly reaches the ultimate user, the consumer. Alcoa mines bauxite and converts it into aluminum, which it sells to a can manufacturer. The can manufacturer converts the aluminum into cans, which it sells to food manufacturers. The food manufacturer packs the can with food which it sells to a wholesaler, who in turn sells it to a retailer, who finally sells it to a consumer. Thus the *output* of the system is products and services to the consumer. An opposite flow in the form of money payments from the consumer for the product purchased reaches the various elements back through the system.

A marketing system is for an *economy* as a whole. It is the *means* by which all of the goods and services flow to the consumer from the various stages of manufacturing and all of the funds flow in the reverse direction from the consumer to each of the preceding stages of distribution and manufacturing.

Such a system is essential to the efficient flow of the product to the ultimate consumer. One way that efficiency is affected can be shown simply in Figure 1–1, where *M* refers to the manufacturer, *R* to the retailer, and *C* to the consumer. The upper portion of the figure illustrates a part of a marketing system that has no middleman. Each manufacturer must contact all three consumers, and hence *nine* contacts are required for every producer's product to be available to every consumer. The lower portion, which includes a retailer, requires only six contacts, of which the manufacturers must make only three. If we assume, as in the typical case, that the manufacturer's contact is by a salesman, the cost savings that result from utilizing the services of a middleman can be readily recognized. Other functions of the middleman contribute further to economical distribution. The nature of this system is important because the economic welfare of an economy is strongly determined by its efficiency and sensitivity to the changing needs of consumers. For the manager, it affects his entire marketing operation in the company.

To convey the nature of this complex system, we will examine that part of the marketing system that relates to a single industry—an industry's *dis-*

FIGURE 1–1
How the middleman lowers cost

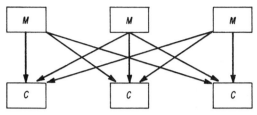

Number of contacts = 3 x 3 = 9

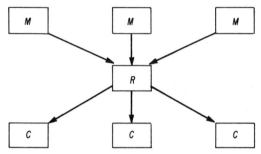

Number of contacts = 3 + 3 = 6

tribution system. Further, only a part of that system will be considered because we will include only the most immediate level of production—the manufacturers producing the consumer goods—and omit the earlier stages in the production process.

The distribution system of an industry

Hierarchy in a distribution system. The interaction of parts of a distribution system is also complex, as implied in Figure 1–1. Figure 1–2, though simplified, clarifies this interaction by considering two characteristics of the marketing system: hierarchy, or levels, and geographic space, or plane. *Hierarchy* is shown by the different levels at which the parts work: manufacturer (A), wholesaler (B), retailer (C) and consumer (D). In this figure, we assume that all manufacturers in the industry use the same distribution system. Each manufacturer sells to wholesalers, each of which, in turn, sells the product to a set of retailers, and, finally, each retailer sells to a set of consumers.

The concept of market *plane* is essential because (as in Figure 1–2) it shows the geographic dispersion of each of the respective parts— manufacturer, wholesaler, retailer, and consumer—over the United States, but with each set on a different plane. This dispersion, particularly in a

FIGURE 1–2
Distribution system of an industry

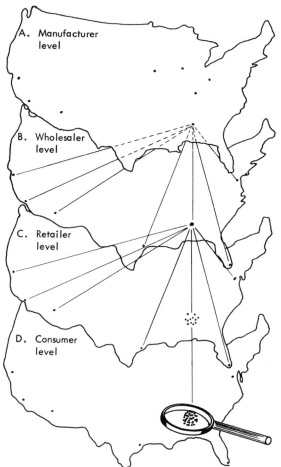

The diagram focuses upon Birmingham, Alabama,
only to illustrate the flow of a consumer product from
level to level over the entire continental United States
(except for Alaska). The number of wholesale establishments, retail stores, and household units shown
for Birmingham is far less than the actual number.

country as large as ours, renders the marketing problem infinitely more
difficult because of the variety of conditions found in different geographic
areas.

Figure 1–2 represents the production and distribution of a particular
product, such as a radio set or a jar of coffee.

MANUFACTURER LEVEL. Each manufacturer, for example, General Electric or R.C.A. (shown by a dot on level A) sells a brand. Assume that each manufacturer produces in a single plant.

A producer of radios in Birmingham, as shown in Figure 1–2, must somehow conceptualize his ultimate market, his potential consumers. Here the real complexity of a marketing system begins to be apparent. We can see that his market information may be less than perfect. If consumers do not like his brand or his way of marketing it, he will be in serious difficulty, because they will turn to his competitor's products. Further, these disgruntled consumers have no ready means to tell him why they are dissatisfied; the easiest thing for them is to buy another brand providing a satisfactory competing brand is readily available. He must somehow conceptualize these consumers in order to understand why they are deserting him and to conceive reasonable solutions to the problem (for example, price is too high, the advertising doesn't tell them enough, his retailers are out of stock because his salesmen are ineffective). The conceptualizing task is difficult because the consumers are myriad, literally millions in fact, and they are not all alike. They can be remarkably different in various parts of the country; for example, those on the West Coast like dark, heavy coffee, while those in the East prefer it light. The densities of people—how closely they live together—are also highly varied; contrast the New York area with the southern part of Utah. Further, these people differ not only geographically but also demographically—some areas have relatively younger or older people, more women, more blacks, and so forth. They also differ psychographically, or in how they respond to marketing effort.

WHOLESALER LEVEL. You will recall from Figure 1–2 that the manufacturer at Birmingham sells to wholesalers throughout the country. A wholesaler's role is to _collect_ products from a number of manufacturers, to _sort_ these products into groupings that serve the retailer's needs, and then to _disperse_ them geographically by shipping the groupings of products to the respective retailers. In one part of the country the consumers want only electricity-powered radios, in another, both electricity- and battery-powered, and in a third, only battery. From the wholesaler's view, each wholesaler competes in the process of carrying out these functions with other wholesalers. He must persuade as many effective retailers as possible to handle his product. He bargains with his supplying manufacturer for a satisfactory buying price and with his retailer for a satisfactory selling price. His market area is more restricted geographically than that of the manufacturer (as is shown in Figure 1–2) because the wholesaler is expected to supply a retailer quickly when the retailer needs the product; the manufacturer is typically too far away to provide this fast service.

To conceptualize their markets in order to achieve effective market planning, both wholesalers and manufacturers need detailed information on and explanations for the geographic location of customers. For this the wholesaler uses such concepts as urbanism, economic regions, and standard metropolitan areas. These are especially helpful in delineating the dynamics of marketing because market potential is in effect a *moving* target, as economic conditions fluctuate, consumers needs change, and populations move.

RETAILER LEVEL. The retailer's general function, analogous to the wholesaler's, is to *collect* products from a number of wholesalers, to *sort* these products into groupings that meet consumers' needs (such as in a grocery store), and to *disperse* the products geographically. The difference is that the retailer disperses directly to the consumer.

Each retailer in the C level of Figure 1–2 competes with other retailers in his market area. He too bargains for a satisfactory price from his wholesaler and from his consumer, but government rules can limit this. Much of the bargaining is hidden, however, and occurs slowly through the myriad ways the retailer employs to adjust his margin of profit.

CONSUMER LEVEL. The magnifying glass on level D of Figure 1–2 shows how each retail store serves many consumers. The consumer compares the price, product, and service of different retailers in deciding which brand to buy. This ultimate user of the product is the focus of attention of the manufacturer's marketing manager, whose task is to translate the company's offering into a description—a "package" of ideas—that fits the consumer's way of conceptualizing according to his needs and then to translate these needs back to the production manager so that the factory's output will more closely conform to them.

Because the marketing manager is so far removed from the consumer, in both a geographic and an emotional sense, he may become preoccupied with the intermediate levels (the wholesaler and retailer, for example) and tend to ignore the consumer. But if he does this for long, he does it to his sorrow. When the consumer finds a better brand and shifts to it, a marketing manager's sales may not reflect it immediately because inventories of his brand will be accumulating at the retailer and wholesaler levels; neither of these anticipate the change in consumer purchases and so fail to adapt to it by reducing their buying. When he does catch on to what is happening, the damage is often done. Winning back consumers can be costly. A few bitter experiences of this type teach a marketing manager that unless his product pleases the consumer his efforts at good wholesaler and retailer relations may go for naught.

SUMMARY: INDUSTRY DISTRIBUTION SYSTEM LEVELS. The function of the marketing system is to collect, sort, and disperse the product in meeting the needs of the consumer. Both wholesalers and retailers perform these functions. The wholesaler buys from a number of manufacturers; this serves to collect geographically. He sorts the products of these various supplying manufacturers in such a way as to meet the needs of particular retailers; this disperses these assortments geographically. Retailers collect, sort, and disperse in an analogous way but at one level lower in the system and to a much more restricted market geographically.

Market potential is a concept essential to an understanding of the marketing process: Expected purchases of all brands in a given area for a given period.

Diversified needs of an adequate marketing system

Thus far we have considered only one distribution system and only one *channel*, one route, within that system—manufacturer to wholesaler to retailer to consumer. In actuality, there is a large number of other possible channels. A manufacturer also often uses more than one channel for the same product and so has a marketing channel system made up of more than one channel. In North Dakota and Utah, where population is sparse, for example, he will use a wholesaler, while in New York, where population is concentrated, he will sell direct to the retailer. A variety of possible channels is shown in Figure 1–3.

This variety is needed to meet such varying circumstances as geographic concentration of buyers, distances, value of product, physical nature of product, and financial capacities of buyers and sellers. Channel 1 in Figure 1–3 makes use of a mail-order arrangement. Sears, Roebuck and Co. first came to national prominence by performing this role. Channel 2 is used by Avon (cosmetics) and Fuller (household brushes). Oil companies often own their own service stations; they illustrate channel 3. Jewel Tea Company, in distributing by truck direct to the consumer in parts of the country, is the "wagon retailer" of channel 4. Large sellers serving large stores in major cities represent channel 5. Channel 6 can be illustrated by the food industry, where a full-service wholesaler may sell to subjobbers, or, in more familiar terms, limited-service wholesalers. Clothing represents channel 7 when a sales agent collects from a variety of manufacturers and in turn sells to a wholesaler who sells to both subjobbers and retailers. In channel 8, the manufacturer has his own branch offices scattered over the country, usually staffed by salesmen who sell to retailers; as indicated by the dashed line, this channel is often used for *industrial* products. Channel 9 is fairly obvious in consumer goods, and 10 is widely used with industrial products. This list of alternative channels is by no means exhaustive; for example, the alternatives shown here for industrial products are quite incomplete. The mill supply house, which corresponds to the wholesaler in consumer goods, is missing. The manufacturer's agent, widely used in industrial marketing, is also omitted.

Evaluating a total marketing system

It is much too premature to attempt to evaluate a marketing system here. More will be said in Chapter 16, but we can set the stage so that the

FIGURE 1–3
Manufacturers' alternative marketing channels

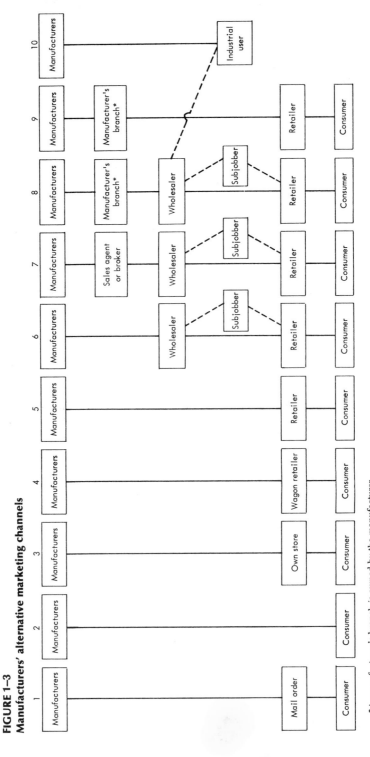

°A manufacturer's branch is owned by the manufacturer.
Source: Adapted from John R. Bromell, *Primary Channels of Distribution for Manufacturers* (Washington, D.C.: Department of Commerce, July 1950), p. 3.

reader will have some points of leverage for thinking about evaluation as he considers the details of how a marketing system works.

One important but perhaps nonobvious point is that the level of marketing activity of an economy appears to grow with the standard of living. Perhaps this is because a more complex society increases the need for the manufacturer to communicate directly with the consumer. At the same time, better communication technology encourages this communication, and there are more new products to require it. To illustrate, we can contrast the standard of living in the Soviet Union and the United States, as in Figure 1–4. The differences are remarkable in most cases, showing up

FIGURE 1–4
American and Russian standards of living

	New York	Moscow		New York	Moscow		New York	Moscow
Beef (1 kilogram)	45	196	Oranges	8	138	Refrigerator	32 hours	343 hours
Chicken (1 kilogram)	16	260	Vodka (one liter)	120	604	Washing machine (automatic)	53 hours	204 hours
Ice cream (plain vanilla)	22	177	Toilet soap (small bar)	2	25	Television, color	147 hours	1,111 hours
Milk, fresh (one liter)	7	32	Medium car	762 hours	7,907 hours	Telephone rent (per month)	52	246
Eggs (one doz.)	17	162	Diapers (10 cotton)	46	983	Haircut, men	46	39

The New York Times, *February 2, 1971, Sec. E, p. 5.*

Costs are expressed in time spent on the job by the average industrial worker in New York and Moscow. All figures are for minutes, except where otherwise indicated.

greatly in appliances and least of all in the labor-intensive task of cutting hair. Even in the Soviet Union, however, for many years a form of trademark has been required so that a consumer can identify the factory that produced a malperforming item. In recent years, as its standard of living has grown, the Soviet Union has been moving significantly toward mass advertising, though on nothing yet that approaches the American scale.

The criterion by which we have tended to judge our marketing system historically has been a growing standard of living. Earlier generations in the United States felt that this criterion would give people the satisfaction they wanted, as is the case now in the less developed countries. When the standard of living is low, a growing standard probably accomplishes this. But when the standard is high, people begin to want their marketing system to satisfy other goals as well.

One of the new goals is sensitivity to the consumer's need for improved products, which becomes especially important in an economy of rapid technological change. Its application in the Russian and Yugoslavian economies was pointed up by Khrushchev in a fascinating description of an exchange he had with Tito:

> I also asked Comrade Tito if they had much of a problem with fashion-conscious young men and women chasing after tourists, trying to buy all sorts of trinkets off them, especially around the hotels. "In our country," I said, "we are ashamed to see our people buying and bartering and begging from foreigners. How do you deal with this problem?"
>
> "We don't really have that problem here," said Tito, "and I'll tell you why. When some item becomes fashionable among our young people, we buy the necessary equipment for a factory and start manufacturing the item ourselves. Of course, consumer tastes are always changing, but all you have to do is use your head and make sure your industries keep up with fashions and adapt to changing consumer demands."[2]

This goal became especially important in the United States following World War II, which initiated a period of exceedingly rapid product change that changed the nature of much of the consumer industry. But success in meeting this goal helped to precipitate new problems and a corresponding new set of goals that have to do with what traditionally has been thought of as the *means* of marketing. These are concerned with adequacy of information to the consumer and the effects of marketing upon the basic character of Americans. These goals give rise to such questions about marketing as: Does it make Americans more materialistic and more cynical?

That these emerging criticisms should develop in the postwar technological environment is not surprising. Food is a prime example. Traditionally it came basically from the soil. We had developed a culture which included rules for wise eating. Almost suddenly, edible things can be made by chemistry (for example, protein can be derived from crude oil). But we have neither the culture to guide us in the consumption of foods from these sources nor the time for the thousands of years necessary to build it up by trial and error. If we are to maintain our standard of living, we must investigate these new products. To do so we need an enormous amount of information, which it is the role of the manufacturer to provide.

---

[2]Nikita Khrushchev, *Khrushchev Remembers*, trans. Strobe Talbott (Boston: Little, Brown & Co., 1970), p. 391.

He uses the most effective means he can—often television. Television is an intrusive kind of medium; it is no wonder that the public becomes concerned about its effects on children or on basic human values. It allegedly causes people to buy things they do not need, thus littering the earth with the trappings of a materialistic civilization it has abetted, if not created. Similarly, appliances add immensely to the standard of living but entail serious problems of service and repair, even to the point where they are replaced rather than repaired when they fail. New toys bring vastly greater opportunities to please the kiddies, but when combined with another technological change—television—they open up equally vast opportunities for deception.

These changes are having significant and perhaps profound implications for the nature of American marketing. New laws are passed frequently and new administrative rules such as those from the Federal Trade Commission are being issued continually to meet these changing conditions. Consequently, marketing should be approached, even by the manager, from a socially evaluative point of view.

Because most of the criticisms of the marketing system focus upon the consumer segment, they might seem irrelevant to those engaged in industrial marketing. This is not so. Many industrial companies are now producing consumer products or contemplating that possibility. W. R. Grace first entered foods when in 1966 it

... was on the lookout for ways to get a good return on its investment. A consumer division seemed the answer, and the company began investing in a number of consumer-oriented acquisitions which now include F. A. O. Schwarz, toy retailer, and John Meyer of Norwich, a ready-to-wear manufacturer, as well as grocery operations.[3]

Further, for many industrial companies, what happens in the ultimate consumer market is a major consideration in the success of their sales. Government regulations applied to consumer markets will also inevitably "rub off" on the industrial markets, thus stimulating criticism there. Finally, if the consumer marketing end of the system fails to perform adequately, the whole system will probably be called into question.

Before addressing ourselves further to criticisms of the marketing system, however, we should obtain a better understanding of the system and how it works, in some detail. This examination is particularly necessary because some of the well-intentioned criticism springs from the premise that all marketing management decisions are well-informed, rational choices. A commonly held view is that modern psychological research techniques enable the seller to attack the vulnerabilities of the consumer and render him helpless. If this premise is not valid, it may be

---

[3] *Advertising Age*, August 30, 1971, p. 200.

that one of the major areas of improvement in the operation of the American marketing system can come about through better management of the marketing operation of the companies that make up some of the central elements of the marketing system.

Aside from the possibility of improving internal management in terms of its own objectives of better meeting society's needs, we must somehow change the system if it is not performing adequately, as judged by society. To change it requires that the rules influence managerial behavior in an appropriate way. Thus, as regulators we must understand the manager's decision process. This is complicated by our lack of knowledge, as we will see below in discussing public policy as an environmental influence on decision.

MARKETING MANAGEMENT: DECISION, PLANNING, AND CONTROL

Introduction

In considering how the individual selling unit in the marketing system operates, we will investigate the question: What is marketing management? Some readers will be students who intend to be in marketing management, others already are marketing managers, and still others may be in related activities that bear on marketing management in either a managerial or a regulative capacity. To meet all their needs our main objective in this book is to develop a structure, a "theory," of managerial marketing around which they can organize their reading and experience in order to arrive at a better understanding of it.

This understanding can serve two objectives. First, it will help them obtain new insights from the experiences they will be acquiring on the job in the future. Inevitably they will develop from experience some such structure to serve this crucial need anyway, so they can profit from new experience and new knowledge. To acquire such a structure from experience alone, however, is a slow and often uncertain process. Formal education can help them to speed this up so they grow in marketing skill much faster. Second, understanding of marketing management will permit a better grasp of the role of marketing in economic development, which many countries are so earnestly seeking. This structure is culture-free and can be applied to any environment. In general, study of marketing management leads to a better evaluation of marketing activity in terms of its performance in meeting the consumer's needs.

Marketing management is the process of decision making, planning, and controlling the marketing aspects of a company in terms of the marketing concept, somewhere within the marketing system. Before proceeding to examine some of the details of this process, comments on two aspects will be helpful background.

The *marketing concept* is simple in principle but often very difficult, if not impossible, to fully implement. Adam Smith's comment cited above is most consistent with it. The concept is that a company can more effectively serve its own objectives if it will integrate the various aspects of its marketing activities explicitly so as to meet the preferences of its *customers.* To one unfamiliar with company practice the need for implementing the concept and the capacity to do it would seem to be so obvious as not to merit discussion. This is typically not so, however, for many reasons which will be presented in the following chapters.

This process of marketing management takes place "somewhere" within the marketing system. Having seen the marketing system portrayed, you know that "somewhere" can be within any of the many, many companies—manufacturing, wholesaling and retailing—that make it up. Marketing management is practiced in every one of them.

Assume, to simplify, that we are concerned only with the manufacturing level in a direct sense because the manager we are considering occupies a marketing management position there. What is the nature of each of the three elements making up the marketing management process: decision making, planning, and control?

Marketing decision making

ADAPTATION OF CONTROLLABLE TO UNCONTROLLABLE. The manager makes decisions about things he can control—the *controllable.* In very general terms, what does he decide? Roughly, he decides the kind of a product to produce, the kind of a distribution system to use, the price to charge, advertising messages and media, and the salesmen's message to customers on whom they call.

In making these decisions he learns from experience to use an operating principle which simplifies his task and avoids substantial frustration. It might be called the "law" of marketing management, like other rules of behavior such as Aristotle's Golden Mean and the Golden Rule. This "law" of marketing management states: Since some things are controllable and others are not, separate the controllable from the uncontrollable and don't waste your time and energy trying to change the uncontrollable. Rather attempt to understand it so you can adapt the controllable to the uncontrollable in such a way as to satisfy your company's needs as effectively as possible. The application of this law is an art in which analytic tools from science can aid.

As suggested by the discussion of the marketing system, there is a complex of more or less uncontrollable forces operating on the manager. These can be summarized, as in the outer hexagon of Figure 1–5, as *competition, demand, nonmarketing cost, structure of distribution, public policy,* and *company organization.* Underlying these are, of course, the much more fundamental forces of technological, social, political, and economic change. While over the long term these factors will shape the nature of the

FIGURE 1–5
Elements of marketing management

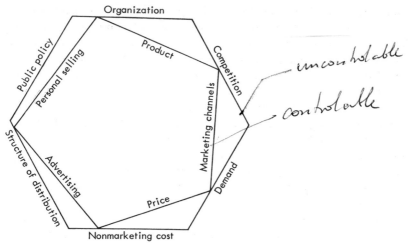

uncontrollable forces, the manager is forced by such aspects as convenience and lack of adequate data to concern himself mainly with the immediate uncontrollable item.

The inside pentagon of Figure 1–5 portrays the controllable elements,
the ones about which the marketing manager can decide. The art of marketing management is the effective adaptation of these elements to the uncontrollables in the marketing environment so as to optimize the company's welfare. This optimum welfare can be thought of as the maximum
area attainable in the inner pentagon within the constraints of its environment, the outer hexagon. A recent consulting experience by the author
can illustrate the abstract idea of how a change in the market environment
creates a need to adapt.

A large paper company had developed a copier machine which had
proven quite profitable as long as the company could require the buyer to
use its paper in the copier. In 1969, however, the Federal Trade Commission (FTC) ruled that a tied sale—the practice whereby the manufacturer
requires the buyer of its copier to use its paper alone—was not legal in this
industry. Thus a change in an uncontrollable feature, public policy,
created a problem. The usual solution—the customary way of adapting—is
to buy the retail stores which distribute its machines. When the machine
is sold to the user, he can be urged to use the company's own paper. Unfortunately, in this case the company had a long-term objective of expansion via merger, and to attract merger possibilities, the stock earnings
ratio of the company had to be high. To invest in retail stores would have

required a heavy outlay of funds and a long period of development before a satisfactory return could be obtained. Consequently, when the recession of 1970–71 occurred, the company encountered serious financial problems.

CONTROLLABLE FEATURES.   With Figure 1–5 for perspective, we will first examine each of the controllables. These relate to (1) product or service variation, (2) selection and management of marketing channels for distributing the product, (3) setting prices, and (4) fixing and allocating the promotional budget to advertising and selling.

1   *Product variation.*   A company's modification of the nature of its offering is achieved through product and service decisions which are essentially of two types. Some decisions are concerned with *change* of an *existing* product to conform more nearly to the demands of the market. These changes may be superficial or fundamental (for example, the use of a new package as opposed to a revolutionary redesign of the product). Other decisions concern *dropping* or *adding* an item to the product line. These decisions of product change and change in product line are common, since few companies in the United States produce a single product. They are also serious decisions for most firms. A marketing manager must be constantly on the alert to exploit new-product opportunities and to avoid continuing an unprofitable item.

2   *Marketing channels.*   All companies must choose the set of channels they think will be most effective. The possibilities, as we have seen, are almost unlimited. Selecting the correct channel requires careful analysis, particularly since the decision usually involves a heavy investment of time by managers and salesmen and goes far in fixing the rest of the marketing plan for some time into the future. The spatial aspects of the structure of distribution, for example, the geographical concentration of buyers in each market, will make a great difference in determining the best set of channels for a particular situation.

3   *Prices.*   Prices must be set. Competitors' prices typically establish significant limits to the range of choice, but there is usually some discretion. There are many pricing problems. Not only must a number of products be priced, but if a marketing channel other than direct-to-user is employed, consideration must often be given to the prices set at each level of the marketing channel. Finally, some buyers may receive a different price (or discount as it is usually called), based on such factors as the quantity they purchase.

4   *Promotion.*   Most companies must use some type of promotional effort. The function of both types of promotion—*advertising* and *personal selling*—is to provide potential buyers with information about the product: its quality, its availability, and its price. A salesman may well perform other functions, such as delivery and repair, but, to simplify he will be viewed here as a conveyer and receiver of information. Thus advertising and personal selling are alternative methods of performing the function of

conveying information, but a particular blend of the two may be more effective than either of them alone. In many companies promotion decisions require much of the marketing manager's time.

Advertising is concerned with deciding how much advertising to use; what media to use (newspapers, radio, television, direct mail, billboards, car cards, point-of-purchase display, etc.); the frequency with which the advertisements will appear (daily, weekly, monthly, etc.); and the message to be employed (this involves the artwork and copy prepared for printed media and the commercials prepared for radio and television). Personal selling deals with the selection, supervision, and training of salesmen; the allocation of salesmen to territories; and the evaluation of salesmen.

"Promotion" is also often used in the trade literature in a restricted sense of special pricing arrangements to retailers and consumers.

UNCONTROLLABLE FEATURES. The uncontrollable or environmental elements that the decision maker must adapt to, as shown in the outer hexagon of Figure 1–5, are not uncontrollable in an absolute sense. Instead they can best be viewed as controllable, but only at a *cost*. They are (1) demand, (2) competition, (3) nonmarketing costs, (4) structure of distribution, (5) public policy, and (6) company organization.

Company demand is the expected sales volume of a brand or service for a given period of time, with given marketing practices and under given environmental conditions. For instance, the sales of company A last year were $1,259,613,000. Undoubtedly, this sales figure would have been different had the company used different marketing practices or had the environmental conditions surrounding the company been different. The analysis of demand is the study of buyer behavior, which is the source of sales. In recent years the economist, the general psychologist, the social psychologist, and the sociologist have made contributions to the understanding of buyer behavior. (These contributions will be summarized in Chapter 3.) Demand is the marketing man's special province—on this topic he should be the recognized authority in his company. For this reason he should be a key member of overall planning groups in the company.

Competition is the degree of rivalry among companies in terms of the number and size of the companies in the industry and other market characteristics that limit a marketing manager's freedom to maneuver. These market characteristics, which will be described in Chapter 2, make up the *structure of competition* that a company faces, and they determine the kind of rivalry that will appear in a market. The rivalry may be stable, for example, or it may be highly chaotic, as exemplified in a "price war." How competitors are likely to respond is often one of the critical considerations in a marketing manager's decision in such matters as where to position a brand.

Marketing decisions usually involve some estimate of *nonmarketing* costs. The marketing manager, however, is concerned only with those cost outlays that are affected by his decisions. For example, assume the problem is to decide whether to establish an advertising budget of $100,000 or $125,000. At least two costs are involved: the cost of the advertising, which is a marketing cost, and the cost of producing the quantity of product necessary for the additional sales volume resulting from each of the advertising expenditures, which is a nonmarketing cost. Both costs are affected by the marketing manager's decision, but only advertising is controllable from his point of view. The cost of producing the additional units he must take as given, and thus it is an environmental constraint. Just as there are several significant concepts of demand, there are numerous cost concepts, each one having its use, as will be elaborated in Chapter 4. Moreover, in dealing with cost, the marketing manager usually must rework the conventional cost data found in his company in order to make it useful for his purposes, and therefore he must be familiar with appropriate cost concepts.

Another uncontrollable feature is the industry's *distribution* system. It is made up of all of the marketing channels currently in use by the industry, and a manager must decide which channels are best for his needs. The spatial features of the market, for example, the geographical concentration of buyers, are key dimensions of the structure of distribution. Because the concept of a distribution system was explained earlier it will not be dealt with in the discussion of environmental constraints in Part II. Instead it will be covered as a part of the management of marketing channels, Chapter 14.

Becoming increasingly influential in marketing decisions is the law, which embodies *public policy*. It is the rules of the game laid down by public bodies to influence the company to market in such way as to better serve the public interest. In some decisions, public policy is the consideration bearing the most weight. For instance, under certain conditions the Robinson-Patman Act prohibits charging different prices to different buyers. This may seriously limit a company's freedom in setting prices. Also, the FTC is continuing to be concerned with deceptive advertising and is questioning whether advertising adequately informs the consumer. Public policy also exerts an unobtrusive but pervasive influence which must be considered in long-term predictions concerning marketing channels. The efforts of the antitrust agencies to limit such things as exclusive dealing and the practice of vendors selling only to certain buyers instead of to all buyers, for instance, will probably result in a greater number of available marketing channels.

Unfortunately, the current state of the art of regulating marketing does not permit us to deal effectively with it. True, we do have a fairly adequate formal way of looking at competitive practices called the market structure concept, and we will use it in Chapter 2 on competition. But for the newer area of consumer information and the one which is currently in the greatest state of change, we have almost no structure. For marketing per se, regulation is much the most important area of public policy. It is very complex because, like all public policy, it involves bringing society's values to bear upon the phenomenon of marketing practices. Our less-than-ideal solution is to delay extensive discussion until the end of the book and then to devote the last two chapters to it.

Finally, there is *company organization*. The uncontrollable factors that we have been discussing up to now are the more general, global kinds of influences. For the manager, however, nothing is much more important than the fact that he makes his decisions in an organization. It dominates the criteria by which he makes his decisions and influences the information he applies to these criteria in coming to his decisions. Until this central nature of organization is recognized, he can engage in marketing management only in a superficial way. It is like talking about modern physics and chemistry without considering the concept of the atom. Chapter 5 is devoted to organization.

Marketing planning

Decisions are basic. Yet individual decisions are only the ingredients in the central activity of a marketing manager, which is to *plan*. Individual decisions are put together in a mosaic which provides the systematic, coherent, comprehensive, and unified approach to marketing a brand that is represented by a *marketing plan*. Constructing the *annual marketing plan* for a brand or group of products is one of the major tasks of marketing management.

There are a variety of plans, but the annual plan is considerably the most important. It is a detailed description of each of the decision areas for the coming 12 month period. Its full significance can be made much clearer in the context of company organization considered in Chapter 5. To give some grasp of its magnitude of detail, however, you might bear in mind that the annual plan for Instant Maxwell House coffee at General Foods in 1966 was a 200-page typewritten document. Literally, a book.

Marketing control

A plan is a statement of what the marketing manager intends to do. A central question always facing him once he has executed a plan, however, is the retrospective one: How well did it do, in fact? How successful was I?

Control attempts to answer such questions by providing a *measure* of performance, such as market share. A *standard* for that measure of performance is also required. Is 10 percent a "good" share, or does 20 percent represent "good" performance? In addition, he must have a *feedback* system which tells him the market results of the plan—sales computed as a share—compared to the standard. Finally, he needs these measures regularly, and so he develops a *market monitoring system* by which he regularly evaluates and from which he makes such adjustments as will keep his performance within acceptable limits. He thus keeps his marketing operation under *control*. Repeatedly, we will have occasion to discuss the problem of control, particularly in Chapters 6, 7, and 8. The central points made here are intended only to serve as an introduction. It is, however, the chief means by which a marketing organization maintains sensitivity to the market, which is essential to its own welfare and to its capacity to meet society's needs.

Summary: Application of marketing management process

To put the somewhat abstract notion of the marketing management process to work requires considerably more concepts and information. These concepts are detailed graphically in Figure 1–6. Most of the essential elements of marketing management are presented in an integrated way in this model of the marketing decision process.

At the top of the diagram is *company objectives*, which give overall guidance to all the firm's activities, including marketing. Stemming from company objectives are *marketing objectives*, which are more specifically tailored to marketing activities, as will be described in Chapter 5. Given these specific marketing objectives, the manager proceeds to analyze his market so as to identify the marketing opportunities he has (*market opportunity analysis*) and uses this analysis to begin the imaginative task of formulating possible courses of action. He analyzes his market externally by examining the elements of his environment (*analysis of environmental influences*), particularly buyer behavior (*analysis of buyer behavior*), to see what opportunities they offer him. He has found, perhaps, that it is helpful to divide his potential consumers into low-income and high-income groups and then to examine his market on a segment-by-segment basis (*market segment analysis*). From this analysis he selects those segments he believes should constitute his best market targets (*selection of market targets*), and he will try to sell to these instead of to everybody—he uses the rifle instead of the shotgun method.

Notice also that from his analysis of environmental influences he may reconsider a decision already made and change his view not only of market opportunity but even of marketing objectives. He might conclude, for example, that a market share of 20 percent is much too high and all he can really expect is 10 percent. It is even conceivable that the still earlier decision as to company objectives would be reconsidered. The anticipated smaller market share, for example, might suggest that the growth objective of the company is unobtainable or that profit should be given greater weight than was originally intended.

FIGURE 1–6
Marketing decision framework

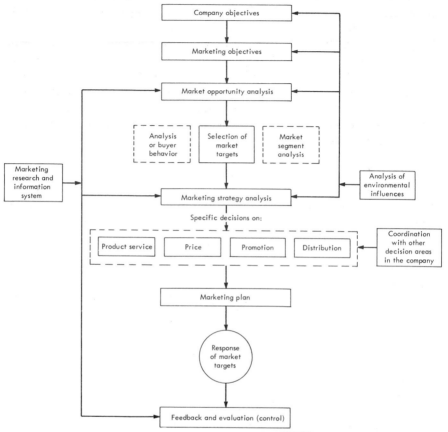

Source: Developed by David W. Cravens, the University of Tennessee, 1970.

To the available marketing alternatives he applies *marketing strategy analysis* to decide which ones he should consider with some care. Marketing strategy is a vitally important but subtle concept. It consists of a set of rules agreed upon with higher management. These rules serve as part of the marketing manager's frame of reference and thus act as general guidelines in directing his decisions. The chairman and president of the Purex Company recently stated that "The Purex *strategy* is to put out a product with a minimum of advertising, then depend on promotions to grocers at favorable prices and the appearance of the package in the price advantage."[4] The rules implied in this statement put severe limits on the

---

[4] *The New York Times*, October 10, 1971, p. F7.

alternatives in marketing decisions that marketing people in the Purex Company can consider.

In applying his strategy, the marketing manager makes his decisions about *product and service, price, promotion* (advertising and selling), *distribution* and channels in a systematic and integrated way such as to constitute a *marketing plan.* In formulating this plan he must, of course, secure *coordination with other decision areas in the company.* After formulating the plan he initiates it and then observes the *response of market targets* by means of *feedback and evaluation* in order to determine whether the marketing operation is performing adequately and therefore is in *control.*

The repeated analyses carried out in the foregoing processes—market opportunity analysis, marketing strategy analysis and feedback and evaluation (control)—are often supported by *market research,* which is the systematic collection of data to support decision, planning, and control. Much of this information is made available through a computerized *information system.*

While this summary offers highly useful perspective and details on the process by which the marketing manager adapts to his environment, it is a simplified view. The remainder of the book will fill in details on the marketing management process and the nature of the problem of evaluating a marketing system in terms of social objectives.

DISCUSSION QUESTIONS

1. What is the marketing process?
2. Why is there a need to evaluate a society's marketing system?
3. Do you believe that a manager should concern himself with social evaluation? If so, why? If not, why not?
4. What are the controllable and uncontrollable elements of marketing management?
5. Marketing strategy is a subtle but vital element of effective marketing management. Why should this be so?

part II

Environmental constraints

To CONCEPTUALIZE a marketing problem we must, as marketers, learn how competitors' activity affect us, how buyers respond to our marketing effort, what the cost of marketing effort is, and how our individual position in the corporate hierarchy shapes the picture of the marketing process. In studying the marketing system, we will treat each of these four conditions as an environmental constraint and view each of them as having a structure. In this way we can adopt a general approach and say that structure generates behavior, or more specifically, that structure with its input represents a process which generates an output. We will see this best illustrated, perhaps, in buyer behavior, where information is the input, a set of variables such as attitude and the relations among them constitute a structure, and purchasing behavior is the output.

Ideally, all four structures—competition, demand, cost, and organization—would be dealt with simultaneously, because each one intimately relates to the other three in a number of ways, and all enter into a marketing decision. To do so would make exposition impossible, however. The order of consideration was chosen to reduce the problem of repetition, although it cannot be eliminated.

Chapter 2 emphasizes competitors' responses to one anothers' marketing decisions and focuses upon buyers' responses and costs only insofar as needed to explain competitive behavior. Nevertheless it is clear that the way buyers conceptualize the products sets the framework for competitive action.

Chapter 3 will focus upon the buyer's response to market variables.

25

Competition will be left implicit, except for the concepts of product class and evoked set, while costs per se will be ignored.

Chapter 4 sets a theoretical framework for understanding costs. Empirical measurement techniques for the identification of relevant costs are presented on the assumption that the marketing manager's objective is in some sense to maximize profits.

Chapter 5 provides a structure for explaining how the organization shapes managers' decisions. This influence process has important implications for both better management and better conformity to the needs of society. For example, the chapter suggests a partial answer, at least, to why the concept of a computerized marketing information system should have foundered so badly.

2

Structure of competition

RATIONALE FOR MARKETING

A RATIONALE for marketing management from the viewpoint of the manager can endow the concept with greater logic and meaning. The purpose of marketing as used here is to inform the buyer. Terms like "sell" and "persuade" carry connotations of power that are incorrect. Marketing effort in the sense of providing the right information to the right person at the right time can have an effect that will "influence" the buyer. However, the process can be more accurately phrased as one "that will help the buyer make up his mind."

The pervasiveness of the communication function of marketing may not be obvious, however. An examination of the communicative nature of each of the elements of the marketing mix will make this clear. Advertising and selling are obviously intended to tell the buyer something. What is sometimes forgotten, however, is how easily and painlessly they provide information to the buyer as contrasted with his having to search for it. Other promotional devices communicate, too, but less obviously— for example, point-of-purchase display. Even price communicates some important but varied information. When a buyer is not well informed about the brand, price tells him what the product is in the sense of what product class it belongs in; here it is an *identifier*. When he is not only poorly informed but also has no other ready source of information, it tells him something about how good the brand is; it is an *evaluator*. Most commonly, price tells him how much he will have to give up of other things (foregone opportunities) if he buys the brand; it is a *constraint*.

Marketing channels also communicate in that they tell the buyer how conveniently they can show him a brand physically if he goes to buy it. The physical appearance of the brand always tells him what it is explicitly so that he can identify it in the future. The buyer also can draw on other experience in order to make interpretations about whether the brand or product is good or bad. A red tomato connotes more flavor than a green one.

Buyers need information; they are psychologically uncomfortable if they are forced to buy when it is inadequate. It is not always obvious why buyers have this need. Even when frequently purchased brands haven't changed for a long time, however, the need for information does not diminish. New people come into the market, and newlyweds establish homes for the first time. Accustomed buyers occasionally have a need for change or variety. If the same kind of food is eaten three times a day, its appreciation and value are rapidly depreciated. Over time the way products are used tends to change. Bicycles, once instruments of transportation, became means of enjoyment and now are widely used also for physical fitness. Many products are not purchased frequently; during the interim between purchases they are forgotten, and memory must be refreshed. Since World War II the increased pace of technological change has speeded up new-product introduction, thus confronting the buyer regularly with new brands. Finally, a person buys things for their symbolic role, to identify himself to others and to serve his self-concept. In a society with a high standard of living, there are almost infinite ways that basic human wants like hunger can be satisfied. The need of buyers to identify themselves thus takes a higher priority in choice. Communication itself is thought to help build this kind of value into a brand. The Marlboro cigarette is "better"—more satisfying—because it gives the smoker a sense of being a he-man riding a horse alone on a mountaintop, and he thinks he might appear this way to others also.

Thus the provision of needed information to the buyer constitutes a guiding rationale for marketing management. Given that the buyer needs information and that the function of marketing is to inform the buyer, the marketing manager is faced with the decision of how much to spend and what means to employ to that end—what marketing mix to use. Chapter 3 is devoted to the consumer's need for information in his purchasing decisions and details how the seller can benefit by providing it. Chapter 4 considers concepts necessary for obtaining an estimate of the cost of obtaining the benefit to the company that is provided by the consumer buying its brand.

This chapter, within the framework of this rationale for marketing, will set forth concepts of competitive structure and describe the *process* by which the conditions of competitive structure generate competitive rivalry. This rivalry gives an urgency to the necessity that the marketing manager meet the buyer's need. It is the driving force that generates much marketing activity, as in the following example: "Stung by a series of marketing setbacks at the hands of Procter & Gamble, Scott Paper Co. has put into operation a sweeping reorganization of its packaged products division at a time when P & G is starting to knife into Scott's East Coast toilet tissue business."[1] The marketing decision maker—president, marketing manager, or brand manager—has little or no control over these competitive conditions. When he does not have control, he must strive to understand these conditions so he can adapt effectively to them. From this understanding he hopes to be able to predict the consequences of a given competitive structure.

A competitor is one who sells a product that in *the view of the buyer* is substitutable for some other brand. A buyer has a set of needs or motives. He perceives a certain set of brands as meeting these needs. This array of brands can be conceptualized as a *product class*. Thus, when we speak of "industry" we view it as defined by the product class, not as defined by the U.S. Census or some other equally arbitrary method. The seller of one of the brands in the product class must share his sales with competitors. Competitive structure gives an objective view of the process by which this sharing is accomplished and so provides a framework of strategy formulation.

It is useful to think of two levels of competition: within class and within evoked set. First, there is the market-positioning view of competition, which considers the position of one brand in relation to other brands in the product class. A recent trade paper headline asked, "Is this the era of positioning?" Much attention is being devoted by marketers to the effectual positioning of their brands, an indication of the importance of the concept of a buyer-determined product class.

To obtain a more concrete understanding of market positioning, it is helpful to think in terms of an operational measure in which the technique of nonmetric scaling is applied. An oversimplified way of describing the technique in this instance is to ask buyers to consider whether there is greater difference between brands A and B than between C and D, between brands A and C than between B and D, and so on, until all pairs in the class have been compared. By computer manipulation, the results will show how far apart each of the brands is to the other brands, as judged by the buyers. To the extent the brands are "close" to one another they are substitutable, and competition can be thought of as intense.

Figure 2–1 illustrates the idea of competitive positioning. Brands A and B are close together but quite some distance from C and D. The next step is to ask what position the buyers would like best. This *ideal* position can also be obtained, in principle, by nonmetric scaling. The ideal point for

---

[1] *Advertising Age,* July 26, 1971, p. 1.

FIGURE 2–1
Competitive positioning

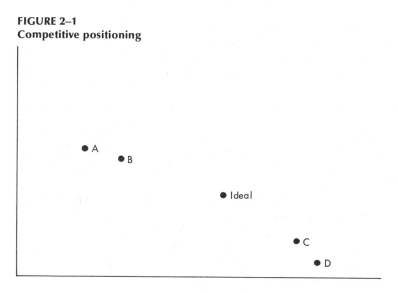

positioning a brand is shown in Figure 2–1 to be some distance from competing brands. The technique has two significant limitations. First, it does not tell us specifically what the dimensions are, and we must infer them from other knowledge we have about the characteristics of the various brands. Second, for meaningful results a number of brands must be used, and this imposes a burden on the respondent. Thus, samples must be small.

One of the more obvious ways to position or reposition brands is through product change and the use of marketing efforts to communicate that change to buyers. Just how this can best be done is not known because not enough research and experience have been devoted to it. How much can advertising alone, for example, move a brand in Figure 2–1? One point should be made, however. Who the various competitors are—A, B, C, and D in Figure 2–1—makes a lot of difference in positioning a brand. A common dictum is: Don't place yourself near a strong competitor! The headline, "Coffee Marketers' Nerves Atwitch at Folger Market Expansion Rumor" suggests the concern about a potential competitor.

The second level of competition is due to the fact that buyers typically do not consider all possible brands in a product class when they contemplate buying a brand. To simplify their lives they consider only a few, which constitute the buyer's *evoked set*. In a study by Brian Campbell, out of a product class of about 15 toothpaste brands the average number of brands considered was 2½.[2] This evoked set tends to cause buyers to

---

[2]Brian M. Campbell, "The Existence and Determinants of Evoked Set in Brand Choice Behavior" (Ph.D. diss., Columbia University, 1969).

focus upon price. They know enough about these few brands to be able to compare them on other dimensions and to let price be the relevant choice criterion. This is the situation we associate with *Routinized Response Behavior* (see Chapter 3), and it can result in intense competition indeed.

An operational measure of evoked set is to ask buyers what brands they would consider buying. Especially if the brands meet the buyers' *aspiration levels*, as described in Chapter 3, price competition is likely to be intense among these particular brands because the buyer is not motivated to search for a better brand when his aspiration level has been met. A measure of the degree to which a buyer's aspiration level is satisfied could be obtained by the nonmetric scaling technique described above. Here, however, the buyer is asked to position his "ideal brand" as well as all other brands in the product class. The distance between the available preferred brands—evoked set—and his ideal brand could be a measure of satisfaction of aspiration level.

Obviously, we would not expect all buyers to be alike on these various operational measures. Different buyers have different motives. This helps explain the powerful role of market segmentation if it can be meaningfully accomplished, as described in Chapters 3 and 8.

LEVELS OF RIVALRY IN THE DISTRIBUTION SYSTEM

The discussion so far suggests that competition refers only to rivalry among companies on any one of the four planes of the marketing system referred to in Figure 1–2. Manufacturers compete with manufacturers on the same plane, wholesalers with wholesalers, retailers with retailers, and buyers with buyers. Typically the most important rivalry occurs on the same plane, but rivalry between different levels does happen, and it is sometimes enough to make a great difference. The wholesaler strives to buy from the manufacturer as cheaply as he can and to sell to the retailer as profitably as he can. In several industries the wholesaler has increasingly been caught in the middle between strong manufacturers and large retailing chains. The focus in this chapter will be upon rivalry on a given plane—*horizontal competition.* Rivalry among levels—*vertical competition* —will be treated as influencing the intensity of competition at a given level.

MANAGERIAL SIGNIFICANCE OF RIVALRY

The unremitting pressure of the actions of rival companies creates many of the problems that a manager must solve, and his attempts to counter the moves made by these rival companies involve some of the most sophisticated problems of marketing, in both a long-term and a short-term sense. Market planning requires anticipating the actions of competitors, and, insofar as possible, preventing them from anticipating your actions. This is usually accomplished by keeping your own plans confidential. Occasionally, outright deception may be used.

Two large midwestern companies, for example, produce the equipment for high-voltage electricity transmission lines and compete with each other by bidding for sales. This requires the bidder to name a price without knowing his rival's price. One source of information used by company A to find out about company B's pricing plans is to quiz the mutual supplier of metal as to his knowledge of company B's intentions. The supplier usually picks up considerable plant gossip in his calls. Company A went one step further, however, by telling the supplier that it intended to use much higher towers in a construction project than was actually planned. Company A hoped that when company B received this information about the higher towers, company B would conclude that, because of the cost of the additional tower height, company A would name a higher price in its bid for the contract. Thus, company B would be encouraged to bid a higher price, and so increase company A's chances of getting the contract. There are obvious ethical problems in deception.

The actions of a company depend upon what it *expects* its competitors to do. The necessity of acting upon such expectations leads to the state of *mutually recognized interdependence,* with emphasis on the world "mutual." If one, but not both, recognizes that interdependence exists in their marketing, the competitive problem is not nearly so serious. This state of *mutually* recognized interdependence is important for three reasons. First, when it exists major and even violent changes in competitive intensity can occur quickly. Second, it is much more complex than when the interdependence is not recognized. If you will play out an interaction between two sellers, A and B, in your mind, you will readily see why this is so. Finally, it characterizes and complicates most of the situations in the American economy in which marketing decisions play a major role. As transportation and communication have improved historically and more companies have come to serve the national market, interdependence has increased.

Competitive interdependence is more prevalent than it usually appears to be. Not all the members of an industry compete directly, but interdependent behavior is nevertheless created by a series of geographically

FIGURE 2–2
Overlapping markets increase interdependence

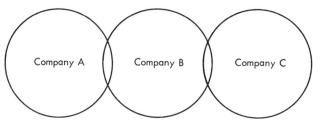

linked markets. Figure 2–2 illustrates this idea. Company A does not compete directly with company C, yet company A's behavior is conditioned by what it thinks C will do, because any significant change on A's part will be transmitted to C via B's behavior. Distance and the consequent freight costs may tend to seal off markets from one another, but a certain amount of overlap generally exists.

Finally, the *intensity* of competitive rivalry is recognized by managers, scholars, and public policy makers alike, but they may not agree on an operational measure of it. For this, the concept of a *brand-switching matrix* can serve. It describes the degree to which buyers switch among brands over some period. Table 2–1 lists, on the left side, the brands bought last

TABLE 2–1
Brand-switching matrix

Last purchase \ This purchase	Chase & Sanborn 1	Sanka 2	Nescafé 3	Instant Maxwell House 4	Folger's 5	Others 6	Total
Chase & Sanborn 1	57	3	3	35	2	19	119
Sanka 2	5	72	11	33	9	19	149
Nescafé 3	8	11	144	47	15	31	256
Instant Maxwell House 4	29	39	45	636	37	101	887
Folger's 5	4	8	9	53	195	27	296
Others 6	11	37	23	114	27	403	615
Total	114	170	235	918	285	600	2332

time, while across the top are listed those bought this time. Mrs. Jones bought Sanka the last time and Nescafé this time. Consequently, her purchase falls in the third column and second row cell of the table. By looking at the distribution in the second row we see how greatly Sanka buyers shifted on the next purchase. To the extent that a sample of buyers from the market when so analyzed falls on the diagonal from upper left to lower right (1–1 to 6–6), competition would not be intense. This is called a state of brand loyalty. A manager is often surprised the first time he sees a brand-switching matrix of his market to find how much switching actually occurs. If in the past he has observed a fairly constant market share, he has probably been unaware of the great amount of switching activity hidden by this figure.

DYNAMICS OF COMPETITIVE STRUCTURE

At any point in time the competitive structure of an industry determines the competitive behavior of companies in that industry—how you respond to your competitor's marketing effort and how they respond to yours. This structure also sets a framework for understanding ongoing marketing activity. Because a company's competitive structure often changes, a new framework is continually evolving. These changes, however, can often be anticipated and planned for. In fact, a new brand that represents a new product class displays a slight systematic pattern of change.

The instant-coffee market provides a concrete illustration. The structure of competition and the consequent competitive behavior varied sharply in that industry in the 20-year period between 1946 and 1966. The instant-coffee product class was initiated by Nestle with the introduction of Nescafé in the United States about 1940. With time, more brands entered the market, and until 1961 the market continued to grow, as shown in Figure 2–3. This growing market prevented the most difficult, keenest competition, but a number of other changes occurred in the structure of competition intrinsic to the product's life cycle that were later to have seriously adverse consequences for the profits of companies in the industry. First, as the product technology in the industry stabilized, fewer product changes were introduced. Second, every competitor acquired pretty much the same technology, and their costs became very similar, if not identical. Third, and as a consequence of the first two changes, all brands became very much alike, so that the consumer was less able to distinguish, and he came to use price as the basis of comparison. Fourth, as the product class became widely used, everyone knew about it. Changes were communicated by word of mouth, and consumers became better informed, especially as interbrand differences tended to disappear. Thus price came to the fore as the basis for judgment.

All of these developments served to sharpen competition, which in turn eroded profit margins. Finally, as seen in Figure 2–3, in 1962 the growth curve for the product class turned downward in absolute terms. Coffee became a less primary beverage, especially for young people, as they turned to the new soft drinks. The consequence was excess capacity in instant coffee, because as sales declined fixed plant remained the same. Every company strove to increase its sales in order to utilize its plant fully

FIGURE 2–3
Growth and decay of instant-coffee market

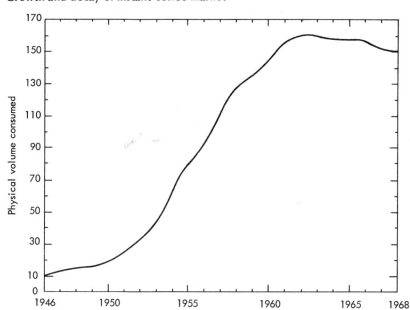

and reduce *per unit* cost of its brand. One tempting way to increase sales was by cutting the price. One company could increase its sales only by decreasing its competitors' sales by more than the industry decline alone would have caused. Competitors responded by cutting price even more. Profit margins tended to evaporate when caught between falling prices and rising unit costs.

Some of the larger companies anticipated these events and initiated product-development research. This research culminated in "freeze dried" coffee. We can expect that it, too, will in time repeat this cycle. Other actions than new-product development are possible, some legal, others not.

The cigarette industry offers another kind of an example of the changing structure of competition. The growing acceptance of a product class was not so important here as was shifting economic conditions. Advertising accounted for most of the 86 percent increase in American Tobacco Company's market share in the six-year period from 1925 to 1931 foreshadowing the Great Depression,[3] as shown in Table 2–2. American's share of the market went from 21.18 percent in 1925 to 39.40 percent in 1931. The company's absolute sales almost trebled, increasing from 17

---

[3]W. H. Nicholls, *Price Policies in the Cigarette Industry* (Nashville, Tenn.: Vanderbilt University Press, 1951), p. 58 ff. The information about shares of market is in terms of production rather than sales; absolute data are in terms of sales.

TABLE 2–2
Percent of nation's cigarette production

Year	Major companies			
	Lucky Strike (*American*)	*Chesterfield* (*Liggett & Myers*)	*Camel* (*Reynolds*)	*Old Gold* (*Lorillard*)
1925.............	21.18%	26.61%	41.60%	1.90%
1926.............	19.32	29.44	41.22	1.66
1927.............	21.84	29.49	38.46	3.79
1928.............	28.72	25.03	33.72	7.01
1929.............	32.47	26.95	30.40	7.48
1930.............	36.46	25.02	28.51	7.47
1931.............	39.40	22.73	28.43	7.03

Source: W. H. Nicholls, *Price Policies in the Cigarette Industry* (Nashville, Tenn.: Vanderbilt University Press, 1951), p. 62.

billion cigarettes to 46 billion. Apparently there was little rivalry in any other dimension than advertising, except perhaps in personal selling, and least of all in price. This experience suggests that advertising was effective as a marketing tool.

Later, however, during the depression decade, advertising was found to be ineffective. By using price (a package for 10 cents), the economy brands increased their share from 0.34 percent in 1931 to over 14 percent in 1939. Of the four big companies, the American Tobacco Company suffered most, losing market share from 39.4 percent in 1931 to 22.7 percent in 1939.[4] Knowledge of the precise conditions that made advertising an effective tool in the period 1925 to 1931 and an ineffective one in the period 1931 to 1939 can be helpful in choosing between advertising and pricing in the design of the marketing plan.

This long-term view of an industry as defined in terms of the buyers' concept of product class sets a dynamic framework for the examination of a brand's competitive situation in more static terms. This short-term view is what we tend to think of when we use the concept of competitive structure as a tool of analysis for acquiring a better understanding of competition as a part of the company's environment.

ANALYSIS OF COMPETITION

Introduction

The basic principle of this analysis is that the structure of competition leads to certain kinds of competitive behavior and to certain consequences: structure causes behavior and behavior causes consequences. Hence, a discussion of competition raises three kinds of questions.

---

[4]Ibid., p. 91.

The first is concerned with the *structure of competition.* Why do the companies in any industry exhibit a particular type of rivalry? The marketing manager must have an understanding of the cause of this behavior in order to gain insights into the competitive behavior in his industry that will aid him in predicting future competitive behavior. All of the major things that determine an industry's competitive behavior, taken together, are called the structure of competition.

The second deals with *competitive behavior*. How do the companies constituting an industry behave in relation to one another, with respect to price? Do they tend to use price rivalry, or do they follow a "live and let live" policy of very limited price rivalry while perhaps competing on other dimensions? Or do they go so far as to work out formal agreements not to compete on any dimension?

The third considers *competitive consequences*. What are the consequences of any given type of behavior? Often called "performance," the issue here is the effect of a particular kind of competitive behavior upon company objectives such as profit and growth.

We will discuss competitive behavior first before turning to structure of competition and to competitive consequences, although this order does somewhat reverse the causal relation. In this discussion of competitive behavior, we will, to simplify, assume a single-brand company, unless otherwise indicated. The consideration of multiproducts merely complicates the analysis and hides important but subtle mechanisms.

Competitive behavior

In the typical market, companies have conflicting attitudes. In the first place, each company would like the industry to be as profitable as possible; the greater the industry profits become, the greater will be the absolute value of a company's share of industry profits, other things being equal. Thus agreements not to compete on price are encouraged, because with the price higher than it otherwise would be, industry profits can be much greater. On the other hand rivalry is also encouraged, because each company wants the largest possible share of the total market, and price cutting can be an effective temporary device for increasing a company's share. An examination of competitive behavior is essentially an analysis of these two types of conflicting pressures and the pattern of behavior that emerges from their resolution.

Five patterns of competitive behavior can be distinguished: (1) perfect collusion, (2) effective collusion, (3) limited collusion, (4) price leadership, and (5) chaotic competition.[5]

PERFECT COLLUSION. Perfect collusion among competitors involves

---

[5]For an application of this analysis to five industries, see John A. Howard, "Collusive Behavior," *Journal of Business*, 27 (1954): 196–204.

(1) complete *coordination on all competitive fronts*, not only price. It necessitates the establishment of a mutually satisfactory sales quota (expected market share) for each company. Such extreme collusive behavior probably appears somewhat alien to the American student of business; in fact, it is seldom, if ever, found in the United States, where stringent antitrust laws discourage arrangements among companies to avoid price rivalry. It is rarely found even where public policy is much less stringent—for example, in Great Britain.

The reason for its rarity is fairly obvious: Significant intercompany cost differences exist in most industries, and when the differences are sufficient, perfect collusion requires that production be transferred to the most efficient companies if total profits for the industry are to be maximized. If such transfers take place, the inefficient companies are then handicapped in bargaining for their share of the market whenever existing arrangements expire, because production personnel will have been disbanded. These inefficient companies would be "disarmed" competitively, and so they prefer to carry on at least some degree of competition, even though the law may not require it. Conceivably, the inefficient companies could be paid to remain out of the market in perpetuity, and although such arrangements have been made, they are unusual because of the inability of the participating companies to agree on the value of such an arrangement.

(2) EFFECTIVE COLLUSION.   Effective collusion exists when companies set identical prices and divide the market among them but do not agree on other, nonprice competitive dimensions such as industrial research, advertising, salesmen, and the like. An agreement to share the market in a certain way is usually essential to effective price agreements; otherwise, the temptation to shade the price secretly in order to sell more becomes too great. Even with market-sharing arrangements, extreme rivalry on the nonprice dimensions encourages competitors to break over the boundaries of the markets that have been allocated by the market-sharing agreement.

Effective collusion has been fairly common in Great Britain in the past, and examples of it have been discovered by the antitrust agencies in the United States. Except in local areas where the federal antitrust laws do not apply, effective collusion is probably uncommon.

(3) LIMITED COLLUSION.   Limited collusion implies the type of intermittent behavior that first involves price agreement and then price rivalry that occurs when fuller collusion is weakened by internal dissension within a group of companies and by secret price shading. Its key characteristic is the absence of market-sharing arrangements. As the files of the antitrust agencies readily reveal, this type of behavior is often found in American industry.

(4) PRICE LEADERSHIP.   In a large number of American industries a considerable degree of price coordination among competitors—often called tacit

collusion—takes place in the complete absence of any overt collusion. The pricing behavior among four cigarette companies discussed above (American, Liggett & Myers, Reynolds, and Lorillard) from 1925 to 1950 illustrates this tacit variety of collusion, which by definition occurs without explicit or formal agreement. Throughout this 25-year period, prices to the wholesaler were almost identical among the four companies, even though formal collusion was not apparent. Advertising rivalry, however, was vigorous during the period. Price changes are minimized in these industries in order to limit possible instability, but the changing costs and demand conditions resulting from a dynamic economy, especially those reflected in the Great Depression, force price changes.

Price modifications arising out of cost variations or shifts in demand usually take place through price leadership. One company becomes the accepted leader, and no one changes price until the leader changes; then all companies follow. The fact that prices were identical among the large cigarette companies for over a quarter of a century is explained by leadership. An essential condition is that the leader be able to lead *upward* price changes, since any company of significant size can usually force an industrywide price decline by simply cutting its price.

Price leadership is often necessary to avoid market instability when price changes are made. An interesting question arises as to why a particular company is the accepted leader in the industry. There are essentially two kinds of price leaders in an industry: the dominant-firm variety and the barometric variety. A *dominant-firm price leader* is a company that has a dominant share of the market; in the extreme case, the industry is made up of this one large company with a competitive fringe of many small companies. The competitors can sell all they wish at the price set by the leader, so there is no reason for them to cut prices below this company's. Alternatively, if the small companies set a higher price, they will lose sales to the leader. In this situation, the leader estimates its most profitable combination of price and sales volume, using its known costs of production and subtracting from industry demand the volume it estimates its competitors will offer at its proposed price. Then it proceeds to set this price.

The *barometric price leader*, on the other hand, derives its name and position from the fact that its actions in setting prices are believed by the rest of the industry to be a good barometer for them to follow. The other members realize that the price set by the leader is a satisfactory one and that it acts with tolerable promptness when a change in market conditions suggests the need for a different price.

American Viscose has been the leader in the rayon industry for many years. Prior to the depression it held the leadership position because of its dominant share of the market: for example, in 1924 American Viscose had 73 percent of the market when its nearest rival held 11 percent. Since the depression its share has fallen sharply—in 1945 it was 30 percent. The price leadership of American Viscose was maintained after World War II because other members of the industry respected its good judgment, as demonstrated by its success over many years in estimating market conditions. It became a barometric leader.

Price leadership covers a great variety of behaviors and a large proportion of American manufacturing industry. Consequently, it is useful to think of three levels of price leadership analogous to the three levels of collusion: perfect, effective, and limited. A large share, as in the rayon industry encourages perfect price leadership: followers follow without exception. Effective leadership is more common, however: they follow most of the time. Limited leadership, where they follow occasionally, is probably the most common.

CHAOTIC COMPETITION.   Chaotic competition is another type of behavior often found in a market. An identifying characteristic of chaotic competition frequently is that after the price leader has cut his price, the follower will cut below the lowered price instead of merely meeting it. This behavior arises under one of the following conditions: (1) when interdependence is not mutually recognized, and one or more of the companies do not know that there is strong interdependence between their actions and the behavior of competitors; (2) when, especially in situations where mutual interdependence is recognized, wrong predictions are made as to how competitors will react; (3) when there are significant differences among the companies as to the beliefs each holds about which price will best serve the interests of the industry; or (4) when a company feels fairly sure that it has strength enough to win. The experience of a large midwestern producer of electrical equipment illustrates the case of a company that failed to realize the extent of mutual interdependence between its actions and those of its competitors. In 1952 it brought out an improved product but maintained the usual price in the industry. A period of severe price competition ensued when it began to gain share as a result of the superior product. On the basis of this experience, when the company again brought out an improved product two years later, it raised the price above the going price in the industry.

The more extreme form of chaotic competition, usually called a "price war," is not likely to occur for a long period because losses will force a truce. A truce will be brought about in a way which depends upon structural conditions (as discussed in the following section). The periodic price wars observed in local retail gasoline markets are illustrative of chaotic competition.

A dramatic and unusually well-reported example of a price war took place in June 1951 among the leading New York department stores, mainly Gimbel's, Macy's, and Abraham & Straus. It grew partly out of the policy of "fair trading" practiced by manufacturers to fix minimum prices at which the retailer could sell. This quotation from *The New York Times* suggests the drama of the event:

PRICE WAR SET OFF IN STORES: SOME GOODS REDUCED 30%

Thousands of women shoppers snapped up bargains yesterday when a full-scale price war developed among leading New York department stores. One hour after Macy's offered 5,978 items for sale at 6 per cent less than so-called "fair-traded minimums set by manufacturers," Gimbel's began to meet the cuts.

By noon, Abraham & Straus in Brooklyn cut prices on some of the items offered by Macy's 10 per cent and more. Macy's soon undersold A. & S. by 6 per cent in line with its traditional cash savings policy, and Gimbel's again matched Macy's. Hearn's, Bloomingdale's, Namm's and many other stores joined in the battle reluctantly.

. . . As rival stores met its prices, Macy's consistently went 6 per cent below them. By closing time, the original 6 per cent cut was a dimly recalled memory. Some reductions went as far as 30 per cent. From 3:00 P.M. on price cuts were made almost on a half-hourly basis.[6]

The effect of this rivalry on prices can be observed in Table 2–3 by comparing the actual prices charged at the end of the first week of the "war" with the fair-trade column, which shows the prices before the price rivalry began. Bayer aspirin prices probably were the most dramatic. The fair-trade price was 59 cents per 100 tablets, as indicated. At the end of a week the price had been cut to 12 cents, as shown in the table, and by June 14 it was as low as 4 cents. The cost to the store per 100 tablets is believed to have been 43 cents, which, if true, indicates that at the lowest point the seller was losing 39 cents on each bottle.

The losses, however, were not as serious as the price cuts might suggest, because the milling crowd of customers bought many items on which prices were not cut. Customers were also attracted to the event from much greater distances than usual. The event was probably an effective means of unloading heavy inventories accumulating in anticipation of heavy consumer buying for 1951—buying that did not materialize as expected. Moreover, it was confined to fair-traded items, which are subject to a high markup. Finally, Macy's may have viewed it as an essential cost in teaching competitors not to attempt to compete with it on price. Nevertheless, Macy's was the only department store in favor of a price war; the other department stores were quite embittered by Macy's action in precipitating it, and some went so far as to propose legal action against Macy's.[7]

Different industries will exhibit different types of competitive behavior, and even within a given industry, behavior may vary from time to time. If the analysis set forth in this chapter is to be helpful to the market-

---

[6] *The New York Times*, May 30, 1951, p. 7.
[7] *The New York Times*, June 4, 1951, p. 1, and June 7, 1951, p. 26.

TABLE 2–3
Price changes in a price war

Item	Fair trade $	Gimbels Open $	Gimbels Close $	Macy's Open $	Macy's Close $	A. & S. Open $	A. & S. Close $
Dormeyer mixer (4200)	46.50	28.19	28.19°	†	†	28.19	28.19
RCA 45 record attachment ...	12.95	8.19	8.19	8.19	8.19	8.19	8.19
Webster three-speed player ...	88.24	59.99	59.99	56.39	56.39	56.39	55.49
Waterman fountain pen	3.95	2.11	1.98	1.94	1.94	1.98°	1.89
Underwood typewriter.......	68.60	44.95	44.95	44.95	44.95	44.95°	44.95
Novel *From Here to Eternity*	4.50	1.64°	1.64°	1.74°	1.74°	1.69	1.69
Proctor steam iron	15.45	‡	‡	12.17	12.17	12.15	12.15
Coffeematic percolator	29.95	19.13	18.88	19.13	19.13	18.98	18.88
Regina waxer	64.50	44.39	37.55	37.55	37.55	37.55°	37.55
Bayer aspirin (100's)........	.59	.12	.12	.15	.12°	.15	.12
Ronson lighter	6.60	‡	‡	3.76	3.76	3.70	3.70
Ronson lighter	8.25	†	†	7.74	5.39	5.35	5.35
Ronson lighter (butane)	13.50	†	†	10.29	10.29	10.25	10.25
Sunbeam hedge trimmer	43.50	35.24	32.19	32.19	32.19	32.19	32.19
Rainking No. K sprinkler	8.50	7.49	7.49	7.49	7.49	7.49	7.49
Rainking No. H sprinkler	7.65	5.96	5.59	5.95	5.59	5.95	5.59
Rainking No. D sprinkler	5.95	4.94	4.64	4.94	4.64	4.89	4.59
Rainking nozzle	1.39	1.31	1.21	1.31	1.31°	1.29	1.19
Koroseal hose, 25 feet........	5.75	5.06	4.76	5.06	5.06	5.05	5.05
Koroseal hose, 50 feet........	9.80	7.41	6.94	6.94	6.94	7.39	6.89
Koroseal hose, 75 feet........	13.85	12.22	11.46	11.46	11.46	11.45	11.45
Kaywoodie pipe	4.00	‡	‡	3.29	3.76	2.89	2.89
Kaywoodie pipe	10.00	8.41	8.41	8.21	7.91	7.95	7.75
Lake golf cart	6.95	†	†	5.62	5.62°	4.98	4.98
Dunlop tennis balls (3)	1.75	†	†	1.29	1.21	1.29	1.19
Swank jewelry.............	5.00	†	†	3.21	3.02	2.98	2.98
Glass fishing rod	9.95	†	†	6.98	6.95°	5.00	5.00
Jack Kramer tennis racket	18.50	†	†	9.98	9.98°	8.95	8.95

° Latest price reported; item out of stock.
‡ Not reported.
† Item out of stock.
Source: *The New York Times*, June 7, 1951, p. 26.

ing manager, it must aid him in understanding the competitive behavior in his industry. The next section will be devoted to a discussion of the objective market characteristics that, taken together, make up the structure of competition.

Structure of competition

One of the leading authorities on market organization has noted that "It seems probable that if Firestone, like God in another context, had not existed, the structure of competition in the tire market would have created him."[8] This observation points to the fact that the competitive behavior found in an industry does not spring so much from the personalities of the

[8]Edward S. Mason, "Price and Production Policies of Large-Scale Enterprise," *American Economic Review*, Supplement, Part 2, 29 (1939);71.

executives in that industry as from the structure of competition within which the industry operates.

The opposite view is sometimes found in marketing literature. An analysis of the men's clothing industry, for example, states, "The root of the industry's problem . . . is its 'basic inferiority complex'—a chronic fear of cutthroat competition which leads it to underprice its products to the point where there is no margin for promotion, for profit and for expansion."[9] The implication of the quotation is that if the executives in the industry were rid of this unfortunate personality trait, industry profits would be higher. Analysis suggests that an examination of the competitive structure of the men's clothing industry would provide a more meaningful and actionable explanation of this behavior than would Freud.

There are several dimensions of competitive structure. As indicated above, their effect upon competitive behavior is dependent on their influence upon the *degree of mutually recognized interdependence* among the actions of different companies in a given market. The dimensions from traditional economic analyses are number of firms and degree to which the product is somewhat different among the firms. From these two dimensions economists deduce five market structures:

1. Monopoly. Single seller of a product class.
2. Pure oligopoly. Few sellers selling an identical product, where "few" is defined in terms of whether mutual interdependence is recognized and "identical product" means that all buyers' motives are alike. This implies that the aggregate response function for the firm is the same slope as for the product class and that buyers are perfectly informed.
3. Differentiated oligopoly. A few sellers each with a somewhat different product. This means that the buyers of the different brands can have varying motives.
4. Monopolistic competition. Many sellers with a somewhat different product.
5. Pure competition. Many sellers with an identical product.

Implicit in each of the five cases is the condition of "many buyers." To include "few buyers" (oligopsony, for example) would immensely complicate the analysis. Except where otherwise indicated, we will continue this simplifying assumption.

These categories that result from combinations of the dimensions are useful, but for practical purposes they are usually incomplete. They are especially incomplete for the ubiquitous oligopoly case, because there is no theoretical or analytic "solution," that is, there is no stability in the theory except under some highly unrealistic assumptions such as implied in the classic Cournot solution that will be described below.[10] In the real

---

[9]*Advertising Age,* July 2, 1956, p. 6.

[10]William Fellner, *Competition among the Few* (New York: Alfred A. Knopf, Inc., 1949).

world, however, stability does in fact occur, which we can easily verify if we look around; companies typically are not continually changing their prices.

To explain the stability that we observe among oligopolists we must, as William Fellner has so well pointed out, recognize the additional conditions that exist to bring it about. The most relevant dimensions of these conditions are: (1) number, size distribution, and brand differentiation of the companies selling brands in the product class, (2) number, size, and kind of buyers, (3) marketing channels used, (4) degree of spatial concentration of the market, (5) public policy, (6) company organization, (7) movements of industry demand over time, and (8) cost conditions. The first six dimensions are static and explain how, over time, tacit agreements and stability result. The last two are more dynamic and destabilizing.

NUMBER, SIZE DISTRIBUTION, AND BRAND DIFFERENTIATION OF COMPETITORS.   The number and size distribution of the companies constitute one of the most important structural dimensions. The fewer the sellers in a product class, the greater the likelihood that interdependence will exist among the companies and price will be avoided as a competitive tool, as far as possible. Multiproduct competition is more common, however, and it can be more complex than the single-product competition implied above. Assume company A has a very large share of product X and an average share of product Y, while B has a small share of X and an average share of Y. If so, B can be price aggressive in X because it knows that for A to meet its price for X, A will have to spend a lot of money (either in advertising or lowered price) and thus will have less to spend on Y. This will make A vulnerable in Y to B's effort. Assuming single-product competition, the more an industry is characterized by *one* large firm and *several* small ones in product class, the easier it will be for the large company to act as a price leader, since it can enforce its leadership more effectively. This leadership is likely to prevent periods of "price fighting" when prices must be changed as a consequence of changed cost and demand conditions.

Price leadership (usually of a noncollusive nature) becomes even more common where a *few* companies—oligopolists— make up the entire industry. Most economists believe that as a consequence profits are higher. In comparing the profits of 40 industries, Joe S. Bain found the profits to be significantly higher in industries where eight sellers had more than 70 percent share of the market than in industries where they had less than 70 percent share of it.[11] This belief has become more firmly fixed since Bain's study. Most economists would also expect the rivalry to occur in new-product development and advertising. Quite recently, however, the ar-

---

[11]Joe S. Bain, *Barriers to New Competition* (Cambridge, Mass.: Harvard University Press, 1956), pp. 195–99.

gument has been advanced that product development occurs on dimensions of the product that are not important for the consumer but, rather, those that are trivial from his point of view. This belief is apparently based on the evidence that the largest firms (over 5,000 employees) do not appear to be more inclined to research and development than medium-size firms (1,000 to 5,000).[12]

A common situation is for two essentially antagonistic *groups* of companies to exist within an industry: a few large companies and several small ones. It appears that two blocs tend to be formed, one composed of large companies and another of small companies, and that some degree of interbloc competition is generated. The bloc made up of the smaller firms resorts heavily to price competition. There is some clear evidence of this tendency in the British economy, where in the past collusive arrangements have been legal, but not in the sense of being legally enforceable. Since trade associations are the vehicle through which collusion is usually carried out in Britain, there are sometimes two separate trade associations.

Finally, the degree of difference between each brand and competing brands is important. These brand differences, as it is often put, dull the sharp edge of competition. This implies that the objective is to make it more difficult for the buyer to discriminate among brands and so to confuse him. We believe that a more meaningful way to look at it is as a problem in market segmentation, our next topic.

NUMBER, SIZE, AND KIND OF BUYERS. Just as on the selling side of the market, the number of participants on the buying side makes a difference. If there are many buyers, the loss of one to a seller is typically not tragic, and so he does not readily lower price in order to hold or acquire a customer. The size of the buyer also matters. If it is large—an oligopsonist or even a monopsonist—the seller is more likely to cut price and so trigger serious competitive behavior to hold or acquire the company as a customer.

The buyer has two characteristics other than size that particularly influence competition: level of information and motive content. The more a buyer is capable of making intercompany product-quality comparisons, the more likely he is to turn his attention with confidence to other features of the purchase, such as price, and to select products accordingly. When buyers become price conscious, pressure is put on selling companies to use price as a competitive tool. The lowering of price by one or more selling companies usually means that competitors will follow.

There is an enormous range in the level of buyer knowledge among the various product markets. One extreme is illustrated by the consumer

---

[12]R. R. Nelson, M. J. Peck, and E. D. Kalachek, *Technology, Economic Growth and Public Policy* (Washington, D.C.: The Brookings Institution, 1966), pp. 68–69.

buying a new type of appliance, perhaps his first television set, which has both highly technical and aesthetic features. He does not even know what criteria to judge it on; as you will see in Chapter 3, he is in the stage of *extensive problem solving*. He is faced with a wide variety of choices, and he buys the product class most infrequently. Many features of such a purchase are not amenable to an objective evaluation, even if a consumer had the time to make all possible comparisons and the budget to pay a testing laboratory. He often is forced by the pressures of other obligations to take only a limited time in which to make the purchase decision. He cannot conceivably be well informed. At the other extreme is a simple, cheap product such as bread that is bought very frequently. In most cases this would involve well-informed *routinized response behavior*. A buyer's need for information also varies greatly over the life cycle of a product.

The second buyer characteristic, differences in motive content, leads to the demand for differentiated brands mentioned above. If these homogeneous segments can be identified, the company can, by directing its marketing effort at these target customers, obtain a market protected from competitors. This possibility arises because there are often economies of scale in producing product so that a company must maintain a certain minimum level of production to obtain low costs. It may be able to identify a segment that offers a demand that matches its optimum production capacity. The company may also, by adding something to the product, be able to serve this segment better. Or it may be possible to remove an attribute from the product that the buyers in the segment do not value, and thus reduce costs and cut price.

MARKETING CHANNELS. The greater the length of the marketing channel in terms of the number of middlemen to which each manufacturer sells (e.g., wholesaler, retailer, and contractor), the greater the chances for price rivalry. As the number of links increases, the number of prices that must be tacitly coordinated among competitors if price rivalry is to be prevented, or at least minimized, is increased correspondingly. Moreover, it may be difficult to force the wholesaler and retailer to observe the prices agreed upon by the manufacturers.

When manufacturing companies in the same industry use *different* marketing channels, the problem of coordinating prices among themselves becomes even greater. The rubber-covered cable section of the electric cable manufacturing industry in Great Britain has for several years been more competitive than other sections of the industry.[13] The major reason appears to be that it sells through wholesalers and retailers, whereas the other sections of the industry sell directly to the buyer and therefore have fewer prices to coordinate.

---

[13]Monopolies and Restrictive Practices Commission, *Report on the Supply of Insulated Electric Wires and Cables* (London: Her Majesty's Stationary Office, 1952), pp. 32–39.

SPATIAL DIMENSIONS.   The spatial features of the market are embodied in the geographic locational pattern of competitors and buyers. The overlapping-market aspect of this pattern was shown in Figure 2–2. It is possible for a company to be almost isolated from the influence of its competitors because of prohibitive shipping costs due to weight, bulk or perishability of the product. This isolation is seldom complete, however. The other extreme is represented by companies located adjacent to each other and selling to buyers located in the immediate area. The spatial pattern of the market exerts a strong influence on the degree of interdependence among the competitive actions of the companies involved.

PUBLIC POLICY.   Historically, the antitrust laws have had as their objective the enforcement of price rivalry. They undoubtedly serve to discourage formal price agreements. It would be naïve, however, to assume that formal agreements are, in fact, completely eliminated, and it would be even more naïve to assume that coordinated behavior is prevented. Also a portion of the law (the Robinson-Patman Act, for example) actually limits price rivalry, as we shall see in Chapter 15.

COMPANY ORGANIZATION.   In the short term the nature of the competing organizations also shapes the nature of competition. Over the long term, however, these organizations can be modified to represent a better adaptation to the competitive environment.

The goal structures of the competing companies can shape the nature of the competitive behavior in a market. A company that has as a goal to grow faster than the industry and that effectively transmits that goal down through the corporate hierarchy to the pricing decision can cause great instability, especially if the competing companies have good information as to their respective shares of the market.

The goal structure illustrates the primary problem of a company organization in obtaining effective pricing in an intensely competitive market. The idea will be introduced here but developed at greater length in Chapter 5. The organization structure must be so arranged that it can make well-informed decisions quickly and in terms of the company's goals. If the decision takes place too high in the organization, it may not be well informed in terms of current market information, and therefore it will not be made quickly. If it is too low in the organization, the decision may lack perspective (for example, fail to recognize that cutting price in one area will spread to other areas) and so take a view that is too short term in orientation. Such behavior is also more likely to be inconsistent with higher goals in the company. A central problem in oligopolistic markets is to prevent miscalculation of a competitor's intent.

MOVEMENTS IN INDUSTRY DEMAND.   Movements in industry demand over time are a critical influence upon competitive behavior. "Beer Sales Down, Rivalry Up" is a typical headline from a business periodical. These movements are mainly of three types—cyclical, secular, and seasonal.

Cyclical movements. The business cycle has been substantially dampened by a government policy of full employment, but it still exists. Its effect varies among products, with capital goods and consumer durables generally being most sharply affected. When the business cycle brings a decline in industry sales, an increase in the sales of any one company can take place only at the expense of competitors' sales, and mutual interdependence consequently increases. Changes ordinarily occur in cost as well as in demand, which increases the need for price changes. This necessity opens the possibility of intercompany disagreements about the correct price and misunderstandings about the intentions of the participants, especially since antitrust laws keep these agreements at the tacit level instead of permitting them to operate at the overt level. Both levels are conductive to chaotic competition.

A dramatic example of the effects of a cyclical change in demand upon competitive behavior occurred in the heavy-electrical-equipment industry price war in January 1955. Price cuts in this industry, which deals with products like enormous generators and motors used in the largest public utilities, were reported as 50 percent and more. It has been estimated that as a result of this price war the industry suffered a $200 million decline in gross sales during a three-week period. The dominant source of the "war" appeared to be the 1953 recession, supplemented by the fact that the backlog of postwar demand was being satisfied. Another dimension of the competitive structure, the size distribution of buyers and sellers, was also relevant in this situation; the public-utility industry segment is made up of buyers large enough that they can play off even such sellers as General Electric and Westinghouse against each other.

Some economists also argue that the effect of price on total industry sales for some products, especially capital goods, varies directly with the business cycle—buyer's respond more to price cuts during prosperous periods than in periods of depression.[14] If so, for such products as capital goods, price is less effective as a tool for expanding industry sales in periods of depression. Finally, as general business declines, consumers probably become less willing to try new products, preferring to confine their purchases to those that are familiar. Product competition is then less useful as a device for increasing market share. Companies selling cyclically sensitive products will resort to almost any means to avoid price competition, knowing that price rivalry will probably result in heavy damage to each company.

Alternatively, as the level of business conditions improves, companies tend to discontinue collusive practices that they had taken on during the depression as protection against chaotic competition. In post-World War

---

[14]See, for example, Richard B. Heflebower, "The Effect of Dynamic Forces on the Elasticity of Revenue Curves," *Quarterly Journal of Economics*, 55 (1940–41): 652–66.

II Britain some companies voluntarily discontinued collusive practices initiated during the depressed interwar period.[15]

Secular movements.   The secular or long-term aspect of demand as a dimension of the competitive structure determining competitive behavior is also important. Figure 2–3, the instant-coffee market, showed a secular increase in demand and the beginning of a secular decline. A secular decline occurs when either technological change or a shift in consumer motives causes buyers to discontinue certain purchases. A good example is the bituminous coal industry, which, though it received a temporary boost from World War II, over the long term has been losing to other sources of power such as oil and electricity. A current example of an increasing secular demand is the television manufacturing industry.

The effects of secular changes in demand upon competitive behavior are similar to those of a cyclical nature, except that because secular declines are more or less permanent, some of the companies making up the affected industry must eventually go out of business. They may be able to shift their manufacturing and distributing facilities to other products, but if the equipment is highly specialized, continuous losses may be required to eliminate the excess capacity. Such industries are said to be "sick." Fortunately, the rapid growth of the American economy has kept this problem to a minimum. When excess capacity has occurred, the remedy has usually been to discontinue capital investment. The growth of the economy has usually solved the problem, although the adjustment may be painful for some companies.

Through a careful demand analysis, a company can fairly accurately predict whether the industry will be "sick" or whether the decline in demand is only temporary. If serious excess capacity is likely, management is faced with only two alternatives: to escape with as little loss as possible or to seek government help. The answer to the problem is, of course, to produce new products, and so to move to a new industry.

Seasonal movements.   Seasonal fluctuations in demand will probably have a destabilizing effect upon competitive behavior. Retail gasoline sales, for example, may vary as much as 20 percent seasonally. Typically this effect is not nearly so serious as cyclical and secular declines, however.

COST CONDITIONS.   Cost conditions exert an influence upon competitive behavior. The stability of costs is important; for example, manufacturing companies using such metals as zinc are subject to ever-changing costs because of fluctuating zinc prices. To compensate for the fluctuating costs, prices of their products must often be changed so they can maintain satisfactory profit margins.

The proportion of fixed costs is another factor that must be considered.

---

[15]Howard, "Collusive Behavior," p. 202.

Fixed costs are those incurred irrespective of the levels of production and sales. A company will ordinarily continue to produce and sell as long as the price is high enough to yield a revenue that covers current operating costs, even though little or nothing is contributed to overhead (fixed costs). The distinction between fixed and current operating costs will be further clarified in Chapter 4. The argument as stated here assumes that variable and marginal costs are similar in magnitude over the relevant range of variability of production (for the validity of this assumption see Chapter 4). In companies where there are large amounts of capital equipment, such as those manufacturing steel, fixed costs are high relative to current operating costs. If price wars break out in this situation, price can be driven to an extremely low level before the companies with higher current operating costs stop producing. In such industries, companies are exceptionally careful to avoid price as a means of obtaining sales. They often adopt some mutually satisfactory pricing arrangement to prevent rivalry, such as the basing-point method of pricing discussed in Chapter 10.

Competitive consequences

The consequences of the eight dimensions of competitive structure described above can be summarized as general observations. The fewer the number of companies, for example, the greater the tacit collusion or coordination on competitive dimensions. Even with a very few companies, however, a miscalculation can lead to serious rivalry, especially if supported by other dimensions such as declining industry demand or large buyers.

Direct selling (no middlemen), high fixed cost, and spatial scattering of competitors all discourage rivalry. Company organization can operate either way, depending upon its nature, as we will see below when we consider two models of the competitive process.

Public policy is typically intended to encourage rivalry, but in some cases it may have the opposite effect. An example is the Robinson-Patman Act, to be discussed in Chapter 15.

In general, the effects of rivalry are to erode profits. Yet it may bring growth, because the lowered prices tap new demands that did not exist for the higher prices.

Several possible courses of action in intensely competitive situations are implied in the analysis of the competitive structure. Rapid, well-informed pricing is one possible response. By responding quickly, the manager avoids losing customers and indicates to price-cutting competitors that their gains will be short-lived, thus discouraging price-cutting behavior in the future. If well informed about his costs, the manager will not cut prices lower than necessary and will avoid misleading competitors so that they do not engage in dangerous miscalculations. Effort devoted to identifying market segments in which the company has a particular advantage can be highly useful. Minor product improvements such as a modification of the package to better serve a segment can give some, but often temporary, protection from rivalry. Advertising skill in discovering and developing new, dramatic appeals to the relevant segment can also help.

These courses of action can be taken at the brand manager level. It is also important to note that they have strategic implications—doing things today which make a more favorable market for tomorrow—even though we tend to think of the brand manager as making decisions only at the operating level. Much of the efforts of the marketing manager and the president are devoted to changing the structure, ideally in such a way as to create a favorable future environment for the brand manager. The marketing manager operates largely via product development, typically of a completely new product but in a product class familiar to the buyer that will truly better fit the motives of the buyer. This is a very effective way of gaining protection, and, since World War II, it has become the common course of action in the American market, as we will discuss in Chapter 13. A new distribution system which lowers cost or improves availability and service can also be effective. Price agreements among competitors are also possible at this level. They are illegal, however, and unless joined with market sharing are not greatly effective.

The president has even greater options for changing the structure of competition itself. Mergers which reduce the number of competitors and increase relative size, are one way. Federal antitrust agencies follow this activity carefully, especially among the larger companies, and impose severe legal limits, as we will see in Chapter 15. This course of action, however, should not be confused with the merger movement of the past decade, which was much more of a conglomerate nature. Expansion was in new-product classes instead of in market share of existing product classes. By directing the construction of new plants the president can also affect the level of cost and even the fixed/variable cost ratio. He can locate the new plant so as to be more favorably situated to serve customers. In addition, he can change the organization to affect the competitive structure in ways that will be spelled out more fully in the next section. He can work through trade associations to bring about favorable changes in public policy. Finally, he can completely change the company organization, such as by going to a brand manager type of organization that will unify the marketing of company brands.

These actions by the marketing manager and, especially, the president can be very important indeed in bringing about a more favorable future environment for the brand manager. But to achieve a fully synchronized view about a brand so that the resultant decisions really do function to set a favorable future competitive environment for the brand manager is not easy. A well-thought-out marketing strategy for a brand can enormously help to bridge the distance in point of view and resolve the problems confronted by the president and the brand manager.

Marketing strategies are related to the competitive structure by a number of concepts. First, *segmentation* is used to identify market(s) in which the company has a particular advantage so that in serving them it can enjoy protection from the sharpest head-on competition. Second, these market(s) become its *target market*. The characteristics of the customers in the target market are examined carefully to determine the attributes of the brand that will best serve their needs. If, for example, the target market is people over 50 years of age and in the higher income brackets, the brand attributes for a food could be mild in flavor and nonfattening. Third, with this information the marketing manager examines the competitive situation in terms of the possible market *positioning* of his brand. Using a Figure 2–1 type of analysis with mildness as one dimension and nonfattening as another, he might find that company A is already serving that market segment, and he knows that company A is a very tough competitor with marketing skill and good cash reserves. If this is the case, he would reconsider this segment as his target market. On the other hand, if he found a competitive "hole," a vacancy, at this segment, he would proceed.

Fourth, the target market characteristics and the corresponding competitive situation become the foundation in formulating a *strategy*. Thus, the general range of relevant brand characteristics is defined, as is the general range of marketing mix elements. Fifth, considerations of profit and growth lead to the selection of the specific elements of the *marketing mix*. Sixth, these marketing mix elements become the foundation of the *marketing plan*. Finally, the strategy not only serves as a *guide* in selecting the marketing mix, but when the strategy is agreed upon with the manager's boss, the strategy becomes something of a *standard of performance* by which his boss judges his behavior in evaluating his performance.

In summary, as regards the respective roles of the brand manager, the marketing manager, and the president, the role of the brand manager's position is almost entirely operating. He is concerned with current operations. His small strategic role is in the search for identification of and exploitation of market segments. The position of the marketing manager entails almost no operating role. On the other hand, he has a substantial strategic role, especially in the new-product area and to a somewhat lesser extent, perhaps, in the channel area. Finally, the position of the president is a heavily strategic role.

MODELS OF THE COMPETITIVE PROCESS

To focus the idea of structure determining competitive behavior much more sharply, we will construct two models incorporating different structural conditions for yielding stability of the competitive process.[16] The two models of the process have differing assumptions about the nature of the conditions:

1. A model of a single-product company in which price changes tend to be *infrequent* and reaction to competitors primarily *passive* might have the following organization characteristics:

a) Price is determined by a committee of equals.
b) Communication chains between the decision-making unit and the primary sources of information are long (both upward and downward).
c) The unit making the actual price decisions does not have the responsibility for establishing the criteria for price decisions (that is, the decision-making unit is decentralized and is subject to dicta from above with respect to price policy).
d) Demand information is channeled through a cost relay point with consequent overemphasis on cost in relation to demand.
e) Firm policy information is channeled through a cost relay point with similar consequence.
f) Information on competitors is channeled through a cost relay point with corresponding consequence.

2. A model of a single-product company in which price changes tend to be *frequent* and reaction to competitors tends to take the form of *price leadership* might have the following organizational characteristics:

a) Price is determined by the individual.
b) Communication chains between the decision-making unit and the primary sources of information are short (both upward and downward).
c) The decision maker for specific price decisions also has the responsibility for establishing the criteria for price decisions (that is, the decision-making unit is centralized).
d) Cost information is channeled through a demand relay point with consequent overemphasis on demand in relation to cost.
e) Firm policy information is channeled through a demand relay point with similar consequences.
f) Information on competitors is channeled through a demand relay point with corresponding consequences.

In order to make explicit the implications here for the analysis of the behavior of the manager, consider the predicted behavior in a classic situation of two firms possessing the characteristics listed above, as indicated

---

[16]R. M. Cyert and J. G. March, "Organizational Structure and Pricing Behavior in an Oligopolistic Market," *American Economic Review*, XLV, 1955, 129–39.

by the Cournot duopoly model. Because this model is highly simplified, it enables us to see certain aspects more clearly.

The Cournot model says: Let there be two duopolists in the market. Assume that company 1 has the organizational characteristics of the first model above and company 2 the organizational characteristics of the second model. Following Cournot, let there be *no costs* and let all buyers of the product class have the *same motives.*

The market demand function is defined to be:

$$p = 25 - = \frac{x_1 + x_2}{3}$$

$$\text{where } p = \text{price}$$
$$x_1 = \text{output of firm 1}$$
$$x_2 = \text{output of firm 2.}$$

It is further specified that each duopolist *expects no reaction* on the part of the other in response to a change in output, which is to say that mutual interdependence is *not* recognized. This can be described mathematically as follows:

$$\frac{dx_1}{dx_2} = \frac{dx_1}{dx_2} = 0 \, (\text{conjectural variation terms}).$$

The Cournot market solution is reached by setting marginal revenue for each duopolist equal to zero (i.e., the point of optimal production under the assumption of no costs) and solving the resulting equations.

$$px_1 = 25x_1 - x_1 \frac{(x_1 + x_2)}{3}. \tag{1}$$

$$\frac{dpx_1}{dx_1} = 25 - \frac{2x_1}{3} - \frac{x_2}{3} - \frac{x_1}{3}\frac{dx_2}{dx_1} = 0. \tag{2}$$

$$x_1 = \frac{75}{2} - \frac{x_2}{2}. \tag{3}$$

Similarly,

$$x_2 = \frac{75}{2} - \frac{x_1}{2}, \tag{4}$$

and thus,

$$x_1 = 25 \tag{5}$$
$$x_2 = 25$$
$$p = 8.33.$$

Hence, with each company selling 25 units at 8.33 there is stable competitive behavior.

Let us explore some of the implications of the two models. Assume that the market demand increases, such that

$$p = 30 - \frac{x_1 + x_2}{3}.$$

Under the assumptions previously outlined, it is predicted that company 1 will tend to (1) be slow in changing its perception of the market demand, (2) underestimate demand when its perception does change, and (3) give a positive value to the conjectural variation term. Thus, company 1 might have expectations with regard to the market demand function and assume that if he changed his price, his competitor would also do so. We describe the latter as recognizing that interdependence exists, and so the conjectural variation term is 1.

$$p = 25 - \frac{x_1 + x_2}{3}.$$

$$\frac{dx_2}{dx_1} = 1.$$

Contrarily, it is predicted that company 2 will tend to (1) change its perception of market demand quickly, (2) overestimate demand, and (3) not expect competitive interdependence. Therefore it will give a value of zero to the conjectural variation term. Thus company 2 might have the following estimates of key information:

$$p = 100 - x_1 - x_2.$$

$$\frac{dx_1}{dx_2} = 0.$$

Under these conditions, the market solution deviates significantly from the standard Cournot solution:

$$x_1 = 10.$$
$$x_2 = 45.$$
$$p = 11.67.$$

The effect is to make company 2, with sales of 45, dominant in the market at a price of 11.67.

Note that the solution above will be stable only if the new production level and the resultant profits are acceptable to the controlling management group in each of the two firms. If, for example, the controlling management group of company 1 is not satisfied, it may demand a reorganization of the company. Specifically, it may insist that its organizational structure be more like that of company 2. Such a reorganization would have obvious consequences for the estimation of demand and so forth, with a resultant impact upon the market. [17]

SUMMARY

The analytic concepts associated with competitive structure and related to the idea of brand positioning and target markets are central ideas in strategy formulation. The basic notion of the chapter is that competitive structure determines competitive behavior, which, in turn, determines how sales in the product class are shared. This has consequences for the achievement of individual company goals. Later chapters will describe the conditions of competitive structure and provide concepts and techniques for analyzing them.

The competitive structure sets a broad framework in which a variety of forces that impinge upon marketing decisions can be organized. It brings together demand, cost, competition, and organization in one central focus. The structure is especially useful when combined with the various levels of decision in the organization hierarchy. By means of it we can see that much of the decision activity at higher levels is actually directed toward the profit possibilities in the future for the lower levels. Specifically, the president's decisions can improve future opportunities for the marketing manager, and decisions by both the president and the marketing manager can improve opportunities for the brand manager. The strategy is directed to improving the environment for the operating activity that is carried out by the brand manager. We also see here, however, why the brand manager searches avidly for favorable market segments. Segmentation is a way of relieving sharp competitive pressures.

Though market structure itself can be viewed as this broad framework of strategy formulation, it can also be specified in much more detail. Marketing strategies can appear in the form of a model, with behavior correspondingly specified in a more precise way.

DISCUSSION QUESTIONS

1. What do we mean by brand positioning? How is it accomplished?
2. What do we mean by target markets? What is their relation to market segmentation?
3. Explain the relation between competitive structure, competitive behavior and competitive consequences.
4. Describe the types of competitive behavior and illustrate each from your reading or experience.
5. The analysis of competitive structure is said to be a broad framework for formulating marketing strategy. Explain.

---

[17]The work here is developed further in Howard P. Tuckman and L. Peter Holmblad, "A Modified Simulation of Cyert, Feigenbaum, and March's Duopoly Model," *Management Science*, July 1972, pp. 694–705.

MARKETING ANALYSIS OF DEMAND 3

Structure of demand

THE MANAGER'S VIEW

THE STRUCTURE OF DEMAND deals with how the buyer responds to the forces that determine his behavior. The purpose of this chapter is to explain the *process* by which the buyer responds to these forces. We will focus upon the marketing variables but will not be confined to them. To simplify the discussion we will assume that the buyer is exposed to only one seller's marketing effort and thus avoid the complications of competitive effort. Also, in presenting the process we will first assume that all buyers are alike and then examine how they are different in order to approach the problem of market segmentation. In dealing with the structure of demand, the marketing manager is confronted with the difficult problem of conceptualizing the buyer. He must do so in enough detail to understand the buyer, which requires that he know something about how the buyer thinks. Yet he must conceptualize him in simple enough terms to fit him into the quantitative terms of the company's financial framework.

The powerful influence of the company's financial accounting system, in fact, forces the manager to conceptualize all relevant issues in financial terms. Therefore, it is necessary to develop a quantitative financial description of buyer behavior. This is helpful for a manager contemplating such marketing action as an advertising expenditure intended to influence buyer response. He should also know the empirical content of each of the curves summarizing buyer responses for his market, as shown in Figure 3–1.

57

On the vertical axis are given the various amounts he could conceivably spend, the *cost*, in other words, and on the horizontal axis are the sales figures, the revenue from *all* customers that would accrue because of those expenditures. These relations are thus aggregate *response functions*, or curves. They are very important ideas, and we will use them throughout the book (especially in Chapters 7 and 8, where they will be dealt with quantitatively). Some of the details of the content of the curves, such as the *number* and *size* of buyers as measured by volume of individual purchases, however, are sacrificed in this method of describing buyers.

FIGURE 3–1
Response functions for controllable factors

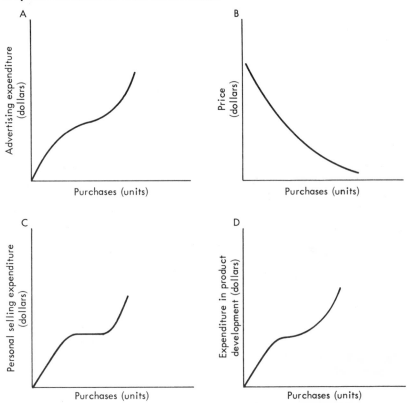

These two dimensions, number and size of buyers, are obviously essential for the manager's volume planning. A few big buyers are treated differently from many small ones, but for the purpose of bringing the buyer's response into the financial framework of analysis, the differences will be ignored.

A marketing manager, however, must put more meaning into these curves if he is to use them as guides in developing his marketing plan. The solution consists of two parts. First, he can treat marketing as a problem in market communication and describe the *purpose of marketing effort* as being to *communicate with the customer*. Second, he can use a theory of communication to connect the information, through a number of intermediate variables, to the buyer's purchase. He can either use a formal, explicit theory such as will be set out in this chapter or he can, from long experience, develop his own intuitive theory of the market, as illustrated concretely in Chapter 5 by the example of a petroleum company manager setting prices. By using the explicit theory he will learn his market much faster and probably much more accurately. Equally important, he can then communicate with others about it and so obtain a well-understood, integrated program that can be more effectively carried out.

The function of marketing cost as described by the curves in Figure 3–1 is to put information into the market—to affect the variable *information available* in Figure 3–2 which is the barest rudiments of a model of the buyer. The function of buyer *purchases* in Figure 3–1 is to create sales which generate the *revenue* indicated in Figure 3–2. In this way, the manager's necessity to conceptualize things in financial terms is linked to the theory of buyer behavior. This connecting system, or highly simplified model, describes a single typical or representative buyer instead of all the buyers in the market. Therefore, if we have a representative sample of the population, we can generalize our results to the population.

FIGURE 3–2
The model and the manager's way of conceptualizing

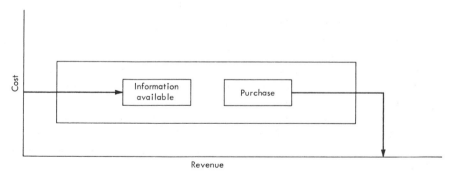

Because the connecting links between information available in the market and purchase are missing in Figure 3–2, we have only a "black box," which is not very useful. We can begin supplying these missing links, however, by asking and attempting to answer the question: Why

does the buyer buy? First, however, we will clear up some essential terminology.

There is a great variety of buyers in a market: consumers who buy for
themselves and for households, and those who buy for organizations such
as manufacturing companies, retailing and wholesaling establishments,
educational institutions, hospitals, and government agencies. For convenience, we will classify all buyers as either consumer or industrial. All
buying decisions have elements in common, but the traditional distinction
between consumer and industrial (organizational) buying can be de-
fended on the following grounds:

① First, users, official buyers, and makers of buying policy in the
purchasing organization are usually different people. True, a woman
buying for a household may be buying for someone else, for example, a
child, and she and her husband may have agreed beforehand on "policy,"
but the difference in degree compared with the industrial buyer is so
great that it becomes a difference in kind.

② Second, those with power to influence the buying decision in industrial
buying are often more diffuse and less easily identified or accessible than
are consumers.

③ Third, the total offering rather than just the product becomes the focus
of the industrial buyer's attention; factors such as presale and postsale
service, training offered, and so on are likely to affect the buying decision.
In consumer buying the brand is sometimes completely divorced from the
producing company in the buyer's mind: He does not even know the name
of the company that produces the brand, and the brand name (Jello, for
example) carries the complete burden of identification.

What shall we call the thing being transferred? Should we use the
term "product," "service," "supplier," or "offering" as the focus of attention? For the consumer, the term "brand," is customarily used, as distinguished from the term "product," which refers to product class, the array
of brands or products that are closely substitutable for one another in the
buyer's needs. For the industrial buyer, the term "product supplier-offering" is more appropriate because of the importance of the total offering,
including such things as the seller's reputation for technical services and
delivery. The industrial buyer contemplates the total offering and the suppliers who can provide it. Thus, the services provided typically differentiate the industrial goods seller more than they do the consumer goods
seller.

We must also consider who this person, the buyer, is. The term "buyer"
refers to any person who exerts influence over the purchasing decision.
But this is much too vague. Literally interpreted, it would, in an organization, include the whole board of directors, since they determine the
overall objectives and policies from which individual purchasing decisions stem. The individual organizational purchasing decision is a way of

carrying out some aspect of company objectives which, in turn, should be congruent with the still higher objectives embodied in overall company objectives. But from the point of view of the seller, buying power resides in those who *directly influence* the buyer's *choice.*

Finally, following the marketing concept of Chapter 1, we will take the buyer's point of view.

THE BUYER'S VIEW

Why does the buyer buy? When asked in terms of the buyer's view, this is a surprisingly subtle question that requires equal subtlety in answer. There are many levels at which it can be asked and answered. The famed bank robber, Willie Sutton, was once asked why he robbed the bank. Willie replied, "That's where the money is!" From Willie's view of the world—his frame of reference—this was a perfectly honest answer. To him, the issue was not whether to rob, but instead, *given* that you are going to rob, which is the best place to rob: a home, a filling station, or a bank? The moralist would like Willie to have answered the question at the motivational level. Why did he rob instead of earning an honest living? In this book we will be more general than either Willie or the moralist and ask why the buyer buys at a number of levels and attempt to answer the question for each of them. The evidence for the answer given here is contained in a variety of sources. We are confident that the theory set forth is substantially valid, although the relationships are probably a little more complex than this discussion suggests.[1]

Buying situations can be summarized into three major types, according to how much information the buyer needs. In the first situation, the buyer needs relatively little information; this is *routinized response behavior* (RRB), because it is assumed that the buyer is purchasing a familiar brand. In the second, he needs considerable information; this is *limited problem solving* (LPS), where it is assumed that the buyer is confronted with an unfamiliar brand but one from a familiar product class. Finally, *extensive problem solving* (EPS) requires him to develop a new product class concept and he needs a great amount of information.

These three categories—RRB, LPS, and EPS—are useful because the manager can fit his particular problem into the appropriate case and proceed to analyze it with the respective concepts. Further, they conform closely to the traditional product categories that have been taught for many years in elementary marketing texts and that have been useful for developing retail store strategy: convenience goods, specialty goods, and shopping goods, respectively. These are described as follows:

Convenience goods: those goods for which the consumer, before his need

---

[1] J. U. Farley, J. A. Howard, and Donald R. Lehmann, "After Test Marketing, What?" in *Proceedings of the Business and Economic Statistics Section*, Washington, D.C.: American Statistical Association, 1970 pp. 288–96.

arises, possesses a preference map that indicates a willingness to purchase any of a number of known substitutes rather than to make the additional effort required to buy a particular item.

Specialty goods: those goods for which the consumer, before his need arises, possesses a preference map that indicates his willingness to spend the additional effort required to purchase the most preferred item rather than to buy a more readily accessible substitute.

Shopping goods: those goods for which the consumer has not developed a complete preference map before his need arises, requiring him to undertake search to construct such a map before he purchases.[2]

ROUTINIZED RESPONSE BEHAVIOR

There are two *general* levels at which the question as to why a buyer buys can be asked: in terms of the product class and in terms of the brand. This is illustrated in Figure 3–3, which describes the process by which a

FIGURE 3–3
Gasoline buying decision

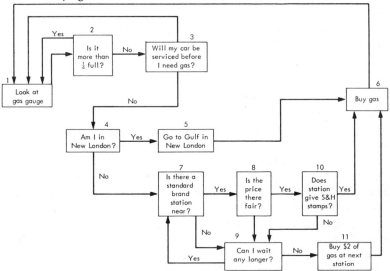

Source: J. A. Howard and J. N. Sheth, *The Theory of Buyer Behavior* (New York: John Wiley & Sons, Inc., 1969), p. 134.

retired banker's wife in New London, New Hampshire, buys gasoline for her car. Her choice process is not completely idiosyncratic by any means; it is very similar to others that were studied at the same time.

When she gets into her car she habitually looks at the gas gauge (box 1)

---

[2]L. P. Bucklin, "The Informative Role of Advertising," *Journal of Advertising Research*, 5 (1965): 11–15.

and, if it is less than one-fourth full, she decides that she needs gas (box 2), the product class. It may be, however, that she will have her car serviced tomorrow, and if so, it is more convenient to get gas then (box 3). These three boxes, however, only explain why she buys the *product class*, the set of brands that are closely substitutable in satisfying the buyer's needs.

The "why" question here is in terms of her needs (motives). She has a *hierarchy* of *motives* that she would like to satisfy at any one time. Obviously she cannot satisfy all of them. Instead she satisfies the most urgent or most *intense* one at the moment. When she saw her gas gauge at less than one-fourth full, the intensity of the motives relevant to using her car was increased enough to precipitate action.

The second-level question in this case is, Why does she buy a *particular* brand? The answer to this is more complicated, but it is much the more common question asked by the marketing manager. She responds differently according to whether she is in New London, as indicated by box 4. If she is, "go to Gulf in New London" (box 5) implies that she has a personal preference for Gulf. This preference is contained in her image or concept of Gulf and each of its competitors. It is the mental trace of the attributes of each brand that are relevant to her. "Image" is sometimes used in a rather loose way; as Blaine Cook, senior vice president, TWA, said in speaking of some market research, "Image is an ephemeral sort of thing."[3] The term is used here, however, in the same sense as psychologists use the term "concept," which is coming to be an accepted way of explaining human thinking. As Patrick Suppes, the philosopher-psychologist-mathematician put it, "the theory of information processing and concept formation might even give quantum mechanics and molecular biology a run for their money for the title of most important scientific development of the twentieth century."[4]

If she is not in New London, more variables enter explicitly into the decision. She now conceptualizes her problem in terms of "standard brand stations" (box 7), of which Gulf is but one. A relevant question concerns whether she prefers Gulf in New London because of the particular station or the nature of the gasoline per se. In choosing a brand away from New London, other, more economical, considerations enter in, such as price (box 8) and availability of trading stamps (box 10). The evaluations of these situational attributes—availability, price, and stamps—constitute *impersonal* attitudes. They are impersonal in the sense that she does not care about, for example, the level of the price per se. It is only that, to the extent the price is high, she has less money to spend for other things.

The elements that explain how the lady buys gasoline when she is in RRB and which underlie Figure 3–3 form a set of variables (such as pref-

---

[3] *Advertising Age,* June 5, 1972, p. 63.
[4] *Information Processing and Choice Behavior,* Technical Report No. 91 (Stanford Calif.: Stanford University Institute for Mathematical Studies in the Social Sciences, 1966), p. 27.

erence and impersonal attitudes) that constitute a theoretical system. This system can be applied to all markets, and it will be, quantitatively, to a consumer nondurable product in Chapter 8. To show the nature of this theoretical system we will first answer the question: What was the psychological process that triggered the lady to action when she observed her gas gauge?

Figure 3–4 shows this process. She received some information from her gas gauge which affected the value of information recalled (the symbol F^R is used to refer to "facts recalled"). Emphasis is placed on recall because to be most useful these variables must be measurable, and recall is a commonly used measure. The information that is recalled could have come from a great variety of sources. The company pays for some sources (such as by its marketing effort) as was illustrated in Figure 3–2, the manager's way of conceptualizing the problem.

In Figure 3–4 there is a *motives* box. M^C refers to the content of her motive(s); for example, she desires to achieve, or, as we say, she has an achievement motive. M^I refers to the intensity of that motive, how badly she wants to achieve. The increase in information affects the intensity of

FIGURE 3–4
Triggering of buying decision

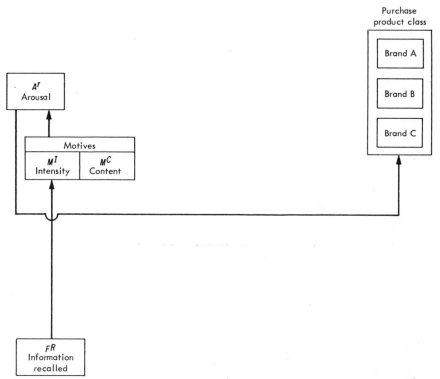

the lady's motives (M^I) and causes her to put energy and attention to buying gasoline instead of to the multitude of other things her motives are driving her to do. This intensity, in turn, triggers *arousal* (A^r), which is a general state of readiness to act. It is readily measurable in the laboratory by various electrical devices. Arousal, in turn, triggers her to contemplate buying *some* brand in this product class, as shown at the right of Figure 3–4, but not any particular brand.

She will confine her attention to the three brands shown even though there are a number of other brands available. These are her *evoked set*, a simplifying mechanism that she takes advantage of. To consider all brands available each time she contemplates buying gasoline would be an inefficient use of her time. She has many, many things she wants to do other than buying gasoline.

How does she decide which of the three brands to take? By the definition of RRB she already has a well-formed concept of each brand. Her *impersonal attitudes* (A^I) may change, however, as a result of the information received, as indicated in Figure 3–5. She may find, for example, that the price is different than she anticipated from her previous experience.

FIGURE 3–5
Brand choice in routinized response behavior

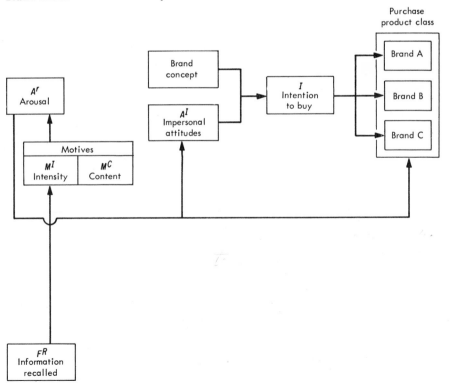

The sum of these impersonal attitudes for each brand and the preference represented in her concept of the brand together generate *intention to buy,* shown as *I* in Figure 3–5. She will buy that brand for which she has the strongest intention.

Intention is a very useful idea because it can be measured at any point in time, whereas purchase can be measured only when it has happened. To the extent purchase is infrequent, intention is a more useful idea for understanding buying behavior. Intention and purchase may not agree perfectly, however, because sometimes after the researcher has gotten her attitude toward brands and before she purchases she will receive unanticipated information which will change her impersonal attitudes.

Returning to Figure 3–2, you now can see the possibility of a complete linkage between the manager's cost—his expenditure on advertising, for example, which affected the buyer's information recalled—and the consequent revenue, or purchase in the case of RRB. In terms of the lady buying gasoline, for instance, the marketing manager of Gulf could spend money on road signs which say "*X* miles to good Gulf gasoline." This information would then affect the buyer's impersonal attitude by indicating the expected degree of availability of the brand, which in turn could affect intention and purchase as shown in Figure 3–5.

In order to explore somewhat carefully the nature of the RRB case, now that we have already worked through one example, we will examine the industrial-buying counterpart of the lady buying gasoline. A study of the purchase of industrial fasteners done in Pittsburgh, Pennsylvania, in 1961[5] shows an RRB case also, but this is a somewhat more complicated buying process. Since the buyer spends eight hours per day at this task— his job—we would expect it to be more involved than that of the lady who only incidentally buys gasoline. Box 1 in Figure 3–6 indicates that the buyer has received a request from the plant for fasteners, which triggers motives relevant to the product class (as in Figure 3–4). Here you will see why the term "product supplier-offering" is more accurate for industrial buying than the term "brand."

Most of the boxes contain questions; for example, in box 2, the buyer asks himself, "Is delivery date less than lead time?" There is a subtlety about this question, however. It implies that he takes one piece of data and compares it with another: the delivery date on the purchase order is compared with the lead time required by the plant, plus the current date. Consequently, the question is really an implicit *information-processing rule.* Further, a *decision rule* stemming ultimately from motives and the total purchase situation is implied between each of the boxes containing an information-processing rule: If the delivery date is not less than the

[5] J. A. Howard and C. G. Moore, Jr., *A Descriptive Model of the Purchasing Function,* unpublished monograph, University of Pittsburgh, 1963.

FIGURE 3–6
dustrial buying: Filling a particular purchase order

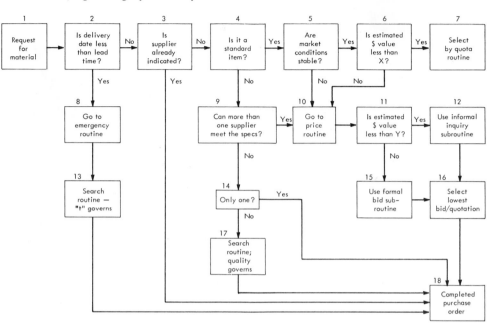

lead time, ask whether the product is a standard item (box 4). We also observe here the role of price as a constraint on purchase, because if it is a standard item, price questions begin to be raised, as in boxes 5, 6, 10, and 11. The rule is an important idea; as the distinguished psychologist George A. Miller has observed, in studying man "we should probably grant (rules) the same status that mathematical equations have (in the natural sciences)."[6]

Boxes 10, 12, 13, 15 and 17 refer to various kinds of routines. This was done to simplify the diagram. A "routine" is a series of steps (or boxes) necessary to perform a particular task. Had each routine been shown in detail, Figure 3–6 would have contained many more boxes.

A *stop rule* can also play an important role in the buyer's decision process. Although an example is not shown in Figure 3–6, it could be that, when the buyer felt a need for the product class (box 1) and proceeded to make his decision, he found the answer "Yes" in box 2, and then in box 13 found that the fastener (or motor, or whatever), was simply not available. For the diagram to be complete, there should be a line out of box 13 to

---

[6] G. A. Miller and David McNeill, "Psycholinguistics" in Gardner Lindzey and Elliott Aronson, *Handbook of Social Psychology* 2d ed: Reading, Mass.: Addison-Wesley Publishing, 1969, p. 667.

another box that directed him to notify the initiator of the request that the product class was unavailable. As far as the act of purchasing is concerned, this notification would imply, "Do nothing!" This implicit rule is what we mean by a stop rule. It is an important element because it incorporates the *nonpurchase* of a product class that we often observe and therefore should be able to explain.

The rules implied in Figure 3–6 are the impersonal or professional attitudes used to evaluate the offerings of the suppliers that fall within the buyer's evoked set. In box 2, for example, if, for the supplier in question, the date that he can make delivery is, in fact, less than lead time ("No"), the rule is to ask "Is supplier already indicated?" (box 3). These rules are the means by which the buyer's motive content (M^c) is translated into actual choice, as in Figure 3–5. Referring back to Figure 3–2 again, we see how the marketer's cost expenditure is related to buyer behavior.

More specifically, however, we should consider how a supplier should behave in selling to this buyer in conditions of RRB. Where the official company buyer chooses the supplier and potential supplier A's offering has no strong differential advantage, there will be a natural reluctance to change from current supplier B to supplier A. For supplier A to even fall into the buyer's evoked set, the salesman from supplier A should regularly call on the buyer. There is evidence that frequent interaction is likely to increase interpersonal sentiment in the direction of increased liking.[7] A buyer wishes to identify with an "attractive" salesman and is rewarded by the salesman's comments of appreciation at receiving an order.

Supplier A, while selling an identical product to supplier B, might have a net differential advantage in his total offering. In such a situation, the credibility of the company is important in getting a favorable first hearing, but once this "toe in the door" is obtained, the quality of the salesman's presentation is important in getting a favorable purchase response. However, an official company buyer may fail to see the significance of the difference in offering. The problem then for supplier A is to reach the executive who has formal authority to specify the offering or who can advise or recommend to those who do. Here, however, we are moving out of the realm of RRB into LPS, which we will explore next.

LIMITED PROBLEM SOLVING

When a buyer is confronted with a new, unfamiliar alternative but one that is in a familiar product class he is in Limited Problem Solving (LPS). He must learn about—form a brand image or concept of—the unfamiliar brand. This obviously requires more information than that required to

---

[7]G. Homans, *The Human Group*, London: Routledge and Keegan Paul, 1951; P. B. Wall, "Proximity as a Determinant of Positive and Negative Sociometric Choice," *British Journal of Social and Clinical Psychology*, IV (1965), 104–9.

buy when he is in RRB. Here we will use the term "brand" to describe the alternative, merely to simplify. It could be described just as well as "product supplier-offering." IN RRB only the intensity of motives and impersonal attitudes can be affected by information, as indicated in Figure 3–5 above. In this new situation the marketing manager can profitably allocate more funds to marketing effort to communicate the additional needed information.

Brand-concept formation can best be explained by breaking a brand concept into its three component parts, as shown in Figure 3–7: *brand comprehension* (B^c), *personal attitude* (A^P) and *confidence* (C). *Brand comprehension* is the buyer's denotative, descriptive, nonevaluative understanding of the brand. It is the means by which he identifies it enough to know which product class to put it in. He also uses it to talk with his friends about the brand in order to find out more about it. Physical dimensions such as "big" or "small" often serve this role.

Personal attitude is a connotative, evaluative dimension. It has to do with things that matter directly to the buyer in meeting his needs. It can

brand concept

FIGURE 3–7
Formation of brand concept

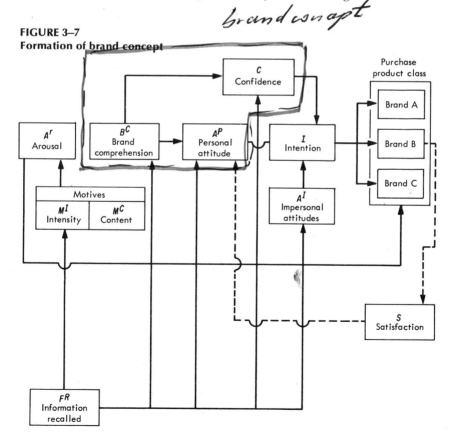

FIGURE 3–8
Multidimensional personal attitude: Consumer rating of brand of instant breakfast

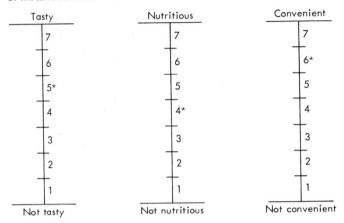

be contrasted, of course, with the impersonal attitudes discussed earlier that also operate in RRB. The singular form "attitude" implies a summary or single dimension, such as a like-dislike scale. A multidimensional measure is more useful and more accurate, however. This more complex measure is illustrated in Figure 3–8, where Mrs. Jones is asked to rate a brand of instant breakfast. She gives it a 5 on tastiness, a 4 on nutrition, and a 6 on convenience. Tom Dillon, chairman, BBD & O, dramatically, knowledgeably, and realistically described the bases for such attitudes in paper towels:

> They are, of course, not a basic human need. People mopped up and dried things with rags for centuries, and it is unlikely that they dreamed of paper towels. . . . It is also a product which has been continually improved. . . .
>
> To an average man no doubt all paper towels look alike. With male logic it may be hard for him to see why paper towels should not be sold solely on a price and quantity basis, if, indeed, there is any moral basis for selling them at all.
>
> But to a mother of three subteen children who have a dog, the prospect of a washload of rags every day is not inviting. To her a paper towel is a necessity and she has quite firm personal opinions about what characteristics that paper towel should have.
>
> Some will be most concerned with the strength of the paper towels. Some will have more concerns about absorbency. Some will be concerned with softness. Some will give more consideration to decorative aspects.[8]

Thus Mr. Dillon gives us something of a more realistic feel for attitude

[8] Thomas O. Dillon in *Public Hearings on Modern Advertising Practices* Federal Trade Commission, October 22, 1971, pp. 324–25.

dimensions. Incidentally, the single-dimensional versus the multidimensional notion applies just as well to impersonal attitudes. In point-of-purchase (P-O-P) display we often see information to serve both personal and impersonal attitudes. *Business Week,* for example, points out a *Progressive Grocery* study which indicates that P-O-P display including advertising and price upped sales as much as 100 percent and never less than 15 percent.[9]

There are two kinds of dimensions to a personal attitude. One is functional and relates to the capacity of the brand to satisfy the buyer's physiological needs (such as those implied in the three scales in Figure 3–8). A second kind, however, has to do with the buyer's social relations. He wants to be viewed as important, in some sense, to other people. Also, he wants to think highly of himself, of his identity and who he is, always in relation to someone else. This subtle type of need relates to his self-concept. It probably plays a relatively more important role in an advanced culture with a high standard of living that gives greater freedom in the way people satisfy their basic physiological or innate motives. It is important also because much of the criticism of marketing effort, especially of advertising by social critics, is aimed at this type of effect.

Finally, *confidence* is the buyer's certainty in judging the quality of the brand in terms of his needs. It has nothing to do with quality per se, but merely measures his confidence in his ability to judge the quality, irrespective of the actual quality level of the brand.

Each of these component parts of a brand image is formed by receiving information from information recalled, as indicated by the arrows in Figure 3–7. Also, as indicated there, brand comprehension affects personal attitude, which affects intention. Brand comprehension also affects confidence which in turn partially shapes intention. Finally, as in RRB, intention influences purchase. The same triggering process operates as in RRB.

However, we have omitted from our description a key idea in LPS: the *satisfaction* (S) derived from buying and consuming the brand. "Consuming" is used here in a broad sense to mean any utilization so as to gain satisfaction, such as by wearing clothes or having your friends view the recent acquisition of a painting. It is indicated in Figure 3–7 in the lower right-hand corner. The arrow assumes brand B was purchased. The dashed line indicates it is a feedback in which the buying process feeds back upon itself.

The concept of satisfaction completes the view of LPS, in which the buyer is confronted with a new brand in a familiar product class. But how about the case where the buyer is confronting a radically new alternative, as Carnation Instant Breakfast was or the Amana home electronic range has been to most housewives? This entails Extensive Problem Solving.

---

[9] *Business Week,* January 8, 1972, p. 38.

EXTENSIVE PROBLEM SOLVING

When such innovations as Carnation instant breakfast and Amana home electronic ranges are introduced, the housewife has no brand comprehension dimensions to identify them by and no personal and impersonal attitude dimensions with which to judge them. In each case she has to form these dimensions in order to develop a *product-class concept.* Because this is a much greater learning situation and requires considerably more information than does LPS, it is designated *extensive problem solving* (EPS). Unfortunately not nearly enough is known about the process, partly because the basic research in concept formation has been largely confined to the denotative aspects (brand comprehension), instead of relating to the evaluative dimensions of the concept.

The dimensions of personal and impersonal attitudes are called *choice criteria.* They are formed when the buyer brings his motives to bear on the brand itself and on the purchasing situation. The simplest way to show them diagrammatically would be by arrows in Figure 3–7 running from motives to personal attitude and to impersonal attitude.

We know that, in general, the human has more difficulty forming concepts about abstract things than about concrete things. This characteristic undoubtedly carries over into buying behavior and makes it more difficult for the buyer to form a concept about a service than about a physical brand. The significance of this becomes apparent when we note that more than 60 percent of our labor force is now engaged in producing services, as compared with 25 percent in 1890.[10] Some service companies such as airlines and banks are attempting to add concreteness to their image by having their employees wear "career apparel."[11]

EPS raises new questions about buyer information. All of the discussion so far has implicitly assumed that the buyer passively accepts all information he is exposed to. In fact, the buyer is quite active in regulating his information input. He must select. He is continuously confronted with millions of bits of information and even under the best of conditions is capable of taking in only a very, very small proportion. If you try to recall what you remember from when you first entered this room, for example, you will find it isn't much. If you then look around the room carefully, you will see how much more you were exposed to that did not enter your sensory system to a point where it can be recalled. Then if you close your eyes and recall what you saw, it will be immensely more than when you first entered the room, but still not all that is "out there."

Two forces operate to regulate the input of information to the buyer. As in the simplified diagram of Figure 3–9, one force is the buyer's uncertainty (confidence), which feeds back to arousal, his state of awakedness. To the extent the buyer is confident, he is less likely to take in informa-

---

[10] *Science,* August 20, 1971, p. 679.
[11] *Christian Science Monitor,* June 30, 1972, p. 6.

tion. The second force is related to the importance of the purchase to the buyer (motives). To the extent it is an important purchase in some sense— socially, economically, or physically—the buyer is more likely to look for information, to search. This effect is reflected in the intensity of the buyer's relevant motives; and it is indicated in Figure 3–9 by an arrow from motives to arousal.

FIGURE 3–9
Information-regulating mechanisms

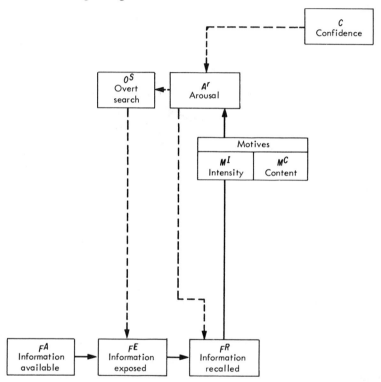

Arousal facilitates information input in a number of ways. First, it affects recall by regulating the buyer's receptors. You may have seen a reference to research done a few years ago by advertisers on "popping pupils," in which the amount of pupil dilation in response to an ad was used as a measure of advertising effectiveness. Arousal (A^r) also affects memory (F^R) directly. This is not well understood, but greater arousal, up to a point, seems to cause material to be more firmly imbedded.

Second, if the first means does not suffice to give the buyer the information he needs from his normal pattern of exposure, he physically searches. This is expressed by an arrow in Figure 3–9 from arousal to *overt search*

(O^s). Overt search involves talking with friends about the brand, reading additional advertising sources, and perhaps even reading *Consumer Reports*. In this sense, overt search is a simplification of a variety of behaviors.

The buyer's *level of aspiration* also has an effect on information search. He searches until he finds something that meets his needs. He has some idea of "how good" it must be, how high it should come on the attitude scales if it is to be satisfactory. How high that is depends upon the buyer's aspiration level, which is not a completely fixed quantity. It, too, adjusts over time. To the extent he is in a favorable environment—has no trouble finding what he needs— his aspiration level will tend to rise. Contrariwise, to the extent he is not in a favorable environment, it will tend to shift downward.

The concept of a product class is important in a practical sense. It is the basis of brand competition, as we saw in Chapter 2. One problem that companies have is to correctly identify or measure, which is to say they must learn exactly what they are competing with. There is also some competition among product classes as shifts in preferences are created by long-run social and economic changes. The women's lib movement, for example, is credited by clothiers with shifting women into lower price clothing, even among those in the high-income brackets. Pantsuits are more important and bras less important.[12]

MARKET SEGMENTING VARIABLES

Casual observation indicates that all buyers of a product class are not alike, even though we have been assuming this in order to simplify. Differences in buyers are, in principle, differences in motives, but we have limited capacity to measure motives directly. In any event, associated attitudes and habits may be just as important as motives in differentiating buyers. There are obvious geographic differences (some people live in the South and others in the North), demographic differences (some are young and some are older), and psychographic differences (some have one set of needs and others have other needs). *If* these *measurable differences* happen to also indicate differences in the *response curves* shown in Figure 3–1, they offer opportunities for the company to market differently and more profitably than if the differences are ignored and all buyers are treated alike. This can be more profitable because it can offer a market protected from competition and the erosive effect of competition upon profit margins.

Treating buyers all alike—exposing them to the same marketing mix—is called *undifferentiated* marketing, is illustrated in Figure 3–10. Assume that in all three diagrams the dots represent buyers arranged on two

---

[12] *The New York Times*, May 7, 1972, p. F7.

dimensions of some type, for example, age and income. In undifferentiated marketing it would make no difference what age or income level they were; we assume they all would respond alike to the marketing effort.

FIGURE 3–10
Types of segmentation strategy

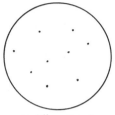 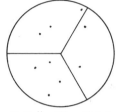 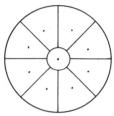

Undifferentiated   Partially differentiated   Completely differentiated

On the other hand, the manager may believe that the market is made up of three homogeneous groups, according to the two dimensions. This is called *partially differentiated marketing*. He selects one or more of these as his *target market(s)* and proceeds to develop a marketing mix particularly appropriate to it. He has thus *positioned* his product in terms of that segment. The positioning concept, which implies a recognition of competitive influences, was introduced in Chapter 2.

The marketing manager may decide, however, that each buyer is a distinct entity and for maximum profitability should have a separate mix. This is called *completely differentiated marketing*. Such a practice is not common except in the industrial market, where a company uses salesmen and sells to only a few buyers. The salesman can have a good knowledge of each of his buyers, which is to say he can intuitively infer the relevant segmenting dimensions or variables. He can also negotiate individually with these buyers.

Companies follow the practice of segmenting much less than they would like to, for three reasons. First, segmenting obviously adds to cost. Additional versions of a product reduce the economy of mass production. At a minimum, the sheer management time devoted to the task is costly. This can be thought of as the more general problem of whether the segments are accessible: Two housewives like different cleaning strengths in their wall cleaners, but are the segments accessible enough to justify the cost of differentiation? Most segments are usually accessible in one way or another, but sometimes only at exorbitant outlays of funds.

Second, the differences in response curves among the segments are not sufficient to justify the cost. In considering segmentation, there is often the implicit assumption that measurable differences—geographic, demographic, and psychographic—always coincide with differences in corresponding magnitude of response curves. This need not be so.

This leads us to the third and related reason. Companies follow the segmenting practice less than they would like because they don't know what the segments are. They almost never know the shape of the response curves. In fact, the research to date is somewhat discouraging because it raises questions about how important demographic and psychographic differences are, as we will see in Chapter 8. Small intersegment differences in response, however, could be important economically. Other research approaches may be more fruitful. The validity of segmentation research itself is currently an active area of research.

Confusion is added to the situation by research often misnamed "segmentation research" by companies in which it is carried on. Lack of a theory of buyer behavior and the new availability of multivariate statistical techniques in the past decade have driven company researchers to do the obvious: They attack differences among buyers to get leverage in constructing an understanding or ad hoc theory of their market. When you know nothing about any phenomenon, marketing or otherwise, the natural beginning point is to examine differences in the hopes of teasing out causal relations. With the theory set forth in this chapter, you can approach the market-segmenting problem more directly by asking: Where does the segmenting variable impact upon the system, at purchase or earlier in the process? This possibility will be shown in Chapter 8.

In all of the discussion of segmentation we have been quite vague about what the actual segmenting dimensions are. Unfortunately, this accurately reflects the state of the art of segmenting. You are forced to be empirical and think in terms of ad hoc rather than general dimensions applicable across a number of product classes. The psychological literature provides some hints about general dimensions, but these largely remain to be explored systematically by basic research.

SUMMARY

The contents of the black box between marketing outlay intended to create revenue and the realization of that revenue, as pictured in Figure 3–2, are a set of psychological mechanisms that make up a process. This process is the underlying structure of demand.

A more complicated structure may be necessary, however. In describing the buyer's psychological process we assumed that all buyers are alike. Obviously this is not so—there are geographic, demographic, psychographic, and other differences. Whether these differences reflect differences in response curves, however, is quite another matter. And it is response curves only that are of importance, as we will see in Chapter 7. If differences in response curves do exist, a structure that will incorporate them is essential.

Recognition that differences among buyers can exist introduced the possibilities of market segmentation. Segmentation also considers the ideas of target markets and market positioning as essential concepts of marketing psychology. An alternative strategy to segmenting the given market is to expand the product class and thus to enlarge the market.

DISCUSSION QUESTIONS

1. At the outset of Chapter 2 it was asserted that "sell" and "persuade" are misleading. After reading Chapter 3, do you agree? If so, why? If not, why not?
2. Explain the relation between structure of demand, response functions, and the consumer's decision process.
3. There are three levels at which we can explain *why* people buy: Routinized response behavior, limited problem solving and extensive problem solving. Show how the explanations differ at each level from the other two levels.
4. What is the relation between a buyer's motives and choice criteria?
5. What must be true of buyer response curves for segmentation to offer potential to the manager?

4

Structure of cost

INTRODUCTION

STRUCTURE of nonmarketing cost, the third noncontrollable element in the marketing manager's environment, consists of the structural elements and the relations among them. Using cost inputs, this structure embodies a process that generates a cost output. To make this general concept applicable, a number of supporting concepts and their definitions are necessary. It so happens that the same concepts needed for nonmarketing costs are appropriate for marketing as well. The purpose of this chapter is to describe these supporting concepts and how to use them.

To many readers, however, there is probably a prior question. Why devote considerable time to a somewhat abstract discussion of cost? Historically, marketing personnel have not been much concerned with cost in their decision making. Volume of sales has been by all odds the primary criterion of decision in marketing. Why, then, should we be concerned with a seemingly little-used set of concepts?

There are at least five reasons why we can expect a much greater emphasis upon cost in marketing decisions in the future than has been laid to it in the past. First, in the past 20 years higher management has devised, in the brand-manager concept, ways of granting considerable authority to lower level marketing personnel without losing control. The central instrument for providing both freedom for the individual and control by higher management is the marketing plan. Decision close to the market has the advantage of being based on better market information. In the interests of the corporation, the more important a decision, the more essential it is that it be made in terms of the company's goals, and profit is almost always one of these goals. But this possibility has been limited because essential data—demand and cost—for profit-directed decision making have been lacking.

Second, in the past, marketing management has had little knowledge of demand data, of the probable effects of marketing effort on sales. Splendid intuitive judgments were made, but these are next to impossible to quantify. Present developments (described especially in Chapter 8) give us hope of quantitatively determining these effects. Until these tools were available, it was useless to consider profit-directed decision making in marketing.

Third, the cost of deriving appropriate cost data for each brand has been a very real barrier to the utilization of cost in marketing decision. For some time now the guiding theory and necessary statistical tools have been available, as we will see illustrated later in this chapter. The cost and time to apply them, however, were not justified until cost systems began to be computerized as they are now. This development has astoundingly reduced the cost of deriving the appropriate estimates. Because of this, at least two companies now intend to provide appropriate cost data even to the salesman level, the lowest line unit in the marketing operation.

Fourth, computerized marketing information systems are clearly on the horizon. Many companies are attempting to develop them. Such a system brings together cost, demand, and related data and converts it into a more useful basis for decision. Chapter 6 is devoted to just this topic.

Fifth, one of the real problems in decentralizing decision in marketing and expecting it to be profit directed is, of course, the motivation of lower level marketing decision makers. In part, this can be accomplished by rewarding on the basis of profits. Perhaps even equally important, however, are the manager's personal motives and goals. Does he have a personal intrinsic desire to achieve profit? Quite recently there has been a basic shift in American values toward new areas of social concern such as pollution control. To an extent, these are motivating lower level employees to personally want their companies to engage in social betterment. Obviously this can be done in a private-enterprise system only after some minimum level of profit has been achieved. Insofar as this new motivation continues and corporate leadership is able to tap and stimulate it, there may be a demand from lower levels of marketing management for the concepts and appropriate information necessary in profit-directed decision making.

For these reasons in particular we believe that cost will be an increasingly important element in lower level marketing decision, such as at the brand manager level. We know of one of the largest marketing companies that is now devoting an extensive program to instilling brand managers with a profit orientation and providing them with the necessary concepts and data to comply with it.

Since a structure is a system of interrelated parts, we must determine the component parts of the structure of costs. The parts can be described in terms of four elements that determine the way all costs in a company are distributed by its accounting system. For example, the *cost structure* causes input costs to be *distributed* in such a way as to generate a reliable *brand* cost estimate. Three of the structural dimensions can be easily visualized in a three-dimensional diagram, as in Figure 4–1, which can be quite helpful in comprehending the general concept of structure of cost. These three dimensions are *cost inputs, organizational units* (*divisions* in the figure), and *cost outputs* (*brands* in the figure). The fourth element will be dealt with below.

FIGURE 4–1
Cost structure

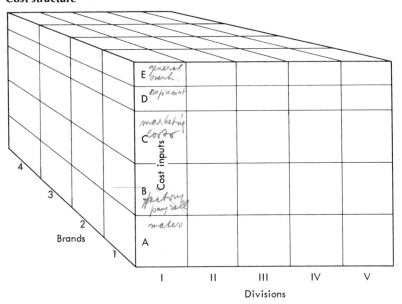

The more specific terms—divisions for organizational units and brands for cost outputs—are used to add substance and clarity to the discussion of cost structure. Cost is meaningful only in terms of the particular organizational unit affected, because many costs are incurred in a company that do not have relevance to all its units—production machinery, for example, is bought for a particular division. Assume we are concerned with division I, the Maxwell House Division of General Foods.

What cost inputs are incurred? Raw coffee must be purchased (A—materials); people must be paid (B—factory payroll); some marketing cost will be involved, such as advertising and salesmen (C—marketing costs); production equipment must be charged off (D—depreciation); general company overhead such as the president's salary must also be charged against the product (E—company overhead).

Managers in a marketing area are usually concerned with making decisions about a particular brand. Let us say it is brand 1, Instant Maxwell House, for example. Hence, in Cell IA1 are the material costs of the Maxwell House Division for producing Instant Maxwell House for some given period such as a month. In this way we derive the content of each cell in Figure 4–1, and the sum of column 1 for division I is, of course, the total cost of producing the given number of units of the product during a specific period.

Implicit in this three-dimensional structure, however, is a fourth, very important dimension—the physical, engineering, or technological *relation* between cost inputs and the cost outputs generated by the cost structure. This relation leads to the crucially important differences in cost due to changes in the rate of production of a given plant or other unit of activity. To produce X number of 4 oz. containers of Instant Maxwell House will require Y number of pounds of raw coffee. This physical relation can be described in mathematical terms. A marketing decision maker wants to know this relation because the price of raw coffee fluctuates. If he is drawing up an annual marketing plan, he must have an estimate of what the new price for raw coffee (the cost input) six months from now will do to the cost of producing the brand. Figure 4–7 below will illustrate a regression analysis which relates total cost to individual brands as a means of separating fixed and variable costs for individual brands in a multiproduct company. The same regression analysis can be used to identify the engineering relations between individual cost input items and the cost of the individual brand.

Hence, as the cost (prices) of input factors change, such as in the case of raw coffee, the division may find it profitable to make use of the economic principle of substitution. This could mean, for example, substituting a certain amount of cheaper coffee in the production, which would reduce costs.

The physical relation itself may change as new technological developments occur. In production, new machinery can lower the cost of production. In marketing, as television began to cut into radio, the physical relation between units of advertising message and buyer behavior probably also changed. A change in the physical relation is what we mean by a *change in the cost structure* itself instead of *change in the price of the cost inputs*. This distinction is essential to bear in mind, and confusion often arises in practice because it is not carefully maintained.

In the following pages we will deal with how to get those numbers in the cells of Figure 4–1 that are appropriate to our needs. To obtain the facts needed for marketing decision making and planning, we must have a set of sharp cost *concepts* and a way of *measuring* their empirical counterparts.

COST CONCEPTS

Introduction

For two reasons we are taking on a very difficult problem when we attempt to obtain relevant and reasonably accurate figures for the cells of Figure 4–1. First, marketing cost inputs such as advertising, salesmen, price, and channels are not well understood in terms of their *effects*, their consequences for sales. Because of this lack of knowledge, accountants have not been willing to treat them as they would other cost inputs. If a piece of machinery is purchased, its cost is written off over the life of the machine instead of being paid for, in an accounting sense, during the year of purchase. On the other hand, if a large advertising campaign is developed and executed this year, the accountant would not be willing to treat it in the same way, even though he might be intuitively convinced that the campaign run this year would gain sales for future years as well. Thus, heavy marketing expenditures cause current profits to be understated, which creates a bias against marketing effort.

Second, the marketing decision maker has great difficulty even with nonmarketing costs because, historically, accountants have been concerned only with financial reporting. Cost-reporting systems were designed to meet this need. Cost estimates, however, are now also required for managerial control, public regulation, and decision making. As these new needs for cost estimates arose, the traditional system was merely modified to accommodate them. Consequently, the decision maker has had difficulty in understanding the logic of the existing system and in adapting its output to his needs. We will examine each of these four needs for cost data so that we can better perceive the problem of the decision maker.

By *financial reporting* is meant, essentially, the construction of a periodic profit and loss statement which provides information for management, stockholders, unions, and the government.

Control of company performance is achieved in a large measure through the use of cost data because cost is used as the criterion of that performance. Obviously, such a vital function must receive the accountant's attention. Confusion arises, however, because "cost control" is a commonly used term which sees only the problem of cutting costs, of keeping costs at a minimum. Writing of business in general, *Business Week* stated, "The key phrase in the second quarter of 1971 was cost cutting."[1] On the

---

[1]*Business Week*, August 14, 1971, p. 47.

other hand, in using cost as a measure of performance, such as in comparing a salesman's actual expense with his budgeted expense, we are concerned with how well the salesman is doing his job—which is to sell.

Cost data are important in government *regulation*, such as in income tax reporting, but they figure most clearly in instances of direct price regulation. In this connection the important fact is that cost is what the regulating agency says it is, irrespective of what may seem logical and proper to management. The taxing authorities have the same effect. The marketing manager is more likely to encounter the use of cost data for government regulation in the "cost proving" required by the Robinson-Patman Act. According to this act, differences among prices charged to different classes of customers are justifiable if based on differences in costs incurred in serving the customers. (For qualifications to this statement and for other methods of justifying price differentials, see Chapter 15.)

Finally, cost estimates are required for *decision making*. "Direct-costing" systems have been adopted by companies partly on the grounds that they provide the appropriate cost estimates for many decisions.

The important point in this discussion of the four uses of cost data is that the "cost" required for each use is usually of a different magnitude. This is one of the major reasons for the ambiguity of the term "cost." With this background in the nature and uses of cost data, it should be compellingly clear that a market executive must be thoroughly familiar with cost analysis; *he alone* knows the cost facts he needs because he *knows* better than anyone else the *alternatives of choice that he is comparing.* Hence, it is essential that we carefully develop some guiding concepts that will help the manager to understand this uncontrollable element of his environment.

Incidentally, the rest of the chapter may appear to cast the accountant in the role of the villain. The intention, however, is to prepare you for the problems you will encounter. An imaginative, sympathetic, articulate accountant can be of immense help.

Two general concepts

Two of the most basic concepts in cost analysis are classification criterion and the relevancy criterion.

CRITERION FOR CLASSIFYING COSTS. For most marketing decisions, cost information must be assembled, or classified, on a particular basis. For example, if the decision is to choose between two marketing channels, the appropriate costs must be classified according to channels so the alternative channels under consideration can be compared. The accountant sometimes uses the term "segments of the company" to describe these bases for classifying costs. Some of the most commonly used bases, segments, or criteria for classifying costs are brand, geographic area, marketing channel, method of solicitation, delivery, groups of customers, and size of order. In Figure 4–1, the brand criterion was used because it is often needed and it is more easily understood than are some of the other bases. The decision to be made determines the appropriate classification criterion.

CRITERION OF COST RELEVANCY. A Navy recruit is often beset with problems as to how he should behave; the often-stated principle is, "If it moves, salute it; if it doesn't, paint it!" Similarly, in making a cost estimate for a particular marketing decision, one of the major problems encountered is deciding which cost items should be included and which should be omitted. A marketing manager thinks that one of his products is unprofitable and should be dropped. He presents this proposal to the president, who immediately asks, "Why?" The manager is then confronted with the need for compiling a defensible cost estimate. Obviously the first costs to be included are raw materials and labor directly used in producing the product, as we saw in Figure 4–1. Then less clear-cut items are encountered, such as marketing costs in cell I1C; and finally such things as executive salaries (cell I1E) must be considered. The question of what cost items should be included is, without exception, answered by the relevancy criterion—include only *those cost items* that will be *affected by the decision.*

The criterion of cost relevancy, which will be used throughout the following discussion, is emphasized because there has been considerable confusion about marketing costs. As mentioned above, cost data are often used for marketing control purposes, for which purpose quite different estimates are usually made than for decision making. Also, teachers of marketing have often concerned themselves with consideration, in various ways, of whether distribution costs too much in an economic welfare sense. In their concern they have attempted to establish the two categories of "distribution costs" and "production costs" and to assign certain cost items on a *permanent* basis to one or the other of these categories.

Specific cost concepts

The next task is to set forth those specific cost concepts that render operational the idea of cost structure and its underlying concepts of classification and relevancy criteria. These specific concepts bring together the *accountant's view* of the problem and the *theory of cost* from economic analysis, in order to focus both on marketing decisions. A knowledge of accounting terminology will enable the marketing executive to work more effectively with the accounting department. For the sake of brevity, however, some terminology found in the cost accounting literature will be omitted. The concepts appropriate for present purposes are summarized in Table 4–1.

OUTLAY VERSUS OPPORTUNITY COSTS. Opportunity cost is a central con-

TABLE 4–1
Cost distinctions

Concepts			*Basis of distinction*
Outlay	v.	Opportunity	Nature of the sacrifice
Future	v.	Historical	Degree of anticipation
Short run	v.	Long run	Degree of adaptation to present output
Variable	v.	Fixed	Relation to output
Incremental	v.	Marginal	Type of added activity
Traceable	v.	Common	Traceability to a part of the company
Direct	v.	Indirect	Traceability to different products

cept in all cost analysis for decision making. Cost may be an actual expenditure (outlay cost), or it may be the price that the input's service would command in the most productive alternative use (*opportunity cost*). To use the productive services of anything for one purpose is to sacrifice the opportunity of using those services for other purposes. The cost of these services, then, is the most productive foregone opportunity. The opportunity-outlay distinction is of great practical importance, although sometimes its application is complex.

The opportunity-outlay distinction applies in the use of limited factory facilities, for example, in a decision whether to eliminate a brand from the product line when the factory is producing at capacity. In computing the cost of the brand being considered for elimination, the manager should include an estimate of the profit that would result if these limited factory facilities were used in producing the most profitable alternative brand. If the existing product still shows a contribution to profit after this inclusion, the brand should be continued.

The opportunity-outlay distinction can also apply to parts or materials in computing costs of production. Often the materials were purchased when their prices were lower, or they were obtained at a special bargain price. In either case their cost in producing the product should be their current price on the market rather than the actual cost outlay made by the company in purchasing them. This is because the foregone opportunity here is to sell them in the current market. The accountant employs the term "replacement cost."

Opportunity cost is always the appropriate concept. However, because outlay cost often measures opportunity cost, outlay cost can also be used. The marketing executive should be on the alert to detect discrepancies between the two and to use estimates of opportunity cost when a discrepancy does arise.

FUTURE VERSUS HISTORICAL COSTS.   The distinction between future and historical costs is obvious but important, although it is often ignored in practice. Cost data provided by the conventional accounting department are only *historical,* yet a decision involves only *future* costs. Historical costs can be particularly misleading because they are familiar and so possess a subtle sense of rightness. Although experience may throw considerable light, it is all too easy to assume that the past completely illuminates the future. Typically, the cost structure does not change quickly, but the items going into the structure may. The wide fluctuations that occur in the price of such raw materials as zinc, copper, and tin offer good examples of why large differences in product cost may occur over time. With new products, even the cost structure may change, because as experience is gained in producing the item the cost will decline. In marketing a new product, decisions such as price will often be based upon the much lower cost that will be attained from both volume and experience rather than upon current costs.

SHORT-RUN VERSUS LONG-RUN COSTS.   Economic analysis sets forth three periods of activity: market, short run, and long run. Market applies when the rate of output is constant; short run when the scale of output (plant capacity) is constant but rate of output can be changed; and long run when the scale of output as well as the rate of output can be changed. These concepts of time guide the manager, steering him clear of the pitfalls created by the ambiguities of the term "cost." They distinguish between operating and strategic marketing.

The time horizon of the manager's decision partly determines the amount of the cost estimate. Differences in the time horizon introduce an array of crucial concepts that make up the core of cost theory. These concepts, which can be applied to an enormously wide range of practice, are shown in Figures 4–2 and 4–3. Assume, since cost theory has been devel-

FIGURE 4–2
Long- and short-run average cost curves

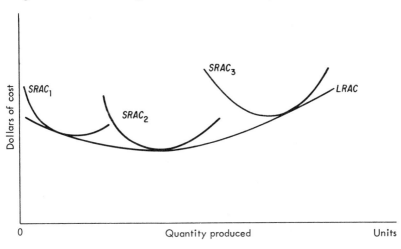

oped in terms of production, that the graph in Figure 4–2 represents the facts from a manufacturing plant. Only for the moment, however, must you adjust your thinking to production instead of sales. The curve labeled *LRAC* shows the average total cost per unit of product at various levels of output *when the scale of output is changed*, that is, when the capacity of the plant is modified. Thus, scale of output means roughly the same thing as what the manager means by capacity. The term "capacity," however, is ambiguous because production can almost always be increased somewhat, although the increase may bring lessened efficiency, or, stated differently, may bring rising costs.

Each *short-run average cost (SRAC)* in Figure 4–2 represents a factory *with a given scale of output* and shows the total unit costs that would result from changing only the level of production. The curve *LRAC* is usually referred to as the "envelope curve" because it envelops all of the various possible plant sizes or capacities, each of which is represented by a short-run curve. The *LRAC* curve is made up of an infinite number of *SRAC* curves, and it shows the total unit costs at all possible scales of output over the range of production included in the graph. Thus the term

FIGURE 4–3
Marginal and average cost curves for a given plant

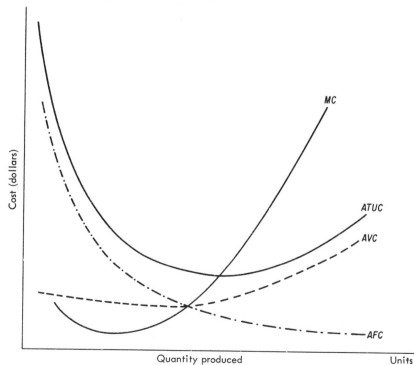

"economies of scale" applies to the behavior of total unit cost related to the scale of output—the envelope curve.

The distinction between short run and long run is essential to an understanding of cost theory because it contains the distinction between variable and fixed costs and related concepts upon which so much of decision rests. As indicated, short run refers to a period of time that permits adjustments in the rate of production only, whereas long run refers to a period of time long enough to adjust the scale of output as well. The distinction should not be confused with the calendar-time distinction of short term and long term that was used in the discussion of demand analysis, although in Part III (for reasons set forth there) we will treat them as synonymous.

Let us examine the short-run average total cost curves of Figure 4–2 more carefully. One of these curves is reproduced in Figure 4–3, where it can be seen that short-run average total cost, labeled $ATUC$ (average total unit cost), is the sum of the average fixed cost (AFC) and the average variable cost (AVC) at various levels of output. Although AFC varies with the rate of production, the total fixed cost does not change—a given amount is merely spread over more units as production expands. This "spreading the overhead" through greater utilization of a given capacity is often, in practice, confused with economies of scale. Total variable cost, however, does change with output.

Finally, while *average* total cost ($ATUC$) pertains to the cost of producing *each unit* of a given output, the term "total cost" means the cost of producing *all the units* of a given output. The change in total cost that results from producing an additional unit is called the "marginal cost" (MC). Mathematically, marginal cost is the first derivative of the total cost, but we can deal with it verbally.

Marginal cost is the key to an understanding of the *profit-maximizing principle*, which is a central idea used throughout this book. Table 4–2 illustrates how these costs, particularly marginal cost, are computed. The table should be worked through carefully to insure that you comprehend this essential cost concept. The average fixed cost and average variable cost can be computed by dividing each figure in columns 2 and 3 by the appropriate quantity figure from column 1. The reader should carefully note in column 5 that marginal cost is the *change* in *total cost* that results from an additional unit of production.

Variable versus fixed costs. The dichotomy of variable costs and fixed costs conforms precisely to the short-run fixed and variable distinction of cost theory where the variation is a consequence of changes in the *rate of output*. The fixed costs are constant in total, but when divided by the number of units and thus expressed as averages, they vary inversely with output.

Limited empirical evidence suggests that average variable cost may

TABLE 4–2
Short-run cost relationships

Quantity (1)	Fixed cost (FC) (2)	Variable cost (VC) (3)	Total cost (TC) (4)	Marginal cost per unit (MC) (5)	Average total cost per unit (ATUC) (6)
0.........	150	0	150		Infinity
				——50	
1.........	150	50	200		200.00
				——25	
2.........	150	75	225		112.50
				——15	
3.........	150	90	240		80.00
				——10	
4.........	150	100	250		62.50
				——20	
5.........	150	120	270		54.00

sometimes be roughly equal to the marginal cost of cost theory within narrow ranges of the level of output. An example will be presented below to support this observation. The evidence is strong enough to support the use of average variable cost as a workable approximation of marginal cost over the usual range of production in many, but not all, decision situations.

Equality of average variable and marginal cost is important because marginal cost is the appropriate decision input but average variable cost is more easily measured. When the two are identical, average variable can be used as an estimate of marginal cost.

Finally, it is easier with the concepts now at hand to clarify the point made in Chapter 2 that the fixed/variable cost ratio makes a difference in the intensity of competition. If in Figure 4–3 we think of price as being represented on the vertical axis, as well as cost, we can imagine a great number of prices that would cover AVC but not ATUC. The company will continue to produce as long as AVC is covered, so unprofitable competition can continue until the plant must be replaced. Replacement of the plant will entail additional fixed cost; when faced with this decision, management, if it is profit oriented, will close it down.

INCREMENTAL VERSUS MARGINAL COSTS. With the incremental-marginal distinction we are no longer confined in our thinking to the idea of a factory and changes in rates of production; *the incremental-cost concept generalizes the marginal-cost concept to any added activity.* The concept of marginal applies only to one more unit of production whereas in practice we use incremental terms for additional units of any activity. These distinctions are important because marketing decisions often involve several additional units of an *activity* other than production. A company with a sales force must decide how to allocate the salesmen geographically. In making the decision, the marketing manager should have an estimate of the incremental cost of *adding sales effort* to each territory in order to compare it with the additional (incremental) revenue that will accrue as a result of the additional sales effort. We will do this in Chapter 7.

The incremental-cost concept should not be applied blindly, however, because some marketing decisions, such as product change and marketing channels, imply long-run commitments. Costs ordinarily classified as fixed become incremental when a longer period of commitment is implied in the decision. The decision to expand a marketing organization by adding a direct sales force will obligate a portion of the marketing manager's time for as long as this direct-selling approach is continued. He cannot avoid devoting some of his attention to directing and evaluating the force. A correct estimate of the incremental cost required for the decision would include some portion of the marketing manager's time, and it would require an approximation of opportunity cost.

TRACEABLE VERSUS COMMON COSTS.   A traceable cost is one that can be identified, *as a practical matter*, with a part or segment of the company; this "part" may be anything, such as a brand, department, or plant. The distinction is important in marketing decisions, since by far the greatest number of companies are multiproduct, and cost estimates are needed for each of the products. One of the constantly recurring decisions is the problem of the most profitable *product mix* (the "best" combination of products) because the mix can usually be altered by changes in price or promotion. The need for the traceable-common distinction is so prevalent in marketing that it will be developed in detail.

The reader may raise a question as to why, if in a concrete marketing problem the incremental cost has been approximated, he should concern himself with the traceable-common distinction. It was stated previously that incremental cost gives us the correct answer. The reason is that if cost records are regularly maintained so as to separate traceable from common costs on a *continuing* basis (e.g., in by-products), incremental costs can be estimated more easily for various decisions. A special cost study which may be costly and time-consuming will not be needed for each decision.

Strictly speaking, common costs arise because of technological reasons alone. One kind of common cost involves joint products, such as in the pork-packing industry, where two hams inevitably accompany two shoulders (at least with a normal hog). In practice, common costs also arise because the company accounting system throws together many costs in the process of classifying them for financial reporting purposes. Here we see illustrated a point made at the beginning of the chapter about how the traditional financial reporting system has merely been adapted to decision-making needs. In the development of a product unit cost, accounting practice allocates all unallocated costs, or "overheads," as they are often called. When such cost data are used in making decisions, they can lead to serious errors in the profit estimates of marketing decision alternatives. The accountant typically prepares what is termed "a historical, fully allocated, average unit cost" which has essentially three constituent parts: (1) traceable costs, (2) variable common costs, and (3) fixed common costs. The practical problem, then, in estimating the cost of an individual brand in a multiproduct company is to determine the "correct" allocation of the *variable common costs*. Traceable costs pose no problem, and fixed common costs do not vary with the decision and so can be ignored.

Under certain conditions the conventional accounting practice of full allocation can lead to serious errors, but in other instances it is not too damaging. If a large proportion of the costs are traceable, and these costs are also variable in the short run, then overheads are small and conventional accounting practice will yield a rough workable approximation to the average variable cost of theory. When overhead costs are large and partly fixed in relation to output, cost estimates that have been derived through full allocation are not at all satisfactory, and decisions based upon them may not at all tend to maximize profits.

Three possible situations are encountered in estimating the costs of an individual brand:

1. The brands are related in a situation of what is termed "joint products" —an increase in the production of one brand causes an increase in the production of one or more other brands.
2. The relationship is one of "alternative products"—an increase in the production of one brand is necessarily accompanied by a decrease in the quantity of the related brand.
3. The products are not related—the quantity of brand A has no influence upon the quantities of brands B, C, and so forth.

Joint products are illustrated in the production of iron, where steel inevitably accompanies iron. If one product is much more important than the other in the sense of contributing greater profit, the less important product is called a "by-product"; in time, the position of the two products is often reversed. In the joint-product situation, there is no logically satisfactory method of estimating the cost of the individual products; the costs are said to be indeterminate.

Alternative products typically arise because of limited factory facilities or other limited inputs, such as materials or labor. Here, the concept of opportunity cost is usually appropriate in estimating the costs of individual brands, because the major cost is the foregone opportunity to produce the alternative brand.

Unrelated brands perhaps are the most common. The cost of each unrelated brand can be determined, in principle, by systematically varying both the total volume of production (all products taken together) and the proportions of the various brands making up the product line. In the ordinary production situation, however, the variation in production may not be great enough to reveal the cost information. The conditions under which the principle can be used will be illustrated in Figure 4–7 later in this chapter.

A practical solution to the problem of estimating costs of an individual product is to isolate the common variable costs as a total by regression analysis, and then to allocate these costs to individual products by using some approximate measuring method. A number of methods can be used to allocate the common variable costs. First, if there is a traceable-cost item which in total is highly correlated with either total output or the variable common costs to be allocated, this item can be used as the basis of allocation. An example might be materials. The method provides a workable close approximation to the incremental cost of each product. Second, the relative size of total traceable costs of each product can be used as the basis of allocation. Third, a method which is more consistent with conventional accounting practice is the separate allocation of each variable common-cost iter. according to the traceable-cost item that appears to be most closely related. Electric power might be allocated on the basis of machine hours, inventory expenses on the basis of direct materials, and indirect labor on the basis of direct labor.

DIRECT VERSUS INDIRECT COSTS.   The distinction between direct and indirect costs is used by the accountant as *one application* of the traceable-common distinction. Direct costs are those that can be traced to a particular *brand*. Since almost all marketing decisions in one way or another focus upon the brand, you can see why the direct-indirect distinction is so useful. The method of tracing is usually inspection and judgment. Through direct costing, the traceable-common distinction with *respect to brands* has been incorporated into many company accounting systems.

Summary: Cost concepts

In summarizing this extensive review of cost concepts, we can say that the marketing manager typically wants an *opportunity, future, traceable* cost. Thus, in Figure 4–1 the data in cells I1D and I1E would be ignored because these costs—depreciation and general overhead—would presumably not be affected by most marketing decisions. Cells I1A, B, and C contain the relevant information. Whether, for example, it is a short-run or long-run estimate ordinarily depends upon your position in the company. If you are a brand manager, you usually want a short-run cost estimate, but if you are a marketing manager or president, you typically want one that is long run.

COST MEASUREMENT

Unless we can measure cost in a particular instance, we are severely handicapped in using the profit-maximizing principle. Development of a computerized marketing information system would be impossible.

The first essential in measurement is that the concept be appropriate to the situation. As was long ago said, "Better to have a crude measure of the right concept than a precise measure of the wrong concept." It is precisely for this reason that we devoted so much space to developing cost concepts. Which one is appropriate depends upon the nature of the particular instance.

Three examples are set forth here in order to concretely attain the goal of focusing upon marketing decisions the tools of the accountant and the methods of cost analysis derived from economics. The preceding discussion has necessarily been general in nature and perhaps elusive. As we have noted, the marketing manager faces major obstacles in using cost estimates because of the way in which accounting systems are constructed and the way in which accountants typically view the problem. The first example is presented in order to contrast the two accounting views. The second deals with a more conventional marketing problem—the use of cost data in selecting alternative marketing channels. The third example of a food processing company is an "ideal" case representing somewhat atypical conditions which nevertheless illustrates the use of statistical analysis in measuring costs. These examples will aid in bridging the gap between cost concepts, the accounting department's information, and the marketing manager's growing needs for cost data, especially if he contemplates a computerized marketing information system.

Example 1: Conventional accounting methods contrasted[2]

Example 1 contrasts the two basic approaches to decision making and illustrates some of the principles of cost analysis. It also points up the problems in terminology that a marketing manager may face when he attempts to work with cost data from his accounting department.

The two approaches are the *net-profit method* and the *contribution-to-profit method*. The key difference in the two approaches is that with the net-profit method, fixed costs are included in the decision, whereas with the contribution-to-profit method, fixed costs are omitted and only direct costs are included.

Table 4–3 contains the data from a company's annual operating statement. The upper portion of the table represents the contribution-to-profit approach, in which only direct costs are assigned to each product. If we

---

[2]Adapted from "Assignment of Non-Manufacturing Costs for Managerial Decisions," National Association of Cost Accountants, *N.A.C.A. Bulletin*, 32 (1950–51): 1135–73.

were to add all the costs of product A ($270,000) and divide it by the number of units produced, we would have the typical product cost. As described earlier, this is "a historical, fully allocated, average unit cost" which is used in the net-profit approach and is inappropriate for marketing decisions involving change in volume of sales, as they typically do. This cost concept is inappropriate because it contains three types of costs: (1) traceable costs, (2) variable common costs, and (3) fixed common costs.

TABLE 4–3
Net profit versus contribution to profit

	Total $	Product A $	Product B $	Product C $	Product D $
1. Net sales	1,000,000	300,000	200,000	100,000	400,000
2. Less variable cost of sales .	580,000	120,000	155,000	45,000	260,000
3. Manufacturing margin . . .	420,000	180,000	45,000	55,000	140,000
4. Less variable selling and advertising expenses	120,000	60,000	15,000	25,000	20,000
5. Merchandising margin . . .	300,000	120,000	30,000	30,000	120,000
6. Less fixed expenses					
7. Manufacturing					
8. Direct	20,000	20,000			
9. Allocated per Schedule A	50,000	20,000	5,000	10,000	15,000
10. Selling and advertising					
11. Direct	20,000				20,000
12. Allocated per Schedule B	50,000	25,000	12,500	12,500	
13. Administrative Allocated per Schedule C	80,000	25,000	10,000	10,000	35,000
14. Total Fixed Costs	220,000	90,000	27,500	32,500	70,000
15. Operating Income	80,000	30,000	2,500	(2,500)°	50,000

°Loss.
Source: Adapted from "Assignment of Non-Manufacturing Costs for Managerial Decisions," in National Association of Cost Accou tants, *N.A.C.A. Bulletin*, 32 (1950–51): 1169.

Variable cost of sales (line 2) is the direct proportion of manufacturing costs, and variable selling and advertising expenses (line 4) are likewise direct. You will recall from the earlier discussion that "direct" is an accounting concept in which traceable costs are assigned to each product by a process of inspection and judgment. Thus, if you were managing product A, lines 1 to 5 pose no problem. Presumably all the costs are traceable to product A.

Lines 8 and 11 pose no problem because they are traceable to manufacturing and selling, respectively, but not to the product, and so are clearly fixed. Lines 9, 12, and 13, however, do raise questions because they contain arbitrary allocations rather than being traceable. It is unlikely that such allocations would match the actual incremental cost from dropping the product.

As an example of the consequences of these accounting approaches, let us say that the management of this company is faced with the decision to drop one of the products. This situation could arise when a company, unable to secure adequate capital to expand, is confronted with a growing demand for its products. Product C is clearly the candidate if the net-profit approach is used, since the product has been yielding an annual loss of $2,500. This is true, however, only because someone arbitrarily said that $32,500 of total fixed costs (line 14) should be allocated to product C. In the absence of other evidence, the correct answer, which can be obtained only through the contribution-to-profit approach, is a toss-up between products B and C (line 5).

In summary, the net-profit approach is designed to serve the needs of financial reporting, but typically it is not useful for decision making. Contribution to profit, or marginal income as it is sometimes called, is the appropriate concept for decision.

Example 2: Cost estimates and a marketing decision[3]

Example 2, which illustrates the use of cost estimates in making a channel decision, is taken from an actual company experience. The marketing manager in this company doubted the profitability of one of the company's four marketing channels. Though he had his vague suspicions, there was no concrete evidence to support or refute them. He wanted to determine the profit contribution of each of the four channels, which required that estimates of revenue and cost be made for each channel. The task was simplified because no significant changes had occurred or were anticipated in costs or prices. Therefore, it was hoped that historical data could be projected into the future with confidence. Estimates of revenue for each channel were easy to make because the same product was sold to the four channels, and the price was the same among the channels.

The application of the criterion of relevancy of costs to a decision (discussed early in this chapter) required two steps: (1) determination of the proportion of total distribution costs that were variable, and (2) allocation of the variable proportion of these total distribution costs among the four channels.

TOTAL VARIABLE DISTRIBUTION COSTS.   There were four distribution expenses: selling, office, warehousing and shipping, and delivery. Each was analyzed to determine its proportion of variable costs. Monthly data for the past year were used, and it was assumed that the accounting data did

---

[3]Adapted from Charles H. Sevin, *How Manufacturers Reduce Their Distribution Costs*, Economic Series No. 72, Department of Commerce (Washington, D.C.: Government Printing Office, 1948).

FIGURE 4–4
Relation between number of sales calls and selling expense (Formula: $14,000 fixed per month + $3 per 100 sales calls)

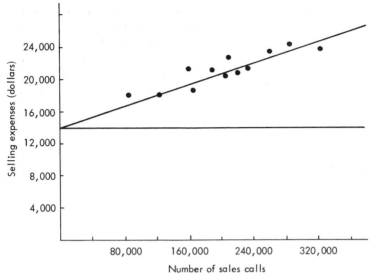

Number of sales calls

Source: Adapted from Charles H. Sevin, *How Manufacturers Reduce Their Distribution Costs*, Economic Series No. 72, Department of Commerce (Washington, D.C.: Government Printing Office, 1948), p. 44.

not contain arbitrary allocations of costs. Figures 4–4 and 4–5 show the analysis of selling and office expenses, respectively. For example, in Figure 4–4 the total selling expense for each month was plotted as indicated, and a free-hand line was drawn through the points. This line intersected the vertical axis at $14,000, and the slope of the line was such as to yield the variable cost of $3 per hundred sales calls, as indicated.

The same graphic regression analysis was applied to each of the expense accounts. As Figures 4–4 and 4–5 suggest, the variable proportion of selling expense was $3 per hundred sales calls, and that of the office expense was $208 per thousand invoices.

In summary, each of the four distribution expense accounts was analyzed on the following bases:

Selling expense .... Number of sales calls
Office expense .... Number of invoices
Warehousing and shipping expense .... Number of cases handled
Delivery expense .... Number of deliveries

The final task in this first step was to make an estimate of unit production costs, because sales varied among the four channels. Labor consti-

FIGURE 4–5

Relation between number of invoices and office payroll and other office expense (Formula: $8,750 fixed per month + $208 per 1,000 invoices)

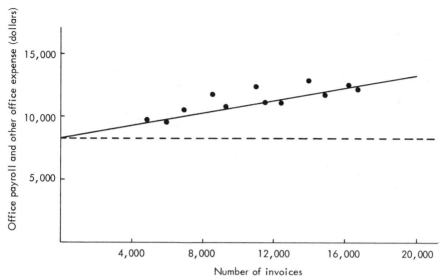

Number of invoices

Source: Adapted from Charles H. Sevin, *How Manufacturers Reduce Their Distribution Costs*, Economic Series No. 72, Department of Commerce (Washington, D.C.: Government Printing Office, 1948), p. 44.

tuted by far the major proportion of production costs, however, and clearly the direct labor proportion of labor would vary with different volumes of production. It was suspected that a proportion of indirect labor also varied with volume, so the analysis shown in Figure 4–6 was carried out.

ALLOCATION TO CHANNELS.   The variable proportions of the four distribution expense items and of the production cost were then allocated to each channel by merely multiplying the unit variable cost in each channel by the number of units appropriate to that channel. Selling expense was allocated to channel A, for example, by multiplying the number of sales calls that had been made in that channel during the year by $0.03.

The cost estimates were then summed and brought together with the revenue estimates to yield the data summarized in Table 4–4. According to the analysis, the customers in channels A and B are making a contribution to profit, but the company is merely "breaking even" on customers in C and is losing $50,000 annually on customers in D. A decision must be made: first, should channel D be dropped? Clearly, unless something can be done to increase the profitability of those customers, the company would increase its profit by eliminating them, even though the decrease in sales will create excess capacity both in plant and personnel. It is also conceivable that dropping one product may damage or increase the sales of

FIGURE 4–6

Relation between direct and indirect production labor cost (Formula: $100 fixed + 27.3 percent direct labor per month)

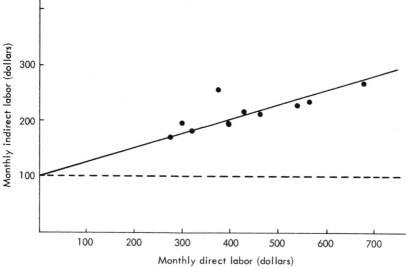

Source: Adapted from Charles H. Sevin, *How Manufacturers Reduce Their Distribution Costs*, Economic Series No. 72, Department of Commerce (Washington, D.C.: Government Printing Office, 1948), p. 45.

other products, but in this case the sales in one channel had no effect upon the sales in other channels. After a careful examination of the customers in channel D, it was concluded that nothing could be done to increase their profitability to the company. Top management was opposed, however, to creating unemployment because of its long-term effect on labor relations— a consideration not included in the cost analysis.

TABLE 4–4

Sales, variable costs, and profit margins by channels (before changes in channels, 1946

Channels of distribution	Sales	Variable costs°	Profit margin	Percent of sales
A	$750,000	$400,000	$350,000	47
B	250,000	100,000	150,000	60
C	300,000	300,000	—	—
D	200,000	250,000	(−50,000)†	(−25)†
Total	$1,500,000	$1,050,000	$450,000	30
Less: Nonvariable expense			300,000	—
Net Profit...............			$150,000	10

° Production plus distribution costs.
†Loss.
Source: Adapted from Charles H. Sevin, *How Manufacturers Reduce Their Distribution Costs*, Economic Series No. 72, Department of Commerce (Washington, D.C.: Government Printing Office, 1948), p. 43.

The picture of channel C as shown in Table 4–4 was not satisfactory even though, according to the analysis, the company was "breaking even." The marketing manager was fully aware that the method used for separating variable costs gave only crude answers. The elimination of channel C, for example, would relieve him of certain supervisory activities that were a very real cost and yet were not included in the estimates. For- tunately, analysis of the customers in channel C revealed that if the low- volume customers were eliminated, the profit contribution of channel C would increase substantially.

There was still the unemployment problem, which would be further aggravated by dropping some of the customers from channel C. Examina- tion of the customers in channels A and B suggested that, if the promo- tional effort were increased, enough additional sales could be attained to compensate for the customers dropped as a result of eliminating D and some of the customers in C. This was done, and the following year's results are shown in Tabel 4–5. The improved profit position, however, is by no means conclusive evidence of the soundness of the decision. Profit is the consequence of many forces.

TABLE 4–5
Sales, variable costs, and profit margins by channels (after changes in channels, 1947)

Channels of distribution	Sales	Variable costs°	Profit margin	Percent of sales
A	$ 825,000	$415,000	$410,000	50
B	315,000	130,000	185,000	59
C	120,000	110,000	10,000	8
Total	$1,260,000	$655,000	$605,000	48
Less: Nonvariable expense			310,000	—
Net profit..............			$295,000	23

° Production plus distribution costs.
Source: Adapted from Charles H. Sevin, *How Manufacturers Reduce Their Distribution Costs*, Eco- nomic Series No. 72, Department of Commerce (Washington, D.C.: Government Printing Office, 1948), p. 46.

Example 3: The statistical analysis of product cost—an ideal case[4]

The analysis of product cost of a middle-sized food-processing firm in this example illustrates the application of cost theory by means of statis- tical analysis applied to accounting data in order to arrive at a cost es- timate required for a marketing decision. This approach has been made much simpler by the computer.

One of the cost concepts commonly needed in marketing decisions is incremental cost (the marginal cost of cost theory) where the variation is

---

[4]J. Johnston, "Cost-Output Variations in a Multiple Product Firm," *The Manchester School of Economic and Social Studies*, 21 (1953): 140–53.

in the rate of output. The decision whether to increase advertising depends in part on what the incremental cost will be at the new level of sales. Usually, price and product decisions also require an estimate of this concept.

Marginal costs in a multiproduct company can be estimated by means of statistical regression analysis under ideal conditions in which there is, in a short period, sufficient variation in both the proportions of products manufactured and the aggregate output. These ideal conditions existed in the food-processing company as a result of normal week-to-week seasonal fluctuations in both the volume of sales for each product and the total sales volume. Since such fluctuations occur less frequently in most companies, a longer period of time is required for an adequate number of observations. With the longer period, other changes might enter to confuse the cost-output relationship, but this is a matter to be determined for each case. The cost data were adjusted for changes in the prices of raw materials because these fluctuated over the period under study.

The company's accounting system was a good one because it yielded weekly data on the physical production of each product and total direct-cost data for each product, subdivided according to the four cost categories of materials, labor, packing, and freight. The question may be raised as to why it was necessary to go to the trouble of applying statistical analysis if the accounting system gave these data. The answer is that the direct costs are developed in the accounting department according to their *traceability*, and traceability is determined by *inspection and judgment*; therefore, traceable costs may contain elements of fixed costs and omit elements of incremental cost.

TABLE 4–6
Empirical statistical analyses for separate products

Product	No. of weeks	$Y=$	a	bX
A	37	$Y=$	3.5	$+0.1115X$
B	37	$Y=$	-5.9	$+0.1620X$
C	36	$Y=$	181.6	$+4.9293X$
D	29	$Y=$	4.7	$+0.4165X$
E	24	$Y=$	16.9	$+3.6432X$
F	14	$Y=$	13.8	$+3.4448X$
G	7	$Y=$	72.2	$+4.0384X$
H	18	$Y=$	-31.5	$+5.4472X$
I	14	$Y=$	-90.6	$+5.0368X$
J	20	$Y=$	8.4	$+0.1192X$
K	17	$Y=$	-0.7	$+0.0920X$
L	16	$Y=$	-16.2	$+0.9687X$
M	20	$Y=$	168.1	$+1.5711X$
N	9	$Y=$	1.2	$+0.1111X$

Source: Adapted from J. Johnston, "Cost-Output Variations in a Multiple Product Firm," *Manchester School of Economic and Social Studies*, 21 (1953): 143.

FIGURE 4–7
Cost-output relationships

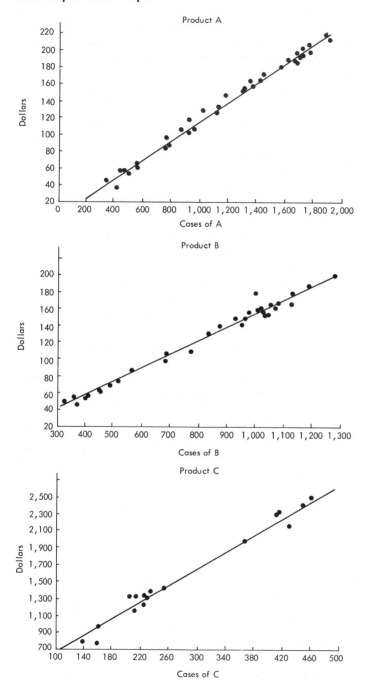

Source: J. Johnston, "Cost-Output Variations in a Multiple Product Firm," *Manchester School of Economic and Social Studies*, 21 (1933): 145.

On the graphs in Figure 4–7, the dots represent weekly data. A linear function was fitted statistically to these weekly data for each product. Only three of the products are shown there, but the equations for all 14 products are presented in Table 4–6. Y indicates total deflated direct cost, while X indicates output.

It is clear from the graphs of products A, B, and C that a linear relation provides a good fit. The graph shows the total variable-cost relation; since it is a straight line, average variable cost does not change with output. Although average variable cost is not shown here, it can easily be derived merely by dividing total variable cost by the number of physical units at any level of output. In this case, it can be concluded that marginal (incremental) cost and average variable cost are identical because a constant average variable cost indicates that the increments to total cost are constant. This provides additional evidence (other than that found in other statistical cost studies) for the point made earlier that average variable cost may be used as an estimate of marginal cost.

Although in this instance only direct costs were used in the analysis, total costs (direct plus indirect) could have been used as well. The element of indirect cost is shown by the Y-intercept when total costs are used. In Figure 4–7 the regression line passes either through or close to the origin for each product, A, B, and C. This tendency for the Y-intercept to be close to the origin suggests that the accounting system of the company closely approximated the "variable" and "fixed" cost of theory in classifying its accounts as either direct or indirect. Also, it suggests that there are no variable common costs, or put another way, that all variable costs in this company are traceable to a product. A negative value for the Y-intercept would imply that not all elements of variable cost were included in the direct cost; thus the value of the Y-intercept can serve as a criterion of whether the accountant's direct cost in a particular case can be used for decision making. The limitation of the criterion is usually that, in practice, no observations will be close to the origin; therefore, the regression line must be extrapolated beyond the range of observations, which is a risky procedure.

SUMMARY

The concept of cost structure is the basic one to be used by the manager in examining the third uncontrollable element of his environment, nonmarketing costs. Supporting concepts provide him with the particular cost that he needs—an opportunity, future, traceable cost. A special case is direct cost, where the costs can be traced to the product.

These concepts were applied in three examples to show how costs can be measured for planning purposes. The supporting concepts were carefully considered because a large increase in the use of cost data by marketing decision makers can be expected. Developments in organization, demand analysis and measurement, cost measurement, marketing information systems, and possibly even managerial values will bring this about.

DISCUSSION QUESTIONS

1. Describe the concept of cost structure.
2. The conventional accounting cost of a product is "a historical, fully allocated, average unit cost." Compare this cost concept with the one that is appropriate for a brand manager who is deciding whether to change his price.
3. The conventional accounting cost of a product contains three types of costs: traceable costs, variable common costs, and fixed common costs. Which of the three would you accept as clearly appropriate for decision making?
4. If the cost of raw materials changes, would you look upon the change as affecting the cost structure or the brand unit cost generated in the structure? Explain.
5. Will the most profitable price necessarily cover company overhead?

5

Structure of
marketing organization

INTRODUCTION

WE HAVE BEEN REFERRING to the marketing manager or decision maker, as
a generalized person. Who he is specifically makes a great deal of difference in what he does and how he does it. The question of *who* he is can
be answered by where he is in the organization, as shown by his position
in the organization chart. *What* he does in that position—the role he
serves—is defined by standard operating procedures. *How* he performs
that role in that position is defined by his decision process, which has as
its central element an information-processing rule, which describes the information he needs to perform that role in that position.

Hence, if we are to understand how a complex organization is coordinated so as to behave in a goal-directed way, we must know the manager's
decision process. Equally important, if we are to understand the role of information, market research, and computerized marketing information
systems in decision making, we must also understand the concept of a
decision process. We can refer to our earlier analogy with modern physics
and chemistry and speak of the decision process as the molecule and the
information-processing and decision rules as the atoms. As molecules can
be put together in an infinite variety of ways to form physical objects such
as chairs and tables, so can decision processes be put together in an
infinite number of ways to create different organizations.

For anyone intending to work in marketing, hardly anything is more
important than that he understand a company organization. We saw, for
example, at the end of Chapter 2, by contrasting two pricing models, how

104

the nature of the organization can shape the decision outcome. But an organization also has many more personal effects than this. More young men encounter difficulty from inability to adapt to the organization than from any lack of technical expertise. If a new member does not understand the organization he will fail to *anticipate* the many peculiar things that can happen. Once he observes these events, he will be likely to explain them to himself as due to either the dishonesty of the people or their stupidity, or both, unless he understands that an organization can encourage this "irrational" behavior. His explanations will probably be wrong and can unfavorably affect his morale and effectiveness. Then, too, *where* he is in the organization—his position in it—profoundly shapes the nature of his job and his identity: this position strongly determines the way in which he sees marketing management problems and how he identifies the controllable and uncontrollable factors.

The design of an effective organization is an age-old problem, but its central significance in all human affairs, not only in companies, but in governments, churches, and universities as well, has become much more appreciated as we have attempted to (1) aid the developing countries to industrialize, (2) make big government more efficient and sensitive to the citizenry's needs, and (3) sensitize the marketing operation of a company to the buyer's needs. The need for change—for redesigning the existing marketing organization—has probably quickened of late. The impact of the computer is just beginning to be felt, and its full consequences are yet to become apparent. The recent splurge of mergers to form conglomerates has sharpened interest in the design of marketing organization, as more conglomerates face falling profit margins (as in 1970–71) and require radical reorganization to survive. Consumers, too, are demanding organizations that are more sensitive to their needs.

DESCRIBING THE MARKETING ORGANIZATION

The marketing organization as well as the company organization of which it is a part can be described in at least three ways: (1) as an organization chart, (2) by its standard operating procedures, and (3) as a decision process or group of decision processes.

Company organization chart

Most commonly, the company is portrayed by a hierarchical chart, an *organization chart*. The example shown in Figure 5–1 is that of a simple divisionalized company. It is one of the most common types, especially among the larger heavy marketing companies such as in the packaged goods industry (for example, General Foods and Procter & Gamble). The description here is fairly typical, but there is variation across companies and often across divisions in a given company.

The lines in Figure 5–1 represent authority: who reports to whom and who tells whom what to do. In a large company there are many levels. Three levels, however, can usefully be conceptualized as a simplified basis for the marketing management process of decision, planning, and control. These three levels are *president*, *marketing manager*, and *brand manager*.

FIGURE 5–1
Company organization chart

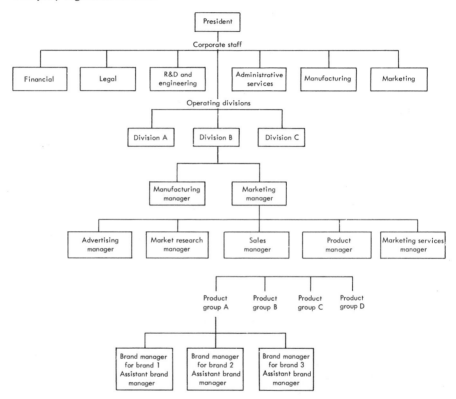

Each of these three levels represents a quite different decision situation. The higher the level, the longer the *planning horizon* of the decision maker at that level. We must recognize deviations, however. The president, for example, will sometimes be exceedingly short term in his decisions in order to meet quarterly dividend requirements, which influence his cost of capital. The amount of *risk* involved in the decision tends to increase with the length of the planning horizon. The types of *data* and the types of data *analysis* also tend to be different among the three levels.

In most organizations a considerable portion of the activity confronts a fairly stable environment, largely because it is selling an established, unchanging product, and therefore decisions tend to be fairly repetitive. This tends to be a *steady-state* activity, which means that relative to other activities of the company not much adaptation is required to keep it well adjusted to its environment. The steady-state part is organized differently than are more innovative parts. Such companies as General Foods, General Mills, and Procter & Gamble have found it useful to decentralize the authority involved in running the steady-state portion of the activity because of the difficulty higher level managers find in keeping adequately informed about a wide array of production technologies and markets. They have appointed "little presidents" to take charge of some portion of the activity, typically a brand, and called them *brand managers*. The brand manager is responsible for bringing together all the marketing activities of a particular brand. His major responsibility is to develop the marketing plan for that brand, and the marketing plan is a central feature of corporate management.

One of the serious questions in the so-called "little president" arrangement is how much authority to grant the brand manager. He usually feels that he should have more authority than he does.[1] To grant additional authority, however, may lead to suboptimization—he tends to sacrifice higher level goals by optimizing immediate goals because he lacks the experience and position in the company to give him the necessary perspective. The marketing plan is one instrument by which higher management can give him authority without losing control, as we will see later.

The *marketing manager*, as a part of his responsibility, brings together all of the individual brand marketing plans and develops an overall marketing plan. At the same time he begins the process of reconciling the overall marketing plan with the plans from the other parts of the division, such as the production plan and financial plan, although brand managers also play a role in this. This administrative role is less important for the marketing manager, however, than his strategic role as an *innovator*. Brand managers run the steady-state portion of the organization, whereas the marketing manager is in charge of major change, although within the limits set by the president. In modern marketing the greatest area of change is product innovation, but marketing channels also represent significant innovation.

We might consider why the marketing manager could not perform the coordinating task. Perhaps the brand manager is excess baggage, unnecessary overhead. An example will show why he is not. Assume the product is instant coffee, Sanka. It is now January and a "5 cents-off" promotion is planned for May in California. Arrangements must be made for printing the special labels, for the plant to pack the jars with the labels, for distribution to have them at the warehouse in California on time, for the

---

[1] *Advertising Age*, May 10, 1971, p. 62.

salesman to arrange special deals so the retailer will stock an extra amount, and for the advertising to be run. If these tasks are left to the respective functional areas—promotion, production, distribution, sales, and advertising—which are responsible for all brands, the chances are very high that something will go wrong, "that something will fall between the stools." In summary we can say that the marketing manager is largely responsible for the strategic aspects of a given brand and for the administrative aspects of all brands in his division taken together, while the brand manager is responsible for the operating aspects of a particular brand.

The *company president* is involved with marketing issues, too, but in a much more general way. He looks at the marketing activity as an investment problem, as another way of utilizing and obtaining a return on funds. The marketing details do not concern him because they are his subordinate's responsibility. It is essential to separate the internal from the external implications the company's marketing activities will have for him. The *internal* or managerial aspects of marketing tend at the president's level to become submerged in the total ongoing activity of the company, which is described in a financial plan. The president is also deeply and specifically concerned about the *external* implications of marketing. This interest is due to public policy, as contained in legislation, administrative decrees, and the feeling of the public that certain company marketing practices are not beneficial to society.

We will assume that the president alone is concerned with public policy. While he has the major responsibility, however, every marketing decision maker must be aware of some aspects of public policy and take them into account in his decisions. The necessity for this concern with public policy has become clearer since the "electrical conspiracy," when a number of individual executives were given prison terms for participating in an alleged price-fixing arrangement. Prior to this, the manager assumed that he would not be held individually responsible, since the company would pay any fines levied against it as a result of his decision making. He no longer has this protection; he can now be held individually responsible.

These three levels in the corporation are arbitrarily labeled as the brand manager, the marketing manager and the president. Together they serve as a vehicle to convey some complex ideas about the consequences of organization for the marketing management process. These particular positions are not set out in all organizations, of course, and in few of them are their activities detailed quite so sharply as implied here. Nevertheless, functions that each carries out are performed by someone in every company. We will emphasize the differences in activity among the levels in order to deal with important marketing problems that are usually ignored in marketing texts.

Standard operating procedures

The organization chart tells us only about a man's position in a company organization. A second way of describing a company organization, and one that tells us considerably more, is by its standard operating procedures (SOP). An SOP is a description of each person's job, *what* he is supposed to do in performing the task of his assigned position. It is what others in the organization can expect him to do. In sociological terminology, it is his role. When SOP's are well understood, each person can proceed to do his job confident that he knows what others whose activities interact with his will do. The SOP gives cohesion and direction to the company organization.

By describing the SOP of each of the three levels—president, marketing manager, and brand manager—we can obtain a clearer picture of the concept of an SOP and contrast the nature of the job at each of the levels. A nondivisionalized company is assumed here; a divisionalized company has a marketing manager for each division reporting to the general manager or president of the division.

THE PRESIDENT. The president's internal marketing responsibilities are of the propose-dispose type: major policies are proposed to him from below and he decides or "disposes" of them. Typically, he does not distinguish between marketing, production, or finance alternatives. For him they are always cast in financial terms and represent uses of funds, with a certain expected return on those funds. Usually, an investment such as a contemplated new product involves all aspects—marketing, manufacturing, and finance—simultaneously.

The president's external responsibilities have multiplied many times as companies have become larger and more open to public scrutiny and have impinged on more elements of public policy. He alone can speak for the corporation and interpret its purposes and functions to the many publics it touches upon. Probably nowhere has this been more true than in marketing-oriented consumer goods companies in the past five years, as the consumer movement has burgeoned and lawmakers have been sensitized to the needs of the consumer.

THE MARKETING MANAGER. To say the task of the marketing manager is "to administer all brands and innovate" is not enough. In order to examine the marketing manager position, we will set forth the following SOP:

1. Basic function

   To plan, organize, direct and control the marketing operations of the company to produce optimally profitable income; to study present market needs and to project future market needs and trends; to guide the company in the development of products and services that will enable it to achieve its objectives for profitable growth.

2. Duties and responsibilities
   a. Policies

   Participates with president in developing corporate policy.

   Develops and administers marketing policies to supplement the more general corporate policies.

   b. Market intelligence

   Provides for continuing study of company's markets.

   Identifies, classifies and quantifies the market by significant segments and changes in these particular segments.

   Measures customer attitudes and awareness to the company's and competitor's products.

   Determines the impact of advertising programs.

   c. Planning

   Develops short-term and long-term objectives.

   Submits these objectives to subordinates and works out a general strategy to achieve them.

   Adjusts annual plans as required.

   Based on his market studies, submits to producing division the need for new products.

   Develops plans for introduction of new products.

   d. Execution of plans

   Delegates to his managers responsibility and authority for carrying out approved plans.

   Provides coordination and supervision needed to ensure the marketing organization is working together toward achieving objectives.

   Sees that marketing objectives and plans and any changes are communicated throughout the company.

   e. Control

   Insures that plans he develops, when executed, accomplish what they are supposed to, and the first step is to find out what they did accomplish, which requires measuring performance.

3. Authority

   Has authority to carry out marketing plans as approved by the president within the framework of corporate policies.

   Has authority to select and employ advertising, market research and other agencies within budget limitations.

   President reserves authority to give final approval for new products.

   Has authority for hiring, firing and transfer of personnel within his own department.

4. Relationships

   Reports to president.

   Positions supervised: advertising manager, market research manager, sales manager and the various product or brand managers.

a) Lateral relationships

Works closely with other functional managers in developing plans, executing plans and measuring performance.

b) External relationships

Maintains top level contacts with major customers.

Maintains memberships in industry and professional associations.

Maintains contacts with government departments, agencies and legislative personnel.[2]

Many companies have initiated the marketing manager concept with difficulty because it involves subtle relationships. However, if (1) his job is spelled out (the SOP is very explicit), (2) this description is widely *known* throughout the company, and (3) it is also widely *accepted* in the company, the marketing manager can usually operate effectively. These three conditions are emphasized because difficulty in introducing the marketing manager concept has arisen when not enough attention is given to them.

THE BRAND MANAGER. The brand manager's SOP is particularly important because many readers may aspire to be assistant brand managers as their first jobs out of business school. The brand manager plays a dominant role in the success or failure of an ongoing brand. His importance is shown in a full-page ad by *Parade* addressed to brand managers which appeared in *The New York Times*.[3]

It appears that more and more industries are adopting the brand manager type of organization: ". . . some banks are even beginning to create product manager structures that could have been lifted straight out of General Electric's small appliance division."[4] The automobile industry is moving in this direction, at least as indicated by a goal of John Delorean, manager of GM's Chevrolet division: ". . . he . . . is looking forward to the day when each car line will be put under the direction of a project manager who will have total developmental responsibility for it."[5]

A brand manager is charged with the marketing responsibility for one or, at most, a few products instead of all of the company's products. He sets almost no policies; planning is his major responsibility. As a part of this function, he does the following:

1. Recommends to the marketing manager new-product plans and priorities. Interprets market needs and required product cost and performance characteristics to those departments concerned with product package development and design.

---

[2] Victor P. Buell, *Marketing Management in Action*, (New York: McGraw-Hill Book Co., 1966), pp. 23–27.

[3] *The New York Times*, September 21, 1971, p. 33.

[4] *Business Week*, June 24, 1972, p. 78.

[5] *Business Week*, September 18, 1971, p. 64, and *Advertising Age*, March 20, 1972, p. 54.

2. Works with market research department in estimating market potential of his products.
3. Works with production and finance departments, providing them with sales forecasts.
4. Works with the marketing services manager and warehousing, inventory, and transportation departments on inventory plans by field distribution points.
5. Works with sales and advertising managers in developing sales, advertising, and promotion plans for current and new products.
6. Recommends pricing policies and strategies to the marketing manager.
7. Studies the effectiveness of distribution channels and recommends necessary changes to marketing manager.
8. Develops plans for the organization and staffing of his department.
9. Maintains complete knowledge of his products and their applications and continually appraises their advantages and disadvantages.
10. Recommends to the marketing manager the products that do not produce satisfactory profits to be dropped from the line.

This description highlights a major characteristic of his role, which is the number of people he works with.

As for execution, the brand manager works closely with the interested departments—sales, advertising, distribution, pricing, marketing services, manufacturing, and warehousing and inventory control—to insure that the marketing plan is being carried out. As for control, he prepares necessary reports on such performance criteria as sales and profit status of his brand, recommends corrective action when needed, makes periodic field checks to observe sales performance and competitive behavior, and reviews order backlog and inventory reports.

As to authority, he is a staff executive and issues instructions only as the agent of the marketing manager. His effectiveness in administering his products is achieved through the quality of his marketing plans and his ability to coordinate the activities of the other departments that carry out his plans. If performance is lagging in one of the relevant departments, such as sales, advertising, or market research, and he is unable to remedy the situation by talking directly with the individuals involved, he gets corrective action through the marketing manager. Practically, however, he learns to avoid using this court of last resort any oftener than he must, because frequent use of it implies to his superiors that he cannot do his job well. Finally, as for relationships, he reports to the marketing manager, and he often has two assistant brand managers and perhaps even an associate brand manager.

Internally, he works closely with all relevant departments in formulating and carrying out plans and measuring performance. He is a member of the marketing management committee and the product planning committee. Externally, he maintains contacts with a representative group of customers and channel-of-distribution executives to develop firsthand information on market needs, competitive actions, and product acceptance. He also participates in trade and industry associations.

CONSUMER VERSUS INDUSTRIAL PRODUCTS. There are subtle but significant differences in the marketing operations of consumer and industrial companies. A discussion of the brand manager's role provides an opportunity to clarify these. In an industrial company the brand manager is known as a *product manager*.

The marketing organization of one of America's leading aluminum companies is shown in Figure 5–2. Its mill products division (products that require further processing from ingot aluminum) has a marketing position called industry manager for consumer durable goods shown as one of the six *industry managers* in the second column. These people are

FIGURE 5–2
Marketing organization for industrial product

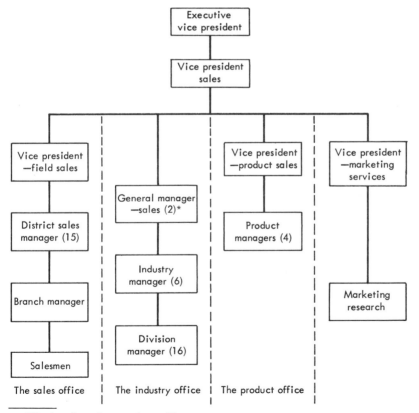

*Number of people occupying position.
Note: Vertical position on chart does not necessarily depict level of responsibility.
Source: "Approach to an Industrial Marketing Information System," J. U. Farley, J. A. Howard, and J. Hulbert, *Sloan Management Review*, 13 (Fall 1971).

essentially *marketing* managers of particular *markets*, each defined as an industry. The consumer durable goods "industry" is made up of manufacturers of major appliances, housewares, furniture, notions, boots, and sporting goods. A salesman calls on one of these companies, for example, and encounters stiff price resistance for aluminum products. When he does he transmits upward the request for a price reduction through the district sales manager for his geographic area, who in turn passes the request to the industry manager for consumer durables at the home office. The details of this process are shown in Figure 5–6 below.

At the same time, the company has a product manager for foil, fin stock and packaging sheet. Much of the aluminum material used in satisfying the market presided over by the industry manager for consumer durable goods is fin stock, such as that used in the fins on modern aluminum baseboard residential heating units or the coils in refrigerating units. The product manager for foil, fin stock and packaging sheet is responsible for seeing to it that the factory produces fin stock in the right amounts and at the right time to meet the various "industry" markets where it is used. Another major responsibility of his is to insure that it is produced to meet the needs of these markets in terms of quality. He is alert to technological changes which suggest product-improvement possibilities and to the necessity of working closely with production to insure these improvements are initiated as quickly and effectively as possible. Thus we see that in industrial companies, the "brand management" function can be separated into two different positions: the industry manager, who is market oriented, and the product manager, who is more production oriented. The SOP for each is quite different.

There appears to be a number of reasons for these differences in consumer and industrial companies. First, the contact with the buyer in an industrial company is typically by a salesman with less use of both advertising and intermediate distributive agencies analogous to the retail store in the consumer market. This occurs because the magnitude of the sales is large enough to justify the cost of a sales call. Also, each industrial customer "consumes" a number of the seller's products, so management attempts to develop a marketing organization which enables one salesman at one call to meet *all* of each buyer's needs insofar as the company's product line permits. Finally, production requirements seem to be more influential in shaping marketing activities in industrial companies. Typically, the technology of production is much more involved and costly, and production scheduling is more difficult. Because a plant can usually produce more than one product, a major problem is to decide on a quarter-by-quarter basis in which plant each product is to be produced. Further, profits depend heavily upon the company's ability to keep each plant "full" of the most profitable products.

Consumer goods companies occasionally find it useful to use the "industry" or "market" concept, such as by having one person in charge of an ethnic market. This is rare, however.

SUMMARY: SOP. We have described three SOP's—president, market manager, and brand manager. Now we can contrast them in terms of the basic art of marketing management described in Chapter 1, separating what is *given* from that which can be *changed*. Of the three, the president has the greatest latitude for change, as is indicated by comparison of Figure 5–3 with Figures 5–4 and 5–5. His dimensions of adjustment (the heptagon) are *organization, channels, product, price, advertising* and *selling,* and perhaps, by working through his trade association, even *public policy.* His "givens" (the square) are *demand, cost, competition,* and *distribution system.* He is far removed, however, from the details of operating marketing and leaves them to the marketing manager. He reserves the right to make the final decision on marketing innovation, but the actual innovation is initiated, planned, and carried out by the marketing manager. He tends to view marketing as just another problem of deciding where to put funds. Hence, it can be said that in optimizing the area of the

FIGURE 5–3
President's decision situation

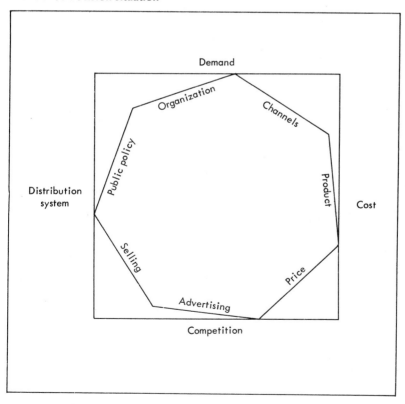

heptagon he plays *the investment game,* which implies a *long-term* planning horizon.

The marketing manager is somewhat more limited. His dimensions of adjustment (the pentagon) are *product, channels, price, advertising,* and *selling,* as shown in Figure 5–4. But he must take the hexagon—*public policy, organization, demand, cost, competition,* and structure of *distribution* —as given. He tends to play *the innovation game and the new-product game,* in particular. Like the president he has a *long-term* planning horizon. He often delegates much of the details of the innovating process, but he retains direct and immediate responsibility for it. He also has an important administrative role in selection, supervision, and training of his people.

FIGURE 5–4
Marketing manager's decision situation

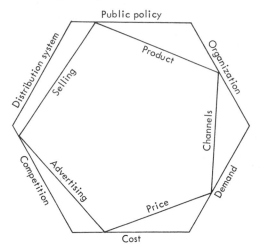

The brand manager is still more limited and can change only *price, advertising,* and *selling:* the triangle. As shown in Figure 5–5, he must take the octagon—*product, channels, organization, demand, cost, competition, distribution system,* and *public policy*—as given. He tends *to play the short-run marketing planning game* and he has a *short-term* planning horizon. He is responsible for making *recommendations* about innovation, but not typically for carrying them out.

In summary, the number of "givens" (uncontrollables) and the number of avenues of action (controllables) is different in each of the three positions, and the planning horizon is also different: as you ascend the hierarchy, the planning horizon increases. But there are four uncontrollables in all three positions: buyer behavior, (demand), competition, nonmarketing cost, and distribution system.

FIGURE 5–5
Brand manager's decision situation

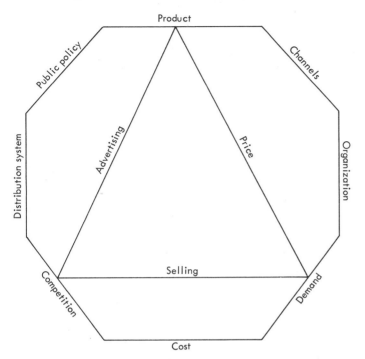

Decision process

The third way an organization can be described is as a mass of interrelated decision processes. Each person at any level in the company through training and experience learns habitual ways of making decisions as he goes about doing his job. The decision process is a set of internalized rules (existing in his mind) which guide his behavior, as described in his SOP. SOP's typically tell the position occupier what to do, and decision processes tell him how to do it.

The concept of an individual person's decision process may seem too detailed to be useful, especially when discussed in the complex context of a large company. To give it concreteness, Figure 5–6 illustrates how, in the aluminum company, price is adapted to meet changing market conditions, as mentioned above. The circle in the upper left-hand part indicates that the salesman calls on a customer who may request that the price be lowered. The arrow out of the circle "up" through the organization triggers a whole series of possible events which culminate in either the price being changed or the customer's request being refused. You should work through it carefully, step by step, to obtain a grasp of how a particular company's decision about price is made.

Each question in a diamond-shaped box is asked by some person—salesman or manager—and also answered by some person. In this way we

FIGURE 5–6
Request for temporary price reduction

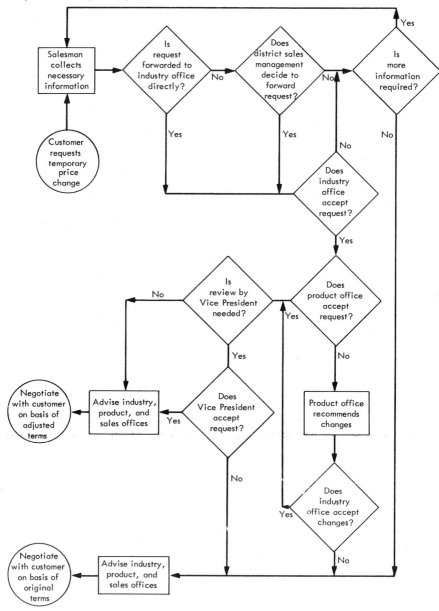

Source: "Approach to an Industrial Marketing Information System," J. U. Farley, J. A. Howard, and J. Hulbert, *Sloan Management Review*, 13 (Fall 1971).

arrive at a sharper definition of the concept of decision process. It is the process by which an individual *raises a question* and *answers it himself*; the *answer* to the *question* is the *decision*. This example shows the significance of the decision process as one way of describing an organization. Later a tested example of a petroleum company's marketing executive's decision process for setting prices will be presented to make this subtle but vitally essential concept more meaningful.

Summary: Describing the marketing organization

Each of the three ways of describing a company or marketing organization—organization chart, SOP, and decision process—is useful under different circumstances. They are not competing, but supplementary. Each one alone is a little like the three blind men and the elephant: it offers a *correct* but *incomplete* view, and therefore a distorted view, which if taken literally can be misleading. The conditions under which each is appropriate will be described after some of the ideas introduced here have been more fully developed.

COORDINATING MARKETING ACTIVITIES

It is a commonplace that for a company to operate effectively it must be well coordinated. Yet to design a company organization that will insure its activities are coordinated is most difficult. Further, marketing activities are more difficult to coordinate than most others in the company. Here we begin to see one of the reasons why the marketing concept introduced in Chapter 1 is so difficult to implement.

One of the functions of a person's role in a company is to coordinate, as indicated earlier by the SOP's. Imagine all 600,000 employees of General Motors Corporation behaving in such a way that what each one does is workably consistent with what everyone else in the company does! This is indeed an accomplishment. Suppose that today a man at a machine in Danville, Illinois, produces a part which will be put into an automobile steering mechanism in Saginaw, Michigan, four weeks from now, which in turn will become a component part in a car being assembled in Lordstown, Ohio, one month later and that the resulting car will be sold to Mr. Jones in Boston one month after that. At each production point, flows of materials and instructions to people must be reasonably coordinated to meet an anticipated customer's need: John Jones will want a red hatchback Vega coupe in Boston three months hence.

But the most difficult problem of coordination occurs in the Boston activities: marketing. In production—Danville, Illinois; Saginaw, Michigan; and Lordstown, Ohio—physical objects are involved which can be easily identified, counted, and communicated. This fact substantially facilitates coordination. In marketing we deal with the abstract, with information which is very difficult to identify, much less to count.

The new car is, among other things, designed to give extra convenience, more convenience than competitor's cars. How is this fact conveyed to Mr. Jones, the anticipated customer in Boston? A whole series of events contributes to that communication. First, the car designer has tried to build this advantage into the car. Second, the marketing department must take this fact and fit it into the requirements of a total marketing strategy. Third, this strategy is communicated to the advertising agency, which develops the copy and the media plan. Fourth, marketing then includes this copy and media plan in the total marketing plan for the new car. Fifth, the agency arranges with the television network to run an ad which portrays the convenience virtue of the car at a time when Mr. Jones is probably watching TV on that station in Boston. Sixth, for reasons developed in Chapter 3, even if Mr. Jones is watching that particular TV show, the chances are small that he will see the ad.

The essential point of this description of car production and sale is that almost nothing concrete is involved in the series of marketing events; everything is an abstraction—information or *ideas* largely transmitted by word of mouth. The opportunities for poor communication and therefore bad coordination are truly enormous, much more so in marketing than elsewhere in the company.

Coordination has become increasingly difficult as companies have become larger. They were able to grow larger by increasing specialization of labor: When a person specializes in a task he can learn through repetition to do it faster and better. Hence, they were able to reduce costs, to operate more economically. Many jobs in companies have become more specialized, or to put it another way, new specialized jobs have been created: budgeting specialists, market researchers, operations researchers, and systems analysts, to name a few.

On the other hand, this very act of specialization makes coordination more difficult. These specialists, each with its unique body of jargon, concepts, and techniques, raise real barriers to communication laterally across the company and so hinder coordination. The technical training of these specialists may also give them a loyalty to their profession that transcends their loyalty to the company and causes them to use goals that are inconsistent with those set forth by the company. Thus, greater size increases the need for coordination but at the same time makes it more difficult.

If marketing coordination in a company is such a difficult problem, how does it get accomplished? Coordination is accomplished either through *plan* or *performance feedback*. A key aspect of control is feedback, as was indicated in Chapter 1. In fact, coordination is but the organizational manifestation of effective control. Actually, both plan and feedback are used in endless combinations. At least logically, however, the two are clearly separable, and therefore we are fully justified in treating them as alternative ways of achieving coordination.

In coordinating by plan, a course of action—a plan—is drawn up which incorporates all aspects of the anticipated marketing activities connected with a product. This plan tells everyone involved in marketing the product *when* and *what* to do with sufficient *lead time* for them to carry out their actions so as to merge it smoothly with related actions. Thus, implied in planning is *forecasting* sales, which in turn requires forecasting the market environment. One of the major tasks in introducing a new product to the market, for example, is to forecast the brands sales accurately and so insure that when the consumer advertising begins in that market, the product is available in adequate quantities on the shelf of the consumer's regular retail store. If the product is available and the advertising isn't, the retailer may get discouraged and refuse to carry it any longer. If the advertising is available but the product isn't, consumers will try to buy it, find it unavailable, and lose interest in it. They may buy a competing brand; in any event, they are probably more likely to ignore future advertising about it than even those who did not try to buy it. This state of affairs also leaves the retailer unhappy with the company. If the brand manager of this new product develops a plan which the sales manager and others agree with, coordination should occur, unless someone's judgment is wrong.

In coordinating by feedback or market monitoring, on the other hand, the action is taken without regard to a plan, the results are monitored and fed back to the manager, and then necessary corrective action is taken. In the example above, if the advertising gets to the market first, corrective action consists of speeding up the flow of product to the retail stores and/or delaying advertising. The limitations on feedback as an effective coordinating device can readily be imagined. In Figure 5-6, which illustrates pricing by feedback, we see the great demands laid on the organization's communication network in carrying out the pricing activity by this method. Feedback coordination also results in a different kind of organization.

The crucial need for planning can be inferred from the example, as can the principle that the more complex the activity the greater the need for planning. Company size is usually correlated with complexity of activities. Thus larger companies tend to be more complex and require greater planning. Throughout the rest of the book the process of planning will be the center of focus. Feedback will be seen as serving to correct the current plan and guide future planning.

Planning is never perfect—"the best laid schemes o' mice and men...." Managers set up control systems (as suggested in Chapter 1) which imply evaluation of performance, and feedback information about performance is fed to management. A sales manager receives every Monday morning a computer printout which tells him how much each of his salesmen actually sold (standard) the previous week, and, for each salesman, how this amount compares with how much he was expected to have sold (norm).

His corrective action will then consist of investigating why the "shortages" occurred, taking action to prevent them happening again, and rewarding those salesmen fortunate to have the "overages."

An unapparent but important fact is that planning enables higher level managers to delegate authority without losing control. This view is splendidly put by a distinguished practitioner, Clarence E. Eldridge:

> The most serious and difficult problem with which marketers have to deal today involves the delegation of marketing authority. Growth has become a way of life with most marketers, and more or less inevitably the time arrives when decentralization, in one form or another, becomes the only course to follow. This means the delegation of responsibility and authority.
>
> Either because the need for middle- and lower-echelon marketing personnel has grown more rapidly than the supply, or for other reasons, there is a quite general lack of complete confidence in the maturity and judgment of product managers and other marketing executives to whom authority should theoretically be delegated. The result is that higher levels of management are of necessity withholding part of the very authority which—if the advantages of decentralization are to be realized—should be passed down the line.
>
> The problem is a difficult one: how to delegate without losing control on the one hand, and without running the risk of unsound marketing decisions and actions on the other.
>
> This problem was far from the minds of those who, thirty-odd years ago, conceived the idea of the marketing plan. Nevertheless, by fortuitous circumstance the marketing plan is tailor-made to contribute, more than any other single factor, to the solution of this problem. It cannot by itself solve the problem, nor can anything else. But the plan can make it possible to live with the problem, to relieve upper management of some of the burden which decentralization was designed to remove from their shoulders, to permit management to retain all the control it needs in the discharge of its responsibilities, and at the same time to permit the product manager (or other lesser executive) to assume a greater degree of responsibility and authority than ever before.[6]

Note, however, that in the second paragraph the author omits the subtle need for coordination. It is not so much that brand managers are less competent than desired but that they must coordinate their activities with those of the rest of the company. Top management ordinarily feels that brand managers lack the perspective and experience they themselves have in identifying the need to coordinate.

THE MARKETING PLAN

Planning, as indicated above, is the central task of most managers, and the marketing plan is one of the first things with which a brand manager becomes acquainted. We will briefly discuss the concept, the construction, and the implementation of this central instrument of marketing. In *con-*

---

[6] *Printer's Ink*, March 10, 1967, p. 43 ff.

cept, the annual marketing plan is a description of the state of marketing affairs with respect to the brand, the implications of this description for action during the coming year, and the detailed action that should be carried out in that year. The marketing plan is the heart of the brand manager's job. It has six major elements: description of the situation, the problems and opportunities in this situation, the objectives of the plan, the complete marketing program, the necessary appropriation, and the estimated profit contribution to the company. These are examined in detail below:

1. The statement of the facts is the foundation element of a plan because everything in the plan depends on correct understanding of the facts. Every relevant fact should be included:
   a) Objective appraisal of brand competition, consumer attitudes and costs.
   b) Sales history—growth pattern.
   c) Competitive situation.
   d) Pricing—does it give a competitive advantage? Is it adequate for profit?
   e) Recent history of expenditures on marketing.
   f) Past advertising strategy.
   g) Market targets.
   h) Consumer wants and needs to be satisfied by the product.
2. Problems and opportunities, opposite sides of same coin, are related to the statement of facts. Every problem revealed by facts should be listed with the opportunity it creates.
3. Objectives are described in terms of the company's specific intermediate objectives, namely those that apply at the brand manager's level in the company, such as:
   a) The consumer's awareness of the advertising and of the brand.
   b) His intention to buy.
   c) His purchases.
4. The complete marketing program is a description of all the marketing activities designed to overcome the problems and exploit the opportunities. Alternative strategies should be stated and evaluated for:
   a) Advertising.
   b) Selling.
   c) Pricing.
5. Recommended marketing appropriation.
6. Forecast of sales volume, cost, and profit.

The *construction* of an annual marketing plan requires a great amount of knowledge, quantities of data, and intense thinking about all aspects. As anyone finds who attempts it, planning is a trying, demanding process because it is always an extension into the unknown: the future. It requires great imagination that is highly disciplined. Market research can be helpful. The young man with an MBA often finds his first job is as assistant brand manager, whose task is to work with the market research department in utilizing existing research and to plan new studies that will provide some of the quantitative underpinnings of the annual plan.

The *implementation* of a plan can be easy or difficult, depending in large measure upon how well it was prepared in the first place. There are two major aspects of a plan: how sound it is in terms of fact and logic, and how well those affected within the company by the plan have been brought into the planning process so that the final document represents a true consensus. The second, or political, aspect is just as important as the first. True, unless the first condition is valid, the second cannot recoup it, but a splendid plan in terms of content is useless unless there is enthusiasm for its execution on the part of all involved.

In addition to building the marketing plan and executing it, the brand manager will want to control the plan. Therefore he builds measures of performance into his planning system to tell him how well it worked. These measures will usually bear some relation, at least, to the objectives. Examples of measures of performance are market share, number of people aware of brand, and volume of sales. From feedback information, problems can hopefully be identified, corrective action taken, and a modified plan developed as the period of the plan unrolls.

The discussion to this point has been in terms of a plan—a mosaic of decisions. In the following section we will speak of making decisions as though they were isolated and ad hoc, one at a time. This immensely simplifies the discussion, but the reader must bear in mind, first, that most of the decision making occurs in connection with drawing up plans. Thus individual decisions are not really isolated from each other as much as our discussion will seem to imply. Second, he must recognize that decision making is a continuing process. A set of decisions represented in a plan is made; if approved by higher executives, the plan is initiated, continually monitored, and modified by new decisions.

TYPES OF MANAGERIAL DECISION PROCESSES

Just as the molecule and atom are basic units of physical matter, the decision process and its component decision rules are basic units of organization. Since we are interested in management, the basic unit becomes the manager's decision process, specifically the marketing decision process.

By classifying managerial decision processes into the three types developed in Chapter 3 it is possible to bring out useful differences in decision-making situations. They are: (1) routinized response behavior (RRB), (2) limited problem solving (LPS), and (3) extensive problem solving (EPS). In conventional organizational literature these could be referred to as structured decision processes, semistructured decision processes, and unstructured decision processes. They differ according to the amount of energy and effort the executive devotes to acquiring and processing information as the basis for his decision. The first requires the least information and the last, the most information.

Routinized response behavior

A manager makes use of routinized response behavior whenever the decision is made repetitively, such as when he has been in the position for some time and the market is fairly stable. The key point is that he has had sufficient information and experience to form a strong image or concept in his mind of each of the alternatives faced in the decision. This image implies (1) that he can readily identify the decision when it appears, (2) that he is using well-established choice criteria for judging alternative solutions instead of being confronted with new alternatives for which he must develop new criteria in order to judge them, and (3) that he is confident of his ability to evaluate them. It is helpful for expository purposes to break the discussion of the decision process into two parts, individual choice and group choice, and to focus upon individual choice first.

INDIVIDUAL CHOICE.   As an example of individual choice, consider the pricing decision process of a vice president in charge of four states in the distribution operation of a large petroleum company. The description of this carefully researched decision spells out in more detail what is implicit in the variety of decisions shown earlier in each diamond-shaped box of Figure 5–6. Think of it as *one* of the several links in the chain of decision processes shown there. Above him is the home office, below him are the district sales managers, and reporting to them are the salesmen who call on the retailers of gasoline service stations. A part of the vice president's responsibility is to set the wholesale price of gasoline—the price to the station—in every pricing area in his four states. He is limited to changes of no more than 4 cents; for changes of greater magnitude he must refer to the home office. A pricing area varies in size depending upon the population density. In a large city there could be five or six pricing areas, but outside the city, a whole county might constitute a single area.

A manager's actions become so habitual that he doesn't realize what he is doing and usually can't tell you how he does it. As this executive said when approached to cooperate in building the model shown here, "I don't know how I do it, and I don't think you can find out!" Although he is unconscious of them, these habits are obviously important, for these reasons:

1. They tie a company together smoothly so that it works without friction and thus they coordinate company activities; they enable him to fulfill many of his *role* responsibilities with unconscious ease.
2. They provide the basis for controlling his own activities, as we saw in discussing the marketing plan.

3. They specify the information he needs to do his job and that is essential in designing a market research project and a marketing information system.

We can now begin to see the crucial but subtle importance of the decision process. This situation might be referred to as an example of the iceberg principle: what is apparent and above the waterline, as in the organization chart, is not nearly as crucial as what is hidden below it—the decision process.

A flow chart of the process (shown in Figure 5–7) describes it precisely. To gain a working understanding of it, you should work through it carefully, step by step, utilizing the symbols shown at the bottom of the figure.

Box 1 says, "Watch the wholesale (w) price (P) of the initiating (i) com-

FIGURE 5–7
Model of pricing decision process

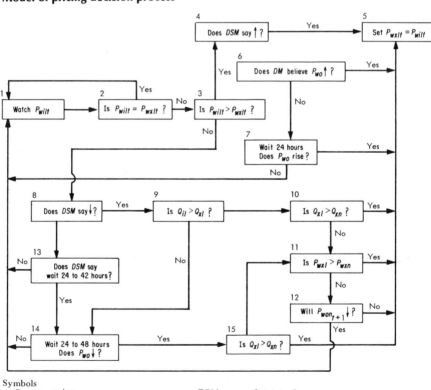

Symbols

P	=	price	DSM	=	district sales manager
w	=	wholesale	DM	=	decision maker
i	=	initiator	x	=	decision maker's company
l	=	local market	o	=	other major competitors (neither i nor x)
n	=	nearby market	Q	=	expected physical volume of sales
t	=	time			

petitor in the local market (l) as of today (t)." It shows the triggering event, a competitor's price change, which causes the manager to think about pricing instead of the dozens of other things that the pressures of his job might cause him to think about. Box 1 also shows the importance of competitors' actions. Box 2 asks, in effect, "Has the price changed?" If it has changed (box 3) whether the price is an increase or a decrease makes a substantial difference, as we will see later. Let us take the increase first.

The decision maker (DM) asks the district sales manager (DSM) his view of whether the price should be increased (box 4), which is an example of how the decision maker ties the company together. His decision process is intimately tied to DSM's and this coordinates parts of the organization. If DSM says "yes," then DM changes price (box 5). DM always likes a high price if it doesn't lose sales to a competitor. He believes, and without doubt he is correct, that the sales of all brands of gasoline together in the retail market will not be much affected by price changes within a fairly wide range, at least in the near future. DSM, however, usually takes a conservative view on "upside" changes because he is judged by gallons sold, not profit contributed. If DSM says "No" (4), DM asks himself whether the price of other competitors will be increased (6), that is, "Does the manager (DM) believe that the wholesale (w) price (P) of other competitors (o) will increase?" If yes, then he changes the price (5), that is, he increases his price. If no, he waits 24 hours to see if another major competitor (P_{wo}) increases his price (7). If yes, he raises price (5). If no, he does nothing (I).

Increases make up a simple process, but when we turn to decreases we are confronted with a more complex picture. This is because DM is profit centered and believes that the generic demand for gasoline is inelastic. Hence, price declines are to be avoided, if possible, because profit always suffers unless market share increases greatly. Further, his competitors are not likely to accept the large share losses implied by his share gain. Instead they will tend to retaliate with price cuts.

Beginning with Box 3, DM asks DSM his opinion (8). As noted above, this is the way the company organization is tied together. If DSM says yes, DM asks himself (9) whether his competitor's share is greater than his share in the local market, because size of share is an indicator of market power. If the answer is yes, DM asks himself (10) whether his own share is greater in the nearby market than in the local market.

If his local share is greater than in the nearby market, he drops the price (5) because, if the price cut spreads later to the nearby market, the loss will not be so great with a smaller share. If his local share is not greater than his nearby share, then DM takes a still closer look and asks himself whether his local price is greater than his nearby price (11). If it is, he cuts his price in the local market because that will merely bring the local market price *down* to what the nearby price already is. If it is not—if his local price is equal to or lower than his nearby price—he goes to (12) and asks himself *directly* whether the nearby price will be lower in the near future for some other reason not contained in box 10. If no, he then cuts because this cut is not likely to spread to other markets via the nearby market. If yes, he holds (1) because of the fear that this cut will merely lead to a cut in the nearby market, which box 10 shows is large and costly.

Back to Box 9 where we took the yes route above, let us go to the no route: The initiating competitor's share in the local market is equal to or less than *DM*'s. He decides to wait 24–48 hours to see whether any other major competitor cuts its price (14). If no major competitor cuts, he sits tight (1). If one does cut, *DM* asks himself whether his share in the local market is greater than it is in the nearby market (15). He does this for the same reason as before. He is fearful that the price cutting will spread to other markets, that it cannot be contained.

This example taken from actual company experience and tested for validity gives a clear picture of a decision process. The concept is essential in considering the use of data for decisions, market research, or a computerized information system. With this idea of information requirements in mind, let us examine the boxes more carefully, such as box 9: Is $Q_{il} >$ Q_{xl}?

First, this question implies an *information-processing rule*: "Take two pieces of information, Q_{il} and Q_{xl}, and compare them to see which is the greater." Clearly, then, *DM* needs these two pieces of information. Hence, the box specifies the pieces of information needed for decision.

Second, between each box a *decision rule* is implied, for example, take a look at box 7: "Wait 24 hours: Does P_{wo} rise?" If P_{wo} increases, the implicit decision rule is, "Raise my price!" (5). If P_{wo}, does not increase, the implicit decision rule is, "Do nothing!" (1).

Information processing and decision rules are also the essential elements in Figure 5–6, but they are less fully described there than in Figure 5–7

We can now summarize some conclusions about the nature of the decision process.

1. Decision processes are the glue of the organization that holds it together; they coordinate the parts. Consequently, changing an organization may cause it to come "unglued" in unexpected and usually disturbing ways because old decision rules are not appropriate for the new situation.

2. Decision processes are exceptionally subtle because managers don't know they have them. It is difficult to change them because the manager doesn't understand what is being asked of him. This fact is important for all executive training. It is especially relevant in persuading managers to use new types of data, such as in implementing computerized marketing information systems, because it is difficult to iden-

tify the information that the system should provide to managers. As a consequence these systems tend to be built without giving adequate consideration to the decision maker's needs, and then the builders are surprised to find they are not used.

3. Decision processes involve personal attitudes implicitly and impersonal attitudes explicitly. Implicit in his choice are his personal likes and dislikes. Impersonal attitudes make up most of the content of Figure 5–7, as would be expected in a formal organization. The choice criteria which underlie attitudes, however, are binary here instead of continuous, as implied in the discussion of the buyer in Chapter 3. Probably the greater complexity of the decision here and the time pressure forces the decision maker to simplify his choice criteria into binary form.

GROUP CHOICE. Many marketing decisions involve other people in the company, as we have stressed throughout. With structured decisions, however, where the manager has had many experiences making the decision, there is no group choice in any meaningful sense. True, other people are consulted, as we saw in Figure 5–6, but their views are taken as constraints—impersonal attitudes—as when the *DM* consulted the *DSM* in Figure 5–7.

Limited problem solving

Limited problem solving (LPS) exists when the manager is confronted with a new alternative but one which is similar enough to others that he can evaluate it against previously established personal and professional choice criteria, as described in Chapter 3.

CHOICE AMONG ALTERNATIVES. To think about an alternative—to evaluate it—it is necessary to have earlier created an image or concept of that alternative. In RRB, this image already existed for each alternative considered because each one had been considered in the past. Now we are considering new alternatives, however, and we must go one step further. We must attempt to understand something about how a concept or image of an alternative is created; we have already learned something about this in discussing buyers in Chapter 3. Just as we saw in Chapter 3 that a brand concept has three elements, so does the concept of an alternative have three components: a descriptive, an evaluative, and a confidence component. Common observation suggests that a manager describing an alternative uses many terms that have no evaluative content for him in a personal, nonprofessional sense. He is merely identifying it. His mental counterpart of these identifying attributes make up the *descriptive* component. The *evaluative* component is his mental counterpart of the attributes by which he judges whether the alternative is good or bad for him. These mental counterparts of the attributes are his personal attitudes which flow out of his directly relevant motives. The *confidence* element is the degree of confidence the executive feels in his judgment of the "goodness" of the alternatives in terms of his personal and professional attitudes. Presumably, the three components are formed roughly together, with the descriptive preceding the evaluative and the evaluative somewhat preceding the confidence.

In addition, he has a set of impersonal attitudes, which we saw expressed in Figure 5–7. We also could see in that figure the major difference between consumer decision and managerial decision, the dominance of impersonal attitudes, and specifically the organizational influences in shaping these impersonal attitudes. Further, we expect that confidence in his ability to judge the alternative on impersonal criteria is much more influential than his ability to judge it in terms of personal criteria.

As to the decision maker's sources of information for developing an image, the normal company communication network may be of little value in this regard. Insofar as internal company sources are relevant, extra effort and time will probably have to be devoted to getting the facts.

GENERATION OF ALTERNATIVES. One question, and a very important one, is: Where do new alternatives come from? The pricing decision discussed in connection with Figure 5–7 is an exceptionally simple case relative to some decisions, because new price alternatives in this situation are particularly easy to generate. Taxes and custom, for example, strongly encourage even-penny prices. Also, the profit contribution of another price is easy to compute. Since total consumption of gasoline is little affected by changes in price and costs do not vary with volume, it could be, however, that competitors would respond *differently* in the new price range to the decision maker's moves than they did in the former price range.

Most new alternatives, however, are more difficult to generate. In fact, some top executives take the view that the major part of their job is to generate new alternatives. They leave to subordinates the job of developing a new alternative and testing it.

We cannot say as much here as we would like to about the nature of the process by which new alternatives are generated. In *generating* new alternatives a manager's personal attitudes serve as a framework for defining alternatives that are acceptable to him personally. These *acceptable* alternatives are then tested against his impersonal attitudes, as in the gasoline pricing example. Here we begin to get an inkling of the possible conflict that may exist between an individual and the company: his personal and impersonal choice criteria must be formed, in addition to the attitudes that come from placing the alternatives on the criteria. Search effort is a critical part of such decisions.

Extensive problem solving

When confronted with an EPS situation, the manager has no criteria—neither personal nor professional attitudes—by which to make the decision either to generate alternatives (personal goals) or to test alternatives (professional goals). One way of conveying some of the subtleties of this type of decision is again by an example.

The new-product decision often involves most of the complications in EPS. A new-product choice does not necessarily involve an unstructured decision; for example, it may be made frequently enough that criteria do exist. Typically, however, such a choice does involve an unstructured decision. The new product is a good example for other reasons, too. The fate of a company can significantly hang on the success of a new product. Since World War II, initiating new products has increasingly been the route to satisfying the company goals of profit and growth. Also, the decision often has severe organizational implications, as we shall see in discussing new products in Chapter 13.

EPS decisions require more information than do LPS decisions. Personal and impersonal choice criteria must be formed, in addition to the attitudes that come from placing the alternatives on the criteria. Search effort is a critical part of such decisions.

SEARCH EFFORT.   Searching for an alternative solution to a need, particularly one that cannot be judged on familiar choice criteria, can consume a great amount of valuable time. How much the manager will search at any given time depends upon the confidence element of his concept of this alternative—his confidence in judging its value. In general, the lower the confidence, the more he will search. He will continue to search until his confidence achieves a *satisfactory* level. If his confidence is quite low, however, he may give up using a rational approach and vacillate or simply rely on related past behavior—which is to do it exactly as he did before.

But what is a satisfactory solution? The answer to this lies in the concept of aspiration level. A manager from his experience develops an *acceptable* level of satisfaction of his personal and professional attitudes which we call his *aspiration level*. It sets the level of satisfaction that an alternative must provide before the search is terminated. Over time, however, the aspiration level changes, but typically only at a slow pace. If he is repeatedly successful in finding solutions with relative ease, his aspiration level will rise. If, on the other hand, he has experienced a series of situations where he has had difficulty meeting his aspiration level, it will tend to decline.

In addition to how much he searches, it is also important to know where he searches.

GOALS AND MEANS-END CHAIN.   Unstructured decision involves the task of forming personal and professional choice criteria toward the alternative. Therefore we must consider where personal and professional choice criteria come from.

Personal criteria are generated from the manager's relevant motives, as was discussed in Chapter 3 in the buyer's decision process. Little need be added here. Impersonal criteria, particularly certain aspects of them, are quite different for the manager than for the consumer buyer. For the industrial buyer, the discussion here will strongly supplement Chapter 3. A manager is typically assigned goals by his superior from which, as well as from his relevant motives he generates his impersonal criteria. In Figure 5–7, for example, we could assume that the home office had assigned to the manager (*DM*) some such goals as growth with a minimum profit. From these interlinked goals and motives to achieve and exercise power, for example, he developed the criteria we saw expressed there in binary form.

How are goals formed? The concept of the *means-end chain* helps us answer this question. In principle, at each level in the organizational chart shown in Figure 5–1, the participant accomplishes his role by breaking it into parts. He then assigns each part to a respective person. In Figure 5–1 we saw how the marketing manager breaks his role into advertising, market research, sales, product, and marketing services. He assigns to each of these managers a goal to give them a sense of direction and by which he can evaluate them. Their goals are thus means to satisfying the marketing manager's goal. Thus we have a means-end chain extending from the top of the corporation to the bottom. This we can call a goal structure.

Goal content is more important than you might think. First, its obvious role is to help him choose among alternatives. Second, and much more subtle, it influences the very information he takes in. A manager, like all humans, is exposed to far more information than he can possibly handle. In fact, his intake capacity is rather limited, and, consequently, he must *select* his information. This he does to a large extent *unconsciously*, and goals influence what he selects. He takes in the most "relevant" information, and since his goals largely define the problem, which in turn specifies the information that is relevant, they determine to a significant extent what information is relevant and therefore what is admitted to his sensory system.

The dominant goals at the top are, typically, profit and growth, although other goals undoubtedly exist. More specifically, these dominant goals are growth with a minimum profit constraint. Neil H. McElroy, chairman of Procter and Gamble, states, "We don't run the business for a consistent earnings growth per share. We run it for a consistent growth in volume, then we set out to bring some of that into the net column. You can't make money unless you do the business." [7] This statement, however, is not inconsistent with striving to give stockholders what they want, which is steady growth in earnings per share.

As we descend the hierarchy, goals must become more specific. What

---

[7] *Business Week,* July 19, 1969, p. 53.

are the goals at the brand manager level, for example? More will be said about this later, but for the moment, to illustrate, we can refer again to P & G, where the brand manager is responsible for volume but not profit.[8]

Earlier the means-end chain was said to operate in principle, but the nice tidy relationships among different goals at different levels implied by the concept often do not prevail. A recent survey of corporate chief marketing executives, however, indicated that setting goals is their major task.[9] Even if a consistent goal structure exists at one time, over time it encounters changes and runs the chance of becoming inconsistent among levels.

Also, that goals are used to evaluate people implies that the managerial behavior at each level is consistent with the goals, which may not hold true. First, the manager at each level must translate the goal assigned to him into operational criteria, or, as we put it earlier, into impersonal choice criteria. We saw these illustrated in Figure 5–7 and concluded there that these impersonal criteria probably did serve the goal assigned him quite well. The example in Figure 5–7, however, was a highly repetitive decision. The congruence between impersonal attitudes and assigned goals may in actuality be much less than perfect, largely because of the complexity of the problem of lack of data (which will be emphasized in Part III) and the limitations of human mental capacity.

Second, goals are not always the evaluative criteria applied to the manager in the role. In one large marketing-oriented company, the goal assigned to the brand manager was sales volume. When asked how he was evaluated, he referred to the following criteria:

1. Ability to put a logical marketing plan together.
2. "Well-buttoned-up" marketing plan—few unanswered questions.
3. Capacity to work with staff areas.
4. Tendency to meet deadlines.
5. Satisfactory advertising copy from the agency.
6. Personal presence and poise.
7. Cohesiveness and dynamism of people in his brand group.

Third, as mentioned earlier, a manager may find himself in conflict between the impersonal attitudes required to serve the goals assigned and his personal attitudes. This problem became particularly apparent in the decade of the 1960s as young people came to question many institutions, particularly private business. This analysis can be carried further and broadened. Any member of the company is given certain *inducements*, such as a salary, to persuade him to work for the company. In return for these inducements to work for it, that is, to accept a role in it, he agrees to

---

[8] Ibid., p. 58.
[9] *Advertising Age*, December 20, 1971, p. 2.

carry out the job—to make *contributions* to the company. The activities that contribute, however, usually also have some negative utility for him: They require his time, which can always be put to other uses. Performing the activities also often places him in personally uncomfortable situations; he may be selling a product packed in a plastic container which pollutes the environment because plastic is indestructible. Thus, in a direct sense, inducements relate only to personal choice criteria. They must satisfy his personal motives in order to be effective. As long as his personal satisfaction from the inducements exceeds the contributions required of him, he will stay, occupy that role, and so, via his professional choice criteria, serve the company's goals. When this is no longer so, he will leave.

IMPLICATIONS OF INCONGRUENCY OF GOALS AND CHOICE CRITERIA. Obviously there are many implications of incongruency among goals, between goals and evaluative criteria, and between personal and professional choice criteria, and we could not hope to discuss all of them here. We can merely illustrate.

There is the "spend up to budget" behavior, for example, which characterizes some companies. A brand manager has graphically described how at the end of the year he wildly spent money for promotion for next year because "it was considered suicidal in nature to underspend one's promotion budget." If it were not spent, his budget for the following year was reduced by higher management by that amount.[10] Current organizational arrangements sometimes encourage this kind of seemingly dishonest and suboptimizing behavior.

A manager's future in the company can be tied to the success or failure of the product. If it is highly successful, it may propel him into a divisional managership at a young age. This possibility, however, causes other executives who are competing with him to wonder if there are ways of increasing their own opportunity and even of diminishing his. The incongruencies that could exist are obvious. As one company president wrote not long ago, "The energies of the more talented, more aggressive, more ambitious employees often seem to be taken up with internal problems of power, prestige and position."[11] Out of this "pull and haul" can emerge a bargaining relationship between competitors for the presidency. This bargaining is usually implicit. In much too simple terms we can say that it will come to be understood between them that "If you will help me become president, I will help you become executive vice president." On the other hand, out of the experience the manager might decide that the *inducements* implied in his current role are insufficient to balance his *contributions*, which exact a personal cost of him, and so he

---

[10]*Advertising Age,* August 14, 1970, p. 81.
[11]Thomas M. Ware, "An Executive's Viewpoint," *Operations Research,* 7 (1959); 3–4.

will leave the company for greener pastures. This example is a bit stark and perhaps unpleasant, but it is realistic in *any* organization, be it government, religious, military, business, or university.

SUMMARY

Each of three views of organization—organization chart, standard operating procedure, and decision process—serve different purposes. In an understanding of information requirements, market research, marketing information systems, goal structure, coordination of activities and the nature of management training requirements, the decision-process view, with its underlying concept of rule, is most productive. If the issue is one of the nature of the manager's role, the standard operating procedure is the most useful. If you are concerned about the manager's identity—his position—and such things as length of decision horizon, the view provided by the organization chart is the most revealing.

Because of the great differences among the levels in the decision process and the role of the position, most of the rest of this text will be structured by level: Part III, the brand manager, Part IV, the marketing manager, and Part V, the president. Yet as we work through each of these three positions, we will find that the three views are essential supplements of each other. Otherwise, in viewing the marketing system we would be like the three blind men and the elephant.

DISCUSSION QUESTIONS

1. Describe each of the three general ways of viewing an organization that includes the marketing operation.
2. Great stress is often placed on a marketing plan and its content. Why is a marketing plan so important?
3. What vital pieces of information about the marketing operation can you infer from a manager's decision process?
4. In most academic discussions of decision, the alternatives are accepted as given, yet generating new alternatives is probably the most crucial task in the corporation. According to this chapter, how are new alternatives generated?
5. Discuss the problem of insuring that goals assigned to a brand manager, for example, are consistent with both his choice criteria and the criteria by which he is in fact evaluated.

part III

The brand manager

IN EVERY company marketing organization there is a large element of the stationary or steady state in which only minor changes are needed to keep the system going and in harmony with its environment. Some kinds of companies, such as those in the package-goods industry, have found that this stationary-state portion of the company, such as established brands, could best be separated from the rest of the organization. In such cases the steady-state portion is separated on a brand-by-brand basis and a brand manager placed in charge. This tendency to use a brand manager type of organization is probably growing, as indicated in Chapter 5.

Other companies have not found it organizationally desirable to separate the steady state from the more dynamic activities, however. Nevertheless, they still must manage these steady-state activities, and the material in Part III is just as applicable to them. In fact, by seeing the two different types of activities so sharply demarcated, the managers in these enterprises may see both of them more clearly and understand them better. The two types of activities differ in time horizon, magnitude of risk, type of data, and kind of data analysis needed for planning.

The chief distinction between the two types of marketing management activities is the time horizon. A conceptually general and practically workable distinction is not easy to phrase, however. In Chapter 4 we saw the economists' short-run versus long-run distinction as indicating whether a change in capacity is involved. It is a very general and useful criterion, but only on the cost or supply side of the decision problem. It has, unfortunately, no corresponding relevance on the demand or buyer-behavior side. For this we refer back to Chapter 3. Here there are at least two reasonable alternatives. First, change in evaluation of brand in terms of the buyer's impersonal attitudes could be the short term and change in terms of his personal attitudes could be the long term. Second, change in terms of personal attitudes could be the short term and change in the weighting of his personal attitude could be the long term. The organization and financial planning structure of a company typically distinguishes according to calendar time, a year or less versus more than a year.

We are faced with the task of bringing these ideas of time together, recognizing that they are quite disparate and that at times we may find them conflicting. Nevertheless, we can adopt a workable alternative. We will refer to decisions and planning as *short term* when they involve a year or less and as *long term* when they involve more than a year. This calendar time will probably not be too inconsistent with the temporal distinctions of the cost and demand sides.

In companies, the brand manager is typically concerned with short-term decisions. He is free to negotiate with his colleagues on changes in advertising, price, and selling effort within the limits set down by the plan, which in itself is drawn up within the framework of a given strategy. These are his controllables, as indicated in Figure 5–5. He is responsible for submitting recommendations on the more strategic variables of product and channels as well (for example, he may recommend a line extension), but he is not responsible for their performance. A brand manager is placed in charge of a new product at the idea-stage, but he works closely under the supervision of the marketing manager.

The brand manager's uncontrollables are also in Figure 5–5. We have examined the structure of competition, demand, cost, and organization, in Chapters 2 to 5, respectively. The concept of a distribution system and marketing channels was briefly presented in Chapter 1. Public policy is delayed for consideration until Chapters 15 and 16, for reasons stated in Chapter 1. Something of the nature of product change introduced in Chapter 1 and the changes in buyer behavior relevant to changes in product constituted a substantial part of Chapter 3. It will mostly be developed, however, in Chapter 13.

In Part III, Chapters 6 to 8 will deal mainly with the brand manager's information problem. Each of the succeeding three chapters (Chapters 9 to 11) is devoted to an area of decision: advertising, price, and selling. Chapter 6 presents the organizational setting within which the brand manager plans the activities in these three areas. The concept of a marketing information system (MIS) is described as an ideal arrangement for planning, an ideal toward which companies strive. A central element of an advanced MIS is a normative decision model, which is presented in Chapter 7. In turn, a central part of a normative decision model is aggregate response curve, which was developed theoretically in Chapter 3 and will be discussed empirically in Chapter 8. Emphasis is also placed in Chapter 8 upon the market research techniques necessary to provide the data for an aggregate response curve.

6

Marketing programming and control: Marketing information systems

INTRODUCTION

RECENT DEVELOPMENTS in marketing information technology place marketing management on the threshold of quantitative decision making to an extent seldom anticipated even a few years ago. This chapter introduces the concept of *quantitative* marketing management, which will be further developed in Chapters 7 and 8. Because the *utilization* of quantitative marketing management is complex and not well understood, Chapter 6 presents a model to provide perspective and a broad comprehension of the *process* by which quantitative marketing management is *applied*. This process includes market research, marketing models, and the marketing information system.

Planning is the chief task of the brand manager, and the product of that planning effort is a marketing plan (described in Chapter 5 in some detail). The term "programming" is used to mean ways of making the combined managerial choices implied in fixing the financial aspects of the total marketing plan and the proper mix of the elements making it up. These are all also implied by the term "plan." Advertising, pricing, and selling are the controllable elements for the brand manager.

Market planning consists of a variety of techniques. First there are the techniques having to do with how to make the choice once the alternatives have been specified and the relevant facts collected. This we call *decision technology*, which is dealt with in Chapter 7. Second, there is the *computer-associated technology*, which is the programs—the software—needed to support the extensive kind of data storage, retrieval, and analysis implicit in modern decision technology. These are discussed in the present chapter. Third, there are the buyer-behavior concepts, the techniques of data collection and the data processing techniques required by the computer and its associated technology to make them conform to the needs of the decision technology. This last body of techniques we call *market research technology*, which is presented in Chapter 8.

We will examine each of these groups of techniques to see if they are consistent with one another. Our major goal is to present these areas, which make up the "new marketing technology," in an integrated and systematic way. Because all three technologies must be applied in an organizational setting that strongly shapes their operation, however, we will examine this organizational setting first.

ORGANIZATIONAL SETTING

In discussing modern programming techniques the degree of possible rationality tends to be exaggerated. Organizational pressures usually force compromise of this rationality to a greater or lesser degree. We discussed the major reason for this in Chapter 5: the lack of congruency among organizational goals set for the decision maker, his impersonal attitudes, and the criteria by which he is evaluated.

As noted in Chapter 5, the brand manager has little delegated authority and much responsibility. He *must* depend upon others, especially the sales manager, advertising manager, and market research manager, or their people just below them. For this reason the position is a splendid training ground for effectiveness in higher management positions. Almost every facet of the brand manager's marketing plan is a joint decision with someone else. Consequently, he must be prepared to spend a great amount of his time in conference with these people and learn to be effective in that environment. In these conferences he will sometimes feel that the heart—the coherency and unity—of his creative marketing plan has been compromised away.

Why should these relations be difficult? Mainly because different parts of the organization have different goals. Also, as we saw in Chapter 5, for a given person the assigned goals, impersonal attitudes, and criteria for his evaluation are sometimes incongruent. Some examples from the experience of a brand manager with one of the large food companies can convey more concretely the nature of the problem. His most difficult relations are with production. He introduced a new package, for example, which upped the cost of production and inventory. Production opposed this. Production is evaluated by standard costs, and the new package would increase its actual cost relative to its standard costs. Next most difficult are relations with research and development (R & D). R & D does not think in terms of "will it sell; will the consumer like it?" Instead, it places a high value on making a "good" product in technical terms, and this can often be a serious handicap because the cost of the product forces the company to "price itself out of the market." On the other hand, R & D is more in favor of change than is production. Relations are also difficult with the sales manager because he has only so many resources—salesman man-hours—and the brand manager will always, in his eyes, want more than what he feels is a fair share. Relations with market research are the easiest. In fact, there seems to be a growing tendency to recruit brand managers from the market research department. That brand managers are more similar to market researchers than they are to advertising and sales personnel in terms of attitude toward risk has been documented by R. M. Edelstein.[1]

From these examples we can infer that the problem is in large part one of differences in goals, although there are probably some personality differences. The brand manager often is not adept at dealing with these personality differences in the way that sales people, for example, are because he has usually had no direct line experience. It is not clear whether the differences Edelstein found were basic personality differences or whether they came about because of working in different organizational environments.

Communication can help overcome differences in view resulting from minor differences in organizational goals, however. Another way of facilitating relations among the various people is for them to exchange jobs for a year or so.

One of the most effective ways of dealing with these relations is for the marketing manager to formulate a clear, concise statement of strategy. A brand strategy can give the plan an inherent logic which can be very persuasive. Procter & Gamble reports that the lack of such a statement is often the source of a brand manager's problems in dealing with sales-zone management and the advertising agency. A strategy is vital, competitive, and informative, however, and sometimes a brand manager may hesitate to reveal it too widely.

Another way of limiting the brand manager's often frustrating experiences in securing group decisions is for the brand manager to enter the conference well armed with quantitative evidence to support his views. Many will go along with him merely because he has given them an answer to use in case anyone questions them. Even if the marketing plan is contrary to what some others want, these people will agree because, if he is well armed, they fear that in a showdown, when the problem is taken "upstairs" to the boss, he will win the argument. Still another possibility is for the brand manager to give more latitude to the sales department, for example, when price changes must be made rapidly.

When there are substantial goal differences, however, it ultimately

[1]R. M. Edelstein, "Risk Taking and Group Decision Making among Business Professionals" (Ph. D. diss., Columbia University, 1971).

becomes a matter of departmental goals being sacrificed to overall company goals. To avoid this sacrifice, the brand manager will need good evidence that, in fact, the company goals will be served by his plan. This evidence can only be had by working closely with the market research department, represented by the department analyst assigned to the brand.

Even this relationship with the research analyst can be frustrating, and often it is. Most of the responsibility for the failure will probably lie with the brand manager; he will fail to define his problem precisely enough so the analyst can get him the facts that will answer his questions. He will fail to communicate his frame of reference. In other words, the analyst will not know the questions the brand manager is asking. As market research technology improves, this gap between the brand manager—the man of action—and the researcher will lessen, but it will always be considerable.

Advertising, too, often involves difficult organizational problems. Effective advertising is difficult to identify before it is run, and group decision encounters problems of differing evaluations of an uncertain quantity, especially with large-volume brands and new brands. Also, advertising usually has to be approved by a number of people up and down the hierarchy, sometimes including the president himself. Worse yet, the advertising is conceived and produced by still another organization, the advertising agency, with its own unique values and points of view. If the brand manager is to get his plan accepted by the other people with whom he must coordinate his activities, he will need facts that help him predict the consequences of various marketing plans. Only in this way can he select the best one in terms of his goals. In sum, he must anticipate and estimate the reactions of three diverse sets of critics: buyers, channel members, and higher administrators.

Typically, he will make estimates about the effects of advertising (dollar amount, media, and copy) pricing (various types of discounts and the relations among the prices of different but related products sold by the company), and sales effort (with many consumer products, when and how to get shelf space, and with most industrial products, what to say and how to say it in order to cause the industrial buyer to want to buy it). Chapter 7 will discuss techniques to increase the rationality of the plan, and Chapter 8, the market research technology needed to obtain the facts required.

To the extent that the brand manager is not merely a "brand watcher" and the plan is, in general concept, truly creative as opposed to merely building on the previous year's plan, the task of coordination with the research analyst, and everyone else for that matter, will be more difficult. In terms of the kinds of decision situations and consequent decision processes discussed in Chapter 5, this will be Extensive Problem Solving, and the brand manager will have to form new goals. New criteria for evaluating alternatives will have to be developed. If, on the other hand, he begins with the previous year's plan, the task of planning will be simpler and will subject him to less obvious risks. However, if he is truly evaluated in terms of foregone opportunities—profits he would have earned had he chosen the best alternative—his performance in the second case will often not measure up to what a company should expect of its brand managers; he will not have been innovative. Unfortunately, in large organizations the "punishments" for a mistake can sometimes be out of line with the rewards for innovation.

Thus a large part of the job of the brand manager is to relate effectively to others. One way to summarize its importance to the brand manager is in terms of alternative organizational strategies that he could employ. First, he can work with those around him and essential to him in an open, frank, cordial manner as he strives diligently to obtain their ideas. When he uses their ideas, he rewards them by telling them so. Doubtlessly more imaginative and effective marketing plans can emerge through this strategy. It is time-consuming, however, and it will make the manager appear less omniscient and omnipotent. Second, he can be a tough individualist, giving no quarter and doing everything possible within the rules to look effective to his supervisors. With this strategy he may well be rated more highly, but to achieve it he must be very articulate, and if he slips, those around him will not support him. Contrasting strategies such as these are highly oversimplified, but they demonstrate the importance of differences in behavior.

The brand manager's *role* in the organizational setting relates more sharply to quantitative marketing management. If his dominant goal is profit and his planning horizon is short term, the task of obtaining meaningful quantitative results can be clearly structured. The use of profit goals at lower levels in the corporate hierarchy is now possible because the computer can provide accurate cost data on a product-by-product basis, as described in Chapter 4.

In developing the concept of a marketing information system (MIS), we must build, step by step, to the sophisticated system shown in Figure 6–6. Because this figure incorporates ideas that are quite complex to the newcomer, we will begin with the simplest possible ideas, as in Figure 6–1 below.

We will use the MIS as a model to serve three functions. First, it will be an expositional device to give us perspective in this exceedingly complex picture of programming and control in the context of quantitative marketing management. Like all models, however, it is a simplified picture of reality, with a number of key assumptions that are sometimes not recognized. Much of the current literature fails to make these assumptions explicit. When this is done, we begin to see the sources of the very serious problems that are now plaguing brand managers as they attempt to introduce the new marketing technology.

Second, the MIS as described here is far more than a mere expositional device. In a very real sense it is an ideal that companies can strive to achieve. If it is properly designed and implemented, it can vastly increase the quality and timeliness of marketing planning. It provides ways of describing the elements and criteria for evaluating plans.

Third, by showing the various stages in the introduction of an MIS, the model provides an understanding of the possible *path* of development that companies can anticipate in fully adopting the new marketing technology.

In summary, the MIS makes three contributions: (1) use of models as a means of describing very complex phenomena, (2) a picture of a desirable goal, and (3) a path for achieving that goal.

MARKETING INFORMATION SYSTEMS

Introduction

With the increasing use of the computer, companies are becoming more interested in the development of a corporatewide, integrated *management information system*. The purpose of such a system is to bring all of the flows of recorded information in the entire company into a unified whole. Thereby it is hoped that the manager's capacity to plan and control the company's activities will be improved. Such a system is often seen as a marked improvement over current procedures.

As companies have attempted to introduce such a system, however, a consensus seems to be growing, especially among some computer hardware manufacturers, that a more realistic approach is to begin with smaller systems, such as one in marketing, or in production. As *Business Week* recently put it, "Skeptics are backing off and asking whether one big system is such a good idea after all." [2] The reason for this change in view is the growing awareness that these smaller subsystems, such as one for marketing, can perhaps be conceptualized in enough detail to be operational, whereas, in the current state of the art, the larger systems probably cannot. The human mind simply cannot grasp the whole management operation with sufficient clarity and detail to permit it to be structured and modeled. New concepts will probably have to be developed to aid us in thinking about such a complex phenomenon. In the meantime, management can proceed to develop the smaller systems. In building the smaller systems too, we can benefit by learning from the mistakes that were made with global systems.

Historical background

The problem of computerizing a marketing information system is so complex that some basic ideas about the development of computers in management are necessary to simplify the discussion. [3] When computers

---

[2] *Business Week,* June 5, 1971, p. 62.

[3] Russell Ackoff, "The Evolution of Management Systems," Management Seminar for Advertising Agency Executives, Columbia University, January 10, 1970.

were first introduced into business, they performed a very simple kind of symbol manipulation: the conversion of data (facts) into information. Data becomes information when the symbols of which data consist are converted into usable form. Clerks carried out this task before computers came into the business scene. A man who wants to know what his current bank balance is, for example, consults his checkbook stubs, which represent his previous bank balance and all deposits and withdrawals made since. By adding and subtracting these facts—manipulating the symbols— he determines his bank balance.

The first job of the computer in business was to mechanize this clerical labor. The systems designed to perform this task were put to work to do a variety of what we call bookkeeping jobs such as preparation of payrolls and purchase orders. It was soon found, however, that the information produced by the early data processing system generated more questions for the user than the clerical systems did. This occurred especially in the early payroll systems. Contrary to what was expected, clerks continued to be employed after the computer was introduced. Now, however, they performed a new function: that of answering questions. What was happening was that to answer the user's questions, the clerks were retrieving the raw data and *reprocessing* it to extract more information from the same set of facts.

In the auto industry, the clerk formerly showed only the breakdown of new-car buyers by brand of car purchased. From auto registrations, his source of data, the clerk could easily show the former owners of each kind of car. By imaginatively putting together two previously unrelated facts, he generated additional information.

Table 6–1 shows, at the bottom of the first column, the total number of

TABLE 6–1
Cars previously owned by current buyers of Olds Regular

	1968 sales	
Make purchased	*Number*	*Percent*
Loyal:		
Oldsmobile Regular	45,310	45.8%
Other Olds divisions	8,185	8.2
Chevrolet Division	8,765	8.9
Pontiac Division	5,982	6.0
Buick Division	11,840	11.9
Cadillac Division	2,238	2.2
Total	82,320	83.0%
Disloyal:		
Ford Corp. product	3,943	4.1%
Chrysler product	9,171	9.3
AMC product	750	.8
Foreign	2,912	2.8
Grand total	99,096	100.0%

Oldsmobile Regulars sold in 1968. In addition, however, listed at the left are the cars that these buyers formerly owned. Of those who bought an Oldsmobile Regular, for example, 11.9 percent had formerly owned Buicks (Buick Division) cars. In addition, we see by the "loyal" and "disloyal" groupings the contrast between how many remained in the General Motors group and how many went to another company for a car. Of those buying an Oldsmobile Regular, 4.1 percent had formerly owned Ford Corporation cars. With this breakdown, management could begin to ask sharper questions, for example, why did people trade up so much more than they traded down, as suggested by the number going to Buick instead of to Chevrolet? From these data managers can begin to form new hypotheses about the nature of the dynamics of the auto market.

This type of experience led clerks to seek *additional* data to feed into the information reprocessing. Thus they could provide still more sophisticated information which the management of American industry was learning to use. As a result, computerized systems were developed which generated, stored, retrieved, and processed data in such a way as to answer specific questions addressed to them. These systems are called information systems, and the computerized files which play a central role in such systems are called data banks. This type of system is shown in Figure 6–1 where (1) the user receives data from the data bank, (2) the additional data causes him to generate new questions, and so (3) he initiates new inquiries. These three activities—inquiries, data, and new inquiries—are represented by the *two-way* flow connecting the *user* and the *data*

FIGURE 6–1
Information system

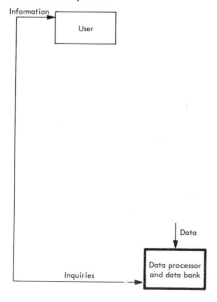

processor. The source of the data in the figure is not given but is shown as being fed into the *data bank* from some unspecified outside source, which will be discussed later.

The next stage in the development of the MIS was to pay attention to a particular class of *users* of the information generated by data processing systems and to develop the system so as to best serve the needs of that class. This class of users was the *managers* of the companies using the systems. In this book we are concerned with a particular kind of manager —a person who manages the *marketing* activity—and in this part of the book we are focusing on the *brand manager*. The simple marketing information system discussed first is a useful step toward understanding the more comprehensive system.

Simple marketing information systems

A new principle is needed if we are to find out what a marketing information system (MIS) is all about. This is the principle of a *loop*. This loop, as shown in Figure 6–2, connects the *brand manager* to the computer by a two-way flow as before, but the system is extended here. Figure 6–1 is not a loop in that the manager does not act and obtain information on the consequences of that act from the computer. Now, as a part of the system, he issues instructions to the *marketing operation* he is managing, as shown in the circle in Figure 6–2. The operation could be made up of a large field sales force, a network of company warehouses, a network of company-owned retail stores, or any element of marketing activity owned by

FIGURE 6–2
Simple marketing information system

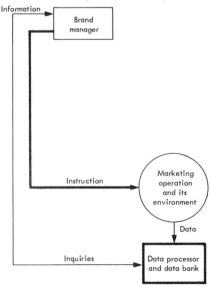

the company. The *environment* of the operation, also shown in the circle, would be different according to the nature of the operation. If the operation, for example, was a network of company-owned retail stores, the environment would be the retail customers surrounding the stores.

Further, the loop is almost completed by the flow of information from the operations environment into the *data processor and data bank*. A concrete example of this flow from the market could be the data from a panel of 1,000 customers who report their purchases of each company's brand and other data specified by the theory of buyer behavior on a periodic basis, such as monthly. Finally, the loop is completed by the same two-way flow from data processor to brand manager (user) shown in Figure 6–1 and serving the same purpose as there.

What does this loop mean? The facts that flow from the environment into the computer are those specified by the systems designer. They are the ones that can be processed to provide the information required by the brand manager's decision rules. The information required by his decision rules, you will recall, is specified by his intuitive information-processing rules, shown in Figure 5–7 of Chapter 5. This is such an important point that we will illustrate it. In box 10 of Figure 5–7 the information-processing rule is: "Compare my share in the local market with my share in the nearby market to decide which is larger." The decision rule is: "If it is larger, change my price to equal the initiator's price; if it is not, ask myself the question in box 11." From his information processing rule we know precisely what information he needs: he needs market-share data in the local and nearby markets. One of the major tasks in designing a simple marketing information system is to identify these rules so as to know what facts will best serve him (best "fit his head") and, therefore, what facts should be stored in the computer. The failure to consider the user's needs adequately has been one of the frequent tragedies in most attempts to construct an MIS.

In summary, what we have been observing in a simple MIS is action and feedback on the results of the action. This is the concept of coordination by feedback used in Chapter 5. The brand manager wants, for example, weekly reports of the sales of his brand by geographic segment such as sales territories. The computer printout each Monday morning lists for each territory the actual sale, the expected sales as forecast in the marketing plan, and the differences between them ("overages" and "underages"). He then selects those territories with deviations, particularly in the downward direction, and puts his intuitive process to work thinking through why these might have occurred. He often telephones someone in those "poor" markets for additional information. As a consequence of the analysis he may wish to modify his marketing plan for the rest of the year.

With these facts and his intuitive judgment, he decides whether to take any action, and if so, which action is best. He then proceeds to implement the chosen action. As a result of his implementing the decision, the relation between the marketing operation and its environment changes. He needs then to know the nature and consequence of the change. Since he knows what action he took, he can, by simple analysis of the data, attempt to infer what the causal process was that occurred. This analysis takes place on the flow of facts into the computer from the operation and its environment, and the results of the analysis come in the form of information from the computer to him. This is the meaning of the loop: (1) action, (2) market facts, (3) facts converted into information, (4) information evaluated by the brand manager and new decisions result in new action, (5) new action leads to new facts, and so on, ad infinitum.

This MIS is termed "simple" because it only provides the manager with the information he already uses in his conventional *intuitive* way. It merely gives him *more* data much *quicker*—and also much *cheaper*, if the computer system is well managed. It does not take over any of his functions, since he does not learn a new approach; the information feeds his own personalized idiosyncratic system. He:

creates the system in his own image. Many companies (McKinzey's Golub says) have a policy of rotating operating executives every two years. It may take a year to design a small MIS and another year to put it in, he says, and by that time there's a new executive at the helm and a whole new set of problems.[4]

It is not known, however, just how idiosyncratic these decision processes are. Therefore it is not known how much changing managers requires changing the system. John A. Howard and W. M. Morgemoth found different divisions in the same company using identical decision processes, however.[5]

If the brand manager wishes, this simple system can be elaborated to simplify some of his functions. Each of these possible elaborations will be developed in a separate section below. In each of them, however, the *concept of the loop*—action, feedback, and new action—remains the *central idea*.

Marketing information systems with plan evaluation

The first new element added is one that permits the system to evaluate the marketing plan. It is a *decision model,* or a computer program based on an explicit set of rules, usually mathematical. It replaces the kind of intuitive rules we saw, for example, in Figure 5–7 of Chapter 5, which now tend to be the basis for the brand manager's managerial behavior. Such subtle mental habits are not easily changed.

---

[4]*Business Week,* June 5, 1971, p. 63.
[5]J. A. Howard and W. M. Morgenroth, "Information Processing Model of Executive Decision," *Management Science,* 14 (1968), 416–28.

If the brand manager has an adequate decision model programmed for his system, he can feed into it his goals and his marketing plan, which incorporates his estimates of buyer behavior, cost, and competitive information relevant to a particular course of action. The output of the system will then be an evaluation of that plan in terms of his goals. Such a system is shown in Figure 6–3, where solutions to marketing problems—*proposed plans*—are transmitted to a *decision model* programmed in the computer. The decision model queries the computer for the necessary data, which the computer receives from the market *(environment)*. The model evaluates each plan in terms of its contribution to the brand manager's objective of company profit. The profit results are fed back to him as *evaluated plans.*

FIGURE 6–3
Marketing information system with plan evaluation

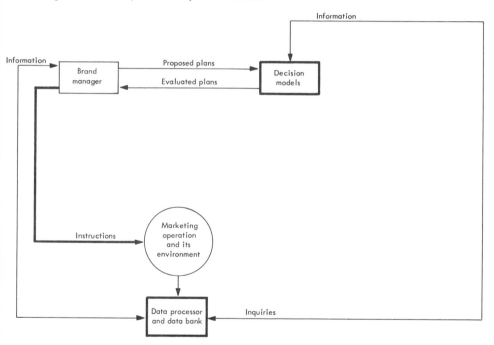

In this way he can, in principle, receive estimates of the profit consequences of each of the plans and so avoid the *cost, delay* and *risk* of tipping his hand to his competitors as a result of trying out a plan in the field. Armed with this new information, he can choose which marketing plan he prefers and initiate the action that is represented in the preferred plan.

The decision model is the crucial new element of this system. It is a major departure from the intuitive decision rules that have characterized marketing management since trading activity first began, perhaps in a Stone Age cave. The success of this system, however, hangs on the efficacy of its constituent parts. It requires certain decision technology, ideally certain formal optimizing models to be described in Chapter 7, a central element of which is aggregate response curves introduced in Chapter 3 and explained at length in Chapter 8. A formal model is necessary for the dimension of action, such as advertising, that is being tried out. A level of advertising that is optimal when analyzed alone may not be so when analyzed in the context of the other two dimensions of price and sales effort that are assuredly just as much a part of the plan. This is the problem of the optimal marketing mix. Once the optimal mix is obtained, it must be allocated to market segments. These decisions are not as simple as they might seem, and they will be discussed further in Chapter 7.

If the ideal of a formal optimizing model is not available to perform each of these tasks, carefully developed simulations may help. It is impossible to gauge the opportunities being sacrificed when you do not know the best answer, however.

Assuming the decision technology is adequate, the decision model is feasible only if the market research technology is advanced enough to provide the aggregate response curves for market segments required by the models set forth in Chapter 7. For this, Chapter 8 probably provides much of the future answer, but let us anticipate it some here in order to obtain a fuller appreciation of the MIS. A very elaborate system providing information on a large sample of individual buyers is being proposed. At a minimum 60 pieces of unchanging information would be collected on 1,000 consumers for market segmenting purposes. Then, each month another set of 40 pieces would be collected. Thus every month 40,000 pieces would be collected, and by the end of the year almost 500,000 would have been accumulated. This is an awesome amount of data.

Marketing information systems with control subsystems

The system can be elaborated still further to include some or all of the *control or monitoring function*. The decision model need not necessarily come first in chronological development, as indicated here. Provision can be made in the system for assisting in the control function without the decision model. Historically, the control function was automated first in most companies.

The essential role of control was described in Chapter 5. But the difficulty of developing a control system which identifies the *correct* problem in sufficient *time* for *remedial* action to be taken was not sufficiently stressed there. More will be said later on this complex issue.

The desirable level of performance is shown in Figure 6–4 by a line from *brand manager—prediction of performance—*to *memory and comparator,* which receives *reports on actual performance* from *data processor and data bank* and compares the actual level with the desired level. Memory and comparator are, of course, terms which refer to computer programs that perform the tasks.

FIGURE 6–4
Marketing information system with control subsystem

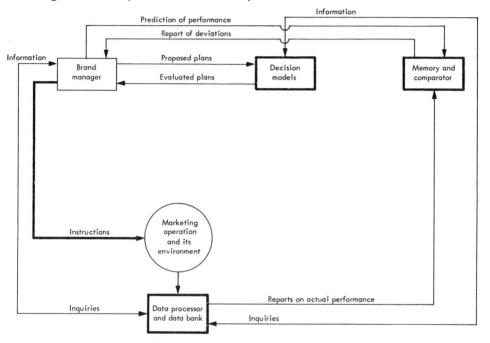

In quality control, as you know, a band of variation in the controlled dimension or variable is established as acceptable. When its value exceeds either the upper or lower limits, the "system is out of control": something has gone wrong. In the same way here, when the actual level is less than the desired level the brand manager is notified. This is the familiar "management by exception" rule.

If, for example, the consumer's actual awareness of a brand is the control dimension and if, as revealed by the monitoring system, it is less than this desired level as shown by *report of deviations,* the computer will notify the brand manager or personnel in the MIS area. The manager can then proceed to determine why the deviation exists between desired and actual, which in turn will guide him in taking action to correct it. Thus he will not be burdened with excess information about the market, and he can devote his time to "problems," to the more urgent issues of the day. The system described in Figure 6–4, however, is confined to identifying *current* problems, not future ones; a key question is whether it will notify him in time for him to take remedial action. There is a solution to this timing difficulty, however, and we turn to it next.

Marketing information systems with problem-identifying subsystems

The next step is *future* problem identification, which allows for more lead time in planning corrective action. It may be possible to develop a set of symptoms which will indicate to the brand manager here and *now* that something is likely to be at an unsatisfactory level not now but at some *future* date. The concept of the *symptom identifier* shown in Figure 6–5 which, again, is a computer program, is in principle similar to the quality-control idea in production departments. The same raw facts are used for its operation as are required by the system of Figure 6–4.

Here we go a step beyond the control concept of the previous section by modifying this simple quality control idea to include a warning system which tells the manager to *expect* a problem, not now, but later. The central idea is the concept of a *presymptom*. Symptoms of symptoms—presymptoms—are identified by the fact that though the system is still "in control," the values of the controlled variable are showing a *trend* instead

FIGURE 6–5
Marketing information system with problem-identifying subsystem

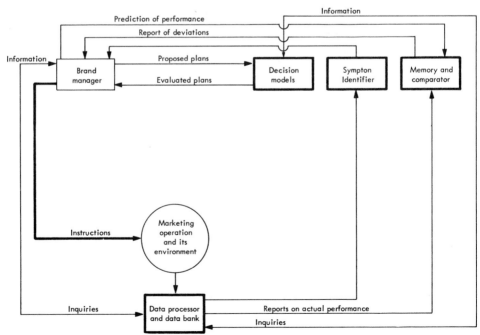

of being random. This would be especially applicable if our brand manager was confronted by a new competitive brand and wanted to monitor its market share.

This trend will, at some future time, take the values outside the control limits. Further, and equally important, this *time can be estimated* so that the brand manager knows the amount of time he has available within which he must take corrective action. Thus, having been warned of possible problems at a given time in the future, he will be in a much better position to deal with it.

Marketing information systems that make decisions

The final type of marketing information system is included mainly to give a complete picture. *Practically it should be approached with great caution*, because it is doubtful whether in many marketing situations the marketing technology—decision, computer-associated, and market research—is sufficiently well advanced to perform this task. Its use may expose the brand manager to undue risk.

For certain repetitive, relatively unimportant decisions, the computer can be programmed to actually make the decision which could be shown by *instructions* from *decision model* to *marketing operation and its environment*. To do this the heavy arrow of Figure 6–6 from decision models

FIGURE 6–6
Marketing information systems that make decisions

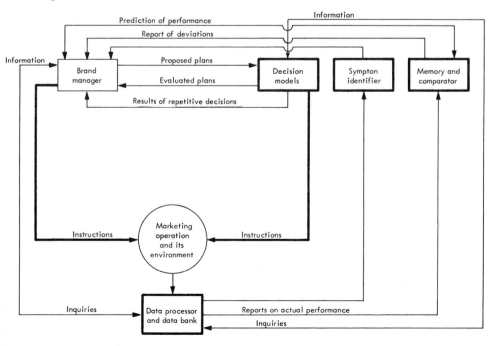

to marketing operation and its environment could replace the heavy arrow from *brand manager*. Once the decision is made, the system reports the results, as implied in Figure 6–6 by the line *results of repetitive decisions*.

So far as we know, there is no such system yet operating in the marketing area of a company. We understand, however, that such a decision-making system does exist in inventory control, which is usually a much more predictable system. Marketing logistics—the physical movement of the product—holds possibilities. If such a system were feasible, the brand manager would be relieved of the unrewarding task of performing a mechanical function; he would be free to think more systematically about the remaining decisions not handled automatically by the system and he would, in principle, thus be able to do a more effective marketing job. These remaining decisions, which are the nonrepetitive and even the important repetitive ones, constitute a large share of all his decisions. They probably deserve much more time than he is now giving them.

Finally, this system can be modified slightly to not only make the decision but also to report only those results of the computer-made decisions that are less than satisfactory, as judged by some predetermined standard. This would require inserting an additional processing step between decision models and brand manager in Figure 6–6. In other words, he would have both the present and future control systems to rely upon.

CONCLUSIONS

If the kind of marketing information system shown in Figure 6–3, one with plan evaluation, were feasible, it would free the brand manager to do the more creative work of (1) developing new kinds of plans, (2) rethinking his basic marketing strategy, and (3) helping plan the market research needed to improve and update the system itself so that its accuracy would be increased.

Is it feasible? In considering this question, we will anticipate the next chapter and assume the brand manager has short-run profit as his objective. The hardware computer technology is clearly capable of performing all of the operations implicit in the complex system in Figure 6–6, thus enabling the brand manager to move from the intuitive decision rules of Chapter 5 to a more explicitly rational process such as that described in Chapter 7. The software, however, is just being created, and its development has awaited a conceptual breakthrough in buyer behavior to guide its evolution. We will see what we believe is the nature of this conceptual breakthrough in Chapter 8. Fortunately, cost theory is in good shape, although specific new developments will follow also from the work on the buyer-behavior model, because cost analysis is meaningful only in terms of estimates as to the effects of the cost expenditure. The lack of these estimates has been a serious deterrent to the development of systematic cost accounting in marketing. Still lacking is an adequate theory of competition, although the concept of market structure (as discussed in Chapter 4) is useful. You will recall from Figure 5–7 in Chapter 5, for example, that competitive information was the major input in pricing gasoline in that particular market.

In discussing the computer's task, we see more fully the nature of the planning and control processes in marketing. Also, as we will see in Chapter 7, the decision technology is with one exception adequate, at least in principle, as long as short-run profit is the brand manager's goal, or at least if his role can be so constrained that short-run profit can be used as the dominant goal.

Figure 6–7 provides a summary of some of the benefits of an MIS. We will see in Chapter 8 evidence for hope of going beyond those outlined there as new benefits become apparent.

The system shown in Figure 6–5, that of a marketing information system with problem identification subsystem, is an ideal for marketing practice. Underlying it, however, are a number of assumptions, some implicit and others that have been made explicit above. The assumptions show the limitations of the system and help explain why such systems have been slow in coming.[6]

If the assumptions or preconditions are not satisfied, there will be problems of the type now being encountered in many companies. The brand manager will probably have to settle for the simple MIS (Figure 6–2), which utilizes his own intuitive decision rules. Unfortunately, such a system may be highly personalized, so that, when he is promoted, a new system will have to be developed to accommodate his successor.

The assumptions underlying development of a marketing information system are listed below. They are not elaborated, however, because in Chapters 7 and 8 we will have occasion to develop them further.

1. An effective control system is available that can be applied to marketing.
2. Decision techniques are, in principle, adequate.
3. Aggregate buyer response functions can be derived.
4. Short-run problems can be forecast and described well enough to estimate the raw data that will be required to support the system.
5. Raw data are stored at a low enough level of aggregation (for example, individual observation of buyer such as a purchase transaction) to provide answers.
6. All traditional short-run problems capable of being subjected to quantitative treatment can be accommodated within the system.

---

[6]See A. E. Amstutz, "Market-Oriented Management Systems: the Current Status," *Journal of Marketing Research*, November 1969, p. 91, for a careful and well-supported evaluation of the state of the art.

7. No organization problems exist. For example, brand managers will, instead of being fearful and threatened, feel free and comfortable learning fundamentally new information-processing and decision rules.
8. All possible alternatives of action are considered.

FIGURE 6–7
Benefits possible with an MIS

	Typical applications	Benefits	Examples
Control systems	1. Control of marketing costs.	1. More timely computer-reports.	1. Undesirable cost trends are spotted more quickly so that corrective action may be taken sooner.
	2. Diagnosis of poor performance.	2. Flexible on-line retrieval of data.	2. Executives can ask supplementary questions of the computer to help pinpoint reasons for a sales decline and reach an action quickly.
	3. Management of fashion goods.	3. Automatic spotting of problems and opportunities.	3. Fast-moving fashion items are reported daily for quick reorder, and slow-moving items are reported for fast price reductions.
	4. Flexible promotion strategy.	4. Cheaper, more detailed, and more frequent reports.	4. On-going evaluation of a promotional campaign permits reallocation of funds to areas behind target.
Research systems	1. Advertising strategy.	1. Additional manipulation of data is possible when stored for computers in an unaggregated file.	1. Sales analysis is possible by new market segment breakdowns.
	2. Pricing strategy.	2. Improved storage and retrieval capability allows new types of data to be collected and used.	2. Systematic recording of information about past R & D contract bidding situations allows improved bidding strategies.
	3. Evaluation of advertising expenditures.	3. Well-designed data banks permit integration and comparison of different sets of data.	3. Advertising expenditures are compared to shipments by county to provide information about advertising effectiveness.
	4. Continuous experiments.	4. Comprehensive monitoring of inputs and performance variables yields information when changes are made.	4. Changes in promotion strategy by type of customer are matched against sales results on a continuous basis.

Source: D. F. Cox and R. E. Good. "How to Build a Marketing Information System," *Harvard Business Review*, 45 (May-June 1967): 145–54.

DISCUSSION QUESTIONS

1. It was asserted that organizational pressures usually force compromise of rationality to a greater or lesser extent. Why should this be so?
2. What do we mean by a "loop" in a marketing information system (MIS)? Explain in some detail.
3. Compare and contrast the decision model used in an MIS with the gasoline-pricing decision model described in Chapter 5.
4. What is a control system? From your observation, to what extent do brand managers achieve the degree of control implied in the MIS?
5. Describe the benefits alleged to result from an MIS.

7

Marketing programming and control: Formal decision techniques

INTRODUCTION

THE MARKETING INFORMATION SYSTEM (MIS) developed in Chapter 6, particularly as it was shown in Figure 6–5, presented an ideal approach to marketing programming. It implied, however, that decision models which focus the profit equation (profit = revenue − cost) on the brand manager's planning and control activities are available for each of the dimensions of action. Are these available in fact? Is the decision technology up to the requirements posed by the MIS?

The purpose of this chapter is to attempt to answer these questions by presenting some of the models and the nature of the problems encountered in their use. Specifically, models for optimizing a single marketing input, for optimizing the marketing mix, and for optimizing the allocation of a marketing budget to segments will be discussed. These formal models assume away one of the most important practical aspects of marketing management: the generation of alternatives of action. In an ongoing operation, two steps preceding the generation of alternatives are the warning that a problem exists and the formulation of the problem.

Most of the formal models also assume that maximum short-term profit is the brand manager's goal. We will accept this assumption throughout this chapter up to a point. This simplification will enable us to concentrate on the appropriate apparatus for meeting the minimum profit constraint which probably will in the future tend to become more a part of his goal. When we reach the section on sales as a goal, however, the complete goal of maximum sales volume with minimum profit constraint and some of its consequences will be described in precise terms.

CONTROL OF MARKETING PLAN

We will begin by examining the realism of the assumptions that the ideal system of Figure 6–5 made about the nature of control. There we assumed that control comes after the marketing plan is initiated. Although this is true in practice, for a number of reasons which will become clear in this and the next chapter, control in fact occupies a primary position.

Ideally, the system should be specific enough that when it triggers the indication that some kind of a problem exists, the particular area of the problem is identified. As the president of North American Rockwell put it in criticizing past practices of the company, "there was no system to show you quickly when you were in trouble, and if there was any action to take, what action."[1] The problem should be automatically *formulated*, and the control system should indicate not only that a problem exists but also what kind of a problem it is. It could indicate, for example, that the advertising medium is unsatisfactory. If this happens, the decision model should then proceed to evaluate all possible alternatives of media.

Thus the control system would identify that a problem exists and *formulate* the problem in the sense of indicating in what area of the marketing plan there is a deficiency, while the decision model would specify the alternative solutions and evaluate them in terms of maximum short-term profits. This assumes away the practical problem of time lag: the brand manager must be notified in sufficient time to make the change in the plan and to execute it, a fact which was incorporated into the MIS of Figure 6–5. In this way a new marketing plan would be ready for execution. This highly idealized version of control was implicit in the MIS of Figure 6–5.

The brand manager currently does not have the luxury of such a system. He has a control system which warns him about some of his problems, but he finds out about these problems in other ways, too. Further, his control system is general; it may operate, for example, in terms of market share. Any of the three variables—advertising, price, or sales— could be the "problem." The system is not specific enough. Finally, his decision models will not test *all* alternatives. These three aspects of his decision process—becoming aware of problems, formulating the problem, and deciding upon the alternatives to be tested—are now largely intuitive. Thus a large intuitive gap exists between the brand manager knowing he has some kind of a problem and the utilization of a decision model.

Fortunately control is receiving increasing attention, both because the problem is becoming greater and the techniques for dealing with it have

---

[1] *Business Week*, July 15, 1972, p. 44.

improved. The problem is more urgent, for one reason, because the marketing environment has become more dynamic, especially with the increased flow of new products developing out of the expanded research expenditures since World War II. Thus a market requires more careful and regular monitoring. Also, as companies have grown, they have more *people* to control or evaluate. Because the brand manager supervises so few people, however, he is almost entirely concerned with evaluating his *plan* and obtaining diagnostic insights rather than with controlling people. For this reason we have said nothing about controlling people here. When such a problem exists, it can obviously arise either because the plan was incorrect in the sense that it did not "fit" the uncontrollable environment or because the plan was correct but improperly executed. To incorporate the evaluation of the execution into the system greatly complicates it. Finally, the power of adequate control has probably become better recognized.

New control techniques are helping to define the practical problem of control more clearly. These techniques have developed out of quality control and servomechanism or feedback theory generally. Control, which involves a considerable and rapid flow of data, raises some sophisticated statistical questions.[2] We can expect more attention to the control problem in marketing.

MARKETING STRATEGY AND ALTERNATIVES TO BE EVALUATED

Logically, the number of alternatives to be considered can be literally infinite, for example, if price alternatives are 16 cents and 17 cents, 16.5 cents is always another alternative. But the interpolation implied by this example is not the difficult problem, because if we know what the sales are at 15 and 16 cents, experience causes us to be comfortable drawing a straight line between the two points. Even here we must be careful, however, because "crossing the decile," such as 39 cents to 41 cents, can create a major decision. Extrapolation is quite another matter, however. If we know the sales for a 15-cent price and a 17-cent price, what do we estimate they will be for a 10-cent price? The human mind is simply incapable of handling a large number of alternatives. The computer can, if it has the necessary program.

To get data of the effect of any variable such as price for even a short range of variation is quite expensive and may not always be feasible. To the extent that we consider a wider range of alternatives, the cost of the market research becomes greater.

The brand manager has some simplifying devices for dealing with the

[2]J. U. Farley and M. J. Hinich, "Tracking Marketing Parameters in Random Noise," *Marketing and Economic Development* (Chicago: American Marketing Association, 1966), pp. 365–70.

problem of limiting the number of alternative plans he considers. He has a strategy, that is, he works within a framework of the *brand strategy*. When his product was introduced, considerable thought was devoted to where to "position" it in relation to other brands in the product class. When Maxim coffee was introduced, General Foods was deeply concerned about whether to position it "close" to existing brands. By naming it Maxim, it probably gained strength, but this ran the risk of "cannibalizing" existing brands carrying the Maxwell House name. The concept of "closeness," as we indicated in Chapter 2, is in terms of how similar the buyer perceives the brands in terms of how he thinks about them in talking with others (brand comprehension) and in terms of how well they each serve his needs (attitude). As the brand manager considers the positioning of his brand, he is simultaneously segmenting his market to identify target market(s). He infers the brand attributes peculiar to the natures of customers in each segment. Then, by considering together segment needs and possible positions along with his own competitive strengths and those of the competitors he would be "close to," he chooses a strategy. A *strategy* is a set of rules which *delimit* the *number* of alternative *courses of action* (plans) to be considered and which is usually agreed upon with higher management. Thus, through a strategy the number of alternatives is reduced to a manageable few.

An example of a marketing strategy is found in women's clothing. There a company can take a low-price–low-quality strategy or a high-price–high-quality strategy. Once this strategy is fixed, the kind of retail store it will be sold in, the size of the retail margin, the level of advertising, and so forth are seriously delimited. If it is a high-price–high-quality brand, it will be sold effectively only in "quality" stores with a high markup and substantial advertising. Bobbie Brooks, Inc., with $150,000,000 in sales and an ad budget of $1,500,000 aimed mainly at teenage girls, apparently has taken this route.[3]

Thus a strategy can be defined at various levels of generality. The more general and the less specific it is, the greater the latitude it offers the brand manager. It permits greater play of imaginative effort. On the other hand, being less restrictive, it does not offer him as much guidance.

The term "strategy" as used here is consistent with the meaning of "strategic" as opposed to operating or tactical as it is used in the title of this book. In this sense, strategic refers to longer term and ordinarily higher level decisions. The effect of strategy is to limit the alternatives that are available to people lower in the organization.

Typically, once a new product is well on its way to complete introduction—all test markets are finished and "roll out" over the country is almost accomplished—it is released to the complete control of the brand

---

[3] *Advertising Age*, July 27, 1970, p. 3.

manager. Prior to this point he has ostensibly been in charge, but the marketing manager has held a tight rein which limits the brand manager's freedom of choice. Thus the brand manager inherits a strategy which was formulated during the introduction and roll out. He will continuously monitor it to see if certain major conditions have changed. If they have, he will contemplate a new strategy and attempt to get the concurrence of the marketing manager. There is some evidence that brands tend to be "restaged"—a new strategy is developed—about every three years.

PROGRAMMING

In presenting a set of principles for marketing programming and investigating their application, it will be assumed that the facts are known with certainty instead of with uncertainty. Statistical decision theory has been developed in recent years for dealing with uncertainty in a systematic way. Because it is probably more justified with long-term decisions, however, it will be introduced in Chapter 12.[4]

Principles of programming

We have seen, in Chapter 5, how a pricing decision is made intuitively (Figure 5–7). Here we will present a more formal approach, but you will recognize that the heart of the current managing task is to bring together the intuitive and the formal into a meaningful pattern. Only a very few decisions—choices among given alternatives—can be handled in a completely formal way. From his intuition, however, the manager should be able to make quantitative estimates that can be treated formally. When this is done, the results could be considerably better than from intuition alone. Further, major developments in cost and demand analysis are now under way which will convert a considerable portion of what is now intuitive into a more formal approach. The precise nature of these developments will be discussed later after we have had an opportunity to build a background which will contribute to their meaningfulness. But we must recognize there is a *creative* element in market planning, the act of selecting alternatives to be considered, which will remain intuitive forever. To merge these formal and intuitive approaches into an effective working arrangement is difficult, and the attempt will inevitably create serious tensions when first introduced into a company.

Formal methods are appropriate under two conditions. The first is when it can be assumed that the brand manager's professional goal is to make the greatest possible profits, specifically short-term profits. As stated in Chapter 5, short-term profits may, in some companies, be in fact the goal. Probably more often in current practice, the brand manager is given

---

[4]Rex V. Brown, *Decision Theory: Useful Tool for Marketing Managers,* Marketing Science Institute, October 1969.

an expense budget and the goal of maximizing his sales (market share) within the constraints of the budget. The computer is making cost data more specific and more generally known, however, and so profit maximizing will probably become a much more common goal at the middle lower levels. The second condition is when the relevant inputs to the decision—cost and revenue—can be quantified. In many cases, this may not be entirely possible, but the brand manager can make subjective estimates. Then too, important nonquantifiable factors can be treated as additional constraints on the decision. If, for example, two alternatives differ on a nonquantifiable factor such as the effect of competition, profit estimates can be computed which leave the choice to be made on only two dimensions, profit and this nonquantifiable element, thus immensely simplifying the choice.

SHORT-RUN OPTIMIZING. The logic of short-run optimizing is important in *conceptualizing the problem, obtaining the appropriate facts, processing the data,* and *interpreting the results.* As noted in Chapter 4, it helps the brand manager communicate with accountants and others in the organization that he needs to work with in order to get the facts. But this logic is rigorous, and there seem to be severe limits on how much it can be simplified while retaining the essential elements. It can be discussed in terms of graphs or symbolic equations, or both. Because everyone can understand graphs but some lack the mathematical exposure to work comfortably with equations, we will use graphs.

Figure 7–1 spells out a set of universally applicable guiding principles by which the brand manager selecting the best plan for any decision can quantitatively manipulate the variables that will achieve his goal of maximum profits. To accomplish this, we bring together competitive relations (Chapter 2), the concept of an aggregate response curve (Chapter 3), and cost analysis (Chapter 4). These three elements are the central features of the brand manager's environment. Because this logic developed historically in terms of price setting, we will first deal with it in this artificial setting and then generalize it to a realistic and appropriate form for all other decisions.

By short-run decisions is meant those in which some costs do not change. Thus, for the purposes of this particular decision, the unchanging costs are fixed. This idea of the fixed/variable distinction (from Chapter 4) becomes a central concept in the analysis. The short-run, average-cost curve that results from making this distinction is related to marginal cost (MC), as shown in graph A of Figure 7–1, where dollars of the unit cost are shown on the Y axis and volume of sales on the X axis. We assume that all production is immediately sold so that sales are identical with production.

The specific nature of these relationships was spelled out in Table 4–2 in Chapter 4, and it may be helpful to review it. The average variable cost and the average fixed cost have been omitted for the sake of clarity. It should be remembered, however, that the level of marginal cost is related to total cost only insofar as total cost is influenced by one of its constituent elements, variable cost. The other component of total cost, which is fixed cost, is not affected by changes in the volume of output.

FIGURE 7–1
Decision concepts

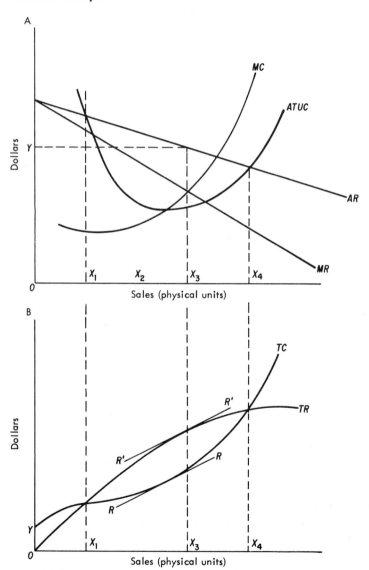

AR in graph A is the sum of the response curves of individual buyers, or the aggregate response curve, to price, and so it relates total purchases to the level of price. It represents the responses the brand manager anticipates buyers will make to different levels of price. Thus, price is shown on the *Y* axis. From Chapter 2 it is known that *AR* also depends upon the behavior of the company's competitors. For the sake of simplicity, assume that the company is in an industry with a competitive structure that encourages price leadership behavior and that the company happens to be this leader. Thus, any price change by this company will be followed immediately by all competitors.

In Figure 7–1, the line labeled *MR* is "marginal revenue," the counterpart of marginal cost (*MC*). Marginal revenue is the change in total revenue divided by the corresponding change in units sold. *MR* falls faster than *AR* because in order to sell an additional unit, the price must be lowered. Thus, the return from each unit is decreased as a result of selling the one additional unit, assuming, of course, that price changes are passed on to consumers by the middleman and that there is no discrimination among buyers. Therefore, the addition to total revenue from selling that additional unit is less than the price of that unit. The physical quantities of production and sales are assumed to be equal; there is no finished-goods inventory.

The most profitable operating position for the company—the maximum *contribution* to company *profit*—is at that price which will permit the brand to sell at such a rate that the level of sales is where marginal revenue equals marginal cost. For example, if the company portrayed in graph A of Figure 7–1 was producing and selling at a level of OX_2, it could increase its profit by expanding production, because at OX_2 marginal cost is less than marginal revenue. The additional units would add less to total cost than the additional sales would add to total revenue. Profit could be improved by lowering price and by increasing sales and production up to OX_3. Beyond OX_3, marginal cost is greater than marginal revenue—additional units will add more to total cost than they will add to total revenue. Finally, if production is expanded beyond OX_4, the company will be operating at a loss because average cost (*ATUC*) exceeds the price (*AR*). Any level of production between OX_1 and OX_4 is profitable, but OX_3 is the most profitable. To illustrate the application of the profit-maximizing principle, the level of production is set so that *marginal cost* (*MC*) equals *marginal revenue* (*MR*). This rule of price setting which yields the maximum contribution to profit is termed the *short-run optimizing principle*.

Let us turn now to a much more useful, realistic, and universally applicable version of the principle. Graph B of Figure 7–1 represents the identical situation described in graph A, but the facts are shown in total figures instead of averages. These figures can be obtained from graph A by multiplying the quantity at each level of production by the price (AR) to get total revenue (TR), and by the average total unit cost ($ATUC$) to get total cost (TC). The transition to graph B is, however, more significant than a mere exercise in arithmetic because this new form can be generalized to all kinds of short-run decisions. In this form, the logic of profit maximizing can be applied meaningfully to the wide range of nonprice marketing decisions, including advertising and selling; for example, "dollars of advertising" can replace price on the vertical axis of Figure 7–1. Thus, the "total figures" of graph B are more useful than the "average figures" of graph A. Then, too, management usually tends to look at the problem in the form of graph B.

Price is less clear in this form, however, since it is reflected in the slope of TR and must be computed accordingly. It can easily be converted into the same type of problem for allocating funds as in advertising and selling, however. In firms in the package-goods or grocery industry such as General Foods, General Mills, and Procter & Gamble, a budget is established for price cutting, or "dealing" as it is called. Wherever the brand manager decides to reduce the price on his product, that budget is reduced, or "spent," by the quantity sold at that reduced price times the amount of the price reduction per unit. The brand manager treats this budget in the same way as he does his advertising and sales-force budget. (This procedure, incidentally, casts B in Figure 3–1 in the same form as the other three subfigures there.) Hereafter, we will speak of a "dealing budget" in considering the role of a price cut in the marketing plan as identical to that of advertising and sales effort, namely, an expenditure of funds. Both can be handled the same way in graph B of Figure 7–1.

The corresponding relationships between graphs A and B are indicated by the dashed lines. At a level of production and sales in graph B less than OX_1 or greater than OX_4, the company would be encountering losses because total costs would exceed total revenue. Any level of production between OX_1 and OX_4 would yield a profit, but OX_3 is the most profitable level. When "total figures" are used, the marginal values are indicated graphically by the slopes or mathematically by the "rates of change."

In order to use the profit-maximizing principle in deciding at which level to produce and sell, the level of production must be found where the slopes of the total-cost curve and the total-revenue curve are equal. Geometrically this position can be determined by drawing two parallel lines (RR and $R'R'$) which will indicate the maximum profit position when one line is tangent to TR and the other is tangent to TC. The distance between TR and TC, which indicates profit, is maximum at this point. This principle of identity of slopes between TC and TR—the short-run optimizing principle—is important to remember because it will be used in this and succeeding chapters.

A widely used management tool called the *break-even chart* describes a set of facts similar but not identical to those shown in Figure 7–1. The break-even chart assumes the lines are straight. It is useful in solving marketing problems, especially in quickly communicating the problem and solution to others in managemenт. It is also helpful in the creative task of formulating alternative courses of action and serves as a first step in setting up feasible courses of action for the second stage of the problem-solving process—estimating the revenue and cost consequences of those alternatives. It has the conceptual weakness, however, of being cast in terms of *net profit* instead of contribution to profit. For this reason it can be highly misleading for short-term analysis.

In practice, the short-run optimizing analysis shown in graphs A and B of Figure 7–1 also has its limitations. Historically, information about the demand relation (aggregate response curve) has usually been lacking. Much of it has been qualitative, and when it was quantitative, the whole range of values for any given demand relation was seldom known. These "gaps" existed in the information because it was difficult to predict the actions of either buyers or competitors. Analogous problems were encountered on the cost side, but usually they were not so serious. Stated in mathematical terms, the limitations of the model were: the demand and cost functions often could not be described with sufficient precision, the functions were not continuous over the relevant range, and the functions were not differentiable.

Recent developments, however, appear to make the optimizing model more practical. First, demand measurements are more feasible. The buyer-behavior theory that was set forth in Chapter 3 and will be applied in the next chapter augurs well for the future. Second, the theory of cost (as presented in Chapter 4) has long been available, but the sheer economics of separating cost according to its components in a large company has been insuperable. The computer is changing that, however. Two large companies, at least, have already made the decision to make available (even to salesmen) on a regular basis the incremental cost of each relevent product. Clearly, this capacity can serve the brand manager.

These developments in furthering the trend toward quantitative marketing management will obviously bring organizational changes. Incentive arrangements can be designed to incorporate the profit goal, and a tendency to further decentralize can be expected to develop.

Application of optimizing principle to single marketing input

To return to the problems of developing the decision model required by the MIS of Figure 6–5, we will consider some applications of this profit-maximizing concept. We will first show how the optimizing concept is applied to a *single marketing input*, namely, advertising, and then how it applies to planning, which requires that all marketing effort—the entire marketing mix of advertising, price, and sales force—be dealt with simultaneously. Finally, the problem of allocating that total effort to market segments will be discussed.

The profit-optimizing principle can be used in formulating decisions as to how much should be spent in advertising, as shown in Figure 7–2.

FIGURE 7–2
Optimizing single marketing input: Advertising

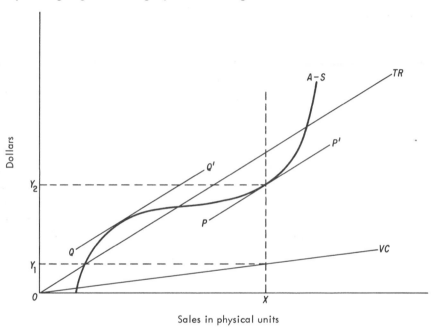

Sales in physical units

A–S is the *aggregate response curve* to advertising (as presented at the outset in Chapter 3), and it relates response of buyers to the amount of advertising (Y_1Y_2) injected into the market. Consequently, advertising is a cost that must be related to other relevant costs in making a decision according to maximum profit.

Hence, total variable cost is the advertising expenditures (A–S) added to the nonadvertising variable cost (VC) shown as Y_0Y_1. An example is production cost in relation to the various volumes of sales that the respective advertising expenditures will yield. TR is the total revenue that would accrue with various sales volumes at a given price. To obtain the advertising expenditure (Y_1Y_2), a line is drawn parallel to the total revenue relation (TR) and tangent to the combined advertising-sales relation and nonadvertising variable cost (A–S). The tangent line is shown as PP'.

In this way the short-run optimizing principle is applied to the choice among alternative advertising budgets.

Another point of tangency that would be parallel with total revenue is shown by the line *QQ'*, but it is a *minimum* profit position. As shown in Figure 7–2, at the level of advertising where *QQ'* is tangent to A–S, the combined cost of advertising and nonadvertising variable cost is greater than the sales revenue (*TR*) that would accrue, and thus it would be more profitable for the company to spend no money for advertising. Admittedly, the sales volume would be small, but it would still be more profitable than if advertising were used.

Obtaining the empirical content of the A–S curve will be dealt with in Chapter 8. The relation also implies some assumption about the nature of competitive behavior described in Chapter 2. Finally, estimates of nonadvertising cost can be obtained, as discussed earlier in this chapter and presented, with examples, in Chapter 4.

This presentation of the problem of setting an advertising budget may seem too abstract to be useful. Yet it does point up the questions that must be answered if advertising budget decisions are to be made optimally and if the advertising is primarily expected to have a short-run effect. This formal approach has two advantages: it provides an optimum answer, and it does so in one step.

Application of optimizing principle to planning: The marketing mix

How do we bring all the marketing inputs together—advertising, price, and selling—into an optimum mix? A total marketing budget can be built up by optimizing each input and adding them together, providing they are independent of each other in their effects. This independence assumption is examined below. Alternatively, the total marketing budget can be set intuitively in terms of the overall strategy discussed above. This total is then treated as an allocation problem which involves solving simultaneously the three relations involved in the marketing mix. This simultaneous solution can be accomplished by linear programming techniques, which are appropriate for resource-limited problems, whereas marginal analysis is appropriate when there is no limitation of resources.

Like all mathematical techniques, linear programming is subject to certain limitations which can sometimes preclude its use. One of these is implied in its name: the relations must be linear. For many problems, however, this is probably not a serious limitation. A second restriction is sometimes more serious. Linear programming assumes that the three elements—advertising, pricing, and selling effort—are independent of each other. This condition implies that pricing, for example, will have the same effect on purchases irrespective of the levels of advertising. We are quite sure that in some situations this is not true; for example, there is good evidence that price will have differing effects depending upon whether it is advertised, and so the independence assumption can be invalid. For many cases, however, the assumption holds and the technique is adequate.

In summary, the marketing mix problem is solvable under some conditions, probably not uncommon ones. We are left with the task of allocating to market segments, which appears to be becoming increasingly important.

Application of formal model to allocation to market segments

For many years, sales managers have recognized that a salesman usually gets better results if he is given some direction instead of being left completely free to call upon whom he wishes. Ideally, of course, this direction merely gives him information about what customers are more likely to buy, and he is left free to use it in pursuing his own goals. If the organization goals are properly structured, this procedure will suffice. Usually, this "allocation" of the salesman, this guiding him where to go, is geographic in some sense—a salesman spends more of his time in Indianapolis, Indiana, than in Paducah, Kentucky, for example.

Geographic allocation, however, is only a special case of the very general problem of allocating marketing effort among any kind of market segments. Allocating total marketing effort to geographic area is, in principle, no different than allocating advertising to different advertising media, setting prices to different markets, and so forth. In fact, geography has tended to become a less important criterion of allocation. As we will see, it was with the problem of setting of prices to different geographic markets that the principles of market segmentation were first delineated.

The idea of market segmentation has recently received increasing attention. Its relevance was discussed in Chapter 2 and its nature in Chapter 3. Events are taking place which make it more necessary for the brand manager to pay more attention to its potential. An example is fractionation of media such as the possibilities for CATV and even TV casettes.

Any discussion of the guiding principles by which the brand manager should take advantage of market-segmenting possibilities may seem far removed from reality. People differ in many ways, and thus many criteria are available by which buyers can be grouped so as to render them more homogeneous than they would be if all the individuals were simply thrown together. These are the purchase rates of different buyers; demographic variables such as age, income, size of family, and life cycle; physical characteristics such as skin and hair texture; psychographic characteristics such as attitude toward a brand and intention to buy that brand; and media habits, such as whether buyers listen to television a lot and read many newspapers. In industrial markets the criteria would be expected to be quite different from the consumer criteria listed above. And herein lies much of the heart of the problem of market segmentation.

Without doubt, buyers can be grouped by any or all of these characteristics, but as we will see, the characteristic that matters for allocation purposes is the shape of the buyer's response curve for each of the segments, as emphasized in Chapter 3. In the next chapter we will discuss getting the data necessary for allocating marketing to market segments.

PRINCIPLES OF ALLOCATION. Economic theory of the partial-equilibrium type provides the clearest available statement of the principles of allocating marketing effort to market segments. You will recognize these principles as those associated in economic discussions with price discrimination, but at this point we are not concerned with economic or social welfare judgments.

Assume that, as in Figure 7–3, we have five geographic markets that are completely separate and independent. Let us put to work our profit-optimizing concepts presented above. For *each* market there is a demand curve (*D*), or aggregate buyer-response curve, and a marginal-revenue curve (*MR*). The markets are arranged from left to right according to increasing elasticity of *D* and consequent *MR*. There is only one marginal-cost curve (*MC*) that is common to all five markets. To array the markets according to elasticity of *D* and *MR* is to place them in decreasing order of profitability. The most profitable market will be served first, the second most profitable next, and so forth. Obviously, this also results in ordering according to decreasing price per unit. The company can always sell more

FIGURE 7–3
Optimum price setting to segments

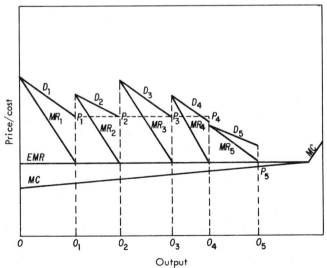

Output

Source: Eli W. Clemens, "Price Discrimination and the Multiple-Product Firm," *Review of Economic Studies*, Vol. 19 (1950-51), p. 5.

in market 1 by lowering the price, as indicated by D_1, but the question is: Where should the price be set in market 1 so as to have the most profitable combination of price and sales volume in the combined five markets?

To answer this question we must consider all five markets, and the optimizing rule is: *Set the price in each market so as to distribute the company's production and sales among the five markets in such manner that (1) marginal revenue is the same in all markets and (2) this common level of marginal revenue is equal to the common marginal cost.* The level of the marginal-cost curve (MC) changes at different levels of sales on the O axis, as shown in Figure 7–3. The specific marginal cost is that level in market 5 where MR_5 intersects MC, the least profitable market. Thus the prices are set so that the level of marginal revenue in each market is equal to the equal-marginal-revenue curve (EMR). The EMR line is derived by identifying the MR and MC intersection of the least profitable market and then aggregating the marginal-revenue curves of the five markets to this level. Thus, the optimal price that the brand manager should set in each market is P_1, P_2, P_3, P_4, and P_5, respectively.

We began the analysis by assuming that the company in Figure 7–3 had already decided to serve these five markets, and the only question remaining had to do with how to set the optimal prices. Often the issue, however, is whether the company should attempt to serve a particular market at all. If MC were lower, it would intersect with MR_5 at a higher level of production and sales. Prices should move down as the EMR lowered correspondingly. If MC was enough lower, the next least profitable market (market 6, not shown here) would be served. The rule is: Serve each market as long as the price exceeds marginal cost, which is the additional cost of serving that market. In Figure 7–3, price is just a little above marginal cost in market 5. If our company were confronted with a rising MR it would ration the product to market 5. The EMR would move up, prices would move up correspondingly, and market 5 would receive a smaller volume at a higher price.

R.C.A.'s cut in the prices of their recordings a few years ago illustrates this principle of setting price differentials. The prices on most types of the slower speed recordings were sharply reduced, although a few were left the same, but the price of 78 rpm recordings was actually increased. Let us assume the marginal costs of producing and selling the two types of records were approximately the same. The 78 rpm records were considered obsolete, and purchasers of these recordings were thought to be insensitive to price. They were being purchased only by consumers who had playing sets that, when worn out, would be replaced by newer types that do not use 78 rpm records. Most of the 78 rpm playing sets still in use were probably the expensive kind and of superior performance; therefore, the record price was small in relation to the quality of the service. Thus price provided only a limited deterrent to purchase. On the other hand many people were buying the slower speed equipment, and the higher record price could have discouraged them.

The experience of the management of a title and trust company also illustrates the application of market segmentation. The company's stock in trade is to search the legal titles for real estate to insure that they are clear of legal claims. In the past, it had priced the service according to each title searched rather than offering a quantity discount. A group of 15 attorneys interested in land that was lying vacant and unused because of back taxes approached the company requesting a special rate. This land would have gone unrecovered if the regular title fee had been charged because it would have been impossible to sell the lots at a profit; the delinquent taxes plus the title clearance fees would have made them too expensive. By setting a lower price to the 15 attorneys, additional sales of the company's services were obtained. It was estimated that 3,000 lots were recovered each year as a result of the segmenting.

To summarize the principles of allocation to market segments, certain conditions are essential for such allocation to take place. First, the *aggregate response curves* must be different from segment to segment. If they are not, no profit will be gained in such allocation, and the time and effort devoted to it will be wasted. Second, the boundaries between the segments must *seal off* one segment from another. In the case of price differences, this condition requires that buyers be unable to buy in the cheap market and then in effect "export" it to the higher priced segments. This can be a problem in the package-goods industry selling to large chains with stores widely dispersed geographically. More generally, the condition requires that there be no across-boundary effects. Given these conditions, the decision rule is to set the prices in such a way that the marginal revenue in each market is equal to the marginal cost that is common across the segments, as indicated above. If the cost varies across segments, marginal revenue must equal marginal cost in each market.

ALLOCATION TO ANY SEGMENTS. A more complex set of ideas can be used to put these principles to work in allocating any kind of marketing effort, not just price. Obviously, once a total optimal marketing expenditure is set, there remains the question of how to allocate it to market segments where the aggregate response curves differ among the segments.

An alternative approach to the one suggested here of setting the total marketing budget and *then* allocating it to segments is to allocate first and then sum the individual allocations to achieve an optimal *unconstrained* budget. The aggregate response curve we use to set the optimal budget assumes that the marketing budget was optimally allocated to segments in the first place.

The principle of formal allocation is merely an extension of the short-run optimizing logic we have been discussing, but now we must think in terms of market segments and use the principles of price discrimination. An illustration will make this clearer.

The rule for an optimum allocation to market segments is that the *ratio of the variable cost of marketing effort to sales in each territory should be equal.* This rule is developed as a consequence of two assumptions, which will be explained subsequently. It is illustrated in Figure 7–4, which shows two territories and the relation between variable marketing cost and sales in each. The allocation to each market is $2,000 when the appropriation is the same in each market. It is clear that, by reducing the expenditure in territory 1 and increasing it in territory 2, total sales can be

FIGURE 7–4
Comparison of two allocations of marketing effort

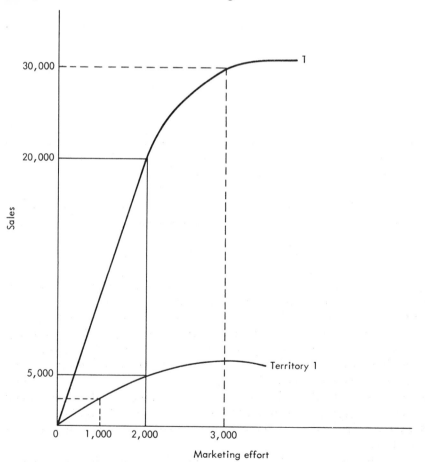

increased without increasing total expenditures. For example, by reducing expenditures in territory 1 from $2,000 to $1,000 and increasing them in territory 2 from $2,000 to $3,000, total sales can be increased by $7,500, even though total expenditure remains the same.

The brand manager, however, must decide *how much* of a shift in marketing cost among his territories is necessary to achieve the optimum allocation. A method for answering this question for any number of segments has been developed,[5] but for the sake of simplicity it will be assumed that there are only two sales territories, as in Figure 7–4.

First, for some representative past period we need to know the relations between total variable marketing effort and sales in each of the two territories which, of course, are the aggregate response curves to total marketing effort. We assume that this relation is described by a_1, a_2, and α in the following equations:

$$f_1(x_1) = a_1 x_1^{\alpha}. \tag{1}$$
$$f_2(x_2) = a_2 x_2^{\alpha}. \tag{2}$$

These equations define the assumptions under which the model operates, but they are less important in practice than Equations 3, 4, 5, and 6, which actually tell the brand manager how to compute the optimal expenditure for each of his territories. In Equation 1, $f_1(x_1)$ is the cost of marketing the x_{1st} article in Territory 1. Likewise in Equation 2, $f_2(x_2)$ is the cost of selling the x_{2nd} article in Territory 2. The exponent α indicates the shape of the aggregate response curve. With a_1 and a_2 solved by Equations 5 and 6 below, the following equations can be used to obtain an approximation of the optimum allocation:

$$\dfrac{A}{\left(\dfrac{a_1}{a_2}\right)^{\frac{1}{\alpha}} + 1,} \tag{3}$$

$$e_2 = \dfrac{A}{\left(\dfrac{a_2}{a_1}\right)^{\frac{1}{\alpha}} + 1.} \tag{4}$$

In Equations 3 and 4, A is the total marketing expense to be allocated, and e_1 and e_2 are the allocations to the respective territories.

Let us work through the example, which is graphically portrayed in Figure 7–5. Last year, when the total marketing effort of $4,000 was allocated equally between the two territories, the company sold $16,000 in

[5]John A. Howard, *Marketing Management*, 2d ed. (Homewood, Ill: Richard D. Irwin, Inc., 1963), Appendix.

FIGURE 7–5
Optimum allocation of marketing effort: An example

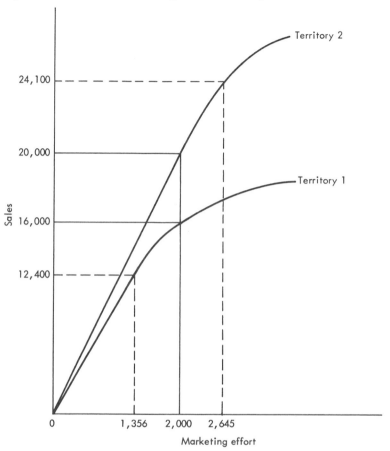

territory 1 and $20,000 in territory 2. Let us assume that experience suggests that in each of the two territories the exponent, α, is 0.5. First the brand manager obtains the value for a_1 in Equation 1, in which E_1 is last year's expenditure and x_1 is last year's sales in territory 1:

$$a_1 = \frac{(\alpha+1)E_1'}{x_1'^{\,\alpha+1}} = \frac{(1.5)(2,000)}{(16,000)^{1.5}} = .001485. \tag{5}$$

$$a_2 = \frac{(\alpha+1)E_2'}{x_2'^{\,\alpha+1}} = \frac{(1.5)(2,000)}{(20,000)^{1.5}} = .001060. \tag{6}$$

Using Equations 3 and 4, the optimum allocations, e_1 and e_2, of the total appropriation, A, can be computed:

$$e_1 = \frac{A}{\left(\dfrac{a_1}{a_2}\right)^{\frac{1}{\alpha}} + 1} = \frac{4,000}{\left(\dfrac{0.001485}{0.001060}\right)^{\frac{1}{0.5}} + 1} = \frac{4,000}{(1.401)^2 + 1} \cong \$1,356,$$

$$e_2 = \frac{A}{\left(\dfrac{a_2}{a_1}\right)^{\frac{1}{\alpha}} + 1} = \frac{4,000}{\left(\dfrac{0.001060}{0.001485}\right)^{\frac{1}{0.5}} + 1} = \frac{4,000}{(0.714)^2 + 1} \cong \$2,645.$$

The optimal allocations to territories 1 and 2 are $1,356 and $2,645, respectively. The important question is how much sales will be increased by the reallocation of marketing effort between the two markets. Under the new allocations, territory 1 yields sales of $12,400 and territory 2, $24,100. The total new sales are $36,500, exceeding by $500 the sales obtained under the method of equal allocation of expenditures to territories.

As a final step, the condition for optimal allocation can be checked. At the beginning of the discussion, the rule given was that the ratio of variable marketing effort to sales must be the same in all territories. In territory 1, the ratio is 0.1093; in territory 2, 0.1097. They are only slightly different; whereas, under equal allocation, the ratios were 0.125 and 0.100, respectively.

The method may yield only an approximation of the optimum allocation because it has been assumed that the value of α (0.5) was known and that it is the same in both territories, and (2) it has also been assumed that the underlying factors which determine the relationships between variable selling cost and sales have not changed significantly. The crucial task in using the model is, of course, to estimate α, which describes the shape of the aggregate response curves, and this problem is discussed in the next chapter. As for the constancy of the functions, the brand manager will have ideas about whether they may have changed. In general we would expect considerable stability in them.

Various operations research models have been developed in recent years to perform this task of allocating marketing effort.[6] In fact, in the quantitative literature they have taken center stage. Often not obvious is that most of them basically depend upon the marginal optimality conditions that we have used throughout this chapter. Now that more managers are becoming familiar with them, data are available, and the computer's data processing capacity can be utilized, we can be sure that a more critical view will be taken of their usefulness. These allocating models are of two kinds: one allocates a given budget most effectively, as does the example shown here, and another allocates it most cheaply to achieve a given set of goals. Company policy in the given situation determines

[6] O. A. Davis and J. U. Farley, "Allocating Sales Force Effort with Commissions and Quotas," *Management Science: Application*, Part II, December 1971, pp. 55–63.

which method is appropriate. In some cases the brand manager is given a budget, and in others he is assigned a set of goals, of which he can optimize one and treat the others as constraints.

SALES AS A GOAL

Max Sales
st $\pi^* \geq \pi^0$

After following the rigorous logic of profit maximization, the reader may wonder how it can be reconciled with a volume or growth goal, which we know occupies so much of management's attention. The purpose of this section is to show how this reconciliation is achieved.[7] It also indicates when the profit-optimizing framework is appropriate for the brand manager and when it is not.

As indicated in Chapter 5, profit is probably a primary goal for most companies, but it is a minimum level which in financial terms is the cost of capital. More specifically, it is the opportunity cost of the funds employed in the brand, the rate of return on the project which will leave unchanged the market price of the company's stock.[8] In most normal situations, brand managers achieve the minimum and so are free to pursue the second most important goal, which is growth. Thus a realistic goal for most brand management is *maximum sales volume* in dollar terms, with a *minimum profit constraint*. Other constraints more or less unique to each situation may also operate.

In the economist's frame of reference, where (as we saw in Chapter 4), the activity is always production, there is an output which will maximize the volume of sales. It occurs when *marginal revenue is zero*. This is shown in Figure 7–6, where dollars of cost, revenue, and profit are shown on the vertical axis and output or physical volume on the horizontal axis. The maximum sales is at the OQ_s output. At that point an increase in output achieved through lowering price will not increase total revenue. Price is represented by the slope of TR. The area of the rectangle OQ_s, R_s, P_4 is larger than at any other volume, as you can estimate from "eyeballing it".

This volume, however, will not maximize profit. The brand manager's maximum profit output will be only about 60 percent of that amount, which is OQ_p. If his minimum profit constraint is only P_1, however, the output that maximizes sales revenue will easily satisfy the constraint. At this level his sales-maximizing price will be O_sR_s/OQ_s, that is, the dollar sales divided by the number of units.

On the other hand, if his minimum profit constraint is OP_2, output OQ_s will not yield adequate profit, and sales will have to be reduced to OQ_c

[7]William Baumol, *Economic Theory and Operations Analysis* (Englewood Cliffs, N.J.: Prentice-Hall, Inc., 1961), chap. 10.

[8]J. C. Van Horne, *Financial Management and Policy* (Englewood Cliffs, N.J.: Prentice-Hall, Inc., 1968), p. 110.

FIGURE 7–6
Sales maximization with minimum profit

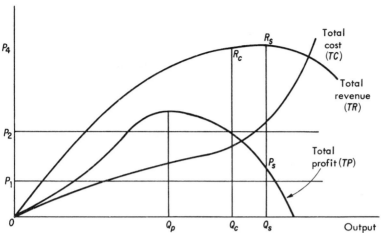

Source: W. J. Baumol, *Economic Theory and Operations Analysis* (Englewood Cliffs, N.J.: Prentice-Hall, Inc., 1961), p. 199.

which is just compatible with the minimum profit constraint. Thus, his profit-maximizing output is usually smaller.

If we take into account his decisions in the marketing plan other than the output decision, the equilibrium points in which the profit constraint is effective (OQ_c instead of OQ_s) can normally be expected to occur. We will use advertising expenditure as an example, but it applies equally well to dealing or selling.

In Figure 7–7, the horizontal axis represents amount of advertising and the vertical axis, total sales and total profit.

The shape of TR assumes that increasing advertising will, at least to some extent, always increase sales, but after a point diminishing returns are expected. If all other costs are added to the advertising cost, we get the line which shows the product's total costs (TC) (production, distribution, and selling) as a function of advertising expenditure. By subtracting these total costs from the level of dollar sales (total revenue) at each level of advertising expenditure, the total profit curve (TP) is obtained.

Here the brand manager's profit-maximizing expenditure is OA_p, at which TP is the maximum M. But if his minimum acceptable profit level is OP_1, the constrained sales-maximizing advertising outlay is OA_c. Thus it will always be better for him to increase his advertising until he is stopped by the profit constraint. Now we see why an unconstrained sales-maximizing output in Figure 7–6, will ordinarily not occur. Advertising can always be used to increase sales to a point where profit is driven to the minimum acceptable level.

FIGURE 7–7
Advertising and sales maximization

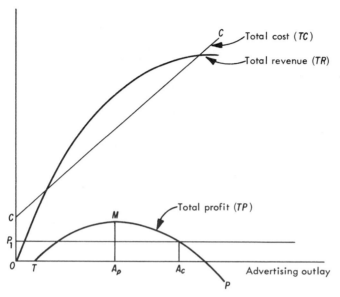

Source: W. J. Baumol, Economic Theory and Operations Analysis
(Englewood Cliffs, N.J.: Prentice-Hall, Inc., 1961), p. 200.

Thus to the extent that maximum sales level is less than minimum profit
level, profit becomes less relevant and the elaborate profit-maximizing apparatus becomes less essential. The brand manager is freer to concentrate
on that second goal of growth. Here we see why, in discussing objectives
with brand managers, the outside observer often comes away with the impression that profits don't matter, that growth is the overriding objective.
In most industries in normal times, growth is the central objective.

This apparent contradiction comes about mainly because brand managers are volume evaluated by the marketing manager. Up to now they
have not had the apparatus or appropriate data to maximize profits, even
if their bosses wanted them to. Now we have hope of supplying the data
through the new marketing technology. To use the apparatus however,
will require a restructuring of the brand manager's goal. This problem of
restructuring goals was illustrated a number of years ago in the company
whose decision process was described in Figure 5–7. The pricing decision
was pushed down to the district sales offices. Unfortunately, everyone
connected with the district sales offices had historically been evaluated in
terms of volume of sales. As indicated in discussing the intuitive decision
process of Figure 5–7, industry demand was probably quite inelastic. The

drive for volume was continued, and the results in an inelastic market were disastrous for profits. Within a short time the company found it necessary to pull the decision back up. Had the reward structure been changed and a training course initiated to teach profit maximizing, the results would probably have been different.

Are there other conditions under which the profits versus growth issue comes out sharply as it does with recession versus prosperity, for example? There are. Thinking back to Chapter 2, you will recall the discussion of instant coffee and the product cycle curve shown there in Figure 2–3. You will also recall that in the early stages of the cycle, profits were high, but as the cycle matured the growth curve levelled off and profits declined. Thus, with new products, the growth goal supersedes the profit goal, in the sense of getting management's attention. As the life cycle of the product matures, however, profit more and more comes to the fore. The brand manager with freedom to act is more likely to find himself in this latter position because, as the brand matures, he is likely to be obtaining more authority. For this reason, the profit-maximizing apparatus may be appropriate for brand managers. When the brand manager has freedom he has acquired it mainly *because* the product has stabilized and the marketing manager feels secure in turning it over to him. In the growth stages, however, the marketing manager will keep closer control and a more watchful eye, than he will when it has stabilized. Over the life of the product cycle, the two volumes—sales-maximum and profit-maximum—are typically quite different at the outset. As the product class stabilizes, the two volumes for any brand in that class tend to become the same.

SUMMARY

The role of formal programming or analysis in solving three basic marketing problems—optimizing a single marketing input, optimizing the product mix, and optimizing the allocation of marketing effort to market segments—has certain limitations. The techniques, with the exception of those for control, require as inputs the empirical content of the aggregate response curves shown in Chapter 3. The lack of these has been the Achilles heel of most of the formal models: the essential data have not been available. Chapter 8 is concerned with just this issue.

The assumption of independence of marketing inputs—advertising, price, and sales effort—raises some serious questions. One suspects that in many, if not most, cases the assumption is violated to some extent. Obviously, this is an empirical fact to be determined for each case, and methods set forth in Chapter 8 may indicate the extent of this. The simultaneity problem encountered in setting an optimum total budget and an optimally allocated budget also must be solved.

Controlling the marketing plan is a relatively virgin area in terms of formal control techniques. The role of marketing strategy in delimiting the alternate plans to be evaluated and in deciding upon the total marketing budget represents one of the most creative areas of the brand manager's activity. The growth goal also has implications for the appropriateness of profit-maximizing models.

It is questionable whether the available decision models are up to the requirements laid upon them by the ideal marketing information system. Unless ths aggregate response curve is derivable, they clearly are not. Even if they are, there will still be a large element of the intuitive in marketing management, but hopefully this will be mainly of the creative type instead of the routinized behavior that probably now characterizes much of the brand manager's work.

DISCUSSION QUESTIONS

1. Compare the brand manager's control system described here with that presented in connection with the MIS of Chapter 6. What are the differences?
2. What is a brand strategy and why is it important?
3. Under what conditions is it possible to use the formal decision technology described in this chapter?
4. How can you reconcile the formal decision technology with the heavy emphasis upon growth which is obvious in almost any top-management discussion of company objectives?
5. What do you conclude about whether the decision technology is equal to the demands laid upon it by an MIS?

8

Marketing programming and control: Market research

INTRODUCTION

MARKET RESEARCH has limitations in providing the data required by formal decision techniques, as well as untapped potential. Company organization is perhaps the most serious of these limitations. Also, the brand manager has no formal control system. These limitations are compounded by the subtlety of the research process which, after all, is a process of human thinking. This chapter will attempt to clarify this subtlety by examining the process in seven steps.

In general, market research is directed toward helping the brand manager infer how and why his customers are responding to his marketing plan so that he can improve that plan. There are, however, three special problem areas: market segmentation, forecasting, and market monitoring. We will examine these as a step to a discussion of ideal market research, in which the development of structural models now becoming feasible is explained and illustrated.

The typical company practice in brand management and its supporting market research is remarkably far removed from the potential picture presented in Chapters 6 and 7. The speed with which these ideas are being effectively introduced into practice is astoundingly slow compared with the anticipations expressed in the management science literature, a fact emphasized by experienced market research directors. The MIS has now been talked about for more than 10 years. This is not because of lack of talent. Even limited contact with marketing managers and market researchers in progressive companies provides evidence that they are usually well staffed by imaginative, well-trained, and highly motivated people.

The ideal system proposed in Chapter 6 would test out all alternative plans and then evaluate the results in terms of specific areas of malperformance. Such a system would require market research only in the design of the system in the first place; thereafter, the system would run on its own, identifying problems and freeing the brand manager to create better marketing plans. Yet practice is quite different; large research departments are a characteristic of marketing-oriented companies, and everyone in them seems to be busily doing something. They could be working on long-term, strategic problems for the marketing manager and president, for example, and so doing work not relevant to the brand manager. A large proportion of research effort is for new products, but by no means all of it.

The best place to begin looking for an explanation of the discrepancy between the ideal and reality is the brand manager's lack of a formal control system. As we noted in Chapter 7, this is far from ideal. He usually has no trouble finding problems, which are but disguised opportunities, but for him to find the most crucial problems is quite another matter. To the extent that the system does warn him, does it warn him in time? The presymptom concept of Chapter 6 can, in principle, do this, but whether it will suffice empirically is a question to be answered. Once he finds he has a problem or an opportunity the control system tells him little or nothing about the nature of it. Thus, he has the intuitive and highly important task of formulating the problem. Once he formulates it, he must intuitively decide upon the range of alternatives to be considered, although his marketing strategy can help focus his attention on this somewhat. Finally, his decision models leave him with some logical problems, particularly the need for estimates of response curves.

Given this state of affairs, where does the market research analyst fit into the process? Does he sit back and wait until the brand manager comes to him and says, "Joe, here are the alternatives I want tested"? One suspects that if he did take this passive role, the market research department would soon be dismantled. If the analyst is to take a more positive role, it must be determined just what that role should be. To accomplish this, we will begin with the nature of the organizational relations between the brand manager and the researcher. Since he does not have a formal control system, we must examine the organizational setting within which his intuitive control process operates. Clearly, what the market research process is depends upon *where* in the brand manager's total decision process the analyst operates in the particular case. If you were the market analyst assigned to the petroleum company decision maker setting prices as described in Figure 5–7, you would agree that which box in that process you are supposed to get the data for would make a lot of difference in the nature of what you do.

MARKET RESEARCH ORGANIZATION

Market research must be planned, executed, and utilized in the context of a company organization, a real barrier to its effective functioning. If this organization orientation is ignored, it is easy to exaggerate the extent to which market research data influence decisions. A General Electric executive in one of the company's divisions recently said,

In the eleven years I have been here we have gone through three cycles of utilizing market research. First, we would make almost no decision not supported by market research. Within a year or so we paid much less attention to it, in fact, almost ignored it. A year or so later we were back again with a "gung ho" rational approach. This cycle has been repeated three times. Why it has happened this way, I am not at all sure.

Market research, however, has become an increasingly important activity, especially at the brand manager level, as a more rational managerial philosophy has evolved, as new managerial decision techniques have developed, and as new marketing research techniques have appeared. Its current importance is suggested by the fact that many companies have market research directors who often have a substantial number of analysts reporting to them and who typically report to the marketing manager. The activity burgeoned after World War II and has continued to grow in the years since. An American Marketing Association Survey, for example, reports that between 1963 and 1968 the number of companies with research departments increased by one third and market research budgets increased 93 percent, with research in wholesale and retail establishments increasing 167 percent.[1] In fact, the rise of market research has probably been a major factor in the development of the brand manager position. A decision maker closer to the "facts"—lower in the organization—was needed to take advantage of these more plentiful and more reliable facts. Yet research expenditures are still small in relation to the magnitude of the risk. Also, they are quite vulnerable to cutbacks when the company's profit picture becomes less favorable.

The brand manager's link to the market research department is typically through a research analyst who is assigned from that department to serve that brand. The potential that the researcher can bring is considerable. Logically he can help anywhere in that extended intuitive process of problem or opportunity recognition to the process of choosing among alternatives. Also, he can bring to the decision not only data but an objective, analytic point of view. If well accepted by the brand manager, he can contribute immensely by challenging pet ideas.

For a number of reasons, however, this link between the brand manager and the research analyst is a difficult one, and analysts who fill the

---

[1] *Advertising Age,* June 30, 1969, p. 14.

role effectively are not easy to find. First, there are few or no company guidelines for such an interactive, highly personal relationship.

Second, because the brand manager's decision process is intuitive, he doesn't know its contents, as we saw in the study of the pricing decision described in Chapter 5. To the brand manager the decision process is merely common sense. To someone such as an analyst with a different experience and training background, the same facts can represent quite "uncommon" sense. The brand manager cannot articulate his decision process and thereby guide the analyst. The analyst must intuitively identify the brand manager's intuitive process in order to work effectively with him.

Third, the brand manager may have major organizational reasons for not informing the analyst as fully as he might be expected to. A brand manager in one of the nation's largest companies, for example, was unwilling to tell his market research staff the nature of his strategy for a major new product. He was fearful it was incorrect and, if so, might plague him later. Also, he did not want his competitors to know about it.

Fourth, the analyst often has a fairly heavy scientific training which does not fit him for this "intuiting" responsibility and for his role in such a complex, intimate, and idiosyncratic relation.

Fifth, the brand manager, like most managers, has little time for extended thinking: He is too busy "putting out fires." This time pressure renders interpersonal relations with the analyst more difficult. At the same time, however, it provides an opportunity. If the brand manager will permit it, the analyst can do some of his thinking for him, but the manager must have faith in the analyst and the roles of each must be well and sensibly worked out. Nevertheless, the time pressure leads to a low quality of research, often referred to as "quick and dirty research."

Sixth, there is a large turnover in jobs among both brand managers and market analysts. One survey indicated, for example, that 70 percent of the brand managers had been in their positions less than two and one-half years.[2] As the research director of one of the largest research departments put it, "Unfortunately, developing mutual respect and confidence takes time and often just as the relationship matures and is beginning to pay off in good communication and good work along come new responsibilities for either the brand manager or the researcher."

Finally, there is a tendency to use outside suppliers. In fact, many so-called market analysts are people with little technical skill who spend their time as a "purchasing agent" buying research services.[3] As computers have developed and market research has burgeoned, specialization of labor has inevitably prompted the development of specialist firms to provide data. A few imaginative people usually head the firms, but the na-

---

[2] *Advertising Age*, May 10, 1971, p. 62.
[3] *Advertising Age*, July 17, 1972, p. 39.

ture of data processing encourages these supplier firms to use standard procedures, often carried out by fairly low-quality labor. This is the way to reduce costs, but, unfortunately, it inhibits innovative research. This problem has been furthered by such companies merging and going public. As R. F. Casey, senior vice president of Benton and Bowles, put it:

Hardly a major supplier has resisted the urge to merge and go public. This has resulted in the virtual disappearance of the innovative, personal and often studiously professional research business. I yearn for research experimentation; close-in, hard thinking as to research solutions to particular problems. The corporate structure of the research supply business does not now seem to be such as to provide that kind of thinking.[4]

From these limitations we can understand why market research directors and brand managers vehemently complain about the inability of the analysts to aid in the most crucial step of all, formulating the problem, and often about other aspects of their functioning as well.

In addition to the difficulties posed by the interactive relation between the brand manager and his marketing analyst, there are some other organizational characteristics which inhibit effective market research. The brand manager is fearful of using new techniques for developing research answers to support his arguments because people above him who read his marketing plan will not understand them. As a marketing research director said of the brand manager, "He is reluctant to employ new techniques for fear that the recommendation will be rejected through lack of understanding of the methodology rather than the weakness of the supporting facts."

The market research function itself is new, springing up largely after World War II. The most convenient man was often grabbed to head it up, and it became largely a reflection of his personality. "Not surprising, then, that many research departments just 'kinda grew' like Topsy—or that their self-defined role, traditional ways of doing things, and staff capabilities have come to be, to some degree, out of sync(hronization) with the urgent needs of marketing people today."[5] At the same time client companies have been taking over to a substantial extent the market research function that advertising agencies performed for them in the fifties and early sixties. Top management is now, however, beginning to raise serious questions about whether the function is effectively performed, and even more important, how to evaluate it (what criteria to use) in order to decide whether it is. This questioning view augurs well for the future, especially because top management will in the process think through what it really does want market research to do.

---

[4]*Advertising Age*, October 12, 1970, p. 76.
[5]*Advertising Age*, July 17, 1972, p. 39.

AN OVERVIEW OF MARKET RESEARCH PRACTICE

Introduction

The brand manager can better utilize the analyst assigned to him if he is familiar with some of the details of the research process. As he knows, there are three types of required information: buyer, competition, and cost. Historically, market research has dealt mainly with the first. When decisions are intuitive, this separation of activities works reasonably well. But as parts of the process become formalized and especially computerized, the three types must be brought together and integrated, as implied in Chapters 6 and 7. We will be conventional here and confine our discussion to the buyer side of the problem. In principle the market analyst would perform in the same way with facts about competition and cost.

Once the purpose of the study has been well formulated and the alternatives have been stated, there are a number of questions the researcher either implicitly or explicitly asks himself in his attempt to approximate the aggregate response function. By "asking them implicitly" we mean he takes the action without realizing that he has made a decision. These questions are: (1) What variables will I use? (2) What instruments shall I use? (3) How shall I collect the facts? (4) How shall I store the facts? (5) How shall I process the facts? (6) How shall I interpret the results? and (7) How shall I present the results? Each of these steps involves some very subtle issues, since market research technology has expanded rapidly, especially in the past decade. We will avoid discussing many of the more sophisticated techniques, however, because we want to get at the heart of the research process. For the experienced researcher most of these steps are taken intuitively and repetitively; he too is in Routinized Response Behavior.

Definition of variables

The early decisions in the research process in particular ought to be made explicitly and carefully. Moreover, they should be made in close and continued discussion with the brand manager. In the first decision, what variables to use, the researcher has from his experience and reading developed a set of beliefs about what causes what in buyer behavior. He has an implicit theory which he applies in each case to develop an ad hoc theory about that situation. The pressure of getting on with the job, however, seldom if ever gives him the opportunity to articulate these beliefs so that he can share them with the brand manager. Much less does he have the chance to test them to see if they are really true. Further, generalizations—general truths not tied to a specific set of conditions—are quite sparse in practice, as the Federal Trade Commission hearing on advertising in late 1971 so well documented.

During the past 10 years, however, the published research has burgeoned and generalizations have become more common, although practice lags. It is now possible to fashion a buyer-behavior theory (Chapter 3) which can guide the researcher. It explicitly postulates certain constructs and the causal relations among them. If a brand manager is to use the theory fully he must collect facts which represent each construct. Thus, for every theoretical construct he must have an empirical counterpart. True enough, the precise relations—the shapes of the functions—depend upon the concrete situation, but the theory gives him strong guidance (hypotheses) about what to expect. Further, in some parts of the system it is possible to develop fairly firm estimates of these parameters. The purpose of the theory, then, at this stage is to specify the constructs and their realistic counterparts or operational definitions, which in turn specify the facts that he should collect. This assertion is a subtle but important idea that will be illustrated below in the section on problem areas. In current practice it does not receive nearly the attention it deserves.

Construction of instruments

In seeking to determine what instruments should be used to measure the real-world counterpart of the theoretical construct, we could ask, in different words: What is the operational definition? The term "instrument" refers to devices such as ways of asking questions of the buyer and kinds of rating scales the buyer is asked to complete. In current practice these tend to be selected somewhat haphazardly. The theory goes some distance in specifying them in general; for example, if brand comprehension, a construct from Chapter 3, is being measured, paired comparisons of pairs of brands are probably appropriate, but if attitude is being measured, adjectival scales are usually better.

The idea of a scale is an important one, especially the adjectival scale. Increasingly we have learned that the human is able to place—to rate—his subjective view of brands. Although it contains substantial error, his capacity to do this is essential. A great variety of scales exist, but the principle is always the same and very simple. The consumer is confronted with such a question as "How much do you like brand A? Will you rate on this scale from 0 to 7 with 7 being the most and 0 the least how much you like it?" The next question could be more specific. Assuming it is an instant breakfast, the consumer could be asked, "Would you rate this brand on how nutritious you think it is?" In this way an adjectival rating is obtained. Such subjective scales seem to have the important quality of being equal interval: In his rating the consumer is able to judge the brand in such a way that the psychological distance between any two consecutive numbers is the same as between any other two consecutive numbers. This property enables us to apply most of the standard statistical techniques to the data derived in this way.

The specific content of an instrument, however, must often be defined as the consumer conceptualizes it, not as the company's data system consolidates it or the research supplier provides it. The content of an adjectival scale, for example, will obviously be different for automobiles than for bread. Depth interviews and word association techniques are possible means of obtaining this specific content for all brands in the product class.

Scales are but one aspect of the more general problem of questionnaire construction which in some form is used in all but the direct observational method of collecting data. The development of a questionnaire may seem simple, but it is an art to obtain the precision desired and to avoid biasing the respondent by an improperly phrased question.

Collection of data

There are many ways to collect the data. We will classify them as in Table 8–1, which sets forth 16 possible ways to accomplish this task.

As shown in the column headings, we can think of all methods as either *surveys*, where we do not deliberately manipulate to get information but instead collect the data from the buyer during his normal ongoing pattern of behavior, or *experiments*, where we do manipulate the stimuli that impinge on the buyer and so create behavior. For an experiment to be meaningful, however, we must more than manipulate, such as could occur when a new product is introduced. We must have at least two versions of a brand, for example, to have a comparison. Otherwise there is no control, no sharp basis for comparing alternatives, and the power of experimentation is lost.[6] By this definition a conventional test market is not an experiment. Only one level of each of the variables, such as product, advertising, or price, is tried out.

Experiments are much the more powerful, but they encounter difficulties in field application. Two of these are cost and delay. Another serious problem often not recognized in marketing is that the lack of a theory has prevented much generalization, as has been emphasized by Hanz Zeisel.[7] Thus surveys are by all odds the most common. In fact, experiments are rare. The experimental design, however, is very useful as a standard by which to evaluate the degree of control attained in survey studies.

Surveys and experiments can be either *cross-sectional* or *longitudinal*. In a cross section, data is collected on a person only once. In longitudinal studies, the same data are collected at more than one point in time from the same person. This latter type is often called panel studies, a term coined by Professor Paul Lazarsfeld, a pioneer in market research. In eco-

---

[6] J. A. Howard and H. V. Roberts, "Experimentation and Marketing Research," (unpublished ms., 1957).

[7] Hans Zeisel, "Tools of Causal Analysis," in Leo Bogart, ed., *Current Controversies in Marketing Research* (Chicago: Markham Publishing Co., 1969), pp. 102–11.

TABLE 8–1
Classification of methods of collecting data

| | Surveys | | Experiments | |
Application of methods	Cross-sectional	Longi-tudinal	Cross-sectional	Longi-tudinal
Direct observation	1	5	9	13
Mail.	2	6	10	14
Telephone.	3	7	11	15
Personal interview	4	8	12	16

Source for classification: Harold W. Fox.

nomics, the term is "time series." Longitudinal investigations provide greater power because of the ability to identify change and therefore get at causation more easily. Also, by using the *same* people over time the error is reduced. Analysis is more complicated, however.

The row headings in Table 8–1 indicate four ways in which these methods can be applied. *Direct observation* occurs in situations like a retail store where an unknown observer observes the customer selecting an item from an array of brands on the grocery shelf. It also is used in a "focus group session" where a group of housewives are brought together, for example, to discuss buying and using some product class. This session can take place in a room with one-way glass where an observer watches behavior and expressions to amplify and add meaning to the words the discussion leader inside the room is eliciting from the members of the group. Questionnaires are often sent by *mail* to a consumer to be completed and returned, and a series of questions can be asked over the *telephone*. For a *personal interview*, an interviewer is sent to ask questions of the consumer in person. To discuss the advantages and disadvantages in terms of the vitally important dimensions of cost, time, and accuracy of each of the 16 possible methods here for each of the variety of uses to which they can be put would require several chapters.

An actual example can add meaning to this classification, particularly since the same example will be used later to illustrate a structural model. In 1966 the market for Carnation Instant Breakfast (CIB) was disturbed when General Foods introduced Post Instant Breakfast into test market in Portland, Oregon. CIB had been in the Portland market for some two years. In a test market, effort is usually made to simulate as closely as possible what the actual market situation will be like if and when the brand goes national. Post was introduced in June. A mail questionnaire was sent to 1,100 housewives—cell 2 in Table 8–1—three weeks prior to the introduction. Then, in late June, late July, and late September, they were telephoned for information: cell 7. All during this test period each housewife was submitting by mail every two weeks a record of her purchases of

Post, Carnation, and brands in related product classes. This was cell 6. Personal interview is often used, but it is expensive and probably inserts more bias into the consumer's answers than does the telephone.

Data storage

With the development of the computer, large studies involving masses of data are becoming more and more common. Imagine the storage problem, for example, for the approximately 20,000 pieces of data involved in a three-wave telephone panel of 1,100 housewives with one bit of data for each of the six constructs shown in Figure 8–1 (see the section on structural models below) for each person at three different times. This omits segmenting data, for example, which is usually collected only once.

The storage problem is not so apparent in company practice because only a one-shot analysis is typically performed. Time generally does not permit the researcher to go back and test ideas (hypotheses) that emerged from discussion of the results of the first analysis. Current practice could be substantially improved if more attention were given to data storage in order to encourage quick access for reanalysis. The reanalysis of existing data might be much faster and clearly could yield a higher quality of results than the "quick and dirty" original research forced on the researcher by the brand manager's time pressure. Reanalysis, however, requires either a continuity of research personnel who are familiar with past studies or an elaborate library system.

Data analysis

The analysis of the market facts collected so they will inform the brand manager about the response functions he needs to know in order to make his decisions as rationally as possible has become an important field. It has burgeoned as statistical techniques of great variety have been introduced, particularly in the past five years. The purpose here is obviously not to attempt to deal with the field exhaustively but rather to present some understanding of the current research process.

Frequency tables and cross classification are two basically simple and standard means of getting information from facts.

FREQUENCY TABLES.   About the simplest possible way to get information for decision is to arrange facts in a column and group them. This is called a frequency chart. A number of years ago, the management of Spic and Span, a traditional household wall cleaner, was considering whether to attempt to increase sales (growth) and profits by advertising it as a floor cleaner as well. Historically, it had been advertised only for walls and woodwork.

To get some evidence, Buffalo, New York, and Birmingham, Alabama, were selected, and the advertising in these two markets was changed for a year to read "for cleaning floors." In each city 300 housewives were inter-

TABLE 8–2
Consumer survey in two markets

	Pretest (percent)	Posttest (percent)
1. °Used Spic & Span in past 4 weeks	43	52
Had Spic & Span in the house:		
2. Regular size	20	24
3. °Large size................................	16	28
Tried Spic & Span in past 4 weeks for:		
4. Painted woodwork.........................	23	24
5. Painted walls	19	17
6. °Linoleum floors	12	25
Attitude toward Spic & Span for cleaning painted woodwork and painted walls (users only). Housewives made:		
7. Favorable comments only	35	33
8. Unfavorable comments only	12	11
9. Both favorable and unfavorable comments	48	52
10. No specific comment	5	4
Largest unfavorable comments were:		
11. Hard on hands	19	21
12. Takes off paint	11	12
Attitude toward Spic & Span for cleaning linoleum (users only). Housewives made:		
13. Favorable comments only	40	37
14. Unfavorable comments only	9	13
15. Both favorable and unfavorable comments	47	42
16. °No specific comment	4	8

°Significant at 5 percent level.

viewed just before the copy change was made (pretest) and another 300 at the end of the year (posttest). The results, arranged in two columns, are shown in Table 8–2.

In row 6 we see that the percentage of housewives using it for floors more than doubled, thus providing evidence that people could be persuaded to buy it for floors. Equally important, the company was worried that if it were advertised for floors, housewives might come to conclude that if it were strong enough for floors it was too strong for walls and woodwork. Rows 4 and 5 suggest that this fear may not have been justified. One increased slightly and the other decreased slightly.

Obviously, many more comments could be made about the data in Table 8–2, but the purpose here is merely to illustrate. By collecting facts before the change was made, making the change, and collecting facts again after doing so, revealing evidence was obtained. If only the posttest column of figures were available, this data in tabular form would have provided much less information. One-shot or cross-sectional surveys instead of the more expensive before-and-after survey represented in the Spic and Span research, however, can be highly useful if the facts are analyzed in more sophisticated ways than by merely computing percentages, as done here.

TWO-VARIABLE CLASSIFICATION.   The simple technique of two-variable cross classification is widely used; it is typically used as a first step even by the highly sophisticated researcher. To evaluate different levels of advertising is, in some sense, to estimate the aggregate response curve for advertising. The current practice is to compare the purchase rates of a sample of consumers with their recall of having seen advertising about the brand. The simplest way to accomplish this comparison is to *cross-classify* the people in the sample by these two characteristics, as in Table 8–3. The absolute figures do not tell us anything, but since the sample was 100 we can treat the figures as percentages, which simplifies the interpretation.

TABLE 8–3
Cross-Classification

	Saw ad	Did not see ad
Purchased brand	30	10
Did not purchase brand	10	50

According to these data, it can be inferred that advertising had an effect: The proportion of people is much greater in the upper left and lower right cells than in the other two cells. If each cell contained approximately 25 people, we could infer that it did not have an effect.

An experienced manager might say, however, "I am not willing to make this inference because this result might have arisen merely by accident." He would want a test of significance to tell him what the chances were that these results might have arisen through chance. Also, he might ask, especially if he is knowledgeable about buyer-behavior theory, "How do I know that advertising caused the purchase? Perhaps purchase sensitized people to the product so that they are now more likely to see the ads. Thus, purchase causes advertising."

In the Spic and Span case discussed above, it is possible to cross-classify size of package used of a cleaner, for example with whether the consumer used it for woodwork, walls, or floors. In this way, we could find out whether using it on floors would encourage the purchase of larger packages.

Another use for the cross-classification technique is to segment markets, as in Table 8–4. In this way you can discover whether younger people are more likely to buy than older people, for example. If such a difference exists, then age is a possible segmenting dimension. The same analysis can be performed on a competitor's brand. If his percentages are different, an appropriate question is, "Why?" Perhaps the facts suggest an opportunity no one had considered before. If older people are more inclined to buy the brand than the competitor's brand, for example, perhaps with some modification of product design and other marketing effort, the potential of selling relatively more to the older folks can be more fully exploited.

TABLE 8–4
Segmenting by cross-classification

	Under 40	Over 40
Purchase	33	17
Nonpurchase	17	33

Here we see what often happens. Market analysis leads to the suggestion of new alternative courses of action that had not been previously considered. This, the creation of new *alternatives* is a role that market researchers all too often abdicate in practice, largely because of the organizational influences discussed above.

More will be said later about segmentation research.

THREE-VARIABLE CROSS-CLASSIFICATION. A typically somewhat more complicated situation requires three variables instead of two (Table 8–5). Assume we have a sample of 200 people of which 100 have heard our TV advertising at least twice or more (high) and 100 have heard it but little, if any (low). We want to know whether the two-way analysis performed earlier isn't hiding the important fact that different-aged people respond quite differently to our advertising. From the data, one interpretation is

TABLE 8–5
Cross-classification with three variables

	Under 40		Over 40	
	Low	High	Low	High
Purchase	8	35	18	17
Nonpurchase	37	15	37	33

that our advertising is not affecting the older people while the young people are responding to the advertising much more favorably. The power and usefulness of cross-classification techniques have probably best been spelled out in Hans Zeisel's classic little book, *Say It with Figures*.[8]

OTHER TECHNIQUES.   A plethora of multivariate statistical techniques, each appropriate under various conditions, is now available. They are much too numerous and complex to deal with here. One important distinction can be made, however. Some techniques merely indicate whether there is a relation between two variables without specifying whether it is an important relation. Other techniques show how strong, how important the relation is. The first is illustrated by tests of significance and the second by correlation and regression analysis. The second is much more useful; we will see an example of it in the section on problem areas. The transition to this approach can be made visually if we think of Table 8–3 as being overlaid by a Cartesian coordinate chart in which dots "purchased brand" on the vertical axis and "saw ad" on the horizontal axis appear instead of the numbers and a line is drawn that minimizes the distances between it and the points. The slope of the line that best fits the points is the degree of relationship. It is called the regression coefficient. How closely the data fit the line is the correlation coefficient.

Interpretation of findings

How should the results of the analysis be interpreted? In market research the results are often gray, not black or white. For example, the numbers in the boxes of Table 8–3 are often in practice much more similar than shown there. In these gray situations, if an interpretation can be made, a pattern of plausible explanation for the study often becomes possible. An explicit theory such as shown in Chapter 3 can be a powerful tool in choosing the most likely conclusion from among the many in these gray situations and in developing a plausible rationale for the set of facts. Interpretation is an art that can be greatly aided by knowledge of the brand and a complex theory.

Presentation of findings and recommendations

The problem of presentation of findings to the brand manager is one of the most difficult. In principle the answer is easy: The findings should be presented in terms of the presumably actionable questions that he asked when the study was first designed. The brand manager must be able to induce from the facts justification for choosing between courses of action, or better still, be able to accept with confidence and conviction the inductions for action of his analyst. The problem was probably much greater 20 years ago when the manager had little or no understanding of the process of market research. Today, many brand managers are graduates of busi-

---

[8] Hans Zeisel, *Say It with Figures* (New York: Harper & Bros., 1951).

ness schools and have taken courses in market research. Some have "come up" through market research. Nevertheless, the problem still exists because of the different frames of reference of the brand manager and the researcher.

There are five serious difficulties in presenting the results in terms of the question asked by the brand manager. First, as we have suggested in Chapter 5, the brand manager may not be fully conscious of what data he used in a *past* decision, much less what he expects to use in some *future* decision. Part of the reason is that the decision is intuitive and has become habitual. Second, he sees the problem in gross action terms, not in precise raw-data terms as the researcher must see it because he is usually responsible for detailed designing of the study and collecting the best raw facts possible. That is, the brand manager sees the problem in terms of vague aggregate response curves, not in terms of the raw data which when collected and processed might provide the response curves. Third, market research technology has not been able to provide the response curves. The fourth problem, which grows out of the first two, is that the market researcher has to mesh the intuitive, vaguely stated needs of the brand manager with the limited capacities of his research technology. Finally, on any finding that runs contrary to his preconceived notions of buyer behavior, the brand manager will likely be a skeptical audience for the market researcher's presentation.

Summary: Market research process

From this survey of steps in the market research process you can begin to see the large quantity of knowledge, technical and experiential, that an analyst could bring to bear to his interactive relation with the brand manager. This is not to say that most analysts have attained this potential, however.

PROBLEM AREAS

Introduction

Most of the foregoing discussion of the market research process would indicate that much research is directed to throwing light in one way or another on the aggregate response curve. For most companies, three related but different problem areas exist to which research is also devoted:(1) market segmentation, (2) forecasting, and (3) market monitoring.

Market segmentation

The need to identify market segments and to measure the aggregate response curve in each of them was demonstrated in Chapter 7 in connection with allocation of the marketing budget to different market segments. An example of management's interest is shown by a Coca-Cola manager who said that one word explains the recent expansion of the soft drink market, and that is "segmentation" by product types and package size.

... if a bottler does not offer his product in a 16-oz, size he loses 21% of the total market. If he does not have cans, it is another 14%. If he does not have one-way bottles he has lost another 5%, and without quarts, 6%, and with that we just passed the 46% mark. . . . With that knowledge Coca-Cola prepared to compete and be a leader in all segments of the soft drink market.[9]

Even large retailers feel similarly, as C. Virgil Martin, chairman of Carson Pirie Scott & Co., noted: "they (each store) think of their customers in terms of age, education and economic levels, and direct their merchandise and promotional programs to a specific group."[10]

The literature of segmentation usually implies that the purpose of market segmentation research is to provide facts for allocating marketing effort. Another use of segmentation, and probably an even more widespread one, is as a device for *understanding* a market or creating an ad hoc theory. We can illustrate this more subtle use by analogy. A mechanic was attempting to repair a two-cylinder outboard motor that was misfiring regularly. A number of factors could cause this poor performance. Ignition was one possible area. He had an instrument for checking the ignition with a dial which registered amounts of some measure. Unfortunately, he had forgotten to bring the book of directions for the instrument and so did not know which *levels* of readings were good or bad. All he knew was that "up" was good. He was imaginative, however. By testing both cylinders and comparing their performance, he found one much lower than the other. He concluded that this was the culprit and proceeded to examine it carefully. The deduction paid off; he found a break in that cylinder's ignition coil that otherwise would have gone undetected because the break was hidden by the band that clamped the coil to the motor. In the same way, brand managers and researchers usually begin with very little quantitative knowledge about their market. By grouping people according to characteristics on which they differ and comparing them on other characteristics such as purchase rates, it may be possible to identify forces operating that were formerly "hidden" and quite unsuspected.

Market segmentation research is a fashionable topic today because of the immense power it could have in relieving a brand manager of the sharp competitive pressures that erode profits. Further, technological changes now under way in media such as cable television, cassettes, and specialized magazines presage a still greater opportunity to serve a variety of markets by different media. In practice, however, segmentation more often is handled by consumer "self-selection," leaving it to the con-

---

[9] *Advertising Age*, November 11, 1968, p. 68.
[10] *Christian Science Monitor*, August 1, 1970, p. 12.

sumer to select the particular ads for himself from those shown in a mass medium. For example, a number of companies advertising over such stations as WXTV (New York), KMEX-TV (Los Angeles), KWEX-TV (San Antonio) and WLTV (Miami) use Spanish-language commercials. Procter & Gamble now has a 30-man Spanish sales force and a Spanish media specialist and is advertising 18 products over these stations.[11]

Segmentation also has a high degree of plausibility, probably because we know from long experience that people are different. Whether they are *different* in the way that matters, namely, in the *effects* of *marketing effort* upon purchasing *behavior*—upon response curves—may be quite something else, however.

There are three basic problems in segmentation research. One is to identify relevant segments, a second is to measure the surrogate variable, and the third is to measure the aggregate response curve in each segment so as to be able to optimize the allocation of the marketing budget to each segment.

SEGMENT IDENTIFICATION. There is an almost infinite number of ways in which buyers could logically differ, and there is probably a large number of ways in which they do in fact differ. But the basic question always to bear in mind is: Do they differ in a relevant way? "Relevant" is defined, of course, in terms of being related to the buyer's individual *response curve*. This question is raised far too infrequently in current market research practice. So often the relationship is assumed without verification. Those characteristics that we can identify are called surrogate criteria because they serve *in lieu of* some variable that is causally related to the response curve.

Typical criteria used are consumer purchase behavior, demographic variables, other situational variables, physical variables, psychological variables, and media habits.[12] The purchase criteria are often stated in terms of some measure of brand loyalty or amount of multiple-brand purchasing. Because this purchase criterion does not indicate buyer response to marketing variables, it is criticized for not being "diagnostic" enough, for not telling us *why* the buyers bought the way they did. Here we see the conflict between the two different purposes of segmentation research, allocating marketing effort and building an ad hoc theory: For the first purpose segmentation is looked upon as something of a mechanical process, while for the second the "why" question is asked at a fundamental level, for example, "Was it because the advertising copy added to the buyer's confidence?"

Demographic variables include age, sex, income, and style of life, for example. Somewhat related are "other situational" variables which give

---

[11] *Advertising Age*, September 27, 1971, p. 54.
[12] J. A. Lunn, Annual Conference of ESOMAR/WAPOR, 1969 Mimeo.

rise to product requirements and impose constraints upon the expression of these requirements. In other parts of the world, refrigerator ownership can be an example. Physical variables are such things as skin and hair texture. Psychological characteristics are increasingly being used, such as attitude toward (and intention to buy) brands or product class. Another class of psychological variable is personality traits—some people are more introverted and others more extroverted, for example. Media habits consider the nature of the buyer's habits with regard to exposing himself to classes of media such as TV, newspaper, or radio and to specific media within each of these classes.

For segmentation, individual characteristics which are relatively permanent are more useful as contrasted with attitude, for example, which may change in a matter of days in response to a heavy advertising campaign. The practitioner sometimes argues, however, that he doesn't mind using temporary attributes. The argument is that if the relationship is identified, when a new consumer acquires the attribute, he will behave in the same way.

MEASUREMENT OF SURROGATE CRITERIA. Originally there was the practice of using a priori surrogate criteria, that is, criteria that we think apply to most if not all products. Personality characteristics as defined in conventional psychological research were popular. Perhaps because the few published studies showing these characteristics explained little about purchase behavior, there has been a shift toward identifying characteristics specific to the particular product-class market. Also, management, with its experience and imagination, has been drawn in to a greater extent as the study is designed. A. J. Lunn, a member of Research Bureau Ltd., which is a market research arm of Lever Bros., Ltd., pointed out in a letter:

> The most successful segmentation projects are usually those where, from the outset, there is good communication between researchers and research users; where the researchers have a clear understanding of current marketing problems and possible courses of action; where marketing men feel fully committed to the research and where they understand its objectives if not necessarily the intricacies of the methodology employed.

It can be said, however, that this same statement would be equally true of most any market research, although this fact often gets ignored in the hurry of "getting on with the job."

An early exploratory study through depth interviewing—long unstructured interviews—is often quite useful in developing candidates and initial hypothesis confirmation. A great variety of measuring instruments and tools of analysis are in vogue. Measuring instruments refer, for example, to the kind of scale used in measuring attitude. Tools of analysis refer to such things as statistical clustering techniques, which have received a great amount of attention.

MEASUREMENT OF RESPONSE CURVES.   Ideally, of course, the analysis should be by response curves as well as in terms of the more explanatory criteria discussed above. So far as is known, there have been no published studies that do this. One suspects that there are not many, if any, in company files. Consequently, we must conclude that in the overwhelming majority of cases an *intuitive jump* is necessary from the data to action which implies knowledge of and so bypasses the aggregate response curve. Also, we suspect that the greatest usefulness of market segmentation research is to understand the market—to create an ad hoc theory—instead of to allocate marketing effort, its commonly discussed purpose. This somewhat critical view of market segmentation research is not intended to belittle the work, but to clarify the problem which arises because of the great discrepancy between practice and the literature.

Forecasting

The second of our three problem areas is forecasting. The prediction of future sales has in practice been labeled "forecasting". Forecasts can be classified as short term (a year or less) and longer than a year (long term). Long-term forecasting will be omitted here and dealt with in Chapter 12.

The need for forecasting sales obviously varies greatly among products. The product-class sales of a low-price, necessary food item are likely to fluctuate little although brand sales, for competitive reasons, are often much more volatile. With consumer durables such as cars, television sets, and houses, product-class sales fluctuate substantially as a result of changing economic conditions. Industrial products, in general, are volatile and machine tools are, of course, an extreme example.

The need for forecasting also varies with the life cycle of a given product class from the product-development stage, to the testing and introduction stage, to the rapid-growth stage and, finally, to the stead-state stage.[13] At the brand manager level, only the last two stages are especially relevant. In the rapid-growth stage, forecasting is concerned particularly with verifying the growth rate forecast typically made back in the testing and introduction stage and estimating what level of sales will be experienced when the steady state is attained.

In the steady-state stage, the brand manager is concerned with forecasting to set standards to check the effectiveness of the various elements of his marketing mix and to make available to others in the company projections that will aid in profit planning. This broader role for forecasting and the effects of *bad* forecasting on both profit and employment are illustrated in the case of a midwestern plant of a large rubber company. This new plant was supplying a number of industries,

---

[13]John C. Chambers, Satinder K. Mullick, and Donald D. Smith, "How to Choose the Right Forecasting Technique," *Harvard Business Review*, July–August 1971, pp. 45–74.

including the automobile industry. In 1955, because of relatively more profitable sales to automobile manufacturers, it was decided to supply only that industry and to discontinue relations with the others. A 1956 sales forecast estimated that sales would double those of 1955 even though sales were confined to the automobile industry. The forecast proved to be highly inaccurate. A 20 percent cutback in auto production in January and February 1956 caused a 50 percent reduction in the plant's production because the company wished to reduce its inventories. Not only did automobile sales decline but the proportion of cars equipped with the product of this particular plant was lower than anticipated. In May of 1956 it was expected that by the following July production would drop to 25 percent of capacity. Hourly rated employment dropped from a high of 950 to an estimated low of 325 in July. Relations with the plant's former customers in other industries could not be reestablished on short notice.

In the past, forecasting was usually done by a different methodology and with different people than is the research connected with market planning. Economists often do the forecasting. Perhaps there were a number of reasons for this separation in the past, but two in particular stand out. First, the facts were used by such people as production schedulers and profit planners located in a different part of the organization from the marketing decision area. Also, market planning of the detail and continuity now commonly advocated is relatively new. In fact, the improvement in planning procedures has done much to integrate decision-making research and forecasting designed to undergird the marketing plan. Second, the methodology underlying marketing decision was formerly so inadequate that it contributed little to the prediction of future sales. As we will see, new research methodology offers hope of integrating them effectively.

The difference in methodology between that required in the past and that called for by market planning is still quite marked. For example, much forecasting is done by statistical smoothing of such time series data as sales of the product. Exponential smoothing and regression are specific techniques that are very useful, but they are quite different from the kind of analysis implied in cross-classification. The reason for not using the individual analysis implied in the discussion of cross-classification is clear. In predicting sales six months from now for a consumer durable, for example, a sample of individual consumer predictions may be a less reliable indicator of sales than a professional forecaster with a statistical smoothing technique would be. If the product is a durable, by predicting the level of economic activity he may do a better job of predicting *product-class* sales. To this estimate the brand manager can apply his expected market share to derive an estimate of his own sales. The level of economic activity—consumer income—is an important determinant of the consumer's purchases, but the consumer is a poor predictor of it. To expect his intention to buy the product class to accurately reflect the pending downturn or upturn is probably asking too much, although there has been substantial debate on this issue.

As Chambers, Mullich, and Smith point out,[14] forecasting is moving toward the use of "consumer simulation models" which will predict the response of consumers to various strategies. These are what we will call structural models below.

Market monitoring

The purpose of monitoring a market is to serve the control function, as contrasted with planning, although control inevitably shades into planning in practice. Monitoring ideally should not only tell the brand manager he has a problem but it should also reveal information that will shape the nature of the new plan. How the data collection discussed here might fit into an overall information system was shown in Figures 6–3, 6–4 and 6–5.

To monitor a market, some index or measure is necessary. Market share is the most prevalent, but this depends upon whether the entire plan is being monitored or merely one aspect of it, such as advertising. Market share has the advantage of automatically separating the *controllable* from the *uncontrollable*. Except where the brand manager has a very large share of the market, he will be less seriously concerned about his own sales decline if his competitors' sales also decline because if they lose, too, there must be some overall industry effect and therefore one that he cannot do much about. In general, the market share measure filters out short-term abberations which affect all brands similarly, such as weather or number of shopping days. If the brand manager's share alone has declined, this suggests that he is weak on some controllable element of the marketing plan. A generally accepted standard is, "I must do at least as well as my competitors." Thus, market share provides a *standard of performance.* It also provides a somewhat deseasonalized measure. The raw data required for the share index is, of course, buyer purchases of your and your competitor's products.

In some industries, commercial services provide market share figures which can be purchased on a regular basis. In grocery store products, for example, Market Research Corp. of America (MRCA) provides share data from consumer purchases by a consumer panel each month. Nielsen makes it available by auditing a sample of retail stores every two months. Selling Areas–Marketing, Inc. (SAMI) obtains it from a sample of movements of product from the warehouse to the retail store every month. A useful way of analyzing the MRCA data, for example, is by applying a brand-switching matrix (Chapter 2). If this analysis is made month after

---

[14]Ibid.

month, the brand manager obtains a very real understanding of competitive relations.

Probably even more often problems will be identified by accident. After all, the existence of a "problem" merely indicates there is an opportunity to do better. The market analyst will often find that problems exist, and to the extent he does, he will usually be a valued member of the team.

Marketing monitoring leads inevitably to the "why" question. For those markets where performance is unsatisfactory, this involves finding the reason. If the control measures were specific enough, as implied in the MIS of Figure 6–5, they would automatically perform the crucial task of "formulating the problem." Obviously, market share as a control measure does not do this, and neither do other currently available measures. Consequently, the formulation of the problem must be intuitive. If the market analyst understands the brand manager's job and is imaginative, his role in problem identification can be considerable.

Designation of alternative solutions leads inevitably to their evaluation. Questions about which action is better and what the best decision is are the basis for most market research. Thus we see that control research shades into decision research. Further, we see that the market analyst's role can be very limited if he is a passive evaluator of alternatives. It can be very broad if he can serve in the market-monitoring process and actively enter into the earlier stages of the brand manager's decision process.

IDEAL MARKET RESEARCH

Introduction

We speak of ideal market research in the sense that it promises to be able to provide two types of estimates: those of the aggregate buyer-response curves required by all of the formal models shown in Chapter 7 and those of how buyer-response curves differ across market segments so that these segments can be properly exploited.

One way to approach the concept of ideal practice is in terms of empirically derived models. There are two general kinds of such models, estimating and structural, each serving somewhat different purposes. Either of these can be the main element of the essential decision model introduced in Figure 6–3, however. The first can be said to yield prediction without explanation. In principle, the second provides both.

Another classification is aggregate versus individual models. Individual models use data about individual buyers, whereas aggregate models use data aggregated over individuals, such as company sales figures, in which the identity of the individual buyer response is lost.

Estimation models

As the computer's potential has more and more become a reality, market researchers are being pushed to think about building decision models which, as you will recall from Chapter 6, was the central idea in a marketing information system that evaluates alternative marketing plans (Figure 6–3). The essence of these is first, aggregate response curves, and second, the incorporation of competitive behavior and cost. As we have emphasized, the cost data are not difficult to derive with a satisfactory degree of accuracy (Chapter 4), but competitive effects must be handled intuitively (the market structure concept from Chapter 2 can be quite helpful, however). The lack of measure of the aggregate response curves, on the other hand, has presented insuperable difficulties.

An estimating model is one possible solution. In current practice, it is probably most often used with aggregate data. If we were able to develop single-equation estimation models such as the following, there would be much less difficulty for the brand manager:

$$P = f(P_r, A_d, S_E)$$

where P is purchase rate, A_d is advertising, P_r is price and S_E is sales effort. There are obviously many questions about measurement of the variables, but for the moment let us avoid these. Knowing the functional relation implied in the equation above, the cost relation, and the nature of competitive relations, the manager could set the value of these marketing variables at the most profitable level.

The estimation model yields ideal results in the sense that it is in terms that the manager needs: How does advertising, for example, affect the buyer? The relation for each marketing input is the elusive *aggregate response curve*. Also, it shows joint effects, advertising *and* sales effort together, for example. Sales effort may have one effect at a given level of advertising but quite another at a different level.

The estimation model, however, only tells the manager what variables changed together in *that particular* set of circumstances. There is no underlying rationale such as in Chapter 3 to suggest that the relationship might apply to the same product under other circumstances or to different products. To extend it to new situations, that is, to new time periods, may be risky indeed because the estimation model implies no detailed understanding of the buyer. This lack of understanding prevents making the kinds of inferences that are useful, such as the effect of advertising copy and advertising media.

Structural models

A structural model is superior to an estimating model in that it attempts to define a set of equations which corresponds to the actual *casual processes* operating in the market, as we will see in Figure 8–1. Not long ago this general development was referred to as "the more-than-faint rumblings of an approaching breakthrough" by William J. McGuire, a psychologist at Yale University. As he pointed out, it deals with the major problem of measurement in natural settings instead of the laboratory—"the detection of the crucial factor among too many unknowns and uncontrollable variables"—and the major problem in nonexperimental research: "teasing out causal direction among covariants none of which we can manipulate".[15]

A structural model requires the network of causal paths that exist between the constructs, such as those specified in Chapter 3, for example. The empirical counterparts (data) of these constructs must be collected and fitted to the network to determine if it is a valid description of reality. In this way we identify the parameters of the relations among the variables implied in the causal paths. The parameters tell us the weights of the relations and the relative importance of each of the influences. The structural model, thus, must be both *theoretically* correct and *quantitatively* valid. If it is possible to reproduce the correlations that actually exist between the constructs of Chapter 3 and their empirical counterpart in the heads of a sample of buyers, from knowing the relations it is possible to predict what effects a change in one variable in a buyer's head will have on the others.

ESTIMATING PARAMETERS OF STRUCTURAL MODELS. Figure 8–1 portrays a model, a theoretical structure. It is the missing link in Figure 3–2, the way the brand manager conceptualizes his problem. It is also a simplified version of the structure of buyer behavior developed in Chapter 3, showing the learning or cognitive portion with certain constructs deleted, such as satisfaction, impersonal attitudes, and the perceptual aspects. In this simplified form, the application is much easier to understand.

The input to Figure 8–1 is a construct that describes the information the person has retained in his memory; *permanent memory*, it has come to be called (it was facts or information recalled in Chapter 3). *Comprehension* is the person's denotative, nonevaluative understanding of the attitude object, in this case, a brand. *Attitude* is his connotative or evaluative understanding of that object. *Confidence* is his subjective certainty in evaluating it in terms of his motives. *Intention* is his plan to act with respect to it within some specified time period. *Purchase* is the overt behavior elicited by the expected satisfaction from acting, as represented in attitude.

In an application of this model to Carnation Instant Breakfast (CIB) the theory specified the data required for application by means of the operational definitions below. As discussed earlier, the source of all but the purchase data was a telephone interview by General Foods of a sample of 572 of 1,100 consumers in Portland, Oregon in late September 1966, when market equilibrium had been disturbed by the introduction of Post In-

---

[15]William J. McGuire, "Theory-Oriented Research in Natural Settings: The Best of Both Worlds for Social Psychology," in M. Sherif and C. W. Sherif (eds.) *Interdisciplinary Relationships in the Social Sciences* (Chicago: Aldine Publishing Co., 1966).

FIGURE 8–1
Abbreviated formulation of theory

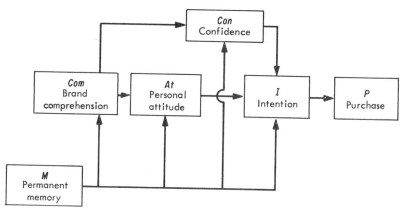

stant Breakfast. Permanent memory for CIB was operationalized as the equally weighted sum of whether the consumer talked with anyone or received a free sample of CIB and his total media exposure (newspaper, radio, TV, and other). Comprehension was the physical facts of the product, such as whether it was packaged in a can, bottle, or box. Attitude was a seven-point scale with "In general, I like it very much" as one pole and "In general, I don't like it" as the other. Confidence was a five-point scale as to how confident he was in judging the quality of the brand. Intention was also a five-point scale, "How likely are you to buy CIB (Carnation Instant Breakfast) within the next month?" Finally, purchase was the number of units of CIB purchased between July 18 and October 1 reported on a standard consumer diary form. These data are assumed to represent equal interval scales.

A set of equations to be fitted to the Carnation data flows naturally out of the theory specified in Figure 8–1. For example, Equation 1 merely puts the arrow from permanent memory to comprehension in symbolic terms. The symbols representing each construct yield the following set of linear equations which show the determinants of each dependent variable:

Comprehension	$Com = \alpha_1 + \beta_1 M$	(1)
Attitude	$At = \alpha_2 + \beta_2 Com + \beta_2 M$	(2)
Confidence	$Con = \alpha_3 + \beta_4 Con + \beta_5 M$	(3)
Intention	$I = \alpha_4 + \beta_6 At + \beta_7 Con + \beta_8 M$	(4)
Purchase	$P = \alpha_5 + \beta_9 I$	(5)

To illustrate, Equation 1 states that comprehension is caused by permanent memory (recalled information). β_1 is the coefficient showing the strength of that relation, and α_1 is the constant. Comprehension and memory, in turn, cause attitude, and so forth.

The equations fitted by ordinary least squares regression to the third wave of postintroduction data yielded the model for Carnation specified by the constants and betas (regression coefficients) in Table 8–6. The idea of a regression coefficient was described above as being analogous to a cross-classification table. In Table 8–6, −1 indicates that the variable in that column is the dependent variable for that equation; for example, in Equation 1 the beta coefficient (β_1) is .85 and it is significant at the .01 level. Specifically, this means that if memory is increased one point, comprehension is on the average increased 0.85 of a point.

TABLE 8–6
Estimates of structural parameters for Carnation Instant Breakfast

Equations	Permanent Memory (M)	Comprehension (Com)	Attitude (At)	Confidence (Con)	Intention (I)	Purchase (P)	Segmenting Variables		Constant	R^2
1	.85°	−1							3.69	.107°
2	.59°	.69°	−1						.65	.358°
3	.53°	.45°		−1					.45	.448°
4	.11†		42°	27°	−1				.33	.663°
5					.30°	−1			−.21	.098°

°Significant at the .01 level.
†Significant at the .05 level.

How do we know this empirically derived model is a true representation of reality? The most important test of the validity of the model is the significance of the beta coefficients. As you will see, all are significant at the .01 level, except for memory in Equation 4, which is significant at .05. Thus we can say it is a valid description of reality. For a brand manager concerned about prediction, however, R^2 in the extreme right-hand column becomes relevant. R^2 is the proportion of variance in the dependent variable explained by the independent variables in that equation. For Equation 1, it is low, explaining only 10 percent (.107) of the variance. Equations 2, 3, and 4 have satisfactory to good R^2s. Equation 5 is low.

Three major characteristics of the abbreviated structure explain at least a part of the unexplained variance and so would increase the R^2s. First, impersonal attitudes are omitted. We know from other analyses that price was a significant variable in influencing purchase. Retail distribution was uneven, and by the end of September the market had begun to stabilize, to regain the equilibrium upset by the introduction of the new brand. Thus, routinized response behavior was probably quite common among consumers; it is here that impersonal attitudes operate. As John C. Maloney has noted: "For a wide array of product classes I have studied, the bulk of purchases is attributable to buyer's choices among an "evoked set" . . . of equally accepted brands, on the basis of factors operating at the time and place of purchase."[16] But most of these situational effects were probably still not correctly anticipated by the consumer. Their effects, then, would be to explain some of the variance in Equation 5.

Secondly, to simplify, segmenting variables were omitted from the analysis, as we see in Table 8–6. This omission is relevant in three ways. Because the theory of Chapter 3 is a theory of *individual* behavior, the analysis implicitly assumes that all consumers are alike. The basic principle of segmenting variables is, of course, to capture individual differences among consumers. Had important segmenting variables been introduced, they would have improved the R^2's of the respective equation. Also, segmenting variables are necessary to yield a "fully identified" simultaneous system. This characteristic has to do with the requirement of all simultaneous systems that there be as many equations as there are unknowns. Finally, the most important point of all from the standpoint of practice, the system has the capacity to identify market segments, which can be so useful to the brand manager.

Third, the advertising signal in this market was weak and a more complicated procedure would have been required to pick it up alone.

USES OF THE STRUCTURAL MODEL. If the data from Table 8–6 are accepted, they can be put to a number of uses. First, if the input were specifically level of television advertising instead of an aggregate measure of information, the brand manager could compute the aggregate response curve required by the decision models of Chapter 7, which in turn were essential to the MIS of Chapter 6. Even with the data in Table 8–6 as they are, the brand manager from other evidence could estimate what levels of advertising expenditure would obtain what levels of permanent memory. Assume that M in Table 8–6 is advertising, let us say in terms of messages recalled. He could estimate how many dollars of advertising effort are required to get each of five levels of recall in the market. Thus, he can relate dollars spent on advertising to advertising recalled in terms of the decision model concept. Having done this, and having already the relationship between recall and purchase from Table 8–6, he could estimate dollars spent on advertising to units of purchase. Thus, we have the advertising-sales relation (aggregate response curve) of Figure 3–1 and Chapters 3, 6, and 7.

Second, it can suggest changes in advertising copy and media. By computing each of the following paths

$$M \rightarrow Com \rightarrow Com \rightarrow I \rightarrow P$$
$$M \rightarrow Com \rightarrow At \rightarrow I \rightarrow P$$
$$M \rightarrow At \rightarrow I \rightarrow P$$
$$M \rightarrow Com \rightarrow I \rightarrow P$$
$$M \rightarrow I \rightarrow P$$

[16] *Contemporary Psychology*, 17 (1972): 347.

and deciding which ones are more powerful, it may be possible to tailor the advertising copy to the most powerful path. This approach enables the brand manager to derive quantitative estimates of the potential of various marketing appeals, especially for advertising, which is one of the central and creative problems of marketing. It should also enable him to deal more objectively with one of the more serious public policy issues. Marketers are charged with promoting irrelevant or undesirable qualities of products. A Coca-Cola representative, for example, recently said that Samson, an enriched soft drink with a high nutritive value, is now being promoted in Surinam as a soft drink rather than "something that is good for you" because he believes there is frequent resistance to nutrition appeals.[17]

Third, the segmenting variables provide indications of protected markets. If age is a significant segmenting variable, the brand manager can perhaps divide people into well-defined separate markets so they can be reached with separate marketing activities. Even if he cannot reach each segment with a separate activity, the knowledge may be useful, as we saw earlier in attempting to infer more about the nature of the market. This diagnostic function is less useful, however, than when he is searching for an ad hoc theory.

Fourth, the variables in the system can be tracked through time and thus provide a means to monitor the market. The detail provided by the number of variables will make it easier to infer why they changed. Thus when unfavorable results occur, it will be easier to find out why it happened than with such gross measures as market share. In a nutshell, the measures of the variables will help "formulate the problem."

Fifth, the data present the same information to the brand manager about competitors' brands as they do for his brand. From the analyses, he will know how effective his competitor's marketing effort is.

Sixth, the system has substantial virtue in bringing together the various steps of the market research process into a systematic whole. It encourages the cumulative development of knowledge.

Finally, the results of the structural model can be used to design and interpret the results of an estimation model for the same market. Estimation models are usually simpler to develop and apply than are structural models; by using one to support the other, the best of both possible models can be obtained: a simpler and more economic model but one with an underlying rationale.

You can now begin to see why the structural model is an ideal answer. But this type of technical development goes much beyond what we find in current practice. Table 8–6 represents a pioneering piece of work, although similar results have been obtained with other bodies of data. Also

---

[17] *Advertising Age*, February 22, 1971, pp. 3 and 117.

very important work in *aggregate* structural modelling has been omitted here to simplify. These types of sophisticated work are merely in their infancy. To fully utilize such techniques a company will have to undergo a major learning process; the organizational barriers to this were emphasized earlier in the chapter. The view of the research director of one of the country's largest advertisers was expressed as follows:

From a practical point of view, our company, and probably most companies have not yet been able to apply this kind of model in the marketing situation. Such an endeavor would require a total commitment from a brand manager and his superiors and a large expenditure in manpower and cost for a significant period of time, probably six months to a year. Since the brand manager's planning horizon is often about just one year, it is very difficult internally to sell this kind of effort.

LIMITATIONS OF STRUCTURAL MODEL.   This type of complex and sophisticated research raises many questions, as indicated by the assumptions necessary. We assumed that the relations are linear; that there are no feedback relations in the behavior of consumers (recursive); that the theory is undebatable; and that all input variables are included. A number of assumptions were made in connection with the use of multiple regression. It was also assumed that the data elicited by the operational definition used (the nature of the questions asked the consumer and the nature of his replies) are congruent with the theoretical concepts of Figure 8–1 and that differences among consumers at a point of time really capture the changes that occur over time (cross-sectional analysis). An introductory textbook is not the place to deal with the validity of such assumptions or the consequences insofar as they are not valid.

CONCLUSIONS

Current market research practice, in general, tends to be considerably short of the requirements being laid upon it by modern decision theory and computer technology. Admittedly, a number of organizational problems that were discussed at the beginning of both Chapters 6 and 8 would delay the introduction of the ideal MIS even if it were available in fully operational form.

Only quite recently have we had any hope of obtaining the crucially essential aggregate response curve of marketing inputs. Some work remains to be done in making this approach more operational; nevertheless, it faces up to the problem in a way that earlier procedures have not.

Even if the market research technology was technically and economically operational, there still might be a logical problem in the decision

---

[18]Frank M. Bass among others has done interesting work here.

models. They assume the marketing inputs are independent, but we believe they often are not. This is a current deficiency.

For these reasons regular market research staffs will have a steady and growing demand for their services in aiding the brand manager. This activity will be in addition, of course, to work directed to *long-term* marketing problems, which are not dealt with at all in these chapters. Also, public policy research will probably expand. Further, one suspects that if the full ideal MIS were available to the brand manager the market research departments would be even busier, because he could never plan his information needs precisely. For example, he is likely to underestimate the degree of disaggregation he will need in his system. All these needs will probably be changing as changes take place in markets and marketing technology and the brand manager finds new needs to be satisfied in the process of acquiring experience with the system.

Perhaps most important of all is the inadequacy of the brand manager's control system. He will need help in finding *important* problems, formulating them in actionable terms, and deciding on meaningful ranges of alternatives. Always, he must do these things quickly.

Top management appears to be taking a more critical view of company market research. In the long term, this will clearly contribute to better research.

DISCUSSION QUESTIONS

1. How effective are the relations between the research analyst and the brand manager? Why aren't they more effective?
2. What do we mean by an adjectival scale, and why is it important?
3. One of the most useful tools in all of marketing research is the idea of cross-classification. What do we mean by it and why is it so useful?
4. Market segmentation is an eminently plausible idea, but why is it so important to distinguish between any differences among buyers and differences that matter? Explain.
5. Distinguish between estimation models and structural models.

9

Advertising management

INTRODUCTION

ADVERTISING is widely misunderstood as a function because, while it is so evident to the public, facts about its effects have been sparse. Advertising usage also varies considerably across industries and even among companies within a given industry. A summary in Table 9–1 of total advertising growth by gross industry classification documents how it has varied historically across industries.

TABLE 9–1
Estimated U.S. advertising expenditures; 1947–70 (in millions of dollars)

Year	Total	Agriculture, Forestry and Fisheries	Mining	Construction	Manufacturing	Transportation, Commun., Other Public Utilities	Wholesale Trade	Retail Trade	Trade Not Allocable	Finance, Insurance, Real Estate	Services	Business Not Allocable
1947	4,241	94	6	55	1,815	88	345	1,171	104	170	358	35
1948	4,907	105	8	68	2,041	104	393	1,434	116	218	402	18
1949	5,331	123	10	78	2,171	114	400	1,567	119	259	477	13
1950	5,864	138	10	89	2,412	118	452	1,706	114	304	509	12
1951	6,497	165	13	106	2,683	142	505	1,805	124	377	566	11
1952	7,161	173	16	120	2,983	156	523	1,912	139	492	637	10
1953	7,784	144	18	141	3,290	157	609	2,145	163	441	666	10
1954	8,080	135	18	132	3,466	172	637	2,175	170	484	681	10
1955	8,997	142	20	141	3,842	194	715	2,407	195	586	748	7
1956	9,674	138	20	149	4,151	212	782	2,548	201	626	838	9
1957	10,313	123	22	166	4,555	244	854	2,592	166	674	903	14
1958	10,414	117	20	158	4,623	261	834	2,550	171	720	949	11
1959	11,358	112	22	201	5,067	284	915	2,707	217	787	1,031	15
1960	11,900	132	27	184	5,322	318	935	2,875	165	892	1,039	11
1961	12,048	137	28	192	5,355	323	950	2,835	125	960	1,130	13
1962	12,919	146	30	209	5,734	379	985	3,070	123	1,041	1,192	10
1963	13,639	148	29	210	6,080	409	950	3,298	103	1,083	1,320	9
1964	14,824	148	26	206	6,698	446	909	3,716	90	1,172	1,406	7
1965	16,175	152	24	231	7,553	512	1,009	3,940	55	1,260	1,433	6
1966	17,511	171	23	238	8,148	586	1,037	4,291	40	1,357	1,615	5
1967	18,004	176	22	250	8,325	602	1,030	4,398	35	1,410	1,751	5
1968	19,054	180	22	265	8,835	633	1,103	4,640	30	1,506	1,835	5
1969	20,507	190	20	280	9,630	684	1,158	4,870	30	1,640	2,000	5
1970	20,838	195	20	280	9,750	705	1,175	4,980	28	1,670	2,030	5

Source: *Advertising Age*, June 7, 1971.

Only about 40 percent of each of the figures in Table 9–1 represents national-brand advertising. A large proportion is institutional, such as that put out by a company attempting to build an image as a progressive firm, and almost a fourth ($3,740,000,000) is retail, which is local instead of national. Even national advertising is spread over many, many brands. Maneloveg of McCann Erickson pointed out in 1971, for example, that out of 108 brands handled by his agency, only six spent over $5 million annually, six from $2.5 million to $5 million, 23 from $1 million to $2.5 million, and 73 well under a million. He went on to say, "The vast majority of brands are spending in the lower category."[1]

The purpose of this chapter is to describe and explain advertising strategy and the advertising decisions made within the confines of that strategy. Partly because of the unique position of the advertising agency, organization plays an especially strong role in advertising management. After the nature of strategy formulation is discussed, each element of the advertising decision—budget, media, temporal allocation, and copy—will be investigated. The emphasis is on mass advertising, but the discussion is not confined to it. Such specialized advertising as direct mail and point of purchase is also included, for example.

COMPANY ORGANIZATION AND ADVERTISING PLANNING

The brand manager's most essential requirement is to have a solid enough grasp of the rationale for his marketing plan and enough quantitative support that he can see it through a maze of organizational relationships without compromising the heart out of it. Nowhere is this problem more apparent than in the planning and execution of advertising. For a number of reasons, "there appears to be little or no basic predetermination of exactly what it is that the advertising is supposed to accomplish," as one executive with many years' experience in one of the large, progressive, and profitable petroleum companies has observed. The average number of people who review or approve ads in a company is 5, but it ranges from 1 to 15. Further, company organizational pressures encourage an executive to say no when he is unsure rather than yes; that is, to err on the negative side. Then, too, the brand manager has been receiving increasing authority in advertising decisions at the expense of the staff advertising man, but he is low in the hierarchy and often not familiar with advertising.

The problem of gaining approval for a plan without losing its integrity is more strongly reflected in advertising because the decisions involve not only the brand manager's own organization but the advertising agency as well. The relationship is not an easy one. In a recent survey of its

---

[1]Federal Trade Commission, *Public Hearings on Modern Advertising Practices,* Washington, D.C., October 26, 1971, p. 470.

members, the Association of National Advertisers (ANA) found that only 46 percent felt that their advertising was as effective as they knew how to make it. Further, 28 percent blame only themselves and their agency not at all, 8 percent blame their agency, and 64 percent blame both, but, interestingly enough, when it comes to remedial action 24 percent would change the agency and 14 percent their company.[2]

The relationship is complicated by the lack of objective standards for evaluating the agency's services, especially its product (creative work), which has been a major factor in continuing an arrangement for compensating the agency which seems anachronistic and creates suspicions in the client. This is the media commission system: An agency is paid 15 percent of the cost charged by the media. Research by the agency, for example, might be an additional cost. The commission system undoubtedly encourages the client to think that the agency, at least occasionally, recommends additional advertising when it may not be wise or necessary from the client's point of view. The rapid expansion in the use of direct mail once it was made commissionable suggests there may be some truth in this suspicion.

For this reason some agency heads are urging the use of the fee system, in which the media commission arrangement is replaced by a negotiated fee. Since 1960 the Glidden Company, for example, has been on a fee arrangement based on the agency's detailed cost accounting for servicing the company. It is said to work satisfactorily in this case.[3] More recently a survey of 181 of its members by the ANA indicated that 25 percent said they had changed their agency compensation practices and one half went from a commission to a fee basis. The survey report notes, "The increasing use of agencies on a partial service basis is leading to greater reliance on fee methods of compensation. . . ."[4]

Why does a company turn to an advertising agency for help, anyway? After all, it usually solves its own new-product, pricing, distribution, and sales problems. Why not advertising also? The answer: The company needs *creative* help. First, someone must take the brand manager's marketing strategy for the product and translate it into words, pictures, and perhaps music to convey to the buyer the benefit that purchasing the brand will yield for him. Second, someone must decide which—which media and which communication technology required by each medium —can best transmit these elements to the buyer. The translation of strategy into words, pictures, and music is the most creative, but the selection of medium usually plays a strong supporting role. An agency is skilled in assembling these creative people, "creative nuts," as they are

---

[2] *The Development and Approval of Creative Work* (Association of National Advertisers, April 1969).

[3] *Advertising Age*, May 18, 1964, pp. 89–90.

[4] *Advertising Age*, May 22, 1972, p. 1.

sometimes called, and organizing them so as to utilize their rare and highly specialized talent.

The agency usually does more for the client, however, than supplying creative skills. Agencies developed in the first place because of the need to purchase media for clients. They can supply market research to a greater or lesser extent to back up their advertising and can go further to help in new-product planning by determining when the new product should be introduced and how it should be packaged and priced as well as advertised. In some cases the agency is directly involved with the whole market-planning process for both old and new products. Finally, they may go so far as to advise on sales promotion devices and actually prepare directions as to how the field sales force should operate and how physical distribution should be carried out.

FIGURE 9–1
Organization of advertising agency

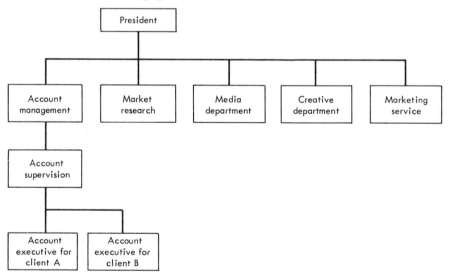

Which of these services an agency does in fact provide for a particular client strongly shapes the nature of the relationship between the client and the agency. In the simplest case, the agency supplies only creative talent for a simple nondivisionalized client. Even here the relations are complex, however.

Assume you are the brand manager in charge of the product (peanuts) and you are developing a marketing plan for the coming year. Advertising is a central element, and you have tentatively fixed a total dollar budget for it. The account executive from the agency calls on you to discuss the advertising input to the marketing mix. The position of the account executive is shown in Figure 9–1, a typical organization chart for a medium-size agency.

Although the creative people from the agency may have some direct contact with you, by all odds the account executive will carry the burden. In a recent ANA survey of its members, they reported that the account group, which is dominated by the account manager, handles key creative matters in 9 of 10 cases. Marketing services is concerned with formulating and evaluating client marketing plans and even strategies. The roles of the creative and media departments should be clear from the earlier discussion. Market research does the research to support the advertising and often does some of the clients' other marketing research activities, although in recent years clients have taken over much more of the research function. Account management is the liaison department which connects the agency to the client and the account executive is assigned to this department. He is responsible for all relations with the client. Occasionally, however, higher level executives in the agency such as the president will call on the client company's president or vice president.

If you have an established product and the brand manager, account executive, and creative man all have had experience with it, the relations can work smoothly. Typically, however, one or more of these conditions are not true. Let us assume the creative man is new, since there tends to be a high turnover of creative people in the agencies. (For that matter, there also tends to be a high turnover among brand managers in the company.) In trying to conceptualize the marketing plan in such a way that he can transmit the problem to the creative man in his agency, the account executive may ask why your strategy is to emphasize the sweetness of your peanuts. He comments that, after all, all of the competitors' brands are sweet, too. The brand manager replies that he has checked his competitors' ads and none emphasize sweetness, and that further his market research department has found that consumers rate all products low on sweetness. After a long conversation, the account executive returns to his agency.

The next day he has a session with the creative man assigned to your account. In order to communicate the nature of the problem to other people in his agency, especially his creative department, the account executive has learned to articulate your strategy, its supporting data, and its implications, as he sees them, for advertising. When he hears the strategy, the creative man explodes, "Who ever heard of advertising sweet peanuts?" The account executive is in a quandary because in the agency the creative man sits at the right hand of the Deity. What evidence can he use? A telephone call to you reveals that in a consumer survey a large proportion of the people said they wanted sweet peanuts. Armed with this, the account executive explains to the creative man that maybe his preconceptions are not quite correct. Perhaps the market has changed and consumers really do want sweet peanuts.

This episode is only one of an endless number of issues that can arise. If some people in the chain of client-agency relationships are new to the product, the problem becomes much worse. Further, and perhaps worse yet, even if you and the account executive agree on a complete set of ads, the marketing manager—your boss—usually demands his say-so. In fact, he is almost sure to reserve the final authority to himself in his delegation of advertising responsibility to you. He might not like the colors chosen, for example. In many companies, the president may also want to approve ads because they might affect current and potential stockholders' views of the company. The president may say that the ads are much too blatant for a "responsible company"—companies liked by bankers—to be associated with them. Because it is so publicly obvious and seen by so many of the company's several "publics," advertising comes under closer scrutiny by all levels than do many of the company's other activities.

Now to a more complex case. What if the agency-client relation involves not only advertising but much of the market research and other services (such as developing trade brochures) to support the marketing plan? In such a case, the evidence must flow from the agency to the client. If your company doesn't do its own research, the chances are that it is fairly unsophisticated. The education job that you and the account executive must do within your company can be profound. On the other hand, your higher level management may recognize its deficiency in evaluating advertising and leave it to the "experts."

Taking a still more complex case, the agency can serve as a marketing counsel advising on the whole marketing plan. It still is not viewed as jointly *responsible* for the total marketing results, however. Here the agency's account supervisor, account executive, and marketing services are tied in with your group product management, advertising management, specialized advertising department, and marketing services. Your task of getting these various departments to work together is not an easy one.

Even more complex is the case of "full partnership," where the agency "shares responsibility" for the total marketing results of the product. Here the agency provides support services on a regular ongoing basis. In a divisionalized company, the relationships are extremely complex because there are more levels in the client hierarchy where communication is required in order to secure coordination and more points where lack of coordination can lead to friction and ineffective marketing results. Even a well-supported marketing plan can be emasculated by compromise at each of numerous levels so that it loses all of its original logic. If the original plan has little logic to begin with, it will end up a meaningless and likely ineffective instrument for achieving the company's goals of profit and growth.

Finally, there is the most complex case. The agency takes the marketing leadership in developing strategies, in coordinating all available skills, in initiating marketing plans, and in providing a full spectrum of marketing services.

In recent years there has been a trend for agencies to place greater emphasis upon the creative and to deemphasize other services.[5] Whether the trend is likely to continue is an open question in which the size of the client company makes a difference. Larger companies are more able to provide their own subsidiary services. The following quotation illustrates the possibilities: "Stunned advertising agency executives learned last week that another major corporation—giant Monsanto Company which spent $9 million for advertising in 1969—will try to do without Madison Ave." The ad managers of each of the company's 35 divisions were required to coordinate their needs through a new advertising group consisting of Franklin J. Cornwell, the advertising director, and three others. This group intended to buy all of the services outside and keep the 15 percent media commissions.[6]

The ANA appointed a committee to study this trend. Its chairman, William Claggett of Ralston Purina, gave his explanation of why it developed in an interim report.[7] As advertising costs, particularly for TV, have risen, there is growing need to measure effectiveness. Another reason is the growing self-sufficiency of the client; he writes his own marketing plan instead of leaving it to the agency. Cost emphasis has encouraged this, but new-product management has also been a factor. The new-product function is being taken out from under line marketing management, and the managers of this new arrangement have the flexibility to work directly with their sources. Also, because new products are not so profitable to the agency, junior people tend to be assigned to such accounts. The client may respond by obtaining "his own creative guy." Finally, the media-buying services are reported to be improving the quality of their work.

This review of different types of client-agency relationships has suggested their complexity and the range of potential problems they offer. Although advertising is difficult to evaluate, this complexity merely emphasizes the necessity for an advertising plan to be as thoroughly thought out as possible and as well documented by research as economically feasible. Then it should not be compromised by organizational complications.

ADVERTISING STRATEGY AND PLANNING

Greater emphasis is probably placed upon strategy formulation in the advertising area than anywhere else in the company. The power of a well-thought-out strategy as a communication instrument was emphasized in

[5] *Advertising Age*, March 16, 1970, p. 74.
[6] *Advertising Age*, June 7, 1971, p. 18.
[7] *Advertising Age*, November 23, 1970, pp. 8–9.

TABLE 9–2
The top national advertisers of 1970: Total expenditures and allocation to nine media (last two zeros omitted in all figures)

RANK	COMPANY	TOTAL	NEWSPAPERS	MAGAZINES*	FARM PUBLICATIONS	BUSINESS PUBLICATIONS	SPOT TELEVISION	NETWORK TELEVISION	SPOT RADIO	NETWORK RADIO	OUTDOOR
1.	Procter & Gamble Co.	$188,417.5	$751.2	$7,362.8	$2.0	$769.2	$50,796.7	$128,444.5	$278.0	$4.1	$
2.	General Foods Corp.	121,509.7	9,140.3	11,858.8	135.0	270.6	49,259.2	44,642.0	5,263.0	502.0	438.8
3.	General Motors Corp.	119,164.2	20,096.0	23,856.4	457.3	4,180.3	8,961.1	32,972.3	20,906.0	2,804.3	4,930.5
4.	Bristol-Myers Co.	110,872.0	1,872.2	20,381.2		4,287.2	23,351.1	57,078.6	2,843.0	599.8	458.9
5.	Colgate-Palmolive Co.	101,480.7	3,169.3	5,018.4		43.3	36,860.9	46,507.8	8,141.0	1,690.0	50.0
6.	American Home Products	90,544.3	3,322.8	7,334.1	78.9	347.7	26,355.8	40,791.8	10,731.0	1,360.0	222.2
7.	R. J. Reynolds Industries	83,986.5	1,661.8	9,731.8	254.3	176.8	14,401.2	52,405.9	4,304.0	804.7	246.0
8.	Ford Motor Co.	79,745.5	11,220.9	14,544.9	1,214.8	1,797.5	7,544.6	31,345.8	7,430.0	1,676.3	2,970.7
9.	Sterling Drug Inc.	73,212.5	1,169.8	10,003.3	162.0	442.8	12,940.1	41,324.0	4,195.0	2,975.5	
10.	Warner-Lambert Pharmaceuticals	73,123.7	223.1	3,108.5		4,334.1	17,853.4	46,200.3	1,087.0	315.6	1.7
11.	Lever Bros.	67,019.8	2,009.1	3,734.9			20,893.2	38,554.9	1,331.0	496.6	1
12.	Philip Morris Inc.	66,703.8	532.6	13,745.7		81.5	11,491.5	36,685.8	2,500.0	833.7	833.0
13.	American Brands	58,572.7	7,397.8	15,438.9	5.4	661.7	2,092.0	31,365.6	899.0	15.6	706.7
14.	Coca-Cola Co.	52,965.8	2,276.3	6,064.6		474.3	16,944.6	15,527.8	10,239.0		1,439.2
15.	Sears, Roebuck & Co.	52,685.0	253.7	13,399.1			18,960.9	15,273.5	4,306.0	59.5	432.3
16.	Gillette Co.	51,805.5	304.6	5,383.6	16.6	114.3	16,320.3	27,479.3	1,817.0	382.9	3.5
17.	General Mills	51,777.5	1,752.0	7,004.1	40.7	395.1	17,940.0	24,152.4	117.0	386.7	13.6
18.	Kraftco	50,073.0	6,307.7	8,897.4	106.9	1,844.2	13,181.1	18,359.3	1,025.0	108.8	308.8
19.	Chrysler Corp.	48,714.1	7,034.2	9,366.4		491.9	3,926.7	21,341.6	4,869.0	930.5	646.9
20.	Distillers Corp.-Seagrams Ltd.	46,986.7	11,883.0	25,825.0		751.2	254.3		202.0	150.3	7,920.9
21.	Brown & Williamson Tobacco Co.	46,700.4	2,800.0	11,457.3		51.6	7,657.6	21,881.9	261.0	1,127.6	2,591.0
22.	Loew's Corp.	46,413.0	3,535.9	5,364.9		46.1	15,536.2	15,903.6	3,319.0	468.0	1,579.7
23.	PepsiCo Inc.	46,060.2	1,566.6	2,896.5	69.7	390.7	13,797.7	16,864.3	9,194.0	64.1	812.7
24.	American Telephone & Telegraph Co.	45,889.9	4,036.0	9,568.9	7.3	2,308.2	11,110.1	12,928.3	4,806.0		1,071.0

25.	Miles Laboratories	42,136.5	906.8	1,845.8	—	614.2	9,594.3	28,937.6	69.0	168.8	—
26.	Kellogg Co.	38,855.0	1,979.8	2,906.0	64.1	145.9	8,490.3	24,934.7			334.2
27.	Rapid-American Corp.	38,807.9	4,767.9	10,811.7	—	761.3	1,788.7	16,210.6	127.0		4,340.7
28.	Liggett & Myers Inc.	36,016.6	3,230.6	12,198.2	5.8	271.6	3,957.3	13,842.6	635.0	247.0	1,628.5
29.	Norton Simon Inc.	35,887.7	4,748.7	8,075.2	—	390.4	10,169.0	9,150.7	1,792.0		1,561.7
30.	International Telephone & Telegraph	34,938.2	1,699.8	5,435.5	—	3,870.0	13,434.9	9,707.5	330.0	18.0	442.5
31.	Goodyear Tire & Rubber Co.	34,409.5	20,599.1	3,320.2	465.9	973.0	2,778.3	6,067.9	108.0	1,293.8	97.1
32.	Campbell Soup Co.	33,179.7	2,533.2	6,859.7	—	525.0	6,388.1	13,590.4	1,897.0	135.2	92.5
33.	S. C. Johnson & Son	32,193.2	489.6	541.1	—		2,111.9	28,803.7	110.0		1.7
34.	RCA Corp.	31,662.4	8,317.6	10,729.6	—	1,365.0	3,953.7	6,367.2	480.0	35.3	414.0
35.	Firestone Tire & Rubber Co.	31,243.4	18,676.4	3,164.3	390.9	576.6	1,833.0	5,681.1	861.0	53.9	6.2
36.	Alberto-Culver Co.	30,278.5	46.3	2,604.3	—	152.7	14,472.8	12,971.0	31.0		4
37.	Ralston Purina Co.	29,942.4	922.6	980.4	448.0	50.0	7,905.9	18,739.1	523.0	246.2	127.2
38.	Schering-Plough Inc.	29,595.9	756.3	3,234.7	10.1	2,056.1	5,172.2	13,966.2	1,368.0	2,171.4	860.9
39.	Johnson & Johnson	27,174.2	116.0	7,312.4	11.5	530.6	9,807.5	7,737.2	1,659.0	—	
40.	Eastman Kodak Co.	26,637.4	2,445.1	7,241.4	6.2	2,898.0	2,208.3	10,994.4	798.0		46.0
41.	Richardson-Merrell	26,253.6	1,990.6	3,591.0	38.1	850.5	6,039.7	13,220.9	508.0		14.8
42.	Pfizer Inc.	26,156.8	46.3	5,119.1	737.6	1,010.5	2,005.4	14,921.6	1,388.0	536.2	392.1
43.	J. B. Williams Co.	25,476.0	797.5	1,885.9	—	60.0	138.4	22,425.0	47.0	122.2	
44.	Heublein Inc.	24,736.3	2,093.2	5,720.4	—	83.4	6,040.4	6,486.9	2,374.0		1,938.0
45.	American Cyanamid Co.	24,543.3	57.4	4,879.8	1,072.3	3,498.1	3,265.4	11,250.6	390.0	118.4	11.3
46.	Volkswagen of America	24,335.7	2,950.0	6,510.5	—	233.4	3,841.0	8,859.1	453.0		1,488.7
47.	Carnation Co.	24,218.3	1,222.9	958.4	69.8	569.2	9,510.1	11,562.1	207.0	102.2	16.6
48.	Standard Oil of New Jersey	24,061.0	2,598.4	2,933.8	165.0	898.1	6,617.7	6,620.4	3,026.0		1,201.6
49.	Block Drug Co.	23,844.0		3,647.9	—	73.6	3,152.9	15,971.6	998.0		
50.	Westinghouse Electric Corp.	23,771.7	4,327.3	8,209.0	33.9	2,500.0	5,335.4	3,211.6	74.0		80.5

Note: Expenditures in major media compiled by Elizabeth C. Graham, editorial librarian, *Advertising Age.* Tabulation copyright by Crain Communications, Inc.
*Magazine figures do not include ad investments in national farm magazines.
Sources: Bureau of Advertising, ANPA; leading national advertisers, farm publications reports,
American business press, broadcast advertisers' reports, radio expenditures reports, Institute of Outdoor Advertising.

Chapter 8. Many, if not most, of the brand manager's problems can be traced to the lack of it. The agency relationship places a further burden on communication. Thus the need for strategy arises in part from the communication requirement. Because of the great difficulty of evaluating advertising, and therefore of evaluating the quality of an advertising decision after the fact, emphasis is placed instead upon the quality of the logic that leads to the decision in the first place.

In practice, at least among the more progressive companies and agencies, the logic is clear. You attempt to segment the market and so identify target markets. You analyze your competition and pick the best among the possible competitive positions. David Ogilvy maintains, for example, that positioning is the most important decision in advertising. Motivating these judgments are, typically, the goals of growth and profit. With these two pieces of information—target and position—you proceed to formulate a strategy out of which flows your marketing plan. The research technology for achieving these two crucial pieces of information may be primitive, but the logic can be impeccable.

Strategy can be described in terms of target markets, market positioning, level of advertising to be used, kind of copy appeals, and range of media. Such a description is really a set of implicit rules which, as we have seen, aids communication. It also provides higher management with a control over the brand manager; he works out an agreement with the marketing manager for example, as to what the strategy will be. Finally, it obviously guides the brand manager in formulating his plan.

Thus we can see how the three main areas of advertising decision—advertising budget, advertising media, and advertising copy—flow out of the framework of strategy to build the advertising portion of the marketing mix. We will examine each of these three areas in this order, but, like all decisions, they should be made simultaneously. To a considerable extent the media and copy decisions are made in an interrelated way.

TOTAL ADVERTISING BUDGET

Introduction

The question here is: How much should be spent for advertising; that is, what should the total budget be? A brief review of the experience of a few companies will give an idea of the general magnitude of the problem. Table 9–2 presents the total national advertising expenditures of the 50 largest advertisers in the United States in 1961 and the allocations to nine major media. A national advertiser is here defined as one who sells outside a single locality. The left-hand column, represents the rank of the company according to the amount of total expenditure.

The data in Table 9–2 suggest that different companies select quite different media combinations. Also, a relatively few companies do most of the advertising. For example, it is estimated that the 100 leading national advertisers account for more than a third of all national advertising.

The decisions that underlie the data in Table 9–2 are now largely intuitive. The remark of the president of a company known for its marketing skill further supports the intuitive nature of the appropriation decision:

Just after I got back from my vacation in Maine, the advertising department presented its proposed budget calling for a total expenditure of more than $6,000,000 next year. If the production people had asked for one third as much, with as little justification of the need for it, I'd have fired them all.[8]

Although the appropriation decision is largely intuitive, it should not be concluded, however, that it is necessarily a bad decision, one that does not serve the company's objectives. As in the example in Chapter 5 of the petroleum company manager making price decisions, a man with experience may be using very sensible, well-based rules without being aware of them. Unfortunately, advertising budget decisions sometimes get made by people with no marketing experience. A few companies have done extensive and systematic research into the matter, such as Anheuser-Busch (number 64 in total national advertising expenditures). Little if any of the results get published, however, because of their competitive value.

Qualitative criteria for estimating effect of advertising

If qualitative criteria by which the effect of advertising can be estimated in order to guide management in deciding the magnitude of the advertising appropriation can be identified, they can be more quickly and cheaply applied than quantitative criteria. The problem is to locate objectively identifiable conditions in a company's market situation that will suggest whether or not advertising will be effective in a given situation. Such qualitative criteria can serve as the dimensions of a budgeting strategy with the three-way benefit of guidance, communication, and control. They can also serve as a framework within which the use of quantitative criteria can be considered. In a multiple-product company, for example, qualitative criteria can be used for deciding which of the products to advertise.

A comparison of British and American newspaper advertising shown in Table 9–3 suggests that the decision to advertise is not a matter of management's whim.[9] The close relation of expenditures between the two countries of the various products listed, indicated by a correlation

---

[8]A. W. Frey, *How Many Dollars for Advertising?* (New York: Ronald Press Co., 1955), p. 1.

[9]Nicholas Kaldor and Rodney Silverman, *A Statistical Analysis of Advertising Expenditures and Revenue of the Press* (Cambridge, England: The University Press, 1948), pp. 17–18.

TABLE 9–3
Manufacturers' expenditures on newspaper advertising as a proportion of manufacturers' net sales of selected consumer goods in the United Kingdom and the United States, 1935*

	Percentages	
	United Kingdom	*United States*
Flour.	1.8	.4
Canned and bottled foods	2.2	2.3
Coffee, tea, cocoa, beef extracts, etc.	3.3	3.2
Cereals, biscuits, and preserves	4.3	6.5
Sweets and toffee	3.6	5.3
Beer	1.8	4.7
Soft drinks	3.6	15.0
Tobacco	9.3	8.2
Soaps, cleansers, polishes, and disinfectants	13.0	13.0
Heating and refrigerating equipment	4.9	5.7
Domestic electrical equipment	5.4	4.5
Radios and accessories	8.6	5.3
Boots and shoes	.9	4.0
Hosiery and knitted underwear	1.5	4.2
Toilet goods	25.0	28.0
Proprietary medicines	37.0	34.0
Motorcars, motorcycles, and accessories	4.2	4.0
Petrol and motor oil	8.7	6.4

° The American figures were obtained from three surveys, two undertaken by the Association of National Advertisers (1931 and 1934 to 1935) and one by Harvard Business School, into the marketing expenses of grocery manufacturers for 1927. The number of firms included in each commodity appears to have been small (from 3 to 41 in the 1934 to 1935 inquiry).

Where these surveys give data for the same commodities for 1935 and an earlier year there does not, in general, appear to have been any great change in the percentages between the two years. The United Kingdom ratios relate to manufacturers' sales exclusive of duty, and the American figures are comparable.

Source: Nicholas Kaldor and Rodney Silverman, *A Statistical Analysis of Advertising Expenditure and Revenue of the Press* (Cambridge, England: The University Press, 1948), pp. 30–31.

coefficient of +0.93, suggests, though not conclusively, that there are certain underlying factors, perhaps psychological, sociological, or technological, that make it profitable to advertise in some situations and not in others. Since the study was confined to the newspaper medium, an immediate question is whether the nature of the media differed significantly between the two countries. Except for radio, which was relatively unimportant at that time, there was little difference in the kinds of media used. Although somewhat out of date, the comparison is probably more valid then than today, when there is so much exchange of marketing "know how."

To be more explicit about what the conditions are that determine the appropriate level of advertising, Neil H. Borden, after extensive research on the economics of advertising, offered the following hypotheses about the conditions under which advertising will be effective: (1) if industry demand is expanding, (2) when there is a substantial chance of differentiating the product, (3) where hidden qualities exist that cannot be judged at the time of purchase, and (4) when strong emotional buying motives exist, such as the protection of health or enhancement of social position.[10]

The buyer-behavior model can be used to elaborate Borden's hypotheses. If demand is expanding as the result of new buyers in the market, these new buyers will be seeking information on which to base their decisions. Information about one brand rather than another can make a difference in which brand they choose. A "substantial chance of differentiating the product" means that the buyers have different needs—the market is made up of different segments—and that the product can be presented in forms (actual product, package, label, advertising, and so forth) which will permit different brands to present different sets of cues to the buyer. To be cues for the buyer, the characteristics of the brand need not be those that an engineer would refer to in writing engineering specifications for a product; color alone might be the cue by which the buyer discriminates.

The "hidden qualities that cannot be judged at the time of purchase" suggest that the buyer will be forced to greater search in making the decision. This effect of difficult-to-judge qualities is illustrated in contrasting countries with a low standard of living and those with a high standard. The choices are much greater and more subtle in the latter. In the former, the consumer needs food. In the latter, food is available in many forms, and for example, in many social settings. The social setting then becomes a part of the want-satisfying capacity of the food. Further, such qualities may remain "hidden" even after the decision and can be either functional or expressive. If expressive, we mean that buying the brand has implications for the buyer's self-concept, how he appears to others and how he expresses himself to others, not just verbally but in his total being. Cigarette, cosmetics, or liquor advertising often illustrates this. These are subtle impressions to communicate because they are so tied up with our most intimate selves and to the social framework within which we live.

"Strong emotional buying motives" is the counterpart of motive intensity. The more intense the motives that are being satisfied by the decision, the more the buyer will seek out information. There may be that rare case of exceptionally high drive which engenders so much anxiety that the buyer will close out further information search and take the most available brand.

Quantitative estimation of advertising effect

The cost of advertising is not difficult to determine, but the contribution it makes to revenue has been slippery indeed to evaluate. The first

---

[10]Neil H. Borden, *The Economic Effects of Advertising* (Homewood, Ill.: Richard D. Irwin, Inc., 1944), p. xxvii.

step in estimating what the revenue contribution *will be* is to ask what it *was* in the past. Advertising research is one answer. Extensive research efforts, particularly by advertising agencies, have been devoted to media and especially message (copy) selection. Not much research has gone into the budget, the amount of advertising.

EFFECTIVENESS CRITERIA. A crucial question in advertising research, as we shall see, is, what criteria should be used to measure advertising effectiveness. Little advertising research has been directed toward determining effect on sales directly by using *sales* as a criterion of effectiveness. Rather the research has been characterized by attempts to *impute* effects on sales by means of an analysis of some more readily accessible intermediate factor (surrogate variable) with which sales effects are assumed to be associated. Four of the more readily accessible intermediate factors used are readership, attitude toward the advertising, awareness of the brand, and attitude toward the brand.

One of the earliest attempts to measure advertising effect was to analyze readership on the unverified assumption that it influences purchase behavior. "Readership" is an ambiguous term that can be applied to the medium (for example a magazine), or to a particular advertisement in a given medium. It can be classified as unaided recall or aided recall (recognition). Further, the term can have various meanings from the standpoint of reading behavior. For example, the Starch Advertisement Readership Service provides information to advertisers in magazines and newspapers about "ad readership" according to (1) "Noted"—the per cent of a magazine's readers who remember that they have seen the advertisement in the particular issue; (2) "Seen-Associated"—the percent of readers who have seen or read any part of the ad which clearly indicates the brand or advertiser; and (3) "Read Most"—the percent of readers who read 50 percent or more of the written material in an ad. Readership studies are used primarily in selecting media and copy.

The central point of readership, however, is that recall is the criterion. By all odds, unaided recall is the most widely used measure in practice for all kinds of media, not just print. This conclusion was borne out in the federal Trade Commission hearings on advertising in late 1971. Yet readership is usually applied with judgment. As a brand manager put it, it is used negatively. If it is, for example, less than 10, where 10 refers to the percent of the sample that recall the ad, the ad is viewed as deficient. If it is high, such as greater than 35, all that is concluded is that the ad is memorable.

 A second possible measure is attitude toward the advertising. Is it good or bad advertising? A series of advertisements is prepared and presented to a sample of people. The one selected by the respondents as being the best is assumed to have the greatest effect on sales.

 A third measure is awareness of the product and brand. Buyers can be surveyed both before and after the advertising campaign and asked how much they know about the product. Any gain in knowledge represented by the difference in awareness levels between the two surveys is ascribed to the advertising.

Attitude toward the brand is the fourth measure. If advertising appears to change reader attitudes—their evaluations of the brand—it is assumed that sales of the brand are being influenced. In addition to these, however, we know from Chapter 3 that brand comprehension, confidence (in judgment) and intention (to buy the brand) could also be used. Information recalled can be operationally defined as unaided ad readership.

In discussing the appropriate criteria to be used in determining the effect of advertising, they will be considered only in terms of their accuracy as a predictor of purchases. The cost of collecting data in each of the criteria of advertising effectiveness will be neglected, but these can readily be obtained in any concrete instance.

The marketing executive would much prefer to know the effect of advertising on sales. For example, awareness of the ad—measured by the ability of the respondent to *recall* (unaided) the ad—has been found to have an indirect effect on sales. Not many serious systematic investigations of any of the four nonsales criteria have come to the author's attention, although they are increasing.

Intention to buy the brand is probably the most accurate single predictor of purchasing behavior, but the evidence suggests it is an imprecise prediction (see Chapter 8). The inaccuracies encountered in measuring such internal variables as intention are considerable. The interviewer collects an expressed intention. Expressing an intention is a form of behavior, and the theory of buyer behavior suggests that the behavior thus represented would be a function of personal attitudes, impersonal attitudes, and confidence. The attitude thus expressed is expected to reflect actual purchasing behavior that may be carried out under quite another set of conditions when it actually takes place later. In addition, the intention is expressed to the interviewer, another human being, instead of to some neutral mechanical receiver (unless the interview is done by telephone), and there is interviewer bias. This respondent-interviewer interaction has many implications for the buyer's behavior; for example, human beings learn devices to use in dealing with others which may cause them to distort the information they give the interviewer. As a consequence it would be surprising if the verbal behavior did not deviate at least some from the purchasing behavior.

Many advertising people argue that attitude toward the product and brand is the most meaningful measure on the grounds that it is more correlated with sales than either recall of the ad, attitude toward the ad, or awareness of the brand. They also contend that it is impossible to measure the sales effect. The Association of National Advertisers, which is made up of the advertising representatives of most of the large advertisers, took this same position. The association first argued that advertising is only one of several marketing forces influencing sales.[11] A multiplicity of causes complicates the measurement problem by making it more difficult to isolate the effect of any one variable because changes in the other independent variables obscure its effect. Also, if the variables interact, the problem is complicated still further because the effect of any one variable depends upon the values of the other independent variables. Neither of these possibilities, however, necessarily renders it impossible to measure the effects of advertising.

The second argument is that carry-over exists. Carry-over apparently means that as a result of the impact of one set of cues (for example, an advertisement) the buyer responds differently to another cue than he would if he had not been exposed to the first. In other words, his continuing behavior has changed as a result of the first set of cues: he has *learned*. Thus, in the issue of when learning would be expected to occur, it would be when the buyer is in limited problem solving and extensive problem solving.

Learning would *not* be expected to occur when the buyer is fully learned, when his concept of the brand is fully formed. He is then in routinized response behavior. Advertising could still have an effect through stimulating motives and giving information which affects impersonal attitudes, but presumably it is temporary. Thus, the carry-over argument would not appear to be relevant to a stable, fully learned market.

Sales as a measure have been used in a few published studies of advertising effect. Julian L. Simon has carefully summarized these around the central question of whether the relationship between advertising and sales is an S-curve or increasing returns. The S-curve is widely believed to exist; you will recall that it was shown this way back in Figure 3–1. Simon concludes:

There is not one single piece of strong evidence to support the general belief that increasing returns exist in advertising. A very few studies suggest that there are increasing returns, but their evidence is weak. Individually, the items of evidence against increasing returns are also weak, except for mail-order tests. But there are a great many studies that show diminishing marginal returns, and I feel their collective weight is much greater than that of the evidence supporting increasing returns. By my reading of the evidence the efficiency of advertising expenditures always decreases, even at the lowest levels, with increased repetition and with increased size of advertisements (though total profits may continue to rise, of course.[12]

Estimation models, described in Chapter 8, were used in a number of the studies summarized by Simon.

---

[11]Russell H. Colley, *Defining Advertising Goals* (New York: Association of National Advertisers, 1961), pp. 10 and 11.

[12]Julian L. Simon, *Issues in the Economics of Advertising*, (Urbana: University of Illinois Press, 1970), pp. 21–22.

STRUCTURAL MODELS. The structural model, which implies causality, was discussed at length and illustrated in Chapter 8. As we know from Figure 8–1, all of the various measures of effectiveness discussed above can be incorporated into the single model. From Chapter 8 we also know that one of the serious problems with structural models currently is the level of noise that was indicated in Table 8–6 for two of the equations by low R^2s. Nevertheless, this approach begins to give us the fundamental understanding needed to impart rationality to the advertising decision.

EXPERIMENTATION. Not only may the structural model, when applied to observational data, encounter too much noise, but there has not yet been enough experience with structural models on longitudinal data to know their usefulness. Structural models using data from field experimentation can probably provide a solution because the inputs of advertising will be varied enough that the effects can be identified. A variety of cable TV arrangements offers possibilities.

Probably Anheuser-Busch has done the most extensive field experimentation of any company up to now. It varied advertising over markets from 150 percent increase above normal to 100 percent decrease. Unfortunately, their results have not been published, but it is safe to say that based upon the findings the company cut back on its annual advertising budget approximately one third. Table 9–2 shows that Anheuser-Busch, 64th, now spends $19,000,000, reflecting this decline.

Methods of establishing the total budget

It may be helpful to compare the profit-optimizing or incremental approach to fixing the total budget developed in Chapters 3, 4, and 8 with two other methods in common use. These are the percent-of-sales and the objective-and-task methods.

PERCENT-OF-SALES METHOD. This method, which is widely used, consists in applying some fixed percentage to anticipated sales for the budget period, such as a year. In effect, the method results in sales determining advertising. This is difficult to justify on a logical basis, since the purpose of advertising expenditure is to influence sales. The popularity of the method is probably due to the fact that little is known objectively about the effects of advertising that can give top management a way of controlling this expenditure, but this method has the virtue of providing such control. It also has the advantage that advertising expenditures will fluctuate with corporate income so that funds will always be available to pay the cost. Moreover, the method makes for stability of competitive relationships because changes in the level of advertising *among* competitors which would encourage unstable competitive relations are unlikely to occur, particularly if all competitors use approximately the same percentage figure.

The indefensibility of the percent-of-sales method on logical grounds probably explains its waning popularity as a rationalization for the way

FIGURE 9–2
Relation between advertising and sales when sales declined

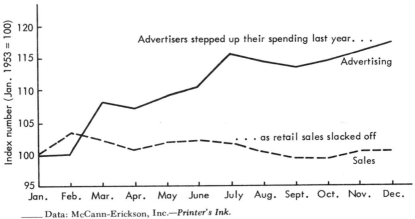

_____ Data: McCann-Erickson, Inc.—*Printer's Ink.*
_ _ _ _ Data: Dept. of Commerce.
Source: *Business Week*, February 13, 1954, p. 42.

the advertising appropriation is determined. The relationship between advertising expenditures and retail sales, shown in Figure 9–2, has been cited as evidence that advertisers are becoming less inclined to tie their advertising to sales. It suggests that advertising continued to increase in spite of declining retail sales. This evidence is no more than suggestive, however, because aggregate data on the volume of advertising are incomplete. Also, advertising schedules are based on expected rather than actual sales.

OBJECTIVE-AND-TASK METHOD. An approach that is probably more common than percent of sales is the objective-and-task method. Under this method, the appropriation is set by the difference between the desired value of some criterion, such as buyer attitudes toward the brand, with advertising and the value of that criterion without advertising. The difference is the objective. The task that must be performed to achieve this objective is then described in terms of the specific advertising actions that must take place, and finally the cost of performing the task is estimated. The essential point is that the statement of objective should incorporate criteria which will permit proof of success, so that after the fact it will be possible to know whether the advertising was a success and achieved its objective.

How well the method works out in practice is suggested by Steuart H. Britt in a fascinating comparison of 135 so-called "successful campaigns" exhibited at the United States Trade Center for Scandinavia in 1967.[13] He

---

[13]Steuart H. Britt, "Are So-Called Successful Advertising Campaigns Really Successful?," *Journal of Advertising Research*, June 1969, pp. 3–9.

stated that the objectives should (1) include a statement of the basic message to be delivered, (2) identify the audience, and (3) describe the intended effect in terms of criteria that can later be used to evaluate its success. In this comparison 64 percent of the campaigns included the first three elements but only 1 percent included all four. Further, 99 percent did not state their objectives in quantifiable terms, and 16 percent did not identify the audience to be affected. Its disadvantage, in practice, appears to be that it does not deal with the question of whether an objective is worth achieving.

INCREMENTAL METHOD. The incremental method is sometimes called the "logical approach" because it places the problem of determining the advertising appropriation into the appropriate framework of contribution to profit. The idea is simple; the aggregate response curve for advertising is determined for a company and then related to the company's relevant costs to obtain the optimum appropriation. The method was discussed in Chapter 7 and illustrated in Figure 7–2.

DESIGN OF MEDIA PLAN

Selecting the appropriate media is the second of the major advertising decisions. The more common types of advertising media are newspapers, business papers, magazines, television, radio, direct mail, car cards, billboards, posters, and point-of-purchase display. How various companies distribute their budget among the media was shown in Table 9–2.

The major media are in a state of ferment. It is predicted that television will decline relatively because of its fast-increasing cost, and radio is expected to increase.[14] The general magazines have suffered seriously in the past decade, but specialized magazines (such as *Car Craft, TV Guide,* and *Skiing*) are becoming much more attractive.[15] Large city newspapers are finding it difficult to attract enough advertising, but suburban papers are in many cases burgeoning.[16] Telephone sales are being used to increase the effectiveness of direct mail.[17] Cable television is on the threshold of large increases, and TV cassettes will soon be available. Currently, there are 4.7 million cable subscribers. Of these, 1.1 million are in the top 100 markets which contain 70 percent of the country's 63 million TV homes. The cable medium thus can be expected to experience substantial growth.[18]

These media changes will have many effects, but one in particular is the further "fractionation" of audiences, the development of smaller, more specialized audiences which will make possible the more precise tailoring of advertising to fit media and audience. This trend will require greater

---

[14] *Advertising Age,* November 2, 1970.
[15] *Business Week,* May 21, 1970.
[16] *Business Week,* August 27, 1966.
[17] *Business Week,* November 27, 1971, p. 86.
[18] *Business Week,* November 27, 1971, p. 79.

attention to market segmentation possibilities. A recent headline, "J(ohnson) and J(ohnson) is Sitting Pretty as Segmented Attack Doubles Baby Powder Sales" points up how baby powder is being advertised for the family, teen-agers, and adults. The accompanying article notes that "Still in the thinking stage are campaigns aimed at blacks and Spanish-speaking segments of the market".[19]

Although we will deal with the selection of media, the first of the advertising allocation decisions, as though allocations to media could be made independent of allocations of the budget over time and to specific messages, this is clearly not possible in practice. For example, if it is desired that advertising appear weekly, monthly magazines are automatically eliminated as possible media, irrespective of their economy. However, a particular combination of four monthly magazines could yield a weekly impact. Likewise it is often asserted, though without evidence, that an advertising message of considerable blatancy would hardly "fit" the staid *Fortune*, for example. For the sake of clarity, it will be assumed that these interrelationships do not exist among various kinds of advertising allocation decisions, except for the relation between media allocation and geographic allocation.

Media selection and the geographic allocation of advertising are so intimately related that, in practice, the two decisions are made more or less simultaneously. A measure of geographic demand (a market potential as described in Chapter 1) is often used in selecting the media for a given area. Measures of market potentials are such sources as *Sales Management's* "Index of Buying Power" and the Standard Industrial Classification method. A mathematical method of allocating promotion expenditures to territories or market segments was presented in Chapter 7. Advertising poses a special problem in the sense that its coverage is fixed by the medium, whereas salesmen can be shifted by the brand manager in collaboration with the sales manager.

The criterion for selecting advertising media is whether it serves a given area better than another medium would. This is evidenced by the two standard criteria often used together in practice for selecting media: reach and frequency. *Reach* is a measurement of coverage. It is an estimate of the number, usually expressed as a percent, of different people who have been *exposed* to at least one advertising message within a given time period, perhaps a week. If a TV program has a weekly reach of 45 percent of the women in the designated area, it means that about 45 percent of the women in that area will be exposed to at least one advertising message each week. *Frequency* is a measure of the average number of times each person who has been reached, as defined above, is exposed to the advertising message. It tells us nothing about the buyer's exposure to *advertising*, only his exposure to media.

---

[19]*Advertising Age*, August 14, 1972, p. 3.

Perhaps in no area of marketing management (with the possible exception of distribution) have there been greater efforts to computerize planning than in media selection. Two general kinds of approaches have been employed: optimizing and simulation.

Attempts to apply the *optimizing* technique of linear programming models to the task of media selection began in the middle fifties. The criterion for making the allocation was typically the simple one of *cost per thousand* readers or viewers exposed to the medium. Because there is some evidence to support the idea commonly held that the relations are not in fact, linear, model builders turned to nonlinear programming techniques. These were of two kinds: iterative or marginal analysis and dynamic programming.[20] The term "iterative" derives from the approach of solving for one medium and then repeating to select the next-best medium, and so forth. The other nonlinear approach, dynamic programming, avoids the linearity assumption but encounters other limitations which will not be elaborated here. All of the optimizing models have the disadvantage of making rather drastic simplifying assumptions without the builder knowing how sensitive or how important the solution is to the assumptions. If not sensitive, the lack of realism presents no serious problem.

The *nonoptimizing* models avoid some of the major simplifications required by the optimizing models. In fact, the nonoptimizing system builder begins by trying to identify what the relevant variables are in the situation. Gensch refers to a heuristic type as well as simulation types.[21] The heuristic type was first developed as a structure from looking at the problem and then putting in parameters based on evidence, when it is available, and using judgment where it is not. Thus, to mathematize the problems, some assumptions had to be made. It has not been successful operationally but, Gensch believes "this mathematical heuristic approach must be recognized as a step in the right direction."[22]

In a simulation model, a great number of calculations are made as though the model were calculating the effects of each alternative in the sample population. One, at the London Press Exchange, has been used operationally since 1964. One here in the United States, designed by Simulmatics Corp., has not been used.

An issue that does not usually seem to get raised is that though the contrived computerized models may not be logically perfect, they may still be as capable of doing the job as well as a human, and doing it more cheaply. From the decision flow chart of Figure 5–7 and other evidence we can infer that, if he can break the task into many small parts and has had much

---

[20]Dennis H. Gensch, "Computer Models in Advertising Media Selection," *Journal of Market Research,* November 1968. pp. 414–424.

[21]Ibid., p. 420 ff.

[22]Ibid., p. 421.

experience doing it, he can probably do it well. Unfortunately, it is not easy to find out whether he is doing it well. Without experience he undoubtedly cannot do so. Even if he can, the task is so complex that one suspects that computerization is much more economical. A fascinating detailed study of two companies' experienced by Marschner shows the problems of allocating media geographically by humans, and its conclusions are not encouraging.[23] Small specialized companies providing this computerized service are being used by a number of clients.

In this discussion of media allocation models we have made some simplifying assumptions. These have mainly to do with what are often called "weighting factors," influences which do make a difference in the decision of which media should be used. Current practice is to attempt to insert subjective judgments of the effects of such factors, thus modifying the simple criterion of cost per thousand of people exposed to the medium. The weighting factors that evidence has shown (or advertisers believe) do make a difference are:

1. Target population weights. Some people are believed to be better potential users of the product than others.
2. Vehicle appropriateness weights. Factors that may affect the appropriateness of a medium are editorial climate, product fit, technical capabilities, competitive advertising strategy, target population receptiveness, and product distribution system.
3. Commercial exposure weights. A person has a better opportunity to be exposed to some media than others.
4. Commercial effectiveness weights. Given that a person is exposed to a medium, he is more likely to perceive (admit to his sensory system) some ads than others.
5. Cumulative frequency weights. This deals with the question of the effect of additional exposures of a given ad, or repetition, as it is often called.

It appears doubtful, however, if these complications tend to be factored in. A retired B.B.D. & O. executive vice-president laments that they are not, that straight CPM (cost per thousand homes) is by all odds dominant.[24]

TEMPORAL ALLOCATION OF ADVERTISING

Another of the basic advertising decisions pertains to proper timing of advertising. One hard fact of life that anyone working with advertising quickly learns is that advertising has limited power. If the person exposed to it has a need for the product, it can be quite effective, other things

---

[23]Donald C. Marschner, "Theory versus Practice in Allocating Advertising Money" *Journal of Business*, July 1967, pp. 286–302.
[24]*The New York Times*, April 30, 1972, p. 25ff.

being equal. Otherwise it tends to be ineffective; the customer ignores it. This is important because the need for many products is more or less seasonal, some entirely so. The advertising must conform roughly to the seasonal pattern of demand.

Management often faces the question of when to begin its advertising to meet seasonal demand. A study of *Family Circle Magazine* readers conducted by a consulting firm revealed that women think of seasonal purchases considerably in advance. The consultant concluded that advertisers were beginning their seasonal advertising too late. The fur-coat industry, which begins to advertise in August, is an example of an industry which advertises well in advance of the time when the product will be used.

When to advertise during the day is another question. In a market survey of coffee drinking it was reported that Sunday morning is when people most enjoy their coffee; a large proportion, 79 percent, drinks coffee then. Yet, it was stated, coffee advertisers tend not to advertise then. A question to be answered is what medium will reach people at that *(optimum)* time.

The expected timing of competitors' advertising is also a relevant consideration in deciding upon the allocation of advertising over time.

Finally, there are the questions of how often advertising should be run and whether it should be at regular or irregular intervals. In an attempt to provide evidence for answering the first question, the effect of advertising on the sales of a consumers' drug product were analyzed.[25] The data were obtained in 1943 from a consumer panel of roughly 2,000 families. It was found that the number of exposures per family to an advertisement during the six-month period varied all of the way from none to sixteen, with an average of seven exposures per family. Some of the conclusions of this study are shown in Figure 9–3. Each point on the family total revenue curve in Figure 9–3 represents family purchasing when other factors are held constant. The shape of the curve shows the effect of diminishing returns. The analysis was not carried to the point of incorporating the actual incremental cost, but to do so would have been a relatively simple step. When only the incremental advertising cost was inserted into the analysis, the optimum number of exposures per family was 12, but this conclusion overstates the case because nonadvertising incremental costs were omitted.

The second question refers to the practice of "pulsing," or intermittent concentrated advertising, versus the use of continuous advertising. Some practitioners argue vehemently that a given budget spent by pulsing will yield more than the same amount spent continuously. Evidence as to the truth of this proposition is limited. Prakash Sethi, using data made avail-

---

[25]Harry V. Roberts, "The Measurement of Advertising Results," *Journal of Business,* 20 (1947), p. 142.

FIGURE 9–3
Family opportunity for exposure to advertising

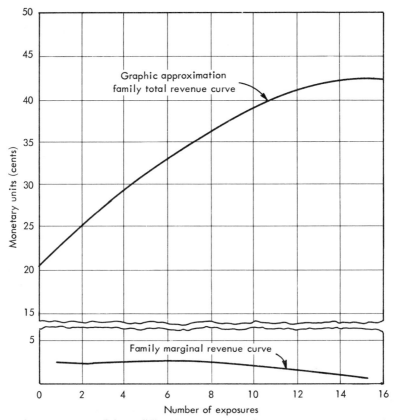

Source: Harry V. Roberts, "The Measurement of Advertising Results," *Journal of Business*, 20 (1947), 142. (Copyright 1947, The University of Chicago.)

able by the Milwaukee Newspaper Laboratory, with matched panels of consumers and analgesics as the product, concluded that in this particular situation pulsing was not successful.[26] It worked early in the test period, but as time went on it became less effective than the continuous application of advertising.

DESIGN OF MESSAGE

Introduction

"Message" is used here to describe the whole advertisement, which in printed media includes both the printed copy and the artwork and in

---

[26]Prakash Sethi, "An Investigation into the Mediating Effects of Socio-Psychological Variables between Advertising Stimulus and Brand Loyalty" (Ph.D. diss., Columbia University, 1968).

broadcasting refers to both the picture and the sound. In practice, a distinction is sometimes made between message content and message presentation, since the former is often provided by the client and the latter by the advertising agency. Content has to do with the ideas underlying the ad, and presentation has to do with the form in which these ideas are presented, for example, copy and artwork. What an ad must accomplish is clearly stated by Tom Dillon, chairman of B.B.D. & O., in describing the task of a 30-second television commercial.[27]

1. It must get the attention of the prime prospect.
2. It must identify the domain of her decision (the product class).
3. It must register the memory of your brand in this domain.
4. It must register in her memory the content of the copy concept.
5. It must link the concept to the brand.

The function of the message in a general sense is to translate the qualities of a brand into the motives or attitudes of the buyer so that he will view the brand as an aid rather than a barrier to achieving his motives. The cost of a brand can be one barrier to motive achievement because its purchase results in less funds for other purchases. Purchasing also requires effort. In addition, the brand itself can have negative consequences, physically and socially, which may tend to offset the positive qualities the buyer expects from it.

Advertising theme or platform

To develop an advertising message which accomplishes this translation of the brand qualities into the motives and attitudes of the buyer, the first task is the formulation of a theme or platform. "Platform" is used in the sense that the actual copy "rests upon it"; the copy is developed from it. We can think of it as copy strategy. The theme or platform is a statement of *the general way that the actual copy will go about accomplishing its task, the avenues through which it will operate*.

Knowing the customers' stage of buying process will do much to set the foundation for the advertising platform. Often in discussions of advertising practice, all effects of advertising tend to get lumped into "motives." As shown in Chapter 3, advertising can have a number of effects upon the buyer. When the buyer is in routinized response behavior, advertising can influence him by telling him that the noninternalized elements underlying intention—his impersonal attitudes toward the brand—have a certain value. Irrespective of his stage of decision, motive intensity can be changed. When he is in limited problem solving, it can change his memory content, which in turn can affect brand comprehension, attitude, and confidence. It is important, especially in the case of attitude, to think of

RRB

LPS

---

[27]Federal Trade Commission, *Public Hearings on Modern Advertising Practices*, Washington, D.C., October 22, 1971, pp. 322–33.

the dimensions (choice criteria) that underlie it and to separate them according to functional or self-concept. Quite different advertising approaches may be required for these two different areas of psychological functioning.

In preparing the platform, the market should be defined and customers identified. If the budgeting decision has been carefully thought through, the market has already been well defined and the customers classified, at least in terms of operational characteristics.

A key element of the theme or platform is the brand dimensions that should be emphasized in the copy. To determine this requires a careful examination of the strengths and weaknesses of competitors' brands. The ideal situation is to have a product that is strong on only certain dimensions, those desired by customers and those on which competitors are weak.

Copy and art work

Once a theme or platform has been worked out, it must be decided what to put into the copy and the artwork. Few useful generalizations can be made about how to prepare an ad. The experienced creative man with talent has many intuitive information-processing and decision rules hidden in his decision processes, but apparently no research has been devoted to attempting to elicit them. It is not an impossible task, however; it has been done with a musical composer, who would seem to be as "creative" as an advertising copywriter or art man.[28]

From buyer-behavior theory we can probably make some fairly good guesses about what ad content would change a number of the buyer variables. To begin with, we can describe how the copy might be decided upon. From psychological research there are some rules we can apply. An implicitly instead of directly stated argument is better if the medium permits the buyer ample time to understand it and he is fairly intelligent. Otherwise an explicitly stated argument is better. If the brand has negative features, the audience is intelligent, and the features are familiar and controversial, it is better to refute them. The spoken word is more effective than the written word, even though the latter is more easily understood. If particular brand dimensions being set forth in the ad are important to the buyer, getting his attention will be easier.

The ad content should be divisible into small, self-contained sections with no more than four or five individual items in any section. The sections should be organized so the various parts fit together into a logical self-ordering structure. Some relationship must be established between the material to be learned and what the buyer already knows, so that one fits neatly within the other. This relationship can be inherent in the nature

---

[28]Walter R. Reitman, *Cognition and Thought* (New York: John Wiley & Sons, 1965).

of the material or it can be brought about by imposing an external structure such as rhymes or music, so that when the buyer hears it he recalls the message in the ad.

If the message is discrepant with what the buyer already knows and has no external structure imposed on it, the greater the discrepancy, the less likely is the message to have an effect. Such a message tends to be viewed as less fair, less informed, less logical, less grammatical, and less interesting than it really is. It leads to Sherif's "assimilation error." If it is similar to the buyer's concepts, he views it as more similar; if it is different from his own, he views it as even more different.[29]

Finally, if the source of the message is clearly identifiable, such as a particularly well-known person speaking on television, the more credible person is likely to have greater effect. This credibility is a function of how much he is thought to know about the subject—his competence—and how much the buyer *trusts* him.

The company behind the brand can also be viewed as the source of impact and thus as having varying degrees of credibility. It was concluded, for example, that doctors in adopting a new drug often depend heavily upon their beliefs about the reliability and scientific knowledge of the company and its "detail man" (salesman) who calls on them.[30]

As to artwork, the Chinese proverb that "a picture is worth a thousand words" is useful to bear in mind. The role of the art element is to support, elaborate, and dramatize what the copy has to say.

SUMMARY

To provide a background for the brand manager as to the nature of the advertising function, this chapter has given special emphasis to his complex relationship with the advertising agency. Managerial issues and advertising strategy were highlighted, and technical aspects, such as media and message, were covered in a way that was designed to enable the manager to evaluate them better. This discussion of advertising management was not intended for the advertising technician.

DISCUSSION QUESTIONS

1. There is a variety of relations between advertiser and advertising agency, each involving a different amount of activity for the agency. Describe them.
2. What is the function of advertising strategy?

---

[29]M. Sherif and C. W. Sherif, "Attitude as the Individual's Own Categories: The Social Judgement-Involvement Approach to Attitude and Attitude Change" in M. Sherif and C. W. Sherif (eds.) *Attitude, Ego-Involvement and Change*, New York; John Wiley & Sons, 1967, pp. 105–39.

[30]R. A. Bauer and L. H. Wortzell, "Doctors Choice: The Physician and His Sources of Information about Drugs," in Donald F. Cox, *Risk Taking and Information Handling in Consumer Behavior* Boston: Graduate School of Business Administration, Harvard University 1967, Chapter 5.

3. What criteria of advertising effectiveness tend to be used?
4. Considerable effort has been devoted to developing quantitative media models. What are the simplifying assumptions that these models make, or what "weighting factors" do they omit?
5. What do we mean by copy theme, copy platform, and copy strategy?

10

Management of pricing

INTRODUCTION
THERE is a mythology associated with pricing that is in part due to its legal and moral implications. To clear the air, these and other complications will be examined first in this chapter, which presents an overview of pricing strategy and the pricing decision, with emphasis upon the brand manager's needs. Three kinds of pricing problems emerge in the discussion: single-product pricing, product-line pricing, and setting price differentials. The legal considerations in pricing, though important, are largely reserved for Chapter 15.

COMPLICATIONS IN PRICING
A surprising number of conditions add complexity to the pricing decision and make it more difficult to decide on a rational course of action in fixing price as a part of the product mix. First, price per se has a substantial communication effect. It tells the buyer how much he will have to forego of something else if he buys the brand. Thus it serves in the role of a constraint, and its effect is captured in impersonal attitudes: Is it a low or high price? As discussed in economic analysis, pricing is confined almost entirely to this role.

In buyer-behavior terminology, when the buyer is in routinized response behavior, he is fully aware of the qualities of the brand, and price is often the dominant criterion of choice. This chapter will largely be concerned with the role of price as a constraint because it is the typical situation for the brand manager. When the buyer is not very well informed about the brand, such as when he is in limited problem solving,

243

price also tells him something about the quality of the brand. Thus it can serve as indicator role that will affect the buyer's attitude and impersonal evaluation. Further, when he is not at all well informed, and is in extensive problem solving, price will often tell him what product class the brand belongs in. Here price serves an identifier role, affecting the buyer's brand comprehension.

Because only the first purpose is usually discussed in the literature, the economics of price determination seem to be unusually abstract and unreal. There are other reasons why pricing is more complicated than the economic calculus would seem to suggest.

Second, pricing has administrative implications. The executive usually hesitates to delegate price decisions to subordinates in the company, yet many price decisions must be made. How many depends largely upon the number of products a company sells and the complexity of the discount structure in the marketing channel. Thus the magnitude of the pricing task often forces delegation. If the executive does delegate, he must formulate price-setting rules for subordinates, which will limit their freedom in setting prices. For example, the decision maker in an example given in Chapter 5 could change price no more than 4 cents. Greater changes had to be referred to the home office.

To complicate matters further, in decentralized companies price has become an integral part of management's control system because the level of profit in the decentralized unit is partially determined by the price that must be paid to other elements of the company for products and services. This gives rise to the problem of setting "transfer prices," which has been receiving increased attention from management.[1] Another administrative aspect of pricing involves the company's relations with its salesmen. In periods of intense competition, strong pressure is exerted by salesmen for reduced prices; pricing may cause friction which is serious enough to affect salesmen's morale. One company has gone to considerable expense to develop an allocation of overhead cost to each product, obviously arbitrary in part, in order to justify to its salesmen the price being charged.

Third, in discussions of the practical pricing problem a certain mythology is often evident that emphasizes the ethical aspects of competitive relations. The managers in an industry often make strong moral judgments against price-cutting competitors. Of all marketing decisions, however, pricing is the most strongly conditioned by competitive relations. Thus the pricer must take such moral judgments with a grain of salt in evaluating how valid they are as an influence on his competitors' pricing behavior.

Fourth, the law impinges upon some price decisions; this not only

---

[1] Jack Hirshleifer, "On the Economics of Transfer Pricing," *Journal of Business*, 29 (1956): 172–84.

complicates the practical pricing problem but also serves to further confuse discussions of the price problem. Obviously, executives will not discuss pricing in a meaningful way if it reveals practices that, when brought to light, might subject the company to prosecution. For example, a large manufacturer selling nationally would hesitate to discuss his precise method of price setting if price were, in fact, set by an industrywide agreement. In addition, illegality carries a stigma. The heavy moral overtones of pricing can account to some extent for the myth that prices are consistently determined by cost alone. Company pricers usually maintain that they set prices based on costs, but when cross-examined will agree that demand considerations also enter into the decision.

Finally, there are a number of practices that are closely related to price decisions but that result in ambiguous instead of clear-cut price changes. Promotional pricing is an example. This is a term applied to the use of deals, premiums, and coupons. A retailer may be given a "special deal" of five cartons for the usual price of four. A consumer is given a premium such as a drinking glass when he buys a box of soap. Retail stores give stamps to customers according to the size of their purchase which can be redeemed in goods. Changing the value of the trade-in has long been common in the retail automobile market; it was also used in the electric shaver market in February 1956 to reduce the price of shavers by almost one half.[2] In the steel industry, charges for "extras" are varied. When demand is high, steel manufacturers may require buyers to accept steel with extra processing even though they do not want it. When demand declines, as occurred in late 1953, this may no longer be required.[3] The executive's desire to simplify the administrative task of changing prices and to maintain stable competitive relations probably accounts for most of these practices, which are alternatives to an outright price change.

Because these complications exist, they emphasize the need for analytic relationships set out in purest form by economic analysis. Such analysis is helpful in cutting through the folklore of pricing practice.

DIMENSIONS OF THE PRICING PROBLEM

On the surface, price seems to be the most definite of the competitive tools, since it is always expressed in dollars. A closer examination will remove this illusion:

A price of, say, iron ore becomes not merely $4.60 a ton but $4.60 per gross long ton of 2,240 pounds of Mesabi Bessemer ore containing exactly 51.5 per cent of iron and 0.045 per cent of phosphorous, with specified premiums for ore with a higher iron content or a lower phosphorous content and with specified discounts for ore with a lower iron content or a higher phosphorous content;

---

[2] *Advertising Age*, April 16, 1956, p. 2 ff.
[3] *Chicago Daily News*, December 16, 1953, p. 59.

samples to be drawn and analyzed on a dry basis by a specified chemist at Cleveland, the cost being divided equally between seller and buyer; 48,000 tons to be delivered at the rate of approximately 8,000 tons per month during April–September, inclusive, on board freight cars of the New York Central Railroad at Cleveland, Ohio; the purchaser to pay all charges involved in moving ore from the rail of the lake steamer to the freight car and other port charges, such as unloading, dockage, storage, reloading, switching and handling; ore to be weighed on railroad scale weights at Cleveland; payment to be made in legal tender or bank checks of the buyer to the Cleveland agent of the mining company on the 15th of each month for all ore received during the preceding month.[4]

Another dimension of pricing is the frequency of the decision. In an oligopolistic market structure which characterizes much of industry, management sometimes recognizes the necessity of making a price decision only under one of two conditions: rising costs or the introduction of a new product. Otherwise the decision has often been made largely by default: "Let well enough alone." Long-term profit considerations dictate fewer changes than do short-term considerations, but in a dynamic economy where demand, costs, and competitive relations at all levels of the distributive structure are subject to almost continuous change, this passive approach to pricing may result in profits being sacrificed. The passivity has probably been caused primarily by the inadequacy of the measuring tools used for making a rational price decision. The tendency has been further aggravated by the spotlight of unfavorable publicity, as illustrated by a headline in one of the business periodicals: "Newsprint: A Rise in Price—and Congress Asks Why." On the other hand, you will recall the oil company pricing decision described in Figure 5–7. There, the manager of just four states made about a thousand price decisions each year.

A third dimension of pricing is the level in the company at which the decision is made. General price setting is done at higher levels, whereas "piecemeal" pricing is done at lower levels. The brand manager in the package-goods industry, for example, typically has little control over the stated brand price but is given a budget for promotional pricing and has correspondingly wide, flexibility in it.

Finally, some kind of an overall view of the pricing process is needed. To provide this perspective it may be helpful to ask how an executive in a multiproduct company would systematically go about setting original prices or reviewing existing ones.[5] He would probably analyze his entire line of products and select certain *typical* products which taken together would be representative of the entire line. Then he would subject each typical product *separately* to the following analysis. Beginning with prod-

---

[4]Reavis Cox, "Non-Price Competition and the Measurement of Prices," *Journal of Marketing*, 10 (1945–46): 376.

[5]For a thoughtful, more concrete analysis, see Alfred R. Oxenfeldt, *Pricing for Marketing Executives* (San Francisco: Wadsworth Publishing Co., 1961).

uct A, for example, he would ask himself: If I change my price to price X
and my competitors *do not follow,* what will be the effect on my sales? If I
change to price X and my competitors *follow part way,* what will be the
effect on my sales? If I change to price X and they *follow all the way,* what
will be the effect on my sales? The executive would ask himself the same
questions about prices Y and Z as well. To help provide the answers to his
questions, he could go through the analysis and then use market research
to provide a more substantial base of information.

Having answered these questions, the executive would then ask himself: What will be the profit contribution of prices X, Y, and Z if the *most
likely* of these possibilities about competitive behavior occurs? He could
use the analytic method of pricing presented below in answering this
question and thereby could decide which of the three prices is best.

After selecting the best price, the executive would ask himself: Should
other elements of the marketing plan for product A—product, distribution
channels, advertising, or selling—be modified? Finally, he would ask: Is
this price legal? He might also ask: Would I be well advised to consider
setting different prices on brand A to different customers? Are there different market segments that offer particularly appealing target markets?
He would try to answer these questions by thinking about why some customers might be willing to pay more than others; for example, some buy in
smaller quantities.

After completing his analysis of product A viewed in isolation, the executive would then proceed with the same analysis to set the prices on
those nontypical products in the line that are *most closely related* to product A. From the process of setting the price of each typical product, he
would probably distill a rule for setting the prices of the related products.
For example, if it turned out that the price of product A happened to be
the direct cost of product A plus 40 percent, he would then apply the rule
"direct cost plus 40 percent" to each of the related products. In the process
of doing this he might find that because of the interrelations of the other
products with product A, perhaps A's new price should be adjusted a
little. Finally, after having thoroughly analyzed A and its related products, the executive would proceed to subject typical products B, C, D,
etc., to the same analysis.

This overview of the pricing process points up the need for clear concepts of competition, demand, and cost. It also indicates the three kinds of
pricing situations: (1) single-product pricing, (2) product-line pricing, and
(3) setting price differentials.

Single-product pricing has to do with situations in which the complications interposed by multiproducts can be ignored. For companies with
only one product, the single-product pricing analysis is directly applicable. Since few companies sell only one product, however, the importance of the concept of single-product pricing lies mainly in providing a
method by which the analyses appropriate to both product-line pricing

and setting price differentials can be developed without becoming bogged down in the details.

Product-line pricing is concerned with setting prices in multiproduct companies in view of the price interrelationships among the company's various products.

Setting price differentials deals with differences among buyers according to their trade status, amount of purchase, location, promptness of payment, time of purchase, and individual situations, such as differences in requirements for certain product qualities.

SINGLE-PRODUCT PRICING

In examining concepts of single-product pricing, we will consider the competitive, demand, and cost factors that have influenced their formation. Then the two methods of single-product price setting, analytic and full cost, will be discussed.

Pricing concepts

Price can be used to increase company sales in either or both of two ways: taking sales from competitors or expanding industry sales. The first method, with which we are concerned here, leads to important questions of competitive behavior.

COMPETITIVE BEHAVIOR. In markets of many and therefore typically small sellers, price is a crucially important instrument because there usually is little if any intercompany difference in products. As a consequence, the demand or aggregate response function is virtually flat, as in market 1 in Figure 10–1. If a seller raises price at all, buyers will tend to shift to other suppliers, and if he lowers it just a bit, he can attract a virtually unlimited number of buyers. He is prevented from following this price-cutting strategy because his costs increase as he expands his output. This is the conventional "pure competition" case. Here we are dealing, of course, with only two dimensions of market structure as described in Chapter 1, namely, the number and size distribution of buyers and sellers.

If we recognize another possible condition of market structure—intercompany differences in the quality of the products and many sellers—the situation will be that usually found at the retail level where in a given location there are a major brand and a number of minor ones. "Private brands" is a term often used to describe the minors, as in the grocery industry. Retail gasoline sales also illustrate this situation. The major's brand is better known and usually has better service stations. As a consequence, he can charge a slightly higher price, perhaps 1 cent more per gallon. Several years ago the permissible difference was 2 cents per gallon. Now, when the difference between his price and his minor competitors' exceeds this 1 cent, he loses sales rapidly. The opposite occurs when he drops below this margin of difference. Hence his demand curve

FIGURE 10–1
Competitive influences on pricing

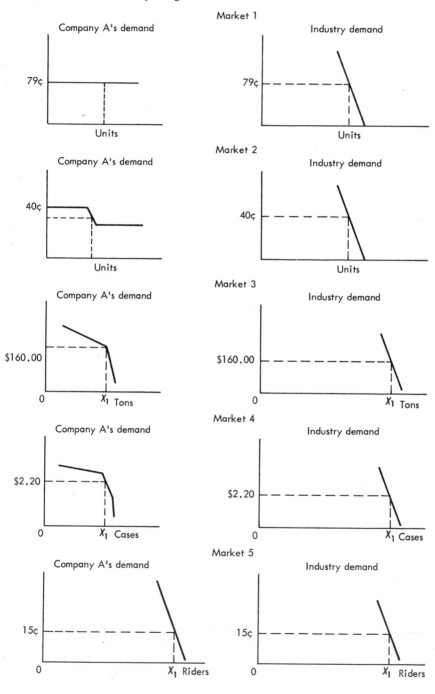

in both extremes is similar to market 1 as shown in Figure 10–1, but in the 1-cent differential range, it is as in the steep part of the demand curve of market 2. This is the case of the "monopolistic competition" of economic analysis.

In Chapter 2, however, it was stated that a company selling in the typical American market can be characterized as an oligopoly, meaning a *few* sellers. Competitive interdependence exists—any price move on the company's part may elicit some move from its rivals. A raw-steel manufacturing company illustrates an undifferentiated oliogopoly. Market 3 in Figure 10–1 presents this situation diagrammatically. In the raw-steel market, there are only a few competitors. They are selling a product that is almost identical among competitors and is directed to well-informed buyers. Competitors react almost instantaneously to downward price changes and without great delay to upward price changes.

Market 4 represents a situation where company A, facing a few competitors, has some independent price discretion. This market, a differentiated oligopoly, can be illustrated by the California Packing Company. This company can reduce the price of a case of No. 6 Del Monte peaches as little as, say, 20 cents per case and decrease the market shares of rivals without eliciting an immediate price change from them. Alternatively, price can be raised as much as 20 cents per case without eliciting at immediate price change from competitors. Above a certain price, such as $2.40 per case, however, the company will immediately lose sales to competitors—retailers are unwilling to pay more because the consumer will turn to competitors' brands if Del Monte is more than 4 cents per can higher. The industry price in this instance is, of course, an average of the different company prices. Still competitors can indeed be a strong force.

The kinked demand curve is one way of conceptualizing the situation shown in markets 3 and 4 in Figure 10–1. This market situation offers some possibility of positioning a brand so that it is a protected "distance" from its nearest competitor. In market 3, company A's competitors will follow it when it changes its price downward, but they will not follow its upward price changes. In market 4, however, company A has *some* leeway in changing prices: Its competitors respond to downward price changes only when a certain minimum price, about $2, is reached. Although the concept of the kinked demand curve is helpful in graphically portraying these situations, it helps only to explain why prices do not change (market 3) or why they change only within certain limits (market 4). It does not explain why prices *do change generally,* which is the more important problem.

Finally, in the municipal-transportation market such as the subway, which typifies market 5, no immediate competitors exist. The possibility of a competitor's price reaction can be ignored, but a price increase will turn riders to other sources of transportation or cause them to travel less frequently. When the New York Transit Authority raised its fare from 10 to 15 cents in July 1953, there was approximately a 10 percent decrease in the number of riders during the first week as compared to the previous year.

Typically, markets of a few sellers can be arranged on a continuum of interdependence in which markets 3 and 5 make up the extremes. Manufacturing companies probably tend to be bunched around market 4, with a much greater number bunched toward the extreme of market 3 than toward market 5. The company that markets a new product in an industry is often temporarily in a situation resembling market 5, but as competitors follow its innovation, the market will become more like 3 or 4. Retail markets, with many sellers, are most often like markets 1 and 2.

Five patterns of competitive behavior that emerge into an oligopoly market were described in Chapter 2. These patterns develop when additional dimensions of market structure are included other than degree of differentiation of product, as shown in Figure 10–1. Although the price leadership variety of behavior is the most common, effective collusion, limited collusion, and chaotic competition may also occur. Perfect collusion is most unlikely. The determinants of competitive behavior will be reviewed here because they can provide a guide to the brand manager in deciding how his price decisions may affect the behavior pattern in his industry.

The problem facing a pricer in an oligopoly market is how to attain the necessary changes in price without causing market behavior to degenerate into chaotic competition. Price leadership, one device by which such changes can be made, can be of two types: dominant firm and barometric. From time to time the role of price leader, often termed the "bellwether" of an industry, may change, and the role may be assumed by another company. The Cleveland-Cliffs Iron Company, for example, had been the leader in setting iron ore prices for many years, but then the Oliver Iron Mining Division of U.S. Steel took the lead by announcing an increase of 20 cents per ton. The reason for the shift in price leadership, it has been said, is that in the past Cleveland-Cliffs was the only major ore producer selling to the general market. Because other ore producers were "captive" and sold only to their owner companies, Cleveland-Cliffs was considered to be in a better position to evaluate the ore market. When U.S. Steel added to its ore capacity, particularly in Venezuela, it had considerably more ore than it could use, and the Oliver Iron Mining Division had to search for buyers. Therefore, the division has been taking a more active pricing role.

The identifying characteristic of a bellwether is its ability to lead upward. Any major company can lead downward in the sense that competitors are forced to follow because they are afraid of losing customers. Some leadership attempts fail. In May 1956, Liggett & Myers increased their price by 45 cents per 1,000 cigarettes. Competitors failed to follow, and within a week Liggett & Myers canceled its increase.

This classification of competitive behavior patterns is not intended to imply that if there is no collusion or effective price leadership, a price change by one company will necessarily result in chaotic competition. Particularly in periods of expanding demand and where intercompany product differences exist, changes in industry price levels occur without chaotic competition developing and without significant price leadership.

The typical determinants of competitive behavior are number and size distribution of companies, product differences, industry demand, number, size and kind of buyers, marketing channels, cost conditions, spatial aspects of the market, law, number of products, and the internal organization of the company. These determinants were discussed briefly in Chapter 2 and elaborated upon in other chapters, although their competitive implications have not always been made explicit. For example, the discussion of demand analysis in Chapter 3 threw light on how demand changes. Chapter 4 discussed the complexities of cost and the possible differences of opinion among competitors as to whether cost has increased enough to risk a price increase. The concepts of structure of distribution developed in Chapter 1 indicated that intercompany differences in marketing channels may exist. The idea of conscious product change mentioned in Chapter 1 implies that significant intercompany product differences may exist. Finally, the role of the internal organization of the company in influencing competitive behavior was explicitly illustrated at the end of Chapter 2.

Since a company must set its prices with future consequences in mind, it should also examine *potential* competition. The following conditions are considerations for estimating this factor:

1. How easy and cheap it is to get into the business, that is, the height and importance of barriers to entry.
2. How much potential competitors know about the profitability of the present producers of the product.
3. Whether the product cycle is approaching the state when the "specialty" is maturing into a "commodity."
4. Whether the other aspects of merchandising competition make the producer an easy mark for an invasion.
5. Whether the buyers are large, highly concentrated, and technically well informed.

DEMAND. The two general problems of demand analysis for pricing purposes are the appropriate demand concept and how to measure this concept.

The demand concept. As is true for any price decision, it is the future demand that is relevant; the exact period in the future to be considered depends upon the length of time for which the decision commits resources. Although price changes typically involve short-term commitments, some can precipitate changes in the basic structure of the industry and so have very long-term consequences.

The two demand concepts, market and company, and the corresponding price-response relations must be distinguished, as in Figure 10–1. Although a company is directly concerned with company demand, consideration of market or product-class demand is also necessary. First, the shape of the response curve for the product class determines what the sales volume for the industry will be when price is changed; thus the market demand has direct effects upon the company's own sales volume. Second, as the previous section on competitive behavior indicated, the nature of the market demand—its elasticity, stability, and so forth—strongly determines the kind of competitive relations that will exist in the industry and that will influence the manager's views of pricing in most industries. Thus, the concept of the company response curve is meaningful in most situations only if some assumption is made about how competitors will react to the price changes under consideration.

In examining the nature of *market* demand, we must first consider the generalizations about factors that determine the shape of the response curve for the product class. These are essential in guiding the use of market research and interpreting its results. As indications of the shape of the market-response curve, deductive economic reasoning has suggested the following characteristics:

1. The characteristics for consumer products are whether a product is a "luxury" or a "necessity", whether or not substitutes are readily available, the importance of the product in the buyer's expenditures, the level of the seller in the structure of distribution, and the extent to which the product can be stored.
2. The characteristics for industrial products are whether the product is used in further production rather than consumed, the shape of the response curve of the end product, and the importance of the product in the manufacture of the end product.

A survey of a number of industry price studies, mainly of agricultural products, suggests some evidence about the empirical validity of these theoretical ideas.[6] Products with good substitutes tended to have high elasticities. The nearer the product was to the consumer level in the marketing channel, the higher was the elasticity. Product storability, however, was not associated with either high or low elasticity. Few industrial products had lower elasticities than farm products. The product elasticities

---

[6]W. Z. Hirsch, "A Survey of Price Elasticities," *Review of Economic Studies,* 19 (1951–52), pp. 56–58.

also changed over short periods of time. Elasticity is a conventional way of describing the shape of the response curve: it is the ratio of a percentage change in sales to a percentage change in price.

Fluctuating economic conditions have a number of implications for pricing. One aspect of the fluctuations is the buyers' price expectations—how buyers expect prices to change in the future and how this will influence their current responses. It is clear that anticipation of price increases will cause some industrial buyers to increase their current purchases. Evidence also suggests that price expectations do make a difference to consumers.[7] The magnitude of the anticipated price change is important, however, and not all consumers behave alike. Buyer expectations about prices are important for the pricer; he may be deterred from changing price because he fears, for example, that a price cut may lead to expectations of a further cut, causing consumers to delay purchases.

Company demand, too, is often sensitive to price change once the buyer is well informed about the quality of the brand, as in Routinized Response Behavior. To this point in the discussion of the shape of the response curve economic analysis has been used, but when we turn to company demand, the structure of buyer behavior (Chapter 3) becomes useful in elaborating upon this view. The model can account for buying behavior which is sometimes superficially labeled "irrational."

Existing users must become *aware* of the new price. The buyer does not *automatically* notice all new stimuli—he may not come into contact with the new information, and even if he does, perceptual bias can operate because he does not expect a price change. Company market research studies have shown the great difference in buyer response between a price cut that is made without being advertised and one that is advertised. This tendency for the level of advertising to affect the response curves incidentally illustrates the situation where two of the response curves shown in Chapter 3—price and advertising—are interdependent. A price change in an important product would also be more likely to be observed than one in a less important item. If the product is subject to periods of price instability, buyers learn to be "price conscious" and to expect price changes; this is observed in the price wars that characterize the gasoline market at the consumer level. "Small" price changes may not be discriminable, and the buyer may generalize his buying response to the new price without being aware of the change. Finally, as suggested above, the buyer-behavior model predicts that more attention will be made to product cues; buyers in Routinized Response Behavior presumably are most sensitive to price changes.

If the sales increase comes from sales to new buyers of the product, time is required for adjustment as these buyers undergo a learning

---

[7]Eva Mueller, "Consumer Reactions to Inflation," *Quarterly Journal of Economics,* 73 (1959): 246–62.

process. For example, if the new product is a food which requires new cooking procedures, consumers must change their habits. A study of meat prices suggested that the short-term price elasticity of pork was -1.0 but the long-term elasticity was -1.5.[8] It has also been estimated, however, that the market demand for fresh California plums had an elasticity of -9.05 on the second week of the season, which dwindled to -0.65 by the tenth week and rose again to -4.84 on the sixteenth.[9] Thus something more than a learning process was involved. In industrial products, an investment in new equipment, for example, may be necessary to take advantage of a price decline in a product being used, and so response to a price change may be delayed.

While discussing the temporal dimension of price changes, it is pertinent to ask which of the optimizing models—the short run or the long run —is appropriate for the pricing decision. Price is usually a short-run decision, but it is conceivable that effects are so long run that the long-run decision model is appropriate. Recently, for example, a company selling welding rods debated whether to reduce its prices. The executives felt that a major price cut could change the basic structure of the industry by eliminating a number of marginal producers. This profound change was expected to affect profits favorably for several years to come. The company decided to reduce its prices. Here the long-term model described in Chapter 12 below is appropriate.

"Psychological" pricing has a variety of meanings. One is the practice of charging slightly less than the standard decimal break in the belief that buyers will respond *much* more favorably to $1.29 for an item, for example, than $1.30. If buyers do respond in the way this practice implies, the response curve in Chapter 3 is a stair-step function. Casual observation indicates that psychological pricing dominates pricing practice, particularly for consumer products but also for some industrial products. One explanation is that a buyer must justify to himself and others the expenditure of money for a purchase. The price of $9.99 enables him to think that he spent $9.00 instead of $10.00 for the product. Housewives in particular are faced with this problem. Some psychologists suggest that there are two kinds of personalities: those who make their decisions based upon internal criteria, and those who depend more upon influences from the environment, specifically influences from other people. If so, the latter type of personality might be more susceptible to psychological pricing because such people feel they must justify their decisions to their friends. David Riesman has popularized these personality types with the terms "inner-directed" and "other-directed."[10]

---

[8]Elmer J. Working, *Demand for Meat* (Chicago: University of Chicago Press, 1954), p. 79.

[9]W. Z. Hirsch, "A Survey of Price Elasticities."

[10]David Riesman, Nathan Glazer, and Reuel Denny, *The Lonely Crowd* (abridged ed.; Garden City, N.Y.: Doubleday & Co., Inc., 1953).

Finally, the "price-quality" association—the quality indicator role of price—is a phenomenon that is widely believed to exist by marketing executives. The buyer imputes quality to a brand according to the level of its price in relation to competitors' prices; if the price is higher than that of its competitors, the buyer thinks it is necessarily a better product. Such a situation probably occurs when the buyer is in Limited Problem Solving and so is not well informed about the brand.

This phenomenon is sometimes described by a backward-sloping demand curve, which is correct for a *mutatis mutandis* type of curve. In a *ceteris paribus* demand curve, however, which is typically used (see Chapter 3), the price-quality association cannot be shown because "quality of the product" also changes when the price is changed. This appears to underlie some of the unwillingness of company pricers to reduce the prices of consumer goods. It operates, however, only when the buyer has no other evidence upon which to base his purchase.[11] The Zenith Radio Corporation was faced with this problem in selling its hearing aid; it found it hard "to convince the public that its $75 hearing aid is as good as others selling for much more."[12] Nor is this phenomenon confined to consumer buyers. In investigating the dental equipment manufacturing industry, a British Royal Commission found a tendency among dentists to identify price cutting with the sale of inferior goods.

Price is but one product cue; however, if the buyer has not had enough experience to evaluate the brand or if the brand is difficult to evaluate even *after* the buying decision has been made, price may be one of the few distinctive cues available. Thus it can serve both as an evaluator and an identifier. A buyer also learns from experience that *on the average* among all the products he buys, price and quality are probably positively related. In addition, some products have social status implications, and these may be subject to the "price-quality" association—the higher the price, the higher the status value.

Measuring response to price   Measurement of response is not easy, especially in an oligopoly market where competitors' response is often difficult to identify and, if competitors do respond, the result is a mixture of company and market effects. There are at least three methods of estimating the effect of price upon sales: (1) the experimental method, (2) buyer interviewing, and (3) the analysis of time series data. The first two methods can be referred to as *crosscut* methods; that is, they are performed approximately at a point in time. The third method uses *longitudinal* data, or data collected over time.

The *experimental*, conventional method without buyer-behavior theory

---

[11] J. Jacoby, J. C. Olson, and R. A. Haddock, *Price, Brand Name, and Product Composition Characteristics as Determinants of Perceived Quality*, Purdue Papers in Consumer Psychology, No. 111, 1970.

[12] *The New York Times*, May 20, 1952, p. 41.

has potentialities for measuring the effects of a price change among many consumer goods. The essential idea is that two comparable markets (the "control" market and the "experimental" market) are selected, price is changed in one of these markets, and then the sales in the two markets are compared after a period of time. The purpose of using two markets is to control, or limit, the effect of influences other than price upon sales. A number of control and experimental markets may be necessary to yield statistical reliability. Also, in order to obtain the appropriate sales information, the sales in these segments of the total market must be isolated from the rest of the market for the observation period, which is often accomplished by a consumer panel or retail audit.

Two examples of the experimental method suggest more concretely the procedure involved. Results of the first example, which consists of two price experiments carried out by a frozen-food packer, are shown in Figure 10–2. The price of a frozen food was cut by two cents for a period of four weeks and then returned to its former level. After another month a three-cent cut was maintained for two weeks. The effect on sales was measured by a consumer panel. It was concluded that the larger cut was more effective and, moreover, that its effect was not so much in increasing the number of buyers as it was in adding to the volume purchased by existing buyers.

The conclusion arrived at in this experiment includes the unwarranted assumption that all of the changes in sales were a result of the price

FIGURE 10–2
Testing new prices

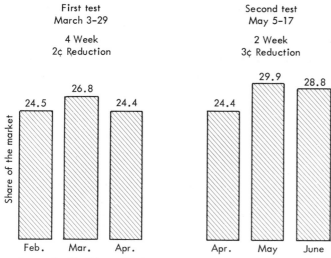

<table>
<tr><td>First test
March 3–29</td><td>Second test
May 5–17</td></tr>
<tr><td>4 Week
2¢ Reduction</td><td>2 Week
3¢ Reduction</td></tr>
</table>

Source: Larkin Osborn, "Market Analysis, a Tool for Developing Business and Controlling Distribution Costs," *Proceedings of the Third Conference on Controllership* (Chicago: University of Chicago Press, 1954), p. 24.

changes. Apparently no attempt was made to compare the sales in the experimental area with the sales in a control area. Another deficiency, for example, could be that the period of time was too short for some of the major consequences of the price cut to work out—perhaps the company was merely borrowing sales from the future.

In the second example, a cosmetic manufacturer was ready to introduce a new product in 1952 and had yet to decide on the price.[13] A limited budget required that the experiment be relatively inexpensive. The cooperation of 15 chain stores (three groups of five each) was obtained, and the experiment was divided into three periods between November 12, 1951, and January 7, 1952. Brand name was the only difference between cosmetics X and Z, the physical product, a cream shampoo, being identical. The experiment was as indicated in Table 10–1.

TABLE 10–1
Experimental method in pricing cosmetics

	Group A stores	Group B stores	Group C stores
Period 1 (Nov. 12–26)	Brand X—49c	Brand Z—59c	Brand Z—69c
Period 2 (Nov. 26—Dec. 3)	Brand Z—59c	Brand Z—69c	Brand X—49c
Period 3 (Dec. 3—Jan. 7)	Brand Z—69c	Brand X—49c	Brand Z—59c

Cosmetic X at 49 cents obtained 18 percent of the market of all brands sold in the stores. Cosmetic Z at 59 cents and 69 cents obtained only 12.2 percent and 11.1 percent, respectively. Store sales records were used as the source of information on sales for the observation period.

The experiment with cosmetic sales was designed to remove some of the nonprice effects on sales by having each of the three groups of stores comparable. For example, three Jewel Tea stores and two National Tea stores were included in each of the three groups. Also, the stores in each group were "matched" according to volume of toiletry sales, geographic area, economic status of customers, and other brands of cream shampoos handled. The experiment was also rotated among the stores, as shown in the table. Selecting the stores so as to obtain similarity in characteristics and rotating the experiments are ways of eliminating the effects of nonexperimental factors. If the stores are randomly selected, the findings can be generalized to the market as a whole with known reliability.

Some questions can be raised about the cosmetic experiment to illustrate the problem of experiment design: (1) Did the use of the two dif-

---

[13]Company security requirements prevent disclosure of more details. Grateful acknowledgment for the information is made to Market Facts, Inc.

ferent brands confuse the effects of price with brand effects? (2) Was there a cumulative effect of price so that the different lengths of the experimental period would affect the results? (3) Did the price policies of the kind of stores used in the experiment prevent the findings from being generalized to the company's other retail outlets? (4) Did the order in which the different prices appeared affect the results? (5) Did the experiment draw from other stores?

The second type of method, *buyer interviews,* can be used in either a simplistic or a sophisticated way. Simplistically, inferences are made from buyers' statements as to what their reactions would be to price changes. In this form the method is subject to limitations, but it may be useful for a price decision. For example, interviews revealed that most buyers of a branded baby food chose it on their doctor's recommendation and were quite ignorant about substitutes and prices. This knowledge, together with other information, led the manufacturer to guess that demand for his product was quite inelastic.

It is possible to use a version of the buyer-interview method in industrial goods by first compiling engineering estimates of the cost savings a buyer can expect from the product. Then, through buyer interviews, the responses of buyers to different prices can be evaluated once the probable cost savings for each respondent have been explained.

The more sophisticated version of the buyer interview is to collect data in terms of the buyer-behavior model where price is one of the impersonal attitudes. This involves a subjective measure of price to which some researchers may object, but it is well to bear in mind that it is those subjective estimates that are conditioning the buyer's decision. Objective estimates per se are irrelevant. The data can then be analyzed in terms of a structural model, as described in Chapter 8.

The third method, *time series analysis,* has received the most attention. A simple approach is to take price and sales data at different points in time and determine the price-sales relationship by the least-squares principle commonly used in regression analysis in statistics. The published studies employing this method have been concerned with the market concept rather than the company concept of demand. Further, most have been confined to basic commodities, and only a few have dealt with products where branding is important.

This method, therefore, has limitations for price decisions in the typical situation of measuring company demand where branding is significant. Competitive relations introduce additional influences that are difficult to incorporate and are so numerous they obscure the effect of price changes. In Chapter 1, for example, it was noted that "product" itself changes over time. The time series analysis method can provide useful background for the marketing manager, but it should be supplemented by either controlled experiments or buyer interviews. A more complex time series approach is to use structural models (as described in Chapter 8) on panel data where variables are lagged.

COST.   Cost increases are often the source of the impetus for a price change. Changes in the level of cost due to any factor might have this effect, but it occurs most often with changes in cost components instead of in the structure of cost. A *New York Times* headline illustrates this: "Shoe Makers Eye the Hide Market—Spring Prices for Footwear Hinge on How Leather Quotations Move."

A more fundamental aspect of cost for pricing is that if a price change is effective, the rate of sale and, probably, the rate of production will be affected. The cost information needed, then, is the relation between the rate of production and cost, which is the marginal cost of economic theory. It may be possible to use the average variable cost of production as an approximation, depending largely upon the magnitude of the change in the rate of production brought about by the price change. This approximation, which was discussed in Chapter 4, is not recommended when large changes in production are involved.

LEGAL CONSIDERATIONS.   The law pertaining to collusion and share of market is a relevant legal consideration in pricing a single product. Prices must not be set by formal agreement among competitors, and an excessive market share may be questioned by the antitrust agencies. The details of legal constraints on pricing are described in Chapter 15.

Methods of single-product pricing

There are two quite different methods of setting price which will be discussed here: analytic and full cost. The adequacy of other pricing methods can be evaluated by comparing them with these two methods.

ANALYTIC METHOD OF PRICING.   The analytic method is merely an application of the short-run optimizing model developed in Chapter 7. There, however, we used the total curves instead of the average curves, which are more revealing for the price decision. The exception to this is where a promotional pricing budget is used, as in the food industry.

Some practitioners would probably argue that the analytic method is somewhat empty of content because the data are not available. In the past this has been a fair conclusion, but the picture is changing. Cost by product can be made available economically by the computer, and the structural model has the potential of providing revenue estimates in many situations. As the brand manager is increasingly assigned a profit goal, with constraints, of course, the analytic method will be appropriate.

A review of the competitive, cost, and demand considerations constitutes the first step in using the analytic pricing method. Long-run considerations of potential competition may cause the pricer to accept a "stay-out" price as the upper limit, however. Such a price is set below the one that will encourage potential competitors to enter the market. The lower limit is set by marginal cost, since a company is better off to drop a product than to keep it if it will not contribute to overhead. The correct level will be that price which results in a volume of sales at which marginal revenue is equal to marginal cost. Figure 10–3 illustrates this with the demand situation of market 5 shown previously in Figure 10–1. P is the ideal price.

FIGURE 10–3
Optimum price with average relationships

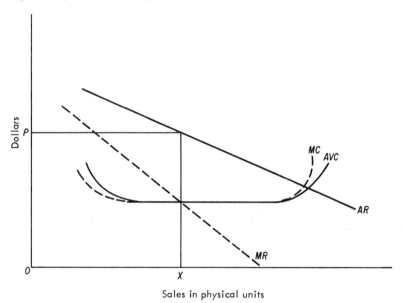

Sales in physical units

To acquire more familiarity with the optimizing tools, assume that we have maintained a price of $1.00 per unit in the past but we feel that perhaps, $0.75, $1.25, or even $1.50 might be a more profitable price. In order to verify this, we take a simplistic experimental approach and select 12 local markets. In three of them we leave the price at $1.00, in three we lower it to $0.75, in three we raise it to $1.25, and in three we raise it to $1.50.

At the end of a month we compare sales in the four groups of markets and find that the average increase in sales (physical units) in the cheapest markets was 20 percent and the average decline in the two higher price markets was 20 percent and 40 percent, respectively. The results are shown in Figure 10–4. The slanted lines represent the total revenues at different prices. The line PP' is drawn through the points representing the volumes of sales at each of the different prices suggested by the price experiment.

FIGURE 10–4
Price-sales relationship

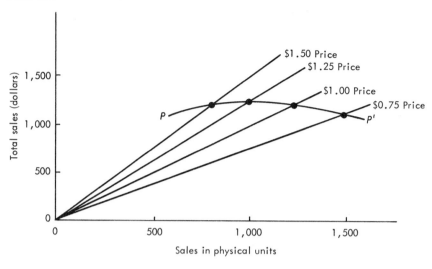

If the average variable cost was $0.25, the unit price of $1.25 would yield a contribution to profit of $1,000 per month, as compared with $937.50 at the unit price of $1.00 or $1.50 and $750 at the unit price of $0.75. The contribution to profit of each price is computed in Table 10–2.

TABLE 10–2
Price, volume, and profit relationships

Price	Sales in units	Sales in dollars	Variable cost	Contribution to profit
$0.75	1,500	$1,125	$375.00	$ 750.00
1.00	1,250	1,250	312.50	937.50
1.25	1,000	1,250	250.00	1,000.00
1.50	750	1,125	187.50	937.50

Ideally, however, we would experiment with a larger number of prices, enough to trace out *PP'* in Figure 10–5. Then we would be in position to set the best price—the "optimum price"—but there are real limits in doing this practically, one of which is cost. To set an optimum price, the short-run optimizing rule directs that we equate marginal revenue (*MR*) and marginal cost (*MC*). Expressed in less technical terms, we would set the price so that our sales would be at the volume where the marginal cost of sales would equal the marginal revenue from the sales. Instead of computing the profit contributions of each price, as was done in Table 10–2, the optimum price can be found directly by drawing RR' tangent to PP' and parallel to TVC, as shown in Figure 10–5.

FULL-COST METHOD OF PRICING.   Full cost, or cost plus, is frequently used as a method of pricing. Strictly interpreted, it means that (1) a forecast of sales is made, (2) based upon this forecasted level of sales, total unit costs are estimated, and then (3) to this estimate is added a percentage markup as profit.

In this inflexible form, the full-cost method is subject to serious criticism: it neglects the influence of competition and demand; it is based upon full cost rather than the appropriate marginal cost; and it involves circular reasoning because price, which influences sales, depends upon full cost, which in turn is partly determined by the level of sales. Figure 10–3 above illustrates typical cost relationships where average variable cost is constant over a significant range. Remember that when AVC is constant it is identical to MC. In Figure 10–5, for example, TVC, or full cost as it is often called, is different for each level of sales.

FIGURE 10–5
Optimum price with total relationships

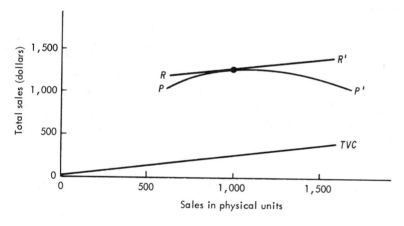

The dangers of full-cost pricing are illustrated by a midwestern manufacturer of cutting tools. One of the company's lines of products became quite unprofitable. An investigation revealed that prices in this line had been set by a formula based upon a cost which was the *average* for all items in the line. A competitor became aware of this practice and cut prices a little on the simple items in the line. This caused buyers to turn to the competitor for these items and to continue to buy from the midwestern manufacturer those that were more complex and more costly but less profitable, because the gross margin, being the average of all products in the line, was lower than it should have been for this type of item.

It is easy to exaggerate, however, the extent to which the full-cost method is inflexibly used in practice. When a company pricer is asked how he sets prices, he will often reply that they are based on cost. When he is more carefully quizzed, however, considerations of competition and demand are revealed. The executives of a company producing certain parts for the jet engines in airplanes typically state that prices are set by tripling the cost of materials going into the part. Closer investigation indicates that price is really established by an analysis of the following items: setup costs, material costs, running costs, testing costs, and *markup*. This last item is very flexible, and demand considerations carry significant weight in setting it. Nevertheless, this company, as well as business pricers generally, perhaps places too much emphasis on cost.

It is sometimes argued, on the assumption that competitors have identical or similar costs, that cost can be used in predicting competitors' behavior. Therefore, by using full-cost pricing, rivalry can be held to a minimum. Industry studies suggest, however, that there are often considerable differences in costs among companies.

PRODUCT-LINE PRICING

Producing a number of products has many more implications for management than the obvious one that more prices have to be established. Since the products may be interrelated both on the demand and the cost side, the problem is to formulate a system or structure of product-line prices that will take the greatest possible advantage of these interrelationships. The product-line pricing problem is much more relevant for the marketing manager, as we will see in Part IV, but it is applicable for the brand manager also.

Pricing concepts

While the same basic concepts apply in product-line as in single-product pricing, the nature of their application is different.

COMPETITIVE BEHAVIOR. Competitive relations are important in product-line pricing because the intensity of competition may vary markedly among members of the line, partly as a consequence of brand positioning. Prices should be tailored to meet these competitive differences. It is usually helpful to divide the problem in two parts: a short-term view which serves as the basis for estimating probable competitive relations with present competitors; and a long-term view which investigates potential competition.

DEMAND. Some automobile manufacturers produce a "prestige" car even though only a few of these units are expected to be sold. This practice illustrates the case where different members of a product line are related on the demand side. Ford has its Continental; Chrysler, its Imperial; and Cadillac introduced the Eldorado Brougham. One purpose of the prestige model is to reflect an aura of quality on the entire line.

"Trading up" is another example of how products are related on the demand side. A customer intends to purchase a cheap model, but as he learns more about the characteristics of the product in the process of purchase, his enthusiasm increases and he ultimately buys a more expensive model than he intended. The practice is conspicuous in the automobile market but is by no means confined to it. Bell and Howell Company brought out a new home-movie projector which sold at one half the price of the established model. Management expected that the new projector would be substituted for the old one. On the contrary, the sales of the established model increased sharply. Although other factors were present, management felt that the primary reason was the trading-up role of the cheaper projector.

The above examples also suggest the possibility of profitably segmenting the market through effective combinations of price and product. This will be investigated further in the section on price differentials below.

Much retail pricing is primarily determined by relations among products on the demand side. A department store will attempt to develop a certain "image" of the store among the public. If the "image" is one of prestige, for example, the setting of prices must be consistent with this image. Price levels are set first, and then products are purchased to be sold at these prices.

COST. The members of a product line are usually related on the cost side through common costs. For example, if one of two products having common costs is dropped, the incremental cost of the remaining product may be increased as a consequence. Changing the level of sales of one product may also affect the cost of another. The analysis of traceable and common costs in Chapter 4 is applicable here.

Methods of product-line pricing

In formulating a structure of product-line prices it is useful to start with some systematic pattern, such as the following:

1. Prices that are proportional to full cost, i.e., that produce the same percentage net profit for all products.
2. Prices that are proportional to incremental costs, i.e., that produce the same percentage contribution margin over incremental costs for all products.
3. Prices with profit margins that are proportional to conversion cost, i.e., that take no account of purchased materials cost. Conversion cost corresponds to the value-added concept.
4. Prices that produce contribution margins that depend upon the elasticity of demand of different market segments.
5. Prices that are systematically related to the stage of market and competitive development of individual members of the product line.

see Oxenfeld.

Cost alone serves as the basis for the first three rules; they are unsatisfactory on the grounds that they ignore considerations of competition and demand. There can be no quarrel with the fourth, if it is interpreted to include adequate consideration of product interrelationships; it is simply an application of the short-run optimizing model to the more complex problem of interrelated products. The fifth rule is designed to incorporate the product-cycle aspects of pricing in the pricing of new products, but it provides little guidance.

PRICE DIFFERENTIALS

To this point the discussion on pricing has dealt with setting prices in a single-product company and with giving consideration to the interrelations among members of the product line in formulating a structure of prices. Conditions of purchase do differ, however, and maximum effectiveness in pricing requires that prices be tailored to conform to these varied conditions. This is the practice of setting prices to market segments, or, specifically, target markets.

The principal bases of systematic, segmented price differentials are: (1) trade status of the buyer (functional discount), (2) amount of his purchase (quantity discount), (3) location of the buyer (geographic prices), (4) promptness of payment (cash discounts), (5) time of purchase, and (6) the buyer's personal situation. *(season)*

Because the first four kinds of price differentials are typically more important, discussion will be confined to these types of discounts. The last two bases give rise to seasonal discounts and informal price concessions. For example, summer discounts are given to industrial users by public utilities supplying gas because an adequate gas capacity must be available during the winter when gas is used for domestic heating, but there is a great surplus of gas during the summer when demand declines. Informal concessions come about because of differences in bargaining strength among buyers. Perhaps much more important is the fact that some consumers are simply more sensitive to price differences than others. Why this should be so has not been well explored.

The analytic method of setting price differentials

Adjusting intermarket price differentials is often critically essential to the growth of a company because they are the means by which the company invades new markets. The play of economic, political, social, and technological forces gives rise to market changes; by adjusting differentials to changing price elasticities the company is able to take advantage of the opportunities these changes create. The principle for setting price differentials to maximize profits is that the price is raised in the inelastic market relative to the price in the elastic market, to such a level that the marginal revenue in each market is equal to the common marginal cost.

This rule was illustrated in Figure 7–3, in which a company has five markets for the same product.

The practical problem of price differentials

The practical problem of setting price differentials involves three phases: (1) determining which markets differ enough in elasticity to justify segmentation, (2) selecting devices for separating and sealing off these segments, and (3) determining the appropriate pattern of price differentials across segments. Differences in elasticity among members of the product line can be estimated by applying the general conceptions of causes of elasticity discussed above under single-product pricing. For example, among industrial products, one member of the product line may represent a small part of the total cost of the end product in which it is used, while another represents a large part of that total cost. The first is likely to have a lower elasticity than the second, which suggests that, relatively, the price should be raised on the first product and lowered on the second.

There are few general rules for sealing off markets. Using different brands and different distribution channels is perhaps the most common device. Particularly in consumer markets, the buyer is often not well informed. Among department stores this is illustrated by the distinction sometimes found between "upstairs" and "basement" prices. Factors such as prestige, the level of information, and convenience probably explain why it is possible to charge different prices on different floors.

The appropriate pattern of price differentials is obtained by approximating, insofar as possible, the optimizing model presented in Figure 7–3, taking into account the interdependence of products on both the cost and demand side.

DISTRIBUTOR DISCOUNTS.   One of the most common patterns of price differentials is encountered in marketing channels. Generally, competition is focused more intensely on discounts to distributors than on end prices to the consumer. This is illustrated in the British electric lamp-bulb industry, where manufacturers believe that the price-sales relation in the consumer market is highly inelastic, making price competition at the consumer level inadvisable.

Industry custom largely determines the specific form of distributor discounts. They may be stated as either *net prices* at each level or *list prices*, to which a pattern of discounts is applied. The discounts may be *single* or a number of *successively applied discounts*, such as "15 percent, 10 percent, and 5 percent off list price."

One of the dominant considerations for an appropriate pattern of distributor discounts is the middleman's procedure for choosing brands. His lack of knowledge as to relative profitability of brands may cause him to think first in terms of gross margin. Then, as a clue to how fast the product will sell, he considers how much advertising the manufacturer supplies in the form of both dealer aids and consumer advertising.

Competition is also a factor in distributor discounts. International Harvester initiated a "Classified Trade Plan" for its truck-parts dealers which provided for a subsidy to those who must cut price in order to hold business. The plan was in response to a sharp increase in independent parts manufacturers since World War II which had led to somewhat chaotic competition among the distributors of truck parts.

In establishing a pattern of distributor discounts, it is essential to have reasonably accurate estimates of the cost the manufacturer encounters in selling to the various distributors. Such data can be persuasive in negotiating with distributors. Other things being equal, the profit contribution to the manufacturer of selling through alternative channels should set an upper limit to the manufacturer's discount to the distributor in each case. A method for determining the profit contributions of alternative channels was explained in Chapter 4.

Cost data may also be necessary to justify price differentials to the antitrust agencies engaged in enforcing the Robinson-Patman Act. There are serious legal implications in setting distributor discounts, largely because dealers at the same level in the structure are clearly in competition with one another, and noninjury to competition cannot be used as a defense. Differences in discounts among levels in the marketing structure are legal. A retailer, for example, is usually given a larger discount—a larger percent of the end price—than a wholesaler. A discount to a nonbroker, for example, a wholesaler or a chain retail organization, however, cannot be justified on the grounds that these organizations are performing the brokerage function. The recipient must be a bona fide broker.

QUANTITY DISCOUNTS. In determining whether to offer quantity discounts and what pattern of discounting to establish, it is helpful to consider the following types:

1. With respect to the way quantity is measured.
   a) Aggregate of all products bought from seller.
      (1) Dollar-value measures.
      (2) Physical-unit measures, e.g., carload discounts.
   b) Separately based on the quantity of individual products.
      (1) Dollar measures.
      (2) Physical measures, e.g., integral case discounts.
2. With respect to the form of calculation.
   a) Incremental, i.e., discounts figured on the increased volume over a specified amount.
   b) Absolute, i.e., discounts figured in terms of total quantities.
3. With respect to number of transactions.

a) Cumulative, i.e., based on aggregate purchases over a period such
    as a year.

b) Noncumulative, i.e., based on the size of a single order.

The considerations in establishing a pattern of quantity discounts are
fourfold: legality, competition, demand, and cost. If the proposed pattern
is legal, the question is whether offering discounts will increase profits.
This in turn raises questions as to whether some buyers will increase their
sales as a consequence and what cost savings will result from the discounts. Practically, the cost savings usually occur in the areas of selling
and distribution expenses rather than production costs.

CASH DISCOUNTS.   The most common type of cash discount is 2 percent
if paid in 10 days, with the full price due in 30 days. Since the motive
behind cash discounts is to speed up collection, they should be considered
as an indirect collection cost. Collection within the time allowed by the
discount will decrease the seller's cost of interest on working capital.
Much more important, however, is the effect on reducing bad-debt losses.
Whether cash discounts actually do make a difference in collection expenses has sometimes been questioned.

GEOGRAPHIC PRICE DIFFERENTIALS.   The problem of setting geographic
differentials in price arises largely because of freight costs. Thus they are
mainly applicable to products for which freight costs are a large part of
variable costs. The law concerning geographic differentials places additional emphasis on the role of cost in setting such price differentials. Geographic differences in competition can also be an important factor
because the strength of regional brands differs greatly. Consumer preferences for many products also vary geographically. Some of the complexities encountered in geographic price differentials can be more easily understood in terms of the market area ideas presented in Chapters 1 and 2.

There are a number of methods of setting geographic differentials:

1. Uniform delivered pricing.
    a) Postage-stamp pricing—distance from the seller to the buyer does
        not matter, analogous to the fact that an eight-cent stamp will send
        a letter anywhere in the United States irrespective of differences in
        the actual cost of sending it.
    b) Zone pricing—distance from the buyer to the seller is incorporated
        into the pricing scheme but only in a rough way. Zones are es-
        tablished, and delivered prices are different among the zones but
        uniform within any given zone. Mail-order houses use zone pricing.
2. Basing-point pricing.
    a) Single basing point—some location (usually a plant site) is selected
        as the basing point and the price to all buyers then is computed by
        adding to an established base price the rail-freight cost from the

base location to the buyer, irrespective of the place from which the shipment is made or, in fact, the method of transportation actually used.

b) Multiple basing point—the principle is the same as with a single basing point except that more than one point is selected and the buyer is charged a price computed from the nearest basing-point location.

c) Freight-equalization pricing—under this scheme all plants become basing points.

3. F.o.b. mill pricing—price is computed by adding the actual transportation costs to an established price, and the buyer selects the method of transportation used.

For many years the automobile manufacturing industry operated on a single-basing-point system. Detroit was the base even though actual assembly was dispersed over the country. The result, of course, was widely different retail prices among areas. When Ford cut the actual prices paid by distant dealers, prices were equalized somewhat, although not completely. To illustrate, prior to a change in pricing, a Los Angeles car dealer paid freight of $280 on a Customline Ford. Under the new arrangement he paid $179. Probably at least two reasons motivated Ford to make this decision. One was the fear of antitrust action because of the "phantom freight" involved—the dealer was paying for freight that he was not receiving. This gave rise to the second, "bootlegging," a practice to which the dealers objected. Because the freight charged exceeded the transportation cost, it was profitable for "bootleggers" to buy new cars elsewhere in the country and ship them privately to compete, for example, with the Los Angeles Ford dealers. General Motors and Chrysler have followed the Ford action in modifying their geographic differentials.

Two kinds of legal problems are raised by geographic price differentials: collusion and price discrimination. Historically, the single-basing-point scheme was used as a collusive device. Companies in the industry would (1) agree upon a base price, (2) agree upon the factory to serve as the base mill, and (3) set all prices by adding the base price to the rail-freight cost from the base mill. Collusion is clearly illegal, and the price discrimination feature may be. There are, however, the usual three defenses for price discrimination: (1) costs are saved, (2) competition is not injured, and (3) it is necessary to meet competition. It has been argued that the only legal geographic pricing method is f.o.b. mill pricing.

SUMMARY

Pricing is probably more laden with folklore than any other area of marketing decisions. One of the reasons for this folklore is the dominant role of competitive relations in setting prices. Pricing becomes meaningful from the point of view of both how it is done and how it should be done only when competitive relations are understood.

A number of pricing methods have been suggested. We suspect, however, for reasons given in the chapter, that the analytic method, applied both to individual brands and to segmented markets, will become increasingly common.

Except for that rare state of monopoly, of all the general market structures differentiated oligopoly offers the greatest opportunity for extensive marketing maneuvers such as positioning and segmenting and the consequent pricing tactics.

DISCUSSION QUESTIONS

1. Oligopoly markets, which are typical of industry, often pose difficult pricing problems. The concept of the kinked demand curve seems on the surface to be very useful in explaining what goes on in practice. Evaluate the concept for the purpose of providing an adequate description of reality.
2. Figure 10–1 shows a variety of market situations. From your experience and reading, select illustrations for each of them and defend your choice.
3. Contrast in detail the analytic and full-cost methods of pricing.
4. Discuss practical situations where products in a company's product line might be related on the demand side.
5. What are the conditions necessary for setting effective price differentials?

11

Management of the sales force

THE SALES FORCE, SELLING STRATEGY, AND BRAND STRATEGY

THE BRAND MANAGER typically has little control over the sales force. Its size, allocation, and maintenance are under the direction of the sales manager, who reports to the marketing manager. Yet, the control the brand manager does have is significant.

True, the brand manager probably cannot control in any way when the salesman makes calls, but he can influence what the salesman does on his calls. Whether he spends his time obtaining more shelf space for brand A instead of brand B, for example, is something of a controllable. If the brand manager has a special campaign in his marketing plan, this should trigger special attention from the salesman in the form of attempts to gain more shelf space and to arrange point-of-purchase displays for his brand. By other dimensions of brand strategy, the manager can make it easier or more difficult for the salesman to get this additional consideration from the retailer. The task will be easier, for example, if the brand manager has specified "dealers' deals" and substantial extra advertising as a part of his plan.

Thus control that may appear quite small can turn out to be important in terms of the sales of the brand. Unless the brand does have extra shelf space and streamers appear in the store window to remind the consumer of advertising in the media, sales can be substantially smaller.

The purpose of this chapter is to portray the activities of the sales force as a strategy, specifically as one element of brand strategy. The nature of the selling process requires a close examination of the role of the salesman. The question of the selling budget—the number of salesmen needed—leads readily into consideration of how salesmen should be allocated. Selection, training, and motivation of salesmen are treated as the general problem of maintaining a sales force. While this is the province of the sales manager, the stakes the brand manager has in its successful implementation make it an area of concern for him as well. Sales strategy is often a key element of brand strategy.

ROLE OF THE SALESMAN

Introduction

In order to fit the salesman's activities into a brand strategy, the brand manager must be acquainted with his role in putting the marketing plan into action. Personal selling has an unusual feature—in most companies there is only limited cooperation between the personnel department and the sales manager, even though both are concerned with selecting and training people. This suggests something about the peculiar nature of the selling job. The former chief of the Division of Occupational Analysis of the War Manpower Commission stated, "We have studied something like 20,000 occupations and we find that the difficulty encountered in devising improved selection techniques for saleswork is probably not equaled in any other group of occupations."[1] Selection techniques may have improved since this statement was made a number of years ago, but the problem still exists.

There are few areas of human activity about which so much is written as personal selling. It has been estimated that nearly a million copies of books on selling are marketed in the United States each year. Surprisingly little is known about the task in a formal sense, however. Like all marketing effort, the personal-selling function is basically intended to communicate, but it often involves a number of other activities. In the case of a frequently purchased item sold in a supermarket, the following activities are part of the salesman's function:

1. Checking to insure that the brand is properly stocked, with no vacant spots on the shelf and with clean, undamaged stock.
2. Investigating whether adequate shelf space has been assigned the brand.
3. Determining the quality of locations given the brand.
4. Arranging promotional material as display.
5. Recording retailers' complaints about "stock returned" and the quantity and quality of the manufacturer's advertising.

---

[1] C. L. Shartle, *Discussion*, Marketing Series No. 39 (New York: American Management Association, 1940), p. 9.

Activities, such as these, however, will occupy a subordinate role in this chapter. They are beginning to be handled by companies that have been established just for this function and that can probably perform them much more cheaply.[2] We will focus on the salesman's interaction with the client, his communication role.

The sales force is an element of brand strategy in this communication role, and as such it can be thought of as one of a number of alternative ways to communicate with the market. For selling to be viewed with advertising as alternative means to the same end of communicating to the buyer is sometimes thought to have become common practice. Therefore,

It is a bit of a shock to learn, from a survey made by the research committee of the Sales Executives Club of New York, that budgets for field sales and advertising are usually derived separately, and that the committee's prime recommendation is that such budgets should be set "in relation to each other since they are elements in a common mix and have to be proportioned."[3]

We seem to have become so entangled in internal administration that we fail to look at the buyer as a whole; we see only part of him, that part we alone are concerned with.

This total or integrated view is especially essential because, first, the sales force is labor intensive, and second, the technology of mass communication is changing rapidly, as we saw in Chapter 9. Consequently, it can be predicted that mass communication will tend to replace the salesman to some extent. The speed of the change is the question. One business writer predicts, "By 1980 the nation's corps of salesmen will have registered a sharp decline per $1,000,000 of business—a decline perhaps on the order of 20% to 25%. By 1990, the nation's salesforce may register another decline of 20% to 25%."[4]

Understanding the salesman-buyer interaction

The integrated view of the buyer's role in the marketing structure is provided by the theory of buyer behavior set forth in Chapter 3. We will elaborate on it here in order to devise a framework for understanding the interaction of salesman and buyer.

The basic idea is that two people will continue to interact as long as they find the relationship mutually satisfying. A salesman calls upon a buyer to sell him a product. During the interaction that ensues each can exhibit a type of behavior that is *rewarding*—reinforcing—to the other. The salesman tells the buyer about a product that will serve the buyer's motives. This satisfaction of the buyer's motives is rewarding to the buyer.

---

[2] *Business Week,* July 22, 1972, p. 46.
[3] *Advertising Age,* March 2, 1964, p. 20.
[4] E. B. Weiss in *Advertising Age,* June 22, 1970, p. 57.

The problem is more complex, however. First, how can the salesman best communicate with the buyer? We know human relations are very subtle and that we are often unaware of what cues about a person we use to conclude that he is credible. Further, human speech is only one way in which this communication occurs.[5] The salesman also communicates by his *body motion*, such as whether he is relaxed or tense. *Eye movement* is important—does he "look you in the eye"? *Paralanguage*—nonverbal speech characteristics such as pauses, hesitations, stutters, and repetitions, also communicate something, as do voice qualities such as pitch, range, and resonance. *Proxemics*—how a man utilizes space—also enter in. Does he stand close to you, at an intermediate distance, or quite distant in talking with you?

Second, how can the salesman reward the buyer? Unless he has had previous experience with the salesman, the buyer needs assurance that the salesman is telling the truth and that the product will in fact meet his needs. The buyer asks himself, "Is he *trustworthy?*" He may also ask, "Is he *competent* to tell me anything about the product?" These two characteristics of the salesman add up to his *credibility*. If he is like me—has the same values I have—I am more likely to trust him. Competence, however, is a matter of knowledge often shown by college degrees, jobs held, and so forth. The more credible he is to the buyer, the more likely is the buyer to conclude that the product will meet his needs. Thus one way in which the salesman can reward the buyer is to give him product information in a credible way. This influence process operates on functional attitudes by *internalization*.

There are two other ways, both social, by which the salesman can reward the buyer. One is by being an attractive person, one whom the buyer likes to know and be with. The buyer then identifies with the salesman and operates on the basis of self-concept attitudes. This influence process is one of *identification*. The salesman may also have power over the buyer, for example, political appointment to local government. This influence process, which is called *compliance*, operates on impersonal attitudes. Thus, three characteristics of the salesman—credibility, attractiveness, and power—are the sources of the influence processes of internalization, identification, and compliance, respectively.

In the light of these subtleties of influence and communication, which are not well understood and so are pursued in an intuitive way, the salesman's task is not an easy one. In fact, it is difficult to find a situation more fraught with uncertainty, and that is why it can be a demanding role.

---

[5] I am indebted to my colleague, James Hulbert, for a most interesting unpublished paper, James Hulbert and Noel Capon, "Interpersonal Communication in Marketing: An Overview," Columbia University, 1971 (mimeo).

From these ideas certain general principles can be stated about the nature of the salesman-buyers relationship. First, an interaction situation that was rewarding in the past will encourage future responses from the buyer or salesman to the extent that the new situation is *similar* to the previous one.

Second, something can be said about the *amount* (quantity) of interaction: the more often within a given period of time one man's behavior (the salesman's) rewards the behavior of another (the buyer), the more often the second person (the buyer) will exhibit that behavior. Correspondingly, if a man has learned to interact by being rewarded and later finds interaction no longer rewarding, he will discontinue responding; his response will be *extinguished*.

The third principle has to do with the value of the behavior. The more *valuable* a salesman's behavior is to the buyer, the more often the buyer will exhibit the behavior rewarded by the salesman.

The fourth, concerns *satiation*, that is, satisfaction of a motive. The more often in the recent past a man has received rewarding behavior from another, the less valuable an additional unit of that behavior is to him, although acquired motives are not so inclined to satiation as are innate motives. Further, satiation is probably temporary.

Finally, over a long period of time a person develops standards about what is "fair" to expect from an interaction situation: how much rewarding behavior the client feels he should give the salesman in return for the rewarding behavior he receives from the salesman. This feeling can be called the sense of distributive justice or ideas about the "fair" allocation of rewards between two people in an interaction situation. When this sense of fairness is violated, the "injured" person may become angry and do things that may not be in his best interest. The buyer, for example, may refuse to interact with the salesman even though it is profitable for him to do so. In other words, he may engage in irrational behavior, behavior that does not serve his motives. Thus the fifth principle is: the more the rule of *distributive justice* fails of realization, the more likely he is to display the emotional behavior called *anger*.[6]

There is, however, a cost—a punishment, a negative reinforcer—of the interactive behavior to each person who evidences that behavior. First, there is the forgone opportunity to do something else. The salesman could have used his time in calling upon a more pleasant client, and the buyer forwent the opportunity to buy the product from another salesman from whom he might have bought it more cheaply. Thus, the more a particular

---

[6]For a more elaborate statement of these principles and their empirical support, see George C. Homans, *Social Behavior: Its Elementary Forms* (New York: Harcourt, Brace & World, Inc., 1961).

mode of interactive behavior *costs* a person, the less of the behavior he will exhibit. Second, the behavior represented in giving social approval is costly to the salesman because to praise the buyer for his good judgment, splendid character, and so forth has the effect of lowering his own self-esteem, especially if the praise exaggerates true characteristics. Cost plays a critical role in the selling analysis because it encourages each person to evidence some *other* behavior—to change his mode of interaction or to interact with someone else—and serves as an opposing force to the reward the buyer and salesman receive from their *current* behavior. Thus, extinction, satiation, and cost serve to encourage each man in the relationship to turn to some *other* behavior; for example, the client may turn to a competing salesman and the salesman to another client.

The discussion so far has been in terms of a short interaction period, but in many sales situations the salesman-buyer relationship is a continuing one. The more social approval the buyer has received from the salesman, the less valuable additional approval becomes; the more time the salesman has received from the buyer, the less useful additional time becomes; and the more approval he has given the client, the more costly further confession of inferiority becomes. Thus, in time, a point of equilibrium is reached in the relationship which continues until there is a change in the underlying conditions.

Such a change often does occur over time. As buyer and salesman become more familiar with one another, they tend to see greater similarities and fewer differences which, in turn, increases their liking for one another. Thus they find each other more attractive, which furthers the influence process of identification. This possibility is important because if each represents an organization, such as is almost always characteristic of industrial marketing, this happy relationship can lead to a sacrifice of the goals of their respective organizations. For this reason one technical company has a policy of rotating the assignments of salesmen every three years.

Both the static and dynamic aspects of this buyer-salesman interaction process can be more fully specified in terms of the variables set forth in Chapter 3. There has not been enough research, however, on these effects in a buying situation to guide us in integrating the effects into the measurement of selling effort and the administration of the sales force. It is obviously an important research area but a difficult one in which there does not appear to have been great progress in the past decade. In one study of salesman effectiveness, it was concluded that:

Personal selling is characterized by a plethora of prescription based only on assertion. In this review it was seen that the researchers, who, commendably enough have tested their models against empirical evidence, generally failed to meet the standards of scientific adequacy set forth earlier. There was little occasion to raise questions concerning strength of association or external validity because few internally valid and statistically significant relationships, based on logically consistent models, emerged.[7]

This framework of analysis will help the brand manager understand what he can and cannot expect of the salesman in handling his brand, and in providing feedback on the brand's performance. One of the goals, for example, in consumer goods is to obtain adequate retail shelf space. The framework suggests that the salesman may be more effective in accomplishing this goal if he can offer additional incentive such as a "deal."

The changing selling environment

The framework of salesman-buyer interaction developed above is one view of the selling process. The environment in which this interaction takes place will obviously condition its outcome. That the selling environment has changed substantially in the past two decades is evidenced by comments from perceptive, well-informed observers, such as the following address by Herbert M. Cleaves, executive vice president of General Foods Corporation:

> One of the changes is epitomized in the composition of many of the daily or weekly sales reports. How the old-time sales manager would shudder to think of a report form that *had no column to list sales*. How can a salesman spend a profitable week and not report any sale!
>
> Let me dramatize that point by inviting you to spend a week with a fictional food salesman. I choose the food field simply because I know it best.
>
> It's Monday morning and our salesman—let's call him Smitty—drives over to the headquarters of a major food chain. On his way in, he slows down long enough to exchange a friendly greeting with the buyer, then moves on through the double doors and down the corridor.
>
> What a change *that* is from just a few years back! Then, Smitty used to spend an entire morning out on the mourner's bench waiting for his brief audience with the very busy, very beleaguered buyer. As often as not, the harassed buyer would stick his head out of the door at noon—or, more likely, make his secretary do the job—and announce: "See you after lunch, boys."
>
> Today, Smitty knows, as he nods his greeting, that the buyer—or, in fact, his secretary—will, as a matter of course every Tuesday morning, take the latest computer card, which indicates inventory levels, and, in the absence of any additional information, she will teletype or phone an order—for, let's say, Jell-O puddings—directly to the order desk at Smitty's distribution sales and service center.

Smitty visits the home economist

Smitty's first appointment this Monday is with the *food chain's home economist*. His objective is to win her approval of a *promotion*—of a recipe—to

---

[7]James Hulbert and Noel Capon, "The Study of Salesman Effectiveness: A Selective Analysis," (Graduate School of Business, Columbia University, 1971), p. 15.

make Jello-O cheesecake. He wants her recommendation for this promotion to be included in the chain's regional and local advertising eight weeks from now. Instead of pitching hard for his product, he talks about the new unique recipe (he knows it is backed by the reputation of his company's consumer test kitchen). He talks about the nutritional values, the ease of preparation, and all the other appeals to consumer needs and wants. In fact, he might even demonstrate to this home economist how the cheesecake is made . . . He emphasizes the impact such a promotion will have on pie crust and cream cheese sales as well as on his own products, Jell-O puddings.

The home economist's questions answered and her approval won, Smitty moves on to the *advertising manager.* There he talks fluently of layouts, visual impacts, advertising exposure, costs and closing dates. He explains what support his company is providing for the campaign. What its advertising coverage will be, not in terms of national figures but in terms of this chain's own marketing area—the numbers of homes reached, the frequency of the message—the whole Madison Ave. story *but told* in terms of Main St.

Next, Smitty carries the ball to the *merchandising manager,* to whom he proposes specific store displays for the promotion. From here he goes on to the sales manager, who supervises all retail store managers. They discuss how best to capitalize on the upcoming promotion and exchange ideas on how to win maximum support at retail. Here, too, Smitty has specific suggestions to make.

On the way out—and by now it may well be midafternoon or later—Smitty drops in on the buyer again. "Jack," he says, "that computer of yours is going to get a workout next month." And he explains the promotion coming up. Like as not, the buyer asks Smitty's estimate on how much more Jell-O puddings to order.

So goes Monday. Tuesday, Smitty spends the day going from store to store in that food chain, explaining to managers the upcoming promotion, relaying headquarters' enthusiasm, telling store managers what the promotion can mean to their sales of Jell-O puddings, cream cheese and pie crust, as well as what impact the increased store traffic can have on the sale of other store items. He spouts ideas on how to arrange display space and makes suggestions for the most effective use of display materials.

That's Tuesday. Wednesday finds Smitty at the customer's warehouse, checking out a suggestion that a new packing procedure for one of the Jell-O products would cut that customer's labor costs. He finds it's true; by packing the boxes top-to-top instead of top-to-bottom, the case can be cut open at the middle and the price stamped on each box more quickly than it could with one layer packed atop another. While there, Smitty observes that carton identifications are printed so small that handlers find it difficult to quickly locate the products they want. Small items, both, but they represent a potentially meaningful reduction of store labor costs for the customer. Smitty relays both ideas to his supervisor who in turn sends them upstairs."

End of the week—and Smitty hasn't written an order

Thursday, Smitty spends in the supermarket outlets of this important customer. On Monday, the chain sales manager had remarked that the sales of the whole category of packaged desserts was unexplainably down. Smitty, in turn, had sold him the idea of a new shelving arrangement for all packaged desserts, including his competitors', which the marketing planners back at his home office had devised and tested as a means of increasing consumer awareness and activity on these profitable items. So, Thursday, Smitty spends talking with store managers and instructing their stock clerks on how to rearrange the package dessert shelves.

Friday, Smitty never leaves the district office. He spends his day with the district sales analyst wrestling with a presentation to a customer he has had difficulty cracking.

So a week has gone by and Smitty hasn't personally made a traditional sales pitch or taken an order. The fact is, because of today's electronic data processing machines and speed-of-light communications, his supervisor knows before he does how well his various marketing efforts are being translated into orders.

So what makes Smitty tick? This week he was part home economist—part advertising man—part merchandising and promotion man—part creative idea man —part materials handling expert—and part financial analyst.

Salesman? Well, hardly! He is more accurately described as "an account manager." No longer is he in charge of a geographical area known as a territory. He is instead the manager of his company's total business relationship with one or more important accounts.[8]

True, this description is of one company in one industry. In another field, General Electric went through a similar development in its major appliance, television, and stereo lines and evolved the term "sales counsellor" to describe the salesman job, in terms very much like those implied by Cleaves.

E. B. Weiss has also offered an explanation for these developments.[9] Much of his rationale has to do with the economics of personal selling, the high cost of a sales call, changing values (such as those of young men who are less favorably disposed to a selling career), and the rise of large retailing organizations, especially those with buying committees.

Implicit in Weiss's thoughtful analysis is a changing model of man. Traditionally, sales management (and higher management, too, for that matter) has had a model of the buyer identical to the one espoused by Vance Packard in *The Hidden Persuaders* (New York: David McKay and Company, 1957). Man is very susceptible to influence if the influencer can just push the right buttons. To Packard, the right button consisted of advertising based upon esoteric psychological information, which he failed to specify. The salesman wasn't sure what the button was, but he was sure that such a button existed if he could just find it. If he didn't find it, it was his fault: he was a failure. If he read enough books on selling or attended enough sales conventions, perhaps he would find out.

The shift has been toward an information-processing model of man.

[8] *Advertising Age*, September 21, 1964, pp. 128–32.
[9] *Advertising Age*, June 1, 1970, pp. 49–50.

You can influence him by giving him information when he needs it. If you give him information about your brand and your competitor fails to do the same for his brand, you have "sold" the customer. Perhaps this nonmotivational view has gone too far, but we doubt it.

The kind of unsystematic observational data represented in Cleaves's statement is obviously incomplete for scientific purposes, but it is nevertheless highly suggestive. In summary, we do not know exactly what the changes in the selling environment have been. Much less do we know what their specific significance is in shaping the reaction to it in terms of the salesman-buyer interaction framework. We do believe, however, that we should not be dogmatic in applying old rules.

HOW MANY SALESMEN ARE NEEDED?

The brand manager can use this framework of the interaction process as influenced by a changing environment to help him understand the question of the size of the selling budget. Ideally, he would estimate the aggregate response curve, assuming independence of other elements of the marketing mix and profit as the goal, and develop an optimum budget. The question, however, is whether it is possible to measure empirically the effect of selling effort in order to estimate quantitatively the optimum sales budget.

A large commercial printing company had not been growing as rapidly as the available demand in its area, in spite of the fact that its sales budget was larger than the average of its competitors. The company devoted $350,000 of its total sales appropriation of $500,000 to the salaries and expenses of 35 salesmen. Management felt that the fault lay in the lack of effectiveness of its sales force. An experiment was devised wherein each of 18 of the company's salesmen was assigned 36 customers, divided into three effort groups—high, medium, and low level.[10] A study of how to develop a method of allocating salesmen geographically could be carried further.[11]

The customers in the high-level group were to receive 16 hours of sales effort per month; those in the medium-level group, 4 hours; and those in the low-level group, 1 hour. Sales effort normally consisted of regular sales calls of about an hour's duration twice each month, entertainment at lunch or dinner, troubleshooting on customer printing jobs in progress, advising the customer on specifications for new works, and planning the sales approach to the customer. Once an account had been assigned a

---

[10]Arthur A. Brown, Frank T. Hulswit, and John D. Kettelle, "A Study of Sales Operations," *Operations Research,* 4 (1956): 296–308.

[11]See John F. Magee, "The Effect of Promotional Effort on Sales," *Journal of the Operations Research Society of America,* 1 (1952–53): 64–74. For a simpler but incomplete statement of the analysis, see John F. Magee, "Application of Operations Research to Marketing and Related Management Problems," *Journal of Marketing,* 18 (1953–54): 361–69.

TABLE 11–1
Intended levels of sales effort

Level of effort	Hours per month	Customers per salesman	Total hours per month
High	16	4	64
Medium...............	4	8	32
Low	1	24	24
All		36	120

Source: Arthur A. Brown, Frank T. Hulswit, and John D. Kettelle, "A Study of Sales Operations," *Operations Research*, 4 (1956): 300, Table II.

given level of effort, it was planned to continue sales effort at that level for three months, except in the face of some disaster to the customer, such as fire, bankruptcy, or strike.

Table 11-1 shows how the experiment was planned. Each salesman's total of 36 customers was divided into the three groups as indicated: high, 4; medium, 8; low, 24. The customers to be administered the increased sales effort were selected by the particular salesmen, subject to the approval of the sales manager. Actual levels of sales effort differed from planned levels because it was not possible to predict precisely how many hours could be devoted to a customer. During the first month, an attempt was made to apply the planned effort with each customer; then the level of effort attained during the first month was applied for each of the three succeeding months.

Results at the end of three months, after the level of actual sales effort had been determined for each customer, are summarized in Table 11–2. The "hours" indicated in the column headings (for example, "Under 5 hrs./month") represent *increases* over the number of hours that had been applied previously to each customer in a given level of effort. The figures in each of the three columns indicate the percent of customers whose purchases had *increased* during the experiment. A buyer was shown as having increased his purchases only if they were above the previous level. If, for example, a buyer increased his purchases from $1,000 to $2,000 in a month, he was not counted as an "increase" again until his purchases exceeded $2,000. The conclusion is that purchases increased *as a result* of the increased sales effort. It was also found that five to nine hours a month of additional sales effort was the most effective amount to apply. This is indicated in Table 11–2 by the proportion of customers that increased their purchases from month to month, as shown in column 3 as compared with columns 2 and 4. The original effort had been 2 hours per month, which, when added to the optimum *increase* of 5 to 9 hours, yielded a total of 7 to 11 hours per month.

This study demonstrates that it is possible to determine the effects of selling effort, although it represents a "hammer and tongs" approach unilluminated by any theoretical ideas. An alternative and probably a simpler way is to use the buyer-behavior model and follow sample buyers, hoping that the number of sales calls will vary among the buyers. The effects of the differences could then be analyzed by a structural model.

TABLE 11–2
Effect of sales on purchases

	Proportion of customers increasing their purchases		
Months since effort increased	Under 5 hrs./month (percent)	5 to 9 hrs./month (percent)	Over 9 hrs./month (percent)
0................	0	10	25
1................	0	24	20
2................	8	37	0

Source: Arthur A. Brown, Frank T. Hulswit, and John D. Kettelle, "A Study of Sales Operations," *Operations Research*, 4 (1956): 301, Table III.

These estimates of sales effectiveness can be combined with the cost of salesmen's salaries and expenses to arrive at an optimal total appropriation figure. As in advertising, the lack of estimates of personal-selling effectiveness has been the stumbling block to rational decisions on the size of the appropriation. Cost data are usually more readily available in sales than in advertising because company records will sometimes reveal when and how often a salesman has called upon a particular customer and perhaps even provide an estimate of how much time the salesman spent with the customer. It is difficult to generalize about whether the short- or long-run optimizing model is appropriate.

Alternatively, and more consistent with practice, the brand manager can use a cut-and-try method. He looks at what other similarly placed companies in the industry are doing in terms of size of sales force and asks how his situation may be different from theirs. For example, his brand strategy may be aimed at a particular market segment that the others do not attempt to exploit. However, this may not make a difference in the size of the sales force best for him. He can go further by doing a systematic analysis of sales force activity, such as John O'Shaughnessy recommends.[12] This will not only help him answer the size question but also provide standards by which to evaluate the sales force once it is fully developed.

[12]John O'Shaughnessy, *Work Study Applied to a Sales Force* (London: British Institute of Management, 1965).

ALLOCATION OF SALESMEN

Another aspect of selling strategy is how salesmen are allocated. Brand managers typically do not have much to do with this decision; it is much more the responsibility of the sales manager, who reports to the marketing manager. If the brand manager understands the problem, however, he can work more effectively with sales-force management. For example, the brand manager may sometimes want more sales time devoted to one type of store than to another.

As an aid toward insuring that salesmen use their time effectively and a basis for evaluating their performance, they are customarily assigned certain customers to call on or, more often all the customers located in a particular geographic area or "sales territory." More than one salesman may cover the same geographic area for a company—one may call on the retail buyers in an area, for example, and another on the industrial buyers located in the same territory. Only geographic territories will be discussed here, but the problem is essentially the same if some market-segmenting basis other than geography is employed. The brand manager may wish to segment by type of retail store.

Three terms and their relationship to one another—market potential, forecast, and quota—are helpful in comprehending the nature of the allocation problem. A *market potential* is the market demand for a *product class* in a given territory under given conditions of the controllable and uncontrollable determinants of demand. The concept of market potential was developed in Chapter 1 in the analysis of the spatial dimension of demand, and allocation on this basis is discussed in the section below.

A *forecast* is the volume of sales of a brand that a company expects to obtain in a given territory. The sum of the individual territorial forecasts is the basis for company planning, such as marketing plans, production schedules, and cash budgets. Territorial forecasts are also essential in planning deliveries from factories to warehouses. A *quota*, on the other hand, is the volume of sales of a brand that a given salesman is expected to achieve in a given territory. Quotas are set in such a way as to provide a maximum incentive. Some experienced sales managers believe that quotas should be set at different levels for different salesmen. The argument is that one man will be stimulated by a quota he cannot attain, while another must have a reasonably attainable quota if he is not to become discouraged and less productive. The failure to distinguish between a forecast and a quota can result in either bad planning or a less effective incentive, or both. If the marketing operation is to be integrated satisfactorily with overall company plans, the distinction is basic.

Allocation by market potentials

Potentials are used for two distinctly different purposes: to allocate marketing effort and to achieve control over the marketing operation. An aspect of control, as explained in earlier chapters, is the measurement of performance. The discussion here will be confined to the allocation of marketing effort—specifically, personal-selling effort. Potentials as aids in control are discussed in the final section under the head "Maintenance of the Sales Force."

Because of their ambiguity, market potentials have serious limitations as devices for allocating sales effort, yet some such device is essential if a sales force is to be managed effectively. The ambiguity of the concept is indicated by the definition of market potential as "market demand for a product class in a territory for a given period of time." As Chapter 1 suggested, industry demand typically is a result of a number of determinants, one of which may be the joint effect of the marketing plans of the companies selling in the territory. In order to render the concept less ambiguous, all of the relevant determinants should be specified. Evidence suggests that only a crude measure can be expected, since these determinants may vary among products, territories, and over time.

How can a company's market potentials be measured to serve as the basis of management decision? Two common methods are *Sales Management's* Index of Buying Power for consumer products and the Standard Industrial Classification method for industrial products. Both provide county-by-county indices, and both can be modified by other indices that are known to vary more closely in some areas with sales of the product class. Selling Areas—Marketing, Inc., (SAMI) data can be used in the food industry, for example, to modify *Sales Management's* "Index of Buying Power."

Some of the difficulties of measurement of market potential are pointed up in a brief examination of the Index of buying Power. First, it does not allow for short-term changes in purchasing power. In fact, estimates of potentials in practice are usually based upon factors that change slowly, such as population, whereas sharp cyclical changes occur in the demand for many products. Moreover, these changes do not occur uniformly over the country. Second, consumer tastes vary from place to place. For example, lamb and mutton consumption is much higher in New England than elsewhere in the United States. Third, it is hard to believe that the sales of at least some consumer products are not influenced by the joint marketing effort of the companies making up the industry. The effect of joint advertising, particularly for a new product, for example, is probably important in influencing sales. Fourth, although the short-term industry demand for meat at retail, for example, is price inelastic, the industry price still has some effect in increasing industry sales.[13]

If an unambiguous definition of potential could be arrived at and it could be perfectly measured, the question is how could it be used as the basis for allocation. The rule usually stated or implied is that *selling effort*

---

[13]Elmer J. Working, *Demand for Meat* (Chicago: The University of Chicago Press, 1954), p. xi.

should be proportional to the potential in each area. But how about an area, for example, where competitors have become strongly entrenched over the years? In practice the solution has been to make intuitive evaluations of the strength of competitors. Thus, even assuming away the two difficult problems of concept and measurement, some intuition must be used. Nevertheless, the sensible use of potentials can contribute to the effectiveness with which the brand manager utilizes the capabilities of the sales force.

A mathematical model was used in Chapter 7 to illustrate the general problem of allocating marketing effort to market segments. Since it was designed for the specific purpose of territorial allocation of salesmen, you are urged to refer to it.

MAINTENANCE OF THE SALES FORCE

Introduction

Maintaining a sales force is a major marketing job. It can be divided into four areas of activity: selecting, training, compensating, and controlling. Motivating is also important, but this is dealt with as a part of both training and compensating. All are relevant to the brand manager.

Hints as to why maintaining a sales force is such a task have been given in the discussion above. The traditional model of man, for example, has probably been a barrier to effective sales management. The salesman has been asked, in effect, to do an impossible job—to "find the right button," a phrase used earlier. The result is that selling can be a frustrating job, a conflict between the salesman's personal attitudes and his impersonal attitudes that have been levied by the organization. High turnover and motivational problems are probably the consequences. Selection, training, compensation, and control are directed to meeting these problems.

Selecting salesmen

One of the obvious ways to lower sales cost is to select men who will be effective salesmen. Selection has received considerable attention from both the executive and the psychologist.[14] The most effective current practice is to describe the job and, from the job description formulate the qualities needed by a salesman to perform this job. Then, through the use of the personal-history statement, the personal interview, and psychological tests, people are selected who appear to possess the qualities specified.

---

[14]For a summary and extensive bibliography, see Earle A. Cleveland, "Sales Personnel Research, 1935–1945: A Review," *Personnel Psychology*, 1 (1948); 211–55. For a highly useful and sobering review of the research in personnel psychology, see Mason Haire, "Psychological Problems Relevant to Business and Industry," *Psychological Bulletin*, 56 (1959): 174–77.

Description of the sales job. Emphasis is placed upon the job description in the belief that each company has a unique selling situation. The source of the job description is illustrated by the experience of Esso Standard Oil Company:

Expert opinion was obtained from our top marketing management and from outside consultants in order to get a complete picture of their understanding of the General Salesman's job. Opinions were also obtained from 11 Division Managements and some 60 District Managements in the field. At this time, the relative importance of some 48 duties of the General Salesman was determined as well as opinions about how the best salesmen go about pursuing these duties. Finally, a number of salesmen were directly observed in action during a typical day's work.[15]

Certain personnel techniques used in production, such as time and motion studies, are sometimes employed in describing the job.

Requirements of the sales job. Esso's experience also provides an illustration of how job requirements can be formulated from the results of the job description. From the various sources of information about the job characteristics, the following areas of investigation were identified:

1. General mental ability.
2. Good health and attitude toward health.
3. Degree of interest in selling.
4. Practical judgment in typical sales situations.
5. General attitude toward people and human relations.
6. Adaptability to daily change (flexibility).
7. Attitude toward childhood, family, past jobs, supervision, and controversial issues.
8. Leadership habits in common situations.
9. Planning and organizing ability (self-sufficiency).

From these qualities, a test was constructed that involved 1,096 judgments by the subject and required six to seven hours for administration. The test was then administered to Esso's 328 general salesmen who had been evaluated by management and ranked accordingly. The completed tests were separated into two groups, those completed by the upper half of the men (best salesmen) and those completed by the lower half (poorest salesmen). From the answers given by the two groups, a test one third of the original length was constructed to be used as a qualification questionnaire in selecting future salesmen.

Unfortunately, important information from the Esso experience is not given. First, what criteria did management use to rank the 328 general salesmen? This reaffirms the fact that throughout the area of personal selling some measure of performance is necessary; to make this measure explicit avoids confusion. Second, did the use of the qualification ques-

[15]William W. Bryan, "A Program for Motivating Salesmen," *Advanced Management*, 20 (1955), p. 18.

tionnaire actually result in the selection of more effective salesmen? Observation suggests that this step, the analysis of the results of the procedure, is all too often omitted. With a large and/or growing sales force requiring a significant number of additions, the method can be validated by applying it to selecting salesmen and then comparing the test performance of the high and low producers in practice.

TOOLS FOR SELECTING SALESMEN.   The analysis of the sales-job requirements in a company should provide a statement of the qualities to be looked for in prospective salesmen. Three tools of selection which can help identify and evaluate these qualities are (1) personal-history statements, (2) psychological tests, and (3) interviews.

Personal-history statements.   The application form, usually called the personal-history statement, is often the first step in screening candidates. An analysis of sales personnel selection was carried out by the Tremco Manufacturing Company, which produces roofing and waterproofing materials and sells to buyers who are, generally, plant superintendents and contractors. The following items were included in the personal-history statement:

1. Age.
2. Height.
3. Marital status.
4. Number of dependents.
5. Average number of years in all previous jobs.
6. Insurance carried.
7. Amount of debts.
8. Years of education.
9. Number of clubs.
10. Reason for leaving last regular job.
11. Years in last job.
12. Experience in maintenance.
13. Average monthly earnings on last regular job.

Earnings were used as the criterion of proficiency. Each of the 13 items was weighed by the responses of 48 salesmen whose earnings for a full year were available. For example, replies to "reason for leaving last regular job" were weighted as follows: still employed, 10; job discontinued, 7; to better self, 5; dismissed, 4; friction or other negative reasons, 2. A critical score, the dividing line between "good" and "bad" salesmen, was established at 62. Tremeo reported that "The experience of the company is that 70 percent of those scoring above 62 are still working (after two years), while only 30 percent of those scoring below 62 are still employed."[16]

---

[16]O. A. Ohmann, "A Report of Research on the Selection of Salesmen at the Tremco Manufacturing Company," *Journal of Applied Psychology*, 25 (1941): 18–29.

This analysis suggests one way in which the personal-history statement can be used, but it is generally agreed that the statement by itself is inadequate. For one thing, it would seem, that if the applicant knew his selection depended upon his replies he would fake appropriate answers. One possibility for using the personal-history statement is to determine sources of conflict within the prospective salesman that might prevent him from adapting to sales work.[17] If psychologist designs and analyzes the statement, it may be possible to use it as a projective technique for evaluating personality characteristics.[18]

Psychological tests. Psychological tests have been widely used in the selection process.[19] In contemplating their use, however, it is wise to bear in mind the role of the measure of performance:

Efforts to select personnel by psychological techniques will stand or fall according to whether a valid and reliable criterion can be found and accurately measured. . . . That it [a valid criterion] is frequently overlooked is nowhere more apparent than in articles, especially those appearing in the nonprofessional publications, concerning sales personnel research.[20]

Tests are designed to predict, but often it is not at all clear as to just what is being predicted.

In practice, psychological tests are justified on the principle that "at least they can do no harm." In other words, there can never be a negative relation between the test results and on-the-job performance, a position which even the most naïve would be unwilling to assume. From a careful gleaning of available studies, two psychologists found a positive relation between intelligence-test scores and job proficiency among "salesmen," but among "salesclerks" there was no conclusive evidence of such a positive relation.[21] In this study, 185 comparisons between intelligence-test scores and job performance were analyzed.

Three types of psychological tests are used: intelligence, personality, and interest. Although there seems to be agreement among psychologists that intelligence is not vitally important for proficiency in selling, it is definite that a certain minimum is required. It has been argued that high intelligence may lead to job dissatisfaction. In considering men for promo-

---

[17]Daniel J. Bolanovich and Forrest H. Kirkpatrick, "Measurement and Selection of Salesmen," *Educational and Psychological Measurement,* 3 (1943): 333–39.

[18]Gilmore J. Spencer and Richard Worthington, "Validity of a Projective Technique in Predicting Sales Effectiveness," *Personnel Psychology,* 5 (1952): 125–44.

[19]According to a survey conducted, apparently, in 1944, only 15 percent of 500 companies were using psychological tests. See J. Robert Hilgert, "Use of Sales Aptitude Tests," *Harvard Business Review,* 23 (1944–45): 484–92. However, a survey more than a decade later reported that 37 percent of the 856 companies surveyed was using them. See *Advertising Age,* July 30, 1956, p. 23.

[20]Cleveland, "Sales Personnel Research," pp. 216–17. For a discussion of the developments in dealing with the criterion problem, see Haire, "Psychological Problems."

[21]Edwin E. Ghiselli and Clarence W. Brown, "The Effectiveness of Intelligence Tests in the Selection of Workers," *Journal of Applied Psychology,* 32 (1948): 575–80.

tion to sales manager, however, there is evidence that intelligence level has useful diagnostic value.[22] Different selling situations may require different levels of intelligence, of course, and there is some evidence to suggest that the intelligence required varies among selling jobs. In an analysis of the salesmen of Burroughs Adding Machine Company, it was concluded that the ability to learn quickly and efficiently is a significant contributor to sales performance.[23]

Personality tests came to have wider currency after World War II.

> The trend has been away from the use . . . [of] intelligence and other types of "problem" examinations and in the direction of personality and interest inventories. The concept of "sales ability," in other words, has shifted increasingly to the idea that "salesmanship" is dependent upon some sort of a social pattern, the outlines of which are still fuzzy.[24]

The Bernreuter Personality Inventory is one commonly used type of personality test. Projective techniques such as the Wechsler-Bellevue, Rorschach, and the Thematic Apperception Test seem to enjoy popularity, but application of these tests is at present limited because they were originally designed to deal with abnormal people, and only a few attempts to validate them have been published.[25]

The social aspects of a salesman's task and his adjustment to the social characteristics of the situation have been receiving increased attention. The social interaction framework discussed earlier here and also the social aspects of the theory of buyer behavior as developed in Chapter 12 are arguments for justification of attention to the social features. Specifically, a buyer's personality can be largely identified by his values, and the theory predicts that people with like values will interact more effectively. One significant part of the process of selecting salesmen is to identify the values of the clientele the salesman is to serve and then select salesmen who possess these values. It has also been observed that people who talk more frequently and more intensely are more persuasive than others and therefore should make better salesmen.[26]

A large number of attempts to use personality tests to screen salespeople has been reported. Researchers appear to agree that a battery of tests, rather than a single test, is required. The results of an attempt to

[22]R. F. Lovett and M. W. Richardson, "Selecting Sales Personnel: The Significance of Various Types of Test Material," *Personnel Journal*, 12 (1933-34): 248–53.

[23]Carl H. Rush, Jr., "A Factorial Study of Sales Criteria," *Personnel Psychology*, 6 (1953): 9–24.

[24]Cleveland, "Sales Personnel Research," p. 248.

[25]For an application of projective techniques to salesmen, see David A. Rodgers, "Personality Correlates of Successful Role Behavior" (Ph.d diss., University of Chicago, 1953).

[26]Eliot D. Chapple and Gordon Donald, Jr., "An Evaluation of Department Store Salespeople by the Interaction Chronograph," *Journal of Marketing*, 12 (1947–48): 173–85.

validate a battery of personality tests are shown in Table 11–3. The battery was administered to a total of 348 applicants, and the analysts' predictions based on the tests were then compared with executive ratings of each man. There was agreement on 253 of the applicants, but disagreement on 95.

TABLE 11–3
Executives' and psychologists' ratings of salesmen

Executives' ratings \ Psychologists' predictions	Satisfactory	Unsatisfactory
Satisfactory	208	45
Unsatisfactory	50	45

Source: Richard W. Husband, "Techniques of Salesman Selection," Educational and Psychological Measurement, 9 (1949), p. 133.

The most widely used measure of interest is the Strong Interest Test. Standard scores have been prepared for 34 professions or vocations, only two of which, life-insurance salesman and real-estate salesman, relate to sales positions. After applying the test to their salesmen and relating the scores to sales performance, some companies prepare their own standard scores for the test. The Strong Interest Test assumes that those in an occupation are proficient in that occupation. A number of analyses involving life-insurance salesmen suggest that the test may be effective. For example, 85 percent of the men who scored A on the test sold at least $100,000 of insurance. Only 51 percent of those scoring B+, 44 percent of those scoring B, and 25 percent of those scoring C did as well as those scoring A.[27] There is some evidence that the Strong Interest Test is a better predictor of sales proficiency among younger men. It has been found, for example, that "For those under 25, a high score gave 3.3 times the chance of success, and those over 30 had 2.3 the chance of success when they had a high score."[28] However, the real question, which is not answered, is how well the test does relative to alternative methods of selection.

A number of available tests are alleged in some sense to measure sales ability specifically. As a rule, no attempt has been made to validate tests of this type.[29]

---

[27]E. K. Strong, "Interests and Sales Ability," Personnel Journal, 13 (1934–35): 216.
[28]Richard W. Husband, "Techniques of Salesman Selection," Educational Psychological Measurement, 9 (1949), 135.
[29]See, however, Martin M. Bruce, "A Sales Comprehension Test," Journal of Applied Psychology, 38 (1954): 302.

Interviews.   Te effectiveness of the interview in selecting salesmen is probably exaggerated; executives often boast of their ability to "size up" a man accurately. As an experiment, 800 visitors at a business exposition were shown the photographs of 10 salesmen and asked to rank them according to estimates of sales proficiency. The ratings did agree among the 800 visitors fairly well, *but* there was no relation between the visitors' rankings and the actual performance of the 10 men. This suggests not only that appearance is a poor predictor but also that people tend to have stereotypes or beliefs about what salesmen should look like. The interview can be a useful tool, but it must be standardized if an attempt at validation is to be made.[30]

APPRAISAL OF SELECTION PROCEDURES.   While the empirical nature of current selection procedures has been emphasized, the theory of buyer behavior can be employed to reduce the number of salesmen's characteristics to be considered in formulating an effective company selection procedure. This is particularly true in the area of personality attributes, which presents some of the most difficult problems of selection. The analytical problem is fourfold: (1) to discover the pattern of the individual's personality structure, motives, and attitudes; (2) to translate this into behavioral terms; (3) to project such behavior into a business setting; and (4) to estimate its probable effect on work performance.[31] When this approach was applied to a company employing 129 salesmen, the analyst developed the following criteria for the salesman's job:

High energy applied to work: Physical energy expressed in motor activity, and aggressive initiative applied to situations and people, are required to keep a salesman "pounding the pavement" day in and day out.

Need for verbal expression: The verbal component of selling is illustrated in some popular sayings: a salesman's job is "to walk and talk"; a real salesman is "always selling something to somebody"; and "a good sales talk is never wasted."

Adequate social skills: Since a salesman's prime function is to interact with people, he requires sufficient social techniques to make him acceptable to individuals of differing social and economic levels and differing temperaments.

Adjustment to authority: In order for a salesman to be loyal to the company and its aims, to follow instructions, and to observe company policy, he needs to keep his own self-assertiveness within reasonable bounds in his relations with superiors.

Realistic ambition: Ambition involves a realistic assessment by the individual of his own abilities and limitations. Successful salesmen usually take their work for granted, enjoy it for its own sake, and are satisfied with its rewards.

Ability to "wear the customer's shoes":   A certain capacity for empathy—for seeing the problem from the customer's point of view—contributes to easier and more effective selling and to building good will.

---

[30]Robert N. McMurry, "Validating the Patterned Interview," *Personnel,* 23 (1946–47): 263–72.

[31]Spencer and Worthington, "Validity of a Projective Technique," p. 142.

Status drive: Various levels of our social class structure tend to generate different kinds of status drive. As a general rule, the strongest drive for a canvassing type of sales seems to stem from an upper-lower- or lower-middle-class background.

Intelligence geared to the job: The lower limit of acceptable intelligence is judged to be approximately bright-normal (estimated Wechsler-Bellevue 110). Above that level, intelligence, per se, appears to be of less importance than the way it is used. What is required is a "practical" kind of intelligence, high enough for the salesman to deal comfortably with business procedures, yet not so high that he will prefer the totally intellectualized approach to problems. The functioning of intelligence depends upon two factors: the individual's personality adjustment configuration, and his cultural pattern. The practical usefulness of the personal-history technique in estimating functioning intelligence consists in its being geared not only to estimated problem-solving ability, but also the effect of personality disturbances and social class background on the way it is used.[32]

This type of analysis would seem to give strength and meaning to a company's research in formulating a selection program. A company with a large number of salesmen and/or rapid turnover has a distinct advantage in formulating selection procedures because research is more feasible.

Training salesmen

Training salesmen has many facets, ranging all the way from incidental comments by the sales manager in his day-to-day contact with his men, to sales conventions, to formal course work. The first two are sometimes termed "motivating" salesmen rather than training them. The method of compensation presumably also performs a motivating role, but compensation will be discussed as a separate problem. Supervision, however, is viewed here as a part of the training problem.

A survey of objectives suggests that sales managers hope to accomplish a number of specific things by training. These include greater sales volume; improved customer relations; greater familiarity with company policies; greater tendency to sell all products in the line; better demonstrations and sales presentations; more encouragement of the customer to use the product properly; fewer lost sales; better merchandising work; reduced customer complaints; reduced number of calls per order; more missionary work; and greater percentage of sales in the high-profit items.[33] Here we can see the potential for the brand manager to play a role in sales force management by participating in the goal-setting process. Some objectives can serve his needs much better than others.

Little seems to be known generally about the qualities in salesmen that can and cannot be improved by training. That learning from experience

---

[32] Ibid., pp. 142–43.

[33] For the sales manager's view of the purpose of sales training, see "A Picture of Hiring and Training Today: A Re-Cap of the NSE Survey," *Sales Management,* February 15, 1950, p. 82, Table 8.

FIGURE 11–1
Learning curve for insurance salesmen

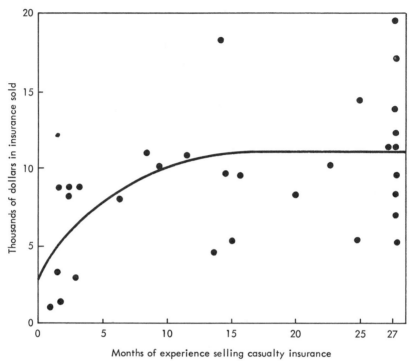

Months of experience selling casualty insurance

Source: Edwin E. Ghiselli and Clarence W. Brown, *Personnel and Industrial Psychology* (New York: McGraw-Hill Book Co., Inc., 1955), p. 80, Fig. 3–2.

does occur is supported, for example, by the data in Figure 11–1, but as the deviations about the learning curve suggest, numerous other factors are operative.

It is generally agreed that training can improve product knowledge and that information about why buyers purchase the product can probably increase sales effectiveness. Some companies go so far as to prepare "canned" sales talks for salesmen to memorize. Company policies can also be explained. However, with respect to personality qualities—the salesman's ability to interact with clients—it is not at all clear whether training will help. Since some personalities are thought to be more persuasible than others, perhaps salesmen can be taught objective criteria by which to distinguish between them.[34]

It may be that the most valuable training the sales manager or supervisor can provide is in helping the salesman understand his role. Defining

[34]See Carl I. Hovland and Irving L. Janis (eds.), *Personality and Persuasibility* (New Haven: Yale University Press, 1959).

that role in terms of a more realistic model than the traditional one would help. A better supported rationale for selling than that now available is needed. The importance of the selling function to the general economic welfare that is frequently emphasized at sales meetings is probably an intuitive attempt to provide this. One often hears "until a sale is made nothing happens."

Training effort directed toward increasing the salesman's identification with the company will probably have a favorable effect upon his performance. Management decisions about training procedures and content can be influenced by a fuller understanding of the nature of the interaction process. Whether this can be transmitted to any but the more intelligent and well-educated salesmen so that it can improve effectiveness is a moot point. The use of well-designed videotapes can help. Ford Motor Company, for example, has recently issued a videotape system for product and sales training to its dealers.[35]

Given a general lack of information as to what training can accomplish, it would seem that evaluation of the effectiveness of training is called for, but surprisingly little effort has been directed at this phase of the problem. One such evaluation of a training course concluded that: "The major deterrent undoubtedly lies in management's reluctance to 'waste time' in testing something it has convinced itself is good. Training programs are uniformly excellent—by expert opinion and proclamation."[36]

With a little planning, an experiment can be performed that will provide meaningful and important evaluations when applied to different facets of the training program. By dividing all or a part of the company's salesmen into two groups and subjecting each group to a different training procedure, differences in effectiveness can be isolated. One study revealed, for example, that one training program was more effective than another for the newer men in the sales force. There are complications in evaluating training programs experimentally, but they are not insurmountable.

The questionnaire method may be effective in obtaining information about salesmen's attitudes to aid in the design of a training program. For example, a questionnaire of 124 items administered by the Libby, McNeill and Libby Company was designed to reveal the following categories of information:

1. Understanding of job goals.
2. Sales training.
3. Company products.
4. Pricing policy.

---

[35] *Advertising Age*, August 14, 1972, p. 56.
[36] S. Rains Wallace, Jr., and Constance M. Twichell, "An Evaluation of a Training Course for Life Insurance Agents," *Personnel Psychology*, 6 (1953); 25.

5. Credit policy.
6. Customer service.
7. Value of advertising and sales promotion.
8. Supervisor's administrative ability.
9. Management's administrative ability.
10. Communication.

The brevity of this discussion does not suggest that training and motivating salesmen are unimportant. It does suggest, however, that not much is known about them objectively.

Compensating salesmen

One of management's major tasks is to formulate rules that will encourage salesmen to develop impersonal attitudes that are congruent with the goals assigned them. "Motivating" the salesman and providing him with "incentives" is the traditional way to phrase this issue. The brand manager is obviously concerned with the salesman's motivation in the sense that the more motivated the salesman to exert effort, the more the brand manager is likely to benefit. He has a specific area of interest, however. Feedback on the brand's performance is especially helpful, and unless the incentive system provides for it, this feedback will be of an inferior quality.

Either through ignorance or lack of congruity between the individual's impersonal attitudes and his assigned goals, a subordinate will behave so as to optimize company goals only if policies are designed in such a way as to encourage him to do so. This is the theory behind compensation methods involving commissions—a salesman who is paid according to his volume of sales is presumed to try harder than if he were paid a straight salary. The inducements-contribution relation, as presented in Chapter 5, is the appropriate principle to use: To the extent that his inducements exceed his contributions he is likely to remain on the job instead of leaving the organization, as well as to try harder to increase his contributions.

Two separate aspects of the problem of compensation are to encourage the salesman to apply his effort as intensely as possible, and to persuade him to apply it in a particular direction. We ordinarily think of compensation as serving only the first role, while supervision serves the second. However, compensation can serve the second as well. Now that computers are making cost data readily available, companies can be expected to begin to provide salesmen with data on each product's profit margin in order to encourage them to sell the more profitable products. This practice has been initiated in at least one company and is being seriously considered in more.

In practice, there is a great variety of compensation methods. They can be roughly classified into (1) straight salary, (2) part salary and part commission, and (3) straight commission. A number of surveys of company compensation systems suggest that about one fourth of the companies use the first method, one half use the second, and one fourth use the third.[37]

Unfortunately, no satisfactory evidence is available to indicate which type of method is more effective under given conditions. It is argued that commission methods are more useful in cyclically depressed periods and that fixed-income methods are more effective in prosperity. The extent of nonselling duties that the salesman performs is probably important in determining compensation. For example, if a salesman does delivery and repair service, the emphasis should be on the straight-salary type.

Certain qualitative criteria have been found to be helpful in designing the compensation plan:

Income and security: By providing a minimum income the compensation plan can yield security to the salesman. It is generally felt that excessive fluctuation in earnings should be avoided.

Incentives: The plan should contain an incentive element; but for it to be effective, it must be understood by the salesmen.

Flexibility: The plan should be designed to meet fluctuations in business conditions. Perhaps both minimum and maximum limits on earnings are essential.

Economy: The plan should be designed to provide an incentive to increase sales but at a cost no greater than competitor's costs. Costs include payments to salesmen, travel, and other expenses, and the expenses of operating the compensation plan.

Fairness: In order to contribute to morale, the plan should appear fair both to management and to the salesman.[38]

One of the largest petroleum companies pays its salesmen a fixed salary on the grounds that a commission system leads to friction among the salesmen. The salary in this case is determined by "merit ratings" and the "job title" assigned to each salesman. Social psychology suggests that one of the key determinants of the type of compensation method to use depends upon the extent to which the company's salesmen constitute a "group" in a psychological sense. If the members of the sales force work together intimately so that group norms tend to develop, a fixed salary or possibly a group bonus method is advisable. In this case, a commission system could create friction. If, on the other hand, the salesmen work individually and have limited contact with one another, a commission system could stimulate rivalry and greater effort. The group aspect, although important, is only one determinant to be weighed against the others that usually exist in a specific problem.

---

[37]Bertrand R. Canfield, *Sales Administration,* 3d ed. (New York: Prentice-Hall, Inc., 1954), pp. 233–34.

[38]Harry R. Tosdal, "How to Design the Salesman's Compensation Plan," *Harvard Business Review,* 31 (1953); 64.

As in other personal-selling problems, a compensation method should be selected by experimenting, if possible, and using behavioral theory as an aid in formulating the hypotheses that are tested in the experiments. This would seem to be especially valid until more is known about the process of personal selling.

Controlling salesmen

In addition to compensation, the sales manager typically has other approaches to a rewarding device for salesmen. The simple idea of praise for a job well done is the most obvious. To the extent that rewards and punishments are used reasonably, they can be effective. A control system is intended to provide information as the basis for administering rewards.

A measure of performance is an essential condition of effective control. Moreover, it is also needed for the development of a selection procedure, which is one of the major ways of increasing sales effectiveness. Although measuring performance is only a means to an end—the increase of sales effectiveness—all too often no attempt is made in practice to evaluate the results of sales expenditure—the salesman's salary, commissions, and expenses.

In practice, a great range of measures is employed, extending all the way from ease of personal relationship between sales manager and salesman (how well the sales manager likes the salesman) to some approximation of contribution to company profit. The first extreme is suggested by a study of the Burroughs Adding Machine Company in which it was found that management's ratings of salesmen and salesmen's performance, as measured by percent of quota achieved, average monthly (sales) volume, and average number of monthly sales, were not closely related.[39] David A. Rodgers came to a similar conclusion from his study of salesmen in the food industry.[40]

Ideally the measure should be directly related to company goals. As one executive stated:

After all, if a man or an office fails to make money for us, then we're in trouble— profits are our ultimate goal and our final test. What's more, when you measure by profitability, you automatically stimulate harder selling on the higher profit items, you take some of the pressures off price-cutting, and you focus attention on local expenses.[41]

It is conceivable, however, that short-term profits can be obtained at the sacrifice of long-term profits. An example is in the acquisition of new cus-

[39]Rush, "Factorial Study of Sales Criteria," p. 18.
[40]Rodgers, "Personality Correlates," p. 92.
[41]Donald D. Couch, *Measuring the Effectiveness of Your Salesmen*, Marketing Series No. 93 (New York: American Management Association, 1954), p. 12.

tomers, which often contributes little to the near-term volume of sales but can be highly favorable to long-term profit and volume.

In order to compute contribution to profit for each salesman, his total sales are compared with the costs that can be traced to his particular operation. The distinction between traceable and common costs was discussed in Chapter 4. If a manufacturing company is involved, the traceable costs usually are manufacturing cost, cost of transporting the product, salesman's commission and/or salary, and salesman's expenses. For a distributive company such as a wholesaling enterprise, the purchase cost of the products sold by each salesman is used instead of manufacturing cost.

A method closely related to contribution to profit is the total gross profit on the sales volume of each salesman, which does not include salesman's commissions nor expenses.

Quotas are more often used in evaluating performance than for any other purpose. Sometimes, however, they are intended to serve as an incentive, and compensation is related to the ratio of performance (sales volume) to quota. Sales managers often adjust the relation between quota and forecast according to the individual salesman's *expected response* to a quota incentive. Some salesmen may be assigned a quota larger than the forecast, while others are assigned quotas that are smaller.

Two sets of records can be used in setting up an incentive system based on quotas: records composed of the sales volume that each salesman is *told* he is expected to achieve, and records of the volume management *thinks* he will achieve. The two sets of accounting records that are often maintained in a company for income tax reasons provide a precedent for this practice. Certainly, the procedure of using two sets of records is desirable if *compensation* of the salesman is to be determined by the ratio between his performance and his individually adjusted quota, and his *evaluation* is to depend on the ratio between his actual performance and the quota management thinks he will achieve. In practice, salesmen's quotas are usually set in some given ration to, or identical with, territorial sales forecasts, without regard to differences among salesmen in personality or other capacities.

If an incentive is to operate effectively, however, the salesman must know its conditions. Whether these individually adjusted quotas should be explained to the salesmen is the question. The explanation would probably create ill will among salesmen, although there does appear to be a trend toward more straightforward relations between salesmen and management.

This decision of whether to recognize intersalesman differences, and if so, how to develop a procedure which will permit the system of intersalesman differences to be administered adequately is the heart of the problem of management's relations with salesmen. A salesman need not necessarily know the performance criteria that are being applied to him. But where management hopes to modify his behavior (which is the purpose of incentives) he must know them, or he will have no basis for changing that behavior. As in all problems of learning, the connection between reward and effort should be obvious to the learner.

Having accepted certain criteria in evaluating the salesmen of a given company, the question remains as to the norm—the desired level—to be set for each criterion. In order to simplify the discussion, assume that a single criterion is being used instead of a multidimensional measure of performance. Specifically, assume it is contribution to profit. What is going to be considered an "excellent," "satisfactory," or "poor" contribution to profit? Typically, it is some average of this year's performance for all salesmen in a similar category of the company. Comparing salesmen with one another suggests, however, that each salesman has had an equal opportunity for sales. This brings us back to the role of potentials, forecasts, and quotas. It may not be possible to make either a satisfyingly accurate estimate of potentials or a prediction of the company's share in each territory, which is the sales forecast. Nevertheless, conditions must to some extent be standardized among salesmen if they are to be evaluated according to their performance in relation to one another. If the selling task, as contrasted with the salesman's performance of that task, is not standardized among salesmen, both the task and its performance are being evaluated, and it becomes impossible to separate the two.

Precision in measuring potentials is an ideal to strive toward, but absolute accuracy is not necessary for the estimates to be useful in many situations. No one satisfactory measure will apply to all products; the fallacy of attempting an all-purpose measure is illustrated by an examination of *Sales Management's* "Index of Buying Power."[42] According to the Index, in 1945 Indianapolis contained 0.527 percent of the national potential and Houston, 0.487 percent, which would suggest that Indianapolis was a better market than Houston by 8 percent. Twelve consumer products were compared between the two markets, and on the average Indianapolis sales were 8 percent higher. When each product was examined individually, however, quite a different picture emerged. For one product, low-priced dresses, Indianapolis was 87 percent poorer than Houston, but for high-priced coats Indianapolis was 58 percent better. Out of the twelve evaluations, *only three came within a 10 percent average differential* in favor of Indianapolis.

It is often suggested that sales performance is multidimensional, which at least implicitly, calls for some type of weighting system as an index

---

[42]Joseph H. White, "Measuring Local Markets," *Journal of Marketing*, 12 (1947–48): 222–23.

of performance. Among practicing sales managers the implicit nature of measuring sales performance is emphasized; that is, they do not verbalize the factors they use in the measuring process, and this failure gives rise to serious limitations. A sales manager can change his norms from time to time—and perhaps even change the factors—without being aware of it or admitting it to himself. Evidence of the discrepancy between management's ratings of salesmen and actual salesman performance suggests that management's evaluations may be quite unreliable. "Rating sheets" have been devised in order to make such evaluations more objective. A rating sheet consists of a list of salesmen's qualities which are considered relevant for the particular company; a range of values, for example, from 1 to 10, is set for each quality. Then, each salesman is placed somewhere along the continuum on each quality, and the resulting scores are summed to provide his total rating.

Personnel psychologists have prepared a number of multidimensional measures of performance.[43] Such a measure can be developed only after a careful job analysis to be sure that the critical features of the job are incorporated. It may be necessary, for example, to include the number of calls made by each salesman so that those activities contributing to long-term market development are not sacrificed.

With the tools of equal market potentials and a measure of performance, a sales manager can proceed to compare performance among salesmen in order to evaluate them. If differences exist, and they typically do, the course of action will depend upon the circumstances. Perhaps a training program for the less effective salesmen is in order. The compensation scheme may have to be modified. Drastic action in the form of discharging a salesman may be necessary; this is a tacit admission that the selection procedure has failed and therefore should be improved.

The brand manager can also use equal market potentials to evaluate the effect of any marketing effort: new products, different marketing channels, prices, and advertising, as well as personal selling. The evaluation is accomplished by varying the marketing plan in different territories; the standardized market potentials permit comparison of the sales results in the different markets with, perhaps, the conclusion that the differences in sales are due to the different plans.

ADDITIONAL COMPLICATIONS

Up to this point, a simplified picture of the salesman-buyer interaction process has been presented. Some important factors have necessarily been omitted. One of these is the stage of the product life cycle. (see Chapter 2). If the product is well established and the buyers are in routinized

---

[43]Rush, "Factorial Study of Sales Criteria"; Bolanovich and Kirkpatrick, "Measurement and Selection of Salesmen."

response behavior, the role of the salesman is much more limited. This tends to be the typical situation for the brand manager. He is confined to providing information that updates the buyer's goal dimensions for his product. At the other extreme, where the buyer is in extensive problem solving, the brand manager has great latitude because he not only provides information that helps the buyer form a concept of his brand but may even influence the buyer's choice criteria. How powerful a role he can play in this respect is not currently clear.

We do know, however, that this influence of the salesman is limited by the buyer's contacts with friends and neighbors, whose influence is often more than offsetting. We suspect that the salesman's credibility, particularly on the trust dimension, is typically not so great. This introduces us to a second complication, the social structure surrounding the buyer.

The role of the consumer's social structure is somewhat understood from systematic research as we shall see in Chapter 13. When we turn to the industrial buyer, however, the evidence is more anecdotal. Further, the salesman is much more important in the industrial marketing mix than is generally true in the consumer market. The retail clerk, for example, typically has only limited knowledge of his products and how they serve the consumer. He is responsible for too many products.

The industrial buyer, as pointed out in Chapter 3, is in a much more rigid social structure. When the industrial buyer is in RRB, the organizational rules that shape his impersonal attitudes are well delineated and accepted. Within this policy framework, the buyer has much latitude and the salesman can play a significant role in updating his impersonal attitudes. We must recognize, however, that the amount of latitude of the buyer varies enormously among product classes, and especially among different companies, although it is fixed over time for any given buyer.

As we move to limited problem solving and extensive problem solving, however, the problem becomes more complicated. To take the extreme case, in EPS the industrial buyer must get a great amount of information from the user of the product for whom he is buying it. There is always a latent power struggle between the buyer and others in the corporation who want more control over the purchasing process. Every person wants as much power as he can get so that he will have freedom of maneuver. The EPS stage opens up an opportunity to reexamine the validity of the existing policy structure.

Let us be more concrete. An industrial buyer wants to be free to choose the supplier not only on the basis of price but by quality criteria as well. Assuming he is adequately informed, he can undoubtedly do a better job of buying for the company than the user can. But the question is whether he is, or even can be, as well informed on quality as the user. The user— such as the designer of a new product for which the component parts are being purchased—is an engineer and typically a specialist in the area. He will argue that he should be free to choose the supplier, since he knows their capacities to meet his specific needs. Given his way, he could reduce the industrial buyer to a mere "order placer." Casual observation suggests that the accelerated speed of technological change since World War II has, in fact, had this effect.

SUMMARY

Because of the magnitude of the personal-selling expenditure in many companies, any improvement is likely to yield a significant improvement in profits. Although intuition plays a major role in this area, there is hope that market research techniques and the buyer-behavior model can contribute to rational decision making. It is true that little is known about the task of selling and its implications for the participants in the interaction of salesman and potential buyer. However, some theory has been developed, and there are isolated studies of significance.

The evaluation of performance bears an especially heavy responsibility in sales-management decisions, and market potentials are usually an essential tool in making this evaluation. For the decision to allocate sales expenditures to territories, however, market potentials have severe limitations.

From this discussion it is clear that the sales force can be a central element of brand strategy: The salesman can make a significant difference in the buyer's behavior when the buyer needs information which the salesman can supply. It is well to bear in mind that the buyer is seldom well informed about all alternatives and that merely telling him about yours will often make the difference in your favor. It might appear that, if this is true, the brand manager exercises so little influence over the sales force that all he can do is take the effect into account in his planning. This is by no means true. He can usually influence the amount of sales time devoted to his brand. Also, by better understanding the sales process, he can shape other elements of the brand strategy so as to affect the role of the salesman. Above all he can, for example, provide deals to the salesman to use as ammunition in his interaction process with the retailer. Finally, the salesman can provide valuable feedback to the brand manager as to how the brand is performing in the market.

DISCUSSION QUESTIONS

1. This chapter stated that the nature of the selling environment has changed significantly, and an essential element in this has been a change in the sales manager's model of man. Explain, and state whether you agree or disagree.
2. Explain the differences between the three concepts of market potential, sales forecast, and sales quota.
3. How would you go about selecting salesmen for a large food company that sells to grocery stores? Contrast your recommendations with those you

would make to Westinghouse selecting salesmen for selling 5 hp. electric motors as replacements in industrial production.

4. There are three standard ways of compensating salesmen: (*a*) salary, (*b*) commission and (*c*) salary and commission. What are the arguments for each one?

5. Because of the heavy cost of a sales force and our lack of understanding of the selling process, control is a major problem. Describe how to set up a system which will give the sales force a modicum of direction.

part IV

The marketing manager's view: Administrative and strategic marketing

THE BRAND MANAGER, the subject of Part III, deals with those portions of the marketing operation—usually a brand—that represent a steady state. Viewed objectively, a steady state is a situation in which minor changes in the system (such as the brand and its associated support—financial, manufacturing, and marketing) will suffice to adapt it to its environment. These are operating decisions. The brand manager, however, is not an objective observer; he is a participant, and he knows that most of the company's profits are generated by steady-state systems. Thus he correctly concludes that he is a vital part of the company. His role is "to maximize profitability of current operations."[1]

Now we turn to strategic decisions, which we have defined thus far as being long term. This definition was adequate when dealing with the brand manager. As we move up the corporate hierarchy, however, a more concise definition is needed. We need one that will enable us to see how and why marketing management has moved to "center stage" in the corporation. According to H. Igor Ansoff, "Strategic decisions are primarily concerned with external, rather than internal, problems of the firm and specifically with selection of the product-mix which the firm will produce and the markets to which it will sell."[2]

In Part IV we are concerned with the strategic decisions taken by the marketing manager. This position, such as that found in a divisionalized

---

[1] H. Igor Ansoff, *Corporate Strategy*, (New York: McGraw-Hill Book Co., 1965), p. 5.

[2] Ibid.

company in the package-goods industries, is used as the typical case. What is said, however, is just as applicable, by and large, to the corporate chief marketing executive in a nondivisionalized company or to the position of general sales manager in many industrial companies.

The marketing manager is heavily concerned with the product line and with new markets. The product line requires attention to the entity as well as to its individual parts—the brands—and to add and drop decisions. He also has another type of decision to make—administrative. While it is true that strategic decisions are, long term, not all long-term decisions are strategic. Some are administrative.

Administrative decisions are concerned with structuring the firm's resources in a way which creates a maximum performance *potential.* One part of the administrative problem is concerned with organization: structuring of authority and responsibility relationships, work flows, information flows, distribution channels, and location of facilities. The other part is concerned with acquisition and development of resources: development of raw-material sources, personnel training and development, financing, and acquisition of facilities and equipment.[3]

In administrative decisions, the marketing manager must concern himself in particular with *marketing* organization, including distribution channels, the location of marketing facilities such as warehouses, and the training and development of marketing personnel.

We will focus upon two major areas of the marketing manager's responsibility—new products (Chapter 13) and marketing channel systems (Chapter 14). The general problem of strategic planning which serves as an introduction to these two areas is the topic of Chapter 12. Both new products and channels represent long-term decisions, but we now begin to make a subtle distinction between them. The first is strategic and the second is administrative, as developed in the definitions above. This distinction will help show the vital role of marketing in *corporate* strategy when we move to the president's perspective in Chapter 15. The concept of corporate strategy has been developed to systematize top-level activity: the generalist's role as opposed to the functionalist's role, with which this book is mainly concerned.[4]

Corporate strategy is a set of rules for guiding the *total* company in the achievement of its objectives. The dominant objective, as we have emphasized, is growth with a minimum profit constraint. It can achieve this growth either through *expansion* or *diversification.* Figure IV–1 shows these alternatives graphically.

The company can expand by *market* development, whereby it seeks

---

[3]Ibid., p. 6.

[4]Ibid., Kenneth R. Andrews, *The Concept of Corporate Strategy* (Homewood, Ill.: Dow Jones-Irwin, Inc., 1971).

FIGURE IV–1
Product-mission matrix

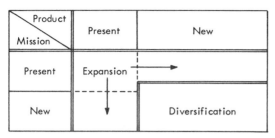

Source: H. Igor Anshoff, *Corporate Strategy* (New York: McGraw-Hill Book Co., 1965), p. 128.

new "missions" for its existing products, as shown by the vertical arrow in the Figure. Or it can expand by *product* development, in which new products are created to replace old ones. This is the horizontal arrow. It can obviously expand by *market penetration,* which is expansion of share of existing products in existing markets; this is not shown in Figure IV–1.

The company can diversify by seeking growth through new products in new markets. This route is, of course, more drastic and risky than expansion because it is on highly unfamiliar ground in terms of *both* products and markets.

The most important point implied in Figure IV–1, however, is that the *product-market concept* is the central focus of corporate strategy, a concept to which all other considerations are subordinated. The marketing function is thus the center of corporate strategy.

As with all strategy, corporate strategy serves three purposes. First, it provides guidance to those within the company who are responsible for applying it. Second, it provides a way of evaluating those responsible for its application. Interestingly, General Electric, which pioneered in the concept of decentralization more than two decades ago, has announced an approach to strategic business planning. A key element is: "Performance of managers is now rated on their adherence to their strategic plans rather than on short-term profits."[5]

Third, corporate strategy serves a communicative role. At this level in the company, however, that role is not internal, as we have been considering it. Its object is the financial market, the source of funds to support the growth objective. It implies a relation between *present* product markets and *future* product markets which will convey to the financial market the idea that investors can be optimistic about the company's future stock earnings.

[5]"GE's New Strategy for Faster Growth," *Business Week,* July 8, 1972, p. 52 ff.

This "common thread" between present product markets of a company and future product markets via diversification is illustrated in the experience of Warner Communications, Inc.:

One of the most dramatic metamorphoses is that of Warner Communications, Inc., which in one decade has gone from coffins and car rentals to the dazzling frontier of cable television. In that same period it has become the 24th fastest growing company on the Fortune 500 list where its 1971 revenues of $373,840,000 give it 294th place.[6]

This company was born in 1961 as Kinney Service Corp., a rent-a-car and parking service with $17,000,000 of revenues. The "common thread" shows in its path of acquisitions, in the following order: funeral service, parking service, rent-a-car, cleaning service, magazine distribution with airlines, magazine publishing, entertainment in the form of managing playwrights, movie production company, and cable television companies.

In the specific place of marketing as the central support of corporate strategy, the brand manager's role is market penetration to support growth. The marketing manager's strategic role is, first, in product development and market development; specifically, he is concerned with new-product ideas, research and development, new-product introduction, balance in the product line, and dropping "dogs." Second, his role is to make administrative decisions that will produce performance potential. These roles we will develop in Chapters 13 and 14. Finally, he can play an important role in acquisition, but this is a matter for Part V.

---

[6] *The New York Times,* August 13, 1972, p. F3.

12

Long-term market programming

INTRODUCTION

THE MARKETING MANAGER plays a dual role. First, he makes administrative decisions: besides setting strategy for and supervising the work of brand managers, he makes broader administrative decisions, as detailed below. Supervision includes insuring that brand managers' plans and the execution of these plans conform to his policies. Second, within the framework set for him by higher management, he makes strategic decisions. Both kinds of decisions involve innovation, and it is the innovative aspect of his decisions that sets them apart from those of the brand manager. These innovative characteristics will be emphasized in this chapter.

The purpose of this chapter is to describe the organizational framework within which the marketing manager innovates and the problems that innovation poses for him. Because his difficulties can be minimized by the use of analytic decision processes, the idea of such processes is developed at some length.

ORGANIZATIONAL FEATURES OF THE MARKETING MANAGER'S ROLE

In examining the organizational implications of innovation, it will be helpful to separate the marketing manager's administrative and innovative roles. There is some overlap between these two categories, however; for example, some administrative decisions, such as channel arrangements, involve innovations.

Administrative role

The marketing manager administers a number of steady-state suborganizations, namely, brands. In addition to brand managers, he manages a number of other people who serve these suborganizations: a sales manager, an advertising manager, a market research manager, and perhaps others, depending upon the particular company. As in all administration, he is concerned with identifying promising people, selecting people, and training and supervising people. In one sense, however, his administrative job is different from others. Brand managers are in key positions, and the company can suffer in years to come if careful attention is not paid to their selection. Because they are in a central line of promotion, the replacement rate is high. Perhaps most importantly, their roles are unique: they are in positions that call for great responsibility to be exercised with limited official authority but have the potential for substantial power, if the brand manager learns to occupy the position effectively.

Specifically, the marketing manager, in his role as the brand manager's supervisor, examines and modifies or approves his marketing plan. Before the brand manager initiates the preparation of the annual plan there will be a planning conference with the marketing manager and tentative decisions will be made, but many changes develop in the brand manager's discussions with others. The finished plan may not resemble the one envisioned by the marketing manager at the time of the planning conference, and he therefore often recommends modifications before he accepts it. This can, of course, complicate matters for the brand manager. He may have striven diligently to get agreement from all interested parties at his level, only to have to go through the process again as a result of the marketing manager's modifications.

Once the various brand managers' annual plans are approved, the marketing manager will combine them into an integrated, coordinated marketing plan. This is made a part of the division's overall plan for submission to the president.

To support his supervisory task the marketing manager wants a control system. Such a market monitoring system simplifies his job and frees him for more imaginative and demanding tasks such as formulating new-product and channel strategies within which his subordinates (the brand managers) will work. Each area will probably have different criteria of performance. For the sales manager of a package-goods company such as a food concern, for example, reports of the size of "shelf facings" in the retail stores may be a useful measure of performance. For the advertising manager it might be consumer ad readership figures. Sales or profit on his product can be the measure of the brand manager's performance. The performance of the market research and marketing services managers is more difficult to evaluate. The marketing manager will supplement these criteria by all manner of information in each case, but his day-to-day and perhaps most important checks can be the standards he regularly applies.

The nature of the marketing manager's information system is much like the one set forth to supply the brand manager's information needs. Criteria of performance, of course, will differ. His system will contain the same boxes as the one described in Chapter 6, but the specific content of those boxes will in many cases be designed to fit his particular needs. Most of the material in Chapter 6 is applicable here.

The identification, selection, training, and supervision of the functional heads—sales, advertising, and research—pose especially difficult problems. The people in these positions can make a great difference in whether the marketing department is an integrated, supportive operation or an ineffectual set of separate fiefdoms.

Finally, the marketing manager must continually coordinate his overall operation with other elements of the organization, such as manufacturing and finance. Of all the areas with which marketing is concerned, the development and introduction of new products may pose the most difficult problems of coordination.

The innovative role

All innovation has potentially severe organizational implications. Because innovations are projections into an uncertain future, they are always risky. They also may affect the professional futures of a number of people, or at least they have the possibility of doing so. This basic combination of risk and large effect often creates very subtle consequences, as can be illustrated by the problems of new-product development and introduction. True, each innovation has its own unique implications, but we emphasize the similarities among innovations for the purpose of concrete analysis.

New products, like all innovations, are important organizationally to the extent that they require new behavior patterns by managers and subordinate personnel. Behavior change never comes easily in an organization, and it is especially painful with new products because the risk, both personal and corporate, can be high. The difficulty appears to differ according to company size, among other things, although some of the large companies innovate so regularly in some areas that the problems may have been largely solved, and Routinized Response Behavior operates.

NATURE OF THE INNOVATIVE PROBLEM. Size has a bearing on the nature of the problem. If the company is small and if the president is the source of the new idea, the task of innovation—the process of gaining market acceptance for the invention—may not be too difficult. Dr. Land and the first Polaroid camera provide an example of a small company's experience in innovation. As a scientist in the field, he knew the technology of this new idea: the instant development of photographs at an economical price. His organization was small, so he not only provided the idea but he could serve as the entrepreneur-administrator as well and keep all of the details of the innovating process at the tips of his fingers. Thus he could force the organization to adapt. This kind of situation may be an important source of new products, but the greatest amount of innovation is now performed by larger companies, in which these principles do not operate. A Brookings Institution study showed that "First, industrial R & D is concentrated in about 400 large firms. Second, R & D is concentrated in a few industries and product lines."[1]

Larger company size introduces very real complications, all having to do with the specialization of labor that makes larger companies possible. This specialization, which was discussed in Chapter 5, makes for great efficiency in producing a standard product. It leads to both vertical and horizontal separations, however, which serve as real barriers to the communication and understanding that is essential to innovation.

The vertical separation erects barriers between the man at the top and the entrepreneur, the one who bears personal responsibility for success of the innovation. Someone lower in the organization who has the entrepreneurial qualities of drive, imagination, courage, and persistence must see the innovation through to success or failure. The man at the top, the president, is too occupied with administering the ongoing organization to do this job. He can manage a large organization only because he is willing to delegate other responsibilities to specialists.

Unfortunately, no human organization—company, church, government bureau, or university—takes kindly to change. Change requires the learning of new decision processes (intuitive information-processing and decision rules, as we saw in Chapter 5), which the manager usually doesn't understand. Perhaps even more important, change disrupts the *modus vivendi.* Able men who must both cooperate and compete with each other inevitably build these arrangements among themselves to make life more comfortable, to add stability to their relations. The nature of this situation can be inferred from the statement of the company president who said, "The energies of the more talented, more aggressive, more ambitious employees often seem to be taken up with internal problems of power, prestige and position." The *modus vivendi* represents established, accepted positions in the corporate hierarchy, positions that are not shown in the company's organization chart. Any threat to them—and change is always a threat—will be blocked in almost any way possible. In sum, the entrepreneur will not be a popular man with others in the company.

Further, even if the entrepreneur's idea are accepted within the company, his chances of failure are high. He cannot forecast with accuracy. He will have to make a jump in his thinking into the unknown in struc-

---

[1]R. R. Nelson, M. J. Peck, and E. D. Kalachek, *Technology, Economic Growth and Public Policy* (Washington, D.C.: Brookings Institution, 1967), p. 65.

turing the problem so that he or his subordinates can prepare demand, competitive, and cost estimates—a jump that is often difficult to defend. We say it is "intuitive."

The problem is especially difficult because the president is obviously also involved in the risk. Yet he cannot know much about the facts of the situation: he has delegated the problem. How does he behave in this situation? He tests the knowledge and understanding of the entrepreneur. He must feel comfortable in accepting the judgment, of the person to whom he has delegated, because he must commit the resources and reputation of the company to the entrepreneur's ideas. He may be tempted or even forced by the pressures of the organization to adopt the mantle of infallibility. If he does so, the solution is easier. Then, if the product succeeds, he can accept the credit. If it fails, the entrepreneur failed, not the president.

The horizontal type of separation is also imposed by the specialization of labor which makes a large organization economically feasible. The ideas for new products no longer come from the president; he has delegated this function, too. In terms of extremes, product ideas are either buyer determined or laboratory determined. Major buyer-determined innovations almost never exist. Usually at least some laboratory work is essential. On the other hand, laboratory-determined innovation is almost sure to be a failure if it is developed in isolation from the market, from the motives of the buyers. In almost all situations, marketing and research and development (R & D) must work together. In this horizontal relation, cross-channel cooperative effort is severely handicapped.

In principle, the problem is lack of coordination. This was discussed at length in Chapter 5, where it was said that coordination can be accomplished by planning or feedback. The innovative activity is too uncertain for it to be planned with dependable results, and feedback will usually not allow enough lead time for corrective action to be carried out. Here the communication problem makes it even less effective. The usual cross-channel problems of communication are intensified by the nature of the three groups involved: laboratory researchers, market researchers, and production personnel.

First, each area, because of its particular kind of activities, is assigned different goals and evaluated by different criteria. These differing goals and criteria not only affect their behavior differentially but their perceptions as well.

Second, each of the two research departments, laboratory and market, is made up of highly trained professionals with pride of accomplishment, their own points of view, and distinctive jargon, all of which impede communication on a subject which is difficult to communicate about anyway: the response of the buyer. Buyer behavior, up until recently, has been difficult to communicate about because there have been few if any widely accepted, much less tested, concepts. In the relationship each side tends to make recommendations securely within their own area of expertise. Once R & D is well along in developing the concept, it is presented to market research in direct, highly specified form. Market research tests the concept with little imagination because it lacks the wealth of background knowledge possessed by R & D. The results of the concept test are presented to R & D in the same direct and specific way. Missing from this flow is the imaginative alternative suggestions that exist in market research as a result of the subtle understandings that inevitably emerge from good research. One *proposes* and the other *disposes*. Each wants to avoid responsibility for a failure, and, according to them, communication with "those other" people is difficult anyway.

It is little wonder that anyone who investigates the problem will quickly find a mass of product failures. Probably no area in the company is as frequently reorganized in search of better solutions as is product development. On the other hand, we must recognize that the problem is not an old one. It grew largely out of World War II, when the enormous power of the laboratory to create new technology became apparent. Unfortunately, in time of war, the demand is clearly defined and economics is almost irrelevant: Get it done at any cost. In the normal peacetime market, economics dominates, and cost is usually a most relevant factor.

POSSIBLE SOLUTIONS.   As companies have become more discriminating, corporate growth is no longer the only sign of success, especially for those in a saturated industry. Even if growth retains its position as the ultimate company goal, technological innovation may not always be more effective than merely being alert to competitors' new ideas and taking them up quickly. Further, not all new ideas are technologically based.

While the uncertainty of innovation has not decreased to any appreciable extent, the potential returns from innovation have increased. Companies have sought a variety of solutions to the problem of innovation. Two that have been tried are change in the organizational *structure*, as broadly defined, and change in *behavior* within the structure.

Change in corporate structure.   Some companies have recognized the important role of the "entrepreneur without authority" discussed above and have given him official encouragement. Usually he emerges as the champion of the new idea and attempts to carry out that role. Unfortunately, not enough of these men are available. The role is too difficult and too uncertain.

Other companies have institutionalized the role of the product champion. A common label is that of the "new venture." A small group, usually from within the company, is selected to initiate the innovation in the form of a new company. It is under the same corporate umbrella but is not bound to the rest of the company at any point below the top level. This venture idea is one of the reasons for the splintering of ad services mentioned in Chapter 9. It has been found that "Venture managers don't want tiers of authority. They want to work directly with their resources (such as advertising agencies). Agencies haven't reacted accordingly."[2] Many companies swear by the venture as an effective innovating device. Once each venture has attained a viable, stable status, it can be brought into the organization by merging it, insofar as necessary, with the various lower levels of the appropriate division of which it now becomes a part.

Change within existing organization structure. If certain conditions are met, deliberate change from within the corporation is possible.[3] The first condition is the existence of *leverage at the top.* Unless there is commitment to change at the top, the organization below is almost sure not to change. And, of course, this top-level commitment implies that top management recognizes its need to change. Top management must disabuse its mind of such myths as "We need more creative men" or "Good ideas come from the top" in seeking the solution.

Second, *a crisis must be perceived.* Only the strongest incentive, such as a belief that a crisis has arisen, will achieve innovation. To bring about change a manager may have to *create* a crisis, such as espousing the belief that "Without new products, we cannot grow further."

Third, *conflict* in the organization is essential. Internal conflict is the organization's response to external threat that demands change. As a result of the conflict, new views emerge.

Fourth, sufficient *time* is necessary. It takes time for a perception of crisis to turn into a sense of the need for innovation. It takes time for the conflicts stimulated by external threat to be resolved. It has been estimated that the minimum time required for a change toward innovation is a year, and usually two or three years.

Finally, there must be a vision that is converted to a *model.* Someone must perceive and articulate the answer to the question, "What would we be, if we were not what we are?" What can top management do to facilitate change? Above all, it can provide a definition of the industry or industries it ought to be in: It can have a *corporate strategy.* Top management can also exhort the organization to strive to change; it can set organizational goals aimed at accomplishing the innovation; it can allocate resources to support the change. In a nutshell, it can have the appropriate administrative decisions made.

If top management accepts one of these courses of action, it can employ a number of different management styles in carrying out the change. Someone, a high-level person, must take the leadership. This is typically a new man rather than an old leader with a new sense of mission. The leader can adopt, in the extreme, one of two styles: authoritarian or cooperator.

---

[2] *Advertising Age*, November 23, 1970, p. 8.
[3] D. A. Schon, *Technology and Change* (New York: Delacorte Press, 1967).

In the first case, after developing a vision of what needs to be done, he seizes authority to carry it out. He brings in aides who support his view and tries to remove those who oppose him. He continually tests his power to carry out these actions. In this process, he creates great dependency; he solves conflict by fiat. He often cannot tolerate able men around him, and so, unfortunately, he is unlikely to leave an able successor.

In the second case, he works to enable others in the organization to understand the innovation process. He neither imposes his ideas on others nor considers himself the principal source of ideas. Instead of creating models of the innovation, he creates models of the *process* of creating models of innovation so that others themselves can create the models. He recognizes interpersonal problems as paramount, and above all, he encourages trust. He works with subordinates as equals and develops a basis for mutual trust which will enable them to run risks with one another and jointly run risks for the organization. The cooperative approach means abandoning the notion of omniscience at the top and the certainty that competency brings success. Such a leader is a hard but a discriminating taskmaster.

The new marketing technology. Another helpful approach to the problem of innovation is to reduce the risk. As indicated earlier, one of the reasons for the organization problems associated with new products is the heavy risk associated with introducing them. If it can be reduced, the organization problems will become less intense. The *modus vivendi* is arrived at through a substantial amount of implicit bargaining among managers. This bargaining can be largely replaced by a rational group decision process if *analytic decision concepts* are utilized. Analytic decision technology, analogous to that discussed in Chapter 7 but for long-term decisions, can reduce the risk both for the group as a whole, because it provides more accurate forecasts, and for each individual, because he can see more clearly how the changes will be likely to affect his status. These techniques are scheduling concepts such as program evaluation review technique (PERT), forecasting techniques, measurement techniques, and choice techniques such as investment analysis. Underlying the application of these techniques are substantive concepts such as the theory of buyer behavior. Together, these concepts are what we can call "the new marketing technology."

Details of such techniques are presented later in the chapter, but we will say nothing more about PERT because its relevance is obvious and it is a simple technique. We will consider first how the techniques are applied in long-term planning. It should be kept in mind that though this discussion and the one following deal mainly with product innovation, the principles apply just as well to all other kinds of marketing innovation, including trade channels.

LONG-TERM PLANNING

Goals

One major difference between the brand manager's and the marketing manager's views is that the latter adopts a longer planning horizon. His long-term decisions and their appropriate programming require a different apparatus, a different set of concepts. The contribution-to-profit goal of the brand manager is not appropriate. Some form of investment criterion is essential: payoff period, internal rate of return, and present value are some examples. But the implementation of these goals via investment analysis raises complex issues, which we will examine here.

A decision concerning an investment (for example, to expand plant capacity) implies moving the company to a new position farther out on the envelope curve of Figure 4–2 instead of operating at a given position on the envelope curve, as we do in short-term analysis. Most long-term marketing decisions involve expenditures that are intended primarily to improve sales rather than to increase capacity, but the decisions are analytically identical. To simplify, we will assume here that the only goal of the marketing manager is to maximize long-term profits. In practice, there is typically more than one goal, but these can be introduced as additional constraints which also must be satisfied.

To evaluate alternative marketing investments, it is necessary to evaluate a stream of revenues over future years in relation to the original cost outlays and any other expected cost commitments during the period. For instance, if a new product is initiated, future sales growth will require additional plant expansion to provide the necessary production capacity, as well as additional funds to support the larger volume of accounts receivable. Thus a stream of future revenues and a stream of future costs must both be evaluated to arrive at a profit estimate to be used in deciding which marketing plan is best. The analytical tools appropriate for making investment decisions are often called capital budgeting, and a particular version of capital budgeting, the present-value method, which is explained below, will be referred to here as the long-run optimizing model.

Some would question whether marketing expenditures should be treated as investments. Many marketing outlays are of the variety that yield at least part of their return at some more distant time rather than within the current year. Advertising is often of this kind. In fact, it is sometimes argued that this is the only way that advertising should be viewed. The cost of developing a sales force is another example. A market area (a sales territory) in which the company has achieved market acceptance should be viewed as a fixed asset. Accounting authorities, however, view the practice of capitalizing these with a jaundiced eye, because the revenue is difficult to forecast. As a consequence the typical practice is to charge off such items as advertising and sales-force expenditures against current income. This leads to understating current profits and overstating profits in future years. For new products it is clear that the expenditure should be viewed as an investment, at least in making the decision.

The new-product decision is a key investment for the company. When a new product is evaluated, one particular *total marketing plan* is being implicitly evaluated—that is, a given level of advertising over the period, a certain personal selling effort, and so forth. With the increased emphasis upon long-term planning in companies, an attempt to evaluate alternative long-term total marketing plans of ongoing products can be expected. This lengthening horizon is partly essential because some of the elements of these plans imply expenditures which logically should be treated as investments. In addition, the longer horizon enables us to deal explicitly, over time, with dependencies that do not necessarily require investment funds. For example, a price decision can over a period lead to a change in the structure of the market in a given industry which will affect the time pattern of inflows and outflows of cash. This possibility, combined with management's longer planning horizon, opens a fertile field for the application of capital budgeting to evaluation of long-term total plans for *ongoing products* as well as plans for new products.

The use of a long-term planning horizon when considering marketing problems forces greater explicit attention to integrating the various elements of a total marketing plan in order to obtain consistency among the parts. The position of the brand manager has arisen from the need to obtain consistent and coherent planning and execution of the plan for individual products or groups of products in companies. A long-term view also can help avoid another temporal inconsistency; it will work to minimize, for example, the possibility that a sales force developed to achieve a market position for a product will be so large that it will represent excess capacity once the position is achieved. By looking ahead, this possibility can be recognized and steps taken to correct it before it happens.

Finally, data that are derived in applying capital budgeting (sales and cost estimates) can be used later as a means of control in appraising the success of the innovation. The estimates made for decision purposes become criteria of performance as the plan is being executed.

In addition to different goals and related investment concepts, long-term planning requires long-term demand estimates, long-term cost estimates, and estimates of future competitive situations.

Long-term demand forecast

The reader will recall the model of buyer behavior in Chapter 3. In principle, it is possible to estimate the values of the segmenting variables over a long-term planning period (such as 10 years) multiplied by a factor for any population increase and thus derive an estimate of future demand. If we could assume the product to be constant and the segmenting variables comprehensive and measured accurately enough, this could be a feasible approach to long-term forecasting. With modern rapid technological change we cannot hope for such stability of structure, however.

Consequently, the more usual alternative is to estimate major determinants of generic or product class. We begin with certain basic forces in the economy, such as demographic, economic, psychological, and technological. The demand for a particular product may be closely related to only one determinant or to several of them. The demand for baby carriages, for example, is closely related only to the birth rate. The determinants are also interrelated. Technology has given rise both to higher incomes and a shorter work week, and the latter has in turn affected the tastes of the buying public. Both the "do-it-yourself" movement and the increased popularity of casual clothing can be attributed in part to the greater amount of time spent away from the job. A systematic approach based on these determinants is essential because, as contrasted with fitting single-equation models to past data and then extrapolating, it provides a much fuller understanding of *why* a certain demand is likely to occur.

DEMOGRAPHIC FACTORS. Demographic factors have several dimensions; the most significant for our purposes are level of population and age distribution. Others are location, which was discussed in Chapter 2, and sex distribution, which has not changed enough to justify attention here but does vary significantly among parts of the United States and among different countries.

TABLE 12–1
U.S. population, 1954–1970

Year	Population (000 omitted)
1954	162,417
1955	165,270
1956	168,176
1957	171,198
1958	174,060
1959	177,261
1960	180,670
1970	205,000

Population growth in the United States has strongly influenced the demand for consumer goods. Table 12–1 shows the large growth in population that has occurred within less than 20 years.

TABLE 12–2
Future U.S. population (projection assumes 1955–57 level of fertility; 000 omitted)

Age (years)	1965	Per-cent of total	1970	Per-cent of total	1975	Per-cent of total	1980	Per-cent of total
All ages	195,747	—	213,810	—	235,246	—	259,981	—
Under 5	21,243	11	24,190	11	28,111	12	31,991	12
5 to 9	20,837	11	22,089	10	25,029	11	28,940	11
10 to 14	19,216	10	20,893	10	22,145	9	25,080	10
15 to 19	17,267	9	19,262	9	20,936	9	22,186	9
20 to 24	13,502	7	17,343	8	19,331	8	21,001	8
25 to 29	11,459	5	13,640	6	17,460	7	19,441	7
30 to 34	11,068	6	11,582	5	13,753	6	17,554	7
35 to 39	11,914	6	11,118	5	11,633	5	13,792	5
40 to 44	12,374	6	11,872	6	11,094	5	11,608	5
45 to 49	11,389	6	12,214	6	11,735	5	10,982	4
50 to 54	10,741	5	11,092	5	11,913	5	11,464	4
55 to 59	9,340	5	10,271	5	10,634	5	11,443	4
60 to 64	7,759	4	8,695	4	9,600	4	9,973	4
65 to 69	6,395	3	6,900	3	7,783	3	8,646	3
70 to 74	4,892	2	5,376	3	5,853	2	6,654	3
75 to 79	3,327	2	3,764	2	4,182	2	4,593	2
80 to 84	1,840	1	2,158	1	2,476	1	2,784	1
85 and over	1,084	1	1,351	1	1,578	1	1,849	1

Source: Adapted from U.S. Bureau of Census, *Illustrative Projections of the Population of the United States by Age and Sex 1960—1980*, Series P-25, No. 187 (November 10, 1958), p. 16.

For long-term forecasting, however, it is *future* population that is appropriate, and there has been a tendency both to overestimate the probable growth of population and to exaggerate its estimated effect. For example, it was estimated that within the 20 years between 1960 and 1980 we could expect our population to increase by almost 50 percent, as indicated in Table 12–2.

Population change often has more significance for many consumer products when examined from the standpoint of age distribution. The extent of the anticipated change in the age distribution is also shown in Table 12–2, which suggests that the number of "over-60" people would be increasing both absolutely and relatively. This caused H. J. Heinz Company to begin market testing as the prelude to adding a line of foods specifically for this market. The Ford Motor Company, believing that the number of teenagers in a family is an important influence in its decision to buy a car, cited the data in Table 12–3 as evidence.

Today, we expect to reach zero population growth by the end of the century, and probably sooner. Current estimates are that the birth rate will have gone down to the replacement rate between 1980 and 1985.[4]

---

[4]Donald J. Bogue, "Demographic Aspects of Maternity and Infant Care in the Year 2001," May 6, 1971.

TABLE 12–3
Influence of children on car buying: Percent among families purchasing new and used cars in first half 1955*

Income	With teen-agers	Children below teen-agers	No children
$5,000 and over	29%	20%	17%
$3,000 to $5,000	18	16	7
Under $3,000	16	13	6
Total	23%	17%	10%

*Based on June 1955 survey.
Source: Survey Research Center, University of Michigan and Ford Motor Company, Marketing Research Economic Studies, March 26, 1956.

Table 12–4 shows both total population and age distribution as they ex-isted in 1970 and are projected to the year 2000 under two different es-timates by the U.S. Census: Series B, which assumes 320 million, and Series E, which assumes 266.

As to the individual industry effects of such population changes, great differences are found among industries. Twenty-seven different models

TABLE 12–4
Changes in population: 1970–2000

Age group	1970 total population (millions)	Percent of total	2000, Series B* projection (millions)	Percent of total	2000, Series E* projection (millions)	Percent of total
Less than 5	17,813	8.7	33,747	10.6	19,651	7.4
5-9	20,562	10.0	30,899	9.5	19,868	7.5
10-14	20,696	10.0	30,117	9.3	20,612	7.7
15-19	19,095	9.3	29,486	9.0	20,748	7.8
20-24	17,190	8.3	26,541	8.1	19,694	7.4
25-29	13,861	6.7	22,052	6.8	18,145	6.8
30-34	11,490	5.6	18,616	5.7	18,240	6.8
35-39	11,099	5.4	21,142	6.5	21,142	7.9
40-44	11,943	5.8	20,971	6.4	20,971	7.9
45-49	12,262	6.0	19,020	5.8	19,020	7.1
50-54	11,129	5.5	16,627	5.1	16,627	6.2
55-59	10,056	4.9	12,826	4.0	12,826	4.8
60-64	8,461	4.1	9,900	3.0	9,900	3.7
65-69	6,920	3.4	8,531	2.6	8,531	3.2
70-74	5,216	2.5	7,767	2.4	7,767	2.9
75-79	3,745	1.8	6,245	1.9	6,245	2.3
80-84	2,378	1.2	3,840	1.2	3,840	1.4
85 and over	1,340	.7	2,453	.8	2,453	.9
Total	205,456	99.9	320,780	98.7	266,281	99.7

* These series differ according to their assumptions about fertility. Series E assumes a gradual movement toward the replacement level.
Source: J. A. Howard and D. R. Lehmann, "The Effect of Different Populations on Selected In-dustries in the Year 2000." Prepared for the President's Commission on Population Growth and the American Future, Washington, D.C., September 21, 1971, Table I.

were fitted to the sales of the 16 industries listed in Table 12–5. When the extrapolation is made from the chosen model, the results are those given in the table.

TABLE 12–5
Relative sensitivity of industries to population change according to rank*

| Industry | 1948–69 data | | | | 1959–69 data | | | |
| | E vs. 1969 | | B vs. E | | E vs. 1969 | | B vs. E | |
	Low	High	Low	High	Low	High	Low	High
Railroads	16	16	12	14	16	16	13	13
Airlines	4	4	10	9	5	4	10	9
Beer..............	12	11	11	10	12	11	8	8
Housing starts	15	14	16	16	15	14	14	14
Mobile homes	2	2	9	11	3	3	12	12
Domestic cars	11	12	2	2	13	15	1	1
Imported cars	1	1	14	12	1	1	11	11
Men's suits	13	13	15	15	14	13	15	15
Frozen foods	5	5	5	5	2	2	9	10
Power boats........	14	15	1	1	9	6	16	16
Credit	6	6	3	3	6	7	3	3
Furniture & household equipment	7	7	6	7	7	8	5	5
Foods & beverages ..	9	9	4	4	10	10	6	6
Clothing & shoes ...	8	8	8	8	8	9	7	7
Steel	10	10	13	13	11	12	2	2
Dishwashers	3	3	7	6	4	5	4	4

* On a scale from 1 to 16. 1 indicates maximum effect and 16 minimum effect by the year 2000.
Source: J. A. Howard and D. R. Lehmann, "The Effect of Different Populations on Selected Industries in the Year 2000." Prepared for President's Commission on Population Growth and the American Future, Washington, D.C., September 21, 1971, Table IV.

In line with projected changes in U.S. population, Rosenau Bros., Inc., the world's largest producer of children's dresses, decided to enter the adult field. The decision came from

a long-standing desire to capitalize on projections of a 50 per cent growth in the 20 to 40 year old female population of the country in this decade. By contrast, Mr. Rosenau noted forecasts for children 5 to 11 years are that the number in this group will remain relatively unchanged.[5]

Managers are often inclined to exaggerate the effects of this decline in population growth on expected sales. Without going into details we can conclude that, if national income continues to grow as it is expected to, even with a zero population growth the consequences will be a high-productivity and high-wage economy with higher standards of living.

ECONOMIC FACTORS. Here we are concerned with long-term changes in purchasing power. Although gross national product is not a precise

---

[5] *The New York Times,* October 9, 1971, p. 41.

measure of purchasing power, it does give an indication of the levels of income.

Another useful refinement of the income factor is the distribution of income among the population. The reduction of the degree of inequality in the distribution of income that has occurred within the past 30 years has had a significant influence on consumer markets. Income and estate taxes have leveled off top incomes, which has had a depressing effect upon the market for such luxury items as yachts and mansions. At the same time, increased wages and high levels of industrial employment have raised the level of income in the lower brackets. Table 12–6 gives the estimated income distribution by the year 2000.

TABLE 12–6
Changes in income distribution (in thousands, using 1969 dollars)

Family and unrelated individuals, income	*Present (1969)*		*Series B_L*		*Series E_L*		*Series B_H*	
	Number	*Percent*	*Number*	*Percent*	*Number*	*Percent*	*Number*	*Percent*
less than $3,000	9,807	14.9	7,125	7.3	7,004	7.5	5,056	5.3
$3,000–4,999	7,729	11.8	7,060	6.8	6,831	7.2	5,739	5.6
$5,000–6,999	8,027	12.2	6,935	6.4	6,739	6.5	5,673	5.4
$7,000–9,999	12,395	18.9	10,371	9.3	10,031	9.4	8,563	7.7
$10,000–11,999	7,329	11.2	7,028	6.5	7,028	6.5	5,300	4.9
$12,000–14,999	7,865	12.0	11,159	10.0	10,987	10.2	8,569	7.9
$15,000–19,999	6,889	10.5	17,590	15.8	16,742	16.1	14,964	13.5
$20,000–24,999	2,745	4.2	14,064	13.1	13,129	12.9	13,975	12.5
$25,000–34,999	1,797	2.7	15,173	14.4	13,790	14.0	19,878	18.6
$35,000–49,999	667	1.0	7,049	7.0	6,272	6.5	12,483	12.0
$50,000–and over ...	438	0.7	3,749	3.5	3,333	3.2	7,103	6.8
Total	65,690		107,304		101,887		107,304	
Median	$8,762		$16,130		$15,694		$19,928	
Mean	$10,362		$19,079		$18,635		$23,642	

*Series B_L is the low-income estimates from the Series B population estimates; Series E_L, low-income estimates from Series E; Series B_H, high-income estimates from Series B.
Source: Computer Projections, President's Commission on Population Growth and the American Future.

PSYCHOLOGICAL FACTORS.   Both buyer psychology and technology are highly amorphous and present problems of measurement. The human being serves as a unit of measurement for the population factor and dollars serve as a measure of income, but there are no satisfactory units for measuring the psychological and technological factors. The two are also often strongly interrelated: new technology creates new needs as well as being created to meet new needs. The psychological factor refers to the buyers' motives (as they were defined in Chapter 3) and the consuming behavior that emerges as these motives drive him to adapt to his total environment—economic, political, and social.

The psychological factor is of obvious significance; for example, British economist, Richard Stone, has said, "On the basis of observations it appears that changes in taste and habits are extremely important over time in determining the amount demanded of many commodities."[6] On a more specific level, a joint study made by Procter & Gamble Company and the laundry industry suggested that, in the middle fifties, less than one half of the bed sheets washed at home were also ironed. This decline in ironing, it was concluded, had an adverse effect upon the sales of home ironers. Technology has increased to a much higher level since World War II. One measure is the amount of industrial research, which is now probably about six times what it was in 1947. Social change, interacting with technology and perhaps precipitating it, has created very rapid change in tastes.

One way to describe some of the consequences of this interaction is that as a society becomes more affluent, so that its basic needs are met, it is free to utilize less immediate utilitarian criteria in buying. David Riesman, in *The Lonely Crowd*, has articulated this point of view perhaps as fully as anyone.[7] In his view there are three kinds of people, according to their sources of values. Each kind is associated with a particular stage of social and economic development. The tradition-directed individual, found primarily in primitive societies, receives his values from the traditions that constitute the culture of his *society*. The inner-directed individual receives his values from the *family*; this quality characterizes the inhabitants of small towns and immigrant groups in large cities. The other-directed person receives his values from other members of his *peer group*. The idea of a peer group is a special example of the concept of social group. It is made up of the fairly intimate members of one's age and social class. This other-directed person is to be found in highly urbanized areas. Since there is a definite trend toward urbanization in the United States, Riesman's thesis suggests that a large proportion of the American population is becoming other directed.

---

[6]Richard Stone, *The Measurement of Consumers' Expenditure and Behaviour in the United Kingdom, 1920–1938* (Cambridge, England: Cambridge University Press, 1954), Vol. I, p. 270.

[7]David Riesman, Nathan Glazer, and Reuel Denney, *The Lonely Crowd*, abridged ed. (Garden City, N.Y.: Doubleday & Co., Inc., 1953).

As to the significance of this thesis for consumption, Riesman argues that in this other-directed society, which is characterized by high purchasing power, consumption occupies a highly significant social function. We communicate with and classify other people by comparing consumption standards. We accept them into our peer group according to whether their standards of taste agree with ours. As Riesman notes, "The proper mode of expression requires feeling out with skill and sensitivity the probable tastes of the others and then swapping mutual likes and dislikes in order to maneuver intimacy."[8] Our knowledge of and ability to discourse on the merits of products, therefore, influences our relative position in our peer group. The implications of this social role of consumption is an explicit part of Riesman's thesis—there are "taste leaders" who determine the products that are accepted by their groups. Most members of the group surrender independence of judgment in order to maintain acceptance by the group. Research carried out since Riesman's work raises doubts about the generality of taste leaders over products, but clearly some people are much more influential than others for particular product classes. Chapter 13 will deal with this.

A more recent development is the shift in values during the past decade, especially among young adults. By "values" we mean motives and associated attitudes. This shift has brought a lessening of interest in material things and more concern with self-fulfillment, in whatever line of activity.

Technological factors. By technological factors is meant new production and distribution processes and new products. Technology is the consequence of a new idea, an invention, as it is put to work and woven into the industrial and social fabric. Joseph A. Schumpeter adopted the term "innovation" to apply to this process of putting the idea to work and made it the cornerstone of his theory of economic growth.[9] Some of the more significant innovations in marketing have been the supermarket and mass communication media, particularly television.

Changes in technology are ordinarily measured through the concept of "productivity," but in this form it is a mixture of many things, such as new machinery, better managerial techniques, and more efficient labor. The concept is useful to the marketing manager in understanding long-term economic growth, cost, and price trends. An average annual increase of 2½ to 3 percent in gross national product has been estimated as due to improved productivity. It varies considerably over time and across countries.

Because predicting the effects of technology for a decade is perhaps not too difficult for the knowledgeable and careful observer, research can

---

[8] Ibid., p. 94.
[9] Joseph A. Schumpeter, *The Theory of Economic Development* (Cambridge, Mass.: Harvard University Press, 1934).

often be expended profitably. After an intensive study of technology for the Twentieth Century Fund, one writer concluded that most major technological changes in industry can be observed 15 years ahead on the horizon.[10] This contradicts the common view that the effects of technology on American industry are dramatically sudden. The idea, the invention, occurs long before successful innovation is possible, because in the innovating process, economic criteria are applied—such as, Will it pay? This is why technological change is rapid during a war. The sharp shift in demand for military goods makes many innovations economically feasible where they were not before and may not be again.

Examples of the effect of technological change are readily observable. In the case of the demand for home ironers mentioned previously, the new synthetic textiles have had an adverse effect upon the sales of home ironers because many of the textiles do not require ironing.

SUMMARY: LONG-TERM DEMAND FORECAST.   The experience of manufacturers of recordings offers an example of the joint effects of these long-run determinants and their significance for marketing strategy. In the late 1930s and again in the spring of 1955, the recording industry experienced sharp price cuts at a time when consumer prices generally were stable. In profit terms these price cuts were probably wise for both the initiating companies (Columbia in the 1930s and RCA in 1955) and others in the industry, since the increase in sales for the industry as a whole more than compensated for the drop in unit price. Not only had long-term changes in demand increased the demand for records, but its price elasticity had also probably increased. Roughly, the significant factors were thought to be the increase in total purchasing power, a shift toward a more equal distribution of income, and population growth. Also, technological change permitted lower unit costs for playing devices, and consumer tastes in music had changed.

The manager must forecast to plan: his choice is whether to do it implicitly or explicitly. If he does it explicitly, there are a number of methods, all of which are less than perfect but when used together and imaginatively produce results that are better than chance. The fundamental determinants of long-term demand—population, income, buyer psychology, and technology—must be considered in any explicit plan.

Cost forecasting

In principle, the methods of cost analysis set forth in Chapter 4 permit identifying the engineering relations among cost inputs and cost outputs at a point in time. Then by predicting the price of future cost inputs and feeding them into this derived cost structure, future costs can be estimated.

---

[10]Irving H. Siegel, "Technological Change and Long-Run Forecasting," *Journal of Business,* 26 (1953): 141–56.

These engineering or technological relations, however, may not remain constant. This is especially true when the innovation is a new product. As it passes through the life cycle, the technological relations are almost sure to change. In general, however, costs are much easier to forecast than demand.

Competitive forecasting

A very important determinant of profits over the life of the innovation is the structure of competition that characterizes the industry. If competition is intense profits will be eroded, as we saw in Chapter 2. At the other extreme, however, the manager might find a specialized segment of the market which conformed in size to his optimum economies of scale and so have a market protected from the rigors of price-reducing competition. To accomplish this strategy would require a fairly good understanding of demand and cost structures and, perhaps, considerable luck.

THE LONG-TERM OPTIMIZING MODEL

Assuming that good forecasts of demand and the competitive and cost consequences of the innovations are available, how can the marketing manager put them together so he can choose between them in a systematic way? The demand forecast provides information necessary to evaluate the project in terms of the growth goal. Investment analysis provides the answer to evaluating the project in terms of the profit goal, which, of course, is much more complex than the growth goal. It is often referred to as the *discounted cash flow* method; the basic principle is to evaluate the *net* flow of cash (the difference between the additions to cash and the deductions from cash) that is expected to result from an investment. The cash flow method is used to select the investment offering greatest profit: the greatest difference between total revenue and total cost. It is particularly appropriate for comparing alternatives with widely varying expected time patterns of inflows and outflows of cash—a condition that often characterizes alternative marketing innovations.

An application of capital budgeting to the product decision in a manufacturing company can provide a concrete illustration of its elements. Bear in mind, however, that the concepts apply just as well to any marketing decision with long-term implications. Assume that the decision has been made by top management to initiate only·*one* of two products, A or B; the problem, therefore, is to choose between them. The cash inflows to the company from product A, exclusive of investment, are summarized in Table 12–7, and the cash outflows from the company for this product are incorporated in Table 12–8.

A long-term forecast of sales is necessary to obtain the data required in column 2 of table 12–7; all of the earlier discussion of long-term demand analysis is applicable here. Also, since the revenue forecasts in column 2 of this table, are in dollars, a price is implied. This price forecast requires some consideration of expected competition, typically a heavy consideration, as was emphasized in Chapter 2. The principles of cost analysis discussed in Chapter 4 and earlier in this chapter are essential in deriving the cost data required for column 3.

TABLE 12–7
Expected cash inflow from product A

(1)	(2)	(3)	(4) Cash inflow before taxes	(5) Depreciation for tax purposes	(6) Taxable income	(7)	(8) Cash inflow after taxes
Year	Sales revenue	Costs				Taxes	
1......$	700,000	$560,000	$140,000	$ 43,800	$ 96,200	$ 48,100	$ 91,900
2......	805,000	620,000	185,000	41,000	144,000	72,000	113,000
3......	850,000	660,000	190,000	37,800	152,200	76,100	113,900
4......	884,000	680,000	204,000	38,800	165,200	82,600	121,400
5......	891,000	700,000	191,000	35,700	155,300	77,700	113,300
6......	924,000	720,000	204,000	32,300	171,700	85,900	118,100
7......	960,000	760,000	200,000	29,300	170,700	85,400	114,600
8......	1,024,000	800,000	224,000	30,100	193,900	97,000	127,000
9......	1,088,000	840,000	248,000	26,300	221,700	110,900	137,100
10......	1,120,000	860,000	260,000	22,900	237,100	118,600	141,400

Source: John A. Howard, *Marketing: Executive and Buyer Behavior* (New York: Columbia University Press, 1963), p. 52, Table 1.

We will make three assumptions: that, at the end of 10 years, both the market for the product and the equipment used in producing it are exhausted; that inventories and accounts receivable are converted into cash; and that accounts payable are paid. All figures are incremental in the sense that they reflect only the consequences of the additional activity that would be encountered as a result of adding the product. The estimated annual revenues from the product are shown in column 2 of Table 12–7, and the associated costs (excluding investment and accruals) are shown in column 3. Column 4 is the difference between columns 2 and 3. The effects of the corporate income tax are reflected in columns 5 through 8.

Under corporate income tax regulations, depreciation of plant and equipment can be charged against income in computing a corporation's income tax. Depreciation is introduced in column 5, since it reduces the taxable income and therefore reduces the taxes that must be borne by the revenue stream expected from the investment. The figures in column 5 are arrived at by the sum-of-the-years'-digits (SOYD) method of calculating depreciation, which gives the greatest weight to early years. Assume that for tax purposes the economic life of this asset is 15 years; thus, for the first year, the depreciation on $350,000 is $43,750, which is rounded off to $43,800. This is computed by summing the years as the denominator and

$$\frac{15}{120}, \quad \frac{14}{120}, \quad \frac{13}{120}, \quad \cdots$$

inserting the particular year as the numerator, that is, 15/120. Then the second year, 14/120 is depreciated, and so forth. Also, it is assumed that a depreciable investment outlay of $350,000 will be required for the first year of operation and that to meet an expanding market, depreciable outlays of $30,000 each will be necessary at the end of the third and seventh years.

In Table 12–7, column 5 is deducted from column 4 to give taxable income shown in column 6, which is then multiplied by an approximate tax rate of 50 percent to arrive at the tax figure in column 7. The data in column 7 are then deducted from column 4 to obtain column 8, which constitutes the estimated *additions to company cash flows* that would result if product A were added.

TABLE 12–8
Present value of product A

(1) Year	(2) Discrete investment, end of year	(3) Continuous cash inflow during year	(4) Discrete cash inflow end of year	(5) 10 percent discount factors	(6) Present value of discounted cash flow
0......	$500,000			1.0000°	− $500,000
1......		$ 91,900		.9516	87,452
2......		113,000		.8611	97,304
3......		113,900		.7791	88,739
3......	50,000			.7408°	− 37,040
4......		121,400		.7050	85,587
5......		113,300		.6379	72,274
6......		118,100		.5772	68,167
7......		114,600		.5223	59,856
7......	50,000			.4964°	− 24,820
8......		127,000		.4726	60,020
9......		137,100		.4276	58,624
10......		141,400		.3869	54,708
10......			$160,000	.3679°	58,864
					$229,735

° Flows occur at one time, rather than throughout the year.
Source: John A. Howard, *Marketing: Executive and Buyer Behavior* (New York: Columbia University Press, 1963), p. 54, Table 2.

Investment outlays are incorporated in Table 12–8 so the net cash flow can be evaluated. Assume that an investment of $500,000 will be required to initiate production of product A. Additional investments of $50,000 each (500,000 units of capacity) must be made at the end of the third and seventh years to satisfy the expanding market. As indicated above, however, only a portion of these investments is depreciable. The investments are shown in column 2 of Table 12–8. Column 3 is, of course, column 8 from Table 12–7, cash inflow *after* taxes. Since working capital of $160,000 will exist at the end of 10 years, this figure is shown as a cash inflow in column 4. Thus, columns 2, 3, and 4 summarize the cash flows that are expected to result if product A is added.

To conclude that product A is better than B, the present-value criterion is used: each flow is discounted by the cost of capital to arrive at a present value, and the product with the highest present value is preferred. By "long-term optimizing principle" we mean the use of the present-value criterion. A 10 percent cost of capital is arbitrarily assumed here. The discount factors shown in column 5 that are appropriate to this cost of capital can be read from the 10 percent column of an interest table that compounds continuously. The asterisked factors, however, are of slightly different nature; they apply to those flows in Columns 2 and 4 that occur all at once, rather than uniformly throughout the year.

The first step in obtaining the present value of the expected flow is to multiply the cash flow by the discount factors. The outflow of cash is viewed as negative values and the inflow of cash as positive values, summed algebraically. Since the present-value figure of $229,735, the summation of column 6, is a positive figure, product A would be a profitable use of company funds. Thus, the rule is that any investment which yields a positive present value should be accepted, provided that unlimited investment funds are available to the company. Stated in this way the decision really involves how much money, in total, should be invested.

However, the typical investment problem at the level of the marketing department, and the one we set out to solve here, is to determine in which particular marketing alternative a given amount of funds should be invested, the total amount of funds to invest having been decided at a higher level in the company. The example here was formulated as a marketing department problem: should the company invest in product A or product B? These are mutually exclusive alternatives. The solution to this problem can be more complex.

If products A and B require the same amount of investment, the above strategy (take whichever product has the higher present value) is applicable.[11] If A and B should require different amounts of investment,

---

[11] A different criterion than the present value, namely the internal rate of return, yields an unambiguous answer. It is computed by finding a discount rate that when applied to the stream of net inflows of cash and to the stream of net outflows of cash will reduce them to the same value. Using this criterion, the rule is to select the alternative with the highest rate of return, but it assumes that all net cash flows (positive or negative) intermediate between the initial and terminal positions can be compounded at the particular rate of return that is calculated for the project. More specifically, it assumes that all positive net flows can be invested at this rate of return and that all net outflows (investments) are borrowed at that rate. The assumption is usually not correct; for example, the positive net cash inflows are usually reinvested at a lower rate. To the extent that the rate is lower, the use of the internal-rate-of-return criterion overstates the actual return. The present-value criterion, on the other hand, assumes that the positive net flows will be reinvested at the cost of capital.

however, the solution is to use another criterion—the present value per dollar invested.

Planning horizon

In the long-term optimizing model considered above, the time period taken as the basis of analysis (the planning horizon for this decision) was 10 years because it was believed that this period would constitute the life of the product. The selection of a planning horizon for making a capital budgeting decision must be judgmental, but the nature of the analysis makes the problem of deciding upon the appropriate planning horizon less serious than first appears because the discount factor causes distant years to have less effect upon the present value than near years.

Imperfect information

Up to this point in presenting the concepts for evaluating an innovation we have implicitly assumed that the manager knew with certainty such things as expected sales and costs of the new product. In fact, the sales figure is typically highly uncertain. Costs are a little less uncertain.

Let us be a little more precise about what is meant here by "uncertain." It could mean that though he is not actually sure the figure will be $229,735 as shown in Table 12–8 above, he does know the *probability* of its being that figure. If so, we say the decision involves *risk*. If, on the other hand, he does not even know the probability of the figure, he is truly *uncertain*. For this situation there are some criteria, but the issues are not clear, and so we will deal no further with it.

A set of useful concepts has been developed for dealing with risky decisions.[12] The first, a *payoff table*, is a statement of the various events that the decision maker thinks will occur for each alternative innovation he is considering and of the payoff associated with each of the various combinations of alternatives and events. By simplifying, the payoff table can be illustrated with the capital budgeting example used earlier. The simplification consists in assuming that we are *uncertain only about the physical volume of sales* that each product will yield and that the price that will be charged and the costs—including the cost of capital—that will be incurred by the company over the next 10 years are known with certainty.

The various physical sales volumes are the *events*, and the alternative products, A and B, are each an *act* that management controls, as illustrated in Table 12–9.

---

[12]For a description of the extent to which these concepts are applied to practice in marketing, see Rex V. Brown, *Marketing Applications of Personalist Decision Analysis* (Marketing Science Institute, July 1971).

Product A alone will be examined, but the analysis would be applied in the same manner to B. One event is the sales volume of 28 million units, which is the physical volume of sales. When multiplied by the unit price of 35 cents, this volume yields the dollar sales figure of $229,735 as the present value of product A, as shown in Table 12–8 above. The act figure for Table 12–9 is the introduction of product A, which will have a present value of $229,735 *if* the event of 28 million units occurs. The mere construction of a payoff table contributes insight to the making of a decision even though the complete analysis is not carried out, since it forces separation of a number of elements which in thinking may tend to be lumped together.

TABLE 12–9
Payoff table for determining conditional values of products

Event: Sales in physical units (in millions)	Act	
	Product A	*Product B*
20...............		
24...............		
28...............	$229,735	
32...............		
36...............		

The second central idea is *subjective probability*. It is assumed that a decision maker, in choosing among alternatives involving an uncertain future, can meaningfully contemplate the alternatives in terms of his own subjective estimates of the probability of each event occurring. The essential idea is that he can analyze his problem consistently in probabilistic terms; whether his estimate of the probability of a particular event agrees with anyone else's does not matter. He might, for example, recall from his experience how many times a similar event occurred one way and how many another. Then by weighting each possible event by its estimated probability, he can apply the theory of probability to his decision. On the other hand, he may merely make an intuitive guess.

Before explaining how the probabilities are assigned, it is essential to point out that the events must be *collectively exhaustive and mutually exclusive*. The first requirement, for example, says he must believe that the sales will be no greater than 36 million units and no less than 20 million units. The second requirement that they be mutually exclusive means that only one of the events will occur, not more than one.

If probabilities are to be used as weights, as in Table 12–10, the probabilities must be assigned according to three basic axioms:

1. A probability is a number between 0 and 1 assigned to an event.
2. The sum of the probabilities assigned to a set of mutually exclusive and collectively exhaustive events must be 1.
3. The probability of an event that is composed of a set of mutually exclusive events is the sum of their individual probabilities.

Another concept of statistical decision theory is *conditional value* (see Table 12–9, in which product A is evaluated). In Table 12–10, column 2 gives the subjective probabilities assigned by the marketing manager to the various events. In column 3 are the conditional values of each event; that is, the value of product A *if* a particular event occurs; for instance, if sales turn out to be 24 million units, the present value would be $67,789. The values in column 3 are obtained on the assumption that in each event the total sales volume in physical terms is distributed over the 10-year period in the same pattern as shown in Table 12–7 and that the same pattern of prices will prevail.

TABLE 12–10
Expected value of product A

(1)	(2)	(3)	(4)
Events: Sales in physical units (in millions)		Value of product A	
	Probability	Conditional	Expected
20...............	0.1	− $ 93,660	− $ 9,366
24...............	0.2	67,789	13,558
28...............	0.4	229,735	91,894
32...............	0.2	391,683	78,337
36...............	0.1	553,133	55,313
	1.0		$229,736

The conditional values are weighted by the respective probabilities to obtain a series of values that when summed yield the *expected value*. To avoid confusion, it is emphasized that the sum of column 4 is the "expected" value of the "act," which in this case is to choose product A. Thus a formal definition of the expected value is: *a weighted average of all the conditional values of the act, each conditional value being weighted by its probability.* It is simply a weighted arithmetic mean, where the weights are given by a specific probability distribution. The decision rule, then, is to *choose* that *act* having the *greatest expected present value.*

In this example of how decisions involving risk can be dealt with, a number of important ideas have been passed over in order to present the method first in a straightforward, simplified manner. The most fundamental idea not previously mentioned is the use of the theory of probability to revise subjective probabilities in the light of *additional information*. The theory for revising subjective probabilities is much too extensive to present here.

Another aspect of decision theory considers the process by which a manager's attitudes are translated into probabilities that he can assign to a collectively exhaustive and mutually exclusive set of events in compliance with the three basic axioms. He could, for example, compare his attitude toward the risk that the sales volume will be 28 million units for product A with his attitude in a lottery in which he chooses from 100 tickets numbered 1 to 100. It is assumed that each ticket is equally likely to be the winning ticket. In this situation, he can imagine that he has two choices. Choice 1 is some number, n, of lottery tickets, of which the prize is $229,735. Choice 2 is $229,735, *if* the sales are in fact 28 million units. Assume that he prefers choice 1 to choice 2; if he does, then in order to arrive at his correct subjective weighting of the probability that 28 million units will be sold, n should be decreased. If on the other hand he prefers choice 2, n is too small. By adjusting the value of n, we arrive at a value for n that makes the executive indifferent between choice 1 and choice 2. This n determines his subjective probability of the event. In this case, the n making him indifferent would, presumably, be 40, since there were 100 total tickets and the subjective probability was .40.

The same logic can be applied to obtain the subjective probability of each of the other possible events, shown in Table 12–10 as 20, 24, and 36 million. In addition, he can apply tests of logical consistency, the simplest being whether his subjective probabilities add up to 1.0.

Once he has computed his subjective probabilities, they can be fed into the analysis. We suspect, however, that because the rewards for taking risk in a large organization are disproportionately small relative to the personal risks taken, there is a high preference for a high probability of success relative to the expected value by some objective measure of probability.

SUMMARY

The marketing manager makes both strategic and administrative decisions. The strategic decisions are critically essential to furthering corporate marketing strategy, with its central focus on the product-market concept. Corporate marketing strategy is composed of rules for achieving the company's growth objectives through new products or new markets, or through diversification, which is a combination of the other two.

To serve this function the marketing manager's role is primarily innovative. Innovation raises subtle and very grave organizational problems because an organization avoids change if possible. Three avenues of solution exist. First, organization structure can be changed. This is illustrated by the new-venture concept.

Second, behavior within the organization can be changed. If top management will exert leverage, a crisis will be perceived, conflict will be created, and the consequent search for a solution can lead to a model. An effective corporate strategy can be that model. It is the speed of technological change that has probably given rise to the urgent need for a concept of corporate strategy.

Third, analytic decision processes can be introduced to avoid the conflict and consequent bargaining that delays change. Investment analysis is one appropriate element of the analytic decision processes. Subjectivist probability is another.

DISCUSSION QUESTIONS

1. Describe the function of the marketing manager and refer back to Chapter 5 to supplement the discussion in this chapter.
2. The new-product failure rate is substantial. Are there organizational reasons why this should be so?
3. The marketing manager adopts a much longer term planning horizon than does the brand manager. What difference does this longer term horizon make?
4. Forecasting demand is one of the more difficult tasks of a marketing manager. How would you go about making a 10-year forecast for subcompact cars?
5. Cost forecasting is typically not so difficult as demand forecasting. Assuming that competitively you will be 10 years from now where you are now, but recognizing that the future is uncertain, what concepts could you use in choosing a new subcompact car?

13

Product innovation

INTRODUCTION

WHAT is a "new" product? Americans often use "new" in a value-laden way: to be new is to be *good*. Consequently, products are often described as new when, in fact, they are not.

A new product is defined here entirely in terms of the buyer's view: if the change in the product being sold causes a change in the buyer's behavior, it is new. If he merely hesitates and thinks about it, it is a *minor* innovation. If he overtly seeks information about it and has known (established) criteria by which to judge it, it is a *normal* innovation; if he has no criteria by which to evaluate it, it is a *major* innovation. This is not a fully developed set of definitions; we will be more precise below.

The serious organizational problems of the marketing manager in product innovation were discussed in Chapter 12. In this chapter we will discuss the problem itself as though it were uncomplicated by organization. We first deal with the nature of the new product's contribution to company objectives. Besides this direct contribution, the new product usually has some "side effects"; this is the problem of the product line. Forecasting of demand for a new product is difficult, especially for a major innovation. Underlying any meaningful attempt to quantify demand is the process of acceptance of a new product from the buyer's view, which we will examine at some length. Thus the accuracy of demand forecast can be improved if it is supported by solid theoretical analysis of the basis of buyer behavior. This theoretical background is even more essential in the formulation of an effective marketing plan for the new product, and we will investigate problems of demand, cost, and competition in the formulation of the marketing plan. Finally, concomitant to the question of adding a new product is the equally serious problem of dropping an undesirable one.

CONTRIBUTION TO COMPANY OBJECTIVES

Product innovation is usually essential to meeting corporate goals because of the growth and higher profit it provides. With no product innovation in an industry, the competing companies tend to force the profit level down, as we saw in Chapter 2. A new product can provide a protected position which will yield a higher profit, although the affect is usually only temporary. Graf and Mueller, for example, show that in the food industry in 1966, the new products averaged a margin of 23.2 percent, whereas established products earned an average margin of only 19.4 percent.[1] The growth contribution is obvious. It is interesting to note the comment of a long-time observer of the new-product scene, R. Conrad Jones, senior partner of Booz, Allen and Hamilton, Inc.:

... the World War II upsurge in new product development—particularly in package goods like those turned out by food producers and pharmaceutical manufacturers—ended in the mid-nineteen-sixties as a combination of wartime inflation and the great wave of acquisitions plugged the growth gap. When the economic problems in the late 1969's and 1970's widened that gap, new products again came to the fore—if not the means—of corporate growth.[2]

Graf also shows the risk side of innovation. Of the new food items presented to the retail stores, only 23 percent were accepted, and this figure excludes those many cases where a product or a concept—an idea about a product—was discontinued before it was introduced to the retail store.[3] Many of these excluded cases obviously represented heavy investments in laboratory research and market research. Consumerism has increased the risk of new-product introduction.[4]

This high risk of innovation complicates what would be difficult organizational problems in any event. Two of these problems of innovation are so subtle they are often not recognized, and solutions are sought to the wrong problems.

First, the risk varies enormously from innovation to innovation. In the case of a minor innovation—where the buyer does not need additional information to make up his mind whether to buy—the process is usually not difficult. At the other extreme, with a major innovation the risk can be

---

[1]Franklin H. Graf and Robert W. Mueller, "New Item Problems and Opportunities," special presentation to Grocery Manufacturer's Association Executive Conference, June 16–19, 1968, Chart S–6869.
[2]*The New York Times*, January 31, 1971, p. F16.
[3]Graph and Mueller, "New Item Problems and Opportunities," p. 2.
[4]*Advertising Age*, November 29, 1972, p. 41.

very high indeed. The company's own experience in innovating is important, too. Even with a major innovation the company may have sufficient experience with innovating that its managers can draw analogies to the new product and apply established rules. Put technically, new-product introduction has become a habit, and they have reached Routinized Response Behavior in their decision making in this area. Typically, however, the risk is severe and the decision is made infrequently enough that it is not routinized.

Second, in well-managed companies fairly strict limits in the direction of new-product development are set from above. Corporate strategy decides "what industries we will be in." Obviously, such a policy cannot be set once and for all in a world of high technology, and there will probably be some tension between the marketing manager and higher management over what this tentative policy should be. Nevertheless it is needed to give unity and coherence to the development of the total corporation, as we have emphasized.

PRODUCT LINE

The marketing manager does not look at a new brand as an isolated contributor to company goals. To him, it is a part of a team, the product line. What the other brands are in that product line makes a substantial difference in the way he views the new product.

First, he must have a total offering if he is to meet competition effectively. Celanese Corp., for example, has had serious problems for several years, such as those that led to the firing of 1,300 salaried employees, partly because of an incomplete product line. It has no rayons or acrylics and instead is heavy in acetates and polyesters, which are oriented to the volatile apparel markets. Fashion change, such as a shift from single-knit to double-knit fabrics, can catch the company in a squeeze.[5]

Second, the new product can affect existing products. A common problem is that the new product will "cannibalize," that is, take sales from existing products. On the other hand, it can add strength.

Third, the existing line members can provide strength to the new member. Merely to carry the related brand name, such as Maxwell House, can substantially improve buyer acceptance for the new brand.

These interrelations characteristic of the product line provide both opportunities and problems in corporate innovation.

FORECASTING AND MEASUREMENT OF DEMAND

Introduction

One of the most essential pieces of information we must have in choosing new products is the estimated sales volume of the product. Other

---

[5] *Business Week,* July 22, 1972, p. 60 ff.

elements in the marketing mix can be dealt with only after the new product has been well specified and sales have been estimated.

To *forecast* demand means to attempt to predict what the sales of the new product will be at some future time. To *measure* demand is to estimate what the effects of the various aspects of the marketing effort will be upon sales. Ideally both processes, forecasting and measurement, would amount to essentially the same thing, because what the marketing manager wants to know *now* is the amount of the sales at different points in time in the *future* and how his *marketing effort* will affect this level of sales at each point in time. As mentioned in Chapter 8, however, the techniques of forecasting and measurement have tended to go their separate ways in development. One of the major reasons for this separation has been the absence, until recently, of a systematic theory of buyer behavior.

A number of approaches to this problem are possible. To convey a notion of the technology involved, we will discuss concept testing, test marketing, and mathematical models.

Concept testing

Concept testing is one way of determining buyer response to a new product before even a prototype of the product is produced. It is used as a forecasting device to provide enough lead time for corporate planning, including that required to develop the new product in the laboratory. It also suggests what the nature of the product should be and how it should be marketed.

The central idea of concept testing as a way of identifying demand for the innovation is to describe the proposed innovation, either in words or sketches, to the customer. The concept is thus symbolically instead of significatively described, and the buyer cannot directly sense the product. If the innovation is not too complex, the buyer may be able to imagine the product and to articulate his conclusions as to its relevance to his needs. If it is complex, the chances of this are much smaller. Concept testing has the major advantage of providing information with more lead time and at less cost than if a significative exposure approach is used. Not only is the information timely and cheap, but it also is not very likely to tip the innovator's hand to his competitors.

An approach used by the auto companies is intermediate between concept testing and test marketing. The new car is shown physically to a sample of consumers, but their experience is limited to visual exposure, with a small amount of exposure to physical effects derived from such things as sitting in it. They are not permitted to drive it.

Test marketing

In a market test the buyer is exposed to the product in an almost completely realistic way. A community or two are selected and the new product is put on sale, with all of the elements of the marketing plan operative. Thus estimates of sales can give fairly reliable forecasts, if the communities are representative. Typically, however, a single community is used, which raises the problem of the unreliability of a sample of 1.

Market testing has the disadvantage of being expensive. It requires not only the marketing cost, but the company must have produced an adequate supply. Further, the data are not as timely as in concept testing, because product development must have proceeded to quite an advanced state and at least some production facilities must have been made available. It will often tip off competitors to company plans, so they can try to destroy the reliability of the test market. As a marketing manager of a large household products firm put it:

> They make special price deals on their own products with the stores, they expand their advertising heavily, and they'll even do things like yanking the number one brand off the shelves temporarily just to foul up sales comparisons . . . one firm even bought up most of the available radio and TV spots when word leaked out we were going into a city for test marketing.[6]

A compromise to test marketing is the "mini-market test" in a few very small communities. It is much cheaper and gets less attention. The practice of R. T. French Co., a food producer, is perhaps typical:

> First, it runs internal research on taste and appearance preferences among inexpensive outside testers. This generally eliminates three out of five product candidates that probably would have failed in full-scale market tests. Next came "mini-market tests" in three to five communities with population of 25,000 to 35,000, at a cost of about $50,000 per product. . . . Usually one of the original five products survives this testing stage. Finally, the survivors of the mini-tests go into standard test markets in two representative communities of 350,000 people.[7]

Market testing, like concept testing, is merely a way of collecting data. It tells nothing about how to analyze the data to determine the magnitude of future demand or how to market the product. Simple analysis gives the percent of repeat purchase, which is a common criterion: the proportion of the sample that buy the product more than once. Market testing is typically used with frequently purchased products. Whether the customer buys again at least indicates the product has some merit and the customer was not persuaded to buy it only by advertising.

Mathematical models

Mathematical models are sophisticated ways of analyzing the data. A variety of mathematical models has been developed to attempt to solve

---

[6] *Wall Street Journal*, May 24, 1966, p. 1.
[7] *Business Week*, March 4, 1972, pp. 74–75.

the forecasting problem. Most of them operate in one way or another on the principle of extrapolating the trend from data such as that collected in a test market.

PRODUCT LIFE CYCLE.   One of the earliest models was the product life-cycle concept, which was often thought of as being amenable to mathematization. The idea was that every product class goes through stages of acceptance; for example, introduction, slow acceptance, fast acceptance, leveling off, and decline. Further, it was thought this pattern was regular enough from product to product that a function could be fitted which could thereafter be applied to test-market data from which an extrapolation could be made.

The idea of a product-class cycle was illustrated with the instant-coffee market in chapter 2. Figure 2–3 showed the physical volume of instant coffee sold from 1946 to 1968, with the usual slow beginning (1946–1950), the period of rapid increase as additional companies entered the field and helped expand the market (1952–1960), the leveling-off period with profits declining as production and marketing became so stabilized that brand differences began to disappear (1962), and the gentle decline thereafter, as new soft drinks and fruit juices, for example, began to replace the product class. A number of approaches to predicting from the life cycle of a product class are possible. One is to use multiple correlation on past data, which explains some 17 to 56 percent of the variance.[8] The same principle has been applied to the life cycle of particular brands, without much success.[9]

STOCHASTIC MODELS.   Following the general principle of extrapolating the trend from test-market or roll-out experience, William T. Massy has developed a more sophisticated model called STEAM.[10] In it, parameters are estimated from the test-market data, for example, and using a Monte Carlo simulation each family's purchase experience is projected forward. With six months of data from a test market it was possible to predict sales reasonably well up to three years in advance, as shown in Figure 13–1.

Massy points out that "Experience shows that disaggregative data (data by individual buyer) must be used when analyzing new product demand".[11] This principle is probably applicable to any demand situation, as indicated in Chapter 8. This is in contrast to the life-cycle approach, which employs aggregate data and so hides the behavior of the individual buyer. A major problem is that in the course of the new-product introduc-

---

[8]E. M. Rogers, *Diffusion of Innovations* (New York: The Free Press, 1962), chap. 10.

[9]Rolando Polli and Victor J. Cook, "A Test of the Product Life Cycle as a Model of Sales Behavior," Marketing Science Institute Working Paper, p. 43–3.

[10]William F. Massy, "Forecasting the Demand for New Convenience Products," *Journal of Marketing Research,* November 1969, pp. 405–12.

[11]Ibid., p. 405.

FIGURE 13–1
Actual versus simulated sales, product B

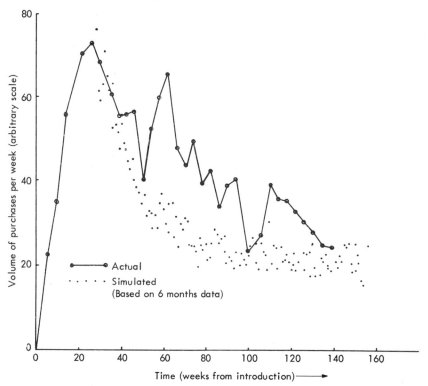

tion, the probabilities of repeat purchase are changing, and buyers differ in terms of how these probabilities change. Massy goes on to say:

> Households should be stratified by depth of trial (i.e., whether they have ever tried the product, and if so, how often) if meaningful inferences are to be drawn from the data. Moreover, useful information is obtained by recording when each trial occurred (or at least when the last trial occurred). The time of the last trial can be a useful predictor of the length of time that will elapse before the next purchase. It is also logically desirable to provide for heterogeneity of households' tastes when building models of buyer behavior—including those designed for new product situations.[12]

The problem is complicated because this extrapolation does not allow for the influences of marketing effort after the test market. All of these con-

---
[12] Ibid.

siderations emphasize the need for a more detailed picture of the buyer if the new-product introduction model is to be useful to management.

Glen L. Urban has attempted to model the behavioral processes in somewhat more detail. He has constructed a total information system for new-product introduction that includes a normative decision model and provides for adaptive control in national introduction as well.[13] Its behavioral processes, however, are somewhat short of the model proposed in Chapter 3. Also, as Henry Claycamp, senior vice president, N. W. Ayer, has said, a model "is only as good as the data that goes into it."[14] Thus theory is not only essential for building a model, it is equally essential for identifying what to measure—what facts to collect. Finally, even without quantification, the theory can clarify intuitive mental processes in regard to the innovation.

THEORY OF BUYER ACCEPTANCE

Introduction

It is clear from the discussion of mathematical models that additional details of the buyer-acceptance process are essential to better forecasting and measurement of a new product. This knowledge of marketing effects will reduce the risk of new-product introduction. (We learned from Chapter 12 that reduction of risk is one way of alleviating the serious organizational problems encountered in any innovation.)

Discussion here will be limited to a physical product, although services have become increasingly important. For example, in the past few years the United States has become the first full-fledged service economy to exist in the sense that more than half of the private, nongovernmental work force is engaged in supply services.[15] There is evidence that an abstract concept such as a service is more difficult for a person to learn, but not much is known about the nature of the complications. This does not imply at all, however, that services do not have equally crucial new-product problems.

The major task of product innovation is to identify needs the buyer has that are not now being served. As used here, a "needs" is defined in terms of the fundamental level we associate with the buyer's motives. The potential to satisfy them comes about either through (1) changes in the buyer, or in his situation, which *creates* new needs or (2) new capacity on the part of the company to meet his existing needs.

New needs are created in a number of ways. An increasing standard of

---

[13]Glen L. Urban, "SPRINTER MOD. III: a Model for the Analysis of New Frequently Purchased Consumer Products," *Operations Research*, September–October 1970, pp. 805–54.

[14]*Business Week*, March 4, 1972, p. 77.

[15]*Business Week*, October 30, 1971, p. 50.

living, for example, is obviously of importance to a consumer. He has more money to spend, and to buy something does not require him to give up something else he has been in the habit of buying. Shifts in social and technical forces affecting him also can create new needs. Women's fashions are a classic example: The miniskirt well illustrates acceptance of these shifts. Fashion designers, however, guessed incorrectly that a new need had been created when the "midi" was unsuccessfully offered in the autumn of 1970. On the technical side, new products create related new needs. The purchase of skiis, for example, creates the need for ski clothing.

New capacity to satisfy *existing needs* can come about either because new ideas for products evolve or because ideas that were formerly uneconomical to produce now became profitable, through cost reduction, product improvement, or market expansion. This allows the company to take advantage of additional economies of scale.

It might seem that to develop a new product, ideally, we would identify these needs and proceed to build the product and market it accordingly. Our imperfect knowledge of buyer motivation does allow us to be explicit in this attempt. However, by focusing upon the buyer-behavior process that is partly generated by such motives, we can get along very well. Further, even if we knew buyers' needs we would still have to know the buyer-behavior process in order to design our marketing plan, as we will see in the following pages.

The description below of the nature of the process of buyer behavior in a new-product context is merely an extension of Chapter 3. This description will indicate what concepts to measure and forecast—what facts to collect—and how to analyze these facts. This analysis can be formal, such as in the application of a structural model as described in Chapter 8. Or it can be informal or intuitive, as in the gasoline-pricing decision process discussed in Chapter 5. Either way, concepts are essential to help the manager think about the problem.

As you recall from Chapter 3, there are three general types of buyer behavior processes: routinized response behavior (RRB), limited problem solving (LPS), and extensive problem solving (EPS). To simplify, RRB and LPS were discussed most fully. EPS not only represents a significant proportion of all new-product introductions but also helps clarify the distinction between minor, normal, and major product innovations. A major new product is one which places the buyer in an EPS state. Since by definition in EPS he does not have criteria by which to judge this new product or service, he must form them. This is to say he must form a *product-class* concept. The product-class concept contains the evaluative criteria by which he judges all brands that he puts into that class in his thinking. To form these criteria he needs much more information than in LPS, and the manager should bear this in mind in designing a marketing plan for a new product.

If the marketing manager fails to view a new product in relation to the company's existing products, the new product can seriously cut into the sales of existing products—"cannibalization", this is called. How the buyer perceives the new product can also be partly determined by the nature of the company's existing product line. If the new product is properly "spaced" with an existing product, "trading up" can be practiced: the buyer is attracted by the new product but in the course of exploring it he may find himself coming to prefer a higher priced product (with a higher profit margin) in the company's line.

We will focus on normal and major innovations, those instances where the buyer needs information to make his decision to try, and then to accept or reject. When he does use information, it is essential to know how he goes about getting it in order to understand the nature of the information and its consequences for his behavior. This is the problem of the buyer's *information acquisition*. What he finds and how he goes about searching depend on the nature of his informational environment. This informational environment—his *sources of information*—also must be examined. There are also individual differences among buyers, thus introducing the possibility of segmenting the market, which is discussed as a part of the marketing plan.

INFORMATION ACQUISITION

Introduction

The buyer's acquisition of information extends from his almost passive role of merely varying the intake of his sensory receptors ("paying attention") to a very active role in which he talks with friends, seeks out different advertisements, investigates several retail stores, and even goes to the library to look up information (overt search).

In this section we will first examine the process of paying attention and then the process of overt search. In the first case we take the buyer's informational environment as given and do not explain why he exposes himself to new information. In the second we examine why he exposes himself to a new informational environment.

Paying attention

The term "paying attention" has a wide variety of meanings. It has become so imprecise as to mean whatever information the buyer takes in because he was paying attention. In these terms it is synonymous with selective perception.

There are essentially two characteristics of information selection. First, the *quantity* of information which the buyer accepts is greatly reduced: he does not take in nearly all that is "out there." The available buyer-behavior evidence indicates that the magnitude of this compression can be substantial. It appears, for example, that during 50 percent or more of television advertising the average viewer is tuning out the entire commercial. He is undoubtedly tuning out parts of it a still higher proportion of the time.

From the more general psychological literature, George A. Miller concludes that man's effectiveness as an information channel and also as a storage facility is poor compared with such inanimate equipment as the telephone and tape recorder.[16] On the other hand, man's coding ability— his capacity for "insight," "judgment," and "ability to recognize a Gestalt (pattern)"—is superb and may never be surpassed mechanically or electronically. The petroleum pricing decision process in Chapter 5 illustrates this coding ability.

In large part this remarkable and even astounding capacity of humans is the result of the second characteristic of the selection process: The buyer is *systematic*, not random, in selecting information. He seems to have a remarkable set of rules by which he selects in order to decrease it to a manageable amount and still meet his needs. This selective process is accomplished primarily by three memories: sensory memory, short-term memory, and long-term or permanent memory.

Through his *sensory memory* the buyer receives all information that is "out there," all information to which he is exposed. It is received in physical form, light waves in the visual mode and sound waves in the auditory. These two modes are by all odds the most important among the five senses. Although this memory is large at any point in time, it is very, very short. If the information is not transferred from it to short-term memory, as implied in Figure 13–2, within a matter of milliseconds, the information is dissipated and lost.

FIGURE 13–2
Central constructs

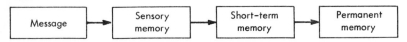

Short-term memory, on the other hand, retains information somewhat longer before the information is lost. Some evidence suggests that if the message is transferred to permanent memory within 18 seconds, the information can be satisfactorily stored. For longer periods, however, it too is an ineffective instrument of storage. Long-term or *permanent* memory is the source of effects upon behavior.

Two characteristics of the human in taking in verbal information are

---

[16]George A. Miller, *The Psychology of Communication* (New York: Basic Books, 1967), chap. 3.

striking. First, he takes it in *much faster* than might be expected. The average skilled reader can process between 300 and 600 words per minute, which is about 10 words per second and 50 to 70 letters. The answer is that he does not perceive letters. He has learned—has in his long-term memory—rules of grammar which tell him much of what to *expect*. A verb is usually followed by an object: "He drove . . . (the car)."

Second, in his memory are stored many associations (such as that apples grow on trees), so he need see only a portion of a sentence: "Apples grow on——." He will immediately and unconsciously fill in "trees" with a high probability of being correct. Thus, this second characteristic of the way he takes in information also requires him to call on his memory, and it gives him enormous power to fill in missing words, adjust for errors in printing and grammar, and overcome interfering sounds and high noise levels.

The key point here is that he can do these things when confronted with a continuous *flow* of information only because he has a memory which contains *both* a language structure and relevant substantive information. Hence, we see the powerful role of material already in memory in acquiring new material, new information.

When he is confronted by a flow of sentences, internal representations of what he thinks he *will* perceive as he processes them are generated. He thus generates *expectations*. These internal representations are generated by the same rules as his speech. What he perceives is compared with the respective representation or expectation. If they match, fine; he goes on to scan the next segment to which he is exposed. If not, he generates a new representation and matches it. The closer the first match is, the more quickly the two will converge on repeat trials. Hence, the efficiency of speech processing is closely related to the accuracy of this first guess. Because of this advance hypothesis—this expectation—about what the message will be, the buyer can tune his perceptual processes to admit certain pieces of information from the flow and reject other pieces.

There are rules by which information is admitted from sensory memory to short-term memory, as in Figure 13–2. We will say little about sensory memory, however, because it is a fair replica of the reality to which the buyer is exposed, at least for our purposes, and storage is so short. The transfer of information to short-term memory is quite another matter, however. If the buyer is familiar with the speech habits of the speaker or the sentence composition habits of the writer, he can more quickly and correctly comprehend the message. Presumably the more sophisticated he is in the use of grammar, the more quickly and correctly he will understand it. If the material is difficult he will be delayed in processing it. A key point is that material is sorted in short-term memory in *meaningful* units instead of representations of the physical message. Although its capacity is small, by *rehearsing* its content the buyer can lengthen the period information is retained. An example of rehearsing is repeating a telephone number as it is dialed.

There are also rules by which information is transferred from short-term to long-term memory, where it can affect behavior. If the material is unfamiliar (the buyer does not have an internal structure for it), simple mnemonic devices which provide an *external* structure for the material can help in the transfer. These devices are used in everyday activity. Rhymes is one: "Thirty days hath September." Another is the method of loci, in which different but related pieces of information are imagined as being located at different points in space, such as in different rooms of a house. If the information is about a brand in an important product class, the buyer may be motivated to utilize one of the devices. If not, they can perhaps be built into the stimulus to facilitate his utilization of them. Advertising often does this with rhymes and jingles. With complex material, however, mnemonic devices will not work because complete memorization is not possible. If the information is familiar (the buyer already has an internal structure to place it in) and the particular product class concept is important, he will probably remember it.

With complex material people remember structure, not details, and it is probably more accurate to say they *reconstruct* the material rather than remember it. What is recalled is shorter than the original, the phraseology is more modern, and the entire message is more coherent and consequential. With the passage of time these errors increase except that the length of the recalled material does not necessarily change.

The existence or nonexistence of cognitive structure has been emphasized in this examination of information and memory. This structure would seem to be made up of associations with both concepts, the brand and the product class. Brand comprehension (denotative meaning), personal attitude (connotative meaning), and confidence in judging the brand constitute the content of the brand concept. There is a corresponding product-class concept.

What the discussion of memory suggests for the manager may be what the experienced copywriter knows intuitively. Even so, knowing something intuitively and knowing it explicitly are two quite different things, as we have emphasized throughout. Above all, the message must be meaningful to the buyer. It must fit his current cognitive structures—brand comprehension, personal attitude, and goals—insofar as possible. To the extent that it does not, mnemonic devices such as music and rhymes can help.

Overt search

In the explanation of why the buyer overtly looks for information, thus exposing himself to a new informational environment, at least 2 other central mechanisms are added—feedback fron confidence to arousal, and stimulus ambiguity to arousal. The principles involve the three roles of arousal, as shown in Figure 13–3. The determinants of arousal include the level of motive intensity, which is directly associated with it, as we saw in Chapter 3. There is also a feedback from confidence in the brand concept to arousal. This is an inverse relation; the higher the confidence, the less the effect on arousal.

FIGURE 13–3
Additional arousal mechanisms

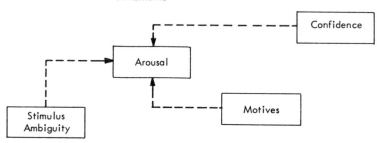

The ambiguity or uncertainty of the information controls the level of arousal as well. The relations here, which are complex but interesting, are portrayed in Figure 13–4. The message can be ambiguous in three senses. Sheer physical ambiguity is one possibility, such as static on the radio and "snow" on the TV screen. Another is that the information is not credible either because the source is not trusted or is considered incompetent. Finally, the message can be a case of fantasy which is supposed to symbolize something.

FIGURE 13–4
Ambiguity-arousal relation

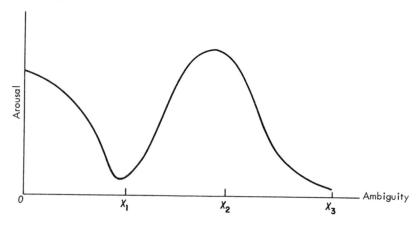

We expect the relation between the buyer's confidence and arousal to be just the inverse of the relation between stimulus ambiguity and arousal. The inverse relation is the X_2 to X_1 range in Figure 13–4, which for most cases is the most relevant. The figure, however, does bring out a point made by detergent industry managers, for example. For some products, the buyer seems, after a period of usage, to shift to another brand for no apparent reason. This phenomenom could be explained by saying that the buyer had reached the OX_1 stage with respect to the brand concept and is becoming bored with it. It is like turkey at Thanksgiving, delicious on Thursday, tasty on Friday, but boring by Saturday and nauseous by Sunday. As a consequence, arousal increases and he looks for a new brand. This is the loyalty-disloyalty cycle.

The consequences of the level of arousal are threefold. We saw in Chapter 3 that it energizes overt behavior. Also, it has an effect on the memory process, but this mechanism is not well understood. Probably, up to a point, increased arousal will cause the message to be imbedded more heavily in permanent memory. Another way to say it is that there will be more associations with material already in memory. Consequently, forgetting would be less. Finally, increased arousal can also energize overt-search behavior in the same way it does overt purchasing behavior.

The implication of the arousal process for management is that neither the brand concept nor the message can be too ambiguous, but also neither should be too familiar.

Search for information about a brand can be related to broader buyer-behavior patterns. General search in the form of shopping can be viewed as a metaplan which triggers and guides a part of the plan that underlies a consumer's plan or intention to buy a particular brand. A consumer probably seldom shops for a single product; he is simultaneously alert to the possibilities of meeting all current needs. The more the purchase of the new product can fit into existing patterns of behavior, the more likely it is to be accepted. Consider, for example, how heavily a housewife's search for cookies is determined by her grocery shopping habits. Shopping for consumer durables is obviously a much more extensive process and is more of a separate routine. The successful elements of the search plan are retained and the less successful ones are dropped. Thus through generalization and by trial and error a buyer develops patterns of search behavior.

CONSEQUENCES OF SEARCH.   The consequence of a buyer's search effort is to change the values of a number of his variables: motives, brand comprehension, attitudes, confidence, and intention.

If attention is high, the buyer acquires a vocabulary to identify the brand and to describe it so that he can discuss it with others and think about it. In the case of a major innovation, when the buyer understands a single brand he is on his way to forming a product-class concept which contains his choice criteria for judging all brands in that class. Technically, he must develop a *linguistic* and *nonlinguistic equivalence,* an equivalence between the label he attaches to the product class and the attributes and behaviors he assigns to that product class. In other words, he must establish an isomorphism between the *naming* behavior and the *culturally patterned* kinds of behavior associated with purchasing and consuming the brand.

Consequently, in introducing a major innovation, manufacturers must emphasize its product-class characteristics as well as its brand characteristics in their advertising and sales effort. Along with other sources of information, this would support *deductive* learning of the product class and brand concepts. Experience with the brand and information about the particular brand would support *inductive* learning of them.

We can make two statements about concept formation of either brands or product classes: (1) Concept attainment becomes more difficult as the number of relevant attributes of the concept increases, the number of values of attributes that it has increases, and the salience of these attributes decreases. (2) Concept formation becomes more difficult as the information load that must be handled by the buyer to solve the concept increases, and the information is increasingly carried by negative instead of positive instances where the information tells him what it is *not* rather than what it is. Different buyers use different strategies for handling the information load, and some strategies are in the long run more successful than others. The segmenting variables discussed below should capture these differences.

The effect of the information on attitude toward the brand, given that the information is credible and favorable, depends on current level of attitude. The higher it already is, the less will any given piece of information increase it. Put more precisely, the amount of change is inversely proportional to the original position; this is the so-called polarity principle. If the manager is using attitude change as a measure of his marketing effectiveness, he must allow for the consequences of this difference in absolute level in concluding whether it has been successful.

Brand loyalty to an existing brand causes the buyer to close out information about the new brand. In addition to posing these perceptual and cognitive barriers, the change in brand may require learning some new overt acts in connection with the purchase or consumption of it, and inertia in this respect also can provide a barrier to change. If so, the particular motivational content of the information—whether it affects the intensity of motives—makes a difference. Too little or too much motivation is less favorable to learning than a medium level of motivation, but excessive motivation is probably a problem only for products that are highly important, economically or socially. Once a series of acts is well learned, however, the higher the motivation, the better the *performance* of this series of acts.

In the face of these barriers to communicating with buyers by symbolic means such as advertising, manufacturers have turned increasingly to sampling and couponing. Sampling is the practice of making available free samples of the new brand. The most obvious effect of this is to eliminate the price barrier and the effort of purchasing the product. Colgate-Palmolive is reported to have distributed free to 80 percent of American households 40 million units of a regular package of Ultrabrite toothpaste at a total cost of about $50 million. Couponing is a similar practice. For example, to introduce Folger's coffee into the Chicago market in 1959, 1.5 million coupons, each good for a free pound of coffee, were distributed. A rule of thumb sometimes used by the manager is to sample only for a really superior product.

SOURCES OF INFORMATION

Introduction

In considering the nature of the buyer's informational environment—the availability of information—and the influence processes that operate in this environment we will use Lasswell's paradigm: who says what to whom, how and with what effects. We will deal here with the *who* and *what* and to some extent with the *how*. The *whom* is obviously the buyer. Some of the *effects* will also be included.

Availability of the information is important because it determines *how much* search effort is necessary to utilize it. To the extent that it is difficult to utilize, the buyer will be deterred. Contrast the effort required of the buyer in perceiving a television advertisement appearing during an attractive show with the energy necessary to obtain facts by reading a copy of *Consumer Reports,* which, if the buyer is not a subscriber, he must get from the public library. This "minimum effort" principle helps to explain how the buyer selects from among given sources of information and why television is an effective medium. The consumer's unsatisfied need for information on new products is probably one of the reasons for the current consumer movement.

The nature of the buyer's information—its content and sources—is quite varied. He obviously receives his facts from a great number of sources: newspapers, billboards, television, radio, his relatives, his friends, members of his family, accidental conversations with strangers; sales clerks; he may go so far as to read *Consumer Reports* in his search for information. The sources can be categorized as follows: buyer sources, commercial sources, and neutral sources. This classification (more than others that exist) focuses attention on factors that the innovating company can influence.

Buyer sources

Buyer sources are interpersonal sources, such as word of mouth, which are not under the control of the seller. These sources are known to be highly effective in new-product acceptance. Because of their complexity, we will examine some additional concepts necessary to deal with them.

The importance of *interaction*—face-to-face relations—with other people in influencing behavior is obvious from everyday life. Even in the critical decision of choosing a family doctor, friends, neighbors, and co-workers are found to be more important sources of information than are professional advice and independent judgment. This influence is transmitted from person to person by word-of-mouth information, and it matters not only *what* the other person says but *who* he is, as well as to *whom* it is said. This influence is the heart of the theory of social structure. Here we deal only with the basic unit of social analysis, the single dyad—the relation between two members, in this case the relation between the buyer and his immediate influencer. Later, in discussing advertising, we will incorporate the full view of social structure, and later still, we will deal with the case where the other person in the dyad is a salesman.

What influence processes operating in the social dyad determine the effect of the "other person" on the buyer? There are three distinct types of social influence, as we saw in Chapter 11—compliance, identification, and internalization. These set a framework for discussing the influence processes which is especially useful for innovation because it emphasizes the nature of the source of information, and in innovation different sources operate at different stages of the acceptance process.

Compliance occurs when the buyer accepts the influence of the communicator—the other person in the dyad—because he has the power to withhold reward or administer punishment. It is sometimes a force in industrial buying. By complying, the buyer does what the source, the other person, wants him to do because he sees this as a way of achieving a desired response from the other person. He accepts the communication not because he believes in its content, but because it will be instrumental in producing a reward or in avoiding a punishment. This *social effect* on his behavior operates through his impersonal attitudes.

Identification occurs when the buyer is influenced by the communication because there is a role relationship with the other person that forms a part of the buyer's self-image. The communicator is a part of the buyer's immediate social structure and the two form a regularly interacting dyad, which implies common interest and activity. Identification is then a way of establishing or maintaining a desired relation with the other, and self-definition—the buyer's own self-image—is anchored in this relation. Thus the *social anchorage* of his behavior is crucial. The effect here operates through the buyer's personal attitudes, but only its self-concept dimensions.

Internalization occurs when the buyer accepts the influence because the other person's values are congruent with his own, and the content of the communication suggests a course of action that is intrinsically rewarding to him. *Value congruence*—the congruence between his motives and those of the other person—is the crucial distinction here. Its effect is via the functional dimensions of his personal attitudes. If the message is congruent with his own value system or motive structure, the buyer will be more sensitive to information. This is what we mean by relevant information. When the information from the other person is ambiguous, the buyer will search for clarification and thus further internalize the message. However, internalization need not be equated to rationality, as defined by some objective standard.

We can now bring together four interrelated and important ideas: expressive behavior, self-concept, role relationship, and attitude change. *Expressive behavior*—behavior which indicates to others the kind of a person the buyer is—appears quite common in some consumer buying and is probably the area toward which most social criticism against advertising is directed. Through expressive behavior a person sometimes unwittingly reveals himself. Expressive behavior that is *intentional* is motivated by the buyer's self-image. Self-image or *self-concept*, which is a constellation of attitudes, links the individual buyer to a *self-identifying* reference group. The desire to maintain this *role relationship* will cause the buyer to change or stabilize his personal *attitude*. The effect is probably to change confidence more than attitude. In an economy where the standard of living is above the subsistence level, the buyer exhibits intentional expressive behavior: to some extent he purchases products because they *express* to others how he would like to appear, not because the products are intrinsically rewarding. He uses the product to act out his self-image, and this self-image reflects his self-identifying role relationship. Thus we have an explanation for the frequently observed phenomenon of seemingly "irrational" buying, which is roundly condemned by social critics. The explanation suggests that the behavior is really quite meaningful. As has been said, ". . . we should not expect a symbol-using animal to be interested in nothing but food and drink."

Commercial sources

Commercial sources represent the information disseminated by the innovating company. In consumer goods, this includes such means as advertising, salesmen, merchandising effort, pricing, packaging, distribution channels, and display, retail and otherwise. These sources are under the control of the seller. To understand their consequences, we must look at them from the buyer's point of view—how the buyer uses them as sources of information. This view can be summarized in the question, "How much does the source reduce my risk and how much does it cost me in money, effort or time to use it?"

The manager has two broad avenues for disseminating information: advertising and personal selling.

ADVERTISING. As indicated earlier, if the social structure—the buyer's neighbors, his friends, and other sources of face-to-face interaction—has absorbed information about the innovation, the buyer will be more likely to try it. Hence advertising can be used indirectly by merely making the brand known on a broadcast basis throughout the social structure, so that the "other person" in the dyad is familiar with the innovation. Without doubt, advertising serves this purpose in consumer products much more than do salesmen. On the other hand, advertisers usually view the buyer as though they were approaching him directly. The first approach is indirect advertising, and the second, direct advertising.

Indirect advertising. In indirect advertising, a commercial source (advertising) is used to influence the buyer's sources of information. Advertising serves the attention-getting function in the social structure, but it is in general less influential than friends in developing a *preference* for the brand. Furthermore, the whole social network, not just the portion represented by the buyer–other person dyad, is influential. One dyad tells another dyad, and so on ad infinitum, as suggested by Elihu Katz and Paul F. Lazarsfeld and others.[17]

The social links by which influence is passed to the "other person" in the dyadic relation and through him to the buyer are the social *network*, the *process* of transmission, and the *content* transmitted. Is this influence merely a link in the transmission activity with no interest in the product class, and if so, how is the buyer rewarded? We can assume that if this transmission behavior was not being rewarded, it would not be carried on for long. To ask this question is to get at the heart of the social structure concept as applied to buying, which has been implicit in all the preceding discussion of interaction. If these are roles in society, the fulfillers of which we label "opinion leaders," they are rewarded for carrying out this information-giving activity by being granted positions of status within the group in which they are fulfilling this role. Their role is one of the set of roles associated with that position in the social system. A role is a social prescription of *some,* but not *all,* of the premises that enter into an individual's choices of behaviors, as we saw in Chapter 5.

One of the simplest explanations of the function of social structure in innovation is the "two-step flow" which, in its most extreme form, holds that there are people in every social group who act as gatekeepers of information flowing into the group. In this extreme form, the proposition is not true. The leader does not confine himself to disseminating information but also seeks information from other leaders, for example. It has been well documented that opinion leaders are more exposed to mass media

---

[17]Elihu Katz and Paul F. Lazarsfeld, *Personal Influence* (Glencoe, Ill.: The Free Press, 1955).

than are nonleaders, but a large proportion of the receivers initiate the conversation with the leader.

Not only are opinion leaders effective. It also appears that introduction by a nonleader has negative effects. Moreover, some of the leaders are probably not innovators themselves. Thus some of the links in the communication network are not buyers and should be appealed to on some basis other than their buying motives.

In making conclusions about the role of indirect advertising, we can say with some evidence first, that indirect advertising does make a difference in product innovation. There are intermediate human links between the person receiving the advertising and the buyer. The reader transmits the advertisement information to the "other person" in the buyer's dyad. The line can be still more circuitous. Second, this diffusion process causes the effect of advertising to be slower but much more powerful in getting attention than it would be if these links did not exist. Third, it is desirable for marketing activity to (1) encourage the "other person" in the dyad to transmit information and (2) attempt to ensure that the information transmitted by these human links is accurate and favorable to the new product instead of inaccurate and unfavorable. Fourth, it is desirable that opinion leaders initiate the use of the product. Fifth, especially with radically new products (major innovations), the initiating seller should communicate in words that will provide the social intermediary with an *adequate vocabulary* to make him effective in transmitting the information. Sixth, if we know the type of influence process that is operating in the ultimate dyad that includes the buyer—compliance, identification, or internalization—we can better predict which of the buyers' variables will be affected.

Thus the social structure is linked to the dyad. The dyadic process itself shapes the flow of information between the broader structure and the buyer in the dyad; it makes a difference, for example, whether the other person in the dyad is an opinion leader. There remains the question as to whether the broader structure itself actually influences the nature of the process in the dyad, other than serving merely as an information input and thereby shaping the nature of that input. This is a much broader sociological issue, too broad to be dealt with here, but from our analysis a number of inferences can be made; for example, the motive represented in the structure will influence what is perceived (and therefore passed on) and how the information is modified (distorted).

Direct advertising.   Most conventional advertising, that is, advertising aimed directly at the buyer, has difficulty in getting attention. Earlier in the chapter we saw the memory mechanisms by which tuning out occurs.

In the case of a normal innovation, direct advertising can be quite effective, if current choice is random within the buyer's evoked set and especially if it meets his needs better than his current brand does. Getting attention will not be difficult, and advertising is easily accessible. Its credibility, however, is probably somewhat suspect.

When buyers are loyal to existing brands, the effectiveness of advertising is severely limited both in first getting attention and then is creating change in attitude, confidence, or impersonal attitudes, because of its questionable credibility. If loyalty is based more on risk because the product class is important (motives are intense) than on the buyer's belief in the current brand's quality, attention to the advertising is more likely.

There is considerable distortion of information under normal innovation. Advertising is often ambiguous, and the buyer has already developed many associations with a particular brand. If he is a loyal buyer, this encourages misperception.

With a major innovation, there are only three conditions under which a message from the mass media will be likely to receive strong attention. These are if it satisfies an obvious or urgent unmet need, the buyer has moved into the disloyalty stage of the loyalty-disloyalty cycle described earlier, or he has learned to look systematically for new products in general, as a purchasing agent might.

If the message does receive the buyer's attention, its credibility is probably not high and it is perhaps viewed as being more competent than trustworthy. On the other hand, the appearance of a product in national advertising does seem to endow it with some credibility, especially if the company itself (the source) has a favorable image. Companies are becoming more concerned about their public image, largely, we suspect, because of management's growing belief that the image significantly affects the acceptance of the company's new products. Above all, advertising is a convenient source of information for the buyer, and its cost to the buyer is low if it appears on his television screen during his preferred TV program or in his regularly read magazine.

Direct advertising, however, is seriously handicapped in introducing a major innovation (in providing buyers with choice criteria), especially if the motives have social implications. It probably tells the buyer little about what criteria are socially acceptable, although showing the brand in a fashionable context may be intended to achieve this. The social network is probably much superior for this purpose. Similarly, if the product itself or its consumption is complex, advertising is handicapped. On the other hand, except for these handicaps, advertising has a relatively easier time with a major innovation than with a minor one because there is less to be unlearned.

SALESMEN.   The analysis of social interaction ought to be particularly appropriate for understanding the salesmen's role because of the nature of the salesman-client relation: it represents clearly purposeful interaction. Yet there is some evidence that this case can differ from that discussed earlier, where the "other person" who supplies buyer information is a friend or neighbor. The salesman may be of a "lower status" than the buyer, except when he is a person of high technical competence. He is also a member of a formal organization, which more strongly influences his behavior than does the looser, informal social structure that characterizes consumer buying outside the family. In industrial markets, both members of the dyad represent formal organizations.

Even in the case of a radically new product—a major innovation—the salesman can usually get at least some attention, especially if he is backed by a well-known and respected company. The salesman's personality, his aggressiveness, for example, makes a difference in his role. Getting attention is about as far as the compliance process will usually take a salesman, however. Perhaps at its best, compliance can only secure trial, although some trade relations (reciprocity) arrangements which give the salesman power may be effective enough to secure adoption.

If the salesman and client have developed the mutually satisfying role relation often found in industrial purchasing and life insurance, identification can probably go far in providing brand comprehension, personal attitudes, confidence, and intention. But if the salesman is of a lower status, the role relationship will probably be less effective in changing behavior.

The problem-solving influence or internalization process is operative to a considerably extent because of the two-way conversation that is possible. Competence—perceived competence—will contribute to internalization because of the salesman's expertise. This seems to occur in mechanical products where the salesman, usually being an engineer, has the technical know-how that the buyer does not have. Some salesmen achieve such a good working relation with their clients that their credibility is exceedingly high, as a result of the combination of both trust and competence dimensions. The salesman is often in a position to help the buyer. An unexpectedly fast delivery can help the industrial buyer to give the impression to his superiors and peers that he is doing his job effectively.

From a study of the drug industry it appears that doctors are influenced in their preference for drugs by the reputation of the company that sells the drug. With riskier drugs, doctors are more likely to be swayed by their preference for a certain company than for a salesman (detail man). This confirms the importance of company image as an influence in the trial and adoption stages of a new product. The influence of the internalization process (problem solving) is probably operative with such salesmen, because doctors state that their preference for a salesman is largely determined by their confidence in him. It is not clear whether it is the competence or the trust components of the salesman's credibility that matter most.

The buyer's search effort in utilizing salesmen is not costless. His time is required in talking with salesmen. True enough, he can be selective, but only if he works for a firm that salesmen visit regularly, which is some-times true only of larger companies.

Because most salesmen-client relations involve organizational buyers instead of consumer buyers, the formal organization instead of the looser social structure is involved. With radically new products this fact is especially important because the buyer is usually several people and al-most always at least two—the buyer and the designer who will use it as a component of the product he is designing.

There appear to be considerable differences between large and small firms in their efforts to obtain information. Large firms are specialized enough to have made institutional arrangements for search, such as having a special purchasing *research* department. The buyer in the small firm, because of lack of specialization, probably thinks of a new product only when he is approached by a salesman, when he observes a competi-tor making use of it, or, of course, when he accidentally encounters it. Also, he is in an environment relatively barren of information because he is so tied down with the details of his position that he can seldom look outward to expose himself to new sources of information. Participation in professional and trade association activities can be important sources of information.

In normal innovation, when a new product is merely a change from an existing brand, the salesman plays quite a different role. Here the buyer has his own criteria by which to judge the new product, but even if he is highly loyal, getting his attention is a problem with which the salesman can probably deal. Some salesmen are much more adept in getting atten-tion than are others. The salesman with high credibility, both competence and trust, seems to have a great advantage because, in addition to getting attention, by indirection he can reduce the buyer's loyalty to his current brand. At the same time he increases his loyalty to the new brand by the process of identification. How important the product is will make a dif-ference.

When the buyer is not loyal to his existing brand (makes random choices from within his evoked set), the salesman would seem to be truly effective in gaining acceptance, particularly if he is credible to the buyer.

Neutral sources

Neutral sources are more objective in the information they transmit. However, they are limited in their capacity to transmit goal information. Choice criteria that require information on product technical performance and price are conveyed, for example, by *Consumer Reports*, which implies that the buyer ought to use these criteria. The buyer will not learn about radically new products from such a source because some time elapses before they are reported upon, although he may learn about aspects of new products representing normal innovation. Also, the use of these sources requires time, effort, and skill. Skill is implied by the fact that people who utilize them tend to be above average in education and in income. The role of skill with language and substantive information was emphasized in the discussion above of information acquisition. Much of the population simply lacks the reading and comprehension skill and the interest to use such sources in their present form. If the product is important enough and the buyer has the skill, the sources play a large role in the buyer's search effort, but they appear to be confined largely to consumer durables.

Women's fashion magazines, on the other hand, do provide not only information about what is recently available but also information relevent to personal choice criteria.

One of the most common neutral sources is news stories, which can play a large role in regard to major innovation, since the radically new is usually more newsworthy. A recent news story on the home electronic range in test market in Chicago is an example. It gave substantial useful information, including people's attitudes, from which the buyer could infer something about socially acceptable criteria in judging it. The credibility of these reports is probably quite high in trust. If they are taken from a scientific report, as many of them are, the competence would be viewed as high. If the intellectual integrity of the editorial policy is questionable, these news stories degenerate into advertising, and perceptive readers come to recognize them as such. Advertising agencies and their clients devote considerable resources to public relations activities that utilize the news-story approach.

DEVELOPMENT OF THE MARKETING PLAN

In the development of a marketing plan, along with estimates of demand, the influence of competition and cost must also be considered. After the appropriate marketing strategy to develop alternative marketing plans is determined, investment theory is used in arriving at a choice among alternative new-product candidates and their respective marketing plans.

Demand

We have already examined demand concepts relevant to new products and how they apply in general terms. The question now is, How are they used to provide a forecast of sales, since current modeling seems less than ideal, and to guide the development of a marketing plan?

These concepts can be used formally in designing a test-market study, in fitting a structural model to the data (as in Chapter 8), and in interpreting the results. From these the forecast of sales and the response curves to the marketing inputs can be derived, and the market segments can be measured. Forecasting can be strengthened by the application of the STEAM model, for example. Ideally, several markets would be used, with different levels of marketing mix in each, and this may be necessary for the resulting model to yield results that will generalize to the national market.

These concepts can also be used informally, even though no systematic market research is done. To use them informally is to use them for thinking about the problem. An experienced marketing manager typically knows quite a bit about his market. He knows whether his new product is a minor, normal, or major innovation. If it is a minor or normal innovation, he probably knows whether buyers buying this product class tend to be loyal to existing brands. He has some idea as to whether the new product is really substantially superior to existing brands or it is an "also ran." He probably has some fairly accurate intuitive judgment as to whether the product class is viewed as important by the buyers.

These four key pieces of information enable the manager to proceed with a subtle, complex analysis. If the product class is important, the buyer's social structure and its ramifications and implications will be scanned. By utilizing the concepts from the information-acquisition processes, he can develop ideas about the nature of the message and how best to deliver it, with salesmen or advertising or both. Whether to use sampling can also be considered. The marketing manager will consequently have ideas about the strengths and weaknesses of each of these approaches to the buyer and can meaningfully consider different ways of evaluating the results once he introduces the product. From the concepts about buyer acceptance, there are almost endless possibilities.

The interesting thing about this informal approach is that precisely this procedure should be gone through as a *preliminary* step to employing the formal model approach. Unfortunately, in too many instances this does not happen, and a more mechanical, less effective study design results.

A central aspect of any demand analysis for a new product is its implications for the product line. These are the extent to which its introduction will affect the sales of the company's existing products and existing products will affect sales of the new brand and whether there are gaps in the product line which it will fill. The experienced manager will have intuitive ideas about these issues, and market research guided by his ideas can often provide reasonably good evidence to help him decide.

Another aspect of demand analysis is the possibility of market segmentation. The marketing manager must know the variables that are likely candidates for segmenting purposes. For a consumer product, these characteristics might be personality traits, social class, culture, time pressure, social and organizational setting, and financial status. In the current state of the art of segmenting, however, selection is mainly ad hoc instead of from a prior list of possibilities. Each new product typically has its own unique set of segmenting characteristics. These ad hoc variables may be manifestations of more basic underlying characteristics, but we don't know. With industrial buyers, the segmenting characteristics are still less clear. For new products the extent to which the buying company is decentralized is undoubtedly a significant characteristic or variable. Larger firms have better search processes than smaller ones.

We suspect that segmenting variables represent the information acquisition characteristics of the buyer more strongly than his information utilization characteristics. Why the effect should be greater is more apparent in the light of the information acquisition processes developed in this chapter. The personality trait of self-esteem, for example, may operate via information acquisition instead of in the more cognitive portion of the buyer's behavior. Capacity to process information is probably related to education, culture, and social class.

Competition

An important element of the demand analysis omitted so far is the positioning of the brand vis-à-vis its competitors. For a normal innovation competitors can usually be identified because they are probably presently existent. From estimates of where the brands of each of these competitors are "located" in terms of consumer perceptions and preferences, a good position can be selected.

With a major innovation, however, competitors are yet to appear on the scene, although the marketing manager usually has some ideas about who the potential competitors are. In the instant-coffee example shown in Figure 2–3, Nestlé could guess rather well who would be competing from its knowledge of the product and marketing process required and the capabilities of existing coffee companies. As indicated in Chapter 2, the nature of the process can often raise barriers to entry that only a large company can surmount. A heavy investment in production facilities or the marketing costs of national distribution can deter a small company.

Cost

Current costs are usually ascertainable by working closely with the production and accounting departments to insure that they understand the appropriate concept and the marketing manager's particular application of it. The projection of current costs to the future over the planning horizon is another matter, however. Both the cost structure and component costs may change. Production engineering can provide some notion of possible changes in cost structure that will be due to changes in production technology. Purchasing can be helpful in estimating changes in the costs of components.

Pricing and channels in marketing plans

In addition to advertising and selling, which were discussed in connection with the buyer-acceptance process and demand, pricing and marketing channels are other components of a marketing plan for a new-product introduction.

PRICING. It is more complicated to price new products than established ones because of the product cycle—introduction, growth, maturity, and obsolescence. Typically, a new product has perishable distinctiveness. When first placed on the market it has a monopoly, but the value of this position to the company is seldom certain. As time passes, three things will occur: (1) improvements in the product will be made, which will contribute to a widened market acceptance; (2) costs of production will be reduced; and (3) competitors will enter the market with a similar product.

Price serves not only as a constraint, but as an identifier and evaluator. It is sometimes used by the buyer merely to recognize it as the brand he thought it was. In the absence of other information, he will use it to indicate quality. Price as a constraint is typically not very important in innovation until the buyer feels that he is capable of evaluating the "quality" of it, its want-satisfying capacities. The identifier role can be relevant with both normal and major innovations, but the evaluator role probably comes out most strongly with normal innovations.

Pricing the new product requires an estimate of just where the product will be in the cycle at various points in time. In addition, the price decision itself will significantly influence the speed at which the new product will pass through the cycle—a high price with consequent high profit will stimulate competitive inroads.

Two extremes of pricing policy can be considered: a skimming policy and a penetration policy. A skimming policy involves setting the price at a relatively high level in order to "skim off" the most profitable customers in the market. It is a good way to recoup quickly the heavy outlay in product research, both technical and marketing, and in the promotion expenditures usually required for new products. It has the disadvantages that market acceptance will be slower, the rate of product improvements will be less, and new competitors will enter more quickly.

A policy of market penetration typically involves a lower price and a longer view. Immediate profit per unit will be less, but profits could be much higher over the life of the product. The choice of whether to emphasize skimming or pentration can only be determined after demand, competitive, and cost factors have been evaluated. Obviously the price plan must be consistent with the total marketing plan for the new product.

While the product-line and price-differential implications of pricing new products have not been discussed they usually exist, and they should influence the decision. A marketing manager cannot make the most effective price decision, for example, without first deciding which channels will be used and what the appropriate discount will be at each level in the channels.

SELECTING CHANNELS FOR NEW PRODUCTS. The theory of buyer behavior in Chapter 3 and the discussion of channels in Chapter 1 suggested something of the nature of the channel problem in marketing a new product. If the buyer is to purchase a brand, he must learn from some source that the product exists, and he must receive the other information he seeks in the learning process, especially in the case of a major innovation. The characteristics of the purchasing situation (the state of the segmenting variables) permit considerable variation in the nature of this learning process. If it is an important product, for example, the buyer will want considerable information, which must be supplied either by the middleman or the manufacturer via advertising and sales effort. Information should also be available to the buyer *after* his decision to reduce his anxiety, especially if it is a product that is difficult to evaluate postdecision. If, however, it is an unimportant product, the buyer will be less inclined to search, and the task will be to make the product as readily available as possible. A nationally known maker of maps and globes, for example, decided to add a toy globe for children to its product line. Traditionally the company had sold its products through stationers, book stores, and book departments of department stores. Because of consumer purchasing habits (the tendency of customers to search for "toys"), the new product had to be sold through retail outlets that commonly sold toys, which required a radically different system of channels.

The seller of a new consumer product contemplates a number of alternatives in attempting to find the combination of middlemen that best meets the characteristics of the new product in terms of how buyers are likely to respond. Although the wholesaler will probably not promote the item aggressively, he does have useful connections with retailers, and his margin is relatively low. If the manufacturer can supply the impetus by advertising to the consumer, the wholesaler may be a desirable alternative. A second alternative is to use a specialty shop, which will probably promote the product more agressively but will demand a higher margin for its services. A third alternative is to sell directly to the retailer. Although direct selling requires a large sales force, the salesmen can be effective in enlisting the retailer's cooperation. He may be persuaded, for example, to use point-of-purchase display. A fourth alternative may be to combine missionary salesmen who will occasionally call on the retailer with the first alternative (the wholesaler). Although the use of missionary salesmen adds to the cost, it may not be as costly as selling directly. Moreover, missionary salesmen offer some of the advantages of direct selling, such as arranging for point-of-purchase display in the retailer's shop and generally enlisting his cooperation.

As a product becomes accepted, its channel requirements often change. Since heavy promotion is required in the early stages of product acceptance, it may be wise for the manufacturer to provide the middlemen with *temporary* incentives in the form of higher margin and sales aids. The middlemen, who are well aware of this, will attempt to negotiate a favorable long-term commitment. If the manufacturer's forecast of the rate of product acceptance is too low, he will have committed himself to an unduly high distribution cost. On the other hand, an overoptimistic forecast will lead to unfulfilled sales expectations by middlemen and their consequent dissatisfaction. A few beer wholesalers (distributors) were persuaded by canned-pop producers to add canned pop to their line. Although the distributor margin on beer is typically about 65 cents per case, the distributors were offered only 20 cents per case on pop, with the argument that the sales volume would more than offset this low margin. Experience indicated that beer wholesalers are not an economically feasible outlet for canned pop—they do not attain the necessary volume.

Decision

The remaining task in developing a market plan is to put all the information about a new product together in such way that it can be used to evaluate growth potential. It can also serve as an input to the investment analysis presented in Chapter 12, and you may find it helpful to refer to the example there. This example set forth what facts are required and how they are put together to compute an estimated rate of return on the funds that would be required to initiate a particular new product.

For frequently purchased products, test-market facts can be analyzed as in Chapter 8 and future sales extrapolated, after giving weight to competition. From competitive considerations an experienced manager can estimate how quickly competitors will enter the market and help to expand the market if the brand is a major innovation. If it is not, competitors moving in can decrease sales. Marketing costs are derived from the marketing strategy set forth. Nonmarketing costs can usually be secured from the accounting department. To complicate matters, all of these estimates must be for the period of the expected life of the product.

DROPPING PRODUCTS

Introduction

The necessity of contemplating the dropping of a product can arise in a number of ways. Probably the most common is "normal product obsolescence," which is a decline in demand caused by a shift in consumers' needs, technological change, or significant improvements in competitors' products. Also contributing to the necessity of dropping a product are past mistakes in developing products as well as mistakes inherited from other managements when a company is taken over through merger or stock purchase. The usual case of a decline in demand is considered here, but many of the methods suggested also apply when the need for a decision arises from other sources, such as past mistakes which were prevalent in the past decade.

Determining need for product change

One of the problems of product elimination in a company producing many products is to know when to investigate the possibility of eliminating a given product. The use of the product cycle in this connection was discussed in Chapter 2. The auto industry has in the past solved the problem in part by the industrywide practice of changing the body style every three years.

Market research techniques can help. Through the use of performance feedback by retail-store audits, warehouse withdrawals, and consumer panels, the marketing manager can determine a significant change in competitive position within 30 to 60 days. Since these data are also required to appraise marketing effectiveness properly, they should not be considered an additional cost. Although these methods may provide adequate information on performance, however, they obviously do not provide the complete answer to the question of product elimination. They merely record changes in the market position rather than anticipating them, and they do not tell why the change occurred—this can only be inferred. The actual cause of the change may be any one of several, and the analysis required to determine the cause takes time.

Buyer-attitude surveys can be useful in revealing the need for product change, but surveys are useful only insofar as the survey designer has meaningful hypotheses, such as structural models, about the specific changes needed. This means that the surveys are usually worthwhile only after preliminary thinking and investigation have been carried out.

Dealer surveys can be helpful. The Chevrolet policy for example, provides for representatives of the division's 7,600 dealers to come to Detroit about four times a year to meet with Chevrolet executives for a discussion of suggested product changes. The extent to which this policy is motivated by the politics of marketing channels, which aim to get dealer cooperation, is not known.

Courses of action

Once it is clear that a decision must be made about an existing product, the alternatives available to a marketing manager are: (1) change the product, (2) sell it in bulk, or (3) eliminate the product.

CHANGE THE PRODUCT. Changing the product is the only alternative, aside from the other two more radical decisions, if the marketing effectiveness and factory-cost levels are already at an optimum. Practically, however, it may be possible to improve marketing effectiveness through such means as price or promotion adjustments or reduction of production costs. When things go wrong, the common practice is to examine factory costs, price, the product, and selling costs.

The marketing research techniques described above, when imaginatively applied, can help in revealing product changes essential to successful marketing. After acquiring this specific information and translating it into product design, the marketing manager can pass the recommended design to the production manager for a decision as to economic feasibility. If it is not practicable, one of the other two alternatives can be considered.

SELL IN BULK. By selling in bulk, promotional outlays can be eliminated. Bulk selling may be a real alternative if the product is one in which keen competition has forced the price down and a big demand exists for it. The attention of the marketing management, a scarce resource, can be freed for other uses.

ELIMINATE THE PRODUCT. The same tests recommended for deciding whether to add a product can be applied in the decision to drop a product. If long-run analyses of demand and cost suggest a profit projection of less than the cost of capital, the product should be dropped.

The human cost of dropping a product can be high: It can mean unemployment. Often this deters a company from this course of action. In a company that innovates regularly with new products, however, it is usually possible to phase the employees for the old product into the production and sale of a new one.

SUMMARY

New products are the lifeblood of companies in many industries. They are required for both growth and profit, but they pose some of the most difficult problems for marketing management. This is especially true for organizational problems. A body of concepts and techniques that can be called the new marketing technology has evolved in response to the manager's needs. This technology is rapidly becoming available, but like all sophisticated tools it requires some skill, which can easily be learned and applied to each new product situation. The underlying concepts, however, can also be used productively in a highly informal way.

The task of deciding when to drop an old product is often discussed along with problems of adding new products. In fact, adding a new product and dropping an old one often occur simultaneously. The concepts and tools for this decision, are the same as that for adding products, and we leave it largely to the reader to apply them to this corollary task. The minimum profit constraint can be a cue to indicate that consideration should be given to dropping the product when the actual profit on it has fallen to a minimum level.

We now begin to see more of the role that the marketing manager plays in furthering corporate strategy and its underlying objectives. More specifically, financial analysts often judge a corporation as to (1) how many new products it has in the pipeline, (2) its track record in product innovation, and (3) its willingness to drop unprofitable products. All of these in large measure are a reflection of the marketing manager's effectiveness.

DISCUSSION QUESTIONS

1. What is meant by concept testing and what is its role in new-product development?
2. When a new product, especially a radically new one (a major innovation), is introduced, the buyer is heavily dependent upon the company for the necessary information to understand and judge it. If so, why should the limitations of his information acquisition and processing be so important? Can't he just read the ads?
3. In a wealthy society such as ours, consumers are free to buy for self-concept reasons, since their basic needs can be met in any one of a number of ways. What is the significance of this fact in designing a new-product strategy and generating a marketing plan out of that strategy?
4. When would you employ an indirect type of advertising and when a direct type?
5. One of the marketing characteristics of companies that financial analysts often examine with great care is whether the company has an effective "drop" policy. Why should this be so?

14

Channel system management

INTRODUCTION

THE choice of the channel system is a major administrative decision. It is one way in which the marketing manager contributes to the company's maximum performance potential, which will enable it to carry out its corporate strategy more effectively.

Chapter 1 introduced the concepts of marketing system, distribution system, and channel system. In developing the concepts of hierarchy and plane as dimensions of a company's channel system, it was shown that agencies in each plane—wholesalers and retailers—perform collection, sorting, and dispersing functions. Part III often dealt with the management of these agencies in a *given* channel system, for example, the role of the salesman in working with the retailer and the use of "dealer deals."

Now we need a fuller grasp of what each type of middleman contributes so as to justify his inclusion in a company's distribution system. The processes of collecting, sorting, and dispersing the products they handle were useful for the broad-brush approach of Chapter 1. Here we must turn to more precise definitions.

Even though a marketing manager may be fortunate enough to develop a fairly optimal distribution system, change in the nature of the environment will in time erode its advantages. Important questions arise as to the nature and source of these changes because they not only pose problems for the company but reflect, among other things, the worldwide trend of economic development. This in turn raises new questions as to the economic welfare of the consumer. Therefore we will pay particular attention to the dynamics of the channel system.

Understanding of these dynamics also is helpful in making a choice among channels. The problem of channel selection is dealt with at two levels: strategy and plan. The strategy of the company's channel system guides the actual decision, the choice of a channel plan.

Logistical systems are usually not under the control of the marketing manager. They have to do only with the physical distribution of the product, as a part of the flow of raw materials into the plant, inventories within the plant, and distribution of the finished product to the retailer. The intimate relation between effective marketing and how well the company's logistical system performs its function, is readily recognized.

Finally, because of potential change, a distribution system needs to be monitored regularly to evaluate its effectiveness.

FUNCTIONS OF MIDDLEMEN

The production of a good and its consumption are usually separated both in space and time. Therefore, someone must perform the functions of *transporting* the product to the distributive agencies, *storing* it, *financing* it, and taking the many varieties of *risk* incurred in the distributive process, as well as *informing* potential customers about it. The need for transporting the good is obvious. Perhaps less obvious is the fact that, typically, a product remains for a period of time in one or more warehouses before it is used; thus it incurs all of the costs entailed in storage, such as interest cost and insurance against fire, pilferage, and other types of risk. Throughout the distributive process someone owns the product, and the owner's funds will be tied up in it, so that he forgoes the opportunity to use these funds elsewhere. There are many noninsurable risks, such as the possibility of a loss resulting from a price decline. In a few instances, such as with agricultural commodities, it is possible to limit the risk of a price decline through "hedging," but these products typically make up a small part of the marketing manager's problems. Another function of the distribution process, to inform potential buyers as to when and where the product is available, is accomplished in part through advertising and personal selling.

For some products, the process of distribution is even more complex than we have implied because the product becomes physically changed en route to the ultimate user. Packaging is the simplest and most common change of product occurring in the distributive process.

The links in the distribution process are defined in terms of the functions middlemen perform. There are four general types of middlemen: (1) agent middlemen, who do *not* take legal title to the goods they handle for the producer, (2) wholesalers, who take title and sell to retailers, (3) retailers, who take title and sell to users, and (4) voluntary chains in which retailers pool their buying in one way or another. There are also numerous kinds of middlemen within each of these types, each filling a specific need for a client who may be either a manufacturer or another middleman. Thus essentially three types of flows can be identified: transactions, ownership, and physical product. Agents are involved only with the first; limited-service wholesalers, with the first and second; and full-service wholesalers, with the first, second, and third. Exceptions to this terminology are found in practice, as the American Marketing Association discovered in its attenpt to obtain general agreement on terminology.

Agent middlemen

Agent middlemen fall into five categories: brokers, commission merchants, resident buyers, manufacturer's agents, and sales agents.

The function of a *broker* is to bring the buyer and seller together. Brokers serve more than one client; they may represent the buyer or the seller. They do not handle the goods; in fact, they seldom see anything more than a sample of them. Usually they cannot bind their client, which means that every transaction must be approved by the client before it is binding on the seller and the buyer can be assured of delivery. The broker is paid a commission for his services. He is useful in an area where a seller finds it uneconomical to use his own sales staff to reach the wholesaler because the demand is too sparse. This often happens when the product is highly specialized.

The *commission merchant* is the same as a broker except that he can bind his client and often takes physical possession of the goods. He is commonly found in the fresh fruit and vegetable industry and also in the textile industry.

Resident buyers are commission buyers who are mainly confined to large central markets such as New York and Chicago. They supplement the purchasing staffs of retail stores, keeping their clients informed of market conditions and buying "fill-ins" after the stores have made their principal purchases for the season. A recent development has been the use of resident buyers by grocery supermarkets.

A *manufacturer's agent* is a substitute for the company's own salesman, often found in the industrial field. He can bind his principal, and he has the exclusive right to a defined territory, although he is closely controlled with respect to price and terms of sale. Typically, he does not take physical possession of the goods, and he sells noncompeting lines for several different companies.

The *sales agent* is a middleman who acts like the company's sales force. He sells the entire output of his client and offers the company various other marketing services, such as financing. The commission that he receives depends upon the amount of services he renders. He is commonly used by small manufacturers selling to a distant market. There seems to be a tendency for sales agents and manufacturers to be integrated. Either the manufacturer assumes ownership of the sales agent's operation or the sales agent takes over the manufacturer.

Wholesaling middlemen

Wholesalers hold legal title to the goods. They are mainly (1) full-function or service wholesalers, (2) limited-function wholesalers, (3) petroleum bulk stations and terminals, and (4) assemblers. In practice the wholesalers of consumer durable products are called "distributors." Wholesalers are sometimes called *full-function wholesalers* or jobbers because they provide a wide range of services—they carry stocks, deliver, grant credit, "break bulk," and send out salesmen. Wholesaling middlemen who sell goods to industrial buyers are often called *industrial supply houses* or *mill supply houses.*

Limited-function wholesalers are cash-and-carry wholesalers, drop shippers or desk jobbers, mail-order wholesalers, and truck or wagon jobbers who do not perform all of the functions of the full-function wholesaler.

Petroleum products require special handling facilities because most of them are liquid. *Petroleum bulk stations and terminals* receive bulk shipments, store for short periods, and disperse their product to filling stations and other retailers and to industrial, commercial, and institutional users.

Assemblers deal in farm products and seafood. They operate at two levels in the distributive chain. First, they serve local producing points where they buy from producers, such as at a country grain elevator or a fishing wharf. Second, at intermediate points in large producing regions, they assemble carloads and truckloads from the local markets for movement to terminal markets in consuming regions. They may serve a storage function and offer finances to the buyer or seller.

Instead of using a wholesaler, the manufacturer may take the alternative of creating his own wholesaling establishments, called manufacturers' sales branches or offices. Customers place orders with the manufacturer's salesmen who work out of these offices. Sales branches usually perform the storage function, and goods are delivered from them to the buyer.

Retailing middlemen

The most common types of retailing organizations are small independents, department stores, chains, supermarkets, and discount houses. In practice, retailers are often called "dealers." There are other kinds of retailing organizations, such as variety stores, (exemplified by Kresge and Woolworth), consumer cooperatives, and automatic vending.

The definition problem becomes more difficult in regard to the retailing portion of the distributive structure. For our purposes, however, reasonably workable definitions will suffice.

Independent refers to ownership—each establishment is separately owned, as contrasted with the chain store, where several establishments are under one ownership. Small independent retailers vary considerably in the extent of service they provide, but they tend to be full service, offering clerks, delivery, and credit. They usually do not promote aggressively, but obtain their share of the retail market through proximity to the consumer and services that often emphasize the element of "personal touch."

Although it is reasonably correct to label a *department store* an "independent," the situation is changing. Department stores have moved strongly in the direction of multiple-unit ownership, although the degree of centralized control varies considerably; some of the ownership groups are very loose. A department store handles a large variety of apparel lines, house furnishings, and housewares. The merchandise is arranged by departments, and purchasing, as well as accounting, is on a departmental basis. The U.S. Census Bureau sets a minimum of 25 employees as the criterion for classifying an establishment as a department store. Department stores historically were located in downtown areas, but there is a strong trend toward the addition of branches in outlying shopping centers. Extensive services are provided, and charge accounts and return privileges, as well as delivery, are emphasized. With many exceptions department stores are characterized by an atmosphere of "prestige," and their promotion, though extensive, is consistent with this atmosphere.

Chains are multiunit retailing organizations that combine wholesaling and retailing operations under one management. They usually maintain a high degree of centralized control. The extent of service rendered a manufacturer varies considerably among chains. At one extreme are Sears, Roebuck and Company and Montgomery Ward and Company, which offer a fairly complete line of services; at the other extreme are chain drug concerns, which provide little service. Chains tend toward aggressive promotion and emphasize price. They often make use of "private brands" —the practice of having a manufacturer produce for them under their brand instead of the manufacturer's. There are local, regional, and national chains.

The *supermarket*, a development of the 1930s, is typical in the food field. It is characterized by large size and a location which provides extensive parking space. Self-service is emphasized. A wide range of food and related grocery store products is stocked, and there is a strong trend to make more nongrocery items available. Aggressive promotion is used to support this operation, which strives to keep expenses low.

The *discount house*, characterized mainly by price competition and limited service, appeared after World War II. Its distinguishing characteristic is a lower markup than that of more conventional retailers. It has been confined largely to consumer durable products, particularly appliances, but is continuing to expand into soft goods, drugs, and cosmetics.

The discount house has probably been most damaging to small independent stores and department stores. In a sense it is a counterpart of the supermarket, as we will explain below.

Voluntary chains

The voluntary or cooperative chain is another distributive organization of major significance. The manner in which this form has emerged helps to explain its role in the distributive structure. A group of retailers wished to centralize their purchases in order to increase their bargaining strength and to cut freight costs through more carload purchases—the freight rate is less for carload (C.L.) shipments than for less than carload (L.C.L.). Group buying can be accomplished on a very informal basis, as by designating certain members to buy particular products for all of the members. This loose arrangement is called a *buying group*. If the group wishes the advantages of more centralized control, the solution is to organize or to purchase a wholesaling concern as a group. The group then becomes a *cooperative chain*. Finally, in order to insure his market, a wholesaler can organize a group of retailers who will buy primarily from him in return for the merchandising services and advice that he offers. The Ben Franklin Stores affiliated with Butler Brothers of Chicago are an example of this latter type of retailing organization, which is called a *voluntary chain*.

A marketing manager groups these agencies into a system he thinks will meet his needs. Before proceeding with more detailed discussion of just how he goes about putting these together, however, an understanding of the dynamics of a channel system is necessary. These changes often occur slowly, and their effects are subtle.

DYNAMICS OF CHANNEL SYSTEMS

Introduction

Change in the structure of an industry's distribution system creates the need to modify the channel system of an individual company. Because the systems of many companies are immensely complex, an understanding of the nature and sources of change in an industry distribution system can aid in detecting the necessity for change at the company level. Better methods for making such changes can be identified and evaluated. Further, because the marketing management task may vary in societies with differing levels of economic development, issues of social and economic welfare begin to emerge.

Changes in the distributive structure occur slowly, but marketing channel decisions involve long-term commitments. Thus the marketing manager must forecast long-term movements, which requires a knowledge of the sources and rate of change. Structural change occurs in response to basic changes in the economy, but it is exceedingly diverse among products. The following description of the process of structural change is intended to suggest the type of situation that may occur rather than to present a specific case analysis. The discussion will be confined to consumer goods because industrial goods typically present a simpler problem and less information is generally available on them.

Structural change

Out of the many changes that have occurred in the structure of distribution in the past several decades, at least one long-term trend emerges in a number of products. This is the tendency for the *manufacturer of consumer goods to absorb a larger proportion of the increasing marketing burden by selling directly to the retailer.* At the same time, he is relieving the retailer of some of his marketing functions. The tendency of retailers is to maintain little more than a large display and a storage room for a wide variety of packaged products and to attempt to make their establishments models of engineering efficiency. The trend to increased sales by manufacturers directly to retailers, although generally accepted by students of the subject, has not been well documented by research.[1] The large retailing organization always has a means of putting a limit on acquisition of power by the manufacturer in this way, however. He can often market competitive products under his own brand name. This is the widely used practice of "private branding."

The shift of marketing functions to the manufacturer accounts for some of the channel problems he must face. A good example was the dilemma of many manufacturers in the late fifties and early sixties who feared that if they sold to discount houses established retailers would discontinue handling their products. If they did not sell to discount houses, however, their volume of sales would suffer seriously. In the heat of the argument, it is often forgotten that similar problems have long plagued the manufacturer and the middleman. In 1890, it was the department store that was "illegitimate," and legislation was sponsored by the established "legitimate" retailers to legislate it out of existence. In 1900, it was the mail-order house; in 1930, the chain store. In the past several years it has been the discount house, although the term is not so often heard today. A reasonable inference is that tomorrow there will be a similar phenomenon, with a different name.

For this trend to be portrayed more meaningfully, it can be abstracted from consideration of certain aspects of economic development in the

---

[1]See, however, Harold Barger, *Distribution's Place in the American Economy since 1869* (Princeton, N.J.: Princeton University Press, 1955), especially chapter 5. Also see a series of four impressionistic but plausible articles by E. B. Weiss, *Advertising Age*, April 18 and 25 and May 2 and 9, 1955. For a detailed description of developments in Great Britain, see James B. Jefferys, *Retail Trading in Britain, 1850–1950* (Cambridge, England: Cambridge University Press, 1954).

United States since 1900. The dimension of levels of economic development is important for a company selling in underdeveloped countries, but it is also relevant to public policy in a country attempting to attain a higher level of economic development from an already well-established base. By setting forth two models, it is possible to represent the extremes in the positions of middlemen and manufacturers, with most actual situations being somewhere in between. By analogy, they also represent the extremes in economic development. The models do not conform precisely to reality, but they do contain the essential characteristics of the phenomena of shifting marketing functions from the distributive agencies to the manufacturer.

One model is termed the "rural general store," which can be considered representative of the American retail structure in 1900. It is still to be found, however, in the more remote sections of the United States and is apparently common to all underdeveloped countries. Because of the low level of agricultural technology, a large proportion of the people must live on the land and be sparsely scattered geographically to produce the necessary quantity of food.

The other model of distributive institution, here labeled the "supermarket," embodies the characteristics of a trend toward a high level of economic development. It is a large store, heavily self-service and with a low profit margin. In 1964, specialty store margins were reported as 43 percent and department store margins, 39 percent, while discount store margins were estimated at 25 to 30 percent.[2] Movement of people to the cities with consequent urban population concentrations is one of the dominant reasons for the development of these institutions.

Currently the supermarket is representative of a large and growing proportion of retailing in the United States. The food supermarket has come to have nonfood departments. The discount or "promotional department store," which was reported in 1964 to be selling 7 percent of all general merchandise, furniture appliances, apparel and food,[3] is a more recent and dramatic development. Essentially the same characteristics are embodied in the large chain drug stores. The supermarket, because of its greater familiarity, will be used as the basis for discussion.

RURAL GENERAL STORE MODEL. The rural general store provides almost all the items needed by its customers—food, clothing, tobacco, agricultural and carpentry tools, and so forth. The number of items offered is not great compared with the supermarket type of retail institution, however, because the standard of living of its customers is low. (The level of income is generally recognized as the criterion for identifying the level of economic development of a country.) A large proportion of the items making

---

[2] *The New York Times,* July 19, 1964, p. 12F.
[3] Ibid.

up this standard is produced at home rather than purchased in a store. The general store offers extensive services; customers' purchases may be financed for as long as a year. Almost every item sold is handled by a clerk, and packaging is a major task.

Brands are relatively unimportant. If the item is branded at all, the consumer takes whatever brand the retailer stocks. Insofar as the consumer has a choice to make, he can seek the advice of the retail clerk, who is readily available. An implicit problem is that the quality of the product may be lower than it should be to serve the consumer optimally. In spite of the low standard of living, there tends to be a seller's market, and the manufacturer does not have to be as sensitive to the needs of his consumers. Further, manufacturers tend to follow an internal incentive system which encourages volume of physical output instead of quality as defined in terms of the customer's needs.

In the Soviet Union this emphasis upon quantity of production has been a serious problem, and each plant is required by law to have a "production mark" placed on its product so those with low-quality output can be identified.[4] A more attractive form of this device, called a "trademark," is required on certain products and for all exports. Considerable resources are also devoted to plant inspection as a means of obtaining a higher quality of production. Thus branding may be used to lessen the costs of maintaining an extensive inspection system. What are considered the "wastes of capitalist marketing," such as advertising, may turn out to be more economical than adding to the costs of inspection. This difficulty of insuring satisfactory quality may be worse in the Soviet Union because of its highly centralized control of production and the consequent divorce of the policies of companies from the influence of information about their markets. We suspect that in large part this market insensitivity to the consumer is a consequence of an underdeveloped economy.

Thus, in the rural general store format, the retailer, rather than the consumer, makes the choice among brands. The retailer possesses an intimate knowledge of his customers which is an aid in planning his purchases. Moreover, careful planning is not essential because the items are relatively imperishable, turnover is low, and consumer preferences for particular brands do not exist.

Engineering efficiency in the physical flow of items, particularly insofar as it saves the consumer's time, is not important because the consumer's influence does not tend to be felt. Alternatives are limited, and the shopping trip has social implications for the buyer that are almost as significant as the economic purpose of obtaining goods. The local retail store is a center of social relations.

---

[4]M. I. Goldman, "Product Differentiation and Advertising: Some Lessons from Soviet Experience," *Journal of Political Economy*, 74 (1967): 346–57.

Changes in method of store operation come very slowly, also because the consumer has no easily accessible alternative place to purchase other than perhaps mail order, which is somewhat less convenient and does not serve his social needs. The market is so small that economies of scale—a concept presented in Chapter 4—prohibit more than one store in an area; thus, competition is not available to provide an impetus to change. Lack of convenient transportation prevents the buyer from going to another community. Because of his relative social isolation, the consumer has only limited access to new ideas; therefore, he does not demand change.

The sources of supply for the general store are a number of wholesalers, located at some distance, each of which regularly supplies a portion of the retailer's needs. Very few of the wholesalers that supply the general store purchase directly from the manufacturer, and there may be as many as three or four levels of intervening middlemen.

Thus, the rural general store satisfactorily served a primitive level of economic development. But change came. These changes had mainly to do with population and technology, but like most forces underlying economic development, their consequences were complex. They will be elaborated later. For the moment let us turn to the other model, the model that these changes made possible.

SUPERMARKET MODEL.   The supermarket, which is large and may be independently owned or part of a chain, offers a greater absolute number of products than does the general store, although it is largely confined to satisfying a small proportion of its customers' total needs. It carries a number of the more widely demanded brands of each product; for example, there may be eight different brands of coffee.

Few services are offered by the supermarket. In many instances, from the manufacturer's *advertising* the consumer knows precisely which brand he will buy before entering the store. If the brand is not available, he may go elsewhere. If the consumer has not made up his mind prior to entering the store as to which brand he will buy, he chooses from among the brands on display according to their location, appearance, information given on the label, and price. This places extremely heavy information demands upon the buyer. To acquire the information required to purchase the market basket that is part of our high standard of living with no help from a clerk, especially one whom the consumer knows and can trust, is very demanding. The situation is fair game for "consumerism."

Another important point is that the retailer exerts little control over which brand the consumer will purchase, and therefore over which manufacturer's brand will be stocked. In buying food and similar small items, the customer walks through the store, placing his choices in a cart which is then rolled out through the check-out line. He pays for his purchases in cash. About the only service a clerk provides is occasionally telling the customer where items may be located, taking his money, and performing the limited packaging function of putting everything into large bags.

In some modern stores, the customer's task is even simpler. Display cases are equipped with pushbuttons the customer presses for the desired item. Alternatively, the displayed item is numbered and a correspondingly numbered IBM card is selected by the customer and handed to the clerk, who places the card in a machine. Either way, the item is dropped from its storage place to an endless belt which conveys it, along with all others selected, to the check-out counter. In another retailing plan, the housewife telephones her order to a computer which "verifies the order, item by item, and quotes various quantity prices—for a single item, several items or a case. The cost of the order is given, and a delivery time is scheduled—at least four hours later and within a two-hour target period." The order is then delivered to her home within the scheduled time.[5]

For larger appliances, delivery and installation services may be offered, in which case the customer will pay extra for them. More likely, the service will be provided by a commercial service company, the distributor, or the manufacturer, rather than the retailer.

The function of the supermarket is basically an engineering and transportation feat. Relative to the general store, it handles an enormous tonnage of products. Large quantities, perhaps two or three carloads of items, are purchased at a time in order to secure quantity discounts and save on shipping cost. This tonnage makes it economically possible to use mechanical equipment as an aid in handling the products. The items are packaged in the most convenient quantities so that a complete box of items is placed on the shelf at one time, which further encourages the use of mechanical equipment. Not only is it possible to be efficient in an engineering sense, but the supermarket operator has no other choice. A few extra miles of driving in the family car to a shopping center provides the consumer with a number of available alternative sources. As a result of mass communication—especially advertising—and social contacts, the consumer is a somewhat well-informed buyer. In Chapter 3, however, we observed the central role of information in his decision process and how lack of information leads to tension and discomfort. He needs much information, especially since many of the products are complex. Uncertainty about the effects of processed foods on health, for example, can complicate buying.

Forecasting demand in order to plan stock purchase is a problem for the supermarket operator. He can know little about his customers personally, and forecasting is complicated by consumer preferences for par-

---

[5] *Business Week*, March 28, 1970, p. 110 ff.

ticular brands. Further, rapid stock turnover is essential to profit. Although it is expensive to carry a heavy inventory, properly timed purchases enable the retailer to buy at lower prices. Among fresh and frozen foods, perishability sharpens the forecasting problem. Forecasting errors resulting in shortages can be corrected through rush orders, but this too is costly. The volume of sales is such that careful analysis of sales will reveal the relative speed at which each brand moves through the store, and these data can be helpful in forecasting demand. To the extent that the retailer has a choice in deciding which items to stock, he uses an effective criterion in the form of "contribution to profit per square foot of shelf or floor space." Given the margin and the rate of flow of an item, the item can be quickly evaluated against alternative items in a manner that is workable, though not precise, since differences in cost of handling among items are omitted.

This shift from the rural general store to the supermarket has major consequences for the nature of the relationships between the manufacturer and the middleman.

Middlemen-manufacturer relationships. The trend of manufacturers to take over many of the functions of middlemen, which has brought about changes in both roles, illustrates Adam Smith's theorem that specialization of labor is limited by the extent of the market.[6] As the market has widened in terms of number of people and greater quantity purchased due to a rising standard of living, the determination of who can most economically perform a given function changes. Often, instead of functions being shifted among existing agencies, new specialist agencies develop to perform these functions, such as advertising agencies, market research firms, and time-sharing computer facilities.

The differences in the roles of the middlemen and the producer in the general store and supermarket models is significant to the marketing manager. The general store, its wholesalers, and their suppliers jointly performed almost the entire marketing function, leaving the manufacturer free to concentrate on production. The retailer made the choice for the consumer; the consumer bought whatever manufacturer's "brand" the retailer stocked. The retailer handled the packaging problem which, as a form of product decision, is now critical for the manufacturer.

When the wholesaler was the only link between the manufacturer and the retailer, he was a full-function wholesaler. He established relations with the manufacturer, made his products available to the retailer, and sometimes financed the manufacturer. A careful study of the Los Angeles grocery market offers quantitative evidence of developments. In 1920 the entire Los Angeles market was served by full-function wholesalers only,

---

[6]George J. Stigler, "The Division of Labor Is Limited by the Extent of the Market," *Journal of Political Economy,* 59 (1951): 185–93.

but by 1946 their share had fallen to 16 percent. Limited-function and specialty wholesalers had taken 18½ percent of the market; retailer buying cooperatives, 30½ percent; chain stores, 29 percent; and direct sales by the manufacturer to the retailer, 6 percent.[7]

In the supermarket type of operation, the manufacturer carries much more of the marketing function. Through consumer surveys and other forms of market research, he determines consumer preferences, settles on the "best" product, and predicts the rate of flow of his brand. He uses informative and appealing packages. Through national advertising, he establishes a reputation for a product of a certain quality, which must be maintained. If a mistake in production is made or the product is found to be injurious to the consumer, he must be ready to rectify it immediately. The items are packed in sizes appropriate to the retailer's needs, largely determined by the rate of consumption of a product and the requirements of mechanical handling equipment.

The wholesaler rarely finances the manufacturer. To the extent that the consumer does not finance himself, he is financed by a specialist company (consumer finance company), seldom the retailer.

The promotion and availability of a new product must be closely coordinated because the retailer has to be convinced of the product's relative profitability before he is willing to devote valuable shelf space to its display. Should the manufacturer's promotion be inadvertently delayed, slow sales will suggest to the retailer that the item is not a desirable candidate for his shelves, and he may remove it before the promotion is effective. Formerly, the retailer played an important role in the introduction of new products because extra promotional effort was required to overcome established consumption habits. Through the dramatic sales appeal made possible by modern mass communication, such as television, the manufacturer can now introduce the product more economically.

Sources of structural change

As implied above, the primary sources of change in the distributive structure are those that lead to economic development in any country. These sources are mainly greater population, with a rising standard of living, and improved technology. Changes in consumer tastes probably have been a significant influence, but their effect is more difficult to evaluate.

POPULATION. A growing number of consumers has an effect on the distribution system because the market becomes larger. A rising standard of living also adds to the quantity of products supplied through the distribu-

---

[7]Ralph Cassady, Jr., and Wylie L. Jones, *The Changing Competitive Structure in the Wholesale Grocery Trade* (Berkeley and Los Angeles: University of California Press, 1949), p. 26. For an analysis of the position of the wholesaler between 1869 and 1929, see Barger, *Distribution's Place in the American Economy*, p. 70, Table 20; p. 132 ff, Table B–5.

tive agencies. The fact that today's consumers must purchase all they consume, rather than producing their own, has added to the tons of products that flow through retailing institutions.

Changes in the locational pattern of population have had major effects. First, intraregional movements of population from rural to urban communities have led to highly concentrated consumer markets which have encouraged the development of supermarkets and discount houses. Eighty-five percent of the total population growth in the decade 1950-60 occurred in the standard metropolitan areas. Changes in 10 leading cities for two decades are shown in Table 14–1. The movement of population to the suburbs, which has slowed, as can be seen by comparing city and SMSA figures for the fifties and the sixties in the table, has been less important in causing this trend. There is evidence in the carpet industry, for example,

TABLE 14–1
Growth of selected SMSA's

	Preliminary 1970 count	Percent of change 1960–70	Percent of change 1950–60
1. New York			− 1.4
New York SMSA			11.9
2. Chicago			− 1.9
Chicago SMSA			20.1
3. Los Angeles	2,782,400	12.2	25.8
Los Angeles SMSA	6,970,733	15.4	45.5
4. Philadelphia	1,926,842	− 3.8	− 3.3
Philadelphia SMSA	4,774,139	9.9	18.3
5. Detroit	1,492,507	−10.6	− 9.7
Detroit SMSA	4,161,660	10.6	24.7
6. Baltimore	893,908	− 4.8	− 1.1
Baltimore SMSA	2,112,105	17.1	23.8
7. Houston	1,212,928	29.3	57.4
Houston SMSA	1,957,588	38.0	51.6
8. Cleveland	739,226	− 15.6	− 4.2
Cleveland SMSA	2,043,939	7.0	24.6
9. Washington			− 4.8
Washington SMSA			37.7
10. St. Louis	608,078	− 18.9	− 12.5
St. Louis SMSA	2,332,425	10.8	19.9

Source: *Advertising Age*, August 31, 1970, p. 12.

that the effect of the movement to the suburbs has operated in just the opposite direction. Bigelow-Sanford Carpet Company adopted in 1954 the innovation of selling through wholesalers rather than direct to the retailer, in part because small suburban stores tend to buy from wholesalers rather than direct from manufacturers.

Second, the interregional population movements which led to great gains for California and Florida, for example, have also had repercussions in the structure of distribution. Some of the movements are shown in Figure 14–1. In the short period of 10 years a few states gained population by more than 50 percent, while several others actually lost population. Some communities in North Dakota, for example, lost more than 25 percent of their population in the past decade. These represent drastic differences in rates of growth, with obvious implications for the distributive structure.

FIGURE 14–1
Geographic population change, 1960–70

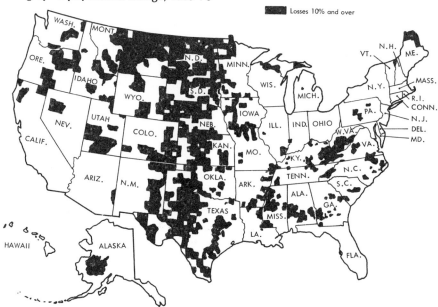

Source: *The New York Times*, February 24, 1971, p. 68.

TECHNOLOGY. The influence of technological change is interwoven with changes in the distributive structure. As agriculture became more mechanized, workers were released from the farms to seek jobs in urban areas. Technology is responsible for the development of almost the whole category of consumer durable goods, on which the consumer typically spends 10 percent and more of his disposable income. One of these technological developments, the automobile, has permitted the consumer to shop over a larger area, so he has more alternative sources, and to buy more on a single shopping trip. Packaging methods and materials usually required in a self-service institution are another result of technology. Mechanical vending has been stimulated by improved packaging, temperature control, slug rejection, and coin-changing mechanisms.

The development of modern mass communication, most recently exemplified by television, aided by CATV and cassettes, enables a single manufacturer to communicate economically with the national market and small highly specialized segments. The use of "preselling" through mass communication by the manufacturer has been supported by historically rising wage costs, which have limited the ability of the retailer to employ the quality of person required for effective floor selling. It has become more economical for the manufacturer to do the selling task mechanically, in the sense of using mass communication, than for the retailer to do it with hand labor at current wage levels. A new product can be introduced to the market with greater speed and economy because mass communication makes dramatic presentations possible. The ease of introducing new products has encouraged efforts toward product "obsolescence" by the manufacturer, whereby he introduces a "new model" which causes the "old model" to be "outdated." Thus extensive personal selling at the retail level is less necessary.

Improved technology of transportation has contributed in many ways to changes in the structure of distribution. Transportation cost historically has been a declining proportion of distribution costs; this decline has been almost enough to offset other forces that tended to increase these costs.[8] As a consequence, the consumer finds it possible to purchase a greater volume with a given income than he would otherwise. Although it appears difficult, if not impossible, to set forth a meaningful conclusion as to transportation costs, particularly since World War I,[9] there have been a large number of innovations in transportation.[10]

By 1920 . . . the United States transportation was already entering an unprecedented phase of technological change that even by 1950 . . . had yet to complete its course. The basic factor bringing about the change was the development of the internal combusion engine, which had been invented several decades before the turn of the century and which had been initially applied to highway vehicles just before and during the 1890's and to the airplane in the subsequent decade.[11]

Innovations in railroad transportation, largely under the stimulus of truck competition, have been faster service, improved loading, greater protection of shipments against damage, truck service from freight stations, piggyback, and containerization. As an example of faster transportation, the railroads had long offered only third-morning service from Florida to New York and from Chicago to New York. When trucks

---

[8]Barger, *Distribution's Place in the American Economy*, pp. 57–58.

[9]Harold F. Williamson (ed.), *The Growth of the American Economy*, 2d ed. (New York: Prentice-Hall, Inc., 1951), pp. 383, 678–79.

[10]Ibid., pp. 667–68.

[11]Ibid., p. 667.

achieved second-morning delivery, the railroads initiated second-morning service for less than carload shipments. Air freight is changing the picture today.

Motorized highway transportation is another illustration of the effect of technological changes upon the structure of distribution. The automobile provides the consumer with transportation that makes it economically feasible for him to travel a distance to shop and also to transport his purchases instead of using delivery services, as indicated above. The automobile and the truck have permitted suburban development without dependence on rail lines. In rural areas, the truck can be said to have wrought a revolution in transportation.

In the food sector of the economy, refrigeration has been one of the major innovations. [12] Frozen foods and year-round fresh foods have become important products at the retail level. Their perishable nature has itself urged direct distribution channels, and these new products have contributed to the volume of purchases by the consumer. The home refrigerating unit has tended to increase the magnitude, and decrease the frequency, of purchases of many food products. Both these changes have contributed to the convenience a consumer obtains from patronizing a supermarket. At one time after World War II it seemed likely that home refrigeration might lead to significantly less food volume passing through retail stores because of the possibility that wholesalers would supply the consumer directly. While this change has not developed, it has been noted that "The patterns of food distribution conceivably might change should a large proportion of American homes be equipped with their own freezing storage."[13]

Summary: Structural change

Perspective is needed in order to assess the significance of the differences between the general store model and the supermarket model which mark the change in the roles of middlemen and manufacturers. We can say in summary, however, that economic development probably makes the consumer better off, but the process raises new problems. Some of these will be discussed in the next chapter.

The movement toward the new type of distribution exemplified by the supermarket is slow. The supermarket and the discount house are not replacing existing institutions, but supplementing them. As with the department store, mail-order house, and chain store, the newer type of distributive unit will become a part of the existing structure, and in the

---

[12] Oscar Edward Anderson, Jr., *Refrigeration in America* (Princeton, N.J.: Princeton University Press, 1953), especially chaps. 7–10, 14, and 16–19.

[13] Ibid., p. 301.

process it will probably modify its own character. The "price-cutting" atmosphere that pervaded the early department store, for example, is a far cry from the "quality" atmosphere it often cultivates today.

This lack of radical changes in the structure is supported by Barger's study.[14] Marketing conditions are too diverse to permit only one kind of distributive institution. Specifically, a portion of customers has always been willing to pay for extra services. This is particularly true for certain products, such as style clothing. Also, immense areas of the United States are obviously too sparsely populated to lend themselves to highly centralized shopping, at least under forseeable conditions of transportation technology. Although the tendency for the manufacturer to bypass the wholesaler has been stressed, evidence of radical change is lacking.

Finally, it may be that the traditional categories of retail stores—convenience, specialty, and shopping—are disappearing. The large "promotional department store" (discount house) might seem to be performing all these services, for example. On closer examination this is probably not so. Korvettes does sell food a la supermarket and appliances, but probably in different locations. These categories tell the marketing manager more precisely what services he can expect a certain type of middleman to render if he is included in the system. This information is obviously essential to any discussion of distribution system design, because these services will affect volume and cost and revenue.

STRATEGY OF CHANNEL SYSTEMS

Some qualitative criteria can help conceptualize the problem of choosing among different distribution systems in broad terms. In the quantitative analysis discussed in this section, qualitative criteria are used first to limit the numerous possible channels so the marketing manager can consider the alternatives in evaluating them. Three dimensions of channel strategy underlie these qualitative criteria. Maximum geographic coverage to reach as many ultimate customers as possible is one dimension. A second is maximum sales from the ultimate customers. A third is minimum cost to make profit results as favorable as possible.

Channels for industrial products

The logic of marketing channels stands out most clearly in the case of industrial products. Manufacturers of industrial products typically sell directly to the user. With machine tools such as drills, punch presses, and lathes, for example, the unit of sale has a high value, as compared with consumer products. Also, considerable information must be transmitted by the manufacturer to the user if the product is to perform most effec-

---

[14]Barger, *Distribution's Place in the American Economy,* especially pp. 28–36 and 65–79.

tively. The extreme instance is that of a custom-made machine, by definition one that is produced to meet a particular customer's requirements The buyer usually has some objectively measurable criteria of selection or product cues, such as volume of production, to apply in choosing between the machines of two manufacturers, and he must have information on these criteria for each of these machines. In addition, some criteria are qualitative and require more communicative effort by the manufacturer. Finally, since the manufacturer must service the product once it is in use, direct channels are encouraged. All of these characteristics tend to justify the seemingly high cost of direct selling when the manufacturer uses his own sales force to call on the ultimate customer.

As the number of buyers increases or the buyers are more dispersed geographically, the manufacturer is likely to use an intermediary, often a manufacturer's agent. Also, as the product becomes more standardized among buyers, its value becomes lower, and the information required becomes less technical, a wholesaler, called a "mill supply house," may be substituted for the manufacturer's agent. The major function, as you will recall, is simply to make the product available when it is needed.

Channels for consumer products

Because channels for consumer products are typically more indirect than for industrial products, the logic behind their design is more complex. Yet, some industrial products are distributed in a considerably more indirect manner than are some consumer products. Small manufacturers often buy certain minor component parts from the local hardware store which has been served by a wholesaler who, in turn, has received the items from a manufacturer's agent. Alternatively, there are direct channels among consumer products. Avon sells cosmetics directly, and Fuller sells brushes in the same way. In small towns, milk often goes directly from the producer (farmer) to the consumer.

QUALITATIVE CRITERIA. Company practice, supplemented by logic and a limited amount of fundamental research, suggests that the following are some of the qualitative criteria—dimensions of channel strategy for selecting the channels for consumer goods:

1. Nature of the commodity.
    a) Perishability-durability.
    b) Magnitude of unit value.
    c) Necessity-luxury. [15]
    d) Consumer habits with respect to place of purchase.

---

[15]The "necessity-luxury" criterion is ambiguous. It has been suggested that a good definition for a luxury is something that some people think others should do without. The criterion is an attempt, however, to incorporate some of the self-concept aspects of consumer attitudes, and it is related to such things as prestige.

2. Structure of manufacturing.
   a) Degree of concentration.
   b) Location of production in relation to user demand.
   c) Width of product line.
3. Structure of retailing.
   a) Number of stores selling mainly this product.
   b) Location of stores in relation to manufacturers and consumers.

The four aspects of the nature of the commodity make considerable difference in the nature of the channel. Perishability is a condition encouraging a direct channel between producer and consumer. Milk is an example. Admittedly a product at the other extreme of the perishability-durability continuum tends to have fluctuating sales, which also encourages direct channels because fluctuations in consumer demand become intensified the further they are transmitted back toward the manufacturer. Yet, this is not nearly so strong a force.

Higher value products tend to directness because they require greater promotional effort to inform the buyer adequately whether the product meets his needs. The source of this tendency to use greater promotional effort is that consumers will be sensitive to information about a product and even search ("shop") for a product of higher unit value, as we learned in Chapter 3.

In terms of the necessity-luxury continuum, necessities lend themselves to indirectness. Consider an example that illustrates the combination high-price–luxury characteristics versus low-price–necessity characteristics. The Parker Pen Company introduced a ballpoint pen called the "Jotter," designed for the mass market, which sold for $2.95, whereas other Parker pens ranged from $5.00 to $12.50. The "Jotter" was distributed through drug, tobacco, and similar wholesalers, but the more expensive Parker pens were distributed directly to retailers.

The character of consumer purchasing habits with respect to place of purchase also is significant. The question is whether the kind of store considered is one at which potential customers shop regularly or rarely visit. A paint company that attempted to distribute a new self-polishing floor wax through company-owned retail outlets failed because consumers tended to purchase floor wax in grocery outlets rather than making a special trip to a paint store.

The structure of the manufacturing level of the industry also exerts an influence upon the method of distribution. The larger the manufacturer—the more it is a concentrated industry—the more profitable it may be to absorb some of the distributive functions and thus bypass the wholesaler.

A second issue in relation to the structure of the manufacturing level is how manufacturing is geographically located in relation to consumer demand. The more widely dispersed the manufacturing level is geographically in relation to consumer demand, the greater the pressure to indirectness through the use of the wholesaler and even an agent. Products must be *collected* by the wholesaler from a larger area at the manufacturing level, which enhances his role in the distributive process. At the opposite extreme—the geographic concentration of production—the tendency is to direct selling, as illustrated by General Electric's location of its major appliance production at Louisville, Kentucky. As a result of this concentration, General Electric now ships directly to the retailer, since freight costs can be cut through mixed shipments. The wholesaler, however, continues the rest of his usual functions.

Another determining feature of the structure of manufacturing is the width of the product line—the wider the line, the greater the tendency to serve the retailer directly, because it is more convenient and economic for him to purchase from as few sources as possible. The manufacturer's personal-selling costs may also be reduced because the salesman can sell more on each sales call. The introduction of new machinery in the British cast-iron pipe manufacturing industry caused the manufacturers to specialize more, to concentrate on a more limited range of products. Thus, technological change encouraged a narrower product line, with a consequent increase in the use of wholesalers.

In the structure of retailing, one important element is the degree of concentration. For example, low concentration—the availability of a large number of retailers—favors using the retailer rather than bypassing him and going directly to the consumer. It is usually easier to use existing channels than to establish new ones.

Another structural feature at the retail level is the location of stores in relation to the consumers and the manufacturer. It is important because the retail locations must provide relatively greater convenience to the potential consumers than would be the case if they bought directly from the manufacturer.

In a study of 93 consumer products sold by independent retailers in Britain, it was found that the following characteristics existed when the manufacturer sold through a wholesaler: (1) unconcentrated manufacturing, (2) unbranded products, (3) large number of retail outlets handling the products, and (4) products of low unit value. Conversely, when the manufacturer sold directly to the retailer, the following characteristics existed: (1) concentrated manufacturing, (2) branded products requiring promotion, (3) fewer retailers, and (4) products of high unit value. [16]

One guide to selecting channels is the classification of products as convenience, shopping, or specialty, based on the amount of effort the con-

---

[16]James B. Jefferys, *The Distribution of Consumer Goods* (Cambridge, England: Cambridge University Press, 1950), pp. 49–52.

sumer-buyer will expend in purchasing the item. He devotes the least effort to convenience items, medium effort to specialty items, and the most effort to shopping items. The theory of buyer behavior incorporates this effect in that types of buying situations—RRB, LPS, and EPS—correspond to these categories. Thus we see retailing institutions being shaped by the nature of the consumer's thinking processes.

As a result of evaluating the dimensions of channel strategy, the manufacturer may decide upon one of two extreme alternatives: intensive or selective distribution. Intensive distribution means that the manufacturer will place his product in every available outlet; selective distribution implies that he will select from among the available outlets rather than using all of them. Although the extremes are seldom used, this way of examining the channel problem may help to clarify the issues in arriving at a stage where more quantitative analysis can be applied.

A third type of policy, called "exclusive distribution," arises when selective distribution is pushed to the extreme of having only one dealer for each geographic area. This middle-man usually agrees to the practice of exclusive dealing, that is, he agrees not to handle competing products. The major advantage of exclusive distribution to the manufacturer is the middleman's willingness to promote the product more intensely; he also may be more willing to carry a complete stock of the manufacturer's line and to provide repair service. The manufacturer's costs are reduced because his salesmen call on fewer accounts. From the middleman's view, exclusive distribution provides territorial protection, which means that competition from other middlemen selling the same brand will be less and he can reap the reward for investing in market-development expenditures. It is believed that the effect of "exclusive dealing" on competition may run counter to the Clayton Act. The effect upon competition can be illustrated by taking the extreme case—if a manufacturer has exclusive contracts with a large number of dealers, a competitor may find it difficult, if not impossible, to enter the market.

The marketing manager can obtain two important results by applying the qualitative criteria discussed above. First, many logical alternatives are found to be unfeasible and can be eliminated. In this way he is left with a manageable few to consider and evaluate quantitatively. Second, elements in the situation which are likely to affect cost and revenue in some way can be identified. It is these elements which must be measured —have numbers put on them—if quantitative analysis is to be applied to the problem of selecting channels.

PROFIT CRITERION IN SELECTING CHANNELS

There is still the task of selecting one basic system. Quantitative analysis involves the application of the profit criterion to the selection. This criterion requires bringing together quantitative estimates of sales volume and costs. The source of such estimates can be the manufacturer's own experience with this or related products, or it can be his competitor's experience.

Certain principles of system design can be helpful in formulating the basic channel system and in avoiding later mistakes. First, the system should provide for access to a given proportion of the market and for a given amount of promotion. The size of the middleman's margin required to obtain the necessary market coverage and promotion should be incorporated.

The problem of providing access to a given proportion of the market is illustrated by a company producing steam traps for industrial use. Management knew that its market was concentrated in the large cities. Since the company had a distributor in each of the large cities, it assumed that the company's market coverage was adequate. An analysis, however, indicated that distributors should be selected according to the industries they served as well as according to geographic area. One distributor in a large city had been selected because he served the mechanical industries, but the paper and chemical industries, each an important market in the same area, were not being served.

Second, the channel system should provide a "feedback" whereby the results of the model, once it is in operation, are explicitly transmitted back to the marketing manager so that he is in a position to evaluate the system's effectiveness rationally. He must know how well the system is operating. Are his sales going into dealer inventories or to the consumer? What is the quality of cooperation from members of the channel? Are conflicts among the channel members at different levels of the channel causing tensions?

The need for a feedback is suggested by the "Good Friday revolt" of Chrysler Corporation dealers in 1953. Representatives of Dodge dealers throughout the country peremptorily summoned top Chrysler officials to a Detroit hotel. They demanded that the price of cars be cut at once and that the dealers be permitted to send a representative to the next meeting of the Chrysler board. The confrontation was repeated in 1966.[17] Chevrolet encountered a similar situation two years later. The mechanics of feedback will be discussed subsequently in connection with evaluating channel performance.

Third, a system design should anticipate repercussions among channels —an undue incentive in one portion of the system may lead to dissatisfaction and tensions in another portion. This often occurs, for example, when a manufacturer is using both supermarkets and small grocery stores.

---

[17] *The New York Times*, October 16, 1966, p. F. 9.

The small stores usually require a higher markup to operate profitably, and the supermarkets, which sell a higher volume of the product, may resent this.

Finally, legal limitations may seriously impair the freedom to choose. The Robinson-Patman Act, for example, presents barriers to freedom of choice because it limits a manufacturer in discriminating among middlemen on either a price or a service basis. Brokerage fees are limited by law. Even though a buyer is relieving the seller of the brokerage function, he cannot be paid a brokerage allowance unless he is a bona fide broker. Also, the Clayton Act limits "exclusive dealing."

Long-run optimizing analysis

The channel system that emerges from applying these principles of channel design should be tested with the additional information implied in the long-run optimizing analysis that was illustrated in Table 12–7 above, which constitutes the final stage of fact finding and analysis. To choose quantitively among alternative distributions systems using the long-run optimizing analysis we must conceptualize the problem in a particular way. In Chapter 13 we saw how this is done for a new product, and we can proceed analogously with the choice among distribution systems.

A planning horizon estimate is required for each alternative system we are considering. System A may suggest a shorter time horizon than system B because if we take A we will have to change sooner than if we take B. System B, for example, could be less affected by technological change and so be expected to be more stable than A. Assume the horizon is 10 years.

With this time horizon estimate for A, we can refer to Table 12–7 to recall the facts we will need. Typically, a company expects to sell a certain volume of its products through its distribution system. This multiproduct aspect of the decision is a complication but does not change the principles of the analysis. To simplify, assume we will distribute only one product. In this 10-year horizon, we will assume that the current product will begin to be replaced by a new product beginning about the fifth year, and there will be an overlap of the two products between the fifth and seventh years where old A is retiring and new A is taking over. A revenue estimate year by year will be required for each product.

The cost estimate is somewhat more reliable, being an amalgam of various component costs. The analysis will appear similar to that implied in Table 12–7. Over and beyond the cost of producing the product and normal selling cost, however, we will have a heavy investment in the early years in salesman time devoted to gaining acceptance of the product in the middleman agencies making up system A. Unfortunately, we cannot depreciate this investment as we did the new product in Table 12–7 because the Internal Revenue Service does not recognize such marketing costs as an investment that affects future revenues. Thus, Column 5 would be irrelevant for this particular expenditure. Another cost element would be the margin that each level of middlemen would require. Incidentally, this level of margin might well have an effect on the price and therefore on the revenue side as well.

From a careful examination of cost and revenue elements, a table in the form of Table 12–8 is completed for each alternative system and a present value computed for each. Ordinarily the system with the highest present value is chosen, except where important elements cannot be justified and must be treated as constraints. These constraints must be balanced against the margin in present value offered by the "best" system.

Short-run analysis

Sometimes it may be logically sound to treat the channel choice as a short-term decision instead of as an investment. This short-term analysis is particularly likely to be appropriate when a channel can be dropped. No investment in negotiation, for example, may be necessary. Further, there are cases where the decision really should be viewed as long-term but the short-term analysis is appropriate as a first step. The procedure for carrying out a short-term channel analysis was illustrated in detail in Chapter 4 especially in Figures 4–4, 4–5, and 4–6 and Tables 4–4 and 4–5. For a more concrete understanding of what such an analysis entails, refer back to that example.

Negotiation

After a company management has accepted a channel system in all of its details, the problem of negotiation remains; it must be accepted by the middlemen making up the system. The economics of the middleman does not permit precisely informed judgments, and consequently there is opportunity for astute bargaining. In addition to the lack of information, conditions may vary among middlemen so that a standard arrangement may not be appropriate for all middlemen.

Negotiation is also complicated because the middleman's sales organization, as well as the middleman himself, must accept the plan. Friction in the channel system may develop from the device of a special bonus to the middleman's salesmen from the manufacturer. Although this bonus is effective from the manufacturer's short-term view, it may encounter the ill will of the middleman himself because it can distort the middleman's sales incentive system.

In the negotiating procedure between the manufacturer and the middleman, the manufacturer makes implied, and often explicit, commitments as to the gains for each middleman in the channel network. Lack of fulfillment of the middleman's expectations can be serious, and the commitments are difficult to retract. Therefore it is important that the original estimates of the system's operation be accurate.

PHYSICAL DISTRIBUTION

The channel system is a *marketing* function and has traditionally been viewed as a responsibility of the marketing operation. With the passage of time the strict communication aspects of marketing management have come more and more to be separated from the physical flow of the goods. One consequence is that it is now meaningful to define marketing in communication terms as we have done in this book. Another consequence is that the concept of the logistic system has emerged. The logistics concept incorporates the physical distribution system and more. It "includes the total flow of materials, from the acquisition of raw materials to the delivery of a finished product to the ultimate user. . . ."[18]

A number of forces encourage this shift of responsibility for physical distribution from marketing to some other department, variously labeled transportation, logistics, traffic, and so forth. One factor has probably been the rising cost of transportation as an element in the total cost of the product. Another has been the development of quantitative techniques such as inventory control and warehouse location, which apply just as well to physical input as to physical output. By combining the two, input and output, in one system, as implied by the logistics concept, greater savings can probably result. The computer is obviously essential to this type of "big systems" analysis.

Although the shift toward the logistics system concept is probably a definite trend, some companies still leave this responsibility to the marketing operation. The physical distribution system is interdependent with the other marketing functions. In fact, establishing a system of warehouses over the country is sometimes an alternative to using a wholesaler. If the manufacturer's own warehouses are not a feasible alternative to the wholesaler, the extent and nature of the network will usually make a difference in which particular middlemen he uses.

The causal relation can run in the other direction, however; the nature of the channel system in use can influence the manufacturer's decision as to the number, size, and location of his warehouses. In this way of looking at the problem, the spatial location of demand by middlemen is taken as given, and the warehouses are located in an optimal way with respect to this location of demand. If the manufacturer is selling direct to the user, as is common in industrial products, this approach, locating warehouses with respect to a given locational pattern of demand, is realistic. Further, warehouse size and locations can usually be changed with greater ease than relations can be severed with some middlemen and developed with others. For example, warehouses can be leased or rented, but to develop effective relations with good middlemen is a costly, time-consuming process.

---

[18]John F. Magee, *Physical Distribution Systems* (New York: McGraw-Hill Book Co., 1967), p. 2.

The optimizing rule for the warehouse location decision is: Determine the geographical pattern of warehouse locations which will be most profitable to the company by equating the incremental cost of warehouse operation with the transportation cost savings and incremental profits resulting from more rapid delivery. The application of this rule can be complex, in part because of the great number of possible locations. Also, the incremental profits from faster delivery to the customer are difficult to compute; in fact, many analyses of warehouse locations make the unrealistic assumption that sales are unaffected by the location. A way to estimate these profits from faster delivery is to have the executive estimate how much of a penalty in the form of air transportation, for example, he would be willing to pay if the alternative were not serving the customer. By making simplifications which are not seriously unrealistic, it is often possible to handle the problem mathematically with the aid of the computer.[19]

EVALUATING THE SYSTEM'S OPERATION

The dynamic nature of the marketing system requires fairly continuous evaluation of a company's system of distribution channels. The problem of evaluation varies among companies. It is a complicated by the fact that usually the channel system and the logistics system are being evaluated simultaneously. A company with only one type of middleman as its channel, say a retailer, is faced with a much simpler problem than one with a number of links in its distributive chain.

The requisite features of any evaluating device are a criterion of performance and a "feedback," a flow of information about the middleman's behavior in terms of this criterion. The automobile industry serves as a simple example because there is only one link in the chain, the retail dealer. The criterion of performance is the number of automobiles sold. Congressional hearings suggest that the criterion was actually more complicated because emphasis was sometimes placed upon selling certain items. Ideally, a dealer's contribution to the manufacturer's profit would be used as the criterion. There is also the problem of setting a standard or norm of the criterion—how many automobiles should dealer A be expected to sell? Prior to congressional hearings on the relations of General Motors with its dealers, General Motors used national averages in setting dealer norms. The dealers criticized this practice as being inequitable. Later, General Motors agreed to relate the norm to an estimate of the potential in the specific dealer's area.

Where there are a number of links in the distributive chain, another

---

[19]For specific warehouse location studies, see William J. Baumol and Philip Wolfe, "A Warehouse-Location Problem," *Operations Research*, 6 (1958): 252–63; and Alfred A. Kuehn and Michael J. Hamburger, "A Heuristic Program for Locating Warehouses," in Ronald Frank, Alfred Kuehn, and William Massy (eds.), *Quantitative Techniques in Marketing Analysis* (Homewood, Ill.: Richard D. Irwin, Inc., 1962), pp. 523–46.

type of feedback may be necessary. The retailers may be willing to prepare reports, but since the manufacturer may not have direct contact with the retailers, he cannot identify them in order to negotiate for the information. A watch company uses the warranty-card system. Consumer panels, retail audits and warehouse withdrawals, referred to in Chapter 7, can be useful, but they are costly.

The complex nature of the relations between the agencies making up the channel requires a more extensive kind of feedback than is typically used.

Attitudinal data expressing the dealer's feelings about the nature of his relations with the company may be necessary. The dealer-attitude survey can be used to provide this more complex information. The survey is probably useful in detecting latent tensions that may be developing in the distributive system. The A. B. Dick Company's experience illustrates this device.[20] A mail questionnaire, part of which is reproduced in Figure 14–2, was sent to the dealers to be completed and returned. It covered the

FIGURE 14–2
Dealer attitude survey

		AGREE	?	DISAGREE
73.	This company's representative seldom makes mistakes in transmitting my orders and requests to the company.	☐	☐	☐
74.	I think this company does all that can be expected to help a dealer manage his operation	☐	☐	☐
75.	This company has a fair policy on discounts	☐	☐	☐
76.	This company's representative is of little help to me in training my sales people when needed	☐	☐	☐
77.	This company's general policy hampers us in making adjustments with our customers	☐	☐	☐
78.	More often than not this company uses the wrong channels in advertising their merchandise	☐	☐	☐
79.	This company fails to do a good job of locating shipping points at strategic places	☐	☐	☐

Source: The Dealer Inventory, Form 755, The Industrial Relations Center, The University of Chicago, p. 4.

following areas: specific relations of the dealer with the company, administrative services to the dealer, company merchandise, sales promotion, product services, distribution system, pricing policies, credit policies, personal relations with the company representative, administrative ability of the company representative, and the technical competence of the company representative.

---

[20]This grew out of a joint research project between the Industrial Relations Center, The University of Chicago, and the A. B. Dick Company. Grateful acknowledgment for use of the material is made to Robert K. Burns, director, Industrial Relations Center.

Attitudinal information is a highly useful supplement to sales performance data because the manufacturer can more easily infer the reasons for current or future dealer performance from dealer attitudes than he can from such behavioral data as sales and inventory levels alone. The two types of information can best supplement each other, however.

SUMMARY

Marketing channel decisions are particularly important because they involve long-term commitments. Industrial products tend much more toward direct channels than do consumer products. New products often require a change in channels as they are accepted in the market. Even more importantly, channel choices are administrative decisions that strongly shape the maximum performance potential of the corporation. This is the potential for corporate strategy to achieve the company's objectives of growth and profit. Specifically, where the brand manager can support these goals through market penetration, the marketing manager can support them through new products and new markets. Channel choices can increase the potential for the marketing manager to utilize these two ways of serving corporate goals.

Qualitative and quantitative criteria for selecting marketing channels, when supported by market and cost research, can go far in imparting rationality to channel decisions. The long-run optimizing analysis is appropriate for this decision.

The manufacturer's network of warehouses is both a consideration in selecting channels and a separate problem for management. Mathematical programming is being used in solving this type of problem.

Change in the structure of distribution has been emphasized because change is taking place, and it brings the need for adjustment. From a company's view, since the change is often imperceptibly slow, the tensions may accumulate to considerable intensity before management is aware that it has a channel problem. An effective feedback is needed to provide data for evaluating performance and to detect the consequences of change as quickly as possible.

Economic welfare questions also are raised by change in the distribution system. To a large extent the changes are typical of those that underlie economic development everywhere, not only in the United States. This development improves the lot of the consumer but also raises new problems for him. These problems will be examined in the context of the U.S. experience in Chapter 16.

DISCUSSION QUESTIONS

1. Describe the variety of middlemen.
2. Change is an ever-present fact in most distribution systems and this change, often subtle though it is, must be recognized in both administering a given

set of channels and designing a new set. What types of changes seem to be illustrated in contrasting the rural general store and the modern supermarket?

3. Why should changes in population influence the management of existing channels or the design of new ones?
4. What do we mean by "exclusive distribution?"
5. Like managing the sales force, we must rely upon continual evaluation and feedback in managing a channel system. Describe how such a feedback operates and explain why we need it.

part V

The president's view: Strategic marketing

In the well-defined scope and growth direction that any corporation needs, objectives are an essential part. In addition, however, a corporate strategy is required. The objectives set the goals, and strategy shows the path to these goals. Strategy focuses upon the market and indicates how growth and profit objectives can be met, either through expansion or diversification.

In Part III the brand manager's role in furthering these objectives was shown to be market penetration. Part IV saw the marketing manager's role as being product development and market development—he is concerned with new products, the product line, and the search for new markets.

In Part V we will examine the president's role in furthering corporate strategy. Because he directly supports the marketing manager in his activities, he furthers corporate objectives. He also is concerned with diversification, which is more radical and risky than market expansion because it involves new products and new markets simultaneously.

We will also examine the president's administrative decisions. His control of R & D expenditures indirectly supports the marketing manager. He works to develop an organization that will be receptive to innovation—new products are a crucial example. Innovation in market research practices may come to be another. One area of administrative decision that is of growing importance is the president's relation to public policy. Except for Chapters 1 and 14, we have largely omitted this topic, in order to simplify the complex task of describing the new marketing technology and marketing's role in the corporate structure. Part VI will develop a rationale for public policy at length.

399

15

The president's role in strategic and administrative marketing

INTRODUCTION

THE PRESIDENT'S responsibilities that have to do with marketing are both internal and external. In performing his internal functions, he is less constrained than the marketing manager and, of course, much less constrained than the brand manager, as suggested by the controllable and uncontrollable conditions of his position set forth in Figure 15–1. Even these uncontrollables are sometimes flexible. While his internal responsibilities are more well known, the external responsibilities faced by the president of a consumer company are just as important, if not more so.

PRESIDENT'S INTERNAL ROLE

Introduction

The internal functions of the president in marketing depend partly upon the size of the company. In the smaller company he is sometimes the source of ideas for new products (as noted in Chapter 13) and thus can have a profound effect upon the marketing operation. In a large company, however, this probably seldom happens. The president's route of advancement will also make a difference. If he came up through marketing, he will pay more attention to it and have a much better grasp of the details.

Aside from these exceptions the president tends "to play the investment game" in marketing. To him the issue is not new brand A or product line X with all of its attendant strategy and planning. Marketing is another investment to be compared with any one of a great number of others the company might make. The marketing identity tends to be lost. In a large

FIGURE 15–1
President's controllable and uncontrollable conditions

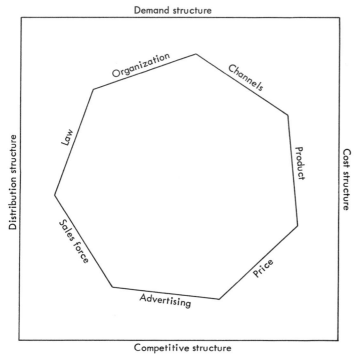

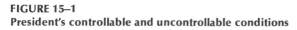

company this is inevitable. Like all humans, the president must simplify a complex world by ignoring small differences.

One implication of this simplifying process is that he may ignore the subtleties of marketing. We believe that this was common in many diversification moves in the past decade. These subtleties in part are due to the fact that marketing knowledge is intuitive and therefore difficult to transmit. When the president fails to recognize them, he may make judgments he would not make were he better informed. This places a heavier burden on the marketing manager, the divisional manager, and the chief corporate marketing executive to communicate the essential elements of the marketing proposal being transmitted for disposal at the president or board level.

One thing to bear in mind in attempting to understand the president is that he, too, is being evaluated. One of the most persistent and demanding criteria applied to him is the day-to-day quotation of his stock in the stock market. Financial analysts influence this by their judgments of his success in formulating and carrying out corporate strategy, which depends heavily on the marketing aspects of his company, as we have seen.

Marketing control function

The president both controls and decides, as do all managers. He controls largely through his response to proposals from below.

The brand manager's proposed marketing plan is sent "upstairs" for approval as a part of the company's total marketing plan, which in turn is a part of the company's operating plan. Out of this operating plan are developed the operating budgets to which all levels must conform and by which all levels are evaluated as a part of the company's financial control arrangements. Except for the unexpected, a particular brand manager's plan receives little individual attention. If it is a product that has had difficulty in the past or an especially important source of profits, it may.

The marketing manager's proposal for a new-product introduction is likely to receive the president's attention, especially because it involves a major long-term commitment of funds and sometimes the direction of company development as well. As a long-term commitment he will view it as a part of his major responsibility of "playing the investment game," of insuring that in *future* years there will be a number of ongoing profitable products from which he can meet the stockholders' demands for dividends. Hence, this new-product proposal will be compared, by means of long-term optimizing analysis, on growth and on profit with alternative uses of those funds to see which will best serve corporate objectives. The president will also want to assure himself that this new product is consistent with the corporate guidelines of directions of new development.

Strategic decisions

Strategic decisions are those that directly serve corporate strategy. As noted in Part IV, this can be accomplished through either expansion or diversification.

DIRECTION OF PRODUCT AND MARKET DEVELOPMENT. In achieving growth through expansion the *direction* of product and market development is crucial. The dominant responsibility of top management is to decide the *future* of a company, to insure that it will be able to meet tomorrow's goals tomorrow. One of the most critical determinants of the company's capacity to do this is whether it has decided what products and markets will enable it to develop so that it will be able to meet growth and profit requirements. This decision, which fixes the product-market environment, strongly conditions other aspects of the company and so sets many future priorities.

This setting of future constraints can be made clearer if it is illustrated with the concept of the industry life cycle. When an industry is first being developed, the companies in it are ordinarily concerned with *future* competitive strength and using newly available technology to establish new product lines. Later internal efficiency becomes the guiding objective, as we saw in the instant-coffee example of Chapter 2. Then the emphasis is upon developing an effective and efficient business organization. This example also demonstrated that as efficiencies were obtained, brands became more alike, resulting in strong competitive interactions that tended to drive the price down. Thus attention becomes focused upon maintaining and even enhancing a strong position vis-à-vis competitors.

Finally, as the industry approaches maturity (as also illustrated in the instant-coffee market), even near-term profit potential becomes dimmed. Additional marketing expenditures to expand share are likely to come out of profits because they will be met by competitors. If there are no new technological breakthroughs on the horizon, the companies will settle for and be satisfied with getting only their share of the industry's growth, but they will attempt to be flexible to meet any unexpected profit opportunities that may come about through the bad judgment or lack of skill of their competitors.

Thus we see that today procedures and directions must be developed which will encourage product innovation efforts tomorrow, which will in turn yield growth and high profits the day after tomorrow.

DIVERSIFICATION. Diversification involves new markets and new products simultaneously. As seen in Figure 15–2, it can occur in either of four forms: horizontal, vertical, concentric or conglomerate. Horizontal diversification consists of moves within the same economic environment. Vertical diversification is forward integration. Concentric diversification has some common thread with the company, either through marketing or

FIGURE 15–2
Diversification alternatives

	New products	
Products \ Customers	Related technology	Unrelated technology
Same type	Horizontal diversification	
Firm its own customer	Vertical integration	
Similar type	(1)*	(2)*
New type	(3)* *Concentric diversification*	Conglomerate diversification

(New missions)

°(1) Marketing and technology related
°(2) Marketing related
°(3) Technology related
Source: H. Igor Ansoff, *Corporate Strategy*, (New York: McGraw-Hill Book Co.), p. 132.

technology or both. Conglomerate diversification has no such common thread.

This common-thread concept was developed in Part IV as essential for communicating to the financial market a sense of optimism about the success of the move. When the president is contemplating diversification, the chief corporate marketing executive should be able to advise him on the extent to which such a common thread is achieved through marketing. This executive should also advise him on the marketing aspects of conglomerate diversification, calling on the wealth of experience represented by his marketing managers.

Marketing's role here is less obvious than it is in product and market development. There is evidence that some of the serious mistakes due to the wave of diversification in the decade of the sixties that came to light in the 1970–71 recession were caused by inattention to the marketing side. Corporate write-offs in 1971 and 1972 were exceedingly high; RCA led the list with $490,000,000. The exact extent to which the failure to seek and utilize internal marketing advice and skill accounted for these mistakes is not clear. But we have no doubt that systematic studies of the diversification mistakes of the sixties will show that a prime cause was a lack of marketing skill applied at the proper time to the analysis.

Administrative decisions

Administrative decisions are concerned with structuring the company's resources in a way which creates maximum performance *potential*. The president makes a great variety of administrative decisions. Three that are particularly pertinent to marketing and often crucial to the future of the company are concerned with R & D, organizational matters, and relating internal policy to public policy.

RESEARCH AND DEVELOPMENT. Scientific research underlies much product development. The decision of how *much* to invest in research and the *direction* in which these funds will be expended is central to serving a corporate strategy which will achieve growth and profit objectives. The role of new products as a source of growth is obvious, and their contribution as a source of profits was spelled out in the beginning of Chapter 13. Obviously, there is a substantial lag in time and space between a research expenditure and a resulting new product that is successful in the market. It makes considerable difference whether the research is directed toward invention—the process of bringing *new technology* into being—or toward innovation—the process of bringing an invention into use. The larger proportion of American company research expenditures is directed to innovation. These costs are somewhat easier to plan than technology-creating costs because their outcome is more predictable. Nevertheless, even they are highly uncertain.

The results of these expenditures lower down in the company hierarchy are as follows:

... the innovative work of a corporation consists in converting uncertainty to risk. This work begins with more information than can be handled and operates on this information at lower levels in the corporation, until clear alternatives of action, together with their probable benefits and risks, can be defined. At this point management can play the investment game—that is, the game of deciding where to put one's bets. The game requires analysis of investment alternatives, estimating markets, costs and technical feasibility, and making investment decisions. The game is played with competitive corporations as opponents. The rewards and punishments of the game can be measured in dollars.[1]

Some of the analytical decision tools that can be helpful where uncertainty is converted to risk in carrying out these decisions were described in Chapter 12.

ORGANIZATIONAL DECISIONS. Organizational changes are almost always approved by the top level and may even be initiated there. Not only does organizational change involve change in "who reports to whom," but factors like changes in goal structure and channels of communications inevitably follow as a consequence.

The effective company organization is a subtle, delicately balanced system of interacting parts, and coordination is the most essential aspect, as discussed in Chapter 5. Coordination often occurs through informal cross-departmental channels that no one but the two people involved knows about. Reorganization can break this link and the consequences of it can then be quickly observed, but the sources are difficult to identify. Presidents are only too well aware of these subtleties, and for this reason reorganizations are typically avoided as long as possible and then decided only at the top level.

In order to be more specific and to simplify, the discussion will be in terms of the packaged-goods, divisionalized type of company instead of a more complex and subtler industrial company such as the metal producer described in Chapter 5.

To determine the principles by which such decisions can be made, we will briefly review and add to some of the points from Chapter 5. The incessant drive for efficiency which a president must pursue leads to greater specialization of labor, which in turn increases the need for coordination. This specialization can take either of two directions, functional or product. Within the marketing operation, for example, one can become a specialist in marketing all of the company's products or a specialist in the production and marketing of a given product.

The specialization approach uses the principle of *differentiation*.

---

[1] D. A. Schon, *Technology and Change* (New York: Delacorte Press, 1967), p. 25.

Groups in the organization become more and more differentiated in terms of the jobs they do, and usually in terms of their formal training for the job. As mentioned in Chapter 5, each group tends to have its own peculiar manner of expression (jargon) and body of principles and techniques. Not obvious but crucial is the fact that each of these groups tends to identify and define problems in its own unique way. What the company responds to in the way of changes in its environment and what it does not respond to are strongly determined by what problem is identified and the particular way in which it is conceptualized. Thus, the specialization that flows from the principle of differentiation can have strong strategic implications.

The alternative and antagonistic *principle integration*, which suggests that the goal of organizing is to achieve a well-integrated organization which facilitates communication.

The amount of communication needed in a company depends upon the dynamism of the company's environment, especially its product market. A dynamic product requires much more communication than does a stable one. This discourages the use of the differentiation principle, and so we have emphasized the integration principle in one key aspect, namely, the development of the *brand manager concept*. He is in large measure an *integrator*. He is merely an example, however, and by no means solves all marketing integration problems.

The key point is that the two principles of differentiation and integration provide useful guides in organization decisions. One of the major decisions the president may have to contend with in the near future in many companies is the extent to which he will decentralize marketing decision making. Will he use a differentiation or integration principle if he decides to decentralize? As discussed in Part III, cost data by brand are now available, and response curves for many products probably will be. This opens up the possibility that quite low-level people—the brand manager, for example—can use maximum profit as a goal. It can avoid the constant battle over profit between higher management and brand managers. In current practice, there is often an inconsistency. Higher management wants more profit from the brand manager but, in fact, he is rewarded by volume because it is a simpler criterion to use, as we discussed at the end of Chapter 7.

Establishing policies that will insure innovation is another area of great importance. The exceedingly difficult organization problem of product innovation was developed in Chapter 12. As we saw there, the president's role was paramount in determining how successfully this can be carried out. Organizing by the principle of differentiation will, of course, inhibit innovation. It is essential that innovation be successful, because, as we have seen, financial analysts are more and more evaluating a company by how many promising new products it has "in the pipeline," its track record in product innovation, and its willingness to drop unprofitable products.

Another area of coming innovation is probably market research, which represents organizing by the principle of differentiation. Chapter 8 emphasized the potential for better market research, but little of this potential is being tapped in practice. As was noted there, for the first time top management is beginning to ask questions about how market research efforts should be evaluated. In time this high-level interest is sure to lead to greater attempts at innovation in market research. Perhaps the problem is in part, at least, as suggested in Chapter 8: Higher management will not accept the evidence from the new techniques because it doesn't understand them. Perhaps, too, there are basic flaws in market research techniques. We may not have considered the psychology of the decision maker and recognized that his problem differs depending upon whether he is in RRB, LPS, or EPS. Several important questions remain to be answered before we can condemn managers at any level.

Finally, consumerism has already forced some changes in corporate organization, and more will probably come. A brand manager, for example, is not rewarded for dealing with consumer complaints. Further, he probably could not handle them if he were, because the problem often lies with production, for example. In other words, we have not carried the integration principle of organization far enough to achieve a desirable accommodation with the consumer's needs. New organizational ways will have to be developed to meet the consumer challenge. Some device of direct communication from the market to top management may be necessary. Some of the consumer-durable companies, especially the auto companies, have been trying the concept of a "hot line"; a telephone number is made available in Chicago, for example, and it is publicized there that any consumer with a complaint can telephone free direct to a unit of the company in Detroit which reports directly to the president.

Relation to public policy

The legal environment of a company, especially in the marketing operation, is often unclear due to the ambiguity of the law and the level of stringency of enforcement. These two conditions leave the president with substantial latitude as to how the company will respond. He must weigh the company's interest, short term and long term, against his own ethical standards in coming to a decision.

. . . . business functions by public consent, and its basic purpose is to serve constructively the needs of society—to the satisfaction of society. . . . Today it is clear that the terms of the contract between business and society are, in fact, changing in important and substantial ways. Business is being asked to assume broader resonsibilities to society than ever before, and to serve a wider range of human values. . . . Inasmuch as business exists to serve society, its future will depend upon the quality of management's response to the changing expectations of the public.[2]

One of industry's statesmen in the marketing area has been C. W. Cook, Jr., chairman of General Foods Corporation. Over an extended period he has devoted considerable effort to leading his industry to accept principles similar to those above.

Another administrative decision the president must make is to what extent he will attempt to change the law, and how he will do so. This is, of course, a part of his external role.

PRESIDENT'S EXTERNAL ROLE

Introduction

The American manager was shaken by the "electrical conspiracy" in which seven highly respected top executives were committed to jail as common criminals. For him the law has acquired a stark personal significance. He can no longer depend upon corporate anonymity to relieve him personally of public condemnation for professional decisions.[3] Still more recently, executives have been jailed for disseminating untruthful advertising.[4] Not all public policy is so drastic, however.

The purpose of this section is to describe the sources of public policy and to introduce a discussion of its content.

Sources and agencies of public policy

Public policy is actually a diffuse complex of limitations emanating from several political units. The federal and state governments are the most important, but occasionally, local laws (those of counties and municipalities) are also encountered. There are different kinds of law at each political level: (1) statutory law, which is legislation; (2) common law, which is the result of court decisions over a long period of time without legislative-policy guides; and (3) administrative law, which is administered by agencies such as the Federal Trade Commission. Various enforcement agencies exist; the Federal Trade Commission and the Antitrust Division of the Justice Department are the major agencies at the federal level. The law is also subject to change.

The precise implications of the law for marketing decisions may be exceedingly difficult to predict, and this uncertainty has led to charges of vagueness. To help meet this objection, the Federal Trade Commission set up "trade practice conferences" to collaborate with industries in formulating lists of practices that will be considered unfair competition

---

[2]Quoted from statement of the Committee on Economic Development, "Social Responsibilities of Business Corporations," by *Business Week*, July 3, 1971, p. 72.

[3]For a thoughtful evaluation by a knowledgeable former executive, see Leland Hazard, "Are Big Businessmen Crooks?" *Atlantic Monthly*, 208 (1961); 57–61.

[4]*Advertising Age*, July 13, 1970, pp. 1 and 99.

industrywide. In these conferences the Commission is concerned with practices that are unfair between competing sellers as well as between sellers and buyers. As an example of the latter, in drawing up rules for the radio-television manufacturing industry, the Commission stated that the word "used" must be placed on the glass container portion that is sometimes reused in making picture tubes. The conferences, which are usually originated by the industry, give rise to "trade-practice rules." These are of two kinds: those that seek to define practices that are illegal in terms of the particular industry, and those that seek to define permissible practices, which in the industry are often termed a "code of ethics."

The following discussion on how the law affects marketing decisions is definitely not intended as a substitute for competent legal counsel. It is offered to convey to the marketing executive a general idea of how his area of maneuver is affected by the legal framework within which he makes decisions. The issues are too complicated and subject to change for the marketing executive to hope to keep abreast of the developments. An attorney's services are also essential in appraising the possibility of enforcement, since one of the major determinants of the significance of a law is the extent to which it is enforced.

Content of public policy

The content of public policy is complex, and a grasp of the details is necessary in order to appreciate its significance. It exerts a pervasive effect upon decision. Since the political and economic aspects of policy are so inextricably bound together in American thinking, we will handle the political with the economic. The economic will be further divided according to the two basic assumptions of an economy based upon a philosophy of economic liberalism: consumer sovereignty and competition. Sociological aspects will be handled under the label of "aesthetics" in the section on professionalization.

CONSUMER SOVEREIGNTY

This body of public policy has mainly to do with the quantity and quality of the information the buyer receives.

Quality

Two features of the law may influence quality decisions: minimum standards of quality of the product itself, and information about that quality. The Federal Food, Drug and Cosmetic Act (1938), an extension of an earlier act, illustrates the first feature by prohibiting the adulteration and sale of food, drugs, and cosmetics harmful to public health. Also, state and local laws apply to the quality of specific products, one of the most common being milk.

The Wool Products Labeling Act of 1939 is an example of the second feature. It requires that articles of clothing or wearing apparel, blankets, and household textiles, made in whole or in part of wool, be labeled so as to disclose the percentage of wool in the fabric as well as the type of wool used. Another example is the Fur Products Labeling Act (1951). The Federal Trade Commission proceeded vigorously against many different forms of misbranding after this area of the law was strengthened by a Supreme Court decision in 1934. Related to misbranding is the information about product quality conveyed by advertising.

In the sixties there were growing complaints about the proliferation of the variety of products, especially their packaging, which allegedly made it difficult for the consumer to choose among brands adequately. Many related issues also surfaced, such as "slack filled" packages. In response to these complaints the Fair Labeling and Packaging Act was passed in 1966. Its major provision was that sellers of packaged items would voluntarily review their product lines and attempt to reduce the number of items by standardizing packages and, if possible, standardizing across competitors as well. Further, the Department of Commerce was directed to report back to the Congress within a year upon the success of the voluntary program. The clear implication was that if the voluntary legislation did not succeed, a mandatory act would be passed. Considerable progress has been made in reducing the number of package sizes, and the Department of Commerce is continuing to monitor the program. A companion piece, the "truth-in-lending bill" was passed later.

Truthfulness

The Federal Trade Commission, first under its original legislation and later under the Wheeler-Lea Amendment (1938), is charged with preventing unfair methods of competition. One of these is false advertising. From its experience, the Federal Trade Commission has formulated standards of acceptability. An example is the category of "permissible puffery," advertising that is not quite truthful but not untruthful enough to be illegal. It is the capacity to deceive rather than actual deception that matters. In a case concerning Chesterfield's advertising, the Commission ruled that Chesterfield's use of "cooler" is puffing, but that "milder," "soothing," and "no unpleasant aftertaste" are illegal. This example illustrates the complex nature of the problem.

Recently, the Federal Trade Commission has begun to require that a company be able to substantiate its advertising claims. It is having profound effects upon advertiser's thinking, and the future suggests even more consequences.

The Commission's new concern with ad substantiation will be effectively complemented by its vigorous efforts, increasingly in the future, to ensure that advertising performs its intended function in the market place, the function of conveying product information in a way that promotes competition among sellers and rational purchasing patterns by the consuming public.[5]

The Fair Labelling and Packaging Act of 1966 also strengthened the limitations upon truthfulness of advertising.

Truthfulness has also been called into question in personal selling. The Federal Trade Commission brought action against U.S. Industries because the salesmen of its distributors were disparaging competitors' products. U.S. Industries was said to be responsible because it provided the brochures used by the salesmen, and the salesmen gave the impression that they were representing U.S. Industries rather than their distributor-employers.

Satisfaction with purchase

What direct recourse does the consumer have when he has bought a product which advertising, salesmen, or any other form of communication told him is better than he in fact finds it to be? In principle, the law of contract gives the consumer adequate protection. Apparently the consumer has been endowed with rather sweeping powers:

Whenever a salesman (or any company communication) makes more than a plainly trivial mistake in describing the merchandise, the customer is entitled to his money back, even if the salesman's error was unintentional. It doesn't make any difference whether the falsity originated with the seller or was simply passed on by him from the manufacturer. Nor does it matter that the customer could easily have investigated and learned the truth. The buyer is entitled to his refund, though he must be prepared to return the merchandise. Further, if the product carries a *warranty* as defined by the Uniform Commercial Code, he may keep the merchandise and obtain from the merchant an amount of money representing the difference between what he got and what he was promised.[6]

In practice, the situation is far less favorable to the consumer. For fear of social criticism he may be unwilling to question the quality of the low-priced items that frequent the supermarket. If he is thick-skinned enough to question, the retailer may refuse to provide restitution.

Should that be the case, the supposed alternative is appeal to the courts. Here he encounters a block, which is financial. The cost of a court suit has been estimated on the average at $1,000. Further, in most states, the consumer pays his own lawyer if he wins, and both his and his merchant's lawyer if he loses. Finally, the problem of recourse is still more complicated if it is a credit sale. If the note is sold to a third party, for example, "the note becomes an almost unassailable instrument for the collection of the money—regardless of the seller's deception or the condi-

---

[5]Robert Skitol, "What Is an Adequate Substantiation?" A.A.A.A. Eastern Annual Conference, June 5, 1972.

[6]Philip G. Schrag, "Consumer Rights," *Columbia Forum XIII* (1970), p. 5.

tion of the product sold by the . . . store."[7] Thus the consumer's protection can be severely limited.

Bait advertising

A number of states have enacted laws that prohibit advertising a false offer that is merely intended to attract the buyer's interest—bait advertising—and other states are contemplating similar action. The nature of the practice is illustrated by the first conviction under the New York law. A sewing machine distributor advertised machines at $29.75, but when the machine was brought to the home for demonstration, it would not work or would break down during the demonstration. The salesman, after telling the prospective customer that the machine was inferior, would then attempt to sell a machine priced at $175 to $300. At the federal level, the Federal Trade Commission has also acted against the practice.

COMPETITION

Because of the much greater amount of legislation intended to affect competition, our discussion of it is arranged by type of marketing decision, with the exception of share of market.

Share of market

In Chapter 2, essentially three ways of viewing competition were noted. First, the *performance* of an industry or company can be examined. Second, the competitive *behavior* of that industry, which consists of the "practices," can be investigated. Finally, the *structure* of competition can be the point of focus. In this third method of viewing competition, one of the key dimensions is the size distribution of the competing companies, which can be measured by share of market.

Share of market is often accepted by the antitrust enforcement agencies as evidence of monopolistic power, since the Sherman Act prohibits the attempt to monopolize or the act of monopolizing. After adducing from a large share of market that "monopoly" exists, the agencies will then proceed to prohibit certain practices—practices that would have been acceptable if the share of the market had not been excessive. Breaking up the company—divestiture—is an alternative course of action, and a classic case is shaping up with IBM.

Usually the share-of-market criterion is applied to the single large company. Another classic of antitrust law is the Alcoa case, the action against the Aluminum Company of America, which, in the court's interpretation, had a 90 percent share of the market. The criterion may also be applied to a collusive arrangement. In 1951, three coat-hanger manufacturers were each fined $10,000 for antitrust violations. It was charged that the three

---

[7] Ibid., p. 7.

companies had 65 percent of the market east of Colorado. As a consequence of the antitrust action the companies agreed not to follow certain practices, such as fixing prices low enough to drive competitors out of business.

An "acceptable" share has never been definitely established but has varied from case to case. A share of 80–90 percent of the virgin aluminum ingot market was unacceptable in the Alcoa case, but United States Steel Company's share of 48.5 percent of their market was acceptable. The Eastman Kodak Company, which had 90 percent of the color-film market, agreed to reduce its share of color-film processing to 50 percent. More recently, in the Brown Shoe Company merger case, market shares were estimated city by city; for example, in 118 cities the combined shares of the merged companies (Brown and Kinney) exceeded 5 percent in one type of shoe, e.g., children's or women's. The companies had integrated forward to the retail level. The Court said that the fragmented nature of retailing caused this 5 percent to be undesirable.

Defining market share can indeed be a complicated procedure. The more loosely the term "product" is defined, the smaller is a given company's market share. It must also be determined what the geographic area to be included in defining the market is, and whether imports should be included. The Supreme Court has found that the "Geographic market selected for determining whether merger is within Clayton Act proscription must correspond to commercial realities of the industry and be economically significant, and while geographic market in some instances may encompass an entire nation, under other circumstances, it may be single metropolitan area."[8] There are other ambiguities, such as in the Alcoa case, where the court included "recovered" ingot aluminum in computing Alcoa's share. Among consumers the nonmetric scaling technique described in Chapter 2 could be used to identify the industry in terms of the product-class construct of Chapter 3.

The consequences for the marketing executive of the share-of-market criterion of illegality is shown in a series of decisions by one of the largest meat-packing companies. The company had 30 percent of the market for one of its products, with a trend toward an increasing share. Fear of prosecution caused the company to increase the price of the product, cut the advertising budget, and begin producing the product for other companies to sell under their brand names. Safeway Stores was alleged to have the policy of achieving only 25 percent of any local retail grocery market, since 50 percent is considered "politically unwise." Some companies wishing to expand have been motivated by the fear of antitrust prosecution to diversify rather than increase the sales of their existing products. Probably much more important, however, is that some marketing prac-

---

[8] 82 S. Ct. 1502 (1962), p. 1506.

tices that would ordinarily be interpreted as acceptable are suspected when carried out by a company with a large market share. "Refusal to sell," for example, might then be interpreted as a device to monopolize the market. In general, the larger the share, the more susceptible the company is to criticism from the antitrust agencies.

Product decisions

Legal limitations are likely to impinge in essentially two areas of product decision other than product quality: the design of the product and additions to the product line.

PRODUCT DESIGN. Much of our law pertaining to competition is designed not to protect the consumer but to preserve competition by protecting one competitor from another, and so limiting the emergence of monopoly that results when one competitor drives another out of business. In designing a product similar to one sold by its competitors, a company is limited by the trademark, patent, and copyright laws. The term "similar" is used here as it is viewed by the consumer, and it is more broadly defined than "style." Although trademarks are only an identifying mark on a product, such as a brand name, they are important. They provide protection for a brand name by limiting competitors' freedom to use it. A long series of court cases has been brought by the Coca-Cola Company trying to protect its trademarks from duplication by competitors. There is always the possibility that if a company does not take legal action against users of its brand name, the name will become identified with the generic product. When this happens the company will not be supported by the courts in later attempts to prevent others from using its brand name; "frigidaire," for example, could come to be applied to all refrigerators.

Since copyright laws relate to literary and artistic works, the burden of protecting the rights of products which concern marketing executives falls mainly upon the patent laws. The action of patent laws is illustrated in a legal decision which forbids copying the design or outward appearance of an established "prestige" product, even if there is no attempt to represent the copy as the original. The case arose when a company produced a much cheaper electrically powered clock similar to Longines-Wittnauer's Atmos model, which was powered by changes in atmospheric temperatures and retailed at $175.

The law is by no means effective in an absolute sense. It does not prevent, for example, "style piracy" in the women's apparel industry, where design is an important marketing tool. Although creators often patent their designs, it is said that patents have serious limitations because the season is over by the time the patent is issued. As a protective measure, a number of years ago the Fashion Originators Guild of America, "a group of leading New York creators," developed a scheme of inducing retailers not to buy unauthorized copies of original styles. If a store broke its pledge, it was "red carded," which meant that manufacturers were directed not to supply this retailer. The plan was effective in preventing style piracy, but the Supreme Court invalidated it because of its collusive nature.

Style piracy was prevented, however, in a case in the furniture industry through a suit brought by Bruswick-Balke-Collender Company against the Kuehne Manufacturing Company. The former designed some school furniture, and upon acquiring orders in excess of its own productive capacities, presented the blueprint of the design to Kuehne as a potential subcontractor. Kuehne refused, but three months later it issued a catalog that included the design.

The significance of the law in new-product decisions is illustrated in the procedure followed by the Illinois Tool Works of Chicago. An executive reports that both the company's patent attorney and outside patent counsel are represented at the monthly meetings of a committee that passes upon new-product projects and reviews progress in research and development.

PRODUCT LINE.   The growing importance of product-line decisions and the expanding volume of law limiting these decisions have developed simultaneously. The interest of the law is prompted by the possible effect of product-line decisions on competition. A new product may be added to the line either through market development or through the purchase of a company with an established product, which is horizontal diversification. Antimerger legislation (The Celler Antimerger Act) enacted in 1950 limits the latter course; prior to that time a company was free to expand through the purchase of another company's assets, unless it violated the Sherman Act. Under the Sherman Act, the acquisition of another company's assets might have been accepted as evidence of *intent* to monopolize. Clearly expansion by the purchase of stock could be questioned. Also, under the earlier legislation, the company could be charged with the attempt to monopolize only if it had already expanded through asset purchase or otherwise. Under the Antimerger Act, however, legal action can be taken against the company either before or after the acquisition, and the process of finding a violation became much simpler than proving "monopoly" under the old legislation. It is said that the purpose of the Celler Antimerger Act is to prevent monopoly rather than to deal with it after it has arisen.

There is not yet enough experience with the Celler Antimerger Act to indicate clearly its general impact or even to set forth sharply defined criteria. From 1951 to 1959 only one in seven acquisitions by the largest 199 companies were challenged. The wording of the statute suggests that whether a merger is illegal will depend upon the effect of the merger on the share of market. In the Brown Shoe Company case the court stated, "The market share which companies may control by merging is one of the most important factors to be considered when determining the probable effects of the combination or effective competition in the relevant market."[9]

In evaluating the effect of the Celler Antimerger Act upon product-line decisions, one of the major questions is how "industry" will be defined in computing share of market. For example, if the industry is defined rigorously so that it includes only identical products, then the act would not affect product-line decisions at all—the merger would merely be adding to the capacity to produce the same product and thus would not influence the product-line decision. Past experience suggests, however, that the industry may be defined more loosely, so that the act can be used to prevent "an addition to product line." If enforcement should take the extreme point of view and be concerned with "conglomerate bigness" rather than "share of market" or the extent of vertical integration, the act could be quite significant. In the Brown Shoe case, "shoes" seemed to be considered the relevant market, although data were discussed which distinguished, for example, between children's and women's shoes.

Under certain circumstances, *tying contracts* are prohibited, which can serve to limit the product line. A tying contract is one whereby the buyer must agree to take some of one product from a seller in order to obtain another product from that seller. An example is the Kodak color-film case mentioned above, in which the consequence of the firm's film-processing arrangement was to force the buyer to take a service he might not otherwise buy from Kodak. Tying contracts enable the seller to dispose of products that might not be easy to sell without such a requirement.

Another limitation on product-line decisions is the Robinson-Patman Act. Because it probably prevents cumulative discounts, which may remove one of the advantages of a wide product line, this act tends to limit the width of the line. Cumulative discounts are based on the total purchases of all the sellers' products for a given period, often a year. For example, a large buyer might receive a discount according to the size of his total annual purchases, even though his purchases included every item in the seller's product line.

Price decisions

Public policy impinges on three major areas of price decisions: horizontal price agreements, price discrimination, and sales below cost.

HORIZONTAL PRICE AGREEMENTS. When price agreement exists among competitors at the same level in the structure of distribution, this is referred to as horizontal price agreement. In contrast to horizontal agreements are the vertical agreements which exist among the different links of the production-distribution process, from raw material to the consumer. Expressed agreements of the horizontal type of either the *level of*

---

[9]82 S. Ct. 1502 (1962), p. 1534.

price or the *methods of setting price* that will result in a similar price among competitors are uniformly illegal under federal and some state laws, with two exceptions. The offense is labeled "price fixing."

The first exception to illegal expressed horizontal price agreements occurs when the price agreements are carried out under the supervision of a governmental agency, as illustrated in the large local milk markets where the federal government supervises pricing at the producer level. The second exception to price fixing occurs when producers of agricultural products make horizontal price agreements, as provided under the Capper-Volstead Act. The Florida Citrus Mutual, a fruit-marketing cooperative, was charged by the Federal Trade Commission with illegally attempting to fix the resale prices of citrus fruit shippers and processors. If the association had confined its membership to growers only, the Capper-Volstead Act would have protected it from prosecution. It accepted handlers, shippers, and processors as members, however.

Agreement as to price alone is not always effective in supporting an industry price at a higher level than it would be without the agreement. For example, if A and B have an agreement not to cut price, A is often unsure whether B is abiding by the agreement. Also, B may be taking sales from A by advertising or some other nonprice competitive tool, so that A feels he must cut his price in order to maintain his market share. Therefore, a horizontal price agreement is frequently supported by agreement on other competitive dimensions. One of the most effective is "market-sharing" arrangements where competitors parcel out the various markets, usually on a geographic basis, and then agree not to sell in areas assigned to competitors. This arrangement was called "effective collusion" in Chapter 2. In 1952 Liquid Carbonic Corporation and four other manufacturers of carbon dioxide agreed in a consent decree to discontinue "allocation of territories."

There are other dimensions of competition in which uniformity of behavior among competitors has been questioned when used in connection with price agreements: credit terms, advertising allowances, allowances for return of containers, guarantees against price declines, and trade-in allowances for used products.

Note carefully that this conclusion of illegality applies to expressed agreements that can be proved by direct or circumstantial evidence. The public-policy objection to expressed agreements is that they result in similar prices among competitors, so that price is eliminated as a competitive device in obtaining sales. Antitrust enforcement may encounter difficulty on this point, however, because the consequences of expressed agreements can conceivably occur even though such agreements do not exist. A company usually cannot permit its competitors to continue charging a lower price, or it will lose customers to them. It must comply immediately with whatever competitors do in their pricing. When a *few* companies are selling in the market, either one or both of two socially undesirable effects may occur in the industry: (1) prices can be excessively high, or (2) they may be inflexible rather than changing to conform to new conditions of supply and demand. The possibility of this kind of competitive behavior occurring through an effective price leader was suggested in Chapter 2. Thus even in the absence of an expressed agreement, unfavorable social consequences can occur, although industry studies suggest that typically they do not.

The doctrine of "consciously parallel action" has been proposed to meet this dilemma of the consequences ascribed to expressed agreements occurring even though the agreements do not exist. The doctrine states that the mere fact that companies behave the same way is not sufficient evidence of illegality. Parallel behavior is only a necessary condition. Another necessary condition is that the market results must be noncompetitive, which is interpreted to mean that the industry or company performance is socially unfavorable. The application of the doctrine of consciously parallel action was illustrated in the Cement Institute case of 1948, where price inflexibility over a long period in a changing economic sense was accepted as evidence of noncompetitive market adjustment. So far the doctrine has had only limited application.

Another development relating to horizontal price agreements gave a new twist to the law. A company may be charged with "conspiring" with its subsidiaries if they compete with each other. In late 1952, the F.T.C. lodged a complaint against Seagram's, Ltd. and its 21 subsidiaries for conspiring to fix prices and hinder competition. A similar complaint was lodged against Schenley Industries, Inc., and its eight subsidiaries. The basis for this new limit upon marketing decisions was a unanimous Supreme Court decision in 1951 which ruled that common ownership is no defense against conspiracy charges. How far this new development may go is yet to be determined.

PRICE DISCRIMINATION. Again, as in product design, price discrimination is an example of policy intended to maintain competition by protecting one competitor from another. It does not apply to the consumer.

The practice of charging different prices to different buyers of products of like kind and quality is called price discrimination. You will recall that a graphic analysis of price discrimination was used in Chapter 7 to describe principles of segmentation. Discrimination may also occur in the form of merchandising aids, advertising allowances, and "free deals" (extra quantities of the product). Much of the law dealing with price discrimination touches upon the marketing channel as well as promotion decisions. The discussion of the law relating to nonprice discrimination will be found mainly in the sections devoted to those decisions.

The legal problems involved in price discrimination have until recently caused marketing managers greater concern than have other areas of law. There is general agreement among marketing people, practicing attorneys, and economists that the law should be changed, but there is no complete agreement as to the kinds of changes that should be made. It is often alleged that the ambiguity of the law and this complexity of the price problem cause the law to be widely violated.

A brief statement of the more common bases for establishing price differentials to customers will add clarity to this extremely complicated subject. *Quantity discounts,* whereby the price is related to the quantity of the product a customer buys, are one of the major kinds of price differentials. *Functional discounts,* which will be discussed in connection with the law and marketing channels, relate price to the trade status of a buyer, such as whether he is a broker, wholesaler, or retailer. *Geographic discounts* result in different prices according to the location of the buyer—the basing-point system is one of the most common geographic discrimination methods. The basing-point method of pricing becomes significant only in the case of products for which transportation cost is a large part of the price, such as steel and cement. It is a method of pricing that permits only *delivered* pricing (the seller pays the transportation) and makes the price to a buyer the *lowest combination* of basing-point price (the price at some previously agreed-upon geographic point) and outbound rail-freight charges. The basing-point location and rail-freight charges are used in computing the price, irrespective of the method of transportation used.

Cash discounts, which relate prices to time of payment, also give rise to price differentials. Another class of discounts consists of those that relate price to the time of purchase, illustrated by *seasonal discounts.* Finally, the "personal situation" of the buyer, such as his bargaining power and negotiating acumen, may lead to price differentials.

The Robinson-Patman Act (1936) closed certain loopholes and considerably extended the scope of the Clayton Act (1914). It provides that price discrimination among goods of like grade and quality is illegal when the product is sold in interstate commerce. Any one of the three following conditions constitutes an exception, however: (1) the differences in price can be justified by differences in cost in serving the accounts; (2) competition is not injured; or (3) the differences are necessary in order to meet competition.

Differences in cost. Cost justification has proved difficult in practice. As the major enforcement agency of the Robinson-Patman Act, the Federal Trade Commission has taken the position that among buyers, price differentials which are greater than the differences in average full costs are illegally discriminatory. Estimates of average full cost are highly ambiguous because they depend upon the inherently arbitrary method of allocating overhead costs, a problem discussed in Chapter 4. For example, a company may allocate no overhead to a less profitable department because if it does, that department will show a loss, and this would be detrimental to morale. Although justifiable for personnel reasons, the practice cannot be justified on any other basis. Many of the complications involved in assembling a cost estimate were also discussed in Chapter 4. There are a number of other complications in measuring cost: many costs cannot be traced to the product; unit costs vary and are indeterminate among the various conditions of sale, such as quantity, location, and channel; and factory costs change, but sales are made from inventory.

Quantity discounts have been cost justified in the past, but in 1951 the Federal Trade Commission ruled for the rubber-tire manufacturers that the quantity for which a discount could be granted must not exceed one carload. Irrespective of actual savings, the "quantity limit rule" overrides any possibility of justifying a greater discount on a cost basis. It was reversed by the court on technical grounds, and apparently no new attempts have been made to apply it.

Competition not injured. In order for price discrimination to be illegal, only a reasonable probability that competition will be injured is necessary; this ruling greatly increases the area of illegality through injury. Injury to competition is assumed when a company sells at different prices to two buyers who are competing on the selling side. Thus, the Robinson-Patman Act applies to "injury to competition" among competing customers and among competing sellers.

Meeting competition. The argument that price discrimination is necessary to meet competitors' prices has become known as the "good faith" defense. In the Standard Oil of Indiana Case of 1951, the Supreme Court ruled that meeting competition justified price discrimination. A seller, however, cannot use this argument to justify cutting a price to a reselling buyer on grounds that this *buyer* needs the lower cost to meet his competition. The F.T.C. has further ruled that the "good faith" defense applies only to "individual competitive situations," and not to "general systems of competition."

In the case of the C. E. Niehoff & Company, a Chicago automobile parts producer, the F.T.C. trial examiner ruled that for the "good faith" defense to apply, the price discrimination must be temporary, localized, and defensive rather than offensive. This position was supported by the Commission. In a later case, however, a court has ruled that offensive price discrimination is not prohibited.

Finally, "meeting competition" cannot justify meeting a price that the manager knows to be illegal or that is of such nature as to be inherently illegal.

Price experimentation. A question of real importance is whether it is legal to experiment with prices in order to secure information for price setting, since price experimentation clearly results in price differentials.

Price experimentation appears to be acceptable in the consumer market where the buyers cannot in any meaningful sense be viewed as being in competition with each other. It is conceivable, however, that if the experiment at the consumer level required changing prices to the distributors and/or retailers, the experimenting company would be charged with price discrimination. It has been reported that in carrying out market tests a food company provides its distributors and dealers with a written statement that it is manipulating price in order to obtain market information.

Salesmen and price discrimination.   It is illegal for a salesman being compensated on a commission basis to sacrifice a part of his commission in order to grant a customer a lower price. One court has ruled that a cost-justification defense is not precluded when the cost savings are accomplished by reason of the seller's commission salesman reducing his commission. It is possible to avoid this problem by discontinuing the sales force and using independent distributors, but these distributors cannot be granted territorial exclusivity.

SALES BELOW COST.   In a number of states there are laws called "unfair sales acts" which make it illegal to sell below cost. An example of the method of establishing these minimum prices is by setting a minimum markup of 6 percent on merchandise cost plus freight and cartage for retailers and a corresponding 2 percent for wholesalers. The enforcement of such laws is, in general, left to private parties; consequently, enforcement has been erratic and in general quite lax. Generally, unsuccessful efforts have been made to transfer the enforcement responsibility to public agencies.

Marketing channel decisions

Public policy has at least two effects on marketing channel decisions: it can influence the manufacturer's relations with the middlemen making up the channel in a given structure, and it can change the nature of the structure of distribution. The first influence, if operative for a long enough period, will lead to the second. The first is illustrated by the "quantity-limit rule," which many of the smaller tire dealers were apprehensive of, even though it was designed for their benefit. They feared that if the tire manufacturers could not grant quantity discounts to the larger dealers, they would refuse to sell to the smaller ones. The trademark law is also important in this respect because under its provisions the manufacturer can have a distinctive brand, which gives him additional bargaining power vis-à-vis the distributive companies in the channel.

If the fears of the small tire dealers were realized, the nature of this section of the tire distribution structure would probably undergo a radical change, an illustration of the second influence. In such a case, a portion, if not all, of the small tire dealers would be eliminated. The more farsighted and financially able dealers would enter other businesses, and the remainder would probably face ultimate financial failure. A company manufacturing auto accessories and thinking of expanding its market would probably hesitate to choose a small dealer whose future is uncertain.

Because of their significance for marketing channel decisions, the implications of the Clayton and Robinson-Patman acts will be discussed below. If the states' "unfair sales acts" were enforced, they would also have an effect both upon the relations between the companies (manufacturer and middlemen) in the channel and upon the structure of distribution.

CLAYTON ACT.   The Clayton Act is significant in prohibiting the *tying arrangements* that lessen competition which were discussed above. It applies to buyers in general, but the rule is particularly relevant to marketing channels. Eastman Kodak, in a consent decree growing out of an antitrust suit, agreed to discontinue a tying arrangement on Kodachrome and Kodacolor brands of its color film. Prior to this agreement, the retail price of either brand included both the cost of the raw film and the cost of developing the exposed film. The government was concerned because Kodak had 90 percent of the color-film market, and this exclusive processing arrangement was alleged to have added to its market power. Now the government requires that Kodak be willing to offer the film and the film processing separately.

Exclusive dealing is similarly characterized by a conditional nature. A manufacturer will sell to a dealer only if the dealer will agree to handle only the manufacturer's products. The condition for illegality is that competition may be injured. One of the major criteria determining this is the volume of business defined in either relative (share of market) or absolute terms. The maker of Revlon cosmetics was found guilty because it had a dominant share and because of the number and importance of jobbers involved in Revlon's exclusive contracts. The effect, according to the Federal Trade Commission, was to close the available channels to competitors. The classic case in exclusive dealing is the Standard stations case, where it was established that a substantial volume of business must be involved in order for the practice to be illegal.

ROBINSON-PATMAN ACT.   The influence of the Robinson-Patman Act on manufacturers relations with members of the marketing channel should make its influence upon the structure of distribution apparent. In general, the effect of this act has been increasingly to prevent change in channel structure by limiting innovations in distribution. The specific provisions of the Robinson-Patman Act relate to (1) price discrimination, (2) brokerage allowances, (3) promotional payments, (4) buyer responsibility.

One important question about the general problem of discrimination is whether a company can refuse to sell to a buyer. If it cannot refuse, prohibition of discrimination can be a more complex problem for the marketing manager. The evidence suggests that a company may refuse to sell to anyone as long as it charges the same price to all actual buyers. The Robinson-Patman Act was intended to prevent large buyers from getting price advantages not open to their smaller competitors. "Refusal to sell" may enable the seller to circumvent this intent because by refusing to sell to smaller buyers, he is then free to set a more favorable price to larger ones.

Another significant point is that price discrimination is illegal only if it injures competition. Discrimination in brokerage allowances, promotional payments, or services are illegal, irrespective of their effect upon competition.

Price discrimination. To the earlier discussion of price discrimination it need be added only that the Robinson-Patman Act is relatively more complicated in its application to channel decisions. The complication arises mainly because distributive buyers at the same level in the structure of distribution are clearly in competition with one another; therefore, the use of the "noninjury-to-competition" defense of discrimination is severely limited. As long as the buyers are not in competition with one another, such as a wholesaler and a retailer, price discrimination is permissible. The legality of functional discounts has been reaffirmed in the Hruby Distributing Company case. One exception to this has occurred, however, in the case of the Kraft-Phenix Cheese Corporation, which was setting the wholesaler's selling price. In this case, the F.T.C. held that since the manufacturer controlled the wholesaler's price to the retailer, all retailers, both those buying direct from Kraft and those buying from the wholesaler, should be considered Kraft's customers; therefore, illegal price discrimination existed.

In addition, many wholesalers also sell at retail; when this occurs, wholesalers must not receive a lower price from the manufacturer for the goods to be sold at retail than the goods to be sold at wholesale. The manufacturer will not clear himself by making only a half-hearted effort to insure that the wholesaler does not underpay. It is apparent that this rule poses serious problems for the manufacturer.

Brokerage allowances. A manufacturer—usually one that does not have his own sales force—can often avoid the use of a broker's services by selling directly to a large buyer. Can the manufacturer pass this saving on by lowering the price to the large buyer who has, in effect, absorbed the brokerage function? The savings that result from bypassing the broker cannot be used by the manufacturer to justify a price differential in favor of a large buyer. The manufacturer is free, however, to substitute salesmen for the broker, and the personal-selling cost may be used to cost-justify a price differential. In the Henry Broch and Company case a broker attempted to give a single buyer a lower price. He did this by absorbing through a lower commission a portion of the price cut, with his principal absorbing the remainder of the price cut by lowering his price. This broker's practice was declared an unlawful brokerage allowance.

Promotional payments and services.   Payments made by the manufacturer to the retailer for joint efforts in cooperative promotional arrangements open possibilities for hiding what is, in fact, price discrimination. The legal rule is that advertising allowances and similar promotional payments may be made only if such payments are made available on *proportionally equal terms* to all other customers competing in the distribution of the product. The same rule applies with regard to services furnished by the seller to the buyer.

This rule poses serious complications. In the cosmetics industry, demonstrators sent out by the manufacturer to the retail stores are an effective means of promotion, but they are probably economical only in the large stores where traffic is heavy. The Federal Trade Commission has suggested that a solution in this industry is to offer the smaller retailers some substitute service. The use of a substitute service was suggested in an F.T.C. action against Lever Brothers, Procter & Gamble, and Colgate-Palmolive-Peet. The practice was to offer an allowance of roughly 20 cents per case of product for newspaper advertising and 9 cents for handbills. Since the small dealers cannot afford newspaper advertising, the F.T.C. lawyers claimed that this resulted in discrimination. The Commission, however, stated that various media were available, and the "proportionality" condition was satisfied.

Payment according to some notion of "value received" by the manufacturer has also been suggested by an F.T.C. attorney, but it has not been applied by the Commission. The manufacturer might, for example, pay the retailer according to his ability to maintain a quota based upon some measure of his sales potential.

Buyer responsibility.   In order to make the antidiscrimination rules effective, the law provides that any buyer who "knowingly" receives the benefit of price discrimination has violated the Robinson-Patman Act. The enforcement of this provision, however, will be difficult, as suggested in the first case that reached the courts, the Automatic Canteen Company case (1953). The Supreme Court reversed the F.T.C. and emphasized the unreasonableness inherent in a provision that in effect requires a buyer to know a seller's costs. However, trade experience or the formation of a buying group in order to obtain volume discounts may be sufficient to prove that the buyer knows that the discounts he receives are not cost-justified.

RECIPROCAL BUYING.   The practice of a company requiring its suppliers to buy their requirements from it has come under fire since 1966, with some very early exceptions.[10] The criticism springs from the fact that the

---

[10]Reed Moyer, "Reciprocity: Retrospect and Prospect," *Journal of Marketing*, Vol. 34 (1970): 47–54.

practice interposes a factor in the buyer's choice that has nothing to do with product quality, service, or price. Some companies have established fairly elaborate "trade relations" departments to administer their reciprocal buying programs.

Most of the cases have arisen when a merger was involved. Outside the context of the merger, reciprocity will probably not be challenged as long as it is not coercive and is not pursued aggressively with an elaborate arrangement of sales and purchase records.

PROFESSIONALIZATION

Among people engaged in marketing, there is often discussion of the need for professionalization of the field. The idea is that if regulation of marketing practices is self-imposed, control through public policy can be avoided. The current state of self-regulation is difficult to assess, and its future is even more uncertain. It must be remembered that things that harass the marketing manager may be desirable from a social welfare viewpoint because they bring cheaper, better products or an easier life for the consumer. An apt statement is, "The greatest of all monopoly profits is a quiet life."

There is a large area, best illustrated perhaps by untruthfulness and poor taste or unsuitable "aesthetics" in advertising, where self-regulation might be more effective than it is. Recently a number of individuals and associations have begun a serious effort to bring about self-regulation of advertising. A disinterested body to decide what is untruthful and to secure enforcement has been suggested. There are many questions to be answered before this can be effectively accomplished. One of the questions is whether the matter of taste should be considered.

Better Business Bureaus, supported by financial contributions from companies, also represent self-regulation, and their efforts are currently being strengthened. In part, at least, their effectiveness lies in the heterogeneity of their membership, which often results in some members being directly damaged by the practices of others. The injured members are more inclined than others to report the practice and to support the bureau in opposing it. The effectiveness of the bureaus and related agencies such as chambers of commerce can be said to have fallen short of the required level of self-regulation.

One source of considerable public concern where self-regulation may play a part is in the influence of advertising and personal selling upon the buyer's standards of choice. An operational criterion of "standards of choice" could be whether the consumer's choice criteria are affected. It is argued that style will come to play a greater role in American consumption and that this will provide the source of standards. It is alleged that by referring to style the consumer can make his purchase judgments independent of advertising rather than having them influenced, if not determined, by the advertiser. It is further argued that in this new era of style, the marketing manager will become more professionalized because he will concern himself with interpreting to the consumer what the style is and interpreting to his company the requirements of the style in terms of product design. Evidence can be cited to suggest that style is becoming relatively more important in influencing purchasing habits. How important it will become and whether it will be developed free from the influence of advertising we do not now know.

SUMMARY

The president has two areas of responsibility: internal and external. His internal functions are both control and decision. His control function arises when he reviews his brand managers' and marketing managers' plans.

His decisions can be either strategic or administrative. The strategic decisions have to do with giving direction to product and market development and with diversification. In strategic decisions, marketing aspects are coming to the center of corporate activity. We believe many diversification mistakes could have been avoided with some attention to their marketing features.

The president's administrative decisions are varied. Attention here is given to R & D, organization, and relating internal policy to public policy. Organizational decisions particularly have to do with goal setting and support of innovation.

One of the serious problems is that marketing literature does not tend to relate marketing to corporate strategy. Perhaps this is one of the reasons that innovation in market research has been so slow in coming. On the other hand, a point of view made up of such concepts as product positioning, market segmentation, marketing strategy, marketing mix, and marketing plan has been developed which will facilitate integrating marketing into the total corporation.

The external responsibilities of the president have to do with public policy. It is taking increasing amounts of his time. Aside from sources and agencies of public policy, the central issue addressed was its content. Two avenues have traditionally been taken: insuring consumer sovereignty and preserving competition. The later has by far received the greater attention. The content of each of these two areas was developed in detail to give the reader an appreciation of the current state of public policy. The discussion pointed up the pervasiveness of the effects of public policy upon marketing decision. Every major area is influenced. Missing, however, was any statement of justification—a rationale—for public policy. For this we turn to Chapter 16.

DISCUSSION QUESTIONS

1. Contrast a president's internal and external roles.
2. What do we mean by the concept of corporate strategy, and what is its relation to marketing activities?

3. What are some of the president's typical administrative decisions that impinge upon the marketing operation?
4. Public policy has increasingly come to play a role in marketing decisions. What do we mean by it, and what is its source?
5. Until recently when advertising became a central public-policy issue, the Robinson-Patman Act was the most significant piece of legislation for marketing decisions. What are some of its provisions?

Part VI

Evaluation of marketing system

THE DESCRIPTION of marketing management as viewed by the manager—the brand manager, the marketing manager, or the president—was completed with Chapter 15. The criteria by which he can judge whether his company is performing well or badly have been established. There remains the question, however, of whether it is performing well in a public-policy sense. This evaluation, of course, requires the incorporation of broader social criteria. The purpose of Part VI is to discuss these criteria.

16

Rationale for public policy

INTRODUCTION

THE CONTINUAL social, political, and economic changes that characterize our society call into question whether the current public policy on marketing activity discussed in Chapter 15 is adequate today. Evidence of this questioning can be seen in data on shifting public opinion. In a large sample of the American population the Princeton Opinion Research Center found in 1965 that 47 percent of the people said new laws were necessary to aid the consumer in obtaining his money's worth. By 1968 that percentage had increased to 58 percent, and by 1969, to 68 percent. Federal Trade Commission activity also has been increasing; Basil J. Mezines reported that it increased almost a third in fiscal 1971 over fiscal 1970.[1] Hence, it is necessary to ask the question implicit in public policy: How does one evaluate a marketing system in order to know to what public policy should address itself, if at all? This was the question raised at the outset of the book.

An evaluation of a marketing system ideally requires a rationale that explains how the system works, incorporates the valid criticisms, and yields actionable criteria. Basic to a rationale for evaluating such an all-pervasive and complex a thing as a society's marketing system is the philosophical framework within which that society views its marketing system, as determined by certain fundamental values.

---

[1] *GMA Monitor,* Grocery Manufacturer's of America, Washington, D.C., August 26, 1971, p. 2.

For the United States the philosophical framework is essentially Western economic liberalism, which places high value on private enterprise. Recent changes in American values, however, are bringing demands that this doctrine of the "unseen hand of the market" be modified, although there are wide divergencies in opinion as to the direction of modification. At one extreme is the argument that the whole concept should be scrapped. At the other is the assertion that our system should not be tampered with, because in following it our accomplishments have been magnificent. It is interesting to note that even the Committee on Economic Development, which is made up of businessmen, asserts, as part of a proposed creed that "Inasmuch as business exists to serve society, its future will depend on the quality of management's response to the changing expectations of the public." This creed (see Chapter 15) has received wide support over the country, with some dissent from both ends of the political spectrum.

The orientation of economic liberalism provides a systematic way of examining the problem. It particularly highlights areas of implicit premises that can be tested through research. This testing of premises is important because much criticism of the marketing system springs from beliefs about consumer behavior that our current knowledge suggests are of doubtful validity. These probably mistaken views characterize both political extremes. The New Left takes something of a Vance Packard view; while the right wing asserts that the consumer is not misled and is perfectly capable of taking care of himself. Insofar as current research methodology permits, the truth of these premises should be tested before any drastic change is made.

Our experience in teaching in the past five years has impressed us with the ability of students to analyze a company marketing problem systematically. When confronted with social issues, however, they are highly unwilling to apply the same systematic thought. In our view, this unwillingness to think objectively about social issues is more or less true of all of us. Further, we believe that teachers of marketing carry an especially heavy obligation to talk and act responsibly in regard to this matter. On the other hand, in the current state of knowledge not all public-policy decisions can be well informed and based on systematic thought. We recognize that many of these decisions will have to be taken without better evidence.

ECONOMIC LIBERALISM

In evaluating a marketing system in terms of consumer needs, economic liberalism makes two central assumptions: companies are competitive, and consumers are capable and well informed and have the desire to choose carefully—traditionally called the doctrine of consumer sovereignty. Economists concerned with competition, particularly under the leadership of Edward S. Mason, have in the past 40 years formulated useful criteria for determining the extent to which an economy conforms to the first assumption. There have long been procompetition sentiments in American life, partly for the economist's reason of efficiency but aided and abetted by an important American value: Small business is virtuous, aside from any efficiency contribution. These criteria have had a strong influence over the years in shaping the competitive aspect of public policy.

On the assumption of consumer sovereignty, economists have been peculiarly silent. Until recently they have not been greatly concerned with developing concepts for dealing with information, and information is a central issue of consumer sovereignty. In principle, the consumer should have the same bargaining power as the seller. With modern technology this obviously cannot be so. In an industry with 10 companies selling to 100 million consumers, the ratio is 1 to 10 million. Even by this superficial measure the consumer is characterized by disparate bargaining power. Gross unfairness is inevitable in most instances. Consequently, a much heavier burden is placed upon the quality of the consumer's information so that he is armed and can protect himself.

Even now consumer sovereignty is receiving only limited attention from economists.

> . . . one branch of pure theory applied the name "welfare economics" to a structure of deductive logic based on an emphatic and rigorous insistence on accepting the consumer's choice between rival offerings as the ultimate criteria, for purposes of economic service of the relative contributions of these offerings to the consumer's welfare. This attitude precluded any inquiry into the conditions making for effective or ineffective exercise of consumer sovereignty or any concern with the problems that underlie the Pure Food and Drug Act or the Federal Trade Commission's requirements of informative labelling.[2]

Faced with this paucity of analytical tools, economists have focused upon the *fact* of buyer choice instead of the *why* of his choice. As Dean Edward S. Mason has so well described it: "Economists are still so mesmerized with the *fact* of choice and so little concerned with its *explanation* . . . that they would appear to be professionally debarred from their important task of developing a social rationale for modern industry."[3] It is only in the past decade that consumer information has come to be accepted as a "problem" by legislators; it is still more lately that consumers have become a powerful political force on this issue. Congressional consideration of "truth in packaging" in 1966 probably marked the major turning point.

---

[2]J. M. Clark, *Alternative to Serfdom,* 2d ed. (New York: Vintage Books, 1970), p. 38.
[3]E. S. Mason, "The Apologetics of Managerialism," *Journal of Business,* 31 (1958), p. 56.

ASSUMPTION OF COMPETITION

The competitive argument of economic liberalism is that if there are many companies competing in the same product class, whether they like it or not the "unseen hand of the market" will force them to serve the consumer's interest. Adequacy of options protects the consumer. The modern concepts for describing this competitive process were largely set forth in Chapter 2 under the general rubric of structure of competition: A particular structure leads to certain kinds of competitive behavior, which have certain associated consequences. The consequences discussed there were in terms of the company's criteria, effect on profits, and growth. In this chapter we are concerned with criteria that matter to the consumer (public policy), not to the company.

Public-policy criteria include profits, but from an opposite point of view. Is there an appropriate level of profits? If profits are too high, this could indicate that prices are too high, but neither should they be too low because such a company cannot long survive to meet the consumer's needs. Another criterion is efficiency: Are the companies producing as cheaply as they might? High profits discourage efficiency. Progressiveness is still another: Do the companies develop new and better products to the extent they should, or do they go so far as to suppress useful inventions to protect an existing market? There is also the criterion of suitability of product: Do the products conform closely to consumer's needs? Finally, there is promotion: Are advertising, selling, and other marketing expenses higher than they need be, and is the price consequently higher because it must cover these costs?

When these criteria are applied to an industry with the somewhat common competitive structure of four firms or less, some conclude that the criteria are seriously violated and action ought to be taken. It is alleged, for example, that four firms or less in an industry is the critical dividing line between competitive and higher-than-competitive pricing, as in the cereal industry.[4] The cereal industry is particularly important because the Federal Trade Commission has announced its intention to proceed against it, in what could be a landmark case. The argument runs as follows: In a concentrated industry, where a *few* companies share the market, these companies tacitly collude and so obtain higher than competitive prices. There is also some evidence that profits may be higher when there are a few firms.[5] But whether the higher prices are *caused* by the "fewness" and, if so, whether four is the crucial dividing line, are less clear.

Further, this protection from competitive forces is alleged to cause

---

[4]Statement of the *Antitrust Law and Economics Review*, submitted to the Subcommittee for Consumers of the Committee on Interstate and Foreign Commerce, U.S. Senate, August 4, 1970.

[5]Joe S. Bain, *Barriers to New Competition* (Cambridge, Mass.: Harvard University Press, 1956).

companies to compete on such undesirable dimensions as "high volumes of advertising" and "a proliferation of surface variations in the basic product, particularly in matters of style and design."[6] This high level of advertising encourages further concentration by differentiating brands. It also serves as a barrier to entry because of advertising economies of scale: Only large firms can afford to use advertising, since it is costly and the outcome uncertain. The principle of economies of scale was presented in Chapter 4. This barrier is supposedly because, the larger the share of market, the more profitable advertising is, since the sales resulting from it are shared with fewer competitors. Why this should be so is not clear. The implication is that advertising contributes nothing to the consumer. This conclusion follows because where the problem of economies of scale in factory size are discussed, no serious consideration is given to the benefits of advertising to the consumer. This argument of the nonproductivity of advertising will be dealt with later.

Finally, it is alleged that firms in a concentrated industry do not compete on "technological progress," which should be interpreted as meaning "socially desirable product development." Why they do not, while competing on advertising and "surface variations" of product, is not clear either, but the proposition seems to be accepted as resting on empirical fact. Some evidence indicates that large firms have no greater advantage than middle-size firms, but middle-size firms do have technology-creating advantage over small firms.[7]

The cereal industry is cited as a particular example of the socially undesirable consequences of concentration, and the recommendation is that it be broken up into smaller companies.[8] This conclusion, as we have seen, is by no means fully supported, but it is persuasive. It organizes a familiar set of arguments—those emanating from market structure analysis—into a coherent statement and extends them to the relatively unfamiliar problem of the adequacy of consumer information. This incorporation of information into the economic apparatus of market structure is much to be desired because it permits a more complete analysis. Others would draw the conclusion that direct controls, such as limiting the level of advertising, may be desirable.

The general train of argument clearly omits two key points. First, it could be that product innovation is the source of both high advertising and high profits. We know from a study of the grocery industry that the profit margin for new products is on the average about 20 percent higher than that for established products. We also know (if not, we soon learn)

---

[6]Statement of the *Antitrust Law and Economics Review*, p. 3.

[7]R. R. Nelson, M. J. Peck, and E. D. Kalachek, *Technology, Economic Growth and Public Policy* (Washington, D.C.: The Brookings Institution, 1966).

[8]Statement of the *Antitrust Law and Economics Review*.

that new products must be advertised if they are to be accepted quickly enough for the innovation to recoup the cost of discovery, development, and introduction.

Second, current profits on a new product are overstated. The courts have accepted the idea that advertising is an investment, as in the Borden Evaporated Milk case,[9] but accounting practice still does not treat it so. When a new product is first introduced the advertising costs are exceedingly high relative to later years in the product's life. Buyers must be told the product exists and what it is so they will know whether it is likely to meet their needs. As a consequence, future years in the life of the product are undercharged. If the cost of advertising were treated as an investment, it (and other introduction costs) would be charged against the product's revenue stream as the stream occurred. Thus future years would be charged according to the size of the revenue stream. Because of this bookkeeping convention any statement of current profits of an *established* product is too high in relation to the products' introductory years, because costs of that product are now being understated.

The role of advertising is thus a central issue in market structure analysis, which constitutes our only systematic rationale for public policy. Consequently, what the role of advertising in the market is, in fact, becomes a crucial question in evaluating the adequacy of our rationale for public policy. Advertising effect would seem to take place via the consumer; for example, the barrier-to-entry argument used in the market structure analysis implies some things about how advertising affects the consumer. How do advertising economies of scale come about? At the current stage of knowledge the question might better be, How *could* advertising economies of scale come about?

To explore some of the consumer information issues that should be a part of any developing systematic rationale, we will turn to consumer sovereignty. The typical disparity in bargaining power between the consumer and the seller forces greater attention upon consumer information.

CONSUMER SOVEREIGNTY

Introduction

The assumption of consumer sovereignty implies that the consumer can and will exercise his judgment. "Can" implies he has enough information to make the choice rationally and that it is in such form that he can use it. "Will" implies that he is willing to devote the effort required to make the judgment rationally. The doctrine asserts that if these conditions hold, and if there are adequate sellers (competition), consumers will discipline sellers and force them to behave consistent with the consumer's interest.

---

[9] *Advertising Age,* July 31, 1967, p. 1.

The assumption that the consumer has adequate information to make buying decisions has in the past decade been called more into question. Ralph Nader has done well in focusing public attention upon the consumer information issue in a number of ways. Particularly important was his request of a number of advertisers to substantiate their ad claims. Their failure to do so led to the F.T.C.'s orders for ad substantiation.[10] Unfortunately, he has not yet developed an underlying rationale to guide consumer policy: ". . . so far there is no coherent Nader program, nor even a common approach linking specific proposals. Conclusions are strewn about haphazardly in otherwise tightly organized reports. We are given a detailed diagnosis but an illegible prescription."[11] Further, it is fairly clear from the previous discussion of competitive structure that the a priori approach implied does not deal adequately with the problem of inadequate consumer information. A more direct approach is needed, because the competitive market structure view assumes the seller has some effective way of identifying the buyer's needs so that he can produce products which conform to those needs. Is this so? Our discussion of market research practice in Chapter 8 raises serious doubts. This direct approach involves examining, first, the consumer's information needs and, second, under "rational decision," how he uses information in the market, with emphasis upon how advertising critics view his use of that information.

Developments affecting consumer information requirements

A number of developments in the past few decades have intensified the consumer information problem. A review of these will throw light on and sharpen the information issue.

First, as the American standard of living has, in general, continued to rise, opportunities for the consumer to buy more products have increased. In fact, there is the *necessity* that he buy more products if employment is to be maintained. But this adds to the burden of the shopper. More scarce time must be devoted to this activity, and some other activity must suffer the loss. In spite of labor-saving devices, the housewife is understandably even busier than was her mother.

Second, the almost fantastic flow of new products means that if the consumer does not carefully cull them to select those that truly contribute to his welfare, in a short time his standard of living will, in fact, be substantially lower. Further, some segments of society are much better qualified than others, psychologically and socially, to make these judgments rapidly and easily.

Third, many of the new products are more complex, and buying them

---

[10]*Advertising Age,* June 14, 1971, p. 105.
[11]*New York Times Book Review,* August 8, 1971, p. 28.

requires more information. This fact is perhaps best illustrated in the case of processed foods. In an earlier period the basic ingredients of foods had been tested in use for centuries as to purity and safety. Our culture provided adequate safeguards. This is not at all true of modern processed foods, where some of the ingredients have existed only a matter of months. The housewife now must add the criterion of safety to those that she already applies in selecting a particular brand. Where is she to find out whether the food is safe for her family? Electrical appliances are another example of complex products requiring substantial consumer information.

Fourth, with the higher standard of living has come the greater possibility of using products for symbolic or what many would call "nonfunctional" purposes. Self-concept is a more neutral term. We no longer eat to keep from starving but merely to enjoy ourselves by expressing ourselves as social human beings. Not only does the act of consuming become social and symbolic, but so do the act of purchasing itself and related activities, as David Riesman asserted so well several years ago in *The Lonely Crowd*.[12]

Rational decision

One way to judge the information problem is according to whether the conditions for rational decision by the consumer are satisfied by current marketing practices. This is also consistent with an emerging view in regulatory thinking: Marketing effort is justified only insofar as it helps the consumer buy better in terms of his own interest.

Of immediate concern are the *limits* of a buyer's information-processing capacity, as discussed in Chapters 3 and 13. A manifestation of this limitation was the political pressure for the so-called truth-in-packaging legislation passed in 1966. The main issue was that the buyer was being presented with too many alternative brands, and the objective was to standardize package sizes so that the number would be reduced. Remaining choices would be comparable, permitting price to be used as the major criterion of choice. Unit pricing, whereby price per unit (volume or weight) of brand is shown on the package, has been a later response to the consumer's limited information capacity.

With the passage of time a more sophisticated view of the consumer problem has emerged in public-policy circles, which emphasizes the *quality* of his information. It is safe to say that over the next several years the focus of regulative attention will be upon information. The basic tenet is that the seller is obligated to inform the buyer. Whether regulation, such as by the Federal Trade Commission, will go so far as to require the seller to provide *adequate* information remains to be seen.

---

[12]David Riesman, Nathan Glazer, and Reuel Denney, *The Lonely Crowd*, abridged ed. (Garden City, N.Y.: Doubleday & Co., 1953).

Because of this new orientation we will focus most of the rest of the chapter upon information, using advertising as an example. Advertising merely displays sharply what is true of all marketing effort: Its major purpose is to communicate. A simplified approach to the informational role of advertising is to examine the comments, of its critics, which presumably should be a part of an emerging rationale. In this way, perhaps, the issues can be seen more clearly.

THE CHARGES OF CRITICS

There is a morass of criticisms about advertising, and it is important that they be recognized and attempts made to answer them. Otherwise they fester and provide grounds for restrictive legislation. Some may well be justified.

Figure 16–1 can be helpful in organizing the discussion. Boxes 1 and 2 can be thought of as "causal" variables and boxes 3 and 4 as "effect" variables. To be consistent with earlier chapters, the boxes should be identified as processes made up of the buyer's mental mechanisms, as

FIGURE 16–1
A framework for analyzing the arguments of advertising critics

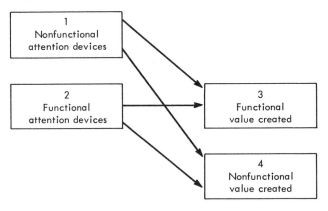

described in Chapters 3, 8, and 13. In this manner, the consumer's perceptual processes are represented by boxes 1 and 2 and his cognitive or learning processes by boxes 3 and 4. Of course, processes per se cannot be objectively validated or tested; only the mechanisms that make up the processes. To relate the criticisms to the specific mechanisms, however, would inordinately complicate the exposition. For the sake of simplicity, the discussion is at the process level.

By considering each of the boxes in turn, the critics' arguments can be classified in terms of the two ways the advertiser creates attention and the two ways he creates value for the product or brand in the mind of the consumer. Explicit definitions are:

1. *Nonfunctional attention devices* are advertising stimuli which imply no assertions about the direct physical and psychological benefits of consuming the brand.
2. *Functional attention devices*, on the other hand, are those advertising stimuli that directly or clearly suggest the physical and psychological benefits of consuming the brand.
3. *Functional value created* is the direct benefit of the product, as perceived by the consumer, which results from exposure to advertising stimuli. Functional values may be classified as either physical or psychological or as real or synthetic. These are not useful distinctions. Broadly interpreted, functional value created is an advertising-induced change in the consumer's belief structure with respect to the capacity of the product or brand to serve his needs through consuming the brand.
4. *Nonfunctional value created* also refers to an advertising-induced change in the consumer's belief structure. In this case, however, beliefs are changed with respect to objects other than the brand being advertised. For example, advertising may influence the consumer's belief structure with respect to (1) the self, (2) the ideal self, or (3) others.

Specific arguments against the methods, activities, and influence of advertisers[13] can be considered with this framework. As in Figure 16–1, they are divided into both functional and nonfunctional devices and value-creation devices.

Attention devices

NONFUNCTIONAL ATTENTION DEVICES. The critic generally does not approve of the advertiser's use of nonfunctional attention devices. Indeed, any activity or method associated with box 1 is criticized. Advertising stimuli of the nonfunctional type, such as mood music, do not relate directly to a *product benefit* that would satisfy the buyer's motive structure; the critic often views such devices as irrelevant, irritable, confusing, and distracting. Because they do not provide information about the brand in terms of criteria that the buyer considers relevant, nonfunctional attention

---

[13]See, for example, J. K. Galbraith, *The New Industrial State* (Boston: Houghton Mifflin Co., 1967); Ralph Glasser, *The New High Priesthood* (London: Macmillan Co. Ltd., 1967); James D. Halloran, *Control or Consent?* (London: Sheed & Ward, 1963); Jules Henry, *Culture Against Man* (New York: Random House, Inc., 1963); James Hulbert, "Advertising: Criticism and Reply," *Business and Society*, 9 (Autumn 1968), pp. 33–38; Ralph Ross and Ernest van den Haag, *The Fabric of Society* (New York: Harcourt, Brace, & World, Inc., 1957); Arnold Toynbee, "Is It Immoral to Stimulate Buying?" *Printers' Ink*, 279 (May 11, 1962), p. 15; and Colston E. Warne, "Advertising —A Critic's View," *Journal of Marketing*, 26 (October 1962): 10–14.

devices are said to limit the consumer's ability to obtain useful information. Nevertheless, they may be pleasing in some other sense, e.g., entertaining.

The criticism that advertising irritates the aesthetic sensibilities often focuses upon the nonfunctional attention device. For example, Galbraith states:

> To assert aesthetic goals is also to interfere seriously with the management of the consumer. This, in many of its manifestations, requires dissonance—a jarring of the aesthetic sensibilities. An advertising billboard that blends gracefully into the landscape is of little value; it must be in sharp contrast with surroundings. . . . The same principles of planned dissonance are even more spectacularly in evidence in the radio and television commercial.[14]

Another example of the nonfunctional attention device is a direct appeal or statement about objects other than the advertiser's brand. The advertiser makes statements about the consumer, about how others perceive the consumer or relate to the consumer, or about a particular life style exhibited by others that contrasts with that of the consumer. The critic generally regards this type of nonfunctional attention device with disdain because he asserts that it is often intended to produce dissatisfaction with self, envy of others, arousal of emotions, and artificially unrealistic levels of material aspiration.

A third nonfunctional attention device has been noted by television producer Eliot Daley: "Sex is just another marketing tool. Use it to tease a would-be buyer of cat food or razor blades or something. Sex: Use as needed to grease the Gross National Product."[15]

Warne suggests that the advertiser makes use of nonfunctional attention devices freely and eagerly. This is deplorable to him: "Practitioners of advertising have eaten the fruit of a new tree of knowledge. Many today openly proclaim their objective to be appeals to the irrational or the irrelevant."[16]

In response to this point of view at least two questions can be raised. Does the consumer know about the brand being advertised? Is he helpless against this onslaught of information? On the first one, it is difficult to argue against using these nonfunctional cues to call his attention to the fact the brand exists if he has not known about it. On the second, the human does have remarkable capacity to tune out, but we do not know whether it is adequate. This capacity to "filter in" the relevant was discussed in Chapter 13. There is some evidence, also, that incredible information tends to be weighted less heavily than credible information. This

---

[14]Galbraith, *New Industrial State*, p. 348.
[15]Eliot Daley, "What Produced These Pot-Smoking, Rebellious, Demonstrating Kids?—Television?," *TV Guide*, Vol. 18 (November 7-13, 1970), p. 10.
[16]Colston E. Warne, "Advertising: A Critic's View," *Journal of Marketing*, Vol. 26 (October 1962), p. 11.

consumer view is implied in responses to a question, "How willing are you to be guided by each of the following sources of information about cars?" The percentage indicates the proportion of the sample that was willing to be guided by each of the respective sources:

Radio	22%	Auto salesmen/dealers	23%
Television	27%	Gas station attendants	45%
Magazines	27%	Garage service men	65%
Newspapers	34%	Relatives	58%
Billboards	22%	Advertising brochures	24%
Friends	66%	Consumer reports	81%
People at work	60%		

How much of this lack of credibility is caused by lack of trustworthiness or lack of competence of the source is not clear.

The current concern among some social scientists over "stimulus surfeit" is probably exaggerated. Alvin Toffler, in *Future Shock*,[17] has contributed to this perhaps mistaken concern, although it seems clear that he is concerned with the rate of change, not the flow of information per se.[18]

On the other hand, the consumer does not pursue his current goals in a mindless, single-purpose way. His ongoing activity that is meeting his current motive structure can be *interrupted*, and often is. Such things as unexpected events, physiological needs, and "loud" stimuli evoked by associations in memory, for example, may lead to anxiety arousal.[19] These need not be just startle responses. They could be an elaborate goal-oriented chain of activity, but the new information received because of them is irrelevant for the original ongoing activity. Further, he may learn something that is irrelevant to his needs if an ad captures his attention *when more pressing needs are absent.* All of us have read magazine articles and ads in a dentist's outer office that we would never have read otherwise. Much of an evening of television watching could be of this type. To this extent irrelevant information will not be tuned out, but we would not expect it to be deep in memory, but rather superficial and capable of being more quickly forgotten. These last conjectures are at the frontiers of behavioral science and go beyond current evidence.

FUNCTIONAL ATTENTION DEVICES. Advertising critics appear to generally acknowledge the need for functional attention devices, but on a limited basis. For instance, they would eliminate the methods and strategies designed to affect the individual's beliefs about the "psychological" benefits of the product. Although the need for those functional attention devices that are related to actual product benefits is recognized, they often are perceived as being innately deceptive if they relate the product

---

[17] Alvin Toffler, *Future Shock*, Bantam Books, Inc., 1971.

[18] Z. J. Lipowski, "Surfeit of Attractive Information Inputs: A Hallmark of Our Environment," *Behavioral Science*, 16 (September 1971): 467–71.

[19] H. A. Simon, "Motivation and Emotional Controls," *Psychological Review*, 74 (1967): 35.

to a "psychological" benefit. The benefit they promise is not viewed as being "real." This distinction between physical and psychological benefits is really meaningless. Perhaps what is being said here is that any benefit that "I" think "you" *ought* not to appreciate is psychological.

Functional attention devices of the physical type are viewed as deceptive only when they promise a physical benefit that the critic does not recognize as being beneficial. An example would be a promise of physical security in an advertisement for a car that the critic mistakenly regards as unsafe. In the case where it is truly unsafe, both critic and advertiser, at least in principle, condemn it. F.T.C.'s policy of asking certain industries to substantiate their advertising claims is a way of clarifying the deception issue. "In his (FTC's Robert Pitofsky) view, it is going to make it 'costly and dangerous' to make unsubstantiated claims. Conversely, by 'deflating the exaggerated ad' he believes it will make it easier for the advertiser with a better product to get his message across effectively."[20]

Value creation

While criticism of the advertiser's methods and actions is quite common, boxes 3 and 4 in Figure 16–1, representing "effects" of advertising on the consumer's cognitive or learning process, seem to be subject to more severe criticism. The critic, instead of discussing the processes linking "cause" and "effect," focuses on dismal phenomena he observes or predicts. Since the "effects" that the critic describes are often considered to be residual, not necessarily intended by the advertiser or even under his control, the arguments associated with value created often do not blame the advertiser for the phenomena he supposedly "causes." Indeed, by hypothesizing residual or unintended effects, the critic may actually add to the impact of his argument; for these "effects," not being readily controllable, seem particularly damaging to the individual, to society, and to culture.

It should be noted that the "effects" associated with functional values created are considered to be more directly under the advertiser's control than those associated with nonfunctional value created, because the former relate specifically to the product or brand. This does not mean, of course, that the advertiser does not also try to influence nonfunctional values. In fact, the advertiser generally believes in their power for many product appeals. He believes, for example, that to tell a child that he will be *seen by others* as big and strong if he eats cereal X is effective. However, the critic would suggest that money spent on appeals to such values is positively detrimental to the consumer's welfare.

FUNCTIONAL VALUE CREATED.   As mentioned above, one of the criticisms of the advertiser is his alleged use of *deceptive* functional attention devices. Associated with this criticism is the belief that, indeed, the con-

---

[20] *Advertising Age*, June 14, 1971, p. 102.

sumer can be quite seriously deceived. Thus the critic may conclude that advertising creates beliefs about psychological product benefits which are, by their very nature, not "real"; or it produces beliefs about physical product benefits which are not "true." This distinction between "psychological" and "real" benefits is useless. Further, we have already seen evidence that to some extent the buyer discriminates source according to degree of credibility.

The critic asserts further that the structure of the consumer's functional belief system is often distorted by advertising, so that even if all the product benefits in his belief system are true, he may give some of them undue importance. Thus it is claimed that advertising changes the relative importance of perceived product benefits. The critic may assert, for example, that advertising causes many consumers to believe that automobile styling is a more important product benefit than automobile safety. But what if the advertiser accomplishes this by *correctly* pointing out that many people do treat styling as more important than they do safety?

A slightly different but increasingly prevalent critical argument maintains that advertising accentuates the importance of the product or brand to the extent that perceived product benefits become dominant in the consumer's overall system of values, as contrasted with aesthetic values, for example. Thus his basic motive structure is modified. If this is the case for a number of products, then the individual's orientation may be labeled "materialistic." On a societal level, then, the critic claims that the aggregate effect of advertising is to distort the value system in the direction of materialism and hedonism. Some critics, such as David M. Potter, deplore the materialism they view as resulting from advertising:

Certainly it marks a profound social change that this new institution for shaping human standards should be directed, not, as are the school and the church, to the inculcation of beliefs or attitudes that are held to be of social value, but rather to the stimulation or even the exploitation of materialistic drives and emulative anxieties and then to the validation, the sanctioning and the standardization of these drives and anxieties as accepted social values.[21]

But is advertising merely a part of the ongoing pattern of activity that transmits current culture? More fundamentally, does advertising really have this effect?

The critics tend to ignore the benefit a consumer derives from advertising in the form of confidence in the brand, which relieves his uncertainty. A Chicago federal court of appeals twice upheld the principle that advertising can bestow value on a brand. It stated, ". . . it (price differential between advertised and nonadvertised brands) represents merely a rough equivalent of the benefit by way of the seller's national advertising and promotion which the purchaser of the more expensive brand expects

---

[21]David M. Potter, *People of Plenty: Economic Abundance and the American Character* (Chicago: University of Chicago Press, 1954), p. 188.

to enjoy.["]22 Carrying the point further, the Soviet Union has found it necessary to develop a trademark which identifies the producing plant. This mark was necessary to prevent the plants from shading on quality when they were directly evaluated in terms of number of units produced.[23] The critic can question whether the uncertainty reduction is worth the cost of the advertising, but he seldom, if ever, raises the question, much less attempts to answer it.

NONFUNCTIONAL VALUE CREATED. It will be recalled that non-functional value created relates to the individual's valuation of objects other than the product or brand of the advertiser. Unfortunately, most critics seem to define the role of purchasing in meeting self-concept needs as nonfunctional. Or alternatively, they seem to underestimate the brands' probable role in serving the buyer's self-concept. There is little doubt from casual observation of such products as cosmetics, cigarettes, and liquor that the self-concept is served by purchasing these products. Whether this is a useful and therefore desirable role has been examined by the psychologist Roger N. Brown. As he has put it, ". . . we should not expect a symbol-using animal to be interested in nothing but food and drink."[24] To maintain effective social relations man must somehow communicate to others things that matter to him, the kind of a person he is, and few could question the crucial part that social relations play in the typical human's life.

When we go a step further and recognize, as we did in Chapter 13, that the human needs a certain amount of variety in his daily life, we observe the fuller implications of even the functional role of purchasing in satisfying the self-concept. The person forced to eat the same food items day after day may find them good at first but then rapidly becoming tasteless. The functional need for variety, which is fairly obvious, gives rise to the individual's need to continually keep up with the changes in the way in which he indicates to others who he is. Thus in a dynamic society he must devote activity to maintaining that self-concept.

The critic judges almost all nonfunctional "effects" as detrimental to the consumer. Regardless of his actual intentions, the advertiser is alleged to change the consumer's evaluative beliefs about objects other than his product. For example, the critics claim he may change the consumer's beliefs about himself, thus fostering dissatisfaction with self or distortion of the self-concept.[25] If advertising truthfully tells a person that he is currently not meeting his social needs, it is difficult to argue against its being

---

[22]*Advertising Age,* July 31, 1967, p. 79.

[23]M. I. Goldman, "Product Differentiation and Advertising: Some Lessons from Soviet Experience," *Journal of Political Economy,* 74 (1966): 346–57.

[24]Roger N. Brown, *Social Psychology* (New York: The Free Press, 1965), p. 568.

[25]Marquis W. Childs and Douglass Cater, *Ethics in a Business Society* (New York: Harper & Brothers, 1954), pp. 168–70.)

used to serve this function. The individual must be aware of this lack if he is to remain well adapted to his group.

Dissatisfaction with self may occur in at least two ways. If dissatisfaction is regarded as a function of the perceived difference between the individual's self-concept and his ideal self-concept (the type of person he would most like to be), then it may increase if the individual's self-evaluation becomes more unfavorable. This would seem to be true in any choice situation where the buyer has an unmet need with respect to his self-concept. Advertising in this role should be acceptable. Dissatisfaction may also increase if the individual reevaluates his ideal self-concept. If advertising causes the individual to feel unfavorable toward himself in some sense, the first type of dissatisfaction may be produced; and if it presents the individual with stimuli that increase his aspirations, the second type of dissatisfaction may be produced. A recent article contains a relevant comment by Charles Revson of Revlon, Inc.: "In the factory we make cosmetics; in the store we sell hope."[26] The critic of advertising would say that the hope stimulated by Revlon advertising may increase the consumer's evaluation of her ideal self, resulting in a relative devaluation of her actual self. Indeed, he may assert that the consumer experiences anxiety and frustration in her attempts to close the gap between the actual and the ideal self.

Advertising is said to produce not only dissatisfaction with self, and accompanying anxiety and frustration, but also a distortion of self, which may be interpreted as the valuing of self for the "wrong" reasons. The critics suggest that the mechanism for this distortion could be direct statements by the advertiser about the individual consumer, statements about the way the individual views others and the way they view him, or statements about the relationship between the individual and physical objects. For example, Action for Children's Television (ACT) asserted that children's television commercials strain the parent-child relationship. This assertion was supported by a survey which found that mothers have unfavorable attitudes toward children's television commercials.[27] ACT quoted a television columnist and critic who stated:

The makers of $15 toys know that Junior must be worked up to fever pitch if he is to have sufficient fanatical gleam in his eye to wrest that much cash from Dad. So pour on the juice. The deafening, super-souped ads for a Johnny Shriek Racer or a Kill-Krush Robot are designed to fill Junior with power-lust. Some ads teach him how to hit Dad for the loot.

---

[26]Theodore Levitt, "The Morality (?) of Advertising," *Harvard Business Review*, 48 (July-August, 1970), p. 85.

[27]Earle K. Moore and Edward A. Bernstein, "Reply Comments of Action for Children's Television," paper submitted to the Federal Communications Commission, April 29, 1970, p. 9.

The implication is that the child is taught by advertising to see himself as a power-seeker, a quality his parents apparently prefer that he not have.

The individual, of course, defines and evaluates himself at least partially in response to his perceptions of others and how they relate to him. If he believes that others (in his society) value him because of his possessions, for example, then this may determine his evaluation of self, his evaluation of the importance of possessions, and his evaluation of others. The critic views advertising as a stimulus that acts to define for the individual the nature of this self-other-object system. This system, as defined by advertising, produces or fosters a value system that is "harmful," either (1) because it results in anxiety and frustration or (2) because it is not consistent with the value system that the critic considers desirable for the individual, society, or culture. Many critics have described this inconsistent value system they believe is fostered by advertising.

Two examples which may be regarded as typical can be noted. One is cited by Frank Whitehead, who considers the consequences of the advertiser's effort:

Even more insidious may be the advertiser's growing ingenuity in linking his product with ideas and images which are in themselves innocuous, pleasurable, even commendable. In consequence of this the concepts of sexual love, manliness, femininity, maternal feeling are steadily devalued for us by their mercenary association with a brand-name. . . .[28]

Another is by James C. Halloran, who describes the society he sees resulting from an advertising value system:

To consume becomes the main principle of life and there is a tendency for emotions and feelings to become more involved with things (goods) than with people. There is little room for altruism, idealism or unselfishness, and it seems highly probable that this concentration on consumption of material goods will produce attitudes unfavourable to responsibility for others and their needs, a mode of thinking which will habitually suppress large areas of our real relationships (including our dependence on others and a sense of community), and inward-turning on the self, away from matters of dispute and social concern, away from responsibility.[29]

There are two questions to be raised in this connection. Does advertising cause people to have certain wants they *should* not have? The second precedes the first—can advertising, in fact, change people's wants, or is it merely instrumental in showing them ways of satisfying their existing wants?

In a recent court decision it was implied that the judge thought advertising does create motives. A U.S. Court of Appeals placed automobile ad-

---

[28]Frank Whitehead, "Advertising," in Denys Thompson, ed., *Discrimination and Popular Culture* (Baltimore: Penguin Books, 1964), p. 31.

[29]Halloran, *Control or Consent?*, pp. 70–71.

vertising in the same category as cigarette advertising by requiring the TV station to make available time for an antipollution group to reply to the advertising. The court is quoted as stating, "Commercials that continue to insinuate that the human personality finds greater fulfillment in the large car with the quick getaway do, it seems to us, ventilate a point of view which not only has become controversial but involves an issue of public importance."[30] The evidence is not at all clear. We do know that other people influence our buying decisions much more than does advertising, but the nature of the causal path is at the moment not clear. The effect could be either through modifying the motive structure or merely serving in an instrumental role. If it does change motive structure, then advertising could well be culpable on these grounds. Instead, it could be that advertising merely stimulates the intensity of a motive which would later show itself anyway: a housewife buys a brand today which an empty container on her shelf would trigger her to buy tomorrow. We would be less concerned about the second effect than the first.

Points not made by critics

There are some additional points about the information role of advertising that do not seem to be covered by the critics. We know that the consumer's tendency to forget information and constant product change result in uncertainty, and we know that this makes a person uncomfortable. We have little direct objective evidence, however, about how much uncertainty is created by what kinds of products under what conditions of purchase. One measure could be length of time required to make the decision.[31] We do have the important evidence in Chapter 8, however, that brand comprehension is positively related to attitude and intention to buy.

The critics seem to neglect the consumer's need for information and the role of advertising in informing consumers about new products. They especially ignore the *cost of information*. Advertising often provides an easy, painless, costless and sometimes even thoroughly entertaining way of obtaining information. In Italy in 1967, for example, there were only 12 minutes of advertising per day in the statewide TV system, on a show called "Carousel." It was reported that "Extraordinarily enough 'Carousel' commanded the largest audience of any program."[32]

Also passed over is the buyer's almost incredible capacity to *tune out* information he considers irrelevant and useful and the consequent and corresponding capacity to tune in relevant information. Further, critics underrate the buyer's tendency to be skeptical, to treat as irrelevant any

---

[30]*Advertising Age*, August 23, 1971, p. 46.
[31]J. W. Newman and R. Staelin, "Multivariate Analysis of Differences in Buyer Decision Time," *Journal of Marketing Research*, 8 (1971): 197–98.
[32]*New York Times Magazine*, July 9, 1967, p. 34.

information that he thinks isn't true. Probably not recognized also is that the consumer has many demands on his time and effort, *information processing is effortful*, and he might buy no differently if confronted with more information.

Whether advertising causes the person to broaden his knowledge of competing brands is an important question. Casual evidence suggests that it does, but this is by no means conclusive. On the other hand, even the best of advertising *is* incomplete: it does not tell the bad features of its own product or the good features of the competitor's offering. There has been discussion in regulative circles of requiring "full disclosure." Most industry representatives agree this is probably not feasible. As Andy Kershaw, head of Ogilvy and Mather, an ad agency, has put it, "The truth, nothing but the truth, but *not* the whole truth."

Even some advertising agencies are concerned that there is too much advertising. Paul C. Harper, Jr. chairman of the board, Needham, Harper & Steers, Inc., recently stated, "It is time the media and our industry acted in concert on this matter. A first step would be a compact to limit the number of allowable messages. A second step in certain high-clutter areas may have to be a cutback in allowable commercial minutes."[33]

Mr. Harper's position raises a number of questions. First, many people do complain that too much of the program time is devoted to advertising. This complaint differs considerably in intensity among social classes. Second, given program-media allocation, is it information about too many alternatives or too much information about given alternatives that is the problem? We must recognize that too much information probably also causes anxiety. It is likely that most consumers would prefer to know about a wide range of alternatives, providing there are differences, in fact, among the brands, including their capacities to satisfy subtle self-concept needs. Differentiating devices which contribute no differences are questionable, as indicated by the concern with "truth in packaging." And even if there are no differences, the advertising can create a difference in that it tells the consumer brand A is backed by a company of some substance because it has the size to justify the expenditure of advertising. As for information about given products, insofar as the buyer's tuning-out devices operate, "excessive" advertising or "clutter" should not be harmful.

Finally, and going beyond advertising, a question not often raised but relevant is whether the general quality of the best in the product class is good enough. Can this be operationalized by a measure of the discrepancy between the buyer's ideal brand and his preferred brand? Of course, this question is only an aspect of the seller's general ability to identify the needs of the buyers to whom he is selling. Earlier in the chapter it was asked whether he could, in fact, identify buyer's needs. Often in Chapters

---

[33]"A Fireside Chat with Commissioner X," September 27, 1971.

2 through 16 there were references to current management's limited ability to do this. We must conclude that although the future looks brighter, this has not been satisfactorily done in the past. If the true effects of "untruthful" advertising and excessive advertising were known, we suspect that much of it would be discontinued in management's own interest.

Another aspect of this ability is whether management can do well in identifying and serving different markets. This is the market segmentation problem, which has become sharper. Only recently has much attention been devoted to it.

Related to market segmentation is the public policy concern about particular market segments. People differ in their capacity (and willingness?) to obtain and use information and thus complicate the doctrine of consumer sovereignty. Currently, there is great criticism about TV advertising for children. It is questionable whether firms have demonstrated adequately differentiated strategies for the ghetto, older folks, and so forth. These people are more limited in their information-processing capacity, but isn't this an aspect of a much bigger question that should not be confused with advertising issues? Or is it an advertising problem?

CONCLUSIONS

In the preceding pages an attempt has been made to describe many of the issues involved in evaluating a marketing system in a technologically advanced society. Evaluation requires a rationale which incorporates the *valid* criticisms, explains how the system works, and yields *actionable* criteria. Advertising was examined as representative of all elements of the marketing mix. The validity of many of the criticisms reviewed is unknown. This opens an immense research opportunity, although some of these assertions probably are not testable in the current state of the art.

Some actionable criteria were proposed. The market structure concept, which has traditionally been the economic rationale, offers one such criterion: number and size distribution of firms. If there are four firms or less of equal size in the industry, action should be taken by breaking up the existing firms into smaller ones, according to the principle being proposed in the cereal case by the Federal Trade Commission. The market structure concept mainly deals, however, with the problem of providing adequate options for the consumers. It does not deal with the other problem of consumer sovereignty: The adequacy and availability of information.

Obviously without a systematic rationale, we do not know whether the correct questions are being raised. We believe that the theory of buyer behavior offers a basis for beginning to develop criteria that will ultimately become a major part of a systematic rationale on the consumer side to supplement that now available on the competitive side.

The task of developing a rationale remains, but the encouraging aspect of the many current controversies is that the issues are being publicly debated. Hopefully, this will also stimulate relevant research so that many statements used in the past will be seen for what they are, unsupported assertions. In this information vacuum, the charges against advertising have increasingly seemed to be regarded as authoritative. Galbraith, for example, is now being cited as an authority on advertising in the most respected scientific circles, such as *Science* magazine. R. S. Morrison uses Galbraith's *The Affluent Society* as evidence when he states, "Indeed, it can be shown that the modern affluent consumer is, in a sense, a victim of synthetic desires which are created rather than satisfied by increased production."[34]

As for an assessment, in terms of efficiency and growth as judged by bits and pieces of evidence, the American marketing system seems to have done rather well. Also, as compared with the rest of the world it seems to have acquitted itself quite satisfactorily. Our supermarkets, discount stores, and specialty shops attest to efficiency and variety. But the complex issues of the buyer's adequacy of information are just now beginning to be explored systematically. Until more is known, no systematic judgment can be hoped for. The issues described here, however, hopefully ask the right questions, and this is obviously important.

This leads to the fundamental question of whether we will come to understand the American marketing system soon enough, or will well-intentioned public-policy measures be taken which will impair its effectiveness before we can acquire that understanding? Deep-seated skepticism of American marketing, especially of advertising, is shared by many influential Americans. This can be illustrated by the former dean of a well-known business school who at one time asserted that teaching advertising in a school of business is like teaching prostitution in a sociology department. He went on to become president of one of America's great universities. His assertion might ultimately be proven to be correct, but his factual basis for it at that time was negligible. Further, facts alone never answer a public-policy question. Values, too, are an essential ingredient.

Finally, insofar as current marketing management is culpable, it is largely because of ignorance, not malintention. At the same time we must recognize the fact that many top managements appear to deliberately violate accepted social standards, to the point that rules with penalties for violation are needed. This may be because they don't know what is happening at the brand manager level in their own companies, or because they fear stockholders will not permit them to follow the Committee on Economic Development's proposed creed cited in Chapter 15 and referred to above. If so, are they correct? Ponder this question.

---

[34]Robert S. Morrison, "Science and Social Attitudes," *Science*, Vol. 165 (July–September 1969), p. 152.

DISCUSSION QUESTIONS

1. What is meant by "consumer sovereignty," and what is its relevance to the task of the marketing manager or brand manager?
2. What is meant when it is alleged that "current profits on a new product are overstated"?
3. Can you offer an explanation of why "consumerism" became an issue when it did, namely in the latter 1960s?
4. Evaluate Professor Galbraith's assertion, "To assert aesthetic goals is also to interfere seriously with the management of the consumer."
5. As someone probably looking forward to being in a brand manager position before too long, what does this chapter mean to you? Is it relevant? If so, in what specific ways?

_____
_____
_____
_____

part VII

Marketing management in nonprofit organizations

THE CONCERN of this book so far has been mainly with describing current and ideal practice in marketing management in a profit-oriented organization. However, this should be viewed merely as an example, a special case, of marketing management, which is applicable to any human organization. All human organizations do have marketing problems. When applied to nonprofit organizations, we call it "social marketing."

17

Social marketing:
Brief comments

Marketing was defined at the beginning of this book in terms of communication processes. As such, it can be seen as a part of all human organizations. Largely because of this commonality, a wide variety of nonprofit organizations is becoming interested in applying marketing principles. At a recent meeting of the International Music Council (UNESCO), for example, a question raised was, "How can one induce the potentially enormous listening and viewing public to take an interest in the better things of music?" In describing this international event the reporter stated, "The word 'marketing' applied to serious music, recurred frequently throughout the sessions."[1]

It is well to bear in mind, however, that an implicit aspect of the definition of marketing is freedom of choice by the client. Like all marketing, social marketing implies changing behavior (in the marketer's favor) or preventing behavior change (to favor a competing alternative). Force of a public or illegal private nature is a way of changing human behavior, but it is inconsistent with marketing. The course of action in changing behavior by marketing is to identify the buyers' needs and then to provide him with an alternative that fits his needs better. Your response may be, "Any stupe can do that!" Remember, however, Chapters 2 to 15. It is difficult for an organization to change behavior in a way that will serve the organization's objectives.

Another implicit aspect of marketing is that a transaction is involved.

---

[1] *Christian Science Monitor*, August 23, 1972, p. 12.

In a transaction, each party gives up something in return for something. Probably with few, if any, exceptions, accepting something involves a cost in some form, even if no more than opportunity cost of time. To the extent the need being served is not important, the client will exhibit fewer of the characteristics of choosing, such as looking for information.

The difference between profit and social marketing does not appear to be marketing techniques and concepts but the underlying assumptions that guide their implementation as discussed in Chapter 1. We have not yet had the experience with social marketing to know what these underlying assumptions are and to know whether they are different. We will examine three aspects: basic marketing concepts, organization, and the "new marketing technology" discussed in Chapter 8.

The *basic marketing concepts* in social marketing of positioning, product class, segmentation, target markets, marketing strategy, marketing mix, marketing plan, and organizational strategy (the social counterpart of corporate strategy) would seem to be relevant to any organization. When applied, these concepts can provide a fairly systematic way of organizing and thinking about a marketing plan.

Organizational problems in social marketing would also seem to be similar. Questions of efficiency inevitably arise. Incongruities among goals, impersonal attitudes, and evaluative criteria must surely be present to weaken the organization's effectiveness. Coordinating different parts of the organization is as difficult as with any corporation. The choice of an integration or differentiation principle of organizing must be made. Control may be more difficult because of less emphasis on the money calculus.

The *new marketing technology* in social marketing, as represented by the theory of consumer behavior and structural models, is just as applicable, at least in some cases. They are being used in family planning in Kenya, for example. True enough, when the client receives an intangible item he probably has greater difficulty conceptualizing it than he would a tangible product. This, however, is true of any service marketed by either a nonprofit or profit organization.

We are confident that it would be a valuable experience for marketers to concern themselves with social marketing projects. It would increase the generality of marketing concepts and offer new ideas. Such attempts should be approached with some caution, however. The track record of those engaged in marketing is not a scintillating one. First, as we have attempted to show in the latter chapters of the book, they have not been terribly effective in relating marketing concepts to the more general corporate-policy kinds of problems. We suspect that many diversification mistakes have been substantially failures in the marketing aspects.

Second, they have been unsuccessful in introducing sophisticated market research techniques into company practice. From the marketing literature one would be led to believe that these in large measure constitute the body of marketing knowledge. Yet that they have not been accepted was well documented by the Public Hearings on Modern Advertising Practices by the Federal Trade Commission in October and November 1971.

DISCUSSION QUESTIONS

1. What do we mean by "social marketing"?
2. In the first paragraph of the chapter a reference was made to the International Music Council. How does its marketing problem, as implied there, differ from a package-goods company selling soap?
3. Attempt to apply the basic marketing concepts of positioning, product class, segmentation, marketing strategy, marketing plan, and so forth to the problem posed by the International Music Council, assuming that you are only concerned with the U.S. "market."
4. Do you feel that the organizational problems may be quite different in social marketing? If so, how?
5. Do you think the note of caution at the end of the brief chapter is justified?

cases

SPIC AND SPAN (A)
Change in copy emphasis

BACKGROUND

In 1951, Procter & Gamble's Spic and Span was already the giant in the household cleaner field, but its sales were severely seasonal, with a big peak at spring housecleaning time and a lesser peak in the fall. It was estimated that three fourths of its volume was consumed in the cleaning of painted woodwork and painted walls, the other fourth being consumed in a variety of cleaning applications.

Nielsen figures showed that Spic and Span was already carried by grocery stores doing 94 percent of the total grocery store volume, so Procter & Gamble could not hope to gain appreciable volume by increasing distribution. Nielsen also showed that Spic and Span accounted for two thirds or more of the powdered household cleaner business. Its chief competitor sold less than one fourth the volume of Spic and Span. No other major national competitors (powder, liquid or paste) were sold for cleaning painted woodwork and painted walls. There were no significant geographic weak spots in its sales. Procter & Gamble had, in Spic and Span, a successful product that had captured such a large share of its market that its growth possibilities seemed dim.

A priori reasoning pointed to linoleum floor cleaning as the logical direction for gaining increased volume. Certainly floors were cleaned regularly the year around, and this application was thought likely to lessen Spic and Span's severe seasonality. The huge spring peak represented a genuine stocking problem. Consumer purchases during the months of April and May were so heavy that the retail shelf stocks (adequate for the other 10 months) were quickly depleted. The sales department had a major job alerting grocers to prepare for the spring bulge with greater reserve stocks, larger shelf-space allocations, and (hopefully) special mass displays.

Consumer use testing of Spic and Span against other floor cleaners proved it to be *equal to, or superior to, competition.* The product would not have to be changed to be sold as a *floor cleaner.* At stake, however, were the profitable sales of Spic and Span for cleaning *painted woodwork and walls.* The change in primary copy emphasis could jeopardize the existing business if the promotion of Spic and Span for floors implied (to the conscious or subconscious) that the product was now too strong for walls and woodwork. If Procter and Gamble appeared to be unduly conservative in evaluating risk, remember that they were gambling with an extremely profitable product.

ALTERNATIVE APPROACHES

1. Convert the copy emphasis at once to take advantage of floor cleaning's big potential.
2. Convert the copy emphasis slowly so the consumer cannot possibly think that there has been a product change.
3. Convert the copy emphasis to floor cleaning in a test market and gauge its effect on the business.
4. Forget the linoleum cleaning story, since there is already a profitable business in painted wall and woodwork cleaning.
5. Launch a companion but separate product designed especially for floor cleaning.

SPIC AND SPAN (B)
Change in copy emphasis

SPIC AND SPAN managers were considering in 1951 whether to change the advertising copy emphasis of Spic and Span from wall cleaning to floor cleaning. Because of the product's success as a wall cleaner, they decided to try the new copy that suggested floor cleaning in a test market before changing it nationwide. The profit foregone by the delay and the cost of the study, they felt, would be much more than offset by the decreased risk made possible by the data from the study.

Two test markets, Birmingham, Alabama, and Buffalo, New York, were selected in order to sample at least some climatic differences. The test was scheduled for the year June 1, 1951, to May 30, 1952. This was necessary in order to compare seasonal consequences. All locally controlled newspaper, radio, and television advertising in these two communities was converted to floor-cleaning copy in May, 1951, and this was continued throughout the year. National magazines, however, continued the wall-washing copy.

A sample of 300 housewives were interviewed in each test market in May, 1951, before the copy was changed, and again in May, 1952. Thus 1,200 interviews were taken, 600 pretest and 600 posttest. The combined results are shown in Exhibit 1.

The interview data, however, did not provide precise information on the volume of Spic and Span involved. It would be possible, for example, to sell a greater number of families but with an actual reduced volume

460

EXHIBIT 1
Consumer survey in the combined test markets

		Pretest	*Posttest*
1.°	Used Spic & Span in past 4 weeks	43%	52%
	Had Spic & Span in the house:		
2.	Regular Size	20	24
3.°	Large Size	16	28
	Tried Spic & Span in past 4 weeks for:		
4.	Painted woodwork	23	24
5.	Painted walls	19	17
6.°	Linoleum floors	12	25
	Attitude toward Spic & Span for cleaning painted woodwork & painted walls (users only). Housewives made:		
7.	Favorable comments only	35	33
8.	Unfavorable comments only	12	11
9.	Both favorable and unfavorable comment	48	52
10.	No specific comment pro or con	5	4
		100%	100%
	Largest unfavorable comments were:		
11.	Hard on hands	19%	21%
12.	Takes off paint	11	12
	Attitude toward Spic & Span for cleaning linoleum (users only). Housewives made:		
13.	Favorable comments only	40	37
14.	Unfavorable comments only	9	13
15.	Both favorable & unfavorable comments	47	42
16.°	No specific comment pro or con	4	8
		100%	100%

°Significant at 5 percent level.

because the heaviest buyers dropped out. Consequently, the Nielsen Food Index was used to augment the interview data. A special "breakout" of the regular Index was made by Nielsen for each of the market areas on a bimonthly basis. The results are shown in Exhibit 2. The numbers represent an index of physical volume necessary because of the different package sizes. The letters at the bottom of the two charts indicate the months.

After analyzing Exhibits 1 and 2, what is your conclusion as to whether Spic and Span should go nationwide with a modified copy which suggests that Spic and Span be used for cleaning *both* walls and floors? Support your conclusion as fully as you can, using the data to document your argument. Do you think the evidence acquired in the test justified the delay and cost? Explain at some length because this decision of whether to do research is a very common problem. Research can be used effectively to reduce risk or to mask managerial indecisiveness.

EXHIBIT 2
Experience in the two test markets

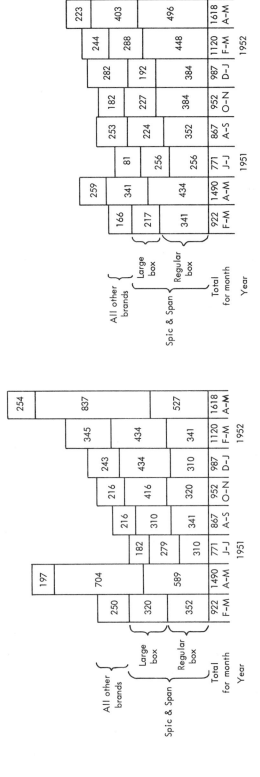

A. Buffalo test area

B. Birmingham test area

THE FEDERAL COMPANY*

THE FEDERAL COMPANY was a medium-sized manufacturer of consumer soft goods. The headquarters marketing staff in Cleveland was responsible for overall planning and direction of all marketing activities, while responsibility for field selling activities was assigned to the managers of the company's six regional branch offices.

David Halsey, Federal's marketing vice president, was experimenting with a new financial reporting format that he hoped would help him make better promotional expenditure decisions. "Our move to profit contribution reporting several years ago was a step in the right direction," he said, "but it didn't go far enough. For one thing, sales are still reported several months after the promotional activity takes place. This makes for some pretty funny profit contribution figures sometimes.

"For another, they still don't tell me whether I'm spending the right amount in each market area. For example, I was pretty sure that we were spending too much in the Atlanta branch, but I couldn't prove it. I couldn't put the squeeze on the branch manager, either, because he was turning in a larger profit contribution than any of the other branches. I want the system to help me answer this kind of question."

The new reporting system had been worked out by Jack McClendon, Federal's controller. "We made a special study," he said, "trying to find out how long it takes before promotional effort pays off. Frankly, the

*I am indebted to Professor Gordon Shillinglaw, Columbia University, for permission to use this case.

results aren't very clear, but they have given us something to think about. For instance, we found that calling on a customer more frequently seemed to increase the average order size as well as the total sales volume. I don't know how far we can carry that, but we're certainly going to follow up on it.

"We did find that the orders received in a month correlate pretty well with the current month's field selling and local advertising expenses. I've talked this over with Dave (Halsey) and we've agreed to report sales and cost of goods sold internally on the basis of orders received. That will mean a little more bookkeeping—the company's financial statements will still show revenues from shipments—but I think the benefits are worth it."

Mr. Halsey explained his experimental report structure to the case-writer. "The main feature of these reports is that they focus on month-to-month changes rather than on departures from the budget. We still get monthly reports of variances from the profit plan for control purposes, but they don't help us much in decision making.

"Let me show you what I mean. Here is last month's report for the Atlanta branch (Exhibit 1). The figures in the right-hand column show the changes from the same month a year ago. I'm not sure that that's the right way to go, but we felt that it would be better than a comparison of two successive months.

EXHIBIT 1
Profit Performance Report, Atlanta Branch

	This month	*Change from same month last year*
Sales (net orders received)	5,000	+ 450
Standard variable manufacturing cost	2,010	+ 181
Standard variable distribution cost	253	+ 22
Gross Margin	2,737	+ 247
Field selling expenses	669	+ 71
Local advertising	523	+ 65
Administration	128	+ 4
Total branch expenses	1,320	+ 140
Branch Profit.	1,417	+ 107
Effectiveness ratios		
Gross margin to sales	.55	—
Field selling and advertising to sales.	.24	—
Branch profit to sales	.28	—
Branch profit to field selling and advertising	1.19	.79

"Our real emphasis is on the ratios at the bottom of the report. The ratios in the left-hand column are conventional percentage figures. Every company uses these. Our big interest is in the ratio to the right, and I don't know of anyone else who calculates this one. It shows the relationship of the *change* in profit or the *change* in sales to the change that has taken place in marketing costs. We call this our 'response function.' At Atlanta, for example, we got 79 cents for every extra dollar that we spent on field selling and advertising. This is the $107,000 change in branch profit divided by the $136,000 change in field selling and advertising costs."

"That means that you didn't get your money back, doesn't it?"

"No, it's a net figure. We've already deducted the $136,000 from the profit figure, so that we're okay as long as the ratio is positive."

"I'm not sure how much good that ratio will do you," said the casewriter. "A lot of other things could have happened, and you can't assume that the increase in sales was all due to the added marketing costs."

"I can't argue with you on that, but we don't take the ratios one by one. What we really want to do is compare the branches, as we do here (in Exhibit 2). This shows that we were wrong about Atlanta. With a profit ratio of 0.79, it is now giving us more of our added promotional dollar than we get in any other branch. In fact, we're considering spending more money in Atlanta rather than less.

EXHIBIT 2
Branch Profit Comparison (dollar figures in thousands)

Results	*Atlanta*	*Cleveland*	*Houston*	*Boston*	*Denver*	*Seattle*
Sales:						
This year	5,000	4,560	3,076	3,249	1,865	2,722
Change from last year	+450	+333	+243	+390	−67	+132
Promotional Expense:						
This year	1,192	684	369	520	375	599
Change from last year	+136	+107	+90	+135	−44	+70
Branch Profit:						
This year	1,417	1,280	831	1,007	634	517
Change from last year	+107	+76	+40	+72	+5	−7
Effectiveness Ratios						
Current Period:						
Gross margin to sales	.55	.52	.42	.49	.58	.46
Promotional expenses to sales	.24	.18	.12	.16	.20	.22
Branch profit to sales	.28	.28	.27	.31	.34	.19
Response function (change in branch profit to change in promotional expenses)	+.79	+.71	+.44	+.54	−.11	−.10

"Seattle and Denver are at the other extreme. Both of them have negative ratios, and we may decide to cut back on our efforts there."

"I don't understand what the negative ratios mean. Why should they lead you to reduce your promotional outlays in those branches?"

"Well, look at Seattle, for instance. We put an extra $70,000 in there, but our branch profit went down by $7,000. That's a negative response to our effort. The extra $70,000 wasn't a very good investment, in my opinion."

"I can understand the minus figures for Seattle, but what about Denver? There your profit actually went up."

"That's right. We spent less than last year, and we lost some business as a result—sales were down by $67,000. Fortunately, the gross margin on the lost sales was less than the amount we saved in marketing expense. That's what a negative ratio means. Whenever I see a minus sign, it tells me that I can make money by spending less on marketing. With a plus sign, I figure that the market isn't saturated yet, so I should put in a little more money. It doesn't tell me how much more or less to spend, but it gives me the direction."

"How do you allow for changes in general economic conditions? It seems to me that these could have such huge effects on the changes that your ratios would lose all their validity."

"We haven't figured out how to grapple with that one yet. One way is to deal with quarterly data instead of monthly data and compare each quarter with the one before instead of the one a year earlier. The drawback there is that seasonal influences are important in our business, and I don't think the figures would be very useful. Another possibility is to adjust the figures in some way for changes in the gross national product or some other index of the volume of business generally. Even without these changes, though, I think we can use the ratios productively. Don't forget that a change in business conditions is likely to affect all of our markets. Other things being equal, a change of this kind would produce either minus signs in all branches or plus signs in all branches. We're looking for differences, knowing that the ratios aren't precise and that all they can do is suggest directions we might want to move."

QUESTIONS FOR DISCUSSION

1. Do you agree that Federal should spend more money in Atlanta and less in Denver and Seattle?
2. Do you think that the new reporting system will provide Mr. Halsey with better information for decision making? What changes, if any, would you make in the system to make it more useful?
3. What other means can you suggest for obtaining information on marketing response functions?

THE NESTLÉ COMPANY

THE NESTLÉ COMPANY INC. was one of the five largest food-processing companies in the United States in the early 1960s. The annual sales volume during this period exceeded $500,000,000. The product line had historically emphasized canned goods of a wide variety. In recent years a long series of convenience foods, such as frozen or dehydrated soups and vegetables and instant coffee, had been added. Over a period of 10 years the latter products had expanded in importance, to the extent that they contributed 40 percent of the net sales.

THE INSTANT-COFFEE MARKET

By 1961–62, both the total coffee market and the instant-coffee segment had reached a plateau of growth. A variety of reasons had been advanced for the state of the total coffee market. Although research was inconclusive, most of the reasons were traceable to an influx of new beverage types (such as instant tea) and new product categories (particularly soft drinks), while coffee was increasingly being regarded as a staple food item. In addition to these trends, instant coffee itself was thought to be affected by the fact that no significant product improvements had been made in the past 10 years, so no further ground-coffee buyers were being attracted.

Coffee buyers (and drinkers) were thought to fall into three distinct groups. In the first group were those who regarded coffee strictly as a hot drink and lacked "fineness" of taste. Instant-coffee users probably dominated this group because convenience of preparation assumed greater significance. The second group consisted of those who were aware of the difference in taste between instant and regular coffees but were willing to sacrifice some taste benefits for convenience. Presumably this group was approximately equally divided in its usage of regular and instant, but with a taste preference for regular (although there was evidence that a minority had come to prefer the taste of instant). The last group, however, placed a high value on taste and would have nothing to do with instant coffee. Although instant was 30 percent to 35 percent cheaper per cup than regular, this was not a major motive for the purchase of instant coffee, since only 10 percent of all coffee buyers were aware of the extent of this difference (and virtually no regular coffee buyers were aware of it).

Instant coffee had gained many users between 1950 and 1960 as the practice of using convenience foods became generally more acceptable. In the process it was felt that it had overcome most of the stigma associated with its use that existed at one time. The extent of the problem was examined in 1950 by a study[1] that effectively utilized projective techniques. Two groups of housewives were giving identical shopping lists, except that one list contained Nescafé and the other, Maxwell House regular. Each group was asked to describe the kind of person that would use the particular shopping list. Almost half of the respondents at that time described a hypothetical buyer of instant coffee (Nescafé) as being lazy, and failing to plan household purchases and schedules well (and 16 percent felt this buyer was not a good wife). Some of the respondents felt it necessary to "excuse" the woman who bought instant coffee by suggesting that she lived alone or had a job. One of the important conclusions was that instant coffee represented a departure from "homemade" coffee and the traditions with respect to caring for one's family.

There was a distinct possibility that many of the feelings reported in 1950 persisted in some regions and rural areas of the United States into the 1960s as well. At the end of the decade a study replicating the 1950 study.concluded, "While the Nescafé housewife of 1968 tends to be differentiated from the Maxwell House housewife on the same dimensions as the 1950 study, the differences have diminished to the point where they are no longer statistically significant. (This may also reflect differences in sample size to some extent.)" [2]

INSTANT-COFFEE MARKET RESEARCH

The stagnation in the growth of the instant-coffee market led to sharply increased competition between brands. Marketing strategies became al-

---

[1]Mason Haire, "Projective Techniques in Marketing Research," *Journal of Marketing*, 14 (April 1950), pp. 649–56.
[2]F. E. Webster, Jr., and F. VonPechman, "A Replication of the Shopping List Study," *Journal of Marketing*, 34 (April 1970), pp. 61–63.

most entirely concerned with expanding individual brand market shares at the expense of other brands. The planning of these strategies required more precise and detailed information about the composition of the market and its responsiveness to different levels of advertising, price, and promotional activity than had been necessary before.

Up to this point the Nestlé Company, Inc., instant-coffee brand group had only required store-audit-type data by Nielsen on market share, relative price movements, and distribution levels by region. However, this revealed nothing about the kinds of buyers the Nescafé brand was attracting, their loyalty, or their responsiveness to price changes, deals, and specific promotional campaigns. The first additional source of information investigated was a national consumer mail panel. This provided quarterly summaries of brands purchased, price paid (including coupons, deals, and premiums used), average size of purchase, and demographic data on 1,000 families for $55,000 per year. However, the panel trial was discontinued after six months when it became evident that the families in it were overly price conscious and were buying a disproportionate share of the lower priced instant-coffee brands. It was felt that this was caused by the reward given to all participants being more attractive to price-conscious people.

The search for a more suitable alternative resulted in the adoption of a telephone interview questionnaire designed to measure consumer awareness, attitudes, purchase behavior, and similar factors. Since the same basic questionnaire was repeated at regular interviews, it provided information that could easily be related to other known market factors such as brand-share movements and advertising expenditures. Relative to the panel, the telephone survey approach had the advantages of less bias (although it was known that it underrepresented the very high and the very low income categories) and a lower annual cost of approximately $36,000. There was, of course, the necessary disadvantage of being unable to follow individual consumers through a sequence of purchases. And regardless of the alternative chosen, it was still necessary to periodically conduct in-store experimentation or one-time surveys to solve special problems. After two years the survey, coupled with the store audit information, had become the basis of the company's instant-coffee market information system.

At the end of the two-year period, five attitude studies or waves had been conducted. Each wave followed the same basic procedure. First, a telephone contact was made with a national probability sample of 6,000 U.S. households. A different group was contacted for each wave, instead of using a continuous panel. The entire questionnaire,[3] requiring 10 to 12

---

[3]Appendix A to this case provides a replication of the wave 5 (February 1964) questionnaire, while Appendix B compares the questions asked in each of the first four waves to those in wave 5.

minutes to complete, was administered to those who answered "yes." When asked whether they had purchased instant coffee within 90 days prior to the interview, on the average,[4] about 40 percent responded that they had bought instant coffee in the past 60 days.

The waves were designed to be conducted in October, February, and June of each year. February and June were chosen to pinpoint the major seasonal differences, since monthly consumption usually declined between 10 and 15 percent in the summer. Another wave was necessary in the first week of October to observe the effect of the new promotional campaigns then being launched. It was the common pattern in the market to do relatively little advertising in the summer and start again in September.

Ultimately it was up to the brand manager responsible for Nescafé brand instant coffee to utilize the results of this monitoring of his market. The wave 5 results had just been tabulated and summarized in a standard format amenable to trend comparisons between waves. (See Tables 1 through 8 at the end of the case for these results combined with the store-audit data for the period.) In preparing the usual position report, based on the data he had received, the brand manager realized he had to keep three basic questions before him:

1. What has been happening in the market during the period between the fourth and fifth waves, and what are the implications for marketing strategy in the coming year?
2. What further analysis (in the form of additional cross-tabulations and other statistical manipulations) should be made on the raw data to refine the understanding of the buyer and the market? In connection with this question, the brand manager was wondering whether some of the models of brand-switching behavior had any relevance to the instant coffee market.
3. Although each wave contained a number of identical questions to ensure comparability, provision was also made for special one-time questions relating to matters of media exposure, packaging, store patronage, and so forth.

In the course of his review of the wave 5 data the brand manager hoped to be able to define some problem areas which could be better understood through special questions placed in the projected wave 6. It was planned that this wave would go into the field in three months' time. Since the respondents to the last wave were known by name, address, and telephone number, the brand manager was wondering whether a follow-up mail or telephone interview to just this group would provide any addi-

---

[4]Actual sample sizes: Wave 5—2455, Wave 4—2415, Wave 3—2319, Wave 1—2548, Wave 2—2450.

tional useful information. The value of the information would have to outweigh the difficulties in generating a reasonable level of mail response, tracing those who had moved and calling back if the telephone were used.

MARKET PLANNING

After reviewing the results of this five-wave analysis, the brand manager for Nescafé was in a quandary. What recommendations for his marketing plan did the findings imply?

He had been following a fairly conservative brand strategy. Price had been used both to maintain distribution deals to the trade and to attract new customers by consumer deals, but neither practice had been employed to the extent, for example, of Chase and Sanborn. Advertising had been substantial, and, whenever possible, new-product ideas formed an essential part of the copy.

In the light of the data obtained from waves 1 to 5 inclusive, should a different marketing mix be employed in the annual marketing plan? If not, why not? If it should, what form should it take? For planning purposes you can assume that the cost of producing a pound of instant coffee is about 50 percent of the price.

INTRODUCTION TO TABLES 1 THROUGH 8

Definitions used in analyzing survey data

A number of specially designed definitions were used by the Nestlé Company, Inc., to make the survey data more meaningful. They are described below in the order in which they are encountered in the tables. All references to question numbers are based on the questionnaire used in wave 5, which is given as Appendix A at the end of the case. "Q" in the following discussion means "Question."

Brand awareness—results of unaided recall, Q1.

Advertising awareness—(same as recall of advertising)—also based on unaided recall. Q2.

Favorable disposition—from Q3 but only using categories 1 and 2, i.e., sum of responses "one best" and "several better" for each brand.

Loyal buyers—defined by Q10. The occasional buyers category for brand X, for example, represents the difference between all those who included brand X in Q7 and those who answered brand X was their usual brand in Q10.

Brand share—This is a disguised figure to avoid revealing critical information based largely on adjustments to company estimates but also incorporates information from published sources, such as the Pan American Coffee Bureau.

Average volume per using household (ounces)—This figure is based on the total number of users (from Q7) of the brand divided into the brand's share of the total number of pounds of instant coffee sold in the preceding two months (for wave 5 this was 13,800,000 pounds).

Brand attitudes—based on Q3.

Brand buyers—those who answered "own brand only" to Q5.

Price buyers—This definition is the result of adding together the following four groups: (1) those who answered "yes" to Q4 and "any brand" to Q5; (2) those who answered "no" to Q4 and "any brand" to Q5; (3) those who answered "yes" to Q4, "own brand only" to Q5, and gave only one brand name in response to Q4a but gave a different brand as their usual brand in Q10a; and, (4) those who answered "yes" to Q4, "own brand only" to Q5, and gave more than one brand name in answer to Q4a.

Current/Most accessible franchise—made up of two groups: (1) those who answer brand X to either Q3a or 3b, plus (2) those who are aware of brand X in Q1 and answer "all alike" to Q3—i.e., they do not discriminate among brands.

Remaining potential—the remainder after the above calculation, split into those who are aware of brand X and those who are unaware (from Q1).

TABLE 1
Summary trends by brand (expressed in millions of instant-coffee-buying households or percent of total market)

Brand	Variable	Wave 1 (February)	Wave 2 (October)	Wave 3 (June)	Wave 4 (September)	Wave 5 (February)
Decaf	Brand awareness	(not asked)	(not asked)	2.8 (13%)	2.0 (9%)	2.3 (10%)
	Recall advertising	1.6 (7%)	0.9 (4%)	0.9 (4)	0.5 (2)	0.7 (3)
	Favorable disposition	0.5 (2)	0.7 (3)	0.7 (3)	0.5 (2)	0.3 (1)
	Loyal buyers	0.23 (1)	0.23 (1)	0.22 (1)	0.23 (1)	0.18 (1)
	Occasional buyers	0.47 (2)	0.47 (2)	0.43 (2)	0.44 (2)	0.37 (1)
	Share of market	0.9%	1.2%	1.3%	1.3%	1.2%
	Average volume per using household	2 oz.	2 oz.	3 oz.	3 oz.	4 oz.
Chase and Sanborn	Brand awareness	(not asked)	(not asked)	8.3 (38%)	9.0 (40%)	9.1 (40%)
	Recall advertising	1.9 (8%)	2.0 (9%)	0.9 (4)	1.4 (6)	1.8 (8)
	Favorable disposition	1.4 (6)	1.4 (6)	1.3 (6)	1.4 (6)	1.6 (7)
	Loyal buyers	0.7 (3)	0.7 (3)	0.7 (3)	0.5 (2)	0.6 (3)
	Occasional buyers	1.4 (6)	1.8 (8)	1.5 (7)	2.0 (9)	2.0 (8)
	Share of market	7.3%	8.6%	7.8%	7.7%	7.6%
	Average volume per using household	7 oz.	6 oz.	6 oz.	5 oz.	6 oz.
Sanka	Brand awareness	(not asked)	(not asked)	7.2 (33%)	7.2 (32%)	7.6 (33%)
	Recall advertising	2.1 (9%)	2.5 (11%)	1.3 (6)	1.4 (6)	1.8 (8)
	Favorable disposition	2.1 (9)	2.2 (10)	2.4 (11)	2.0 (9)	2.1 (9)
	Loyal buyers	1.4 (6)	1.1 (5)	1.3 (6)	1.4 (6)	1.0 (4)
	Occasional buyers	1.4 (6)	1.8 (8)	2.1 (10)	1.6 (7)	2.1 (10)
	Share of market	7.9%	8.2%	7.7%	7.5%	7.1%
	Average volume per using household	5 oz.	4 oz.	4 oz.	5 oz.	5 oz.
Nescafé	Brand awareness	(not asked)	(not asked)	9.8 (45%)	10.8 (48%)	12.5 (54%)
	Recall advertising	3.0 (13%)	3.2 (14%)	2.6 (12)	3.6 (16)	3.6 (15)
	Favorable disposition	1.9 (8)	2.3 (10)	2.8 (13)	2.3 (10)	2.5 (11)
	Loyal buyers	1.2 (5)	1.4 (6)	1.5 (7)	1.6 (7)	1.8 (8)
	Occasional buyers	1.2 (5)	1.6 (7)	2.0 (9)	2.3 (10)	2.4 (10)
	Share of market	9.3%	10.9%	11.7%	12.3%	12.9%
	Average volume per using household	8 oz.	9 oz.	7 oz.	7 oz.	6 oz.
Instant Maxwell House	Brand awareness	(not asked)	(not asked)	17.7 (81%)	19.2 (85%)	20.3 (88%)
	Recall advertising	7.4 (32%)	7.4 (33%)	5.2 (24)	7.7 (34)	8.1 (35)
	Favorable disposition	9.5 (41)	9.0 (40)	8.5 (39)	9.5 (42)	9.5 (41)
	Loyal buyers	8.4 (36)	7.2 (32)	6.8 (31)	7.5 (33)	7.4 (32)
	Occasional buyers	3.9 (17)	4.1 (18)	4.4 (20)	5.2 (23)	5.6 (24)
	Share of market	44.5%	41.1%	39.0%	40.0%	37.7%
	Average volume per using household	8 oz.	7 oz.	6 oz.	6 oz.	6 oz.
Yuban	Brand awareness	(not asked)	(not asked)	6.3 (29%)	5.9 (26%)	6.3 (27%)
	Recall advertising	2.3 (10%)	2.0 (9%)	1.7 (8)	1.1 (5)	1.6 (7)
	Favorable disposition	1.9 (8)	1.8 (8)	1.7 (8)	1.4 (6)	1.7 (7)
	Loyal buyers	1.16 (5)	0.90 (4)	1.09 (5)	0.68 (3)	0.82 (4)
	Occasional buyers	1.16 (5)	1.35 (6)	1.09 (5)	1.13 (5)	1.10 (4)
	Share of market	5.8%	5.5%	5.8%	5.6%	5.2%
	Average volume per using household	5 oz.	4 oz.	4 oz.	5 oz.	5 oz.

TABLE 2
Advertising expenditures by brand (thousands)

Brand	Jan. to June (Wave 1 taken in February)	July to Dec. (Wave 2 taken in October)	Jan. to June (Wave 3 taken in June)	July to Dec. (Wave 4 taken in September)
Decaf (Instant and Regular)	$ 805	$ 410	$ 91	$ 360
Chase & Sanborn				
Instant..........	2,080	1,518	1,290	1,190
Regular	410	425	280	280
Sanka				
Instant..........	720	450	708	295
Regular	1,490	1,720	1,730	2,304
Nescafé (Instant only) .... Instant	2,050	580	1,520	1,120
Maxwell House				
Instant..........	2,308	2,580	2,150	3,020
Regular	1,490	1,380	820	1,060
Yuban (Instant and Regular)	2,300	1,670	1,508	1,230

TABLE 3
Pricing and dealing trends by brand (price—average shelf price per 6-oz. jar deals—percentage of sales in "off-label" dealing)

Brand	Wave 1		Wave 2		Wave 3		Wave 4		Wave 5	
	Price	Deals	Price	Deals	Price	Deals	Price	Deals	Price	Deals
Decaf............	95c	73%	93c	72%	95c	76%	95c	74%	101c	66%
Chase and Sanborn.........	94	76	93	86	95	76	94	75	100	71
Sanka............	91	82	92	74	94	Nil	96	6	103	43
Nescafé	95	77	93	80	95	75	96	68	102	73
Instant Maxwell House	99	39	100	20	104	Nil	102	Nil	107	22
Yuban	107	22	107	18	112	15	111	24	112	31

TABLE 4
Basic regional trends, attitude and purchase behavior

	Total		Region 1°		Region 2°		Region 3°	
	Wave 4	Wave 5	Wave 4	Wave 5	Wave 4	Wave 5	Wave 4	Wave 5
Loyalty (have a usual brand)	74%	74%	75%	74%	76%	76%	71%	73%
Attitudes toward brands:								
One brand is best	53	52	51	52	56	54	55	52
Several brands are better.............	21	23	23	20	16	23	23	27
All brands are alike...	26	25	26	28	28	23	22	21
Price buyers	35	46	35	47	37	45	33	45
Purchasing activity (brands bought in past 3 months):								
Decaf..............	3	3	5	5	1	1	1	1
Chase and Sanborn...	11	11	14	14	10	12	4	5
Sanka..............	13	14	4	4	13	16	32	30
Nescafé ....,....	17	18	22	23	15	15	8	10
Instant Maxwell House	56	56	59	61	57	54	51	49
Yuban	9	8	11	10	6	8	6	4
All others...........	47	51	46	50	50	52	48	54
Sample Base	2,415	2,455	1,237	1,248	578	614	600	593

°Regions are not identified to protect the company.

TABLE 5
Brand share trends by region

Brand	Region	Wave 1	Wave 2	Wave 3	Wave 4	Wave 5
Decaf	1.........	1.5	1.7	2.0	2.0	1.8
	2.........	0.4	0.3	0.4	0.3	0.3
	3.........	—	—	—	—	—
Chase &	1.........	8.7	10.4	9.1	9.0	8.9
Sanborn	2.........	6.7	8.0	7.6	7.6	7.7
	3.........	3.6	3.9	4.3	4.2	4.4
Sanka	1.........	4.4	4.3	4.3	4.1	3.8
	2.........	7.9	7.8	7.3	6.6	6.5
	3.........	12.7	13.6	13.2	13.9	13.2
Nescafé	1.........	12.0	13.7	14.9	15.1	15.8
	2.........	7.3	8.7	9.7	10.5	12.0
	3.........	4.2	5.0	5.0	6.2	6.7
Instant	1.........	46.9	42.4	40.7	41.6	41.9
Maxwell	2.........	41.9	39.4	36.9	38.6	36.7
House	3.........	40.0	39.2	36.5	37.0	36.9
Folger's	1.........	6.9	6.7	7.4	7.0	7.5
	2.........	9.4	9.0	9.5	9.1	10.0
	3.........	9.4	9.5	9.9	9.2	10.4
Yuban	1.........	6.7	6.4	6.4	6.4	7.0
	2.........	6.0	5.4	4.9	5.3	5.8
	3.........	4.0	3.4	3.7	3.8	4.0

TABLE 6
Trends in price consciousness

	Price buyers		Brand buyers	
	Wave 4	Wave 5	Wave 4	Wave 5
Brand loyalty:				
Have a usual brand	47%	45%	89%	99%
Do not have a usual brand	53	55	11	1
Brand attitudes:				
One brand is best	28	26	67	75
Several brands are better	27	36	18	11
All brands are alike	45	38	15	14
Purchasing activity (brands bought in past 3 months):				
Decaf	3	4	2	2
Chase and Sanborn				
Loyal buyers	2	2	3	4
Occasional buyers	17	16	3	2
Sanka				
Loyal buyers	4	4	7	5
Occasional buyers	15	16	3	3
Nescafé				
Loyal buyers	6	6	7	9
Occasional buyers	20	19	5	3
Instant Maxwell House				
Loyal buyers	19	18	41	44
Occasional buyers	44	45	11	6
Yuban	10	11	8	6
All others	71	71	42	44
Bases	(854)	(1128)	(1561)	(1327)

TABLE 7
Sales potentials for leading brands

	Current/Most accessible franchise*		Remaining potential			
			Conscious of brand		Not conscious of brand	
Brand	Wave 4	Wave 5	Wave 4	Wave 5	Wave 4	Wave 5
Chase and Sanborn	17% (65%)	19% (58%)	23%	21%	60%	60%
Sanka	17% (77%)	19% (74%)	15%	14%	68%	67%
Nescafe	24% (71%)	28% (64%)	24%	26%	52%	46%
Instant Maxwell House	65% (86%)	67% (84%)	20%	21%	15%	12%

*Note: Table should be read: 17% of the instant-coffee households, at the time of wave 4, were within Chase and Sanborn's "current/most accessible franchise." Percentages in brackets represent proportion of "current/most accessible franchise" for the brand which is actually being realized by the brand—calculated as follows for Chase and Sanborn in wave 4:

$$\frac{\text{Purchasing activity (see Table 4)} = 11}{\text{Current/most accessible franchise} = 17} = 65\%$$

TABLE 8
Comparison of advertising registration

Brand	Ability of respondents claiming awareness to recall specific ideas	Wave 1	Wave 2	Wave 3	Wave 5
Decaf	Quality claim	23%	7%	7%	7%
	Jingle/description	19%	26%	22%	34%
	Kind of commercial	16	19	1	—
	Value claim	8	9	7	9
	Quality claim	13	4	14	7
	Other replies	9	2	14	10
	Unable to correctly recall specific ideas	29%	36%	43%	36%
	Base: Respondents claiming awareness of Decaf advertising	(181)	(85)	(81)	(70)
Chase and Sanborn	Taste claim	6%	7%	9%	3%
	Flavor and aroma claim	1	3	—	—
	References to couponing	—	—	—	5
	References to package	1	3	—	—
	Kind of coffee	—	—	—	3
	Quality claim	8	7	13	1
	Other replies	13	5	12	12
	Unable to correctly recall specific ideas	72%	75%	66%	78%
	Base: Respondents claiming awareness of Chase and Sanborn advertising	(206)	(213)	(100)	(197)
Sanka	Flavor claim	27%	29%	27%	26%
	Taste claim	9	3	4	—
	Jingle/gimmick	6	4	3	—
	Value claim	2	3	1	3
	Format of commercial	2	2	2	—
	Part of commercial	—	—	—	3
	Quality claim	8	7	7	3
	Other replies	12	14	14	11
	Unable to correctly recall specific ideas	42%	38%	43%	53%
	Base: Respondents claiming awareness of Sanka's advertising	(229)	(274)	(148)	(190)
Nescafé	Base: of preparation	—	—	30%	25%
	Taste claim	51%	38%	8	—
	Flavor claim	4	1	2	—
	Richness claim	3	1	1	—
	Quality claim	4	2	3	7
	Other replies	8	2	9	10
	Unable to correctly recall specific ideas	39%	50%	52%	60%
	Base: Respondents claiming awareness of Nescafé advertising	(339)	(333)	(282)	(378)

TABLE 8 (continued)

Instant	Flavor appeal...................	20%	15%	15%	6%
Maxwell	Value claim	17	34	37	3
House	Premium give-away	8	1	3	4
	References to package...........	7	6	6	—
	Format of commercial...........	3	5	5	2
	Part of commercial	2	1	7	—
	Testimonial	—	—	—	21
	Preparation	—	—	—	17
	Quality claim..................	8	5	5	5
	Other replies	9	2	3	7
	Unable to correctly recall specific ideas	34%	33%	27%	40%
	Base: Respondents claiming awareness of Instant Maxwell House advertising	(822)	(815)	(563)	(861)
Yuban	Richness claim..................	15%	23%	18%	26%
	Representation	4	6	9	8
	Taste claim	3	5	7	5
	Value claim	—	—	6	9
	Flavor claim	—	—	—	6
	Quality claim..................	13	20	6	4
	Other replies	26	7	10	11
	Unable to correctly recall specific ideas	47%	41%	51%	46%
	Base: Respondents claiming awareness of Yuban advertising..................	(261)	(208)	(176)	(170)

APPENDIX A: INSTANT COFFEE USERS QUESTIONNAIRE, WAVE 5

Telephone No. _____

1. What are all the different brands of instant coffee (both decaffeinated and regular type instant) that you know of that can be bought around here? (*Check below*)

    For each one named, ask:

    1a. Which, if any, are decaffeinated (*Check below*)

2. What are all the different brands of instant coffee (both decaffeinated and regular) that you can distinctly recall having seen or heard advertised during the past thirty days either on radio or TV, in magazines or newspapers? (*Check below*)

    For each brand seen/heard advertised, ask:

    2a. What can you recall about the advertising for that particular brand—specifically what are they saying or showing about that brand in their advertising these days? (*Enter below*)

Brand	Q.1 Know About	Q.1a Decaffeinated	Q.2 Seen Advtd.	Q.2a For each brand named in Question 2—"What are they saying or showing in their ads?"
1. Hills Bros.	☐ 1	☐ 1	☐ 1	_____
2. Butternut	☐ 2	☐ 2	☐ 2	_____
3. Decaf.	☐ 3	☐ 3	☐ 3	_____
4. Chase and Sanborn . .	☐ 4	☐ 4	☐ 4	_____
5. MJB.	☐ 5	☐ 5	☐ 5	_____
6. Sanka	☐ 6	☐ 6	☐ 6	_____
7. Nescafe	☐ 7	☐ 7	☐ 7	_____
8. IMH	☐ 8	☐ 8	☐ 8	_____
9. Folger's	☐ 9	☐ 9	☐ 9	_____
0. Yuban	☐ 0	☐ 0	☐ 0	_____
X. Other.	☐ X	☐ X	☐ X	_____
Y. None seen/heard			☐ Y	_____

3. Generally speaking, how do you feel about the various different brands of instant coffee sold around here—do you feel that there is one brand that is better than all the rest, that there are two or three better than the rest, or do you feel all instant coffee brands are pretty much alike?

1 ☐ One best   Ask: 3a. What brand is that? (*Check below*)
2 ☐ Several better   Ask: 3b. What brands are they? (*Check below*)
3 ☐ All alike

4. As you may know, various brands of instant coffee sometimes mark a few cents off their regular price, and some housewives we have talked with take advantage of these reduced prices, while others prefer to stay with their usual brand.

Within the past three months, have you bought any brands that were reduced in price?   Yes ☐ 1   No ☐ 2

If "yes" on Question 4, ask:
4a. What brands: (*Check below*)

5. Do you take advantage of these price reductions only when your own brand is on sale, or whenever you have the opportunity?   Own brand only ☐ 1   Any brand ☐ 2

Brand	Q.3a Best Brand	Q.3b Better Brands	Q.4a Bought on Sale	Brand	Q.3a Best Brand	Q.3b Better Brands	Q.4a Bought on Sale
1. Hills Bros. . .	☐1	☐1	☐1	7. Nescafe . . .	☐7	☐7	☐7
2. Butternut . .	☐2	☐2	☐2	8. IMH	☐8	☐8	☐8
3. Decaf	☐3	☐3	☐3	9. Folger's . . .	☐9	☐9	☐9
4. Chase & Sanborn	☐4	☐4	☐4	0. Yuban	☐0	☐0	☐0
5. MJB	☐5	☐5	☐5	X. Other.	☐X	☐X	☐X
6. Sanka	☐6	☐6	☐6				

6. How many times have you bought instant coffee in the past three months? _____ times.

7. What are all the different brands of instant coffee you have bought during the past 3 months? (*Check below*)

8. Which brand did you buy last (most recently)? (*Check below*)

9. What about the time before that—what brand did you buy? (*Check below*)

10. Do you have what you consider a usual brand of instant coffee for use in your household?   Yes ☐1
    No ☐2

    If "Yes" on Question 10, ask:
    10a. What brand is that (*Check below*)

11. *Ask everyone.* Have you seen or heard any advertising by   Yes ☐1
    any brand of instant coffee in the past thirty days that you   No ☐2
    recall distinctly as being especially *interesting*—that is,
    something which you think would make people very inter-
    ested in that brand of instant coffee:
    If "Yes" on Question 11, ask:
    11a. What one brand's advertising did you think was most
    interesting? (*Check below*)
    11b. What was shown or said in that advertising that in-
    terested you? _____

12. *Ask everyone.* Earlier we talked about brands of instant coffee that are often on sale, or marked off a few cents. Which brands have you noticed recently that were on sale or marked off a few cents? (*Check below*)

Brand	Q.7 Bought in Past 3 mos.	Q.8 Bought Last	Q.9 Bought Next to Last	Q.10a Usual Brand	-.11a Most Int. Advtg.	Q.12 on Sale Recently
1. Hills Bros.	1	1	1	1	1	1
2. Butternut	2	2	2	2	2	2
3. Decaf	3	3	3	3	3	3
4. Chase & Sanborn	4	4	4	4	4	4
5. MJB	5	5	5	5	5	5
6. Sanka	6	6	6	6	6	6
7. Nescafe	7	7	7	7	7	7
8. IMH	8	8	8	8	8	8
9. Folger's	9	9	9	9	9	9
0. Yuban	0	0	0	0	0	0
X. Other	X	X	X	X	X	X
Y. Don't Know	Y	Y	Y	Y	Y	Y

13. How long would you say that instant coffee—either decaffeinated or regular style—has been used fairly regularly in your household?

Less than 1 year ☐
One to 3 years ☐
Four to 6 years ☐
Over six years ☐

14. On the average, about how many cupsful of instant coffee are consumed in your household over a full seven-day week?   No. _____

15. Which of the following age groups comes nearest to your approximate age?
18 to 30 ☐ 1   31 to 40 ☐ 2   Over 40 ☐ 3

16. It would help in our analysis if you would tell me which of the following income groups comes closest to your total family income last year:

$3,000 or less	☐ 1	$7,500 to $10,000	☐ 4
$3,100 to $5,000	☐ 2	Over $10,000	☐ 5
$5,100 to $7,500	☐ 3		

Respondents' first and last names _____
Street Address _____ City _____ State _____
Interviewer's Name _____ Date of interview _____
Unit number _____

APPENDIX B: VARIATIONS AMONG INSTANT COFFEE QUESTIONNAIRES

Approximately 60 percent of the questions asked in the wave 5 questionnaire (Appendix A) were also asked in waves 1 through 4 inclusive and
were coded in exactly the same way. However, the questions sometimes
came in a different order, and various other questions were inserted from
time to time. The specific differences are identified below:

Wave 4

Q1 and Q1a are the same as wave 5.

Q6 through Q16 inclusive correspond exactly with Q3 through Q13
inclusive in wave 5.

Q19 corresponds with Q14 in wave 5.

Q 22 corresponds to Q16 in wave 5.

Also in wave 4 a Q13b was asked: "How long (in months) has that been
your usual brand without interruption?" Also a Q21: "Could you estimate
for me about how much (in dollars) you spent for groceries on the last
trip?"

Wave 3

Q1 through Q11b inclusive correspond exactly to Q1 through Q11b of
wave 5.

Q12 of wave 3 asked: "Have you seen or heard any advertising by any
brand of instant coffee in the last 30 days that you recall distinctly as
being especially irritating—that is advertising that you don't like or that
annoys you?" If there was a Yes response a further Q12a was asked: "What
one brand's advertising did you think was the most irritating or annoy-
ing?"

Q13 and Q14 of wave 3 correspond to Q12 and Q13 of wave 5.

Q15 of wave 3 asked: "How many cups of all kinds of coffee—both instant and regular grind—would you say were consumed in your household
just yesterday alone?"

Q16 of wave 3 asked: "Out of every ten cups of coffee served in your
household, about how many of these on the average would you say were
instant coffee?"

Q17 of wave 3 asked: "What brand of regular grind coffee do you consider to be your usual brand of this kind?"

Wave 2

Q1 through Q3b inclusive of wave 2 (Q1a was not asked) correspond to
Q1 through Q3b of wave 5.

Q6 through Q11b of wave 2 correspond to Q6 through Q11b of wave 5.

In wave 2 a Q10b was also asked (but only if "usual brand" was not
bought either of the last two times): "You said before that you had bought

other brands the past two times. How did it happen you didn't buy your usual brand both of the last two times?"

Q12 of wave 2 corresponds to Q13 of wave 5.

Q13, Q14, and Q15 of wave 2 correspond exactly to Q15, Q16, and Q17 of wave 3 (see above).

Wave 1

Wave 1 is identical to wave 2, with the exception of one question, so that Q5 through Q14 inclusive in wave 1 correspond to Q6 through Q15 of wave 2.

MAXIM ✿

In 1963 the Maxwell House Division of General Foods was the leading company in both the regular and soluble coffee markets. This dominant position was traceable to the company's historic strength in the regular coffee market and the early development and introduction of high-quality soluble (instant) coffees in the early 1950s. As a result of this flavor improvement in soluble coffee, category sales grew dramatically during the middle and late 1950s and were the leading growth factor in the total coffee market of that period.

Not content with this success, General Foods was aggressively developing another new coffee, produced by a process called freeze-drying. This coffee was markedly different in appearance and flavor from either regular or "traditional" soluble coffees. Its growth prospects appeared to many in the company to be as significant as those realized by soluble coffee in the 1950s.

The overriding problem during the initial development period was the high per-unit production cost. By late 1962 the research group assigned to the problem expressed confidence that a freeze-dried coffee could be produced at a "reasonable" cost. Their recommendation to proceed was followed shortly by the assignment of a new-product marketing group to the task of compiling appropriate consumer research and developing the most effective market positioning and strategy for the new brand. During

---

*This case was prepared as the basis for class discussion, rather than to illustrate either effective or ineffective handling of an administrative situation.

1963 this new-products group, headed by Ken Carter,[1] the product manager, worked towards the goal of preparing a fully defined *national marketing plan* by *February of 1964*. This national plan was designed to satisfy two needs:

1. Define the new product's *positioning* and potential share of market impact, as well as its ability to meet the company's *financial* guidelines for new entries.
2. Assuming a favorable decision to proceed with test and/or national market introduction, guide the implementation of these stages.

As the deadline for the completion of the marketing plan drew near, the problem of selecting the best "mix" from many alternatives of *market positioning, name, packaging, pricing strategy, promotion and advertising budgets* became acute.

In defining the optimum market positioning for the new product, three broad potential positions became apparent:

1. A totally new kind of coffee.
2. The best of the soluble category.
3. As good as ground coffee, with the convenience of soluble.

Another vital consideration in properly positioning the new entry was the selection of a name for the brand. The choices included:

1. Maxwell House Freeze-Dried coffee.
2. Freeze-Dried Instant Maxwell House.
3. A name with no Maxwell House connotations.

The basic issue involved was the desire to capitalize on the strength of the Maxwell House name and consumer acceptance at minimum cannibalization risk to other Maxwell House brands.

Each of these positions would require a different marketing approach. Each would also have its own impact on the final share-of-market goal identified in the marketing plan. Each would have to be evaluated in estimating the long-run financial benefits to be gained by the introduction of the new freeze-dried entry. The determination of the most effective market *positioning* would also have direct *effects* on the selection of pricing strategy, promotion, and advertising strategies and budgets used to promote the brand.

The critical task of evaluating all viable alternatives involved and developing the best possible combination, which would be detailed in the marketing plan, was the assignment which Mr. Carter and the men of his product group faced in the closing months of 1963.

---

[1] A disguised name used here to represent the several product executives who eventually worked on the project.

GENERAL FOODS CORPORATION

General Foods grew to its 1964 level of $1,338,000,000 in sales (see Exhibit 1) through a series of mergers and consolidations that had begun in 1926 and had gradually built up a corporate structure containing over 60 plants divided into six major domestic divisions: Maxwell House, Post, Jell-O, Birds-Eye, Kool-Aid, and Institutional Food Service. These divisions turned out a wide array of food products, including Maxwell House, Yuban, and Sanka coffees; Kool-Aid; SOS, Baker's cocoa and chocolate products; Birds-Eye frozen foods; Post cereals; Jell-O desserts; Swans Down cake flour and mixes; Gaines dog foods; Calumet baking powder; Log Cabin syrup; Minute Rice, and many more. To this already broad list of offerings the company was constantly adding new products and establishing such brand names as Awake (concentrated breakfast drink) and Prime (dog food).

Internal organization

Each division functioned as a highly autonomous unit. This decentralized pattern of organization was judged the most effective management method for the corporation's size and geographic spread. Top management maintained a flexible structure of corporate policy designed to coordinate the administration and operations of each division's long-range product plans and new-product development, offering counsel on key decisions.

New-projects policy

An important consideration in the development of the new freeze-dried product's marketing position, objectives, and strategies was the *financial* requirements specified in General Foods corporate policy for new entries. General Foods required each division to submit rate-of-return estimates for any project involving incremental outlays of more than $50,000, specifying its expected payback period (from the date the project became operational to the repayment of the original investment) and projecting the anticipated return on funds employed (using average flows from the first 3, 5, and 10 years of the project's life). This policy statement stressed adherence to the principles of incremental volume decision making and provided explicitly that any new venture's report must include deductions for anticipated incremental losses to *other* General Foods products occasioned by the new project. Top management generally required a specified, projected 10-year average profit before taxes on invested funds, but it allowed the payback period to extend the full 10 years to cover losses accumulated during the market development period.

After reviewing the product group's profit projections and accompanying budget proposals, top management also bore the responsibility for weighing several factors: (1) duration of the period until break even,

EXHIBIT 1

General Foods financial statistics, fiscal years 1958-64* (all dollar amounts in millions, except assets per employee and figures on a share basis)

	1964	1963	1962	1961	1960	1959	1958
Income:							
Sales to customers (net)	$1,338	$1,216	$1,189	$1,160	$1,087	$1,053	$1,009
Cost of sales	838	774	769	764	725	734	724
Marketing, administrative and general expenses	322	274	267	261	236	205	181
Earnings before income taxes	179	170	156	138	130	115	105
Taxes on income	95	91	84	71	69	61	57
Net earnings	$ 84	$ 79	$ 72	$ 67	$ 61	$ 54	$ 48
Net earnings per common share	$ 3.33	$ 3.14	$ 2.90	$ 2.69	$ 2.48	$ 2.21	$ 1.99
Dividends on common shares	.50	.45	.40	.35	.32	.28	.24
Dividends per common share	2.00	1.80	1.60	1.40	1.30	1.15	1.00
Earnings retained in business each year	.34	.34	.32	.32	.29	.26	.24
Assets, Liabilities, and Stockholders' Equity:							
Current assets	$436	$411	$387	$360	$357	$329	$313
Current liabilities	202	162	142	123	126	107	107
Working capital	234	249	245	237	230	222	206
Land, buildings, equipment, gross	436	375	328	289	247	221	203
Land, buildings, equipment, net	264	223	193	173	148	132	125
Long-term debt	23	34	35	37	40	44	49
Stockholders' equity	490	454	419	384	347	315	287
Book value per common share	19.53	18.17	16.80	15.46	14.07	12.87	11.78
Operating Statistics:							
Inventories	$256	$205	$183	$189	$157	$149	$169
Capital additions	70	57	42	40	35	24	28
Depreciation	26	24	21	18	15	14	11
Wages, salaries, and benefits	195	180	171	162	147	138	128
Number of employees (in thousands)	30	28	28	25	22	22	21
Assets per employee (in thousands)	24	23	22	22	23	22	21

*Fiscal 1964 ended April 2, 1964. Other fiscal years ended March 31.

(2) risks, (3) probable competition, (4) quality of forecasts, and (5) period of greatest investment.

MAXWELL HOUSE DIVISION

The organizational structure of the Maxwell House Division reflected its marketing orientation (see Exhibit 2). The division believed that the size, complexity, and competitive nature of the coffee business created the need for a philosophy of vigorous administration and management on a "business within a business" arrangement of product management. Key to the success of this system was having a small group of carefully chosen, aggressive, and mature business managers (such as Ken Carter) literally "run their own business" under general philosophy and strategy guidelines administered by the division's top management. In short, subject to the approval of division management, Maxwell House Division product

EXHIBIT 2
Organizational chart for Maxwell House Division

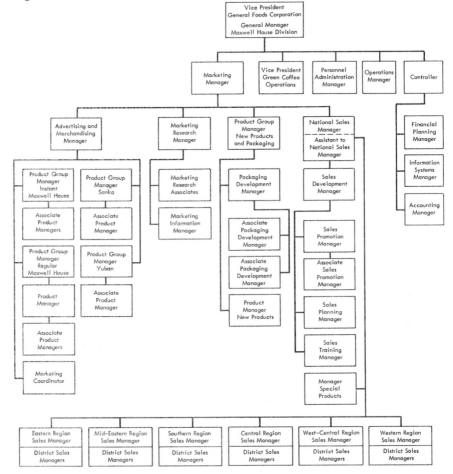

managers exercised the functional responsibility and authority of a "general manager" of a given brand. This "general manager" responsibility required that the product manager *initiate* the development of an integrated, overall plan for marketing his brand, *secure* management's concurrence with this plan, and *follow through* to ensure that each element of the plan was successfully and efficiently executed.

To discharge this "general manager" responsibility to his brand, the product manager had to secure management concurrence on these *primary objectives*:

1. The competitive *position* the brand will occupy in the marketplace.
2. The brand's *profit* objectives.
3. The sales *volume* objectives.
4. The *advertising* strategy and execution.
5. The *promotion* strategy and execution.
6. The *pricing* strategy and execution.
7. All auxiliary plans and operations necessary to realize these profit and sales objectives—including appropriate marketing research plans, product development plans, marketing tests, and so forth.

Finally, the product manager also had primary responsibility for the manpower management and development of his staff, providing day-to-day training of his associates in business methods, techniques, and marketing skills to ensure that each member of the team was contributing to the group's capacity.

This, then, was the general philosophy and framework in which Mr. Carter and his associates operated as they faced the challenge of preparing the marketing objectives and plan for the new freeze-dried coffee product.

THE COFFEE MARKET

Coffee was, without question, the American national drink (see Exhibits 3 and 4). Its position as the largest single beverage category was achieved by a broad demographic appeal and an ability to meet many needs and serve many functions. Thus coffee was seen by many consumers

EXHIBIT 3
Consumption of coffee and other beverages (percentage of persons 10 years of age and over)

	1950	1962	1963
Coffee	74.7	74.7	73.2
Milk and milk drinks	51.0	52.6	52.3
Fruit and Vegetable juices	32.8	41.4	38.3
Soft drinks	29.1	32.6	34.0
Tea	24.0	24.7	24.7
Cocoa, hot chocolate	5.4	4.5	4.0

EXHIBIT 4
Coffee's share of beverage market (index 1961 = 100)

	Consumer $ basis	Liquid consumption basis
1961.	100	100
1962.	95	98
1963.	90	97

Source: Maxwell House market research department.

as being appropriate for most social occasions and at almost every time of day (see Exhibits 5 to 7).

Product-oriented market research

The complex and multifaceted nature of coffee presented many opportunities for research that had immediate value in forming promotional policy and giving direction to new-product development. In particular a series of inquiries into the general motivational structure that underlay *salient consumer needs* and desires for the best cup of coffee were of considerable value in the development of freeze-dried coffee.

Coffee was perceived as having a wide latitude of functions beyond satisfying thirst or providing warmth and comfort. The functions varied as to time of day, mood of the individual, and particular needs at any given time. Some of these functions were: (1) a force to provide energy or stimulation, (2) a tension reliever with an implicit reward and consequently an aid to mental health, (3) a convenience food and a "snack", (4) an appetite depressant, (5) a medication (with apparent emetic qualities), and (6) a "friend" in and of itself. Also, coffee served as a visible symbol of adulthood, and drinking coffee was universally associated with the sociability of a friendly gathering. Other perceptions of the coffee drinking situation were: (1) an opportunity to relax, (2) a thought lubricator to help achieve concentrated thought, and (3) an excuse for sociability. The coffee break had an almost unique status as a reward for work well done or as a legitimate escape from routinized drudgery.

Although consumers perceived coffee in a variety of ways, most agreed on what constituted the important attributes in a cup of coffee. These attributes, ranked according to the number of times they were mentioned, are shown below for two different ways of viewing attributes:

	Attributes desired in everyday cup of coffee	Attributes needing improvement for the perfect cup of coffee
Flavor/Taste	62%	37%
Freshness	46	24
Good aroma	44	21
Gives you a lift	37	18
Relaxing	35	16
Strength without bitterness	30	22

EXHIBIT 5
Trends in coffee drinking, fiscal years 1950–64 (cups per person per day)

	1950	1953	1960	1961	1962	1963	1964 (est.)
Regular:							
At home.........	N.A.	N.A.	1.78	1.90	1.95	1.93	1.86
At eating places ..	N.A.	N.A.	0.25	0.26	0.28	0.22	0.24
At work	N.A.	N.A.	0.18	0.17	0.22	0.21	0.19
Total regular ...		2.31	2.21	2.33	2.45	2.36	2.29
Instant:							
At home.........	N.A.	N.A.	0.52	0.59	0.62	0.60	0.56
At eating places ..	N.A.	N.A.	0.00	0.01	0.01	0.00	0.00
At work	N.A.	N.A.	0.04	0.04	0.04	0.05	0.05
Total instant ...		0.56	0.56	0.64	0.67	0.65	0.61
Breakfast..........	1.03	N.A.	1.11	1.18	1.17	1.18	1.14
Other meals........	0.91	N.A.	0.89	0.92	0.98	0.90	0.85
Between meals	0.44	N.A.	0.77	0.87	0.97	0.93	0.91
Total for day ...	2.38	2.57	2.77	2.97	3.12	3.01	2.90

EXHIBIT 6
Coffee drinking by age groups, fiscal years 1950–64 (cups per person per day: percentage of age group drinking coffee)

	1950		1962		1963		1964 (est.)		% Change 1950–64	
Age	Cups	%	Cups	%	Cups	%	Cups	%	Cups	%
10–14.......	.21	(16.0)	.18	(13.4)	.18	(13.1)	.18	(12.2)	− 14.3%	− 3.8%
15–19.......	1.13	(53.8)	1.09	(40.2)	.89	(37.1)	.71	(31.7)	− 37.2	− 22.1
20–24.......	2.34	(75.2)	2.99	(76.6)	2.70	(69.1)	2.30	(68.4)	− 1.7	− 6.8
25–29.......	2.78	(83.3)	3.88	(85.2)	3.76	(81.4)	3.64	(84.3)	+ 30.9	+ 1.0
30–39.......	3.02	(87.4)	4.50	(88.8)	4.38	(89.7)	4.14	(85.8)	+ 37.1	− 1.6
40–49.......	2.98	(88.0)	4.44	(91.4)	4.27	(90.7)	4.33	(89.6)	+ 45.3	+ 1.6
50–59.......	2.85	(91.2)	3.83	(92.9)	3.75	(89.3)	3.68	(88.2)	+ 29.1	− 3.0
60–69.......	2.22°	(86.0)°	3.01	(89.8)	3.17	(89.8)	3.06	(90.6)	—	—
70 and over ..			2.39	(85.8)	2.40	(86.8)	2.47	(88.7)	—	—

°Figures include all persons 60 years of age and older.
Source: Pan-American Coffee Bureau, based on a national probability sample survey of 6,000 civilians over 10 years of age, taken at midwinter.

EXHIBIT 7
Use of coffee by young people, 1957 (cups per person per day)

Coffee served at home	15–19 Years	20–24 Years
Instant only....................	.74	2.16
Regular and instant	1.04	2.78
Regular only	1.29	2.77

EXHIBIT 8
Coffee consumption trends (fiscal years 1955–64)

Fiscal years	Total coffee Pounds (millions)	Total coffee Equivalent units (millions)	Soluble ratio	Growth of soluble sales versus year ago	High soluble east (millions) Regular units	High soluble east (millions) Soluble units	Low soluble west (millions) Regular units	Low soluble west (millions) Soluble units
1964 (est.)	2,102	174.5	30.0	− 2.1%	63.0	38.2	59.1	14.2
1963	2,171	170.9	31.3	0.2	59.9	38.8	57.5	14.7
1962	2,163	168.8	31.6	5.6	58.4	38.9	57.0	14.5
1961	2,080	163.2	30.9	7.4	57.7	36.6	55.0	13.9
1960	1,984	155.9	30.1	5.3	55.4	33.6	53.5	13.4
1959	1,955	154.1	29.0	9.3	55.7	32.0	53.7	12.7
1958	1,863	147.5	27.7	19.4	54.3	29.3	52.3	11.6
1957	1,738	138.6	24.7	20.8	54.1	25.4	50.2	8.9
1956	1,654	131.5	21.6	21.5	54.8	21.2	48.3	7.2
1955	1,500	120.4	19.4	—	52.0	17.4	45.1	5.9

Most consumers described their optimum cup of coffee as slightly sweet, rich yet smooth, with a minimum of calories.

Because coffee played so many roles so often, a major concern with regard to ground coffee was the bother of preparation—that is, the time consumed in preparation and the bother of cleaning the pot and disposing of the grounds. Also cited by consumers was their inability to achieve a consistently good cup of coffee, whether ground or soluble.

Size and growth of coffee market

During the late fifties and early sixties, the combined instant- and ground-coffee market saw a period of consecutive *increases* well in excess of the 1.5 percent growth rate of the coffee-drinking population (14 years old and over). This growth can be traced to the introduction of a high-quality soluble coffee in the early 1950s—Instant Maxwell House—and subsequently to a general improvement in product quality for other soluble coffees, plus a limited amount of sensitivity to price changes (see Exhibits 8 to 14).

Soluble coffees provided ease of preparation and made it convenient for people to serve coffee more frequently during the day. From 1950 to 1963, between-meal coffee drinking doubled, while mealtime coffee drinking showed small change (see Exhibit 5 above). Even though the between-meal convenience of soluble coffee came at some expense of flavor and aroma, its ease of preparation apparently weighed heavily enough to lead to its rapid adoption.

EXHIBIT 9
U.S. coffee consumption, 1946–64 (net civilian disappearance in billions of pounds of green coffee)

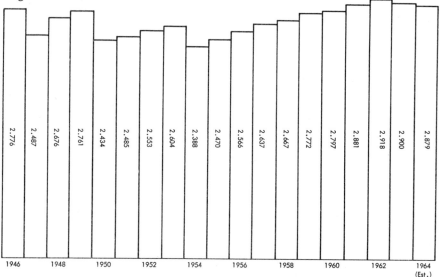

| 2.776 | 2.487 | 2.676 | 2.761 | 2.434 | 2.485 | 2.553 | 2.604 | 2.388 | 2.470 | 2.566 | 2.637 | 2.667 | 2.772 | 2.797 | 2.881 | 2.918 | 2.900 | 2.879 |

| 1946 | 1948 | 1950 | 1952 | 1954 | 1956 | 1958 | 1960 | 1962 | 1964 (Est.) |

EXHIBIT 10
U.S. per capita coffee consumption, 1946–64 (pounds per capita)

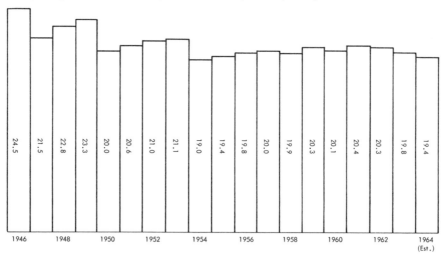

EXHIBIT 11
Annual average prices paid by consumers for coffee (per pound regular; per 2-oz. instant)

Year	Regular	Instant
1952	84.5c	51.0c
1953	86.9	51.7
1954	105.6	60.6
1955	90.1	53.6
1956	93.7	49.5
1957	92.2	45.3
1958	82.1	40.6
1959	68.8	34.6
1960	66.2	32.7
1961	63.8	30.6
1962	61.7	29.1
1963	60.8	28.6

Source: Maxwell House market research department.

By 1962 instant coffee had added .67 cups per day to the average coffee intake, while regular coffee had gained .14 cups per day (see Exhibit 5). Figures also show that the rapid growth of soluble consumption abetted the growth of the total industry until the soluble ratio (i.e., the percentage of total units accounted for by soluble unit sales) stood at 31.3 percent in 1963 (see Exhibit 8).

EXHIBIT 12
What consumers pay for coffee in food stores (average weighted price per equivalent pound)

Year	Regular	Instant
1950	81.0c	73.6c
1955	95.1	93.1
1960	72.6	58.4
1961	70.2	54.7
1962	67.3	52.7
1963	66.2	52.3

Source: Maxwell House market research department.

EXHIBIT 13
Recent trend for regular coffee consumer sales versus price changes (% change versus year ago)

Months	Consumer sales	Consumer prices	
August–September 1963	+ 2%	− 2%	66.5c
October–November 1963	+ 1	+ 1	66.5
December–January 1964	+ 2	+ 6	69.5
February–March 1964		+ 16	76.0

EXHIBIT 14
Comparison of trend for estimated advertising expenditures

Year	Total coffee	20 leading grocery product manufacturers	Coffee expenditures
1958 = Index	100	100	$43 million
1959	88	109	37
1960	117	109	50
1961	119	117	51
1962	106	120	45
1963	104	130	44

Source: Maxwell House market research department.

Market segmentation

Associated with the complexity of coffee buying and consumption were significant variations from the population norm in the behavior patterns of coffee-drinking consumers. Maxwell House marketing executives divided the coffee market as follows:

By user type: Predominantly ground
Predominantly soluble
Dual users

By geographic area: East
                        West
By size of urban area: Over 1,000,000 TV homes
                        250,000 to 1,000,000 TV homes
                        75,000 to 250,000 TV homes
                        Under 75,000 TV homes

The usefulness of this analysis came from the very different patterns of coffee drinking displayed in the East and West. Traditionally, Westerners drank more cups per day than Easterners. Consequently, since light coffee users had converted to instant coffee most readily, the eastern soluble ratio (i.e., soluble/regular units purchased) greatly exceeded that in the West. The East, more populous by half, accounted for half again as many unit sales of soluble. Correspondingly, it contained more densely settled urban areas; cities with over 250,000 TV homes made up 75 percent of its population, while, in the more thinly settled West, they composed 64 percent of the populace. This was important for the introduction of new General Foods' products, since high-quality food innovations seemed to be adopted more readily in the larger urban areas. Exhibits 15 through 19 present the data which Maxwell House had collected to illuminate this market segmentation.

EXHIBIT 15
Coffee drinking by region (cups per person per day)

	1950	1962	1963	1964 (est.)	Percentage change 1950–64
East	2.27	2.91	2.76	2.54	+11.9
Midwest	2.72	3.34	3.30	3.20	+17.6
South	1.91	2.78	2.54	2.61	+36.6
West	2.79	3.52	3.56	3.38	+21.1
United States	2.38	3.12	3.01	2.90	+21.8

Source: Pan-American Coffee Bureau.

EXHIBIT 16
Sales and soluble ratio by area, fiscal 1964 (est.)

	East	West	Total U.S.
Population over 14 (millions)	81.0	53.0	134.0
Total coffee market (units)°	101.2	73.3	174.5
Soluble ratio (soluble/ground units)	42.9	22.9	30.0

°Unit = 48-oz. soluble or 12-lb. ground.

EXHIBIT 17
Geographical distribution of coffee user types

Type of coffee	Total U.S.	Northeast	South	Midwest	West-central	Pacific
Ground only users	37%	24%	40%	34%	49%	51%
Users of both.............	48	57	35	52	42	32
Instant only users	15	19	25	14	9	7

Source: National Coffee Study, 1961.

EXHIBIT 18
Composition of the coffee market by user type

	Percentage of families	Percentage of coffee volume	Percentage of regular coffee volume	Percentage of instant-coffee volume
Exclusively regular	48%	54%	76%	2%
Predominantly regular (60–89%)	14	15	17	12
Instant and regular (40–59%)	5	5	4	8
Predominantly instant (60–89%)	10	8	3	20
Exclusively instant	23	18	—	58

Source: Maxwell House market research department.

EXHIBIT 19
Population by size of urban area (thousands)

Number of TV homes	East	West
Over 1,000,000	42,896	20,454
250,000–1,000,000	41,348	27,071
75,000–250,000.............	22,520	18,116
0–75,000	5,481	8,483
	112,245	74,124

COMPETITIVE POSITION OF MAXWELL HOUSE DIVISION AND POSITIONING OF ITS BRANDS

In 1964, General Foods had a substantial share of the coffee market. Maxwell House Division marketed Sanka, Yuban, and Maxwell House coffees nationally in both instant and regular form, consciously aiming each brand at a distinct consumer need to avoid "cannibalizing" sales to the extent possible.

Sanka was marketed to consumers who sought a coffee that could claim to let them sleep by virtue of its low caffeine content—a selling point that sharply distinguished Sanka from Yuban and Maxwell House.

Attempts were underway in 1964 to reposition Yuban in order to replace its exotic and sophisticated (but apparently unsociable and strange) image with a warm and personable approach designed to establish it as a friendly coffee. The new plan aimed Yuban at the market segment that desired a coffee to please discriminating tastes and could afford to (or would) pay premium prices. Its product planners expected Yuban to attract older (30–50 years), better educated people in the higher income groups (upper 50 percent). Instant Yuban achieved its greatest franchise in the West and Northeast by claiming to be more groundlike than other instants.

Regular Maxwell House, designed to appeal to the majority of ground-coffee users, was sold at popular prices. A promotional goal was to achieve maximum loyalty through intensely competitive promotional programs, including strong consumer advertising. For this brand, the division wished to develop a stronger franchise in the "low soluble" West, where it faced stiff competition from regional brands like Hills and Folger's that had captured strong loyalty. It also sought a way to attract more young users (aged 18–25) to ensure its long-range market position.

Instant Maxwell House paralleled Regular Maxwell House by offering quality at a popular price and claiming greater value than any other soluble coffee. As a foil to the potentially devastating effects of price dealing, Instant Maxwell House continually sought an improved blend which would increase consumer loyalty. The division had also introduced a new 14-ounce jar in an effort to maintain consumer interest and to increase time between purchases so that the consumer might be less responsive to competitive promotion. To increase the number of Instant Maxwell House users in the West, the division used heavy sampling and represented it as offering the "optimum coffee experience."

Exhibits 20 through 22 indicate the strength of the division's competitive position. Its soluble offerings commanded approximately 50 percent

EXHIBIT 20
Competitive position fiscal year 1964 (est.)

	East	West	Total U.S.
Division share:			
Regular	36.0%	13.5%	24.9%
Instant	50.7	47.1	50.3
Volume	76 %	24 %	100%
Gross profit	77	23	100
Advertising and promotion	62	38	100
Merchandising profit	84	16	100

market share in both the East and the West, and Instant Maxwell House sold more than three times as well as its nearest competitor. General Foods regular coffees enjoyed a 36 percent share of the eastern market and a 13.5 percent share of the "low soluble" West, where they encountered strong competition from the well-established regional brands mentioned above.

EXHIBIT 21
Competitive position, brand share, fiscal year 1964 (est.)

Soluble market		Ground market	
Instant Maxwell House	36.8%	Regular Maxwell House	21.4%
Nescafé	12.2	Folger's	15.1
Sanka....................	9.3	Hills	9.7
Chase and Sanborn	6.6	Chase and Sanborn	6.5
Folger's	5.9		
Yuban	4.2		

EXHIBIT 22
Soluble ratio and market share by region

	East	Mid-east	South	Central	West central	West
Fiscal year 1963:						
Maxwell House:						
Instant.....................	39.2	40.2	43.1	37.4	39.4	28.1
Regular	32.1	35.9	32.7	16.1	7.6	8.9
Yuban:						
Instant.....................	7.6	3.3	2.6	2.4	0.8	7.9
Regular	2.2	1.2	0.8	0.5	0.1	4.8
Soluble ratio	39.3	40.2	38.4	27.8	18.9	20.4
Fiscal year 1964 (est.)						
Maxwell House:						
Instant.....................	37.9	38.4	41.1	36.9	36.4	24.4
Regular	33.1	36.9	31.4	16.1	8.8	8.9
Yuban:						
Instant.....................	6.7	3.3	2.3	2.5	0.9	8.2
Regular	2.1	1.1	0.7	0.5	0.1	5.1
Soluble ratio	39.5	39.2	37.0	21.1	18.2	19.7

Development of freeze-dried coffee

Through the middle and late 1950s, the Maxwell House Division had experimented with the use of a special freeze-drying process to produce a new type of soluble coffee. The division's product planners began to focus increased attention on the still embryonic project in 1960, assigning it a top priority spot.

The freeze-drying process, the heart of the new development, closely resembled a technology long used by pharmaceutical firms. It produced a soluble coffee with a unique set of product characteristics. More concentrated than conventional instant coffee, crystalline in appearance, and soluble even in cold water, it offered flavor which rivalled that of regular ground coffee in consumer appeal.

The freeze-drying process began much like other techniques for manufacturing coffee. The manufacturer roasted and ground a carefully selected blend of green coffee beans. Then, as in the preparation of other soluble coffee, he brewed a strong coffee solution at a pressure and temperature somewhat higher than those found in normal home preparation. The next step differed radically from all other coffee-making techniques. At this point, the manufacturer flash-froze the solution. He subjected the resulting solid to a vacuum, and into this vacuum he suddenly introduced just enough local warmth to cause "sublimation" of the frozen solution's liquid content. "Sublimation," a kind of superevaporation, resulted in a solid (ice) becoming a gas (water vapor) without passing through the liquid state. After this dehydration of the frozen coffee solution, the remaining spongelike solids were ground up to ready them for packaging as soluble coffee.

This process departed entirely from the two more traditional techniques. The home-brewed method used to prepare regular ground coffee required only the first stages of the manufacturing process (blending, roasting, and grinding), after which the user brewed the coffee himself in a percolator or dripolator at standard atmospheric pressure, with water heated to the boiling point (212° F). Consumers have long regarded coffee prepared in this manner as the *standard* for good taste and aroma.

The spray-dried method, formerly used to manufacture all instant coffees, required similar initial preparation. But the sealed brewing system worked at supernormal pressure and temperature to make the solution dense enough to afford a profitable yield. When this liquid was sprayed into a column of hot air in a drying tower, its coffee content fell to the bottom in a fine soluble powder ready for packaging. The spray-drying process reduced the coffee's flavor and aroma somewhat.

Freeze-dried coffee suffered from the first of these disadvantages less than did spray dried, since its brewing did not require such intense heat. And there its flavor loss ended. The freeze-drying process saved the coffee from further flavor loss that occurred when spray-dried coffee entered the drying tower. Freeze-dried coffee therefore closely resembled ground coffee in flavor and aroma. The chart (next page) summarizes these and other differences that resulted from the freeze-drying process.

Freeze-dried coffee performed brilliantly when subjected to blind cup taste tests. The freeze-dried coffee was strongly preferred to regular instant coffee, and it was judged to be equally as good as ground coffee.

	Spray-dried coffee	*Freeze-dried coffee*
Flavor:	Less quality than regular No astringency or "mouth feel"	Comparable to regular Some astringency, but less than regular
Aroma:	Very little in-cup aroma	Resembles regular in cup
Appearance:	Powder	Irregular crystals
Solubility:	Fair in cold water Foam in cup (due to air trapped in drying)	Good even in cold water Little foam in cup
Concentration:	Index = 100	Index = 125
Cost:	Index = 100	Index = 135

DEVELOPMENT OF A MARKETING STRATEGY

To make the planning task more manageable, the new-products group assigned to freeze-dry coffee first identified the following basic operating assumptions:

1. That the finished product would possess the flavor of regular coffee and the convenience of instant.
2. That its advertising could make this claim credible.
3. That it would receive backing from advertising expenditures comparable to those invested in other new General Foods products and that these would insure its domination of coffee advertising media.
4. That the product would succeed in maintaining the margin set for it.

These assumptions were necessary to provide a starting point for the setting of goals, to put some constraints on the development of feasible price, advertising, promotion, and position alternatives, and to guide the consumer research program.

Secondly, Mr. Carter arranged a series of meetings with senior division and corporate executives to review these operating assumptions *and* to clarify what was expected of the new product. For the most part these performance expectations were based on requirements for a recognizable success. But success in this context was not merely achieving designated financial goals for the product itself; it also required that the new product should not prosper at the expense of other company brands.

The operating assumptions and the following performance expectations guided the thinking of the new-product group during most of 1963. However, as the time came to solidify the marketing plan, some of these guides looked to be in conflict with others or obsolete in terms of new evidence collected during 1963. Any changes made would have to be justified, since the modified form would serve as the operating goal and performance criteria for the new product. Mr. Carter also suspected that it would be hard to have the expectations scaled down if subsequent research, planning, and market experience showed them to be unreasonable.

Performance expectations

The following are the expectations that guided the initial planning of the freeze-dried coffee strategy:

1. The franchise would be built *outside* that currently held by other division products.
2. The gross margin would be at least *equal* to that on comparable products and better than that on cannibalized business. A necessity to help pay for the enormous investment in new plant and equipment was recognized.
3. The product should endeavor to *increase the soluble ratio*, particularly in the West.
4. The benefits of the freeze-dried process would be exploited *before competition* broadly marketed a comparable product.

Underlying these explicit expectations was a basic requirement that the new coffee achieve a going-year franchise (expressed in terms of share of the soluble coffee market plus people converted from ground to freeze-dried coffee) that would generate enough volume to meet corporate return on funds-employed criteria for new products and still support a campaign that would dominate coffee advertising media.

The product manager's estimate of the going-year franchise, and ultimately its acceptance as a reasonable performance objective, required some very difficult judgments with respect to:

1. The probable rate at which regular and instant users would convert to the new product. A major question concerned the degree to which the "soluble stigma" would make ground users more difficult to convert.
2. The variation in the franchise by market size. The range of the variation would depend somewhat on the extent to which the product was perceived as a premium coffee. Experience with premium-priced coffees such as Yuban showed that the larger urban markets would be more receptive to such an innovation. The question was: How much more receptive? The answer to this question would also weigh heavily in deciding media allocations by market size and type.
3. The effect of the various performance expectations, which are discussed in more detail below.

BUILD A FRANCHISE OUTSIDE THAT CURRENTLY HELD BY OTHER DIVISION PRODUCTS. Because the division already commanded about half of the instant-coffee market in both East and West, a sizable share of the eastern business would inevitably come from *other* Maxwell House brands. Nevertheless, the greatest profits obviously lay in attracting those who had not previously used a General Foods coffee, since this new franchise would directly expand the company's volume and market share. Conversion of customers from other brands was therefore of primary importance.

In projecting profit figures for various marketing plans, Mr. Carter needed a device to predict the comparative likelihood of gains in company franchise as opposed to mere cannibalization. The simplest model considered was one which assumed that the new coffee's usage would come from all other brands in exact proportion to their previously existing market share (in units). Thus if brand X currently held a 12 percent share of the eastern soluble market, the new coffee would gain 12 percent of its eastern soluble target from this brand. Other more complex "cannibalization" models were also considered. Their usefulness was limited because of the lack of evidence that they were any improvement over the simple model.

MAINTAIN A GROSS MARGIN HIGHER THAN THAT ON CANNIBALIZED BUSINESS.   The logic of the simple model determined that if Instant Maxwell House commanded 38 percent of the eastern soluble market, the new product would steal 38 percent of its eastern soluble target from Instant Maxwell House. So, in order to ensure the division an incremental profit to help pay for the tremendous investment required to produce freeze-dried coffee, Mr. Carter suggested establishing a requirement that the gross margin on the new coffee must exceed that on Instant Maxwell House ($2.50 per unit), which in turn already exceeded that on Regular Maxwell House ($2.00 per unit). The higher margin on IMH over RMH reflected the greater cost for plant and equipment required to produce this form of coffee and the need to develop a reasonable return on this investment. This meant that, within reasonable limits which did not distort scale of production on the division's other offerings, incremental profits would result even from stealing Maxwell House customers.

INCREASE THE SOLUBLE RATIO, PARTICULARLY IN THE WEST.   The conversion of regular-coffee buyers to use of the new soluble coffee was a more profitable prospect than the conversion of instant-coffee users for two reasons:

1. The division commanded a lower market share among regular users, particularly in the West, so that conversion of regular users produced cannibalization with fewer drawbacks than did the conversion of instant users (see Exhibit 20 above).
2. Even where the division's new product cannibalized its own brands, the margin on instant coffee ($2.50 per unit) exceeded that on regular ($2.00 per unit), making conversion of the latter the more profitable prospect (by $.50 per unit).

EXPLOIT THE FREEZE-DRYING PROCESS BEFORE THE COMPETITION BROADLY MARKETS A COMPARABLE PRODUCT.   Since the division had spent years developing its new coffee product at a time when the question of its eventual practicability remained uncertain, it had necessarily borne the expense of such exploratory research, which competitors would not need to repeat.

Naturally, the division wished to reap the rewards of its advantage by establishing a strongly loyal franchise before competitors could enter the market.

Mr. Carter estimated that it would take at least two years for any company to develop an offering of comparable quality and make it operational. He reported that while anyone could produce limited quantities of freeze-dried coffee in the laboratory, transferring the technique to a mass-production scale posed difficult problems that required at least two years to solve. He added that, even then, only a major coffee producer could handle such an operation.

Nevertheless, the manufacturing process, having served pharmaceutical firms for years, remained unpatentable. The situation therefore presented the danger that, after cannibalizing some of the division's share, the new brand might then lose share to some especially successful and aggressive freeze-dried competitor, with the net result that the Maxwell House division's total share could actually decline.

Rumors in the trade indicated that one major competitor (Nestlé) and a very few small, North American firms were experimenting with—and were about ready to test, on a limited scale—freeze-dried, concentrated coffees. The quantity and quality of these possible competitive coffees were unknown. Of the firms in question it seemed highly probable that only the Nestlé Company had the technical skill and financial resources necessary to market successfully a freeze-dried concentrated coffee. An interesting aspect of the rumors was the purported Nestlé strategy—to direct its freeze-dried coffee entirely against the soluble market. It would then cannibalize from Nescafé as well as attempt to take share from all other solubles.

On a national level, the competitive position of General Foods's innovation depended on the company's ability to achieve enough capacity to serve a national market. Mr. Carter estimated that new plants could achieve additional volume at the rate of two million annual units per $10 million investment at an operating cost of $6.22 per 48-ounce unit. Each plant would take at least a year to build, plus several months to achieve capacity volume.

ACHIEVING THE GOALS

Mr. Carter recognized that the stringent performance expectations could only be met if the division's marketing efforts found an effective set of appeals to give Maxim a favorable market "position." This meant that he had to decide first what image to seek for the new product, then he had to select a name, a label, a package, and other product features that would successfully conjure up this image in the public eye, and finally he had to decide how to allocate advertising and promotional funds for efficient attainment of these positioning goals.

Positioning

The initial expectations of the new product clearly indicated that it was to meet the following positioning requirements:

1. That it be assigned to a *unique* position, clearly different from the positions of the division's existing brands, so as to minimize cannibalization.
2. That it be differentiated from both other types of coffee so as to establish it as a new *form* of coffee—a third type which offers ground users their customary flavor with new convenience and which allows instant users to retain ease of preparation while improving the taste of their brew.
3. That it be an extension to the Maxwell House line rather than a completely new brand name.

Mr. Carter recognized, however, that the threefold objectives of assigning the coffee a unique position, differentiating it from all others, and registering its association with Maxwell House, while difficult enough to achieve in themselves, complicated the situation still further by conflicting with one another at several points. For example, the more the package emphasized the connection between the new coffee and Maxwell House (a fulfillment of the third goal), the more it encouraged the probability of substitution between the two (a violation of the first). And so Mr. Carter had to handle several dilemmas to achieve the best possible balance among these three goals.

Research on eight product descriptions for freeze-dried coffee is summarized in Exhibit 23.

Name

To balance these positioning requirements Mr. Carter sought a name which would provide an optimum association with Maxwell House without producing so close an identity that substitution would occur to an undesirable degree. Before making his recommendation, he considered two concepts:

1. Using the Maxwell House name directly with some modifier attached.
2. Using a separate brand name that implied its parentage, with only minor emphasis.

For the second concept he considered several alternatives, finally narrowing the choice to three—Prima, Nova, and Maxim. A study asking 463 women respondents to report their association with these names (and a fourth, Kaaba, as a control) and to rate them on various scales produced the results given in Exhibit 24.

Alternatives based on the first concept included Maxwell House Coffee Concentrate, Maxwell House Concentrated Soluble Coffee, and Maxwell

EXHIBIT 23

Research on eight product descriptions for freeze-dried coffee, February 27, 1963

Description	Percent rating as "one of best" on attributes					Would buy	Instant Coffee	Spontaneous associations (Other)
	Flavor	Aroma	Strength	Quality	Freshness			
Extract of coffee	14%	16%	37%	20%	29%	43%	22%	(Flavoring agent, 19%)
Freeze-dried coffee	17	16	17	9	49	48	18	(Frozen, 32%)
Dry frozen coffee	10	7	25	17	46	52	17	(Frozen, 34%)
Crystal coffee	14	14	6	21	40	45	19	(Crystal clear, 47%)
Groundless coffee	12	13	21	21	38	45	29	(No sediment left in cup, 16%)
Coffee concentrate	11	8	39	18	30	51	42	(Stronger—won't need as much, 25%)
Whole coffee without grounds	26	27	30	26	42	52	41	(Whole coffee beans, 26%)
Concentrated crystals of real coffee	22	23	25	23	44	55	44	(Grains/beads of coffee, 10%; concentrated, 10%)

EXHIBIT 24
Study of four candidate names, May 1963

	Maxim	*Prima*	*Nova*	*Kaaba* (control)
Spontaneous association:				
With coffee	22%	5%	4%	14%
With Maxwell House	7	—	—	—
Spontaneous association when identified as coffee:				
Major association	Best/Maximum (37) Maxwell House (33)	High quality (43)	New (24)	Foreign (45)
Not a suitable name	5	6	12	15
Anticipated likes:				
Will like nothing about it	12	13	25	32
Will dislike nothing about it . .	37	31	24	18
Expected Type:				
Instant coffee	34	39	44	26
Regular coffee	51	35	22	34
New third-type coffee	15	21	38	40
Rating index by characteristics: °				
Fresh	148	148	132	130
Fine aroma	135	132	112	118
Highest quality	135	135	110	112
Strong	132	115	100	130
Dark	125	110	102	132
Expensive	118	120	100	112
Modern	112	122	122	112
For men	106	90	90	112

°7-point scale: 4 (mid-point) = 100 index.
Base: 463 respondents (women "heads of households").

House Concentrated Instant Coffee. Of these, Mr. Carter preferred the first or second for their distinctiveness, since research had shown them to be relatively unfamiliar to comsumers, as seen in Exhibit 25. Under "awareness" in Exhibit 25, they were more aware of soluble coffee than they were of either of the other two terms, and yet only 14 percent of the sample had heard of it before.

Mr. Carter rejected the first concept altogether because he felt that use of the Maxwell House name under these circumstances would merely attract current division patrons, rather than new users. He disliked the second concept because of consumer unfamiliarity with the term "soluble." Moreover, reassuring evidence came from a study which indicated that a separate brand name could generate almost as much consumer interest as the familiar "Maxwell House." Subjects who were offered a choice between three gifts—Instant Maxwell House, Regular Maxwell House, or coffee with one of four competing alternative names—chose Maxim or Nova over 50 percent of the time, an acceptable frequency in Mr. Carter's judgment (see Exhibit 26).

EXHIBIT 25
Telephone study on the awareness, association, and connotations of "soluble," April 6–7, 1963

	Soluble coffee	Concentrated soluble coffee	Soluble coffee concentrate
Association			
Instant coffee	36%	50%	52%
Other........................	24	19	18
None—don't know	40	31	30
Awareness			
Heard of before.................	14	7	8
Not heard of before.............	86	93	92
Definition: Unaided			
Heard of synonym	16	19	15
Instant.....................	14	18	15
Other......................	2	1	—
Not heard	44	38	43
Don't know	40	43	42
Definition: Aided			
Regular ground................	34	20	2
Instant......................	37	53	61
Neither—third type.............	29	27	37
Connotation			
Better than instant	7	10	18
Same as instant	12	8	14
Not as good as instant...........	10	10	14

Mr. Carter tentatively chose Maxim because of its easy association with coffee (22 percent in Exhibit 24 above) and favorable connotations (see "rating index by characteristics" in Exhibit 24). He pointed out that Maxim: (1) implies concentration and strength (index = 132), (2) connotes quality (index = 135) and superiority (37%), (3) relates to Maxwell House (33%), and (4) is short, memorable, and euphonious. However, not everyone was equally convinced that Maxim was the best choice, particularly because of the association with Maxwell House.

Jar size and design

Mr. Carter recommended packing Maxim in 2-ounce, 4-ounce, and 8-ounce sizes. He expected the 2-ounce size to encourage purchase on a trial basis, to expand Maxim's shelf facings, and to return a higher margin than other sizes. He selected the 4-ounce size to enable Maxim to offer the consumer a middle-size jar with price and cup yield comparable to a pound of ground coffee (about 50 cups at under a dollar). He counted on the 8-ounce size to offer convenience and economy to heavy users and to attain a price comparable to other brands' large sizes.

As a further aid in distinguishing Maxim from all other brands, the

EXHIBIT 26

Name test—choice of gift product from three alternatives, June 1963*

Product chosen	Total	Percent of users of							
		Regular Ground	Instant	Both	Maxwell House	Regular Maxwell House	Instant Maxwell House	Both Maxwell House	Not Maxwell House
Maxim	53%	41%	63%	56%	52%	47%	56%	53%	55%
Nova	57	45	67	57	53	42	64	55	60
Maxwell House Concentrated Soluble	62	52	71	62	60	53	69	60	63
Maxwell House Concentrated Instant	62	48	73	64	59	47	73	55	64
Regular Maxwell House (average four tests)	28	50	4	29	28	50	5	29	28
Instant Maxwell House (average four tests)	14	3	27	8	16	3	24	15	12
Base (average)	(300)	(100)	(100)	(100)	(150)	(56)	(56)	(38)	(150)

*In four matched tests the respondent was offered one of three products as a gift: Regular Maxwell House, Instant Maxwell House, or a product with one of the four descriptions for freeze-dried coffee.

packaging department designed a jar that differed markedly from everything else on the market. Oval instead of round, it faced the buyer with a shouldered, rectangular shape, topped by a special lug-screw cap, with separate label panels instead of the customary wraparound labeling. Tests showed that this shape was superior to either a square or a round alternative in generating product interest (see Exhibit 27).

EXHIBIT 27
Test of consumer reaction to Maxim square, round, and rectangular jars, January 1964

	Shown square and round		Shown square and rectangular	
	Square	*Round*	*Square*	*Rectangular*
Interest in buying:	59%	58%	55%	64%
Use instant only	62	70	62	78
Use only ground	40	38	40	40
Use both	72	66	64	74
Consider different from other coffees . . .	77	57	85	79
Favorable product evaluations:				
Flavor	71	81	80	80
Aroma	69	79	82	84
Color	83	87	86	89
Strength	75	80	83	85
Overall quality	77	78	83	84
Improvement over other products	80	81	88	88
Favorable packing evaluation:				
Ease of handling	77	88	87	91
Ease of removing coffee	80	88	86	91
Ease of storage	82	86	92	94
Attractiveness	72	75	72	81
Cap style	87	90	88	88
Base: Female heads of households	(150)		(150)	

Copy strategy

Mr. Carter proposed a copy strategy which grew out of his conviction that Maxim did indeed present an inherently superior product, combining the best features of traditional regular and instant coffees and eliminating many of the defects of both. He and his subordinates believed that Maxim's advertising must be directed to convince ground-coffee users that they could continue to enjoy fine coffee flavor with new convenience, as well as to persuade instant-coffee users that they could now make a soluble brew that tasted like regular ground coffee.

To assign Maxim a position as a new type of coffee with the taste of regular and the convenience of instant, he planned to present the new entry as being real percolated coffee, the result of a scientific breakthrough which enabled freeze-dried coffee literally to *become* fresh perked coffee in the buyer's cup.

To overcome the slightly incredible aura of this claim, the copy strategy called for several reinforcing features. It counted on the freeze-dried process story as its "reason why." Tangibly, the coffee's granular form would help establish it as a new type of coffee, and hopefully, the newness suggested by this crystalline shape would help reduce the "soluble stigma" that might otherwise contradict the claim to superior flavor. At the same time, the messages would offer the buyer reassurance through emphasis on the coffee's high quality and by alluding to its connection with Maxwell House—an association which would strengthen the suggestion of quality and lend an atmosphere of authority. Finally, the copy strategy proposed to reinforce Maxim's singular position by pointing to its concentration. The buyer needed to use less, a characteristic which should connote both quality and economy, and, moreover, he would have to recognize this fact when preparing his cupful to avoid excessively strong taste.

Assuming this was the best copy strategy to follow, Mr. Carter then faced the problem of selecting the best means of translating it into complete advertisements. Two executions of the copy strategy submitted by the advertising agency for consideration by Mr. Carter are shown in the Appendix to this case, along with associated testing.

Advertising budget

Mr. Carter felt that the adoption of the operating assumption that Maxim should dominate coffee advertising logically implied the following media objectives:

1. To direct weight against all coffee users 18 and over, especially housewives in households with incomes above $3,500.

Experience with other products had suggested that those with incomes below $3,500 would hesitate to accept a premium-priced, high-quality food product like Maxim. In a test conducted to determine the chief source of coffee-buying decisions, the housewife proved to have made the choice entirely on her own in at least 65 percent of the instant-coffee-using homes and in at least 61 percent of the ground-coffee-using homes (see Exhibit 28).

2. To provide weight sufficient to stimulate maximum trial and repeat usage.
3. To achieve media dominance within the soluble coffee category.

In this respect, the plan "aimed to insure the consumer's attention and awareness of Maxim's introduction by saturing coffee-promoting media in each area in an effort to make Maxim the most salient new food product in the public consciousness."

New-product advertising was typically divided into three periods: (1) a

EXHIBIT 28
Male influence in coffee brand buying decision study, 1962

		Instant			Ground	
Household coffee usage	Total	Use instant only	Use instant and ground	Total	Use ground only	Use ground and instant
Husband asked directly for a brand and wife bought it	18%	18%	18%	16%	15%	17%
(Wife did not buy it). . . .	(1)	(—)°	(1)	(—)	(—)	(1)
Husband mentioned a brand and wife bought it	8	5	8	9	7	10
Husband indicated dissatisfaction and wife bought another brand	15	14	16	20	17	22
Husband bought a different brand	7	8	7	7	6	8
Husband shopped with wife and suggested a different brand and wife bought it . .	8	10	8	9	8	10
(Wife did not buy it). . . .	(—)	(—)	(—)	(1)	(2)	(—)
Husband did none of the above	65%	66%	65%	61%	61%	61%
Base: Total housewives in each group (no male interviews)	(753)	(96)	(657)	(200)	(88)	(112)

°Less than .05%.

2-week *stocking* period (to stimulate consumer—and trade—interest so as to insure adequate distribution), (2) 26-week *introductory* period (to create awareness, encourage trial, and provide reinforcement to secure repurchase), and (3) a 20-week *sustaining* period (to retain initial triers and extend brand awareness over introductory goals).

The final advertising budget for the first year had to be built from these general considerations in a step-by-step process:

1. Since it was assumed that no product trial would come without consumer awareness of the new brand, an awareness objective had to be set for each advertising period. Experience with other comparable new products showed that an overall awareness of at least 60 percent had to be achieved by the end of the introductory period if the product was to be successful.

2. The awareness goals needed to be scaled by market size and by shares expected in those areas. Since bigger shares were expected to come from larger urban markets, the awareness objectives should be correspondingly higher. A reasonable range of awareness objectives during the introductory period is shown below:

Market size (TV homes)	Estimated maximum and minimum feasible awareness (percent of TV homes)
Over 1,000,000	65–75%
250,000 to 1,000,000	60–70
75,000 to 250,000	50–60
0 to 75,000	40–60

3. A critical step would be the conversion of awareness goals into estimates of reach and frequency (that is, the cumulative audience, and the number of repeated messages being delivered to the cumulative audience). Sufficient impact during the introductory period could probably be generated in the largest markets with a reach of 80 to 90 percent and a frequency of once per week. During the sustaining period the frequency usually was cut by half or more; a budget at this sustaining level could probably suffice for the second year. Some adjustments might have to be made during the campaign to combat competitive advertising efforts. Usually this meant outspending the competition by shifting funds into the period of heaviest competitive advertising.

4. There was little question that spot television would be the basic medium to be used. It was already the common media practice in the coffee industry, absorbing an estimated 59 percent of the industry's 1963 budget. Another 20 percent of the industry budget went to network television expenditures.

5. A final problem, resulting from the desire to increase the soluble ratio, was the relative allotment to the high and low soluble areas. The expenditure of the same number of dollars per capita in both areas would certainly result in regional disproportions in terms of dollars per units sold. The question was, How far out of line was the extra expenditure per unit sold in the low soluble area?

Adherence to the initial assumptions of awareness, reach, frequency, and media for the purpose of an "order of magnitude" estimate of the advertising investment produced an expenditure range of $9,500,000 to $12,500,000 in the first year and $6,000,000 to $6,500,000 in the second year. This clearly ensured media dominance (see Exhibit 29) but did not answer questions of adequacy or inadequacy.

Promotions

As a general policy for Maxim, Mr. Carter urged the principle that wherever possible, the brand should direct promotion at the consumer rather than the dealer. He believed that the industry had subscribed to too many trade incentives, many of which proved ineffective, and preferred promotional offers such as free containers, free jars for two innerseals, free enclosed premiums, and so on—offers which exerted "pullthrough" by establishing direct contact with the consumer. This, of course, ruled out cents-off label dealing, which often lost its impact before

EXHIBIT 29
Advertising spending comparison, 1963 (est. thousands)

Product	Total	East	Mid-east	Central	West	South	West central
Total dollars—by region							
Instant Maxwell House ..	$6,490	$1,710	$1,153	$1,048	$ 821	$1,053	$ 705
Nescafé	4,673	1,286	829	748	673	669	468
Sanka.	2,981	675	448	462	520	464	412
Chase and Sanborn	3,243	946	582	574	267	611	263
Folger's	1,627	—	143	192	732	194	366
Yuban	2,440	1,221	433	255	352	162	17
Dollars per thousand population—by region							
Instant Maxwell House ..	$34.33	$40.83	$43.09	$34.01	$25.63	$32.26	$28.29
Nescafé	24.72	30.71	30.98	24.28	21.01	20.49	18.78
Sanka	15.77	16.12	16.74	14.99	16.24	14.21	16.53
Chase and Sanborn	17.16	22.59	21.75	18.63	8.34	18.72	10.55
Folger's	8.61	—	5.34	6.23	22.85	5.94	14.69
Yuban	12.91	29.16	16.18	8.28	10.99	4.96	0.68
January 1, 1964 population (thousands)	189,039.3	41,878.6	26,755.1	30,813.4	32,028.3	32,645.2	24,918.7

Source: Maxwell House market research department.

reaching the consumer. However, some sort of introductory trade allowance and display offer would be necessary in order to ensure rapid distribution.

A great deal of emphasis was placed on a promotional plan that would secure broad product trial. There was a strong belief that a buyer's experience with Maxim would result in a high level of satisfaction and that this was the best way to overcome inhibitions resulting from Maxim's premium price, or the "soluble stigma."

To obtain cost estimates Mr. Carter asked several large promotion houses to quote on the following promotional alternatives:

1. Two-ounce samples with 25¢ repurchase coupon delivered door to door.
2. Mailed coupons redeemable for free jar.
3. Mailed packets of six individually measured servings with a 25-cent repurchase coupon.

The restriction placed on the quotes was that only urban homes with incomes over $3,500 [2] be considered, in accord with the basic media objectives. Comparative projected national costs on alternative promotional techniques are shown in Exhibit 30.

---

[2] This was a total of 34 million homes, of which 25 million were in major urban areas.

EXHIBIT 30

Comparative projected national costs of alternative promotional techniques

Technique	Cost per thousand	Extension
2-oz. jar and 25¢ coupon		
(Base: 25,000,000 homes):		
Product and package	$241.00	$ 6,025,000
Distribution	120.00	3,000,000
Carrier.............................	13.00	325,000
Freeze-dry leaflets	6.00	150,000
25¢ coupon	5.00	125,000
Coupon redemption (25%)	67.50	1,687,500
Scoop..............................	10.00	250,000
Transportation	6.00	150,000
Warehousing........................	5.00	125,000
	$473.50	$11,073,500
Free coupon		
(Base: 9,000,000 homes):		
Coupon .,..........................	$ 6.00	$ 54,000
Freeze-dry leaflets	6.00	54,000
Distribution	10.50	94,500
Postage	27.50	247,500
Coupon redemption (50%)	315.00	2,835,000
	$365.00	$3,285,000
Six single-serving packets and a 25¢ coupon		
(Base: 34,000,000 homes):		
Product	$130.50	$ 4,437,000
Container and top....................	4.50	153,000
Package	26.50	901,000
Handling	25.00	850,000
Postage	39.00	1,326,000
Leaflets	6.00	204,000
25¢ coupon	5.00	170,000
Redemption (25%)....................	67.50	2,295,000
Mailing carton	10.00	340,000
	$313.00	$10,676,000

Pricing

Pricing presented particularly sticky problems. In the first place, Mr. Carter could not hope to set a definite or permanent price for Maxim before actually entering the market, simply because the price of coffee imports had long showed a confirmed tendency to fluctuate violently, by as much as 10 to 20 percent a year, and retail prices for the entire coffee market reflected these fluctuations. Consequently, Mr. Carter tended to view the Maxim pricing decision in terms of both Maxim's premium over Instant Maxwell House and other division brands and the margin generated after accounting for the retailer's markup.

Several other difficulties already mentioned above made the decision for pricing Maxim particularly tough. First, freeze-dried coffee cost about 35 percent *more* to make than spray-dried coffee. Second, pricing had to reflect results of business it took away from the division's other brands. Third, Maxim's concentrated form made the per-cup premium apply to a smaller total volume per ounce. This meant that a smaller jar could be used for 2-ounce, 4-ounce, and 8-ounce sizes, a confusion which might affect the consumer's perception—either favorably or unfavorably.

Indeed, Mr. Carter faced what he felt to be a sharply pronged dilemma, for he realized that with the coffee market's high price elasticity, Maxim might not realize its market share goals (especially for ground-coffee user conversion) if it were priced at a differential high enough to bring an incremental profit on cannibalized business.

To aid in clarifying the problem, several alternative price structures were drawn up—each with a different margin and different premium relationship to Instant Maxwell House and other division brands. Those who were more concerned with the market's price elasticity favored the price structure shown in Exhibit 31. This structure would establish a premium relationship to Instant Maxwell House of 12.2 percent/28.8 percent/43.0 percent for the 2-, 4-, and 8-ounce sizes, respectively, and would yield a higher margin to reflect high investment in plant and equipment. The per-

EXHIBIT 31
Pricing alternatives—Maxim

Brand and size	Retail price	Retail price per oz.	Retail economy vs. next smaller size	Cost° per cup	Maxim per oz. premium
Maxim					
2 oz.	$ .55	$ .2750	–%	2.12c	–%
4 oz.	.85	.2125	29.4	1.63	–
8 oz.	1.59	.1988	6.9	1.53	–
Instant Maxwell House					
2-oz.	.99	.2450	–	1.88	12.2
6 oz.	.49	.1650	48.5	1.27	28.8
10 oz.	1.39†	.1390	18.7	1.07	43.0
14 oz.	1.89†	.1350	3.0	1.04	47.3
Instant Yuban					
2 oz.	.53	.2650	–	2.04	3.8
5 oz.	.99	.1980	33.8	1.52	7.3
9 oz.	1.39†	.1544	28.2	1.19	28.8
Instant Sanka					
2 oz.	.53	.2650	–	2.04	3.8
5 oz.	1.09	.2180	21.6	1.68	(7.5)
8 oz.	1.49†	.1862	17.1	1.43	6.8
Regular Maxwell House					
1 lb.	.87	–	–	1.74	(2.3)‡
2 lb.	1.71	–	–	1.71	(7.0)§

°Soluble, 13 cups per ounce; ground, 50 cups per pound.
†Reflects retail shelf price when label packs of the following are in distribution: IMH, 10-oz., 20c; IMH, 14-oz., 30c; IY, 9-oz., 20c; IS, 8-oz., 10c.
‡versus 4-oz.
§versus 8-oz.

cup cost to the consumer would be close to that of Regular Maxwell House.

A second alternative with a great deal of support was based on the feeling that a higher premium such as 16.3 percent/40 percent/51.9 percent (see Exhibit 32) would not injure consumer acceptance of Maxim. This prediction came from the view that Maxim, as an inherently superior product, might show less price sensitivity than other coffees.

A further alternative, with some potential legal drawbacks of possible charge of price discrimination, was to price Maxim lower in the West. The desired result was to lure a larger number of ground users, since the division had less to fear from cannibalization there.

Choice of alternatives

The final decision on the price level was bound up with the concurrent decisions on positioning, advertising, and promotion. The approach used to consider the logical combinations of these elements was to create a "pro forma" share, budget, and profit projection for each combination.

However, before these projections could be made, a number of problem areas had to be resolved:

EXHIBIT 32
Pricing alternatives—Maxim (higher premium)

Brand and size	Retail price	Retail price per oz.	Retail Economy vs. next smaller size	Cost* per cup	Maxim per oz. premium
Maxim					
2 oz.	$ .57	$ .2850	—	2.19¢	—
4 oz.	.99	.2475	15.1%	1.90	—
8 oz.	1.69	.2112	17.2	1.63	—
Instant Maxwell House					
2 oz.	.49	.2450		1.88	16.3%
6 oz.	.99	.1650	48.5	1.27	50.0
10 oz.	1.39†	.1390	18.7	1.07	51.9
14 oz.	1.89†	.1350	3.0	1.04	56.4
Instant Yuban					
2 oz.	.53	.2650	—	2.04	7.5
5 oz.	.99	.1980	33.8	1.52	25.0
9 oz.	1.39†	.1544	12.8	1.19	36.8
Instant Sanka					
2 oz.	.53	.2650	—	2.04	7.5
5 oz.	1.09	.2180	21.6	1.68	13.5
8 oz.	1.49†	.1862	17.1	1.43	13.4
Regular Maxwell House					
1 lb.	.87	—	—	1.74	13.8‡
2 lb.	1.71	—	—	1.74	4.7§

*Soluble, 13 cups per ounce; ground, 50 cups per pound.
†Reflects retail shelf price when label packs of the following are in distribution: IMH, 10-oz., 20c; IMH, 14-oz., 30c; IY, 9-oz., 20c; IS, 8-oz., 10c.
‡versus 4-oz.
§versus 8-oz.

1. The gross margin and cost projections could be tentatively established from the requirement that Maxim demand a margin greater than that of other Maxwell House coffees.

2. A more difficult problem concerned the state of the market to be expected in the three years following the introduction. Three years was a typical planning horizon for the financial evaluation of a new food product. But even this period was long when it came to estimating future sales trends and competitive responses.

3. A broader policy question concerned the effect of the reduced sales volume of other division brands (because of Maxim cannibalization) on the advertising and promotion budgets of these brands. If these budgets were fixed at 1963 levels, the rest of the division would lose its entire margin on each unit cannibalized. This loss would have to be charged to Maxim profits. On the other hand, if these advertising and promotion budgets were reduced in proportion to the decrease in sales, the incremental loss to the rest of the division would be limited to the customary net profit per unit.

APPENDIX: ALTERNATIVE EXECUTIONS OF THE COPY STRATEGY

Ogilvy, Benson & Mather prepared two television commercials embodying the general copy points outlined above, each with a somewhat different emphasis. The "Freeze-Dried Announcement" stressed the effectiveness of the innovative manufacturing discovery; the "Perfect Percolator Cup" concentrated on the claim that Maxim tastes even better than ground coffee because it has no bitter aftertaste. The agency tested each ad with forced in-home trials. O.B. & M. also submitted two newspaper advertisements (one of which included a 10¢ coupon) stressing the theme that freeze-drying produces a crystalline coffee with the power to turn every cup into a percolator. The agency further suggested outdoor and transit displays proclaiming first "Maxim Is Coming" and then "Maxim Is Here."

1. *Freeze-Dried Announcement*

Announcer: You are looking at an entirely new form of coffee. You are looking at freeze-dried coffee. Tiny, concentrated crystals that have the power to turn every cup in your house into a percolator! This is Maxim, the entirely new form of coffee from Maxwell House. After years of research, it was discovered that freshly brewed coffee could be frozen. The ice could be drawn off in a vacuum, and you would have freeze-dried coffee, concentrated crystals of real percolated coffee. That's Maxim. Rich, full bodied, exactly like the finest coffee you ever brewed. Let Maxim turn every cup in your house into a percolator! Get Maxim, the entirely new form of coffee from Maxwell House.

(Accompanied by appropriate *sound effects*: crystals dropping into cup, water pouring, coffee perking, vacuum being applied, more water pouring and perking; and by appropriate *visual effects*: close-up of crystals on spoon, cup changing into percolator, close-up of jar, perked coffee being frozen and vacuumized, man savoring taste, close-up of label.)

2. *Perfect Percolator Cup*

Pretty Young Housewife: I make better coffee than you do. That's right. I make better coffee than you do. Without a coffeepot. Without a powdery instant coffee. (Slams cupboard door.) But *with* an entirely new kind of coffee! It's Maxim. (Close-up of jar.) And it's fantastic! Maxim turns every cup in your house into a percolator. (Cups turning into percolators.) Yes. Maxim makes better coffee right in the cup than you can brew in a coffeepot. Perfect percolator coffee with none of that harsh, bitter taste you sometimes get with ground.

Announcer: Maxim's secret? A totally new process from Maxwell House turns real percolated coffee into crystals. Tiny concentrated crystals with the power to turn every cup in your house into a percolator. (Repeat visual sequence of cups turning into percolators.)

Pretty Young Housewife: That's why I make better coffee than you do. Unless you've discovered Maxim too.

Announcer: Maxim, the entirely new form of coffee from Maxwell House.

Testing of the strategy

Testing of the "Freeze-Dried Announcement" versus "Perfect Percolator Cut" is shown in Exhibits A1 and A2.

EXHIBIT A1

Persuasion scores	Freeze-dried announcements	Perfect percolator cup
Maxim	17%	19%
Users of instant only	12	22
Users of ground only	16	8
Users of both	23	28
Instant Maxwell House	14	10
Regular Maxwell House	14	19
Connotation		
Maxim different	84	84
Reference to process	46	23
Reference to flavor	20	41
Reference to new different	35	19
About the same	14	22

EXHIBIT A2

	Freeze-dried announcement		Perfect percolator cup	
Recall	Immediate	24 hour	Immediate	24 hour
It's frozen	63%	72%	—	—
It's dehydrated, dried	36	42	—	—
It's perked, brewed	26	22	4%	4%
It's crystallized	18	14	40	40
Eight pots in one jar	36	15	—	—
It's concentrated	15	10	10	10
Tastes like real perked	20	14	16	14
Can make better coffee than you	—	—	20	12
Turns every cup into a percolator	16	7	24	18
An instant coffee	18	8	24	26

MARCHAND (CANADA) LTD.

THE RAZOR BLADE division of Marchand (Canada) Ltd. introduced blister packaging for its products for the first time in May 1961. The new packaging consisted of a printed cardboard backing to which a preformed sheet of plastic containing the product was sealed by a packaging machine. Discussions with suppliers of the packaging equipment and materials had extended over a 17-month period before purchases were finalized.

COMPANY BACKGROUND

Marchand (Canada) Ltd., the wholly-owned subsidiary of Marchand Corp., produced a large variety of high-volume, heavily promoted, durable and nondurable consumer goods. All manufacturing facilities and the head office were located in Windsor, Ontario. The company's divisional organization is shown in Exhibit 1.

The razor blade division

The company's dominant position in the razor blade market was the result of advanced and sophisticated manufacturing skills and aggressive sales and promotion policies. A major marketing strength was the extremely broad distribution pattern. Wholesale drug distributors who covered drugstores, tobacconists, and other small stores provided 75 percent of the company sales. The remaining 25 percent of sales were made direct to chain retailers. In 1960 the company was estimated to have 35 percent of the total shaving market; electric shavers had 50 percent of the market; four other razor blade manufacturers held the remaining 15 percent. The

520

EXHIBIT 1
Organization chart, Marchand (Canada) Ltd.

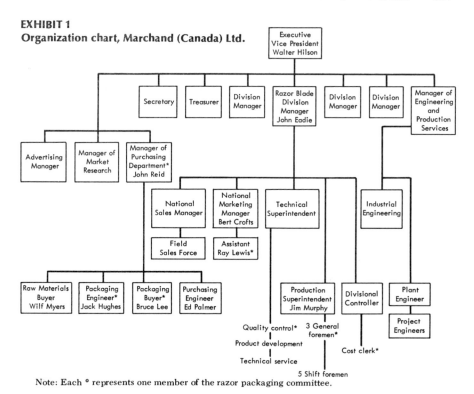

Note: Each ° represents one member of the razor packaging committee.

most severe competition was felt from electric shaver manufacturers, whose share of the market had expanded rapidly between 1948 and 1953.

The division also manufactured and marketed five razor sets ranging from an inexpensive three-piece model to an expensive, gold-plated, one-piece prestige set. All sets were manufactured to extremely high tolerances. Razors had traditionally been a loss item, although as a result of automation some profit was being made. A strong justification for the emphasis on razor sets was the high degree of correlation between Marchand razor ownership and the usage of Marchand blades.

THE PURCHASING DEPARTMENT

The purchasing department served all divisions. The manager, John Reid, supervised the activities of Jack Hughes, the packaging engineer; Bruce Lee, the packaging buyer; Ed Palmer, the purchasing engineer; and Wilf Myers, the raw-materials buyer. Approximately 40 purchase orders were issued each day, ranging in value from $5 to $30,000 and averaging $2,500 each. Often, purchase requisitions from three or four separate departments were grouped either for convenience or to take advantage of quantity discounts. About half the orders issued were routine and were usually handled by Lee, the packaging buyer. Other orders related to changes in materials, specifications, and vendors and took up considerable time. Reid seldom issued more than 1 or 2 orders per day; Palmer and Myers would account for 8 or 10 orders each. Hughes didn't issue orders himself but gave them to Lee for processing.

John Reid—purchasing department manager

To elaborate on his department's role, John Reid said:

In our company, over 50 percent of the sales dollar goes for the purchase of raw materials that we process further and finished products for our own use or resale. In some areas such as raw materials, we have undisputed decision-making powers, subject to the usual controls by top management concerning large expenditures. In other areas we act as the coordinator for points of view of all people interested in the purchase—such as production, industrial engineering, warehousing, and so on. . . . We seem to be in the best position to assess and summarize the pertinent cost factors. Accountants are good on plant costs, but don't understand the total cost picture which considers demurrage, damage, returns, and so on. In either kind of purchase, however, the decision almost always becomes apparent once the significant factors have been defined and quantified. The most indeterminate and difficult part is appraising the long-run performance. For example, what is the sacrifice that a cost cutter makes to get our business? If it's in quality control, what is the cost to us in the final analysis? That's why good working relationships are so important. In case of doubt you go to the company where you know the people, the equipment, the potential, and their weaknesses—and they understand your needs.

Concerning equipment selection specifically, Reid made the following comment;

The responsibility for specification sometimes falls in a gray zone between our department and engineering, when their specification can only be met by one source. Our attitude is that this is either laziness or expediency. By and large few pieces of equipment are so special that they can't be reduced to blueprints.

Reid defined his own job as head of the purchasing department as follows:

Besides some responsibility for major purchases of commodities, such as steel and plastic films, my job is primarily to keep my people fully aware of the long-range implications of their actions. Sometimes they are prone to get carried away with immediate problems and pressures such as processing requisitions and neglect to make complete investigations. . . . At all times we're concerned with cost reductions, and I expect my people to initiate many opportunities.

Reid was regarded by people inside and outside the company as an "enlightened" purchasing agent. A university graduate in science with 16 years' service with Marchand, he was active in a number of community affairs as well as the national executive of the Canadian Association of Purchasing Agents.

He was vitally interested in learning as much as possible about the industry and suppliers he dealt with. To this end he read *The Financial Post* and *Canadian Business* closely and scanned articles of interest in the seven major Canadian and U.S. purchasing, packaging, and plastics magazines. He found direct-mail advertising and institutional material such as internal house organs, employee papers, and company trade papers such as Du Pont's *Packaging Patter* to be more meaningful than normal trade magazine advertisements in developing a good supplier image and "keeping their name in front of me."

In 10 years' time Reid's relations with salesmen had changed substantially as the purchasing department grew from one to five men. Originally, he saw an average of 10 salesmen a day. By 1961, the increasingly technical and longer term nature of his buying decisions meant he saw about two salesmen or groups of salesmen a day, usually by previous appointment or at his request. He preferred technical forums once or twice a year where key supplier people and Marchand technical people met for half a day to review all outstanding problems and plan for the coming period. In this situation he saw his job as ensuring that both parties understood each other completely. For the rest of the time close telephone and mail contact sufficed.

Reid was very emphatic about the fact that the key role of the salesman was to provide service by communicating information quickly and representing the customer's interest to the supplier.

We're a marketing-oriented company, and the need to get promotions set up and into the market in a matter of days creates a real pressure for speed. The supplier must recognize this fact and do a conscientious job of meeting our needs, following up quickly on problems, and keeping us fully informed of the situation. One thing we don't need is a bunch of alibis.

Jack Hughes—packaging engineer

For historical and other reasons within the Canadian subsidiary, the purchasing department also included a packaging engineer who kept in touch with packaging problems in every division. Jack Hughes was a graduate engineer with seven years' experience in industrial engineering and product supervision and three years' experience in his current position.

His view of his job was:

. . . primarily to coordinate the development of new packages for the Canadian company—right from the idea stage to the details of the specifications and the placing of the first order. Some of the ideas I initiate myself to achieve cost reductions. This includes reducing the overlap in our 2,500 different packages. Other ideas stem from marketing innovations or from the production department's desire to change a process. . . . In the future I'm planning to do a lot of getting more uniformity in our suppliers' packages.

Although I pretty well run my own show, I find real advantages in being part of the purchasing department. It provides a flexibility that our parent, with separate groups, certainly doesn't have. Of course they have more factories, people, and other variables to coordinate. It may take them a year to make a change that would only involve a month or so for us.

Bruce acts as a screen for packaging salesmen, so I just talk to those that I've asked in for a specific purpose or that have something new that I can use immediately. Normally when I have a specific requirement I use catalogs and other trade listings to give me leads on possible suppliers. I read all the major U.S. and Canadian packaging and plastics magazines and attend four or five trade shows each year, mainly as a source for new ideas. In these ways I've collected a lot of data, although I'm still finding it hard to keep up to date on all the changes in packaging technology.

Edward Palmer—purchasing engineer

Essentially the purchasing engineer's job was to act as the buyer and a screen against salesmen for the engineering and maintenance departments. Ed Palmer, a graduate engineer, was well suited for this job, having spent 12 years as a project engineer in the engineering department before taking his present job in 1958.

Although most of the requirements were defined by the engineering department, Palmer reviewed 10 magazines a month concerning topics such as materials handling, design engineering, equipment selection, and purchasing in search of new ideas or improvements that might be pursued. In describing the process of selecting possible suppliers, he said:

The big trade directories (Fraser for Canada and Thomas for the United States) handle about 90 percent of any of my problems. In the more difficult situations I'll depend on manufacturer and distributor catalogs and my knowledge of suppliers' capabilities . . . direct mail is of very little use since the information is limited and seldom comes when I'm interested in buying something.

When he looked at the influence of salesmen on his decisions, Palmer concluded that,

. . . in most cases we could do without them. Ideally the supplier should have a good office that is really accessible by telephone when I have a problem, would keep me stocked with good literature and prices, and would have technically competent salesmen who could advise me in case of problems. . . . In my experience, most salesmen don't know much about technical details, and few are of any use in following up orders, keeping us informed about the status of orders, or solving problems quickly.

On some days I will see as many as six or eight men for visits of 20 minutes to over an hour (if, for example, they've been called in to talk with engineering also). About a third are suppliers who already have good relations with us and are calling to service orders or show new products. Another half are people who have never sold to us and seldom call. Sometimes they have a new product and can't understand why we won't try it out. As far as we're concerned, if the product doesn't have immediate application, then we don't have time to try it. The remainder of my callers are various agents and distributors who sell staples such as bolts and ball bearings and can only offer service. There are a lot of these around, particularly now that they're coming from as far away as Toronto.

Over the long term, Palmer expected to see the scope of his job expand substantially:

It will mean eliminating the routines of ordering, pricing orders and grouping orders to save money that any clerk can do in favor of more special work. .... I feel I have as much opportunity as anyone in the company to save money by spending more time on negotiation with suppliers, arranging equipment trials, following new products, and developing Canadian sources of supply.

NEED FOR NEW PACKAGING

As early as 1950, company marketing executives in Canada felt that their most frequently used package, a formed rigid plastic box, lacked eye appeal and display convenience. Between 1955 and 1958 they examined the newly developed techniques of blister and skin packaging, which seemed to offer considerable improvement. The cost of materials and equipment, however, did not seem to warrant a change.

In December 1959, Ray Lewis, assistant marketing manager, returned to Windsor from the annual Canadian Packaging Show and told the marketing manager, Bert Crofts, about a new and inexpensive packaging machine he had seen. Lewis showed Crofts the manufacturer's literature and was very enthusiastic about the possibilities for the machine at Marchand. Crofts agreed and called the packaging engineer, Jack Hughes, to suggest an investigation of blister packs in general.

First informal packaging investigation

Hughes decided to secure a firm quotation from the distributor for the Melville sealing machine seen by Lewis, together with competitive quotes from suppliers of blisters and cards. Hughes also sent the Melville literature to Industrial Engineering for an estimate of sealing and packing times.

BLISTER SUPPLIERS.   After consultation with his manager, John Reid, Hughes decided to ask Multi-Pak Ltd. of Guelph and Service Packaging of Toronto for quotes on blisters. Service Packaging was an easy choice: They had done excellent custom packaging work for Marchand for more than 10 years; they were known to be technically competent; and their salesman made a point of calling four or five times a year. As Reid summarized, "We always think of them in this connection."

Multi-pak was chosen for different reasons. Reid had been aware for several years that they were one of the first companies in Canada to attempt skin and blister packaging at a time when the technology was still changing very rapidly. He had also not heard anything unfavorable about other custom packaging jobs they had undertaken. Consequently he thought that they could probably provide a good quality of formed blisters. Rather than depend on hearsay he asked the opinion of a salesman whom he trusted from long previous association. The salesman, John Doyle of Fairmont Chemical, currently the major supplier to Marchand of polyethylene and cellulose acetate packaging films, had developed a strong personal interest in packaging technology in order to sell more packaging film. Doyle was acquainted with Multi-Pak and judged them to be one of the leading companies in blister packaging.

BACKING CARDS.   Hewson Printers and K. J. Cowan were chosen as possible sources for printed backing cards. These two printing houses had been doing most of Marchand's printing, and the relatively small order didn't warrant requesting quotes from other suppliers.

On January 25, 1960, Hughes gave Bruce Lee, the packaging buyer, the requirements and suppliers' names and asked that quotations be obtained. Since there was no urgency, the letters were not sent until February 19th. Replies were received between February 25th and March 12th and were summarized by Hughes as follows: (1) Melville machine, $1,730; tooling, $150; (2) Multi-Pak, lowest blister quote, $15.80 per 1,000 for 100,000 units; (3) Hewson Printers, lowest card quote, $11.35 per 1,000 for 100,000 units.

Hughes sent the quotes with the sealing and packing times to the divisional controller to ". . . establish and report the cost of this package so it can be used as a guide to compare with other methods of packaging." The controller reported that it appeared there would be a 15 to 25 percent premium for blister packages. Crofts and Lewis found these results "interesting but speculative." No further action was taken, however, as other more pressing projects were at hand.

Second informal packaging investigation

In June 1960, John Eadie, the razor blade division manager, sent a copy of a recent magazine article on skin and blister packaging to John Reid and asked what the company was doing to evaluate these packages. This inquiry was passed on to Hughes, who in turn checked with Lewis. No concrete thinking had been done, and it was decided that the same suppliers should be asked to requote on a smaller razor set package.

During July, Hughes arranged to have some of the company products packed on the Melville machine during a demonstration in Toronto. By the end of August, the new cost information was ready, along with the sample packs. The cost summary was more favorable on the smaller packs.

On September 5th, Lewis wrote to Crofts: "We are writing to recommend that we arrange, if possible, for the loan on trial installation of a machine from the Melville distributor for further in-plant investigation. The trial would give us more accurate industrial engineering times for further costing."

First formal project T-145

In response to Lewis's memo, Crofts and Eadie decided to order a formal study project to cover two promotional items (one was a "deal" combining 15 blades and a safety razor) which were suffering from packaging limitations. It was proposed that 100 units be packaged to gain operating experience.

As a routine measure, Lewis reported the keen interest in blister packaging at the regular semimonthly meeting of the razor division packaging committee on September 15th. This committee, chaired by Hughes, met primarily to keep members informed about current packaging projects, manufacturing and marketing problems, and new products within the division. (See Exhibit 1 above for the actual committee membership.) The meetings usually lasted less than an hour and covered 12 to 20 separate items.

The consequences of Lewis's report to the meeting were immediate and rather unexpected. It transpired that this was the first time the production department had been informed about the interest in the packaging machine and the recommendation for a trial installation. Jim Murphy, the production superintendent, reacted to the report from his representatives on the packaging committee by immediately calling Crofts. Murphy accused the marketing people of ". . . not consulting or informing the production people . . . making all sorts of unfounded assumptions without establishing a proper need." He concluded by saying that he wouldn't have anything to do with the blister sealer until he knew exactly what the machine would be doing, how it would affect his production rates, and that it was the best available piece of equipment from the standpoint of quality control, maintenance, and flexibility of output.

The reaction of Crofts and Lewis was one of surprise, since their attitude was primarily ". . . we're not really specifying a piece of equipment— all we want are some costs." Although they did confess to having made a "faux pas over communications", there was a strongly implied feeling that "Jim Murphy is somewhat against change in general because he has everything going so smoothly right now."

According to Lewis, "For the next week, there was a lot of pussyfooting around. No one was quite sure what to do or wanted to take the responsibility for a decision." Finally Crofts got the production and industrial engineering groups to agree to an in-plant trial where a number of samples could be prepared and the necessary equipment evaluations made. The trial was conducted soon afterward, and all concerned pronounced themselves well satisfied with the construction and performance of the Melville equipment.

The successful demonstration convinced Crofts and Lewis that the Melville sealer was ideally suited to their needs. Furthermore, ". . . we've been looking at this machine for eight months now, why should we delay any longer?" This attitude led to further resistance from the production department, which contended that no specific requirements concerning output, size, and so on had been decided. It also resulted in a negative reaction from the purchasing department. Reid, who until that time had not been directly concerned, questioned the advisability of an immediate purchase in a memo dated September 27th and directed to Crofts. Reid's contention was that "It may be their dollars they're spending, but it's the responsibility of this department to recommend how it should be spent." His memo read:

> I am sending this memo as a cautionary note with respect to Project T–145. The memos received to date seem to be strongly oriented toward the purchase of a blister-sealing machine without a complete understanding of (*a*) the customer acceptance of our product packaged in blister, and (*b*) a full definition of our requirements. We may well find ourselves with a machine that either we don't need after a period of a year, or has too limited an output. Our basic interest in expediency now may result in buying a machine with much too limited an output based on actual market acceptance of blister pack.
>
> We intend to investigate this project from the standpoint of custom packaging which would enable us to test market this package without an investment in equipment as well as to explore to a somewhat limited degree the cost of blister-sealing equipment and the cost of blisters from different sources.
>
> If the blister package is completely acceptable to our customers and more than exceeds your honest expectation, it may well be that our strength would lie in having a completely integrated line for blister forming, loading, and blister sealing.
>
> Should not then our main thrust be directed toward custom packaging and test marketing of these packages, and as a secondary objective canvassing the market for prices of blisters and packaging equipment?

Second formal project T-153

Faced with Reid's arguments, the marketing department agreed to design a new study project to include a comparison of having the packaging sent out on a custom basis versus in-plant packaging. On October 10th, the study was initiated, specifying the target date for distribution of completed packages as January 2, 1961. Earlier quotes provided most of the information required, but because of confusion over the payment of die costs, Hughes was unable to make a comparison until November 10th. Hughes sent the following information to the controller's department:

1. Custom packaging: $34.00 per 1,000, for quantities of 100,000 (Multi-Pak).
2. In-plant costs: $8.28 per 1,000 for blisters (Multi-Pak); $12.75 per 1,000 for backing cards (Hewson); packing times and machine cost submitted previously.

About this time, Eadie was asked about the custom packaging alternative which had been suggested to give the company more flexibility and to avoid an error in equipment purchase. According to Eadie,

> . . . there are just too many production problems for us to be able to do this. However, it does give us an interesting comparison with our own costs. Production people have always taken a very dim view of work being taken away from their people. And, it's hard to explain, but people on the line really feel it is a slap in the face. Equally important is the effect on union relations. This issue has never come up, but there is always the possibility.

In early December Lewis queried the controller's department to find out what had happened to the final cost summary but discovered that the cost accountant was overloaded with more urgent projects. Several days later some unexpected price cutting by Marchand's largest competitor demanded the full-time attention of the whole razor blade marketing group. It was decided that it was neither feasible nor desirable to put the new package into the market during January or February.

Appearance of new suppliers

During November, Hughes kept the packaging study project in mind even though he had already sent quotations along to the controller. Since he was in close contact with the U.S. head-office packaging department on several problems each week and depended on the head office for technical assistance on various packages being developed in Canada, he requested comments on U.S. experience with blister packaging for low-price deals. The reply, dated November 15th, dealt mainly with technical matters of board quality, blister material, and quality control. The end of the letter, dealing with equipment recommendations and commenting on the usefulness of blister packaging, read:

> We have an old vacuum-forming machine, known as an Abbott, which we have had at our main plant for probably six or eight years. While this machine is certainly not the greatest piece of equipment, it has done a job for us in adequate style. I would suggest, however, that if you are entertaining the idea of buying a vacuum former you contact someone like the Vacuum Equipment Company at Chicago. I do not know whether they have a Canadian plant, but I do know they are well established along these lines and produce an excellent piece of equipment for almost any vacuum or pressure-forming operation you might be interested in.
>
> In answer to your last question, I believe the most useful comment on blister

packaging is that generally speaking it is quite expensive, and while we have used blister packing on a number of the kinds of items you are interested in, we usually end up with some other package that is less expensive and sooner or later drop the use of the blister.

I do believe the blister package does a good job and is a popular package on today's market. However, as for the product you have suggested we feel that the blister has not actually added to sales and consequently we find no reason to pay a premium to use a blister package.

Also during November, Hughes followed up on some reports that the purchasing department had received about a Berwin blister sealer. They came from John Mason, a new salesman for Johnson Printers. According to Reid,

Although Mason has only called on us a few times, and we really haven't had very good experience with his firm in the past, he has a fresh approach that is very worthwhile. Not only is he enthusiastic but he has developed a strong technical orientation toward blister packaging—apparently as a hobby. He feels that he can ultimately sell printing by first selling the blister pack idea or at least being in a position to offer good technical assistance. One step he has taken is to ally himself with the Berwin people so he can offer a complete system. This is good for Berwin, too, since it increases their sales representation. In this particular instance it's not going to work because the backing card requirement really isn't big enough to justify quotes from more than two printing houses. However, in our eyes he has definitely overcome the past inertia of Johnson Printers and will be well received in the future.

At Mason's request, a manufacturer's agent representing Berwin in the Windsor area submitted literature and a quotation for a blister-sealing machine and also offered a 30-day in-plant trial. The machine chosen for quotation was designed to handle smaller volumes than the Melville sealer and lacked an automatic indexing mechanism to move the blisters in and out of the sealing area. It was priced at $1,050, compared with $1,700 for the Melville sealer.

Up to this point Hughes had coordinated the contacts with the equipment suppliers. This constituted a minor precedent, since the engineering department, by virtue of its responsibility for equipment specification, was usually involved in equipment-supplier contact at an early stage in the purchase decision. However, due to the nature of the purchase and a heavy work load, the engineering department had declared that it wasn't interested in participating in setting specifications on equipment that might not be purchased. Normally, Ed Palmer would have handled the supplier contacts for the equipment.

Mason also supplied the lead on a new adhesive-coated blister being supplied by Remco Industries, a small plastics fabricator in Chicago. This represented a considerable innovation and potential cost saving, as it meant that the backing board didn't have to be coated. At Mason's request, Remco submitted a quotation that proved competitive with

Multi-Pak and also supplied a number of high-quality samples of their work. Hughes commented,

At the moment I don't know anything about them, although since it's not a critical item, I suspect we can take a chance and not get into trouble. If I have time I'm going to try and visit them in Chicago. . . . The big reservation is that buying from them goes against my principle of using Canadian sources of supply wherever possible.

Final purchase approval

On December 14, 1960, the division controller sent the cost analysis to the razor blade division marketing department. A formal "Request for Addition to Stock" was prepared and approved by Eadie and by the executive vice president, Walter Hilson. The volume was specified at 72,000 units, and the target date for completion of packages and racks was set at March 31, 1961.

Final purchase order

On January 10, 1961, Hughes received a form authorizing him to obtain final quotes based on exact quantities and to choose suppliers for blisters and backing cards. He added Johnson Printers to his earlier list of suppliers for backing cards. At the same time, the engineering department was authorized to prepare machine specifications for Ed Palmer, the purchasing engineer, who would then obtain quotes on packaging machines. The specifications would include such factors as size and cycle time.

Palmer anticipated the receipt of specifications from engineering and asked the Berwin manufacturer's agent to supply a machine for in-plant trial during February. On February 5th, Palmer reported he hadn't yet received the specifications from engineering. Palmer explained:

When I do, I'll send "request for quotations" to four or five suppliers listed in Fraser's directory. I expect there should be quite a number of suppliers, although I haven't looked yet. Actually I don't have much of a feel for the packaging machine market. We seldom buy this kind of equipment, preferring to build most of it ourselves. Also, I don't know when a packaging equipment salesman has been in to see me. I guess they are just too busy calling on the big buyers who are always in the market for more equipment.

Hughes found that the delay in receiving specifications was caused by the engineer being tied up with other projects, and then being away sick. It was decided, finally, to go ahead without the specifications from engineering, to consider only the Melville and Berwin machines, and to go with the cheaper Berwin machine if the in-plant trial was satisfactory. Hughes commented:

Because of the pressures of time we won't be able to canvass other manufacturers or determine whether any other divisions could use blister packaging. If we choose the Berwin machine we'll probably scrap it or trade it for a bigger machine in one or two years as our requirements become clearer.

BLISTERS. In the meantime, the quotes on the blisters had been received, and an order placed with Multi-Pak, the low bidder. Jack Hughes said about Remco Industries of Chicago, "After we get going with the initial order we'll get 150 or 200 of the new coated blisters and test them in the lab. If this blister is as good as it is supposed to be, there will probably be a Canadian company supplying it fairly soon."

CARDS. It was March 15, 1961, before a revised backing card was finished by the art department and sent out for quotes. Johnson Printers, through their salesman, Mason, quoted $9 per 1,000. Next lowest at $12.10 per 1,000 was Hewson, a company with considerable experience in this particular type of work. The highest was K. J. Cowan, a smaller supplier, at $18 per 1,000.

MACHINE. The Berwin machine trial was satisfactory. At a meeting of engineering, production, industrial engineering, and purchasing, it was decided that there was no immediate advantage to the greater speed and flexibility of the Melville machine. In any event, Palmer, the purchasing engineer, had heard nothing from the Melville distributor, since the sample-pack demonstration six months earlier.

The Berwin machine was installed and supplies were delivered in April 1961, and the packaging operations were completed in time for a June introductory campaign. Further orders of material from Johnson Printers and Multi-Pak would be contingent on market acceptance of the blister package.

QUESTIONS FOR DISCUSSION

1. There were frequently substantial differences in points of view about the blister package held by each of the Marchand departments. How do you explain these differences? As an industrial marketer would you have expected them? If so, why? If not, why not?
2. What marketing strategy and plan would you use to sell blister packaging machinery or components to this type of company if you were marketing manager for each of the following companies?

   Melville Engineering Corp.
   Service Packaging
   Johnson Printers
3. Describe in detail your evaluation of the marketing performance of each of the suppliers referred to in the case.

THE BRACE COMPANY
The truth-in-packaging legislation

INTRODUCTION

By the summer of 1966, it had become evident to people in the package-goods industry that a real problem was growing out of some legislation being considered in Congress. This legislation had to do with government regulation of labeling, packaging, and, to a lesser degree, advertising. No one was exactly certain what had brought about the government action, but a few reasons had been hypothesized. Some thought it could be attributed to the Supreme Court decision on reapportionment which concentrated more power in urban areas, where were more vocal and more highly educated people. Others claimed that the legislation was the product of a more highly educated group of consumers in the entire country. A third suggestion was that the problem arose from consumer frustration over the plethora of new products. Also, many conceded that business had not done an adequate job of transmitting information, either through packaging and labeling or through advertising.

At this time the management of the Brace Company, a large manufacturer of breakfast foods whose business was centered around the sales of various kinds of dry, ready-to-eat cereals,[1] became very concerned about the implications of the pending legislation. W. V. Brace, president, and P. Burns, executive vice president, marketing, believed that if the strongest possible legislation were passed, the Brace Company would have to com-

---

[1] The Brace Company is a fictitious entity whose problems and markets resemble those of large package-goods producers generally.

pletely revamp its packaging lines and drastically alter its promotional plans and present advertising campaigns. This would cost the company a tremendous amount of money, easily in the multimillion-dollar range.

Since business interests had been rather ineffective up to the summer of 1966 in combating this governmental action, Brace had requested the opportunity to testify before a congressional subcommittee which was conducting hearings on the advisability of the proposed legislation to regulate packaging and labeling. Two weeks before Mr. Brace was to testify; J. Blackwell, the newly appointed assistant to the vice president, marketing, was called in and asked to research the problem and to clarify the basic issues so that Mr. Brace could speak knowledgeably at the hearings. Several other men in the company brought in what they thought were pertinent data and gave it to Blackwell to analyze. Since actual data concerning the Brace Company had not been gathered, Blackwell was encouraged to use figures on other cereal manufacturers.

THE CONSUMERS' ENVIRONMENT—PROLIFERATION

While doing his research, it became evident to Blackwell that the environment in which the consumer lived in 1966 was much different from that of 20 years before. The major change the consumer faced was that of product proliferation. With the emergence of the modern supermarket and advanced technology, price was being subordinated to innovation of products and packages as major promotional tools. These factors worked to put approximately 4,000 new products on supermarket shelves each year. In 1965, 40 percent of all manufacturing sales were from products not produced in 1950. It was estimated that in 1969 15 percent of manufacturing sales would come from products not produced in 1965. Research and development, the source of innovation, increased 60 percent as a percentage of sales from 1954 to 1964 in 18 large food processors (see Exhibit 1).

While innovation may have led to the expansion of consumer satisfaction and economic growth, it may also have engendered confusion in the marketplace. Not only did the consumer of 1966 face more variety than her 1946 counterpart, but she was also confronted with an increasing inability to differentiate between products due to their increased complexity and subtleties of change. Blackwell found out that there were approximately 8,000 different items in the average supermarket. It could be said that by 1966, product differentiation was a leading means of gaining and holding a preferred market position and that advertising and sales promotion are credited with being the most common way to gain access to customers.

THE CEREAL INDUSTRY

As far as the cereal business was concerned, Blackwell uncovered the following data: In 1964 there were 48,500,000 cereal-using households in

EXHIBIT 1
A. Expenditures for R&D by 18 large food processors

Year	Aggregate sales (*millions*)	R & D expenditures	
		Millions	*Percent of sales*
1954............................	$4,974	$ 18.3	37%
1960............................	5,636	30.3	54
1964............................	6,579	39.6	60
Percent change:			
1954–64........................	+ 32.3	+ 116.7	
1960–64........................	+ 16.7	+ 30.6	

B. Proliferation of cereals, 1954–64

New cereals captured 23 percent of market.
Regular brands decreased share of market from 70 percent to 55 percent.
Number of cold cereals increased from 46 to 79 stocked in
grocery chains.

C. Average number of items offered for sale per manufacturer and average share of manufacturer's cereal sales accounted for by his 5 and 10 largest selling items, 1964

Size of manufacturer	Items for company (*number*)	Share of company sales	
		For 5 items (*percent*)	For 10 items (*percent*)
Largest 4 companies...............	58	35.4	56.9
Next 4 companies	16	52.6	68.2
All other companies	6	86.6	—
All companies (24)	16	39.2	not available

Source: Part A, Robert P. Buzzell and Robert E. M. Nourse, *Product Innovations in Food Processing, 1954–1964* (Boston, Mass., Harvard University Graduate School of Business Administration, 1967); p. 95; Part B, A. C. Nielsen Company; Part C, National Committee on Food Marketing.

which children between the ages of 3 and 12 influenced 70 percent of the sales of the ready-to-eat variety of cereal.

One of the reasons for the proliferation of cereals was a lack of brand loyalty and the introduction of new brands. The National Commission on Food Marketing stated that three out of five consumers buy most popular brands 4 out of 10 times. However, the commission stated, company loyalty is higher than brand loyalty, and company market share is correlated to the degree of introduction of new cereals also (see Exhibit 2). A study by the Marketing Research Company of America put the repurchase rate for cereals at 50 percent.

Cereal companies also attempted to achieve their share of market goals via market segmentation. Arthur D. Little, Inc., stated that "one of the major determinants of a company's market position is not only the number of brands that it has, but also the number of brands that it has in each

EXHIBIT 2
A. Brand loyalty

Product	Strong (chief brand bought 75% of time or more)	Moderate (chief brand bought 40–75% of time)	Weak (chief brand bought less than 40% of time)
Coffee	70%	25%	5%
Laundry detergent	88	9	3
Cold cereal	6	34	60

B. Cold cereal brand loyalty

	Product class					
	I	*II*	*III*	*IV*	*V*	*VI*
Percent of families	52%	10%	10%	10%	9%	9%
Percent of pound volume	14%	8%	10%	14%	19%	35%
Number of brands chosen per year	4	8	9	11	12	15
Number of packages purchased per year	8	21	27	37	52	96

Source: Part A: Benton & Bowles, Inc., 1962.

market segment." Thus it appeared that innovation and segmentation were major product policies for the cereal manufacturers and that both of these strategies required a high level of advertising and promotion to be effective. In 1964, $1.5 billion was spent by food processors on advertising, which was a 4 percent increase over 1963 expenditures (partially reflecting higher media costs). The president of Canadian Kellogg had stated that 17 cents of every cereal dollar went to promotion, advertising, discounts, and incentives, and the Arthur D. Little Company claimed that:

15.2 percent of sales went toward advertising in the cereal business. From 1958 to 1965 advertising expenditures increased 65 percent in the cereal industry. The medium for advertising also changed during the same period of time: television increased from 72.6 percent to 86.3 percent of cereal advertising dollars while newspaper decreased from 15.0 percent to 3.5 percent.[2]

For a more detailed picture of the cereal industry, see Exhibit 3.

THE ROLE OF GOVERNMENT

Blackwell realized that the problem of government action which Brace must recognize was not restricted to cereal manufacturers and the food in-

---

[2]Report of Arthur D. Little to Grocery Manufacturers Association, 1965.

EXHIBIT 3

A. The cereal industry, profit data and revenue sources (in thousands)

		Largest four companies	Next four companies	All other com- panies	All companies
A.	Profit data				
	1964 profit				
	Before tax	$ 77,330	$ 6,007	$ 540°	$ 83,877
	After tax	$ 38,727	$ 3,037	$ 281°	$ 42,045
	Return on sales				
	Before tax	15.6%	8.2%	5.0%	14.5%
	After tax	7.8%	4.2%	2.6%°	7.3%
	Stockholders' equity	$200,118	$26,893	$4,895†	$231,906
	Return on stockholders' equity				
	Before tax	38.6%	22.3%	3.0%†	36.0%
	After tax	19.4%	11.3%	1.6%†	18.0%
	Total assets	$263,051	$33,091	$6,077†	$302,219
	After tax returns on assets	14.7%	9.2%	4.6%	13.9%
B.	Revenue sources, 1964				
	Ready-to-serve cereals	64.0%	43.4%	86.0%	90.8%
	To-be-cooked cereals	36.0%	56.6%	14.0%	9.2%
	Total sales	$491,973	$68,960	$19,368	$580,301

°Five companies.
†Three Companies.
Source: National Committee on Food Marketing.

EXHIBIT 3

B. The cereal industry, output by product category, U.S. 1963

	Ready-to-serve cereals	To-be-cooked cereals	Total cereals
Quantity (thousands of lbs.)	1,293,203	812,400	2,105,603
Share of total	61.4%	38.6%	100%
Value (thousands)	461,531	99,919	561,450
Share of total	82.2%	17.8%	100%

Source: Bureau of the Census.

dustry, either. Rather, it appeared that the federal government had the ability to exercise control over certain aspects of all consumer goods. Theodore Levitt, of Harvard University, was of the opinion that the government was "moving implacably toward the possible destruction of brand-name marketing." Not only did it appear that the government visualized itself as having an obligation to protect the public from big business, but Congress was urged to take action by various committees. In June of 1966 the Consumer Advisory Council decided that mandatory standards should be established to control packaging and labeling. The decision was based on the premise that "the lack of familiarity with many new products, and the varying quality of some, especially when still in the developmental stage, has made shopping and selecting more worrisome not only for consumers but even for retailers.[3]

The shopping environment had changed, as Blackwell learned, and the consumer was faced with product and brand proliferation as well as changes in the dominant distribution outlets for food. The flux in the environment had produced, in the opinion of some, an information gap. Five basic arguments supporting this tenet are as follows:

1. The number of goods and services are increasing.
2. Goods and services are becoming increasingly complex.
3. The growth of self-service forces consumers to rely more and more on information on labels.
4. Technological change is so rapid that knowledge becomes obsolete overnight.
5. Many improvements in the quality and performance of consumer goods are below the threshold of perception.[4]

HISTORY OF GOVERNMENT ACTION

Blackwell knew that the government's effort to control facets of marketing were not the first endeavors in the realm of consumer protection. In 1784, in Massachusetts, a general food law was passed to afford the public a modicum of protection concerning consumption. The real basis for consumer legislation in the United States came during an eight-year period, when, in 1906, the Federal Food and Drug Act was enacted, followed by the Federal Trade Commission Act in 1914. By 1961 it became evident that a new wave of congressional activity was starting to form. Senator Philip Hart (D—Mich.) first introduced legislation on packaging and labeling in that year, but the proposed bill did not pass Congress. From that time through 1966, Senator Hart, believing that the business community had made little effort to police its own affairs voluntarily, promised that if industry would not take steps to protect the consumer, the government would. His promise came to life in 1966 with the "Fair Packaging and Labeling Act" (S 985 and H.R. 15440): "A bill to regulate interstate and foreign commerce by preventing the use of unfair or deceptive methods of packaging or labeling of certain consumer commodities distributed in such commerce, and for other purposes." The bill basically empowered the government to standardize the labeling of the contents of the packages of consumer goods and gave it the necessary flexibility to also standardize the dimensions of packages as well as the weight of the contents within. For the basic aspects of the legislation under consideration, see Exhibit 4.

---

[3]Majority Report on the Fair Packaging and Labeling Act of the Senate Committee on Commerce (89th Congress).

[4]Ibid.

EXHIBIT 4
Extract from Fair Packaging and Labeling Act

H.R. 15440, June 2, 1966. Mr. Staggers introduced the bill.
Referred to Committee on Interstate and Foreign Commerce.

A bill to regulate interstate and foreign commerce by preventing the use of unfair or deceptive methods of packaging or labeling of certain consumer commodities distributed in such commerce, and for other purposes.

.   .   .   .   .

Shall be called "Fair Packaging and Labeling Act."

.   .   .   .   .

Section 2
Informed consumers are essential to the fair and efficient functioning of a free market economy. Packages and their labels should enable consumers to obtain accurate information as to quantity of the contents and should facilitate price comparisons. Therefore, it is hereby declared to be the policy of Congress to assist consumers and manufacturers in reaching these goals in the marketing of consumer goods.

.   .   .   .   .   ◉

Section 4
Labels must conform to the following provisions of the bill:
1. List the identity of commodity, name, and place of business of manufacturer, packer, or distributor.
2. The net quantity of contents (in terms of weight, measure, or numerical count) shall be separately and accurately stated in a uniform location upon the principal display panel of that label if that consumer commodity is enclosed in a package.
3. The separate label statement of net quantity of contents appearing upon or affixed to any package:
   a. If in weight or fluid volume (less than 4 pounds or 1 gallon), shall be expressed in ounces or in whole units of pounds, pints, or quarts.
   b. Shall be legible and conspicuous.
   c. Shall contain letters or numerals in type size which shall be in relationship to the area of the principal display panel of package and uniform for all packages of same size.
   d. Shall be placed parallel to base of box as displayed.
   e. No qualifying words in *label panel.*
   f. Other statements on package about net quantity may not be exaggerating or deceptive terms.

Section 5
1. Authority to promulgate will be in the Secretary of Health, Education, and Welfare (for food, drugs, devices, or cosmetics) and the Federal Trade Commission with respect to other commodities.
2. Promulgating authority can exempt certain commodities where regulations are unnecessary for *adequate protection* of consumers.
3. If promulgating authority thinks that more regulations are needed to *prevent deception of consumers or to facilitate price comparisons,* it can:
   a. Establish and define standards for characterizing size of package which may be used to supplement label statement (may not authorize limit, size, shape, weight, dimensions of packages).
   b. Define net quantity of product which constitutes a serving if necessary.
   c. Regulate discount labels.
   d. Require information and ingredients and composition be placed on package of commodity.

EXHIBIT 4 (continued)

    e.   Prevent distribution of packages of size, shapes, and dimensional proportions which are likely to deceive purchasers in any material respect as to net quantity of contents.

4. If authority determines after a hearing that weights or quantity in a package are likely to impair the ability of consumers to make price-per-unit comparisons, the authority must:

    a.   Publish determination in Federal Register.

    b.   Establish reasonable weights or quantities, or fractions or multiples thereof, in which any such consumer commodity shall be distributed for retail sale.

GENERAL DISCUSSION ON THE BILL

During the summer before the president of Brace was to testify, many members of government and industry expressed their opinions on the subject legislation. Blackwell had obtained the statements and testimonies of these people so that he could arrive at an intelligent judgment for the company's position.

While Congress was deciding the fate of the consumer legislation, much was being said in Washington to urge the passage of the bill. President Lyndon B. Johnson said that:

> the shopper ought to be able to tell at a glance what is in the package, how much of it there is, and how much it costs . . . and the housewife should not need a scale, a yardstick, or a slide-rule when she shops. The housewife should not worry which is bigger: the "full jumbo quart" or the "giant economy quart." The law will free her from that uncertainty.

Paul Rand Dixon, chairman of the Federal Trade Commission (F.T.C.), said, "The goal . . . is primarily to enable the supermarket shopper to make an intelligent choice of products from a cost savings and a quality standpoint." For additional comments on the desirability of consumer protection legislation, see Exhibit 5.

Blackwell believed that members of the administration were in favor of the bill for what it controlled and what it would enable the government to do in the future. Mrs. Esther Peterson, consumer advisor to the president, believed the bill would give the government the power necessary to curb proliferation of packaging, since under the bill standard-size packages could be forced upon companies. William W. Goodrich, assistant general counsel. Department of Health, Education, and Welfare, was in favor of the bill because it would authorize the specification of serving sizes, control cents-off promotions, and generally "bring some order out of the chaos of proliferating package sizes." Winton B. Rankin, of the Food and Drug Administration, was enthusiastic about the bill because he felt it gave authority to standardize the size of certain containers. Dixon, after being aggravated by two similar packages, one labeled 20 ounces and one labeled 1¼ pints, was happy to see control over weights and quantities in

EXHIBIT 5
Statements for consumer protection legislation

CONGRESSMAN EDWARD J. PATTEN:

I do hope, too, we can protect our consumers against what I think are outright frauds in some of the packaging and labeling that I see.

SENATOR PHILIP HART:

[The bill is] aimed at bringing order out of the chaos of the modern marketplace as it pertains to consumer items.

PAUL DIXON, Chairman F.T.C.:

Highest priorities will be given to correcting false or misleading advertising . . . and to deception in sale of . . . food, household equipment, home improvements, and other products of special significance to low-income families and to the elderly.

CONSUMER ADVISORY COUNCIL:

In the marketplace, consumer ignorance and misinformation enable inferior workmanship and poor service to flourish . . . .

the bill. He felt that "the subject bills are aimed at preventing such confusion [about weights and quantities]."

Of course, industry was not overly enthusiastic about the legislation. A spokesman for the National Canners Association warned that the bill "must have sufficient flexibility to enable packers to develop and try out new container sizes that meet shifting consumer tastes and demands." The worry of many businessmen could be seen in a statement by Mr. Minter of the National Confectioners Association: "The bill gives authority to not only standardize weights but to interpret package sizes too." It was the interpretative aspect that had far-reaching consequences.

SOURCES OF CONTROVERSY

Blackwell was also well aware of the lively debate on the legislation which had been carried on during the summer prior to his assignment concerning the bill. The discussions were centered around a few major points. One of these was that the bill made shopping more enjoyable and less time consuming and facilitated price comparisons. (See Exhibit 6.) This argument had two sides to it. First, Mrs. Peterson cited a test by Monroe P. Friedman of Eastern Michigan University[5] which indicated that shoppers were confused by many different alternatives and unable to make intelligent choices (price comparisons) (see Appendices A and B). The advocates of the bill implied that if packages were labeled properly and in standard sizes, consumers would have little difficulty making rapid and accurate price comparisons between products. Industry par-

---

[5]Monroe P. Friedman, "Consumer Confusion in the Selection of Supermarket Products," *Journal of Applied Psychology*, Vol. 50 (1966), p. 529–34.

EXHIBIT 6
The value of legislation to consumers

MRS. ESTHER PETERSON, Consumer Advisor to the President:

... this legislation would help the consumer to buy more wisely and more economically and, may I add, with less frustration than at present.

A poor label with inadequate information can prevent price comparisons and economical shopping, whether or not the intent is to deceive.

JOHN CONNOR, Secretary of Commerce:

When the American housewife goes to the marketplace, she should be able to quickly and easily determine the measure or amount in the container and to compare its price with the prices of competitive products.

[The bill is] intended to enable the public to obtain more complete and meaningful information from labels and packages of consumer commodities.

---

tially refuted this argument when Edward J. Heckman, president of the Keebler Company, said: "The consumer is interested in more than price. Flavor and personal taste are also taken into consideration by the consumer. Price, obviously, is just one factor in the consumer's total concept of value." Similarly, Lee S. Bickmore, of the National Biscuit Company, said, "Especially for our wives' sake, let's not take the fun out of shopping.... Women love to shop and express their taste often in a non-mathematical and intuitive way."

The second side to the facility-of-price-comparison argument concerned the measurement of quantity. Mr. Cohen, under secretary of the Department of Health, Education, and Welfare, said that confusion could not be completely eliminated unless there were price regulations per ounce or per unit and unless there were quality determination (neither were provided for by the bill). Some said that even if price comparisons were easy for the consumer, quality comparisons might be very difficult. Speaking on the quality determination of detergents and soaps, Richard C. Beeson, president of Colgate-Palmolive Ltd. (Canada), said that there was no sure way of telling the cleaning power of various soaps and detergents because of variance in domestic laundry conditions and differences in the soiledness of clothes.

THE DECEPTION ISSUE

Blackwell had uncovered a great amount of controversy on the deception issue of the legislation. The bill would allow the government to seize a product from the market or bar its introduction if the promulgating authority judged that the product was deceptive in either its package form or labeling. While Dixon of the F.T.C. thought that this would protect the consumer from deceptive marketing practices, William B. Murphy, president of Campbell's Soup Company, said that the promulgating authority could call a new package form deceptive simply because it was different (referring in case point to a new triple-condensed soup). A representative of the dairy industry said that the bill would stifle ingenuity and creativity because its deception clauses would lead to standardization.

Mrs. Peterson had said that there was a great cost to the consumer resulting from the confusion created by package proliferation and that the bill would help bring the proliferation to an end via the deception clauses. There were some who denied that package proliferation was deleterious to the consumer. They claimed that the consumer reaped benefits from innovation and a wide latitude of choice. (See Exhibit 7.) Another argument against the deception measures within the bill was posed by the minority opinion of the National Committee on Food Marketing. This group felt that consumers were not entirely at the mercy of food processors and had considerable market power in that "consumers are not misled for long or often on food or household items that are small-unit-cost, daily or weekly purchase, where the seller lives only by his success in attracting repeat business."

EXHIBIT 7
Statements against proposed legislation

NATIONAL COMMITTEE ON FOOD MARKETING (minority opinion):

We assert that these developments, which have emerged in a freely competitive economic framework, have contributed to rising vigor in the food industry and have yielded substantial value to our competitive economy and to consumers.

GROCERY MANUFACTURERS ASSOCIATION:

Successful differentiation eases the necessity of competing strictly on a price and quality basis with competitors of approximately equal production efficiency.

. . . packaging has also provided a wider variety of sizes to meet the increasing variety of sizes to meet the increasing variety of household needs within the constraints of low-cost self-service retailing.

NATIONAL CONFECTIONERS ASSOCIATION:

We have to come up with ideas [new packages]; we can't compete on a brand-name basis.

Blackwell had also come across the results of a marketing research study on the buying habits of consumers, which can be found in Appendix C to this case.

RISKS OF INNOVATION

One of the arguments against the bill emerged from the deception clauses. It was mentioned that the legislation would stifle innovation and creativity in packaging. Blackwell discovered that this argument was taken one step further by opponents of the bill. These people said that the bill would also stifle new-product development by increasing the risk of a new product's success by making it necessary for the product to pass the standards of the legislation.

Introducing a new product prior to any legislation on packaging was tenuous, but the proposed legislation could make it suicidal. (See Exhibit 8.) The difficulty arises from a loss in competitive timing which would occur if a company had to go to the government in order to get permission to bring out a new form of package necessitated by the new product. (See Exhibit 9.) A representative of the National Canners Association testified that "to get an amendment to a standard sometimes today requires years of time [at least a one-year time lag]." William B. Murphy of Campbell Soup Company mentioned that to package new products which are substantially different from present products would doom the new products, since they might not be compatible with the size of the container. (See Exhibit 10.)

A member of the Brace Company supplied Blackwell with estimates on the time necessary to bring out new products, as follows:

Cold breakfast cereal	55 months
Cake mixes	29 months
Frozen dinners	41 months

Also, research and development expenditures cost $122,000 per product for six companies producing 21 new cold cereals.

COST OF LEGISLATION

The final point of contention, Blackwell found, was concerned with the cost of the new legislation. The government did not have any figures to offer on the effects on price levels that the bill would have, but Connor, secretary of commerce said, "Experience has shown that standardization can actually reduce costs and result in savings. Examples are savings in ice cream cartons and molds, can sizes, and paper bags." Mrs. Peterson maintained that the cost of the bill to the consumer would be small compared to the price he is paying for proliferation of packages and the ensuing confusion.

EXHIBIT 8
Risk of innovation

A. FOR THE FOOD INDUSTRY	B. FOR 127 NEW PRODUCTS (1947–1964)
A total of:	22% were dropped after test market.
40% of new products fail after introduction to market.	17% were dropped after regular introduction.
22% of new products fail after test marketing.	30% broke even by end of 1st year.
	44% broke even by end of 2nd year.
8% of new products fail after limited distribution.	61% broke even by end of 3rd year.
	73% broke even by end of 4th year.
9% of new products fail after full distribution.	

EXHIBIT 9

	Product category				
	Breakfast cereal (cold)	Cake mixes	Pet foods	Frozen dinners	Margarine
A. Average number of months in each stage of development					
R & D..................	32	15	11	18	15
Product testing	14	9	9	13	9
Test market	6	6	14	12	10
Limited distribution	5	11	9	12	8
Total months to full distribution	55	29	40	41	33
B. Profiles of typical distinctly new food products					
Preinduction					
Total months to full distribution	55	29	40	41	33
Cost of R & D°	$ 122	$ 27	$ 91	$ 15	$ 65
Cost of marketing research°	$ 60	$ 13	$ 37	$ 8	$ 17
First year of regular distribution					
Sales°	$6,605	$938	$3,943	$416	$6,684
Marketing expenditures as share of sales	51%	61%	49%	20%	30%
Cumulative contributions as share of cumulative sales	− 14%	− 25%	− 29%	− 18%	+ 6%

° In thousands.

Source: Robert D. Buzzell and Robert E. M. Nourse, *Product Innovations in Food Processing, 1954–1964* (Boston, Mass: Harvard University Graduate School of Business Administration, 1967), Table A, p. 107; Table B, pp. 107, 111, and 132.

EXHIBIT 10
Loss of timing

WILLIAM B. MURPHY, CAMPBELL SOUP COMPANY:

Mr. Murphy said that if the bill had been in effect when Swanson brought out frozen food dinners, there would have been a severe loss of competitive timing.

"By the time the problem had been discussed with a number of administration officials and a new or amended regulation had been published in the 'Federal Register' and made the subject of hearings, potential competitors all would have had full opportunity to get on the bandwagon."

Therefore Swanson might not have risked the investment in frozen food dinners, because "eight ounces of poultry would have been too much for an individual dinner, so the only alternative would be . . . to go to Washington for administration approval."

On the other hand, it was estimated that the bill would require Campbell Soup Company to spend $35 million dollars over a total of 70 lines. When asked if he was going to absorb this cost, Murphy, Campbell's president, replied, "Well, I don't think you can. I think you have to pass it on."

See Exhibits 11 and 12 for information on costs.

EXHIBIT 11
Cost estimates

LYLE E. ROLL, KELLOGG COMPANY:

If breakfast cereals were standardized in 8-oz. and 16-oz. packages, Kellogg's capital costs would increase by $8,000,000 and operating costs would increase $3,000,000.

The bill would require 29 different sizes instead of the 11 sizes now existent (slack fill considerations). This would increase manufacturing costs by 4.2 percent which would be reflected by a 5.7 percent increase in the retail prices of cereals.

PROCTER & GAMBLE:

Estimated that changing package sizes for four brands would cost initially $8,000,000, with a $2,000,000 annual increase.

EXHIBIT 12
A. Machinery costs in breakfast cereal production

Equipment	Estimated cost	Rating
Flaking mill	$ 28,000	20 pounds per minute
Toasting oven	50,000	—
Extruder	30,000	30 pounds per minute
Dryer.	100,000	50 feet long
Packaging	150,000	70 family-size packages per minute

EXHIBIT 12
B. Packaging costs by size of firm, breakfast cereal industry

Packaging cost	All companies	Largest 4 companies	Next 4 companies	All other companies
As percent of sales	17.4%	17.6%	15.1%	20.3%
Labor and supervision allocable to packaging	17.0	16.0	20.7	27.9
Packages, containers, case cartons	80.5	82.1	72.6	67.8
Other packaging costs	2.5	1.9	6.7	4.3

Source: National Committee on Food Marketing.

BLACKWELL'S DILEMMA

After analyzing the information he had gathered, Blackwell was still not sure of the arguments the Brace Company should make for or against the Fair Packaging and Labeling Act. He thought that some provisions of the bill might be helpful to the consumer while not overly burdening the industry. However, certain aspects of the bill were quite indigestible to business. He thought that not only would the legislation greatly change the marketing strategy of the food industry byt also, by containing "elastic clauses" which allowed the government to judge what was deceptive and what was not, the bill gave the government a great deal of power which could be expanded to control amost all products in the future.

Despite the arguments that had been proposed by industry against the legislation, Blackwell felt that perhaps even more powerful arguments against the bill could be formed. In any event, Brace was to testify shortly, and Burns wanted the information and cogent arguments outlined for him.

APPENDIX A: SUMMARY OF TRUTH IN PACKAGING IN AN AMERICAN SUPERMARKET*

Purpose

The study attempts to objectively define the issues on the truth-in-packaging controversy by treating consumer confusion as a psychological variable capable of measurement.

Method

Thirty-three young married women at Eastern Michigan University served as subjects, and they were tested in a familiar local supermarket. The women were instructed to select the most economical (largest quantity for the price) package for each of 20 products on sale at the selected supermarket. The women were allowed a maximum of 10 seconds per package to reach their decisions unless there were less than six package types to a product class, in which they were limited to one minute. If there were more than 24 package types to a product class, the women were allowed four minutes to decide. In addition to stating what she believed to be the most economical package in each category, each woman reported to the experimenter accompanying her what information she used in making her decision.

Measures

Three behaviorly based, quantitative measures of confusion in unit-price information were used in the analysis of the data.

Confusion Measure 1:	Indicates the number of women who made incorrect choices for each of the 20 products.
Confusion Measure 2:	Calculates for each product the mean percentage increase in unit price for the women's selected packages compared with the most economical package.
Confusion Measure 3:	Estimates the increase in price which an economy-minded household unit with a specified budget would pay over a constant time period if its purchases reflected the values found for Confusion Measure 2.

---

*By Monroe Peter Friedman, Eastern Michigan University.

RESULTS OF STUDY

Product	Confusion Measure 1[°] (total errors)	Confusion Measure 2 (percentage errors)	Confusion Measure 3[†] (weighted error in dollars)	Estimated annual consumer expenditures[†] (dollars)
Canned peaches	8	2	.00	3.10
Canned peas	5	5	.20	4.10
Catsup	23	13	.28	2.40
Evaporated milk	2	0	0.0	6.60
Family flour	6	2	.13	6.70
Frozen orange juice	6	6	.36	6.40
Granulated sugar . . .	0	0	0.0	10.70
Instant coffee	11	10	.92	10.10
Liquid bleach	32	32	11.70	2.90
Liquid detergent . . .	8	4	.24	6.20
Liquid shampoo	14	63	1.01	2.70
Mayonnaise	8	16	.46	3.30
Paper towels	30	12	.48	4.50
Peanut butter	7	2	.06	3.20
Potato chips	22	1	.05	5.30
Powdered detergent	33	24	2.13	11.00
Soft drinks (cola)	27	17	2.01	13.80
Solid shortening	0	0	0.0	5.50
Toilet tissue	22	5	.37	7.70
Toothpaste	22	16	.69	5.00
Sum			10.15	121.20
Mean	14.3	11.5	.507	6.06

[°] $N = 33$.
[†] Based on a total annual supermarket expenditure of $1,000.

APPENDIX B: PACKAGE CONFUSION: SOAPS AND DETERGENTS
Representative soap packages

Brand	Name	Dimensions	Weight
Tide and Bold	King	$13^5/_{16} \times 9^1/_{16} \times 3^{11}/_{16}$	5 lb., 4 oz.
	Giant	$11^1/_{16} \times 8^3/_{16} \times 3^1/_{16}$	3 lb., 1 oz.
	Regular	$8^8/_{16} \times 6 \times 2^4/_{16}$	1 lb., 4 oz.
Rinso	King	$13^5/_{16} \times 9^{12}/_{16} \times 3^8/_{16}$	5 lb., 4 oz.
	Giant	$11^1/_{16} \times 3^3/_{16} \times 3^1/_{16}$	3 lb., 2 oz.
	Regular	$8^8/_{16} \times 6 \times 2^4/_{16}$	1 lb., 4 oz.
Cheer	King	$13^5/_{16} \times 9^1/_{16} \times 3^{11}/_{16}$	5 lb., 12 oz.
	Giant	$11^1/_{16} \times 8^3/_{16} \times 3^1/_{16}$	3 lb., 6 oz.
	Regular	$8^8/_{16} \times 6 \times 2^4/_{16}$	1 lb., 6 oz.
Ivory Snow	King	$13^3/_{16} \times 9^1/_{16} \times 3^{11}/_{16}$	3 lb., 6 oz.
	Giant	$11^1/_{16} \times 8^3/_{16} \times 3^1/_{16}$	2 lb., 13 oz.
	Regular	$8^8/_{16} \times 6 \times 2^4/_{16}$	13 oz.
Condensed All	Jumbo	$12^2/_{16} \times 8^7/_{16} \times 4^4/_{16}$	9 lb., 13 oz.
	Giant	$9^{14}/_{16} \times 6^{13}/_{16} \times 2$	3 lb., 1 oz.
	Regular	$7^3/_{16} \times 4^{13}/_{16} \times 1^{13}/_{16}$	1 lb., 8 oz.
Salvo (tablets)	Giant	$8^3/_{16} \times 6^{15}/_{16} \times 2^6/_{.6}$	2 lb., 14 oz.

Representative dry cereal packages

Brand	Type	Dimensions	Weight
Kellogg's:	Cornflakes	$12^{1}/_{16}$ × $8^{2}/_{16}$ × $3^{5}/_{16}$	1 lb., 2 oz.
		11 × $7^{10}/_{16}$ × $2^{11}/_{16}-$	12 oz.
		$9^{5}/_{16}$ × $6^{13}/_{16}$ × $2^{7}/_{16}$	8 oz.
	Special K	$10^{9}/_{16}$ × $7^{8}/_{16}$ × $2^{10}/_{16}$	10½ oz.
		$8^{14}/_{16}$ × $6^{5}/_{16}$ × $2^{4}/_{16}$	6½ oz.
	Rice Krispies	11 × $7^{10}/_{16}$ × $2^{11}/_{16}$	13 oz.
		$9^{14}/_{16}$ × 7 × $2^{10}/_{16}$	10 oz.
		$8^{10}/_{16}$ × $6^{5}/_{16}$ × 2	6 oz.
General Mills:	Wheaties	12 × $8^{5}/_{16}$ × $2^{12}/_{16}$	1 lb. 2 oz.
		$10^{11}/_{16}$ × $7^{8}/_{16}$ × $2^{7}/_{16}$	12 oz.
		$9^{7}/_{16}$ × $6^{12}/_{16}$ × 2	8 oz.
	Cheerios	12 × $8^{5}/_{16}$ × $2^{12}/_{16}$	15 oz.
		$10^{11}/_{16}$ × $7^{8}/_{16}$ × $2^{7}/_{16}$	10.5 oz.
		$9^{7}/_{16}$ × $6^{12}/_{16}$ × 2	7 oz.

APPENDIX C: BEHAVIOR AND MOTIVATION SURVEY*

2,431 interviews were conducted concerning food products:

84% of women and 74% of men said people buy well-known brands because of confidence in quality.

54% of men and women said people buy less known brands because of inexpensiveness.

26% of men and 33% of women said people buy less known brands for variety and experimentation.

34% of women had strong preference for well-known brands.

14% of women had strong preference for less known brands.

50% of women had no strong brand preference.

Of those women who decide on a product because of price, 47% preferred private brands and 29% preferred nationally advertised brands.

Of those women who decide on a product because of quality, 69% favored nationally advertised brands and 33% favored private brands.

50% of women look for lowest price brand.

55% of women look for what they consider most popular brand.

40% of women have no concern for brand popularity.

---

*By Arthur D. Little Co. and Opinion Research Center.

index

Index

*This book has been set in 10 and 9 point
Caledonia, leaded 2 points. Part and chapter
titles and part numbers are in 24 point Optima
Medium, and chapter numbers are in 36 point
Optima Medium. The size of the type page is
27 x 45 ½ picas.*